Texts and Studies in Ancient Judaism

Texte und Studien zum Antiken Judentum

Edited by

Peter Schäfer (Princeton, NJ)
Annette Y. Reed (Philadelphia, PA)
Seth Schwartz (New York, NY)
Azzan Yadin (New Brunswick, NJ)

122

Samuel Rocca

Herod's Judaea

A Mediterranean State in the Classical World

WIPF & STOCK · Eugene, Oregon

Samuel Rocca, born 1968; 2006 PhD; since 2000 College and High School Teacher, The Neri Bloomfield College of Design & Teacher Training, Haifa; since 2005 at the Talpiot College, Tel Aviv and since 2006 at the Faculty of Architecture at the Judaea and Samaria College, Ariel.

Wipf and Stock Publishers
199 W 8th Ave, Suite 3
Eugene, OR 97401

Herod's Judaea
A Mediterranean State in the Classic World
By Rocca, Samuel
Copyright©2008 Mohr Siebeck
ISBN 13: 978-1-4982-2454-3
Publication date 3/25/2015
Previously published by Mohr Siebeck, 2008

Table of Contents

Abbreviations... X

Introduction 1
1. *Purpose of the Research* 1
2. *Methodology* 3
   A. The General Framework 3
   B. Main Features: Methodological Introduction 4
   C. Sources 5
   D. The Use of the Horizontal Approach 7
   E. The Use of Comparative Methodology 9
   F. Positivism versus Relativism 10
   G. Inductive versus Deductive Methodology 14
   H. Terminology 16

I. Herod the King: Royalty and the Ideology of Power 19

1. *Herod King of Judaea* 19
2. *Herod and the Jewish Ideology of Rule* 22
   A. Herod and the Heritage of the House of David 22
   B. Herod and the Hasmonean Heritage 29
3. *Herod and the Hellenistic Ideology of Rule* 36
   A. Herod, the Last Hellenistic King 36
   B. Herod's Euergetism: The Expression of Herod's Power
      as Hellenistic King in Foreign Policy 42
4. *Herod, the Client King of Rome* 52
5. *Herod and Juba II – a Comparison* 58
6. *Conclusions* 60

II. The Court of King Herod 65

1. *The Origins of the Court of King Herod* 65

2. The Royal Court of Herodian Judaea 72
   A. The Composition of the Herodian Court 72
   B. Herod's Family (Syngenes) 73
      i. Herod's Brother and Sisters 73
      ii. Herod's Wives 75
      iii. Herod's Offspring and Heirs 78
   C. Herod's Friends (philoi) and the Rest of His Court 84
      i. The Inner Circle of Friends: Ministers and Advisors
         (Ptolemy and Nicolaus) 85
      ii. The Inner Circle of Friends: Orators, Ambassadors,
         and those without Formal Positions 86
      iii. The Outer Circle of Friends: Friends of Herod's Sons 87
      iv. Visitors (Xenoi): Intellectuals, Dynasts, and Political Envoys 87
      v. Herod's Military Household 88
      vi. The Domestic Staff 89
      vii. The Herodian Cultural Circle 91
      viii. Those Who Were Different: Concubines, Prostitutes
         and Catamites 95
3. The setting of the Herodian Court: the Herodian Palace 96
   A. The Herodian Palace: Origins and Structure 96
   B. City Palaces 108
   C. Winter Palaces 112
   D. Fortified Palaces 119
4. Conclusions 122
Appendix I. Herod's Portrait 127
Appendix II. The Gymnasium of Jerusalem 129

III. The Army of King Herod 133

1. Herod and his Army 133
   A. The Ethnic Composition and the Strength of Herod's Army 134
   B. The Structure of Herod's Army 140
2. The Campaigns of Herod's Army 147
3. The Fortifications 153
   A. The Sources of Herodian Fortifications 153
   B. The Evolution of Herodian Fortifications 158
   C. The Types and Distribution of Fortifications
      of the Herodian Kingdom 159
      i. The Herodian Cities 160

    ii. The City Acropolis and the Tetrapyrgia 168
    iii. The Regional Distribution of the Static Defenses
    in the Herodian Kingdom 175
4. Military Colonies and Their Role in Defending
the Herodian Kingdom 188
5. Herod's Navy 190
6. Conclusions 195

IV. The Administration and Economy of the Herodian Kingdom   197

1. The Administration of the Herodian Kingdom 197
    A. The Sources of the Administrative Division of Herodian Judaea 197
    B. The Administrative Division of the Herodian Kingdom 200
2. Taxation and Revenues in the Herodian Kingdom 203
    A. The Taxation System of Herodian Judaea 203
    B. The Income of King Herod 208
    C. Herod's Social Program 210
3. The Division of the Land in the Herodian Kingdom 213
    A. Royal Land and Royal Estates 213
    B. Private Owned Lands 216
        i. The Village 216
        ii. The Manor 222
4. The Economic Resources 227
    A. The Agriculture Products 227
    B. Industry: Glass, Purple-Dye, Pottery and Stone 232
    C. Markets and Internal Trade 234
    D. International Trade: Maritime Trade and the Spice Route 236
5. Conclusions 239

Appendix I. The Languages of Herodian Judaea 240

V. The Ruling Bodies of Herodian Judaea 249

1. The Legal Position of the Ruler in Herodian Judaea 249
2. Herod and the Judaean Ruling Class 251
3. The Ruling Bodies of the Herodian State 261
    A. The Political Constitution of Herodian Judaea 261
        i. The boulē 263
        ii. The ekklesia 266

    iii. The synedrion/Sanhedrin 267
    iv. Outside Judaea: The Greek Cities and the Nomadic Tribes 272
  B. The Courts of Herodian Judaea 273
4. Conclusions 275
Appendix I. The Law on Thieves in Jerusalem and Rome 276

VI. The Cults of the Herodian Kingdom 281

1. The High Priest and Temple Cult in the Herodian Period 281
  A. The High Priest and the Temple Bureaucracy 281
  B. The Temple Cult in the Herodian Period 287
2. Herod and the Rebuilding of the Temple 291
  A. Sources of Inspiration and Parallels for Herod's Temple 291
  B. The Temple and the Temple Mount. 302
3. The Synagogue in Judaea: A Civic Center 306
4. Herod and the Pagan Cults 315
5. Conclusions 319

VII. The Herodian City 323

1. The Herodian Dynasty and the City 323
2. The Urban Features of the Herodian City 325
3. Jerusalem, a Classical City 332
  A. Demography 332
  B. The Water Supply 334
  C. The Leisure Buildings 336
  D. The Private Buildings of Herodian Jerusalem 341
4. Conclusions 347

VIII. Herod's Burial 349

1. The Death of King Herod 349
2. The Burial of King Herod 352
  A. Herod's Funeral 352
  B. Herod's Tomb 354
  C. Herod's Burial. Sarcophagus or Ossuary? 357
3. Conclusions 363

4. Appendix I: Monumental Tombs of the Hasmonean and
   Herodian Period: A Comparative Analysis 364
5. Final Conclusions 370

Bibliography 379
Indices
   Index of Sources 409
   Index of Modern Authors 424
   Index of Names and Subjects...................................429

Abbreviations

ASTI	Annual of the Swedish Theological Institute
ANRW	Aufstieg und Niedergang der römischen Welt
BA	Biblical Archaeologist
BAIAS	Bulletin of the Anglo-Israeli Archaeological Society
BAR	Biblical Archaeological Review
BAR	British Archaeological Reports
BAR International Series	British Archaeological Reports, International Series
BASOR	Bulletin of the American Schools of Oriental Research
BASOR, Supplementary Studies	Bulletin of the American Schools of Oriental Research Supplementary Studies
BEFAR	Bibliotheque des 'Ecoles Françaises d'Athenes et de Rome
CHJ	The Cambridge History of Judaism
DEI	Deutsches Evangelisches Institut
DMOA	Documenta et Monumenta Orientis Antiqui
HUCA	Hebrew Union College Annual
ICS	Illinois Classical Studies
IEJ	Israel Exploration Journal
IG	Inscriptiones Grecae
IMJ	Israel Museum Journal
INJ	Israel Numismatic Journal
JBL	Journal of Biblical Literature
JJS	Journal of Jewish Studies
JQR	Jewish Quarterly Review
JRA Supp. Series	Journal of Roman Archaeology, Supplementary Series –
JRS	Journal of Roman Studies
JSJ	Journal for the Study of Judaism
JSNT Supplementary Series	Journal for the Study of the New Testament, Supplementary Series
JSP	Journal for the Study of the Pseudegrapha
JSPSup.	Journal for the Study of the Pseudegrapha Supplementary Series
JTS	Journal of Theological Studies
JSQ	Jewish Studies Quarterly
LA	Liber Annus
MUSJ	Mélanges (de la Faculté Orientale) de l'Université Saint-Joseph de Beyrouth
NEAEHL	New Encyclopedia of Archaeological Excavation in the Holy Land
NTS	New Testament Studies

NTOA	Novum Testamentum et Orbis Antiquus
OGIS	Orientis Graeci Inscriptiones Selectae
PAAJR	Proceedings of the American Academy of Jewish Research
PEF	Palestine Exploration Found
PEQ	Palestine Exploration Quarterly
QC	Qumran Chronicle
RB	Revue Biblique
REJ	Revue des Etudes Juives
REJ, Historia Judaica	Revue des Etudes Juives, Historia Judaica
RQ	Revue de Qumran
RFS	Roman Frontier Studies, BAR International Series
SCI	Scripta Classica Israelica
SEG	Supplementum Epigraphicum Graecum
SH	Scripta Hierosolymitana
SBB	Studies in Bibliography and Booklore
SBFCM	Studium Biblicum Franciscanum, Collection Maior
SBF, Collectio Minor	Studium Biblicum Franciscanum, Collectio Minor
TSAJ	Texte und Studien zum Antiken Judentum
VT	Vetus Testamentum
WUNT	Wissenschaftliche Untersuchungen zum Neuen Testament
WCJS	World Congress of Jewish Studies
ZDMG	Zeitschrift der deutschen morgenländischen Gesellschaft

Introduction

1. Purpose of the Research

The main theme of this book is a in-depth analysis of Herodian society[1]. The most important facet of this analysis was the relationship between Herod as ruler and the Jewish subjects over whom he ruled, with particular emphasis on the influence of Herodian rule on Jewish society. Yet to understand the relationship between Herod and his subjects, between ruler and ruled, it is necessary, as part of the general background, to undertake a general analysis of Herodian Judaea and its relationship with the Classical world, beginning with Augustan Rome, which was then the center of power, and followed by the main centers within the Mediterranean basin and the Hellenistic East[2]. As such, it is possible to classify this book with other studies dedicated to the encounter between Judaism and the Greek world, most notably those of Bickerman, Hengel, and Momigliano.[3]

I have chosen to focus, not on the beginning of the relationship between Judaism and the Greek world, that is, the early Hellenistic period, but rather on the Herodian period, well after the Maccabees' uprising, a time which is generally regarded as a moment of crisis between Hellenism and Judaism. I will argue that in the period considered, even more so than before, the tie between Judaea and the surrounding Hellenistic world reached its peak in Herodian Judaea. Moreover

---

[1] In this book, I will give a wider chronological frame for the Herodian period. Thus, although King Herod the Great ruled from 40 till 4 BCE, I will take Pompey's conquest in 63 BCE as the beginning of the period analyzed, and will end in 6 CE, with the dismissal and exile of Archelaus. For the earlier Hasmonean rulers, as well as the later Herodian dynasts as Philip, Antipas, and Agrippa I, I will use an even wider background.

[2] In the period considered in this book, the first century BCE – first century CE, the word "Hellenistic" has a socio-political, as well as a cultural meaning. "Hellenistic" therefore can refer to a socio-politic entity that follows in the steps of Alexander the Great's *diadochi* political creations. During this period, these include the Hasmonean-Herodian state in Judaea, as well as the Ptolemaic reign in Egypt, the Nabataean kingdom, and the Parthian Arsacid monarchy in the East. The cultural meaning of the word "Hellenism" is that in all of these states, as well as the Greek East – then part of the Roman Republic and later on the Empire – is that the Greek language, and to a lesser extent, Greek culture, are dominant, or at least are found side by side with native languages and cultural expressions.

[3] See E. Bickerman, *The Jews in the Greek Age*, Cambridge (Mass.) 1988. See also M. Hengel, *Judaism and Hellenism. Studies in their Encounter in Palestine during the Early Hellenistic Period*, London 1974. See also A. Momigliano, *Alien Wisdom*, Cambridge 1976.

in this period Herodian Judaea had a close knit relationship with Rome, which now dominated the whole Mediterranean, including the Hellenistic East. I will contend that Herod, though a Jewish ruler, regarded both Alexander the Great – the embodiment of the Hellenistic ruler – and Augustus as ideal models who were worthy of imitation. Moreover, I will argue that Herod had many things in common with Augustus in particular. Each began his political career at a very young age. Both not only brought an end to a long and bloody period of civil war in their own countries, but the blessing of many years of peace as well. Last but not least, both created a new regime, different from that which had preceded it. These models of inspiration influenced the shape of society in Herodian Judaea as a whole. In fact, Herod pushed Judaea towards major Hellenization, albeit with many elements more akin to Rome than to the surrounding Hellenistic East. Herodian society was therefore permeated by a general trend not only toward Hellenization, but more specifically, toward Romanization, whether forced or spontaneous, as was the case in other provinces of the Roman Empire. This trend of Hellenization was present well before the Herodian period but intensified under Herod's rule. It seems to me that one of the reasons for the intensification of this trend was King Herod's domination of Judaean society, which allowed him to dictate socio-cultural trends to a greater extent than Augustus was able to do in Rome. Herod was an absolute ruler, in the Late Hellenistic tradition, whereas Augustus, *primus inter pares*, needed to respect a Republican framework.

In fact, I believe that a comparative study of Herodian Judaea and Augustan Rome is extremely important, no less important than the more obvious comparative study of Judaea and its Hellenistic Eastern neighbors. Herodian Judaea, like Augustan Rome, possessed a non-Greek native culture, religion and language. Both Judaea and Rome thus faced the challenge posed by the Hellenization of their native cultures. Solutions to the challenge of Hellenization that were discovered and adopted by Augustus in Rome had the great prestige of imperial imprimatur. Moreover, generally speaking, since Augustus often employed his own actions as a model for emulation by upper class Romans, it is reasonable to expect that he was also emulated by noble clients around his empire. Thus, a detailed comparison and contrast of Herodian Judea and Augustan Rome, indicates that Herod, in contrast to his Hasmonaean predecessor, modeled his regime not only on that of Alexander the Great, but on that of his Roman patron.

My research, therefore, is not a biographical study of King Herod. This book does not deal with the Herod's personality nor with his status as tragic figure, as many other scholars have endeavored to do, some of them quite successfully.[4]

---

[4] In my work I fully endorse the tangible evidence regarding the personality of Herod produced by research carried out over more than two hundred years by scholars, including the works of H. J. Jones, S. Perowne, M. Grant, A. Schalit and, more recently, P. Richardson and N. Kokkinos. See W. Otto, *Herodes: Beiträge zur Geschichte des Letzten Jüdischen Königshauses*, Stuttgart 1913. This history of the house of Herod appeared some years after E. Schürer's

Instead, my research deals with Herod as the head of Jewish society in Judaea, and hence this study is first and foremost a study of Herodian society. Other studies of Herod fall into one clear-cut category or another, mainly constituting Biblical and New Testament studies or the history of the Jewish people during the period of the Second Temple. Consequently, Herodian Judaea has somehow been removed from its surrounding context, giving the impression of a reality that was untouched, as it were, by the outside world. Even worse is the illusory impression created of Herodian Judaea as part of the "eternal and unmovable East." In contrast, I attempt in this book to anchor Herodian Judaea as firmly as possible within the surrounding Mediterranean world and therefore within the realities of Hellenistic Roman civilization in order to better understand its multi-faceted dimensions as part of the surrounding contemporary world, and not simply as an entity belonging to a Biblical – New Testament reality.

2. Methodology

A. *The General Framework*

It is worthwhile discussing the methodological approach, or more correctly, the various methodological approaches that I used in writing this book, *Herodian Judaea: a Mediterranean State in the Classical World*. My book has been divided according to various specific topics, following an overall socio-economic approach, dealing primarily with social history and the study of the range of well differentiated social frameworks of Herodian Judaea, such as the court of King Herod, the army of King Herod, the administrative and economic framework of the Herodian Kingdom, its ruling bodies and its cults, the Herodian city itself, and burial practices. The main exception is the first chapter, which is dedicated

---

monumental opus dedicated to Late Second Temple period Judaism. However, once more, the work presented him as an auxiliary implement for theology scholars who wanted to know more about the Murder of the Innocents. The following books are briefly surveyed, beginning with S. G. Perowne, *The Life and Times of Herod the Great*, London 1956. Perowne was a British Mandatory official. The figure of Herod presented by Perowne clearly reflects the sense of failure in trying to mediate between the Eternal East and the Modern West encountered by the British during their administration of Palestine. Another work, A. H. M. Jones' *The Herods of Judaea*, Oxford 1967, is probably the first serious attempt to draw a scholarly history of Herod's family. Though outdated, it is still probably a good beginning. However, the figure of Herod is not that central. A. Schalit's *König Herodes. Der Mann und sein Werk*, Berlin 1969, is really a milestone in many respects, and was published in Hebrew (but not in English!). Schalit's work, however, reflects the cultural background of the early years of the newly born State of Israel. M. Grant's *Herod the Great*, New York 1971, *Herod the Great*, is essentially a popular book, well illustrated, for the general public and without too much scholarly pretension. P. Richardson's *Herod King of the Jews and Friend of the Romans*, Columbia (S. C.) 1996, and N. Kokkinos' *The Herodian Dynasty, Origins, Role in Society and Eclipse*, Sheffield 1998, are the latest books published on Herod and his family.

to the Herodian ideology of rule. It seems to me important to reconstruct and to analyze in detail what Herod had to offer his subjects. This can also explain, notwithstanding various primary sources and the bias of many modern scholars, how Herod succeeded in ruling his kingdom peacefully for forty years and how his presence dominated all of the intersecting frameworks of Judaean society.

B. Main Features: Methodological Introduction

First of all I would like to discuss the primary sources that I have used, including literary as well as material evidence, while writing this book. My methodology is that of comparative analysis that incorporates elements from the realms of anthropology and social studies, more so than from those of history[5]. The positivistic approach of my book uses inductive and deductive methodology, particularly the former, as well as the binary oppositions of Structural Functionalism versus Functional Structuralism. Though the reader may be puzzled initially as to why a book of history, depends on methodologies more properly relevant to a book dedicated to anthropology and social studies, it should soon become clear that this work is not a recollection and analysis of historical events, but it is primarily a study of Herodian society and of the world of the men who lived in late Second Temple Judaea. Each chapter therefore defines such social structures as the court, the army, the administration, and the city. After identifying these social structures, the various cultures and subcultures of Herodian Judaea are defined, exemplified by the discussion on the Herodian ideology of rule, the attitude of the various sects, the Sadducees, the Pharisees, and the Essenes, toward Herod's rule, which constituted a revolution in the religious and political culture of Second Temple Judaea, and last but not least, the burial ideology that stood in

---

[5] In this part of the book, I do not intend to expound on the philosophy of history or on historical methodology itself, but to approach and explain the methodology I have used in writing the book. See, in general, E. Weinryb, *Historical Thinking, Issues in Philosophy of History*, Tel Aviv 1987 (Hebrew). Weinryb discusses the development of historical methodology, beginning with Ranke and Niebhur, pp. 11–14, emphasizing Langlois and Seignobos's approach. According to these French historians, the historian's task consists of collecting the sources, developing an external and internal critique of the sources, discovering factual evidence based on the sources, organizing the synthesis of facts or their interpretation, and then writing the historical synthesis, pp. 14–17. See also C. V. Langlois and M. J. C. Seignobos, *Introduction to the Study of History*, London 1912. Weinryb deals with other problems of historical methodology as well, as the analysis of the history from the bench of the accused, pp. 17–18, the difference between chronicle and history, pp. 19–28, and an acute analysis of historical language, pp. 28–34. For historical thinking and methodology, see also P. Gardiner, *Theories of History*, New York 1959. Gardiner analyzes the development of the historical process, beginning with Vico, pp. 9–205, the nature of historical knowledge, pp. 211–251, the critics of the classical theories of history, pp. 275–342, and the relationship between history and the social sciences, pp. 476–516.

the background of the magnificent funerary monuments, the carved sarcophagi, and the ossuaries of that period.

C. Sources

As in any historical work, my book is based on primary sources, particularly two main types – literary sources and archaeological data. The literary sources consist mainly of Josephus and such Jewish literature as Biblical apocrypha, as the Psalms of Solomon, the Testament of Moses, and Rabbinic literature such as the tractate *Middot*. This is complemented by Greek and Latin authors who deal with the contemporary late Hellenistic period and the Roman late Republic and Augustan Period.

Yet the main source for Herod's rule is Josephus[6], since Josephus and Herod can in fact be considered a unique blend of author and subject. The fact that Josephus dedicates no fewer than four books in his *Antiquities* and one book in *War* to Herod as the most dominant figure, indicates not merely the importance of Herod as subject, but, in comparison with other subjects, most notably the late Hasmonaean rulers, Josephus offers a surfeit of material unmatched by any other contemporary historian. Herod without Josephus would have been consigned to relative obscurity, and our knowledge of his long reign would have been only through later mention of him in Rabbinic literature, along with a few hints in contemporary Greek and Latin authors and in the New Testament. Herod would have been a mute and silent figure, like many of the late Hellenistic Seleucid and Ptolemaic rulers, whose reign is known only through evidence from a few coins and inscriptions. Yet Josephus makes of Herod a ruler whose history is analyzed in detail that rivals that of his contemporary, Mark Antony, or Augustus, and indeed slightly less than figures such as Alexander the Great, Hannibal, and Iulius Caesar. Through Josephus we know much more about Herod than about his other contemporary, Cleopatra VII of Egypt.

Yet my use of Josephus as primary source does not mean that I accept all of his statements about Herod at face value, since most of Josephus' remarks about Herod, a self-conscious member of the priestly aristocracy, are first and foremost a personal statement, and more often than not, hostile. Despite this, Josephus is, on the whole, an objective source, since he based himself on the contemporary writings of Nicolaus of Damascus, which is the main source for the segment of *Antiquities* dealing with Herod. Thus a careful reading of Josephus's *Antiquities*, which is more hostile to Herod than the earlier *War*, allows us to infer that Nicolaus' historical writings were, generally speaking, more favorable to Herod's policy than were those of Josephus, and of course were contemporaneous. *War*,

---

[6] On Josephus see T. Rajak, *Josephus, The Historian and His Society*, London 2002.

where Herod is presented by Josephus in a more positive light – probably a function of his Roman audience or a desire, in the wake of the First War, to valorize a ruler who was without doubt pro-Roman – must be used no less carefully than *Antiquities*. For this approach, Herod scholars are indebted to D. Schwartz's book on Agrippa I and its reconstruction of the various sources used by Josephus when writing about this later Herodian ruler, whose reign was chronologically much closer to Josephus' times.[7] Moreover, even if Josephus is seen to be emotionally involved in judging Herod's rule, he is much less personally involved than in his description of the Jewish War, to which he was not merely a witness, but also a participant. Last but not least, Josephus is not just a source relating to ancient Jewish history, written by a Jew, but a written source that followed the canons used by contemporary Classic historians, including the use of Greek language.

As mentioned earlier, I have used a great deal of archaeological evidence as the basis for my interpretation of Herodian Judaea. More often than not, material culture supplements literary sources and vice versa, and my work is no exception[8]. The material evidence I have used is various and differentiated, and it includes epigraphy, numismatics, and archaeological remains. All these remains, silent witnesses to the past, assume a voice of their own when blended together with literary sources. Thus, while Josephus enables us to reconstruct the composition of Herod's court, it is archaeological data which sets the background through material evidence of Herod's palaces. Another good example is the study of Herod's armed forces. While Josephus can be helpful in reconstructing the size and composition of Herod's army, the various fortifications scattered through Herod's kingdom can be reconstructed only through material evidence. Thus for the study of Herodian Judaea I followed the research model that various scholars have already applied to contemporary Augustan Rome, blending art and material culture with a more traditional general background of general history and literature to give a good sense of the period concerned, as Zanker and Galinsky have already done so successfully.[9]

---

[7] On the reconstruction of the sources used by Josephus for the life of Agrippa I, see D. Schwartz, *Agrippa I, The Last King of Judaea*, TSAJ 23, Tübingen 1990, pp. 1–38.

[8] In this, the use of archaeological evidence, I have followed quite consciously in the footsteps of Rostovtzeff. As Momigliano writes, although the great Russian historian could be more intuitive than logical – in that he did not study, in depth, the problematic of political liberty (but did Mommsendo do any better?); in that he oversimplified the economic structures, in the sense that peasants and slaves were given less than their due; and in that he was unaware of religious problems – his approach to blending history and archaeology deeply modified the historian's approach to Classical history. See A. Momigliano, *Studies in Historiography*, London 1966, pp. 91–104. See also M. I. Rostovtzeff, *The Social and Economic History of the Hellenistic World*, Oxford 1941 and M. I. Rostovtzeff and P. M. Fraser, *The Social And Economic History of the Roman Empire*, Oxford 1963.

[9] See P. Zanker, *Augusto e il potere delle immagini*, Torino 1989, and K. Galinsky, *Augustan Culture, An Interpretative Introduction*, Princeton (N.J.) 1996.

Combining literary and material evidence is like putting together the pieces of a puzzle, though unlike a real, material puzzle whose pieces can always be matched up, in our historical puzzle there is no predetermined image that can guide us to a final, successful, and complete solution and there are many missing pieces, still to be uncovered. Yet by combining literary and material evidence we can succeed in reducing the number of missing pieces and coming closer to a true image of the past.

D. The Use of the Horizontal Approach

The main characteristic of this book is its use of what may be termed a horizontal chronological approach. When writing about history, it is possible to use two main chronological approaches to a subject, one a horizontal and the other a vertical method. The horizontal approach is the study of a determined subject, along horizontal lines, thereby limiting it to a "short" chronological span of time. Although this is limited by the presence of primary sources, which provide the historian, "a priori," with an image of the period which is as complete as possible, it also allows for an "in-depth" analysis of the social structures and cultural background of the given historical period. Moreover this analysis extends spatially, more often than not, extending to the surrounding neighboring cultures. The vertical approach, which has been eschewed in this book, is just the opposite, dealing with a specific topic along extended chronological lines, and spans of time. More often than not, a vertical approach avoids any reference to possible influences on or from neighboring cultures.

In this book, the horizontal approach is characterized by an in-depth analysis of a greatly reduced time frame, that of Herodian Judaea, which spanned a period of approximately fifty years. This time frame, even for the Classic period, can be considered relatively short. Thus, in contrast to a vertical approach, the book isolates a specific period in the history of the Jewish people, from an "a priori" Biblical and early Second Temple Period background, and an "a posteriori" Mishnaic – Talmudic background. Therefore the various social structures and cultures which characterized the Herodian society are analyzed and compared, not to earlier and successive structures present in the Jewish society in Antiquity, but in the light of similar structures that were present in the neighboring Hellenistic and Roman world. The methodology which I employ is not a new one, and has been used by historians such as Bickerman in his reconstruction of early Hellenistic Judaea until the time of the Maccabee's rebellion,[10] by Baumgarten in

---

[10] See Bickerman, *Jews in the Greek Age*.

his reconstruction of the multiplication of the Sects in the Hasmonean period,[11] by Schwartz in his reconstruction of the literary evidence surrounding the figure of Agrippa I,[12] by Gruen in his reconstruction of the political world of Late Republican Rome,[13] and by Galinsky, MacMullen, and Zanker in their studies of Augustan Rome.[14] As this incomplete list of examples suggests, one of the reasons for the horizontal approach in my work is that it has been used more often than not, to analyze the surrounding Classic world, to which I frequently refer.

Yet there are certain limitations to the use of the horizontal approach when it comes to comparative material related to the Hellenistic East, of which Herodian Judaea could be considered an integral part, particularly as regards the use of literary as well as epigraphic, numismatic, and archaeological material. Thus I approached this period, whose chronological background spans three hundred years, horizontally, and not vertically, despite the long time span considered. I believe this to be justified by the fact that social and political institutions, as well as culture, although it certainly evolved, had more often than not been analyzed on a horizontal basis, and not on a vertical basis. The first to use this horizontal approach, on such a long span of time was of course Rostovtzeff.[15] Other scholars have followed suit, even when this collected evidence has comprised a more general study of the period, as the study of the French scholar Will, or Bickerman's magisterial analysis of the Seleucid institutions, or Mooren's study of the Ptolemaic court or simply the thematic collection of papyri, or Nielsen's research of Hellenistic palaces.[16] Moreover, our knowledge of specific spans of time in the Hellenistic period is relatively poor, and thus such a period can still be considered from a horizontal perspective and not vertically. A more cautious approach has nonetheless prevailed in recent years. Good examples of this contemporary trend includes Billow's research on Antigonus Monophthalmos, dedicated to the creation of the Hellenistic state, but which covers a very short span of time, or the research of Sekunda on the Late Hellenistic armies of the Seleucids and Ptolemies, in which the authors reconstruct a social structure within the context

---

[11] See A. I. Baumgarten, *The Flourishing of the Jewish Sects in the Maccabean Era, An Interpretation*, Supplements to the Journal for the History of Judaism 55, Leiden 1997.

[12] See Schwartz, *Agrippa I*.

[13] See E. S. Gruen, *The Last Generation of the Roman Republic*, Berkeley (Ca.), 1974.

[14] See Zanker, *Augusto e il potere delle immagini*, and Galinsky, *Augustan Culture*, or the more recent R. MacMullen, *Romanization in the Time of Augustus*, New Haven 2000.

[15] See Rostovtzeff, *Social and Economic History of the Hellenistic World*.

[16] See E. Will, *Histoire politique du monde hellénistique, 323–30 av. J.-C.*, Paris 2003, E. Bickerman, *Institutions des Seleucides*, Paris 1938, L. Mooren, "Über die ptolemaischen Hofrangtitel", Studia Hellenistica 16 (1968), Antidorum W. Peremans Sexagenario Ab Alumnis Oblatum, Louvain 1968, pp. 161–180, and I. Nielsen, *Hellenistic Palaces, Tradition and Renewal*, Studies in Hellenistic Civilisation 5, Aarhus 1995.

of a short span of time, stressing the impact of the Roman Republican armies on the Hellenistic armies, and their consequences.[17]

E. The Use of Comparative Methodology

A clear cut consequence of the horizontal approach to a determined topic in history is more often than not the use of comparative methodology, and thus comparative methodology as such needs to be defined. Comparative methodology can be presented on two levels. On the first simpler level, it is just the comparison of a certain trend to an identical or similar trend present in neighboring societies. On a more complex level, comparative methodology can be defined as the inference of data in the case study of a certain, circumscribed topic for which part of the data is lacking or unclear, drawn from a very similar trend remarked in a neighboring contemporary culture, which of course shares a certain affinity to the subject being studied.

In this book, the use of comparative methodology is dictated by the fact that in the period considered, Judaea – which constitutes our case study – shared many characteristics with the surrounding Hellenistic East and was politically aligned with the most important Mediterranean power, the Roman Republic. In consequence, I wondered if Herodian Judaea was indeed part of the Mediterranean Classical world, and if the society of Herodian Judaea shared many characteristics with its Graeco-Roman neighbors, even if it preserved, somehow a unique character. A comparison with the surrounding Mediterranean world, I felt, could point to the existence of a certain characteristic, which perhaps might be peculiar to Herodian Judaea, or perhaps shared with its neighbors. Therefore in this book I have used comparative methodology to reconstruct and define not only specific social frames, but have extended it to a holistic study of Herodian Judaea.

My approach is quite simple. I either begin with the analysis of a specific aspect or trend in the broader Hellenistic-Roman world, or I determine if it is reflected in Herodian Judaea, or, vice-versa, starting my analysis from Herodian Judaea and proceeding to the broader Hellenistic-Roman world. In this manner I attempt to determine if any given trend was already present in Herodian Judaea, or if it was already present before the period under consideration, thereby establishing if it reflects a broad trend coming from the outside, or if only some specific influences arrived from outside, or if the trend analyzed is characteristic

---

[17] See R. A. Billows, *Antigonos the One-Eyed and the Creation of the Hellenistic State*, Berkeley 1997. See also N. Sekunda, *Hellenistic Infantry Reform in the 160's BC, Studies on the History of Ancient and Medieval Art of Warfare*, Akanthina 2006.

of Herodian Judaea, with no parallel in the broader Hellenistic-Roman world, and is thus peculiar to Herodian Judaea itself.

The use of comparative methodology is not new to the study of some aspects of the material culture of Herodian Judaea. Thus the relationship between the material cultures of Herodian Judaea and Augustan Italy has been already the subject of a few specific studies, although it has never been the topic of comprehensive and systematic research.[18] While, some specific aspects of the material culture of Herodian Judaea have already been studied and compared to similar aspects of material culture of Augustan Italy, other facets of the material culture of Herodian society are lacking, particularly comparative studies of Judaea versus the Hellenistic East.

F. Positivism versus Relativism

Of all the accepted approaches to historical research – positivistic, moderately positivistic, negativistic, and relativistic – this specific project dedicated to King Herod Judaea can be defined as positivistic. In fact, one of the reasons, or perhaps the main reason why I decided to choose this subject was because I felt that a positivistic approach to this subject would enable me to uncover, at the very least, moderate knowledge of the Classic past. In this regard I believe that my positivistic approach is more optimistic than Schwartz's moderately positivistic approach.[19] However, I must emphasize that my positivistic attitude does not apply to the Classic past as a whole, but only to certain periods within it that

---

[18] Thus there are excellent studies on the following subjects, such as the relationship between the Herodian palace and its parallels in the Hellenistic East and the Roman villa in the West. See G. Foerster, "Hellenistic and Roman Trends in the Herodian Architecture of Masada," *Judaea and the Greco-Roman World in the Time of Herod in the Light of Archaeological Evidence*, Abhandlungen der Akademie der Wissenschaften in Göttingen, Göttingen 1996, pp. 55–73. See also: R. Förtsch, "The Residences of King Herod and their Relations to Roman Villa Architecture," *Judaea and the Greco-Roman World in the Time of Herod in the Light of Archaeological Evidence*, Abhandlungen der Akademie der Wissenschaften in Göttingen, Göttingen 1996, pp. 73–121. On the Italic origin (Rome and Pompeii) of the wall frescoes of the Herodian palaces see K. Fittschen, "Wall Decoration in Herod's Kingdom: Their Relationship with Wall Decorations in Greece and Italy," *Judaea and the Greco-Roman World in the Time of Herod in the Light of Archaeological Evidence*, Abhandlungen der Akademie der Wissenschaften in Göttingen, Göttingen 1996, pp. 139–163.

[19] Seth Schwartz is one of the few scholars writing on the subject who discuss methodology explicitly. In *Imperialism and Jewish Society, 200 BCE to 640 CE*, Princeton (N.J.) 2001, p. 2, Schwartz gives the definition of the method that he used, which he defines as positive. Thus, according to Schwartz, "it is possible to know something about the distant past, although this knowledge can never claim to be more than a sort of hermeneutical model than can help us make sense of the paltry scraps of information that have come down to us." Accordingly, his criterion of research is "moderately positivistic," though he follows a vertical approach, as he considers a certain facet of Jewish history from the second century BCE till the seventh century CE.

can be approached through the horizontal method. Therefore I see a certain relationship between the positivistic attitude and the horizontal approach.[20] I do not think that the negativist approach deserves any prolonged comment, since its basic contention is that there is no way to reconstruct the distant past or to recuperate history and historiography. Of course most historians who follow this approach in fact present us with a careful reconstruction of the past.[21]

On the other hand, the relativist approach to history is deserving of comment, since its methodology can be useful in analyzing and understanding Classic literary sources, including Josephus, who is my main source. The relativistic position still found today among scholars was formulated by Hayden White in his book *Metahistory*. According to postmodern relativist historians, any historical account is not truly an historical or historiographical study, but only a literary achievement. Thus, according to White, the historian performs an essentially poetic act, in which he prefigures the historical field and constitutes it as a domain into which he brings to bear the specific theories he will use to explain "what was really happening" during that particular time frame. The historical account is therefore seen as just one among infinity of possible narratives, distinguished or measured not by the standard of truth, but by rhetorical skill. There is thus no real difference between one historical account or another, since any historical account differs from any others not because of its theme, but because of its literary style. History and historiography are therefore mere rhetoric.[22]

---

[20] I think that there is a certain relationship between the horizontal approach and a positive attitude to past history. Examples of historians who follow a horizontal approach and are positivistic include Zanker in his reconstruction of the material culture of Augustan Rome, already discussed. See Zanker, *Augusto e il potere delle immagini*. Because I am very much aware of the possible fallacy of the positivistic approach if extended to other historical periods I would like to point out that my wide positivistic attitude cannot in any way extend to other, earlier and later periods of Jewish Classic history. Therefore I cannot say that my attitude would be "positivistic" had I been considering the earlier rule of king Alexander Jannaeus or the later revolt of Bar Kochba. In this case, my approach would have been much less positive, or as Schwartz would have defined it, moderately positive. Other periods in Classical Jewish history, not far removed from the period described, such as the Diaspora's Revolts of the Trajanic Period or the second part of the second century CE would have found my approach probably quite negativistic. It is impossible to derive enough from the primary sources for those periods to obtain a good idea of what happened or to begin to understand how the ancients would view these periods and what they thought about them. Therefore I think that it is necessary to add that my wide positivistic attitude is conditioned by the horizontal approach to primary sources.

[21] An important negativistic approach, mainly because it reflects a horizontal analysis, is that reflected in Rutgers' research on the Jewish community of Late Antique Rome. See L. V. Rutgers, *The Jews in Late Ancient Rome: Evidence of Cultural Interaction in the Roman Diaspora, Religions in the Graeco-Roman World*, Vol. 126, Brill 1995.

[22] On Metahistory in general, see Weinryb, *Historical Thinking, Issues in Philosophy of History*, pp. 155–183. Weinryb deals mainly with the Marxist theory of history, as well as the theories of Spengler and Toynbee. See also O. Spengler, *The Decline of the West*, New York 1926 and A. Toynbee, *A Study of History*, New York 1934–1961, and of course E. H. Carr, *What is History?*, Harmondsworth 1961.

White's approach had been criticized by Momigliano and Ginzburg. If the first insisted on the importance of historical facts,[23] Ginzburg accepts in part Hayden's criticism of historical endeavor and tries to find a middle ground between the positivist view of history and the current relativistic mode. According to Ginzburg, historical knowledge is indeed possible, and thus historical sources can be compared to distorted mirrors. Therefore the analysis of the specific distortion of every specific source already implies a constructive element. But a constructive element is not incompatible with proof, which must be considered an integral part of rhetoric. In this he is totally opposed to White, who regards rhetoric as foreign and actually opposed to proof.[24]

I think that White's criticism of history as a literary construction, and thus as metahistory, cannot be dismissed easily, if at all. Although White related

---

White formulated his relativistic theory of history and historiography when trying to explain the historical works of various nineteen century Europe intellectuals, such as Michelet, Ranke, de Toqueville, and Burkhardt among the historians, and Hegel, Marx, Nietzsche, and Croce among the philosophers of history. According to White, the historian performs an essentially poetic act, in which he prefigures the historical field and constitutes it as a domain upon which to bring to bear the specific theories he will use to explain "what was really happening" in it. This act of prefiguration may, in turn, take a number of forms, the types of which are characterized by the linguistic modes in which they are cast. White calls these types of prefiguration by the names of the four tropes of poetic language: Metaphor, Metonymy, Synecdoche, and Irony. According to White, the historical work, which does not differ from that of a poet or a writer, is divided into five stages: chronicle, story, mode of emplotment, mode of argument, and mode of ideological implication. The first stage is the chronicle or the arrangement of events in the temporal order of their occurrence. The second stage is the story, or the characterization of some events in the chronicle in terms of inaugural motifs, or other in terms of terminating motifs, with still others in terms of transitional motifs. The third stage is emplotment. An historian is forced to emplot the whole set of stories making up his narrative in one comprehensive or archetypal story form. According to White, there are four possible modes of emplotment: Romance, Tragedy, Comedy, and Satire. The fourth stage is the mode of argument. Such an argument can provide an explanation of what happens in the story by invoking principles of combination which serve as putative laws of historical explanation. According to White, there are four modes of argumentation: Formism, Organicism, Mechanism, and Contextuality. The last stage is the ideological implication. According to White, the ideological dimensions of a historical account reflect the ethical element in the historian's assumption of a particular position on the question of the nature of historical knowledge and the implications that can be drawn from the study of past events for the understanding of present ones. See H. White, *Metahistory, The Historical Imagination in Nineteenth – Century Europe*, Baltimore (Mar.) 1993. pp. 5–29. See also H. White, "Historical Emplotment and the Problem of Truth," in S. Friedlander (ed.), *Probing the Limits of Representation, Nazism and the "Final Solution,"* Cambridge (Mass.) 1992, pp. 37–53.

[23] See A. Momigliano, "The Rhetoric of History and the History of Rhetoric: On Hayden White's Tropes," *Ottavo contributo alla storia degli studi classici e del mondo antico*, Storia e Letteratura, Roma 1984, pp. 49–59.

[24] See C. Ginzburg, *History, Rhetoric, and Proof, The Menahem Stern Jerusalem Lectures*, New York 1999, p. 1–2, 5, 24–25. See also C. Ginzburg, "Just One Witness", in S. Friedlander (ed.), *Probing the Limits of Representation, Nazism and the "Final Solution,"* Cambridge (Mass.) 1992, pp. 82–96. See also, in concluding, Weinryb, *Historical Thinking, Issues in Philosophy of History*, pp. 389–397 on history as literature, pp. 397–410 on historical narrative, and pp. 411–442 on the rhetoric of history.

only to XIX century historians, it seems to me that his approach it can be transferred to Classic historians such as Josephus, my main primary literary source. Josephus's history can thus be seen and approached as a literary creation. Indeed, more often than not, Josephus's literary style reflects White's four modes of emplotment. As such, Josephus's historical writings can be read as a romance, a tragedy, a comedy, and a satire. The description of the rise of Joseph the Tobiad is a good example of romance.[25] Yet Josephus can resort equally well to tragedy, as in his description of Herod's murder of his second wife, Mariamme, and of his three sons, Alexander, Aristobulus, and Antipater. Likewise, satire is never far away, as in the instance of Josephus's amusing description of Pheroras's refusal to marry Herod's daughter and his wedding to a maidservant. Moreover, the historical writings of Josephus are filled with rhetorical artifices as *topoi*. In this Josephus follows the historical canons of Classical historiography, as Thucydides did before him. Besides, the literary element in Josephus's history or stories is so strong that it can be universalized, or relativized. Therefore Josephus's description of Herod's personal history and his achievements can be, *prima facie*, easily retold as relating to another period and another world. What of Herod as an Italian successful Renaissance warlord? Shakespeare in his rewriting of the Classic story of Anthony and Cleopatra reinvented it as palatable and contemporary for the theatre-going public of Elizabethan England, thereby utilizing an historical plot that could be easily relativized, because of its universal meaning.

Therefore I feel obliged to answer White's criticism of historical endeavor by asking quite seriously, what makes Josephus's literary creation of Herod into a real flesh and blood historical figure who lived in the late first century BCE? It seems to me that it is not Josephus's plot or story line, but rather its background and context that make it real history and not just a literary story. Herod lived in first century BCE Judaea and left his imprints on its material culture: his coins, his inscriptions, as well as his palaces and his huge Temple Mount project make him real, and not merely a literary figure. Therefore it seems to me that the relationship between the literary text and the reality reflected in it transforms the literary plot into real history. Thus if Josephus is indeed a distorted mirror – if we were to apply Ginzburg's central thesis – then the material reality of late first century BCE Judaea is the counter mirror that permit us to reconstruct the reality of that period. In fact, as I have noted earlier, this period is indeed characterized by a wide range of primary sources that are not literary, such as numismatic, epigraphical, and archaeological, that together construct a very detailed image of the period. Moreover, there are relatively high qualitative and quantitative primary sources for the "other" civilizations that characterized the Mediterranean basin,

---

[25] See Josephus, *AJ* XII, 160–228 on the Tobiads. See also D. Schwartz, "Josephus' Tobiads: back to the second century?," in M. Goodman (ed.) *Jews in the Graeco-Roman World*, Oxford 1998, pp. 47–61.

and that surrounded Herodian Judaea, both physically and culturally, mirroring it. In brief, the *realia* described in Josephus's literary creation provide an anchor to reality, and therefore a literary creation can be seen as history. Herod's story therefore is no longer to be regarded as merely universal and relative, but it acquires its specificity, dictated by the archaeological *realia*, free, therefore, from any relativism, anchored securely in reality.

G. Inductive versus Deductive Methodology

In my research I have used inductive and deductive methodology as well. Because my research deals mostly with social and economic history, the inductive approach has been privileged. Inductive methodology involves reasoning from the particular to the general. Therefore I often begin with specific observations and move to a generalization about the observations. The main problem I faced using inductive methodology was to offer premises that can stand up to criticism. Therefore, if my premises were based on literary sources, I tried to present theories and case studies that had already been developed by other scholars and that seemed sound.[26] Moreover, a great number of my primary sources dealing with social and economic history derive from the world of material culture and have already been used in studies by specialist scholars.[27] In fact, inferences about the past derived from present evidence, as in the case of archaeology, count as induction. Last but not least, I must point out that I have frequently used comparative sources as premises. In the use of inductive methodology, I am following the example of other scholars on whose works I have based my research, most notably Shatzman's analysis of the armies of the Hasmoneans and Herod[28]. It

---

[26] See for example E. Gabba, "The Finances of King Herod," *Greece and Rome in Eretz Israel*, Jerusalem 1990, pp. 160–168 and J. Geiger, "Rome and Jerusalem: Public Building and the Economy," in D. Jacobson and N. Kokkinos (orgs.), *Herod and Augustus International Conference – 21st, 22nd & 23rd June 2005*, The Institute of Jewish Studies, University College London 2005.

[27] See, for instance, as a good example of the integration of literary sources and material culture for the study of social and economic issues S. Dar, "The Agrarian Economy in the Herodian Period," *The World of the Herods and the Nabataeans, An International Conference at the British Museum*, London 2001, pp. 17–18, see also J. Pastor, *Land and Economy in Ancient Palestine*, London 1997 and the unpublished B. Zissu, *Rural Settlements in the Judaean Hills and Foothills From the Late Second Temple Period to the Bar Kokhba Revolt*, Thesis submitted for the Degree "Doctor of Philosophy," The Hebrew University, Jerusalem, 2001 (Hebrew).

[28] In the inductive method, the conclusion – really a generalization – may possibly be true if there is no observation which contradicts the conclusion; but it is not necessarily true if there are further observations which could be made. Thus, the inductive method of reasoning moves toward possible conclusions derived from hypothetical connections between premises, or observations, which are selected from among all possible true premises-observations. See as example of inductive methodology. I. Shatzman, *The Armies of the Hasmonaeans and Herod*, TSAJ 25, Tübingen 1991.

seems to me that the advantage of the inductive method is that the premises are more often than not quite correct.

In this research project, I have likewise followed the deductive method adopted, for example, by various scholars such as Schwartz.[29] Deductive methodology, in contrast to inductive methodology, is often described as reasoning from the general to the specific. Therefore the deductive method reasons from certain premises to a necessary conclusion, moving from the rule to the example. If the premises are true, and if the form is correct or valid, then the conclusion is necessarily true. This method is justified when dealing with primary sources that are literary in nature and with political history, which is only a background and not the main topic in this book.

As I have made clear, inductive and deductive methodologies complete each other, and hence I need to move from the general to the particular (deductive versus inductive, and vice versa) in order to obtain the full picture. In the same way, in describing the various frameworks of Herodian society, I often switch from the structure to the function of a defined framework and vice versa. Therefore, since we sometimes know more about the structure of a particular framework than we do about its function, an analysis of the structure of the framework can provide a better understanding of its function. The reverse likewise holds true, since we sometimes know quite well the function of a specific framework, and analyzing it can therefore help us reconstruct its function.

Thus my analysis of varying social frameworks related to the diverse cultures and subcultures that characterized Herodian Judaea calls for an understanding, *a posteriori*, of how the social structures worked through the use of auxiliary social theory, including structural functionalism and functional structuralism.[30] Therefore, as Schwartz and Baumgarten have done so successfully, I have attempted to apply structural functionalism or functional structuralism to my deeper analysis of the social frameworks of Herodian Judaea.[31]

---

[29] Ideally, the deductive method of reasoning is objective in its conclusions, but subjective in its premises. Thus in the deductive method of study, we take for granted the work which others before us have done in identifying and categorizing various parts and their relationships of the subject we are dealing with, and we use this to develop our understanding of the whole system and to generate true examples of the subject. The best example of the use of deductive method is Schwartz, *Imperialism and Jewish Society*, p. 2. The use of the deductive method is totally justified for various reasons. In fact, Schwartz deals with a broad spectrum of time from 200 BCE until 640 CE. Therefore his analysis is forcefully vertical and not horizontal. Moreover, most of the sources used justify an inductive method.

[30] On structural functionalism see E. F. Talcot Parsons and N. Smelser, *Economy and Society*, London 2003 (1956), and E. F. Talcot Parsons, *Structure and Process in Modern Societies*, Glencoe (Ill.) 1960.

[31] One of the main features that Baumgarten and Schwartz adopted from structural functionalism is the study of the distribution of power in a society and its effect on social integration. See Schwartz, *Imperialism and Jewish Society*, p. 3. See also Baumgarten, *Flourishing of the Jewish Sects in the Maccabean Era*.

There is a further reason why I think that the application of structural functionalism is necessary. This type of analysis has been long applied to Greek and Roman history, and since my research takes a comparative approach with respect to the surrounding Hellenistic-Roman world, this is probably the type of analysis best suited to the goals of my research. In fact, the use of structural functionalism can only strengthen the apparent relationship between Herodian Judaea and the surrounding world, using a common social theory of analysis.[32] It is worthwhile to point out that it is occasionally difficult to situate my research totally within this particular social theory or any other type of social theory.[33]

H. Terminology

Last but not least, some notes on the terminology I have used. In this book I needed to deal with Herodian Judaea and the surrounding, contemporaneous Mediterranean world. To differentiate between them as much as possible, I used three different sources for the terminology. Thus the names of persons and sites coming from the Hellenistic and Roman world are transcribed following the *Oxford Classical Dictionary*. To cope with Hasmonaean and Herodian Judaea, I employed the terminology used in the general index of Josephus's *War* and *Antiquities* in the Loeb Classical Library, compiled by L. H. Feldman. For the terminology tied to the Hebrew Bible, external books, Rabbinic Literature, and the New Testament, I used the terminology found in the *Society of Biblical Literature*.

This book is the revised and expanded version of my Ph. D. dissertation which I wrote at the Bar Ilan University, under the supervision of Prof. Albert Baumgarten.

Many people have contributed in promoting the achievement of this book. First of all I would like to thank my Ph. D. supervisor, Professor Albert Baumgarten for all his endeavors, and his constant help and his precious suggestions,

---

[32] See L. Foxhall and A. D. E. Lewis, *Greek Law in Its Political Setting: Justifications Not Justice*, Oxford 1996, as example of structural functionalism applied to Classic studies.

[33] The main limit of structural functionalism as social theory is that it presupposes societies whose social structures remain unchanged for long periods of time. Thus structural functionalism tends to cover patterns of behavior which remain unchanged, which can be problematic. See Schwartz, *Imperialism and Jewish Society*, p. 3. Structural functionalism is a social theory that presupposes long range patterns of stability, but Herod's rule was distinguished as a period of tense social changes, in which new patterns of social behavior developed, while others tended to wane. I have tried to resolve the problem, analyzing case studies in which certain social structures appear to be new, in the light of the later period, after Herod's death, when part of Herodian Judaea passed under Roman direct rule, and these changes were already established and had become dominant patterns. Sometimes I did the opposite in order to understand certain social structures that were typical of the earlier years of Herod rule, but which later waned. I therefore analyzed these structures in the light of the earlier Hasmonean period.

even after I terminated my Ph.D. Without his help my thesis could not have been transformed in a book. My thanks to the precious suggestions and help of Prof. Emeritus, Ehud Netzer, the Hebrew University of Jerusalem, who put at my disposition all his knowledge of Herodian architecture and palaces. My thanks as well to Rav Professor Bonfil, the Hebrew University of Jerusalem, always kind and helpful all along these years. My thanks as well to Professor Gideon Foerster, the Hebrew University of Jerusalem, Professor Jan Gunneweg, the Hebrew University of Jerusalem, Professor Amos Kloner, Bar Ilan University, Dr. Boaz Zissu, Bar Ilan University, Dr. Donal T. Ariel, Israel Antiquities Authority, Monsieur Jean Philippe Fontenille, who put at my disposition his marvelous numismatic collection, and Herkules numismatics, much kind and helpful. Last but not least my thanks to Shifra Hochberg for reading carefully the book's proofs, and for her many brilliant suggestions.

In concluding this introduction, I hope that my research will succeed in closing numerous gaps in the existing research and help to establish much more clearly the position of Herodian Judaea in the context of the surrounding Graeco-Roman Mediterranean world.

I. Herod the King: Royalty and the Ideology of Power

1. Herod King of Judaea

Herod, son of Antipater the Idumaean, was without doubt a parvenu in the history of the Jewish People, a mere commoner who ascended the throne of Judea following the reign of Antigonus, the last Hasmonean king and high priest.[1] The Romans, undoubtedly, would have termed him a *homo novus* – a new, self-made man – on the order of Marius in the Roman Republic, though the patrician ruling class in Rome did not regard *homines novi* any more highly than did their counterparts in Judaea. Both Herod and Augustus rose, respectively, to dominate Judaean and Roman public life and power in the wake of years of bloody civil wars. The civil wars between Hyrcanus II and Aristobulus II following Queen Salome Alexandra's death facilitated the Roman conquest by Pompey in 63 BCE and the division of the Hasmonean kingdom. Another period of civil strife, in the wake of the murder of Caesar, brought Herod to power as sole ruler in Judaea. Herod was the protégé of Mark Antony and the son of Antipater, who had been *epitropos* of Judaea and the political ally of Hyrcanus II the high priest.[2] In Rome, the civil wars that followed the murder of Iulius Caesar in 44 BCE brought Octavian, later known as Augustus, the family heir of the dictator, to supreme power in Rome in the aftermath of a long struggle against the murderers of Caesar, Brutus and Cassius, against Sextus Pompeius, the son of Pompey, and against Mark Antony.[3]

Who was the real Herod? Was he a military adventurer? Was he a successful warlord? Was he merely a Hellenized Jew who, like so many of his contemporaries, succumbed to the charm and fascination of Alexander the Great? And was Herod's rule totally removed from Jewish tradition, as many scholars believe?

Tessa Rajak has analyzed the figure of Herod, as depicted by Josephus in *War* and *Antiquities*. In the first place, she correctly emphasizes that without Josephus there would be no historical recollection of Herod. Moreover, she stresses

---

[1] See Josephus, *AJ* XIV, 121.
[2] See E. Schürer, *The History of the Jewish People in the Age of Jesus Christ* I, Edinburgh 1987, pp. 267–287.
[3] See M. A. Levi, *Augusto e il suo tempo*, Milano 1986, pp. 41–45.

Herod's two faces: the relatively positive portrait that emerges from *War* and its more negative counterpart from *Antiquities*. There is a marked difference in the description of Herod's reign in *War* and in *Antiquities*. In the first book of *War*, Josephus presents a *bios* or biography, which follows all the canons of the Hellenistic-Roman "lives of great men" genre, exemplified by Plutarch's *Lives*. Here, the narrative is developed around specific topics, and at times, Josephus even approximates the genre of Hellenistic romance. In *Antiquities*, on the other hand, the narrative attempts to remain "annalistic," with Josephus writing in the manner of Thucydides, with speeches and documents punctuating the narrative.[4]

In her Ph. D. dissertation, Tamar Landau analyzes the figure of Herod as depicted in Josephus' *War* through the prism of narratology, stressing the rhetorical devices used by Josephus to emphasize and dramatize Herod's life in terms of the binary oppositions of his wholly positive public image and the totally negative representation of his private life. The end result is quite devastating, since. Herod emerges as a quasi-tragic, distant figure, depicted in overtly comic images, with Josephus' malevolent irony ever present.

This dichotomy, however, does not enable the modern historian to obtain a closer, more profound understanding of Herod's personality in the way that Plutarch's *Lives*, for instance, sheds light on the personality of Alexander the Great or Iulius Caesar,[5] since. Josephus exhibits a distinct bias in his depiction of Herod. According to Tessa Rajak, in *Antiquities* Josephus saw himself as the historian of the last Herodian ruler, Agrippa II, and his view of Herod may therefore reflect that of Agrippa II, whose grandfather was murdered by Herod. Moreover, Josephus had both personal and public reasons for his negative view of Herod and Herod's family, including Agrippa II. Josephus regarded himself as a Hasmonean and, as such, he clearly deplored Herod's rise to power. As a priest, he was likewise repelled by Herod's abuse of the high priest's status and its decline within the public sphere.[6]

None of this, however, can explain how Herod was able to retain power and reign undisturbed for nearly forty years. He did indeed create a police state,

---

[4] Josephus' sources on Herod were contemporary sources, as of course Nicolaus of Damascus' *Universal History*, as well as *Strabo's History* and last but not least, Herod's own memoirs. See T. Rajak, "Josephus as Historian of the Herods," *The World of the Herods and the Nabateans, An International Conference. at the British Museum, 17–19 April 2001*, pp. 25–26.

[5] For example Josephus liked to couple rhetorical devices such as *phthonos*, or envy and *euragia*, or prosperity to emphasize the dramatic position of Herod. See T. Landau, "Power and Pity, the Image of Herod in Josephus BJ," *International Josephus Colloquium*, Rome 21–24 September 2003.

[6] See T. Rajak *Josephus, the Historian and His Society*, London 2002, pp. 11, note 3, and pp. 128, 132, 134, 150, 162, 165 on Josephus' relationship with Simon son of Gamaliel. See also S. Schwartz, *Josephus and Judaean Politics*, Columbia Studies in the Classical Tradition 18, Leiden/New York 1990.

and the omnipresence of his soldiers almost certainly discouraged any attempt at rebellion. Augustus retained his power in much the same way in Rome, and the Principate developed into a military monarchy. Undeniably, however, there was a strong consensus in favor of Augustus among all classes of the Roman population, in contrast to Herod, whom most historians present as a ruler who was perceived in a negative light among the majority of the Jewish population of the kingdom.

But was he in fact perceived in this way by his contemporaries? While I do not wish to dispute that the stability of Herod's monarchy relied upon the army, I would like to argue herein that Herod's rule was seen by his subjects in a far more positive light than has been previously considered by other scholars. Herod clearly enjoyed the admiration of the Jews in the Roman and Babylonian Diasporas. Moreover, had he not had the overwhelming support of his Jewish subjects, the Romans would never have appointed him king of Judaea. Augustus' addition of lands to Herod's kingdom, for example, attests to his successful rule. Herod also flourished as undisputed ruler of the Greek East in the tradition of Alexander the Great, and was recognized as such by both the Greeks and by the Roman overlords.

At this juncture, I would like to add a brief note explaining the use of the term Herodian in this work. This term has two main connotations, first as an adjective referring to everything connected with Herod the Great, as well as members of his family who ruled Judaea, or parts thereof, following his death in the first century CE. Thus, the term Herodian refers to King Herod's sons, Archelaus, Antipas, and Philip, to his grandson Agrippa I, as well as to his great grandson, Agrippa II, the last Herodian ruler. The term *Herodian*, when it appears in italics, on the other hand, refers to the supporters of Herod's dynasty, as seen in the New Testament and Josephus.

Last but not least. As my approach is comparative, many of the topics connected with Herodian Judaea have various implications rising all over the Ancient Hellenistic-Roman Mediterranean World. I have severely restricted the discussion in the text, those cases most closely connected to Herodian Judaea, while reserving treatment of the wider consequences for the notes.

We shall now analyze first the ideological background of Herod's monarchy, as well as his ideological message, which was directed toward three different constituencies: his Jewish subjects and the Jewish Diaspora; his Gentile subjects and the Hellenistic East as a whole; and Rome, now the undisputed ruler of the Mediterranean. I shall attempt to answer several questions: What did Herod have to offer his new Jewish subjects? Did he perceive himself as one of the successors of Alexander the Great? And how could his threefold conception of Jewish king, of Diadoch in the manner of Alexander the Great, and of *cliens* king with respect to Rome, stand side-by-side?

2. Herod and the Jewish Ideology of Rule

A. Herod and the Heritage of the House of David

The Roman Senate in 40 BCE recognized Herod as ruler of Judaea. For the Romans, he was Herod, King of the Jews (*Rex Iudaeorum*), and for the Greeks in the East, he was "*Basileus tōn Ioudaiōn.*" Was Herod, for his Jewish subjects, no less than "*melekh ha Iehudim*"?[7]

For the Jews, the world *melekh*, or king, was associated with an ancient and glorious past with which the vast majority of the Jews were familiar, namely the ancient monarchy of the First Temple period. Herod wished to be perceived by his Jewish subjects first as a Jewish king, and then as the successor to the glorious kings of the House of David who once ruled Israel. Thus, from the outset, he endeavored to present himself as the successor to the Israelite kings. As such, Herod could offer his Jewish subjects renewed images of ancient glory that they had never forgotten and that were, indeed, still very much alive as Jewish historians rewrote their ancient history, during the Hellenistic period, for both a Jewish and Gentile public.

It is possible that Herod's desire to connect himself with the distant First Temple Kings of Judaea – his desire to be perceived as a *melekh* – was reflected in his coronation ceremony. Was the coronation ceremony of the Herodian King similar to that of other Hellenistic kings, in which the king received the diadem from the army, or did it reflect and imitate the coronation ceremonies of the Israelite kings described in the Bible?[8] There is no hint in Josephus that Herod

---

[7] Josephus writes in *AJ* XIV 385 that the Roman Senate, under Mark Antony's instigation, decreed that Herod was appointed King of Judaea. Since the decree was in Latin, Herod would have received the title "*Rex Judaeorum.*" Indeed this title was etched on amphorae imported from Italy that were found at Masada. See J. Geiger, "Herod and Rome: New Aspects," *The Jews in the Hellenistic-Roman World, Studies in Memory of Menahem Stern*, Jerusalem 1996, pp. 134–137. On Herod's coins minted at Samaria as well as Jerusalem the inscription "*Herodou Basileos*," or of King Herod appears on the obverse. Thus in the Greek East Herod did bear the title *basileus*, or king. See Y. Meshorer, *A Treasury of Jewish Coins, From the Persian Period to Bar Kokhba*, Jerusalem 2001, pp. 221–224. There is no evidence that Herod was called *melekh* by his Jewish subjects. However Josephus refers to him as Herod as well as *basileus*, for example Josephus, *AJ* XIV, 462. Moreover, Josephus, *AJ* XVII, 197 describing Herod's funeral relates that Herod's body was covered with purple; he had a diadem on the head, above it a crown of gold, and a scepter in his right hand, all attributes of royalty, even for his Jewish subjects.

[8] The coronation ceremony at the beginning of the Israelite monarchy consisted only in the sacramental rite of anointing the ruler with oil on his accession to the throne. In Israel this function was performed by the prophet or by the priest, acting on behalf of the God of Israel. The main ritual act took place when the priest or the prophet, as Messenger of the Lord, poured oil on the head of the one about to be crowned and consecrated him as the chosen one of God. See B. Mazar, *Kingship in Ancient Israel, Biblical Israel, State and People*, Jerusalem 1992, pp. 55–67. It appears that only with Solomon's anointing did a complex coronation ceremony, performed in front of the Temple, develop. The Second Book of Kings describes this ceremony twice: the anointing of Solomon and that of Joash. The two rites were similar. The coronation ceremony

was crowned King of Judaea according to rites described in the Bible. However, Josephus does describe the coronation ceremony of Herod's son, Archelaus[9], in Jerusalem which reflects Jewish elements. Moreover Josephus describes a further coronation ceremony in Jericho, which reflects Hellenistic elements, that was refused by Archelaus, pending the approval of Augustus in Rome.

The Jewish ceremony was held on the Temple Mount after the seven days of ritual mourning following the death of Archelaus' father, as prescribed by Jewish law. After distributing various gifts to the people, Archelaus went up to the Temple Mount, where, in front of the Temple itself, the coronation ceremony took place. Archelaus, was first praised and then sat on a throne. After the enthronement the people acclaimed him as king. This ceremony, as described by Josephus, presents a striking similarity to the Biblical ceremony and is very different from the coronation ceremonies of Hellenistic kings. Like the Davidic kings, Archelaus was consecrated on the Temple Mount, with two notable differences, however, between this ceremony and the Biblical one – Archelaus was neither anointed nor crowned.

Did Josephus ignore this either inadvertently or intentionally? I, for one, do not think so. I suggest that Archelaus was not anointed since this would have been considered no less binding than being crowned, and would certainly have angered Augustus, who, as overlord of Judaea, needed to give his prior consent. Also, Archelaus was not actually crowned, since, like the ceremony of anointment, that was clearly part of the original, binding ceremony. Josephus unequivocally states that Archelaus refused the crown and wished to wait for "Caesar." As client king of Rome, he needed to await formal investiture as king of Judaea by Augustus and could not afford to antagonize the Roman ruler by participating in a ceremony that required the express authorization of Rome. Ultimately, Archelaus was appointed *ethnarch* rather than king of Judaea.

That the ceremony performed in Herodian Jerusalem is really the ancient Jewish ceremony is confirmed by another episode in which Josephus described the Hellenistic coronation ceremony. Archelaus refused the diadem offered him by the soldiers in Jericho. In so doing, he clearly refused a Hellenistic investiture by the army, which was the traditional coronation ceremony of Macedonian rulers. He wanted to be crowned as a Jewish king, not as a Hellenistic king in the Macedonian tradition.

---

of Solomon is described in 2 Kgs 1: 32–38. The coronation ceremony of Joash is described in 2 Kgs 11: 12–20. Solomon was consecrated at Gichon, the spring of Jerusalem. Joash, however, was consecrated in the Temple precinct. 2 Kgs 11: 14. See also R. de Vaux, *The Institutions of the Old Testament, Vol. I - Social Institutions*, New York 1961, pp. 100–113.

[9] See Josephus, *AJ* XVII, 200, and *BJ* II, 1–2. Josephus does not describe Agrippa I's coronation ceremony. He states, however, that, when he arrived in Jerusalem, Agrippa I brought sacrifices to the Temple, that the Nazirites had their heads shorn and that he dedicated his gold chain, given him by Gaius. See Josephus, *AJ* XIX, 293–295.

Figure I, 1 – Coin of King Herod, depicting on the obverse a Diadem with inscribed Chi, on the obverse a Table with three curved legs (TJC 48, Coll. of Mr. J. P. Fontanille).

And yet, the possibility that Herod himself was actually crowned in an ancient Israelite coronation ceremony is perhaps reflected by coins minted during Herod's own reign in Jerusalem. One such coin depicts the royal diadem on the obverse, with the Greek letter *chi* within it; the reverse depicts a tripod. According to Y. Meshorer, the obverse can be interpreted according to the Talmudic passage: "In anointing kings one draws the figure of a crown and with the priest in the shape of the letter *chi*, Rav Menashiah said, like a Greek *chi*." Herod thus wished to stress the cooperation between Jewish kingship, symbolized by the diadem, and the priesthood, symbolized by the *chi*. The obverse of the coin must therefore be a reference to the Israelite king's coronation ceremony, adopted by Archelaus. The reverse probably depicts a tripod, a vessel associated with the Temple in the classical world, maybe symbolic that Herod was crowned on the Temple Mount (cfr. figure I, 1).[10]

The Jews considered the period of David and Solomon, the most renowned of the Jewish kings, to be the most glorious in their history. King David had dominated an extensive empire that stretched from the Sinai to southern Syria, and King Solomon, his son, built the First Temple. Both figures were celebrated in the Bible and later by Hellenized Jews in their art and literature. During the Hellenistic-Roman period, Hellenized Jewish writers in fact valorized the illustrious past of Solomon's reign as a golden age that constituted the pinnacle of Jewish history. By choosing Solomon as his paradigm, Herod could endear the Hellenized Jewish Diaspora to the idea of his rule. For them, as for Greek Gentile intellectuals and the ruling class of Hellenistic-Roman Phoenicia, Solomon was a figure from the Jewish past who shared the same qualities of the ideal Hellenistic king. In Hellenistic Jewish literature, for example, Eupolemus depicts Solomon as a shrewd diplomat who dominated the contemporary Near East through his

---

[10] On the diadem and the *chi* see BT, *Ker.* 5, 2. See also Y. Meshorer, *Ancient Jewish Coinage II, Herod the Great through Bar Cochba*, New York 1982, pp. 24–25. The *chi* perhaps stands for the word *christos*, or anointed. On the tripod, see m. *Šeqal.* 6, 4 and Meshorer, *Ancient Jewish Coinage II*, pp. 23–24. See also Meshorer, *A Treasury of Jewish Coins*, pp. 65–66.

diplomatic skills.[11] Other historians, including Theophilus, Dios, and Menander, depicted Solomon as a figure who tolerated the various pagan cults in foreign lands.[12]

Thus it would be a mistake to attribute to Herod a connection only to King David, whose legendary glamour had already been exploited by the Hasmoneans.[13] Of all the successful rulers of Judah – Solomon, Hezekiah, and Josiah – Herod chose the most magnificent and best known figure as his paradigm: King Solomon. The Jews knew Solomon through the Bible as the builder of the Temple and the ruler who, following David's wars of conquest, brought a long era of peace and prosperity to his vast empire. Solomon was also known as a model of the just ruler, who ensured that his subjects received fair trial, and he was also considered to be a sage and a learned individual, perhaps the most learned person of his age. If the Psalms were attributed to his father, David, later tradition attributed to Solomon a greater number of writings, including the Song of Songs, Ecclesiastes and the Book of Proverbs.[14]

In addition to his reputation for magnificence and wisdom, however, Solomon was likewise notorious for less admirable behavior. His court had a reputation for luxurious decadence, since it was peopled with numerous wives and concubines. In the last years of his reign, in fact, Solomon was accused of introducing pagan cults to Jerusalem to satisfy the spiritual needs of his foreign wives. His actions are contrary to the explicit injunction to kings, in Deuteronomy, not to "multiply horses and wives."

But first and foremost, Solomon was recognized as an absolute ruler, a quality that Herod greatly admired. There was no better paradigm for Herod than Solo-

---

[11] Eupolemus, a Jewish writer in Greek, probably from Hasmonean Judaea, in his book "On the Kings of Judaea" depicted the figure of Solomon not only as the Temple builder, but also as a shrewd diplomat. Only fragments remain of Eupolemus' book. One of them describes the epistolary relationship between Solomon and Vaphres King of Egypt and Souron the ruler of Tyre, Sidon and Phoenicia. Souron is depicted as "subordinate" to Solomon. See E. S. Gruen, *Heritage and Hellenism, the Reinvention of Jewish Tradition, Hellenistic Culture and Society XXXI*, Berkeley (Cal.) 1998, pp. 141–146. In Eupolemus there are various references to the contemporary period. For example there is a clear reference to Leontopolis among the places listed by Vaphres, as the site of the Temple of Onias IV. This is clearly a polemic against the Zadokite priesthood that abandoned Jerusalem to build a new temple in Egypt. The wishful thinking of Solomon is that the Ptolemaic rulers, moved by the proud heritage of the Egyptian Jews, their faithful subjects, would support Judas Maccabaeus in his struggle against the Seleucids, the traditional adversaries of the Ptolemies. See Gruen, *Heritage and Hellenism*, p. 142.

[12] Thus, according to Theophilus, the King of Tyre employed the gold of Solomon to erect a statue of his daughter. See Gruen, *Heritage and Hellenism*, p. 146, note 32. Theophilus is recorded by Eusebius, *Prep. Ev.* 9.34.19. According to the largely unknown historians Dios and Menander, the King of Tyre employed the gold of Solomon to decorate the Temple of Zeus (at Heliopolis?) with a golden column. Dios and Menander are recorded by Josephus, *Apion* I, 112–120.

[13] The Hasmoneans chose King David as their model. See Gruen, *Heritage and Hellenism*, pp. 138–141.

[14] It is not clear if this tradition, attributing to Solomon the Song of Songs, Ecclesiastes and the Book of Proverbs, was already established in the Herodian Period.

mon, since Herod could present himself as Solomon's successor, while providing a corrective to the various mistakes and errors attributed to the legendary Israelite king, and thereby surpassing him in his accomplishments. As such, Herod rebuilt the Temple, and his Temple was larger and more magnificent than that built by Solomon. Like Solomon, Herod entertained a luxurious court, which was also a center of learning, and like Solomon, Herod had many wives. Perhaps most important, however, Herod endeavored to provide his subjects with a long era of peaceful prosperity, as Solomon had done before him.[15]

The best source for parallels between King Herod and the Israelite Kings, especially David and Solomon, is found in Josephus, the most important being the speech attributed to Herod by Josephus in connection with the rebuilding of the Temple. Moreover, since the speech comes from *Antiquities*, it probably derives from Nicolaus of Damascus's writings and is thus a source of primary importance. Josephus likewise mentions Herod together with Solomon in connection with the rebuilding of the Temple. In fact, the first and most significant challenge faced by Herod as ruler of the Jews was rebuilding the Temple into a worthy successor to the one built by Solomon. Here, Josephus clearly makes a connection between the two rulers. In the speech that Josephus attributes to Herod, a speech made before construction on the Temple Mount was begun, Herod clearly compares himself to Solomon, stating that the exiles from Babylon did not rebuild as beautiful a Temple as that erected by King Solomon, and that he would erect a greater and more glorious edifice than the one built by Solomon.[16] According to Josephus, Herod thus underlines his connection to Solomon by rebuilding the House of God as a place of worship surpassing the splendor of Solomon's Temple,[17] a veritable "House for all Nations." As successor to the House of David, Herod could thus claim to dominate the Temple Mount, as did

---

[15] See 1 Kgs, 6: 1–38 and 7: 13–50. For the well-known judgment of Solomon, see 1 Kgs, 3: 15–28.

On the Dream of Solomon, when the young king asked God for an "understanding heart," see 1 Kgs 3: 5–14. On King Solomon's wisdom's "universal" reputation see also 1 Kgs 5: 9–14. Firstly, Solomon built for himself, for his court and for his most important wife, Pharaoh's daughter, various palaces (see 1 Kgs 7: 1–12). On Solomon's various weddings to foreign women and the impressive list of his wives and concubines see 1 Kgs 11: 1–4. On Solomon introduction of foreign cults see 1 Kgs 11: 5–10. On the injunction to a king not to multiply horses and wives see Deut 17: 16. On Solomon horses and chariots see 1 Kgs 10: 26. On the fortifications that the king built at Jerusalem, Hazor, Megiddo and Gezer see 1 Kgs 9: 15. On the historical figure of Solomon see J. Maxwell Miller, J. H. Hayes, *A History of Ancient Israel and Judah*, Philadelphia 1986, pp. 189–217. See also the provocative book of I. Finkelstein and N. A. Silberman, *The Bible Unearthed, Archaeology's New Vision of Ancient Israel and the Origin of its Sacred Texts*, London 2001, pp. 123–149. For a more traditional view from the archaeological viewpoint see A. Mazar, *Archaeology of the Land of the Bible 10,000–586 BCE*, New York 1990, pp. 368–403.

[16] See Josephus, *AJ* XV, 385.

[17] The purpose of Solomon's Temple was to fulfill the needs of the royal court. His Temple is what Hayes and Maxwell-Miller calls a "Royal Chapel." See Maxwell Miller and Hayes, *History of Ancient Israel and Judah*, p. 202.

Solomon, dominating, simultaneously, the figure of the high priest, who ruled Judaea from the beginning of the Second Temple period.

Josephus mentions Herod yet again in connection with the House of David, describing how Herod, short of money, opened the tombs of David and Solomon and found golden furniture instead of money, which he took and most likely melted down. He then began to search for the bodies of David and Solomon, but at that moment "a flame burst upon the two guards sent to search the bodies." The guards were killed and Herod constructed a propitiatory monument on the spot.[18] According to Josephus, Nicolaus of Damascus also notes this monument, but does not mention the attempted tomb robbery by Herod, which Josephus, in any event, characterizes as slander in the form of a literary *topos*, since tyrants in the classical world are known to engage in the sacking of tombs and temples. Examples include Hieron of Syracuse and Gaius Caligula, who plundered the tomb of Alexander the Great. It is highly unlikely that Herod would have considered sacking the tomb, as Josephus would have us believe, and that if he did, that he would find any gold objects in it. After more than eight hundred years, the tomb, whose location was well known to all, would most likely have been robbed earlier. As already noted, Nicolaus does not mention such an episode, and I would suggest that Herod probably beautified the alleged tombs of David and Solomon to underscore his tie with the House of David, and in particular, with King Solomon, Herod's model. Through the building of a monument in Jerusalem – as Josephus saw it – Herod hoped to emphasize his connection with King Solomon and the Davidic dynasty. This was not an uncommon gesture in the Mediterranean world: rebuilding old and venerable tombs of heroes and historical personalities was a recognized way to claim and assert legitimate leadership.[19]

Yet another element – less tangible, but no less a source of prestige in the eyes of his Jewish subjects – may have likewise linked Herod to King David. This was the expansion of the Herodian kingdom, which more or less extended to the

---

[18] See Josephus, *AJ* XVI, 179–184.

[19] There are many examples. The first is Alexander the Great, who laid a wreath on the tomb of Achilles as soon as he landed in Asia Minor. His friend Hephaestion did the same at the tomb of Patroclus. See Arrian, *Anabasis* I, 12. See also R. Lane Fox, *Alexander the Great*, Harmondsworth 1987, p. 113. Augustus erected in the Roman Forum a shrine to his adoptive father Iulius Caesar as Divus Caesar. See *Res Gestae Divi Augusti*, IV 19 and Dio Cassius, *Roman History* LI, 22, 2–3. See also P. Zanker, *Augusto e il potere delle immagini*, Torino 1989, pp. 39, 86. Another good example: Apollonius of Tyana renewed the tombs of the Eretrians, deported to Media by the Persians. See Philostratus, *Life of Apollonius of Tyana* I, 24. See also G. Anderson, *Sage, Saint and Sophist: Holy Men and their Associates in the Early Roman Empire*, London 1994, p. 104. From Judaea come other examples. Herod rebuilt the Tomb of the Patriarchs at Hebron. See J. Lightstone, *The Commerce of the Sacred, Mediation of the Divine among Jews in the Graeco Roman Diaspora*, Brown Judaic Studies 59, Chico, (Ca.) 1984, pp. 70–71. According to Matthew, the Pharisees rebuilt the tombs of the prophets as an act of self glorification. See Matt 23, 29–30.

borders of the legendary kingdom of David, as described in the Second Book of Samuel. As ruler of a great empire, Herod could thus present himself to his Jewish subjects as the successor of King David.

Josephus can help us once more in highlighting the link between Herod and Solomon. As did Solomon before him, according to Hellenistic-Jewish writers, Herod clearly proved himself to be a generous *euergetes* in Phoenicia and in many Phoenician cities and colonies. He erected various monuments in the cities of Ascalon, Ptolemais, Berytus, Byblos, Sidon, the capital city of the legendary Souron, Tripolis, and Tyre, the city of Biblical Hiram.[20] We regard the *euergetism* shown by King Herod to the Hellenized Phoenician cities differently than we do his no less generous *euergetism* to the Greek cities of Syria, Asia Minor, and continental Greece, which will be analyzed later. To the former, Herod displayed his *euergetism* as a new Solomon. To the latter, Herod demonstrated his *euergetism* as a Hellenistic king, successor to Alexander the Great.

Last but not least, it is interesting to analyze the figure of King Solomon as depicted by Josephus in *Antiquities*. An initial reading shows that the figure of Solomon depicted by Josephus follows the First Book of Kings quite faithfully. However, there are some passages that appear to reflect an imaginary Solomon, possibly one who mirrors King Herod. There are, for instance, various feats achieved by Josephus' Solomon that were probably inspired by King Herod, including the rebuilding of Jerusalem's walls; Solomon's sacrifice in Hebron (which is not mentioned in the Bible), where Herod built a structure today known as Haram el-Khalil; the building of the Temple; and Solomon's royal palace in Jerusalem. Both structures, the Temple and the palace, were dominant features of Herodian Jerusalem. We may posit that Josephus' depiction of Solomon, inspired by Herod, goes back to Herodian claims associating Herod with Solomon, and given that Josephus' *Antiquities* were written more than eighty years after Herod's death, it is easy to understand that the figures of the two kings may have merged into one another post facto,[21] without Josephus having been entirely aware of the fact.

Another significant issue is whether or not Herod had Messianic aspirations. Schalit, for example, has underlined Herod's Messianic ideology,[22] but his thesis has met with widespread criticism.

---

[20] According to Josephus, *BJ* I, 422, Herod built *gymnasia* in Tripolis and Ptolemais, a city wall around Byblos, *stoas*, agoras, and temples at Berytus and Tyre, a theater at Sidon, and a bathhouse, fountains, agora and basilica at Ascalon.

[21] See Josephus, *AJ* VIII, 1–211. There are indeed various feats of Josephus' Solomon probably inspired by King Herod. On the rebuilding of Jerusalem's walls, see *AJ* VIII, 21 and 150; concerning his sacrifice in Hebron, see *AJ* VIII, 22–25; on the building of the Temple, see *AJ* VIII, 61–129; and on Solomon's royal palace in Jerusalem, see *AJ* VIII, 130–140. My thanks to Professor Daniel Schwartz, the Hebrew University of Jerusalem.

[22] According to Schalit, as the Pharisees saw clearly that the throne of Israel belonged to the legitimate House of David and not to the Hasmoneans or Herod, the latter, influenced by Pollio

Herod's attempt to persuade his Jewish subjects that he was the successor of the House of David reflected a policy followed by other Hellenistic rulers. The Macedonian rulers of Egypt and Syria likewise assumed the titles of rulers of the ancient Near East. The Ptolemies of Egypt became the Pharaohs of Egypt,[23] and the Seleucids of Syria, though to a lesser degree, presented themselves as the successors of the Great King or of the rulers of Babylon.[24] Unlike the Ptolemies and Seleucids, however, Herod was a native of the region which he ruled. Therefore Herod's own concept of royalty reflected an earlier concept found in the Ptolemaic and Seleucid Macedonian royal houses.

B. Herod and the Hasmonean Heritage

We shall now analyze the relationship between Herodian rule and the Hasmoneans who ruled Judaea before Herod and were subsequently ousted by him. First of all, I shall investigate the Hasmonean ideology of rule and how it was reflected in the various rulers' coins, followed by an analysis of which elements of the Hasmonean ideology of rule were adopted and appropriated by Herod.

From the beginning, the Hasmonean ruler was both a religious and a military figure. Judas Maccabaeus created a new type of Jewish leadership, since he was the military leader of the Jews, and hence a secular ruler, as well as their high priest and theocratic leader. The Seleucid overlords officially recognized the

---

(identified by Schalit as Hillel), developed his Messianic ideology, centered on the building of the Temple. See A. Schalit, *King Herod, Portrait of a Ruler*, Jerusalem 1962, pp. 232–234. See also A. Schalit, *König Herodes, Der Mann und Sein Werk*, Berlin 2001, pp. 471–474. See also A. Schalit, "Die herodianischen Patriarchen und der Davidische Herodes," *ASTI* 6, 1967–68, pp. 114–123. Schalit discusses Josephus' statement that Herod was *theophiles*, or beloved of God. See also E. Hammerschmidt, "Königsideologie im Spätantiken Judentum," *ZDMG* 113, 1963–64, pp. 493–511. According to Hammerschmidt as Herod could not become high priest, he sought recognition as Messiah.

[23] This aspect is, however, mainly a characteristic of the Ptolemies. See G. Grimm, "Le Sérapéion," in *La gloire d'Alexandrie, Musée du Petit Palais*, Paris 1998, pp. 94–98, A. Charron, "La sculpture en Égypte à l'époque ptolémaique," in *La gloire d'Alexandrie, Musée du Petit Palais*, Paris 1998, pp. 170–180, M. Chauveau, "Clergé et temples: rites, richesse et savoir," in *La gloire d'Alexandrie, Musée du Petit Palais*, Paris 1998, pp. 187–192, A. Charron, "Les Ptolémées et les animaux sacrés," in *La gloire d'Alexandrie, Musée du Petit Palais*, Paris 1998, pp. 192–201. A. K. Bowman, *Egypt after the Pharaohs 332 BC–AD 642*, London 1986, is very useful. See pp. 121–203 on the relationship between Greeks and natives and on the temples. C. Préaux, *Le monde hellenistique* I, Paris 1997, pp. 192–195 gives a general description of the phenomenon in the Hellenistic world, pp. 241–259, 264–265.

[24] The Seleucid Empire is still relatively unknown. The best reference to the relationship between the various native peoples, including the Jews, and the Seleucid rulers, is S. Sherwin-White and A. Kuhrt, *From Samarkhand to Sardis, A New Approach to the Seleucid Empire*, Berkeley 1993. On the ideology of kingship see pp. 129–132. On Babylonia see pp. 149–161. See also S. Sherwin-White and A. Kuhrt, *Hellenism in the East: The Interaction of Greek and Non-Greek Civilizations from Syria to Central Asia after Alexander*, Berkeley 1990.

successors of Judas Maccabaeus, first Jonathan and then Simon, as *strategos* and then *ethnarch*, or secular ruler of Judaea. Moreover their position as high priest was also officially recognized.[25]

John Hyrcanus succeeded his father Simon.[26] Although John Hyrcanus' title was only that of *ethnarch*, he considered himself to be an independent ruler, and thus the Hasmonean ideology of rule that he represented comprised a dual image that the Hasmonean ruler presented to his Jewish subjects – that of the high priest who had ruled Judaea from the beginning of the Second Temple Period, and that of Hellenistic king, the image that he presented to the wider Hellenistic world. John Hyrcanus was in fact the first Hasmonean ruler faced with the dilemma of defining the character of his rule. Was he to rule as did the various Macedonian Greek sovereigns or in the manner of the high priest of the Jews, or as both simultaneously? According to Barag,[27] John Hyrcanus was the first Hasmonean ruler to mint coins, doing so around 110 BCE, and his ideology of rule, his iconography of power, is reflected in his coins. The dichotomy of Jewish and Hellenistic ruler that is apparent on his coins was resolved by the adoption of Greek symbols that also have a Jewish significance, such as the helmet, a symbol of royal authority,[28] and the cornucopia, both single and double-crossed.[29] John Hyrcanus adopted the latter as the dynastic heraldic symbol of the Hasmoneans, similar to the eagle as symbol for the Ptolemies or the sixteen-pointed star for

---

[25] See on the first years of Judas Maccabaeus, 1 *Macc.* II, 1–VI, 17. See also Josephus, *AJ* XII, 265–353, *BJ* I, 31–40. See also Schürer, *History of the Jewish People* I, pp. 164–166. On Jonathan see 1 *Macc.* IX, 23–XII, 53. See also Josephus, *AJ* XIII, 1–61, 80–196, BJ I, 48–49. See also Schürer, *History of the Jewish People* I, pp. 174–188. On Simon, the last of the Maccabees see 1 *Macc.* XIII, 1–XVI, 24. See also Josephus, *AJ* XIII, 197–229, *BJ* I, 50–54. See also Schürer, *History of the Jewish People* I, pp. 189–199.

[26] On John Hyrcanus see Josephus, *AJ* XIII, 230–300, BJ I, 54–69. See also Schürer, *History of the Jewish People I*, pp. 200–215. During this long reign began the rift between the Hasmoneans and the Pharisees. See Josephus, *AJ* XIII, 288–298. The Pharisees did not regard the Hasmoneans as illegitimate secular rulers – rather, as illegitimate high priests.

[27] See D. Barag, "New Evidence on the Foreign Policy of John Hyrcanus I," *INJ* 12 1994, pp. 1–12.
See also Meshorer, *A Treasury of Jewish Coins*, p. 26.

[28] The helmet, also found on Seleucid coins, is a symbol of royal authority that emphasizes the tie between the king and his army. See Y. Meshorer, *Ancient Jewish Coinage I, Persian Period through Hasmonaeans*, New York 1982, pp. 66–67. Meshorer ties the helmet to John Hyrcanus II, and he attributes a Roman character to it. See also U. Rappaport, "The Hasmonean State and Hellenism," *Tarbitz LX*, 1991, pp. 481–490. The helmet as symbol of power appears on Seleucid coins. See B. V. Head, *A Guide to the Principal Coins of the Greeks, British Museum Department of Coins and Medals*, London 1959, pl. 27, no. 11, pl. 41, no. 26.

[29] The cornucopia is one of the royal dynastic symbols of the Hellenistic world and was adopted by both Seleucids and Ptolemies. See Meshorer, *Ancient Jewish Coinage I*, pp. 67–68. On the cornucopia on Ptolemaic coins see Head, *Coins of the Greeks*, pl. 33, nos. 22–23, pl. 34, no. 28. The double crossed cornucopia also appears on Nabataean coins. See D. R. Sear, *Greek Imperial Coins and their Values, the Local Coinages of the Roman Empire*, London 1991, for example p. 560, no. 5699.

the Argaead Dynasty. The cornucopia is also found on the coins of all successive Hasmonean rulers. The palm branch also expresses this dichotomy, having similar meanings for both Greeks and Jews.[30] Another symbol found on the coins of John Hyrcanus was the lily.[31]

Judas Aristobulus I, who succeeded his father John Hyrcanus in 104 BCE, adopted both the title of high priest, following the tradition of the early Hasmoneans, and the new title of king. He died after spending but a year on the throne,[32] and Alexander Jannaeus, his brother, succeeded him. The young Hasmonean ruler, like his brother, continued to rule as both high priest and king. It is clear from his coins that the title of king, written in Greek and not in Hebrew, has no Jewish meaning, but it has a purely Graeco-Macedonian meaning. On his coins, Alexander Jannaeus is named King Alexander, clearly the successor of Alexander the Great, who the Hasmonean king attempted to emulate with varying degrees of success. His ideology of royalty was thus clearly rooted in the Hellenistic conception of rule rather than in the Jewish one. Thus, for the Jewish subjects, his royal title had no real value, as it did not relate to any ancestral symbolism of royalty. On the contrary, it seems that the title of king was the fruit of international recognition in the Hellenistic world that the Hasmonean rulers Judas Aristobulus and Alexander Jannaeus so strived for. This legitimacy of rule, however, only had a value for the external Graeco-Macedonian world. For the Jews, Alexander Jannaeus was only the high priest.[33] An examination of the

---

[30] For the Greeks, the palm branch was one of the prizes awarded athletes victorious in competition. For the Jews, the palm branch had a religious connotation connected with the Feast of Sukkot. See Meshorer, *Ancient Jewish Coinage* I, pl. 43, nos. 01–04.

[31] The Jews associated the lily with the Temple. It therefore became one of the symbols of Jerusalem, the Temple-City, ruled by the high priest. John Hyrcanus first struck coins in Jerusalem for Antiochus VII. Later, in his autonomous coinage, he continued to use the lily. It represents his connection with the Temple and probably also his position as high priest. It is important to note that the lily was also adopted as a city symbol by Greek cities, most notably Rhodes. Once again, like the palm branch, the Jewish meaning was paralleled by a Greek one. It could be grasped in the Hellenistic *oikoumene* as the symbol of the city-state/polis of Jerusalem. See Meshorer, *Ancient Jewish Coinage I*, p. 63, pl. 43, nos. 01–04. For the coins of Rhodes in the Hellenistic period that depict the lily on the reverse (Helios is portrayed on the obverse) see Head, *Coins of the Greeks*, pl. 28, no. 31.

[32] See Josephus, *AJ* XIII, 301–319, *BJ* I, 70–84. See also Schürer, *History of the Jewish People I*, pp. 216–218.

[33] On Alexander Jannaeus' reign see Josephus, *AJ* XIII, 320–404, *BJ* I, 85–106. See also Schürer, *History of the Jewish People I*, pp. 219–228. According to Schalit, the Pharisean leadership could not accept that someone who was not an offspring of the House of David could sit on Judaea's throne. See Schalit, *King Herod*, p. 234. See also Schalit, *König Herodes*, p. 474. It appears, however, that what the Pharisees really contested was Alexander Jannaeus' position as high priest rather than his royal title, which was regarded as a valid title of secular leadership. For them as for the rest of the Jews, his royalty was merely a title of power as good as any other. According to D. Schwartz, the Pharisees did not oppose the Hasmoneans as high priests but as kings, as they opposed the linkage of religion and state. This linkage would have brought the former down with the latter. Schwartz bases his theory on various Talmudic texts such as BT,

coins minted by Alexander Jannaeus reveals his dual vision of the Macedonian Hellenistic conception of monarchy, derived from the figure of Alexander the Great, united with the idea of Jewish leadership that inhered in the figure of the high priest. As much as Alexander Jannaeus wished to show himself to the Greek Hellenistic outside world as one of the Diadochi of Alexander the Great, to his Jewish subjects he was first and foremost the high priest, and as such, was not an absolute ruler like Alexander the Great. He had to consult with and respect the decisions of the Council of the Jews and therefore presented himself to his Jewish subjects as willing to share his authority with that body. The wreath, a symbol of leadership and authority in the Hellenistic world, symbolically crowned both him and the Council of the Jews. The choice of Paleo-Hebrew script instead of square writing, then already in use for more than two hundred years, clearly has an ideological meaning. Alexander Jannaeus wanted to show his tie with the Biblical past, and perhaps, the continuity of his rule with that of the Oniad high priests.[34] The most striking symbol appearing on Alexander Jannaeus' coins is the sixteen-pointed star, symbol of the Argaead dynasty, together with the diadem,

---

Qidd. 66 a, a well-known *baraitha* in which the Pharisees ask King Alexander Jannaeus to retain the kingly crown, but to abdicate the priesthood. Schwartz sees the opposite in this source: the Pharisees wish King Alexander Jannaeus to abdicate as king, not as high priest. Another source is BT, *Hor.* 13 a, (see also t. *Hor.*13 a, 2:8, JT, *Hor.* 3: 9–48 b. There it is written that a sage takes precedence over a king of Israel as when the sage dies there is no replacement, but when a king dies all of Israel is fit for kingship and for his succession. Obviously, for the Pharisees there was no problem in a common Jew not from the stock of David ruling as king of Israel, whether he was a Hasmonean or Herod. Moreover, Schwartz adds that as priests, the Hasmoneans could not rule as kings. Last but not least, BT, *'Abod. Zar.* 8 b (also *Šabb.* 15 a). R. Jose writes that the wicked kingdom took over Israel 180 years before the Temple was destroyed. Schwartz stresses that the wicked kingdom was the Hasmoneans, not the Romans of Pompey. See D. Schwartz, "Joseph Ben Illem and the Date of Herod's Death," *Studies in the Jewish Background of Christianity,* WUNT 60, Tübingen 1992, pp. 44–56. And yet in later Rabbinic literature King Alexander Jannaeus appears as Jannai the King in Aramaic as well as Hebrew and not as high priest.

[34] Within ivy wreath on the reverse often appears in Paleo-Hebrew script the inscription "Jehonathan the High Priest and the Council of the Jews", as on the coins of his father. See Meshorer, *Ancient Jewish Coinage* I, pp. 63–66, 69–76. See also J. Naveh, *Early History of the Alphabet,* Jerusalem 1987, pp. 112–124. See also Rappaport, "The Hasmonean State and Hellenism," 1991, pp. 481–490. Symbols likewise emphasize the figure of a ruler split between the heritage of the broader Hellenistic-Greek world and of small and provincial Judaea. Thus, on the obverse of his coins appears the Greek inscription "Alexandrou Basileōs," or King Alexander. See Meshorer, *Ancient Jewish Coinage* I, p. 118. To make his message even more implicit, Alexander Jannaeus also minted a denomination with the inscription King Alexander in Aramaic, the language spoken by the lower strata of the neighboring populations. See Meshorer, *Ancient Jewish Coinage* I, pp. 79–80. And yet, King Alexander Jannaeus minted coins with the inscription in Hebrew "Jehonathan the King" on the obverse. These coins were intended for the Jewish population of the kingdom. See Schürer, *History of the Jewish People* I, p. 227. The inscription Jehonathan the King in Hebrew appears around the eight-rayed star. On the obverse, the anchor is depicted. See also Meshorer, *Treasury of Jewish Coins,* pp. 37–38. Another sub-type of the same coin, found in few specimens, bears a Hebrew inscription on the obverse, which has been interpreted "the king and high priest." Was it a mint mistake? According to Meshorer the coin must be regarded as a mere curiosity. See Meshorer, *Treasury of Jewish Coins,* pp. 38–39.

Figure I, 2 – Coin of Alexander Jannai, depicting on the obverse an anchor, on the reverse the Argead Star inscribed in a Diadem, (TJC, Group K, Coll. of Mr. J. P. Fontanille).

both being symbols of Hellenistic royalty.[35] The inverted anchor that appears on various types of coins minted by Alexander Jannaeus is also a Greek symbol that denotes domination of the sea (cfr. figure I, 2).[36]

Salome Alexandra succeeded her husband in 76 BCE,[37] and as soon as she relinquished the throne to her son, Hyrcanus II, civil war erupted between him and his brother Aristobulus II, ending abruptly through Pompey's intervention in 63 BCE.[38] The last Hasmonean king was Matthias Antigonus, son of Aristobu-

---

[35] Although the sixteen-pointed star is indeed the symbol of the Argaead Dynasty, from which Alexander the Great originated, the eight-pointed star was also considered an equivalent of the sixteen-rayed star. Thus, the simplified Argaead star, together with the diadem, clearly indicates that Alexander Jannaeus did not see himself as merely a Hellenistic king, but as the Diadoch of Alexander the Great. According to Meshorer, the eight-pointed star is merely a symbol with astral connotations that, together with the diadem, symbolized kingship. See Meshorer, *Ancient Jewish Coinage* I, pp. 60–61. Meshorer underlines the importance of the star in later periods. Bar Kokhba was called the Son of the Star in order to stress his Messianic appeal. Moreover the star, together with other astral symbols was common in Jewish art of Late Antiquity. According to Kanael the star is the Jewish symbol for monarchy. This interpretation comes from the Song of Balaam (Num 24: 17), "There shall come a star out of Jacob and a scepter shall rise out of Israel." In any case, both objects are part of the common heritage of the Eastern Mediterranean Hellenistic world. There are other coins that depict the eight-pointed star as a monarchic symbol, such as the reverse of the silver coins of Polemon I King of Pontus (36 BCE–8 BCE). See Z. H. Klawans, *An Outline of Ancient Greek Coins*, New York 1982, p. 192.

[36] This symbol was adopted earlier by the Seleucids. The coins with the anchor were probably minted after the conquest of the various coastal cities around 95 BCE. The inverted anchor was adopted by other Hellenistic rulers whose lands were once part of the Seleucid kingdom. The lily and the cornucopia, already present on the coins of John Hyrcanus I, were also found on the coins of Alexander Jannaeus. See Meshorer, *Ancient Jewish Coinage* I, pp. 62–63.

[37] She was obviously only a queen and not high priest. It is possible that by the end of the reign of Alexander Jannaeus the idea of a Hellenistic king who was also a high priest (and vice-versa) was accepted by most of the subjects. This made it easier for Salome to succeed her husband, thus enabling a woman to rule as queen, following the accepted dynastic rules of the Hellenistic period. Thus, a woman ruled the Kingdom of Judaea as Cleopatra ruled Egypt. See Josephus, *AJ* XIII, 405–432, *BJ* I, 107–119. See also Schürer, *History of the Jewish People* I, pp. 229–323.

[38] See Josephus, *AJ* XIV, 1–104, *BJ* I, 120–178. See also Schürer, History of the Jewish People I, pp. 233–242 and 267–269. Hyrcanus II, stripped of his royal title and various territories,

lus II.[39] At first, Antigonus' coins that were minted in Jerusalem continued the traditional iconography of the Hasmoneans, with the exception of the so-called siege coins, which depict the Menorah and the Showbread Table.[40]

I believe that the Hasmonean ideology of rule – that is, the depiction of the ruler as Jewish high priest with respect to his Jewish subjects and as Hellenistic king with respect to the outside, Hellenistic world – could only partly influence Herod's ruling ideology. In fact, the theocratic tradition was highly problematic for Herod and constituted a serious obstacle to his rule. In the first place, Herod, son of a commoner,[41] was not the scion of a priestly family. Thus he could not become high priest and could not aspire to rule Judaea. In fact, during the first years of his reign, Herod had to face the Hasmonean high priest's claims to the throne of Judaea. However, together with this theocratic tradition, Herod also inherited from the Hasmoneans – particularly from King Alexander Jannaeus – a tradition of kingship rooted totally in the Graeco-Macedonian world and that was completely alien to the Jewish tradition. This Graeco-Macedonian tradition was inherited and expanded by King Herod and will be analyzed in the next section of this chapter, because it is a foreign ideology tied to the wider Hellenistic world. The Hasmoneans, as well as Herod, shared a dual vision of ruler that they themselves invented and fashioned: a Jewish ruler with respect to their Jewish subjects and a Hellenistic ruler with respect to their Gentile subjects and the Hellenistic world. The main difference, of course, lies in the source of inspiration for the figure of the Jewish ruler: the high priest for the Hasmoneans, and the First Temple Judean king – especially Solomon – for Herod.

Herod was influenced by the Hasmonean ruling ideology, moreover, in other ways. He saw as his source of inspiration, for instanced, such Hasmonean rulers as King Alexander Jannaeus, and, in addition, Herod married into the Hasmonean dynasty in order to reinforce his rulership. Last but not least, various symbols found on Hasmonean coins appear on Herod's coins as well. Herod saw himself as the successor to the Hasmonean dynasty, as no less than the ideal successor of King Solomon. Born during the reign of Alexander Jannaeus, Herod was prob-

---

continued to rule over Judaea, Idumaea and parts of Galilee as high priest only. Iulius Caesar later restored the title of *ethnarch* to him.

[39] See Josephus, *AJ* XIV, 330–XV, 10, *BJ* I, 248–357. See also Schürer, History of the Jewish People I, pp. 281–286.

[40] The only "royal symbol" appearing on his coins is the cornucopia, both double-crossed and single, which indicates only his membership in the Hasmonean family. The coins minted by Mattathias Antigonus thus relate only to his role as high priest. His political message was directed to his Jewish subjects in Jerusalem rather than to the Parthian overlords or the surrounding world. The wreath with the Paleo-Hebrew inscription "Mattathias the high priest and the Council of the Jews" appears on the reverse of his coins depicting the cornucopia on the obverse. The siege coins minted in Jerusalem state even more emphatically his position as high priest, as they depict the Shewbread Table and the Menorah, two symbols associated with the Temple, exclusive dominion of the high priest. See Meshorer, *Ancient Jewish Coinage* I, pp. 87–97.

[41] See Josephus, *AJ* XIV, 78 and *BJ* I, 181 on Herod's birth.

Figure I, 3 – Coin of King Herod, depicting on the obverse an anchor, on the reverse a crossed Cornucopias with caduceus (TJC 59, Anepigraphic Variety, Coll. of Mr. J. P. Fontanille).

ably greatly influenced by him, and it is likely that the various achievements of Alexander Jannaeus, including his conquests on the coast and in Transjordan, the extension of the kingdom and his status in the Hellenistic world, greatly affected young Herod. We can surmise that Herod later measured his own success against the achievements of the Hasmonean king. By marrying Mariamme, niece of the Hasmonean high priest Hyrcanus II,[42] Herod attempted to secure his legitimacy in two ways. First, he promoted her brother Alexander to the high priesthood,[43] and thus came to be regarded as part of the Hasmonean family. Second, by marrying Mariamme, he ensured that his future heirs by her, Alexander and Aristobulus, would be of Hasmonean blood. Through them he could guarantee the definitive legitimacy of his dynasty. Herod's selection of Hasmonean royal names for his heirs to the throne is likewise noteworthy.[44]

In a similar vein, Herod minted various coins similar to those minted by the Hasmoneans, to emphasize the continuity of their dynastic policy. Many of these coins depict the anchor on the obverse and the double cornucopia on the reverse (cfr. figure I, 3). The anchor could symbolize Herod's continuation of the last Hasmonean's maritime policy. On the other hand, the message transmitted by the double cornucopia is clear: King Herod's legitimacy was tied to the Hasmonean dynasty, which Herod continued though his marriage to Mariamme and the birth of their children. As successor to the Hasmoneans, Herod felt entitled to depict the double cornucopia on his coins and thus adopted the Hasmonean heraldic symbol. The inscription in Greek within the wreath reads, "Of King Herod," clearly indicating that he, and not the Hasmoneans, was now the master.[45]

---

[42] See Josephus, *AJ* XIV, 467, *BJ* I, 344.

[43] See Josephus, *AJ* XV, 31–41, *BJ* I, 437.

[44] However it is interesting to mention that after the conquest of Jerusalem, Herod carried away the royal ornaments of the Hasmonean kings, probably the Hellenistic diadem and gave it to Mark Antony as a gift, together with plunder from his political foes. See Josephus, *AJ* XV, 5.

[45] See Meshorer, *Ancient Jewish Coinage* II, pp. 26–27. Pl. 2, Nos. 17–21.

3. Herod and the Hellenistic Ideology of Rule

A. Herod, the Last Hellenistic King

Herod's ideology of rule presented various elements shared by earlier and contemporary Hellenistic rulers. I shall first analyze the Hellenistic sovereigns' ruling ideology, and then, how their ideals are reflected in the coins that they minted, which provided a significant venue for the dissemination of propaganda. The Hellenistic ideals of rule were reflected in Herod's ideology of rule, and his coins, as key propaganda tools, played an important role in the Hellenistic iconography of power.

For King Herod, the ideal Hellenistic ruler was the all-powerful Hellenistic dynast, such as the Seleucid and the Ptolemaic rulers. Various Stoic philosophers theorized about the figure of the ideal Hellenistic ruler during this period.[46] A ruler other than Alexander the Great[47] – who served as a major source of inspiration for Herod, as well as for other Hellenistic rulers – was Antigonus Monophthalmos, the true creator of the Hellenistic state. He transformed the political ideal of the Argaead monarchy that ruled tiny Macedonia, a state composed of one *ethnos* and a few cities, into an real state capable of ruling a huge empire composed of various and distinct city-states and *ethnoi*, both Greek and barbarian.[48]

We may well ask if it is possible to create a typology of the Hellenistic king that is valid for all the Hellenistic potentates, including Herod, since all were modeled, ideally, after Alexander the Great and, from a practical point of view, after Antigonus Monophthalmos. According to Préaux,[49] the answer is affirmative. The ideal Hellenistic king undertook the primary and basic responsibilities established a hundred years earlier by the first rulers of Macedonia and continued by Philip II, which may be summarized as those of warrior, protector and feeder of the civil population, and supreme judge.[50] According to Préaux, it is Polybius, who best defines the most important qualities of the Hellenistic king in his funerary oration on Attalus I, these qualities being Attalus' wealth and his martial virtues.[51]

---

[46] Three treatises on kingship written by Stoic philosophers have survived. The Stoic philosophers Cleanthes of Assos, Perseus and Sphaerus of Borysthenes, wrote treaties on kingship. Thus, Seneca later wrote: "the best condition of a state is to be under a just king." See Seneca, *De Beneficiis* 2, 20. See Préaux, *monde hellenistique I*, p. 215.

[47] See Polybius, *History* V, 10. See Préaux, *monde hellenistique I*, p. 182.

[48] On Antigonus Monophthalmos, see R. A. Billows, *Antigonos the One-Eyed and the Creation of the Hellenistic State*, Berkeley 1997, pp. 155–156.

[49] See Préaux, *monde hellenistique I*, p. 181–294.

[50] See Préaux, *monde hellenistique I*, p. 183.

[51] See Préaux, *monde hellenistique I*, pp. 181–185 on Attalus I's qualities of wealth and martial virtues. See also Polybius, *History* XVIII, 41, 3. On wealth as one of the main components of the ideology of the Hellenistic king see Préaux, *monde hellenistique I*, pp. 208–212. As Isocrates (*Nicocles*, 19) recommends, a king must not take upon himself unnecessary burdens, thereby

3. Herod and the Hellenistic Ideology of Rule

Moreover, according to Polybius, Attalus I was also a good father, was faithful to his allies, and was always ready to fight for the freedom of the Greeks. Since the king needed to be victorious in war, he was also required to be the guardian of the various populations in his realm and guarantor of their prosperity by bringing peace, or *eirene*, to the kingdom. Throughout the Hellenistic period, with its constant wars, this remained a fixed ideal, and hence the ruler needed to wage war outside the borders of the kingdom, or in a border area, as in the example of the various wars between the Seleucids and the Ptolemies over Coile Syria fought in this region, and those in other border areas of their kingdoms.[52] Together with victory and peace, another important responsibility of the Hellenistic king was to act as guarantor of the fertility and prosperity of the lands he ruled.[53]

The abstract qualities that were attributed to the king as provider of prosperity, as noted above, also have concrete ramifications. First, a king was supposed to give presents to the Greek cities in his kingdom, and these presents were generally huge quantities of wheat intended for the poorer segment of the urban population.[54] Préaux also emphasizes that the Hellenistic king was a patron of the arts,[55] always surrounded by poets and philosophers and ready to display his own talents as poet, philosopher, and historian. A Hellenistic king was also

---

squandering his wealth, while at the same time, he must live like a king, surrounded by luxury. The negative view of wastage of wealth is repeated in the *Letter of Aristeas*, 205. See P. Green, *Alexander to Actium, the Historical Evolution of the Hellenistic Age*, Berkeley 1990, p. 422. The Macedonian king was first of all a warrior and indeed, a victorious warrior. Only in victory can the charismatic nature of the king display the protection and favor of the gods. The poets praised a victorious king; moreover, a king avid of glory was exalted. All of the Diadochi had to show their quality as warriors, such as Antigonus Monophthalmos and his son Demetrius Poliorcetes, but also kings who had already sat on a dynastic throne for more than a generation, such as Ptolemy IV at the battle of Raphia. A defeated king could lose his throne to another king or to a pretender and end his days in exile or publicly executed. The regent Perdiccas or Antigonus Monophthalmos are good examples. For later periods, Perseus of Macedonia or Mithridates VI King of Pontus are good examples. The Hasmonean rulers provide an equally good example. Alexander Jannaeus, after his defeat by the Seleucid Antiochus, lost both the throne and the loyalty of most of his subjects. Following the conquest of Jerusalem by Herod, King Mattathias Antigonus ended his days on the block of his executioner, the Roman *secator*. On victory as one of the main components of the ideology of the Hellenistic king see Préaux, *monde hellenistique I*, pp. 181–202.

[52] On the Hellenistic king as guarantor of peace see Préaux, *monde hellenistique I*, p. 201.

[53] On the Hellenistic king as guarantor of fertility and prosperity see Préaux, *monde hellenistique I*, p. 201–230. Homer wrote that the fertility of the soil is tied to the good rule of the king. See Homer, *Odyssey* XIX, 111–114.

[54] The generosity of Alexander in this regard was well known. Antigonus Monophthalmos gave no less than 150,000 *medimnes* of barley to the city of Athens in 307 BCE, enough to nourish at least 150,000 persons for a month. Attalus I, the paradigm of later Hellenistic royalty, gave no less than 10 talents and 10,000 *medimnes* of wheat to Sycion (Polybius, *History* XVIII, 16). Not surprisingly, the city voted him a golden statue and an annual sacrifice. See Préaux, *monde hellenistique I*, pp. 202–207.

[55] The Letter of Aristeas is a very good example. See Préaux, *monde hellenistique I*, p. 182.

philanthropos (lover of mankind)[56] and he was supposed to be just (*dikaiosune*). Isocrates stresses that "the king's wish is law," but also that one of the most important qualities of the king is his "justice in judgment." Since the king is the supreme judge, this quality is one of the most important with respect to both the wealthier and poorer population groups among his subjects. The basic expression of the sense of justice is the love of truth (*alētheia*), at least in theory, and thus truth is supposed to be the main source and basic guarantee of justice.[57]

Finally, the Hellenistic ruler is the providential, or perhaps more correctly, the fortunate ruler (shielded by Tyche).

---

[56] See Préaux, *monde hellenistique I*, p. 207. Isocrates (*Nicocles*, 15) already recognized that *philanthropia* is one of the most important royal qualities. From then on, *philanthropia* became a concept requiring fulfillment among both Greeks and barbarians. Thus, Polybius, *History* V, 11 condemned Philip V of Macedonia for not behaving as a good leader should by demonstrating *philanthropia* in time of war. The view expressed in the Letter of Aristeas, 190-192 on *philanthropia* is noteworthy. *Philantropia* is the way of God. Thus, *philanthropia* became an imitation of God that, if followed by the ruler, would bring the ruler nearer to God. *Philantropia* was, according to Goldin, the main ideal in the rule of the Oniad high priests. According to the statement attributed to him in m. 'Abot I, 4, Simon II the Just states that the world rests on three pillars: the Torah or the Law; *avodah*, or the Temple service; and *gemilut hasadim* or *philanthropia*. These are the fundamental and ideal characteristics of Jewish priestly rule. The high priest, who leads the Temple service, is bound to the Torah, the legal code of the Jews. However, if he wishes to be a successful ruler, popular among his subjects, he must go beyond that, showing himself voluntarily as *philanthropos* towards his subjects. The two earlier ruling ideals of the Oniad high priest, a heritage of the Persian period, are now combined with the Greek ideal of *philanthropia*. For the Greek philosophers, *philanthropia* is a voluntary act that goes beyond legal duties. It is an act of kindness that is also a Divine attribute (*eleos, eusebeia, charis*). Thus the entire statement in m. 'Abot I, 4, which expresses the idea of reciprocity, must be read in fact as a political contract between the ruler and his subjects. *Philanthropia* - the exchange of favors and kindness between the ruler and his subjects - is helpful since it keeps the Jews close to the Law of the Fathers. However, Torah, or the Legal Code, and *avodah*, the Temple Service, are no longer sufficient in the new age of humanism, in which the man, and not the gods, stands at the center of philosophical speculations. The concept of *philanthropia* thus expresses a tie of friendship that consists of the bond of mutual aid. *Philanthropia* is the *conditio sine qua non* for a successful interclass relationship and thus for the popularity of the ruler. The Oniad high priest adopted a basic Hellenistic concept as an attribute of rule. See Goldin, "The Three Pillars of Simon the Righteous," pp. 43–58. See also Bickerman, *Jews in the Greek Age*, pp. 258–259, 284–287.

[57] On the wish of the king as law see Isocrates, *To Daemonicus* 36 and Préaux, *monde hellenistique I*, p. 271. On the king's justice in judgment see Isocrates, *Evagoras*, 41. See also Préaux, *monde hellenistique I*, pp. 183, 212. Isocrates, *Nicocles*, 22. For example Arrian, *Anabasis of Alexander* I, 1, writing quite seriously that his main and most reliable source for the life of Alexander were the memoirs of Ptolemy I, adds that he found them truthful, as it is more shameful for a king to lie than for anyone else. It is interesting that Polybius, *History* XIII, 3 scorns Philip V of Macedonia, his bête noire, because during the war he utilized a *ruse de guerre* that did not suit the dignified behavior of a king. Polybius, *History* XXVIII, 18, also reproaches Antiochus IV for the *ruse de guerre* used by him to conquer Pelusium. A possible and practical way for a Hellenistic king to strive for truth is to listen carefully to the complaints of his subjects. The well-known reply to Demetrius Poliorcetes by an old woman who the king would not listen to for lack of time was that he should, then, not be king. See Plutarch, *Life of Demetrius* 42.

3. Herod and the Hellenistic Ideology of Rule

The Hellenistic ideology of rule, as mentioned earlier, is clearly reflected in the coins minted by the rulers. Royal power was symbolized in Hellenistic iconography by the diadem and the signet ring,[58] and more specifically on coins bearing the ruler's portrait. Thus, the ruler's head crowned by the diadem was the most common motif on Hellenistic coins and symbolized royal power. Victory, so important for a king, was represented by the military helmet, as well as by the Macedonian shield.[59] The personification of victory, as well as the military helmet and the Macedonian shield, are depicted on various coins minted by the Hellenistic rulers.

Herod fit the ideal model of Hellenistic ruler perfectly, and the parallel with Attalus I is indeed striking. Herod accrued enormous private wealth, far more than Attalus, and this personal wealth, as well as Herod's *tryphe*, was legendary. This alone made Herod the prototype of the Hellenistic ruler. The luxurious court of King Herod will be analyzed in the next chapter, and his enormous wealth, as well as his sources of income, will be analyzed in the chapter dealing with the economics of the period.

Herod's rise to power was due both to his exploits as a warrior and to his diplomatic facility and generosity. He won military victories over the "barbarian" Nabataeans, and Augustus granted him various territories. Like Attalus, Herod always assisted his friends – the Tower of Hippicus, for instance, was named after a friend of Herod – and he strived to be a good father to his subjects, though few Hellenistic rulers had a worse family life than Herod. He was a most faithful king to his allies, as in the case of Attalus I and the immensely powerful Romans, and was always ready to act as the most generous *euergetes* to the Greek cities outside his kingdom, as we shall see. Herod also acted as *euergetes* within his kingdom, towards his own subjects, Jew and Gentile alike. He erected beautiful monuments in Jerusalem, the capital of his kingdom, and founded Gentile cities within his kingdom, including Sebaste, Caesarea Maritima, and Paneas. Moreover, Herod helped his subjects during the course of the famines of 25–24 BCE and 20–19 BCE.[60] Unlike the Hasmoneans, who, with the possible exception of Salome Alexandra, were not known for such wide-ranging generosity, Herod provided the city of Jerusalem and other urban areas of the kingdom, including the two Greek cities of Caesarea Maritima and of Sebaste, with gifts of wheat during periods of famine. Herod also purchased wheat from Roman Egypt,

---

[58] See Préaux, *monde hellenistique I*, p. 185. It is well known that Alexander, during his last hours in Babylonia, when asked by his generals to whom he would give his signet ring, replied, "to the best." See Lane Fox, *Alexander the Great*, pp. 467 and 471. According to one version, Alexander left his signet ring to Perdiccas.

[59] See Préaux, *monde hellenistique I*, p. 184.

[60] On Herod as victorious commander in the First Nabataean War see Josephus, *AJ* XV, 108–160 and *BJ* I, 364–385. On the foundation of Sebaste see Josephus, *AJ* XIII, 275 and *BJ* I, 64; of Caesarea Maritima see Josephus, *AJ* XIV 76, 121, *XV* 331–341 and *BJ* I, 156, 408–414; on the Temple building see Josephus, *AJ* XV, 380–415 and *BJ* I, 401.

paying for it out of his own pocket. This is probably the explanation for Herod's title *euergetes*, which has been found on a stone weight.[61] Like Salome Alexandra before him, Herod endeavored to bring long periods of complete peace to his subjects and succeeded in doing so more than any previous Hellenistic rulers.

Like Attalus I, Herod was also a patron of the arts, and as we shall see in the next chapter, philosophers, poets, and historians such as Nicolaus of Damascus surrounded Herod. In addition, Herod himself wrote a book of memoirs.

Among his other traits, Herod could also demonstrate *philanthropia* or mercy. When he conquered Jerusalem, for example, he ordered his soldiers to spare the civilian population. He complained to Mark Antony about the merciless behavior of the latter's soldiers when they sacked the city. Later Herod spared two Pharisean leaders, Pollio and Sameas – who, years before, had faced him in the *synedrion*, when he was protected only by his personal guard – in a true act of *philanthropia*. Indeed his *philanthropia* paid off: just as the mother, wife, and daughters of Darius III became unfailing supporters of Alexander, so both Pollio and Sameas later became two of Herod's supporters among the Pharisees.[62]

Herod likewise fits the paradigm of the ideal "just" Hellenistic ruler very well. Evidence for this may be found in Josephus' *War* and *Antiquities*, which never report any acts of injustice by Herod towards his subjects. In fact, Josephus writes that Herod was known to dress as one of the people and was attentive to the mood of his subjects and their views regarding his rule.[63] Obviously the purpose was a practical one, allowing him to know if any of his subjects were rebellious, or if he had committed any act of injustice in the eyes of his subjects. Of course one might ask if the act of spying on ones subjects can be regarded as "love of truth," but Herod evidently disliked false adulation and was prepared to dress as a commoner in order to learn the truth. Ignoring the true mood of one's subjects was very dangerous, he believed, since it isolated the king from the tenor of their feelings towards him.

Herod's Hellenistic ruling ideology is also reflected in the iconographic repertoire of his coins. Like Alexander Jannaeus before him, Herod preferred to depict the diadem alone, without a portrait. The diadem found on Herod's coins underlines the Jewish character of the Herodian monarchy, but also represents a clear symbol of rule for Herod's Greek subjects. Herod's son Philip, who ruled a non-Jewish territory, as well as the Jewish kings Agrippa I and Agrippa II, had no

---

[61] On Herod's help to his subjects during drought see Josephus, *AJ* XV, 299–316. This title is found on a stone weight, dated from Herod's thirty-second year of rule (8 BCE). See Y. Meshorer, "A Stone Weight from the Reign of Herod", *IEJ* 20, 1970, p. 97.

[62] On Herod restraining the Romans in Jerusalem see Josephus, *AJ* XIV, 482–486. On Herod's mercy to Pollio and Sameas see Josephus, *AJ* XV, 2–4.

[63] See Josephus, *AJ* XV, 367. Note the similarity between Josephus' account of Herod and Plutarch's account of Demetrius Poliorcetes. The Essenes were required to report on each other to perfect communal harmony. See Josephus, *BJ* II, 141. Josephus writes that the new Essene will be "perpetually a Lover of Truth," as a spy on other Essenes.

Figure I, 4 – Coin of King Herod from Sebaste, depicting on the obverse a Helmet, on the reverse the Macedonian Shield (TJC 45 c, Coll. of Mr. J. P. Fontanille).

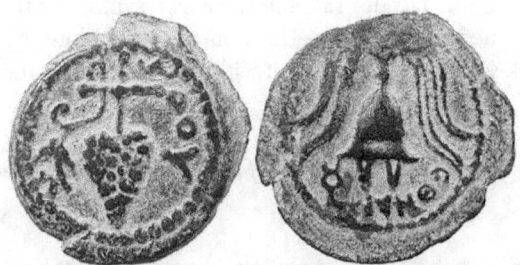

Figure I, 5 – Coin of Archelaus, depicting on the obverse a wine grape, on the reverse a helmet (12611 aehaLG Courtesy, Herkules Numismatics)

problem placing their portrait on the obverse of their coins.[64] The helmet as symbol of rule, as well as the Macedonian shield, representing victory, is also found on the coins of Herod. Thus, on the second of the four denominations minted in Samaria in the third year of his rule, Herod depicted a crested helmet on the obverse and the Macedonian shield on the reverse (cfr. figure I, 4).[65] Archelaus, Herod's successor, also minted coins in Jerusalem depicting the Macedonian helmet, probably as a symbol of his authority as tetrarch (cfr. figure I, 5).[66]

One of the Herodian coins struck in Jerusalem clearly expressed his royal ideology and authority in terms comprehensible to the Greek world. On the obverse it depicts a single cornucopia and on the reverse, a small eagle with cropped wings.[67] This small bronze coin was clearly inspired by larger Ptolemaic

---

[64] See Meshorer, *Ancient Jewish Coinage* II regarding Philip's portrait on coins (pp. 45–46 and pl. 7, nos. 1, 2, and pl. 8 nos. 12–13). On Agrippa I's portrait on coins, see pp. 54–55, pl. 9, nos. 6–6 a. On Agrippa II's portrait on coins, see p. 74, and pl. 11, nos. 4–4 a.

[65] See Meshorer, *Ancient Jewish Coinage*, II, pp. 9–10, 18–20, 22 and pl. 1, nos. 2–2 b. Meshorer underlines the similarity with Roman coins. The Macedonian shield is depicted on a wall of the tomb of Lyson and Callicles at Leucadia in Macedonia. See Romeopulos, *Leucadia - Archaia Mieza*, pp. 41, pl. 39.

[66] See Meshorer, *Ancient Jewish Coinage*, II, p. 33, pl. 5, nos. 6–6 e.

[67] See Meshorer, *Ancient Jewish Coinage*, II, pl. 3, nos. 23–23 c.

and Seleucid denominations in gold and silver. The cornucopia and the eagle do not appear together on the Ptolemaic and Seleucid coins.[68] Generally the cornucopia, as well as the eagle, appears on the reverse, while the image of the ruler is depicted on the obverse. However, as indicated above, Herod and the Hasmoneans did not include their own portraits on their coins, probably to show respect for the sensibilities of their Jewish subjects. The symbolic meaning of the cornucopia has already been discussed. The eagle in the Greek world was the attribute of Zeus, king of the gods, and thus of the ruler of flesh and blood who derived his authority from Zeus. Herod would not have depicted any pagan symbol on his coins. In fact, in the Near East, the eagle was also seen as a divine symbol. Moreover, some of the Jews (obviously not those who pulled down the eagle from the Temple façade) saw the eagle as a symbol of the ruling power, whoever it happened to be. Like the Hasmoneans before him, Herod once more adopted a Greek symbol and invested it with "Jewish" significance.[69]

B. Herod's Euergetism: The Expression of Herod's Power as Hellenistic King in Foreign Policy

As noted earlier, probably the most obvious characteristic of Herod's philhellenism and his conscious behavior as Hellenistic king was his *euergetism*,[70] which found expression in generous gifts bestowed on Greek cities around the Greek world, or *koinē*. Herod's *euergetism* towards the Hellenistic world continued a long tradition of *euergetism* begun by Philip II of Macedonia, who was the first

---

[68] See Head, *Principal Coins of the Greeks*, pl. 20, no. 20, pl. 33, no. 23, pl. 34, no. 24, no. 26, pl. 40, no. 24, pl. 41, no. 29.

[69] The eagle as symbol of the ruling power appears in Biblical texts such as Ezek 1: 10 and 17: 7. In Rabbinic literature it appears in the *Exod. Rab.* 23, 13. See Meshorer, *Ancient Jewish Coinage* II, pp. 29–30.

[70] *Euergesia* was the urge to "do good" by public benefactions. It is possible to distinguish between two types of *euergetism*. Benefactions to one's own city and citizens were generally a characteristic of the polis' *bouleutes* in the Greek East and of the *curiales* in the Latin West. Benefactions to foreign cities or peoples, on the other hand, were the prerogatives of kings alone. Herod engaged in both types of *euergetism*. These gifts consisted not only in economic aid in time of crisis, but also in public and religious buildings erected at the expenses of the benefactor, which adorned the city. The inscription set on the building made clear who the generous *euergetes* was. Moreover *euergetism*, because of its own consecrating nature, was also one of the best ways to underline the *euergetes*' prominence in the political arena. The recipient of the *euergetes*' generosity was the civic body, the polis, rather than individuals. Thus, when the *euergetes* helped the poor of the city, he did so not because they were poor, but because they were part of the civic body. Brown compares pagan *euergetism* to that of the Late Roman Christian bishops, who called themselves *philoptochoi*, or "lovers of the poor." The poor were the beneficiaries of the bishop's charity, but by then the civic authorities of the city were waning and the secular *euergetes*' power ceased to exist after the third century crisis. See P. Brown, *Poverty and Leadership in the Later Roman Empire. The Menahem Stern Jerusalem Lectures*, Hanover (NH) 2002, pp. 3–6.

Hellenistic ruler to make an impressive show of *euergetism* to the Greek world. After Philip II, most of the Greek rulers – the Ptolemies, the Seleucids, the Antigonids, the Attalids and Mithridates VI of Pontus – used *euergetism* as both a form of economic assistance and a means of building and construction, to push forward their political interests and their prominence in the Greek world.[71]

Josephus, illustrating and cataloging Herod's generosity to various Greek cities, provides the perfect definition of the *euergetes*: "He (Herod) seems to have conferred, and that after a most plentiful manner, what would minister to many necessities, and the buildings of public works, and gave them the money that was necessary to such works as wanted it, to support them upon their failure of other revenues."[72]

The most important act of *euergetism* was probably the restoration of the city of Olympia in Elis and of the Olympic Games after years of neglect.[73] According to Josephus, Herod helped to finance the revenues of the Olympic center, probably contributed to the erection of various buildings, restored others, and financed the annual sacrifices. Herod was thus declared *agonothetes*, one of the perpetual managers of the Olympic Games. He appears to have presided over the 50th Olympiad during his trip to Rome in 12 BCE.[74] As with Philip II before him, presiding over the Olympic Games gave Herod enormous prestige in the Greek world, and in restoring the city of Olympia, Herod breathed new life into one of the cultural linchpins of Hellenism. On the other hand, by restoring the Olympic Games, Herod, also promoted the cultural position of the Jews in the eyes of the Greeks. After Herod, the next benefactor of the Olympic Games was the emperor Nero, well known for his philellenism.[75]

---

[71] On Philip II's *euergetism* see "Le dediche macedoni all'esterno della Macedonia" in Ginouvès (ed.), *Macedoni*, pp. 194–196. On the *euergetism* of the Ptolemies see "Le dediche macedoni all'esterno della Macedonia" in R. Ginouvès (Ed.), *I Macedoni, da Filippo II alla conquista romana*, Milano 1993, pp. 202–213. On the *euergetism* of Antiochus IV Epiphanes see W. Bell Dinsmoor, *The Architecture of Ancient Greece*, London 1985, pp. 280–281. On the the *euergetism* of Antigonids see "Le dediche macedoni all'esterno della Macedonia" in Ginouvès (Ed.), *Macedoni*, pp. 196–202. The best-known *euergetes* of the Hellenistic period were the kings of Pergamum. Attalus I, Attalus II and Eumenes II bestowed various buildings upon the Greek cities, the best-known being the Stoa of Attalus I at Delphi, the main oracular center of continental Greece and the Stoa of Attalus II in the Agora of Athens. See M. Andronicos, *Delphi*, Athens 1983, p. 9. and V. A. *The Athenian Agora, A Guide to the Excavations and Museum*, American School of Classical Studies at Athens, Athens 1990, pp. 130–135. On the *euergetism* of Mithridates VI of Pontus see P. Zaphiropoulou, *Delos, Monuments and Museum*, Athens 1983, p. 49.

[72] See Josephus, *AJ* XVI, 146. Josephus records an impressive list of buildings erected by Herod in the Greek world in *AJ* XVI, 146–148 and *BJ* I, 422–428. The list in *BJ* is more complete and detailed than the list found in *AJ*.

[73] See Josephus, *AJ* XVI, 149 and *BJ* I, 426–428.

[74] See Josephus, *BJ* I, 427.

[75] See D. W. Roller, *The Building Program of Herod the Great*, Berkeley 1998, pp. 230–231. On Nero's visit to the Olympic Games in 66 CE see M. T. Griffin, *Nero, the End of a Dynasty*, London 1984, pp. 162–163.

Along with Olympia, Athens was the undisputed center of Greek culture. Greatly damaged during the Mithridatic Wars by the siege and sack of Sulla in 86 BCE, the city required considerable assistance. According to Josephus,[76] Herod donated *anathemata*, or votive dedications in Athens. Hyrcanus II had earlier placed his own statues in the cultic precinct of Demos and the Charites,[77] and thus Herod was not the first ruler of Judaea to confer his *euergetism* on Athens.

According to Roller, it is quite possible, that Herod erected, at his own expense, the Temple of Rome and Augustus on the Acropolis,[78] a round Ionic building constructed of white marble.[79] Moreover, inscriptions from the bases of two statues, both found on the Acropolis, mention Herod first as *philoromaios* and later as *philokaisar*.[80] It is quite possible that these two statues honoring Herod stood near the Temple of Rome and Augustus, whose inscription does not record any *euergetes*. Herod thus wished to legitimize his ties with the source of Greek culture and, moreover, wished to underline his ties with Rome in the most important spot in the Classical world. Once again, his position as king of Judaea was greatly enhanced.

Herod also built in Sparta, once the political leader of the Peloponnesus, but now in a state of severe political decline after the fourth century BCE. As with Athens, there was a long tradition of friendship between Sparta and the Judaean state, going back to a treaty of friendship between the High Priest Onias I and Areus, King of Sparta.[81] Herod also had a personal motive for showing his *euergetism* towards Sparta, since his well-known courtier, Eurycles, came from Lacedaemon, and Herod wanted to show him respect and friendship through consistent acts of *euergetism* towards his motherland.

Pergamum also was indebted to Herod's *euergetism*.[82] The Asian city was not only the seat of one of the most important cultural centers of the Hellenistic world, but also the capital of the Roman province of Asia. The Temple of Rome and Augustus stood at Pergamum. For Herod, it was once again clear that his

---

[76] See Josephus, *BJ* I, 425.

[77] See Josephus, *AJ* XIV, 149–155. See also Roller, *Building Program of Herod the Great*, p. 219.

[78] See Roller, *Building Program of Herod the Great*, p. 220. According to Roller it is quite probable that Herod erected the Temple of Augustus and Rome.

[79] See G. Papathanassopoulos, *The Acropolis, Monuments and Museum*, Athens 1977, p. 47.

[80] On the first statue Herod is named as Philoromaios (OGIS, 414 and IG2.2.3440). The statue was erected in honor of his good deeds and favors to the city. The other statue (IG 2.2.3441) named Herod as *philokaisar* and honored his virtue and good deeds. A similar inscription to IG 2.2.3441 comes from the Agora. See Roller, *Building Program of Herod the Great*, p. 219.

[81] See 1 Macc. 12, 21–23 and Josephus, *AJ* XII, 225–228. According to the letter of Areus, the friendship between Judaea and Sparta goes back to the time of Abraham, as both the Jews and the Lacedaemonians were his descendants. The only possible explanation for this strange letter is that both Sparta and Jerusalem were known in the Greek world to have a peculiar political constitution. See also Roller, *Building Program of Herod the Great*, pp. 236–237.

[82] See Josephus, *BJ* I, 425.

role as *euergetes* towards this city strongly emphasized his commitment to Greek culture and his devotion to Rome.[83]

Another cultural center of the Hellenistic East closely tied to Rome was Rhodes. Herod displayed his *euergetism* toward this city in two ways, by erecting Apollo Pythius' temple at Rhodes and by repairing the Rhodian war fleet. If the first act of *euergetism* benefited Rhodes, the second clearly served the purposes of Rome. The Rhodian war fleet could clear the surrounding waters of pirates, who were the eternal scourge of the Mediterranean during that period of time.[84]

Yet another Greek center where Herod demonstrated his devotion to Rome was in Samos. Agrippa, Herod's *patronus*, had had his headquarters on this Ionian island[85] in 23 BCE, at a time when it was no longer a political or cultural center. Did Herod also finance the cult of Augustus on this island?[86] Herod likewise benefited smaller Greek centers such as Coos, where he funded an annuity and erected a gymnasium,[87] and Chios, where he had the city stoas repaired in 14 BCE.[88] Since Chios was renowned in the Greek world as the birthplace of Homer, the pillar of Hellenic culture, this maybe influenced Herod's decision to help Chios.

Ionia, Lycia, and the rest of Asia Minor,[89] including some small cities of Cilicia, likewise benefited from Herod's *euergetism*, which he displayed toward populations that adopted Hellenic culture but were not of Hellenic stock, such as the Lycians and the Cilicians,[90] no less than the Jews.

Herod also displayed his *euergetism* in Syria, which had once been the political center of the Seleucid Empire and was now a Roman province. His *euergetism* was displayed toward small centers such as Syah and Phasaelus in Batanaea[91] and cities such as Laodicea, where Herod built an aqueduct,[92] Damascus, where he built a gymnasium and a theater,[93] and the huge city of Antioch on the Orontes,[94] where he constructed a well-known colonnaded street, twenty stadia long, with

---

[83] See Roller, *Building Program of Herod the Great*, p. 231.
[84] See Josephus, *AJ* XIV, 147 and *BJ* I, 424. The Temple of Apollo Pithius was situated in the northern part of the ancient city. See also Roller, *Building Program of Herod the Great*, pp. 233–234.
[85] See Josephus, *BJ* I, 425.
[86] See Roller, *Building Program of Herod the Great*, p. 235.
[87] See Josephus, *BJ* I, 424. See also Roller, *Building Program of Herod the Great*, pp. 226–228.
[88] See Josephus, *AJ* XVI, 17-19. See also Roller, *Building Program of Herod the Great*, pp. 223–224.
[89] See Josephus, *BJ* I, 425.
[90] See Josephus, *BJ* I, 428.
[91] See Josephus, *BJ* I, 428.
[92] See Josephus, *BJ* I, 422.
[93] See Josephus, *BJ* I, 422. See also Roller, *Building Program of Herod the Great*, pp. 224–225.
[94] See Josephus, *AJ* XIV, 148 and *BJ* I, 425.

columns of marble, that cut the city in two and formed its north-south axis, dominating the urban structure of the city.[95]

It is likely that Herod built this type of structure in Antioch in order to emphasize his position as king of Judaea in the Seleucid capital. On the one hand, Herod wished to show that a king of Judaea now dominated the Seleucid capital from which Antiochus IV promulgated his terrible decrees against Judaism, and on the other hand, he wished to pacify and benefit a city that was seen still by many Jews as the capital of the wicked Seleucids. Antioch, moreover, was home to a large Jewish community. Herod's act of *euergetism* would clearly have brought benefits to the Jewish population, as well as elevating them in the eyes of their non-Jewish fellow citizens.[96] The colonnaded street, probably a creation of Herod's architects, was to become an important feature in Roman Imperial architecture. From the second century CE, most of the Roman cities in the Near East, including Gerasa, Palmyra, Caesarea Maritima, Aelia Capitolina and those in Africa, such as Timgad and Leptis Magna, had colonnaded streets as their main urban feature.[97]

Herod did not build any structures in Alexandria, nor is there is any record of his *euergetism* there. Since Egypt, including Alexandria, was an Imperial province and hence the personal domain of Augustus, Herod did not wish to undermine Augustus' absolute domination of Egypt. As we shall see later, however, Herod wanted his royal court to outshine the Ptolemaic royal court at Alexandria as the cultural capital of the Hellenistic world.

Herod was a faithful ally of Rome, and his *euergetism* in the Hellenistic world was intended to celebrate his own glory, as well as that of his overlords Augustus and Rome itself. Herod saw himself as the vicar of Augustus in the East, and thus, according to Josephus, he erected most of the public buildings of Nicopolis, the city of victory which had been erected by Augustus at Actium, on the spot where, in 31 BCE, he and Agrippa had defeated Mark Antony and Cleopatra.[98] Strabo describes various public buildings of Nicopolis, such as the *temenos* of

---

[95] Josephus in *BJ* I, 428 do mention only one *stoa*. However in *AJ* XIV, 148 he mentioned two *stoas*. It is much more probable that Herod built columns on both sides of the street rather than on one, which would have been unaesthetic. J. Malalas, 223, the Byzantine chronicler of Antioch from the sixth century CE writes that Herod paved the main street outside Antioch with white stones. According to Roller, the word "outside" means outside the Seleucid foundation of the city. See Roller, *Building Program of Herod the Great*, p. 214. On Hellenistic and Roman Antioch see C. Kondoleon, "The City of Antioch: An Introduction," in *Antioch, the Lost Ancient City*, Princeton (NJ), 2000, p. 9.

[96] On Antiochia's Jewish community see B. J. Brooten, "The Jews of Ancient Antioch," in C. Kondoleon, *Antioch, the Lost Ancient City*, Princeton 2000, pp. 29–33.

[97] On the colonnaded street of Antioch and its influence on later Roman architecture, see H. Hesberg, "The Significance of the Cities in the Kingdom of Herod," *Judaea and the Greco-Roman World in the Time of Herod in the Light of Archaeological Evidence*, Abhandlungen der Akademie der Wissenschaften in Göttingen, Göttingen 1996, p. 17.

[98] See Josephus, *AJ* XIV, 147 and *BJ* I, 425.

Apollo, the gymnasium, and the stadium, which was associated with the games of Apollo Actium.⁹⁹ Archaeological excavations have brought to light the city's *bouleuterion*, the odeon, and two harbors that are 7 km. apart.¹⁰⁰

Which of these buildings were built at Herod's expense? Evidence indicates that since the Actian games were celebrated under the supervision of Eurycles of Sparta, a close friend and courtier of Herod, Herod probably showed his *euergetism* towards the *temenos* of Apollo, the *gymnasium*, and the *stadium*, all of which are buildings mentioned by Strabo and which were connected to the Actian games. Moreover, these games celebrated both Augustus and Agrippa as victors at Actium.

The question arises as to why Herod, rather than Augustus or Agrippa, financed the building of Nicopolis. For Augustus to have done so would not have been a wise political act. Since he presented himself as the bearer and defender of Italic values, as opposed to those of the Greek East, such an act would have contradicted his policy. Augustus could not repeat Mark Antony's philhellenic stand by financing athletic games, a typical Greek institution, in the Greek city of Nicopolis, even if those games celebrated his own victory. Only Herod could show his *euergetism* to Nicopolis without having to overcome any political obstacles. This display of *euergetism*, moreover, did not bring Herod meaningless honor – it garnered him recognition by Rome as the undisputed leader of the Greek world, the eastern champion of Hellenism, as Alexander the Great and Attalus had been. On the other hand, Herod's construction at Nicopolis underscored Roman and Augustan domination of the East, as well as the related role of Herod's Judaea.

Herod's best known acts of *euergetism* were the founding of Caesarea Maritima and Sebaste within his kingdom, though the founding of Caesarea Maritima transcended mere *euergetism* and should be regarded as a typical act of *imitatio Alexandri*, characteristic of most of the Hellenistic rulers. Herod did not establish a mere city there, in the manner of the Seleucids, who founded or re-founded hundreds of cities in their domains. The founding of Caesarea Maritima by Herod was clearly an imitation of the founding of Alexandria in Egypt itself, the most successful and important of cities established by Alexander the Great.

There are many parallels between the two cities that serve to strengthen this thesis. Both were founded as maritime cities, with the harbor very much in evidence, and both were royal cities, with a palace and associated structures situated near the harbor. However there is one major difference. Alexander the Great named his most important urban foundation after himself, calling it Alexandria and thereby setting a pattern for future foundations: Seleucia, Antioch,

---

⁹⁹ See Strabo, *Geography* X, 2, 2. Apollo was the personal god of Augustus. He erected the Temple of Apollo on the Palatine near his mansion in Rome.
¹⁰⁰ See Roller, *Building Program of Herod the Great*, pp. 228–229.

Ptolemais, Laodicea and Philadelphia. Herod, on the other hand, did not name the new city after himself, but after his overlord, Caesar Augustus.

This act has strong semantic meaning. Herod not only wished to underscore his tie of friendship and alliance with Augustus, but wished to show that he regarded Augustus as the true successor to Alexander. Thus, instead of the Tomb of Alexander, the Temple of Rome and Augustus physically dominated the city. Another Alexandrian element lacking in Caesarea Maritima was the huge Serapeum, the temple dedicated to the deities of Alexandria, Isis and Serapis, which was one of the most important structures in Alexandria. The absence of a corresponding temple to the city gods at Caesarea Maritima is because Herod, as a Jewish king, did not wish to build a temple to foreign gods in his own realm. The erection of the Temple of Rome and Augustus can thus be seen as a political act rather than a religious one, and was probably understood as such by Herod's Jewish subjects. Thus, Josephus did not record any indication of rebellion or disrespect on the part of the Jews that could be related to the building of the Temple of Rome and Augustus at Caesarea Maritima or to the Temple of Augustus at Sebaste.[101] Sebaste shares many similarities with Caesarea Maritima, including its name, which celebrated Augustus the Emperor, since "Sebastos" is the Greek for "Augustus." The urban plan of Sebaste was dominated by a colonnaded paved road that cut the city in two, probably inspired by other Hellenistic foundations, such as Antioch, and like Caesarea Maritima, Sebaste was dominated by a huge *temenos*, dedicated to Augustus. Herod thus drew inspiration for the two Gentile cities that he erected in his kingdom from Alexandria and from Antioch, the two most important cities of the Greek East. For Jerusalem, however, the model was the Acropolis of Athens.

A comparison of buildings in the East erected by Augustus and Agrippa and those erected by Herod serves to highlight Herod's unique position in the Hellenistic East. Although Augustus could more freely display his *euergetism* in the East than in Rome, where he was forced to show respect for the Republican tradition, most of the secular buildings that underscored Augustus' rule over the East were erected by others. Most of these buildings bear the name of Iulius Caesar, Augustus' adoptive father, or Agrippa, Augustus' co-regent, and if financed by Augustus, they were dedicated by members of his family and not by himself. Not all of the Augustan *euergetes* were members of the Imperial family, at least strictly speaking. Also quite active were Augustus' *liberti*, who were among the most

---

[101] Agrippa offered a hecatomb in the Herodian Temple of Jerusalem when he visited Judaea in 15 BCE. See Josephus, *AJ* XVI, 14–15. A daily sacrifice was offered in the Temple in honor of the Emperor. This custom, a sacrifice in honor of the foreign overlord, was introduced during the Persian Period and was interrupted in the Hasmonean Period. Herod thus reintroduced this custom, which was interrupted only on the eve of the Great War against Rome in 66 CE. It is possible, though mere speculation, that Hyrcanus II introduced a sacrifice in honor of Rome, and later in honor of Iulius Caesar. Only Herod, on chronological grounds, could have introduced a sacrifice in honor of the Emperor.

important *bouleutes* of their native cities and displayed considerable *euergetism* in locations such as Ephesus and Aphrodisias. This rule does not apply to temples dedicated to his cult alone or to his joint cult with the goddess Rome. It is obvious that Augustus himself did not erect any of the various temples consecrated to him or to him and Rome in the East. These temples, however – erected both in individual cities and at the provincial level, mainly in Asia Minor – were a characteristic of the Hellenistic East, and Augustus accepted them from the outset of his reign. It seems that in Achaia such temples were not built as frequently as they were in Asia Minor.

Although Athens had been the locus and seat of Mark Antony's power, various Augustan structures dominated the Attic city. The Temple of Rome and Augustus dominated the Acropolis, and two temples were erected in the agora. The first, the Temple of Ares, erected at Sunium in the fifth century BCE and transferred to Athens, was dedicated to Gaius Caesar, Augustus heir, as the new Ares.[102] The Southeast Temple, also erected at Sunium, was likewise transferred to Athens.[103] The most important secular building constructed in Augustus' time was Agrippa's Odeon, erected in 17 BCE.[104] The Market of Caesar and Augustus, though it bears Augustus' name, was a project of Iulius Caesar, completed in 12 BCE and dedicated in 9 BCE by Augustus. The building bears the name of Augustus, since it was financed by him, but his name is associated with that of his adoptive father, Iulius Caesar.[105] According to Suetonius, the unfinished Temple of Olympian Zeus was dedicated to the Genius of Augustus.[106]

In contrast to the above situation, Classical Athens greatly influenced the arts of Augustan Rome. According to Zanker and Galinsky, the arts of Periclean Athens significantly influenced the artistic output of Augustan Rome, as indicated by the Temple of Mars Ultor, the Ara Pacis, and the statue of Augustus from Prima Porta. The classicism of the Augustan Age undoubtedly reflected an ideological motivation. Augustus' political ideology was not inspired by the Hellenistic monarchs, as was the case for both Iulius Caesar and Pompey, but by Classical Athens. Hence, for Augustus the art of fifth-century Athens still symbolized the art of the Greek city-state, ruled by a government similar to that of Republican Rome, rather than the art of the successive Hellenistic states, which had been dominated by kings whom Rome fought in many wars.[107] Thus, fifth-century

---

[102] On the Temple of Ares, see AA.VV. *The Athenian Agora, a Guide to the Excavations and Museum, American School of Classical Studies at Athens*, Athens 1990, pp. 114–115.

[103] On the other temple transferred from Sunium, see *Athenian Agora*, pp. 147–150.

[104] On the Odeon of Agrippa, see *Athenian Agora*, pp. 118–123.

[105] On the Market of Iulius Caesar and Augustus, see *Athenian Agora*, p. 28. See also Roller, *Building Program of Herod the Great*, p. 220.

[106] See Suetonius, *Augustus* II, 60.

[107] The portico of the Temple of Mars Ultor was decorated with Cariatydes, like the Erechtheum. The Ara Pacis was decorated with a frieze inspired by that of the Parthenon, which depicted the Panathenaic procession. Augustus' statue from Prima Porta was inspired by the

Athens had a different significance for Herod than for Augustus. For Herod it was a cultural model, the uncontaminated center of Hellenism, devoid of any political meaning. For Augustus, on the other hand, Athens had both a cultural and political significance.

The capital of Roman Achaia was not Athens, but Corinth, a colony founded by Iulius Caesar. The central section of the agora of Augustan Corinth was dominated by the basilica, where the statues of Iulius Caesar and Augustus were displayed. It seems that the *euergetes* were members of Augustus' family rather than Augustus himself. The only member of Augustus' family to have had a temple dedicated to her in Corinth was Augustus' sister Octavia. The so-called Temple of Octavia was erected west of the city center.[108]

At Pergamum, Augustus' *euergetism* was barely manifest. However, his statue in bronze was dedicated in the Temple of Athena,[109] and the Sanctuary of Demeter was associated with the Imperial cult,[110] as evident from a dedication to Augustus and Livia – *theoi Sebastoi* or *dei Augusti*.[111] At Pergamum, the capital of the Provincia of Roman Asia, Augustus preferred, at the outset that his cult be associated with that of the city's deities, Athena and Demeter, which would not have wounded the sensibilities of the Roman citizens living at Pergamum. The most important element of the Imperial cult at Pergamum, however, was the Temple of Rome and Augustus. In 29 BCE Augustus allowed the province of Asia to erect a temple that would be dedicated to him and to the goddess Rome.[112] Here again, Augustus would not be venerated alone. It is worth noting that native Greeks, rather than Roman citizens, practiced the cult of Augustus.[113]

At Ephesus, most of the buildings dating from this period were erected by Augustus' *liberti*. Two of them, Mazaeus and Mithridates, built the South Gate of the Agora in 3 CE.[114] At Ephesus there stood a temple dedicated to Augustus alone, built by the local elite.[115] But Ephesus, though a huge city, was not directly connected to the Roman administration of Asia. Roman citizens living in Ephe-

---

Doryphorus of Polyclitus. See Zanker, *Augusto e il potere delle immagini*, pp. 264–271 and 278–280 on Augustus' Classicism in Rome. See also K. Galinsky, *Augustan Culture, an Interpretative Introduction*, Princeton (N. J.) 1996, pp. 203, 237–238, 356, 360–362.

[108] On Roman Corinth, see N. Papahatzis, *Ancient Corinth, the Museum of Corinth, Isthmia and Sicyon*, Athens 1984, p. 56 on the Basilica, p. 60 on the Temple of Octavia. See also R. Macmullen, *Romanization in the Time of Augustus*, New Haven (Conn.) 2000, pp. 13, 18–21.

[109] See W. Radt, *Pergamon, Geschichte und Bauten einer Antiken Metropole*, Darmstadt 1999, p. 163.

[110] See Radt, *Pergamon*, p. 185.

[111] See Radt, *Pergamon*, pp. 43–46, 121.

[112] See S. R. F. Price, *Rituals and Powers, the Roman Imperial Cult in Asia Minor*, Cambridge 1984, pp. 56, 133, 137, 178, 182, 252.

[113] See P. Southern, *Augustus*, London 1998, p. 107.

[114] See P. Scherrer, *Ephesos, Der neue Führer, Österreichisches Archäologisches Institut*, Wien 1995, pp. 140–144.

[115] See Price, *Rituals and Powers*, p. 134, note 7.

sus had a Temple dedicated to both Rome and to the Divus Iulius, Iulius Caesar having been made a *divus* after his death. Thus the cult of Caesar would not have disturbed Roman citizens as would the cult of the living Augustus.[116]

At Miletus, the only known Augustan building is the Altar of Augustus, near the *boulē* in the agora at the center of the city, and it was clearly not erected by Augustus himself.[117] A Temple of Augustus was also erected in this city.[118] At Teos, in Ionia, there was an Imperial temple, which has been depicted on a city coin,[119] and a Temple of Augustus was also erected at Cyzicus.[120]

The most impressive cultic building, however, probably stood at Aphrodisias in Caria. The Imperial temple was preceded by two porticoes that faced each other, each three stories high. One was decorated with panels showing Republican and Augustan campaigns, and the other depicted various mythological figures and Roman emperors from the Julio-Claudian Dynasty, together with personifications of provinces. Although the complex postdated Augustus, he was amply depicted.[121]

The dichotomy between Roman citizens and local Greeks and their different behavior with respect to the Imperial cult also found expression in Bithynia. At Nicaea the local Roman citizens erected a temple to Roma and the Divus Caesar. At Nicomedia, the local Greeks dedicated a temple to Roma and Augustus.[122] At Antioch it was Agrippa who, in 20 or 15 BCE, created an eponymous district in the city, erected the city baths, as he did in Rome, and restored the theater and the hippodrome. It seems that Augustus built a theater and a tetrapylon at Laodicea, but it was not as important a center as Athens, Pergamum or Antioch, and thus, Augustus' *euergetism* could have been safely displayed there.[123]

In Alexandria, Augustus dedicated the Caesareum, the Roman Forum of the city, which included a temple in honor of his adopted father Caesar. Obviously this temple also served and promoted Augustus' interests, since he was Caesar's adopted son and heir. Augustus did the same in Rome, in the Roman Forum, where he erected a temple to the Divus Caesar, between two triumphal arches that celebrated Augustus' Parthian and Actian triumphs. An Augusteum was erected in Cyrene, where Augustus was venerated together with Apollo and Artemis, protectors of the city. Stoa B5 was dedicated to Zeus Soter, Rome, and Augustus. The well-known Caesareum, once built as a gymnasium, was transformed into the Roman Forum of the city. At the center of the complex, stood

---

[116] See Southern, *Augustus*, p. 107.
[117] See Zanker, *Augusto e il potere delle immagini*, p. 317, fig. 231.
[118] See Price, *Rituals and Powers*, pp. 138, 257, note 38.
[119] See Zanker, *Augusto e il potere delle immagini*, p. 318, fig. 232.
[120] However, Tiberius later penalized the city because it did not finish the building in time. See Price, *Rituals and Powers*, p. 83.
[121] See Price, *Rituals and Powers*, pp. 137–138.
[122] See Southern, *Augustus*, p. 107.
[123] See Roller, *Building Program of Herod the Great*, p. 214 on Malalas, pp. 222–225.

the Temple of Dionysus. Augustus also restored the city agora and the Temple of Apollo. Thus, in the capital of the province of Cyrenaica, Augustus was once more associated with the protectors of Cyrene, Apollo and Artemis, and he was not venerated alone. The Temple of Caesar, as in Alexandria, dominated the Roman Forum.[124]

A comparison of the construction agendas of Herod and Augustus in the East reveals that both erected secular and religious buildings throughout the cities of the Hellenistic East, though primarily in the provinces of Achaia, Asia, and Syria, the most Hellenized regions of the eastern part of the Roman Empire. Moreover in most of the best-known Greek cities – Athens, Sparta, Pergamum, and Antioch – both erected buildings, though Augustus and his entourage built most of them. There were cities where Herod's *euergetism* was more obvious than that of Augustus, and vice-versa. Thus, Herod constructed expensive buildings at Olympia, Rhodes, and Nicopolis, where Augustan *euergetism* was non-existent or limited. On the other hand, Augustus and his entourage displayed his *euergetism* at Corinth, Ephesus, Alexandria, and Cyrene, principal centers of Hellenism, where Herodian *euergetism* is totally lacking.

While both Herod and Augustus erected secular buildings – including fora, stoas, theaters, odeons and bath houses – in retrospect, the most ambitious of these projects was Herod's colonnaded street in Antioch. Herod contributed to the erection of various temples dedicated to the Olympian gods and to the Imperial cult. Though temples dedicated to Augustus in the last years of his reign were a common feature in Asia, most, if not all, were erected by local *euergetes*. It appears that while Augustus himself financed most of the buildings erected in the East, these were dedicated by his entourage. Herod, on the other hand, financed and erected all of the buildings associated with his name.

4. Herod, the Client King of Rome

The tie between Herod and Rome is the last important facet of Herod's ideology. Unlike Alexander the Great and the early Hellenistic rulers, Herod had to face Rome, the Western superpower and effective ruler of the entire Mediterranean basin. Before Herod, various Hellenistic rulers, including the Attalids and the Ptolemies, contracted alliances with Rome. Those who did not, or those who in any way resisted the might of Rome, such as Antigonid Macedonia or the Seleucid Kingdom, were sooner or later wiped off the political map of the East. There was no place in that context for adversaries or enemies of Rome. Thus, the

---

[124] See N. Bonacasa and S. Ensoli, *Cirene*, Milan 2000. On the Augusteum, see pp. 74, 76. On the Stoa B5 and the Caesareum, see pp. 91–96. On the restored Agora and the Temple of Apollo, see p. 25. See also Price, *Rituals and Powers*, p. 142.

more or less equal status that Herod achieved throughout most of his reign, with respect to Mark Antony and, later, Augustus, was unique in the annals of Roman rule in the East. In fact, Herod, and not Cleopatra, was the last real Hellenistic ruler in the Greek East. In contrast to the other Hellenistic potentates before him, Herod could exploit his political position as client king of the Roman state, as *socius et amicus populi romani*, and as personal *cliens* of various Roman public figures.

Herod was not the first ruler of Judaea to make an alliance with Rome. Various Hasmonean rulers, beginning with Judas Maccabaeus in 161 BCE, had signed treaties of friendship and alliance with Rome.[125] This type of treaty, known as *foedus aequus*, granted equal status to the partners, Rome and Judaea. Judaea was thus recognized as *socius et amicus populi romani*, an ally and friend of the Roman people. When Rome recognized Herod as king of Judaea, this treaty, which conferred upon Herod a position of quasi-partnership with Rome, was probably renewed. Herod had two important advantages in comparison to his Hasmonean predecessors, as well as other Hellenistic rulers. First, like his father Antipater, Herod was a Roman citizen, which gave him personal privileges not enjoyed by the Hasmoneans. Second, Herod understood well the importance of the *cliens-patronus* relationship and the advantages that he could gain from such a connection. This personal tie with the rulers of Rome helped him to succeed where other Hellenistic potentates, who were unable to forge such a bond, failed. Herod probably took his obligations as *cliens* very seriously[126] and could thus deal with Rome on several levels. As King of Judaea, ruler of a state, and *socius*

---

[125] The ambassadors of Judas Maccabaeus in 161 BCE signed a treaty of alliance with the Italic power. On *foedera* with allies see M. Cary and H. H. Scullard, *A History of Rome*, London 1986, pp. 169-171. 1 Macc. VIII, 23-29 conserves the text of the treaty. According to the treaty, Rome and Judaea are each bound by the mutual obligation to assist their new ally and their confederates in case of defensive or offensive war. According to M. Stern, there is no motivation to doubt the authenticity of the treaty. Stern connects this episode to the rebellion of Timarchus in the eastern part of the Seleucid Empire. It seems that Timarchus and Heracleides, the leaders of the rebels, influenced the Roman Senate in aiding Judas Maccabaeus to conclude the treaty. This document, similar to other contemporary treaties from the second century BCE between Rome and other peoples, also appears in the Epitome of Justin. See M. Stern, "The Treaty between Judaea and Rome in 161 BCE," *Zion* LI, 1986, pp. 3-28. Jonathan, Simon and John Hyrcanus renewed this treaty, though the last Hasmoneans did not renew it for various reasons. See U. Rappaport, "La Judée et Rome pendant le règne d'Alexandre Jannée," *Revue des études juives, Historia Judaica* LXXVIII 1968, pp. 329-342. When Iulius Caesar granted various privileges to Hyrcanus II, the treaty was renewed. Hyrcanus II was also granted the title of *ethnarch*, the same title received by John Hyrcanus I when he renewed the alliance with Rome. See Josephus, *AJ* XIV, 137, and 143-144 and *BJ* I, 194. Josephus, *AJ* XIV, 145-148 does mention specifically the treaty of friendship between Hyrcanus II and Rome.

[126] Josephus, *AJ* XV, 190, wrote that Herod explained his position to Octavian at Rhodes in 32 BCE on a personal level: "For if a man owns himself to be another's friend (*cliens*?), and knows him to be a benefactor (*patronus*?), he is obliged to hazard everything, to use every faculty of his soul, every member of his body, and all the wealth he has, for him..." See also M. Stern, *The Kingdom of Herod*, Tel Aviv 1992, pp. 39-46.

et amicus populi Romani, who had a *foedus aequus* with Rome and not merely a treaty of friendship and alliance, Herod and his state were on an equal footing with Rome. According to Gabba, Herod's Judaea was in fact one of the few client states that did not pay any tribute to Rome.[127]

The treaty of friendship with Rome, however, had serious limitations. Although, in theory, on equal footing with Rome, Herod was a client king of Rome, and his foreign policy was totally limited by its wishes. Once again, however, Herod's diplomacy and discretion enabled him to extend the borders of his kingdom peacefully through his good ties with Rome. One wonders to what extent Herod's foreign policy was limited by Rome's wishes in comparison to client kings of earlier periods.[128]

A good example of Herod's peaceful extension of his realm is the aftermath of his interview with Octavian at Rhodes, following Mark Antony's defeat at Actium in 31 BCE and the conquest of the East and Egypt by Octavian. Following this interview, Herod received numerous territories from Octavian as a gesture of goodwill. These included Jericho, which had been given by Mark Antony to Cleopatra; the Decapolis region, with the cities of Gadara and Hippos; the Samaria region; and the coastal cities of Gaza, Anthedon, and Straton's Tower, made independent from previous Hasmonean rule by Pompey and Gabinius.[129] In 23–22 BCE Augustus gave Herod the districts of Trachonitis, Batanaea, and Auranitis.[130] Earlier, in 20 BCE, Augustus had presented Herod with Ituraea, the territory of Zenodorus, while visiting Syria.[131]

It is important to emphasize that all of these territories were part of the province of Syria from 65 BCE, when Pompey annexed it to the Roman Republic. It is likely that Augustus believed that since these areas were infested by brigands, they were not ready to come under direct Roman control, since the expense involved would have been too great. Thus he apparently could allow himself to make a generous gift to Herod, his personal client and ally of Rome, and could trust Herod to bring order to these areas. The extent to which Augustus valued Herod as an ally may be discerned through a careful reading of his *Res Gestae*.

---

[127] See E. Gabba, "The Finances of King Herod," *Greece and Rome in Eretz Israel*, Jerusalem 1990, p. 164.

[128] One may recall the foreign policy of the Hellenistic states in the second century BCE, enemies of Rome, such as Antigonid Macedonia and the Seleucid Empire. See M. Cary, and H.H. Scullard, *A History of Rome*, London 1986, pp. 155–156, 159–160 on Antigonid Macedonia and pp. 164–165 and 166–167 on the Seleucid Empire. Also friends of Rome such as the Kingdom of Pergamum and Rhodes, were subject to the wishes of the Roman Senate. Rhodes and Eumenes of Pergamum also experienced Roman displeasure. See Cary and Scullard, *History of Rome*, pp. 165–166. The episode of Antiochus IV, still ruler of a huge Seleucid Empire, when he was humiliated by Popilius Laenas in Egypt, is quite informative. See Cary and Scullard, *History of Rome*, pp. 166–167.

[129] See Josephus, *AJ* XV, 217 and *BJ* I, 396–397.

[130] See Josephus, *AJ* XV, 343–348 and *BJ* I, 398–400.

[131] See Josephus, *AJ* XV, 354 and *BJ* I, 399.

The only Near Eastern king who appears in the Monumentum Ancyranum' inscription is Tigranes III, King of Armenia,[132] who caused Augustus a great deal of difficulty. Herod, in contrast, is not mentioned there at all, and it is obvious why. Clearly Augustus could rely on Herod totally. Armenia was not exactly a client-state like Judaea or Thrace and was a buffer state between Rome and Parthia. Though Armenia was considered to be under Parthian influence, both culturally and politically, Rome tried to reinforce and concretize its influenced by appointing Armenia's king.[133]

As mentioned earlier, one of the keys of Herod's success was his ability to bring this alliance into play on a personal level with various Roman personalities. Herod, for instance, established an advantageous relationship with Sextus Caesar, governor of Syria, when he ruled Galilee in the name of Hyrcanus II. Sextus Caesar not only protected Herod during the "Sanhedrin Affair," but appointed him governor of Coile Syria and Samaria. Part of this relationship was probably a *cliens-patronus* bond that Herod established with Sextus Caesar.[134] It is worth remembering that one can be *cliens* to more than one *patronus*, though obviously the *cliens* has a greater obligation to only one of the *patroni*.

As the son of Antipater, Herod was also the client of Mark Antony, which enabled Herod to become king of Judaea in 40 BCE. It is important to remember that, like Antipater, Herod was also a *cliens* of Iulius Caesar, who granted him and his descendants Roman citizenship. Herod was thus also *cliens* of the young Gaius Iulius Caesar Octavianus, the adopted son of the great Caesar, who took over all of his adoptive father's clients after his death.[135] After Actium, Herod did not cut his ties with Mark Antony's family, though the hierarchy of client-patron obligations did indeed change. From then on, Herod's most important *patronus* was Augustus.

It is probably during this period that Herod began his sincere friendship with Agrippa and became his *cliens*. From 30 BCE, Herod was *cliens* of at least three branches of the ruling family of Rome: Augustus, Agrippa, and the family of Mark Antony. The tie with Agrippa, Augustus' son in law and co-regent, placed Herod in a privileged position. Agrippa's death in 12 BCE appears to have been a setback for Herod, and the temporary damage caused to the personal relationship of Herod and Augustus by the Second Nabataean War would probably not have occurred had Agrippa still been alive. It appears that Herod did not continue any

---

[132] See *Res Gestae* 27.
[133] On Armenia see Cary and Scullard, *History of Rome*, pp. 33 and 368–369. F. Millar, in his book *The Roman Near East 31 BC–AD 337*, Cambridge (Mass.) 1993 does not deal with Armenia. See also E. S. Shuckburgh, *Augustus Caesar*, New York 1995, pp. 167 and 177. This author's judgment is still valid. For a personal view of Augustus on Armenia, see Southern, *Augustus*, pp. 126–127, 174–175. On Augustus' policy in the East till the death of Herod the Great see F. Millar, *The Roman Near East*, pp. 27–42.
[134] On Sextus Caesar and Herod see Josephus, *AJ* XIV, 158–184, 268–269 and *BJ* I, 211–213.
[135] See Southern, *Augustus*, p. 48.

client-patron ties with Agrippa's two sons, Gaius and Lucius, heirs to Augustus, since they are not mentioned at all in the works of Josephus in connection with Herod. Herod was clearly shrewd enough not to enter into client-patron ties with mere youths.

One aspect of the client-patron relationship was to bequeath part of the client's wealth as an inheritance to the *patronus*, and Herod named his *patronus* Augustus as one of his heirs. We may note, tangentially, that Herod's sister Salome had personal clientelar ties with Livia, the powerful wife of Augustus. An indication of this is that Salome willed Jamnia to Livia.[136]

Herod's sons continued the tradition of personal clientelar ties with the *gens* Julio-Claudia. Thus, Antipas was a client of Tiberius. This tie was strengthened with the foundation of Tiberias, the capital of Antipas' kingdom, named in honor of Tiberius.[137] These ties also greatly helped Antipas on both the national and personal levels, since Tiberius was extremely useful to Antipas in his war against the Nabataeans and supported him in his quarrels with his cousin, Agrippa I. As *cliens* of Antonia Maior, Agrippa I was also the client of her grandson, the young Gaius Caesar Caligula,[138] and of her son Claudius,[139] who secured succession to the Imperial throne with the assistance of Agrippa I. Agrippa I maintained a good relationship with Claudius, though the building of the Third Wall of Jerusalem was met with consternation by the governor of Syria.[140] The exact relationship between Agrippa II and Nero remains unclear. Agrippa II became a personal client of Vespasian and his son Titus during the Judaean War, before the former was recognized as emperor. This allowed him to rule vast territories for many more years as *cliens* king of the Flavian dynasty.[141]

Herod's personal ties with Augustus and Agrippa do not, however, entirely explain his success and his privileged position, which may probably be explained by his discrete use of the client-patron bond in his dealings with Rome. First and foremost, Herod saw himself bound to the Roman State rather than to the leaders of Rome, whoever they were, and no matter where his own personal sympathies lay. Thus, Herod served, in turn, Sextus Caesar and Cassius, Mark Antony and Augustus. Each of them, whatever his political position was, represented Rome for Herod, the state to which he owed allegiance as client-king. This position is clear from the speech that he made in front of Octavian at Rhodes after the battle of Actium and the fall of Mark Antony and Cleopatra. Herod took the side of Mark Antony, not only because he owed him allegiance as *cliens*, but also because

---

[136] See Josephus *AJ* XVIII, 31 and Richardson, *Herod King of the Jews*, p. 40.

[137] See Josephus, *AJ* XVIII, 36 ff. and *BJ* II, 168.

[138] For Caligula's bestowal of Philip's tetrarchy, see Philo, *In Flaccum* 6, 40 and for Caligula's bestowal of Antipas' tetrarchy to Agrippa I, see Josephus, *AJ* XVIII, 252 and *BJ* II, 183.

[139] See Josephus, *AJ* XIX, 1–273 and *BJ* II, 204–222.

[140] On Agrippa I see D. S. Schwartz, *Agrippa I, The Last King of Judaea*, TSAJ 23, Tübingen 1990, pp. 145–149, 217–219.

[141] On Agrippa II see Schürer, *History of the Jewish People I*, pp. 471–483.

Mark Antony represented Rome. This speech made a deep impression on Octavian.[142] In contrast to Hyrcanus II, who took an active part on the side of Iulius Caesar in the Civil War between Caesar and Pompey, Herod stayed aloof from all of the civil wars and refrained from taking any side, as much as he possibly could. It can be safely said that Herod supported the side that ruled his own lands, although his support during the civil wars was passive rather than active. Herod benefited personally from his passive stance during the civil wars, since they gave him time to deal with his own problems. During the civil war between Cassius and Mark Antony, for example, Herod dealt successfully with the murderers of his father, and during the civil war between Mark Antony and Octavian, Herod was busy fighting the First Nabataean War.

Within the kingdom, Herod's alliance with Rome manifested itself at various, multifaceted levels. Herod, for example, sent his sons and heirs, Alexander and Aristobulus, to be educated in Rome in the home of Asinius Pollio, another *patronus* of Herod. Since the house of Asinius Pollio[143] was an important literary center during the Augustan period, and since Herod regarded Rome not merely as the political center of the *oikoumene*, but as an important cultural center, he knew that his sons would receive type of education necessary to enable them to rule Judaea. His sons needed to learn Latin, the language of Rome, and the ways of the Roman patrician class; the education of a Hellenistic crown prince was insufficient. Moreover, their stay there was intended to strengthen the bond between the Herodian dynasty and Rome. It is significant that as Herod's overlord, Augustus had the right to choose Herod's heir, but did not exercise that right. Herod chose his heirs himself, though he required Augustus' formal sanction.

The ties between Herod and Rome were reciprocal. When Agrippa arrived in the East in 15 BCE, he visited Herod's kingdom and had sacrifices made in his name in the newly inaugurated Temple of Jerusalem. This visit enhanced Herod's position, as Rome's point man in the Hellenistic East.[144]

Herod's alliance with Rome was also reflected in his coinage. The coins minted by Herod at Sebaste in 37 BCE, for example, reproduced various motifs that appear on Roman Republican coins from the same period. Both the tripod and the apex appear on the first issues and higher denominations. The winged caduceus appears on an issue struck by Mark Antony. Both the aphlaston and the laurel branch tied with fillets[145] that appear on the lowest denomination are part of the iconographic repertoire of Roman coins minted during the Late Republic. The

---

[142] See Josephus, *AJ* XV, 187–194.

[143] On Asinius Pollio and Herod's family, see L.H. Feldman, "Asinius Pollio and Herod's Sons," in *Studies in Hellenistic Judaism*, in *Arbeiten zur Geschichte des Antiken Judentums und des Urchristentums* XXX, Leiden, 1996, pp. 52–56.

[144] See Josephus, *AJ* XVI, 13 and Philo, *Legatio*, 37 (294–297).

[145] See Sydenham, *Coinage of the Roman Republic*, nos. 1289, 1290, 1302 and 1303 (tripod), no. 1358 (*apex*), nos. 1189–1190 (winged caduceus), no. 1311 (*aphlaston*), no. 1187 (laurel branch).

coins of Herod's sons celebrated the alliance with Rome and their clientelar tie with Augustus and Tiberius. The galley on Archelaus' coins probably symbolized his travel to Rome, where he was recognized as *ethnarch* of Judaea by Augustus in 4 BCE. On the coins minted at Paneas by Philip the Tetrarch, half brother of Archelaus, portrayals of Augustus, of Augustus and his wife Livia, and of Tiberius appear on the obverse. On the reverse is depicted the Temple of Augustus at Paneas[146]. Agrippa I's client-patron relationship with the Julii is reflected in the coins he minted during the reign of Caligula at Caesarea. The obverse portrays the head of Caligula or Antonia Maior. The reverse imitates or copies similar Roman themes. The portrayal of young Agrippa II likewise imitates a prototype that depicts the heir to the Imperial throne in Rome as *princeps iuventutis*. Another coin depicts Germanicus, the father of Caligula, on a triumphal quadriga, and another depicts Drusilla, Caius' favorite sister. During the reign of Claudius, Agrippa I minted at Caesarea a denomination that reflected his allegiance as king of Judaea to the Roman state. According to Meshorer, the obverse depicts Agrippa between the personifications of Friendship and Alliance, while the reverse portrays clasped hands, a motif found widely on Roman Imperial coins.[147] Agrippa II's coins depict, as was then usual on the obverse, the head of the emperor: Nero, Vespasian, Titus, or Domitian. The reverse of the coins reproduces for the most part motifs from the Judaea Capta series, mainly depicting the personification of Nike-Victoria or Nike-Victoria writing on a shield. Roman motifs proper also appear on the coins of Agrippa II, depicting on the reverse Moneta and an altar with the relevant inscription in Latin minted in 85–86 CE, similar to coins minted by Domitian in the same years.[148]

5. Herod and Juba II – a Comparison

Both Herod and Juba II of Mauretania were native Hellenistic rulers, allied to Rome. Juba II of Mauretania (25 BCE to 23 CE) was the most important client king of Rome in the Latin West and son of the deposed king of Numidia, Juba II, who lost his throne after the battle of Thapsus in 46 BCE, having taken the side of the Pompeians. At that point Numidia was definitively annexed as a Roman *provincia*. Augustus entrusted the kingdom of Mauretania, annexed by Rome after the death of its king Bocchus III in 33 BCE, to Juba II some years after the victory of Actium in 25 BCE. Evidently, Mauretania was still not ripe to become a Roman *provincia*. Juba, raised in Rome as a Roman patrician, fought at Actium with Augustus. His subjects considered him to be, in effect, an unnatural import,

---

[146] See Meshorer, *Treasury of Jewish Coins*, pp. 85–90.
[147] See Meshorer, *Ancient Jewish Coinage* II, pl. 9. See also pp. 52–57.
[148] See Meshorer, *Ancient Jewish Coinage* II, pls. 11–16. See also pp. 77–78.

since he was raised in Rome and probably did not even speak the native language of his homeland.

Herod, however, was a true native ruler. He had grown up in Judaea and spoke the local languages. Since he was not a priest, however, he was not really part of the traditional ruling class of Judaea, but somewhat of an outsider. Unlike Juba, Mark Antony endowed Herod with his kingdom, and Augustus confirmed him as ruler. Just as Juba was a creature of Augustus, Herod was an ally of Rome, and as such, he kept his distance from Roman civil war as much as possible.

The kingdom of Juba II was composed mainly of nomadic natives, though Augustus had settled colonies of veterans in the coastal cities of the kingdom. Veterans of the VIIth Legion were settled at Saldae, Tubusuctu, and Rusazus; veterans of the IXth Legion were settled at Rusguniae; and others elsewhere. A plausible motivation for so many veterans settling during Juba's reign is that he had no army. Various Italic immigrants likewise settled in Juba's kingdom. These immigrants would have given a Latin character to the kingdom, but would have mixed with the very different local population only with great difficulty.

Herod did not maintain any Roman soldiers in the territory of his kingdom. On the contrary, his soldiers and fleet fought both in Mark Antony's and Augustus' wars as auxiliary forces. Herod also invited foreigners who could readily assimilate into the local population to settle in his kingdom. These included Babylonian Jews in the Galilee and Greeks in the Greek city of Caesarea Maritima.

Juba was bilingual in Latin and Greek, as, most likely, was Herod himself. Moreover like Herod, Juba also supported Greek and Latin culture, building, for instance, a royal library in Caesarea of Mauretania. Juba was married to Cleopatra, daughter of Cleopatra of Egypt, which can explain much about his relationship with Greek culture, since Cleopatra Selene came from Alexandria, the center of Greek culture in the Near East and many Greek philosophers, rhetors, and scientists probably accompanied her.

As for a comparison of the building agenda of the two kings, Juba himself built only within his kingdom at Caesarea in Mauritania, and at Sala. His projects included buildings in Roman and Hellenistic style, such as a palace at Caesarea and a forum at Sala.[149] Thus, Juba's building program cannot in any way be compared to that of Herod.

Both Herod and Juba minted silver coins, though Herod minted Tyrian shekels that followed Greek denominations, or *tetradrachmae*, used in the Greek East, while Juba's coins followed the Roman *denarii*, used in the Latin West. Like Herod, Juba II depicted Roman, Hellenistic, and native motifs on his coins. On the obverse of his coins one finds the portrait of Juba II with the diadem, in the tradition of Hellenistic kings. The iconography on the reverse include Roman motifs such as the Capricorn, the horoscope of Augustus and a hexastyle temple

---

[149] See Macmullen, *Romanization in the Time of Augustus*, pp. 42–44, 46.

dedicated to the Imperial cult. Hellenistic motifs are also present, such as the head of Cleopatra Selene and the single and double cornucopia, always associated with Ptolemaic queens. Native motifs, following Hellenistic iconography, consisted of the personification of Africa, a woman with an elephant headdress, or an actual elephant, and the Tyche of Caesarea of Mauritania.[150]

Juba displayed very limited *euergetism* locally, in comparison to the far-reaching Herodian *euergetism* that extended throughout the Greek East, as well as in his own kingdom. Though there were several points of commonality, Juba was a puppet-king of Augustus, while Herod was a real king, allied to Rome.[151]

6. Conclusions

Herod succeeded in presenting himself both as a traditional Jewish ruler and as a Hellenistic king. There was no deep dichotomy in Herod's ideology of rule, as there was in that of the Late Hasmonean rulers, which had been characterized by a considerable difference between the ideals of the Jewish high priest and those of the Diadoch of Alexander the Great. However, the image of Solomon utilized by Herod for his propaganda, filtered by Jewish Hellenistic historiography and supported by some of the Pharisees, in fact suited the ideals of the Hellenistic king, Diadoch of Alexander the Great. The image of Solomon adopted by Herod was that of a "Judaized" Alexander the Great, and both rulers were kings with the same ideals. Herod could thus project the same ideals of perfect rule onto the figure of Solomon for his Jewish subjects and onto that of Alexander the Great for his Greek subjects and the Hellenistic world.

Regarding Herod and his distant patron in Rome, as much as Herod admired Augustus and what he stood for, he clearly could not imitate him. Herod and Augustus came from very different backgrounds. Herod was the absolute ruler of a Hellenistic monarchy in the tradition of Alexander the Great. Augustus, on the other hand, with an ideology of rule was borrowed from the old Roman republican values, could not present himself as an absolute ruler and was bound to the Roman Republic's constitution. Augustus presented himself as the Restorer of

---

[150] On the coins of Juba II of Mauretania see Sear, *Greek Imperial Coinage*, pp. 591–595.

[151] D. Jacobson points to the relationship between the client kings of Rome in the Augustan period. He underlines the dynastic relationship, for example between Archelaus of Cappadocia and King Herod. Jacobson points out other common features between the various client kings such as the networking between the client kings and their image as Hellenistic kings. In his epilogue, Herod is seen as the most important of the various client kings. Augustus put him in control of a difficult population. Herod's rule was the first step in the policy to assimilate Judaea to Rome and annex it to the Roman Empire. Jacobson points to Caesarea Maritima, one of the capitals of Herod's kingdom that became the capital of the Roman province of Judaea and later, of the Roman province of Syria-Palaestina. See D. Jacobson, "The Roman Client Kings: Herod of Judaea, Archelaus of Cappadocia, and Juba of Mauretania," *PEF 133*, 2001, pp. 22–38.

the Roman Republic, *Restitutor Rei Publicae* and of its former values. Throughout his political career Augustus consistently presented himself as *primus inter pares*, the political position of primacy in the Roman Senate. This concept of rule, or *auctoritas*, the "material, intellectual and moral superiority" of Augustus over his peers, was deeply rooted in the history of the Roman Republic. *Auctoritas*, according to Galinsky is a "higher kind of moral leadership," and the ultimate source of power and influence of the emperor on the moral level. During most of his rule Augustus was a private citizen. Thus his source of power originated in *auctoritas*.[152] The ideals of the Augustan Age were celebrated in the *clipaeus virtutis* offered by the Senate to Augustus in 27 BCE. Four virtues were listed on Augustus' Golden Shield that hung in the new Senate House, the Curia Iulia: *virtus, clementia, iustitia,* and *pietas*.[153] These ideals were rooted in the Italic

---

[152] On the concept of *auctoritas* see Galinsky, *Augustan Culture*, pp. 10–20. In the *Res Gestae* (34, 3) Augustus wrote: "I excelled all in *auctoritas*, although I possessed no more official power than others who were my colleagues in the several magistratures." The *auctoritas* of Augustus is of course reflected in the culture of the period and later. Suetonius (*Augustus* II 100, 3) called the Augustan period *saeculum Augustum*. See Galinsky, *Augustan Culture*, pp. 10–11. According to Griffin, Nero, p. 18, auctoritas is a capacity to get one's way, a political ascendancy secured by force of personality and excellence of achievement.

[153] The meaning of *virtus* was for the Romans first and foremost valor on the battlefield. This virtue was connected to the senatorial nobility, and was the main quality that a member of the senatorial class from the beginning of the Republic had to show. In other words *noblésse oblige*. It was considered somehow one of the justifications for the supremacy of the senatorial class. *Virtus* thus bring *victoria* or victory and *honos* or honor (to which a temple was dedicated in Rome in 205 BCE). *Virtus* could only be achieved through inner moral strife with ongoing effort, this effort being one of the main characteristics of the Augustan ideology. For the Romans, Augustus' *virtus* had the meaning of both the past military achievements in the Civil Wars and against Cleopatra, and the contemporary achievements as *imperator* in the enlargement of the borders of the Roman Empire, mainly in the West. *Clementia* or the impulse to leniency towards civil enemies and foreign hosts alike, was one of the characteristics of Augustus' stepfather, Caesar. This quality so upheld by Cicero, cost him the life. Virgil clearly expressed it in his summary of the Roman national character, *parcere subiectis et debellare superbos*, spare the conquered and wear down the proud (Virgil, *Aeneid* VI, 853). Augustus also showed his *clementia* in his *patronus-clientes* relationship. The young Caesar Octavian's proscription, subject to various reflections in Syme's *Roman Revolution*, did not show any clemency. Octavian was still young and his position in the Roman Republic was barely legal, to say the least. "The purpose does justify the means." See R. Syme, *The Roman Revolution*, Oxford 1939, pp. 187–201. For both Plato and Cicero, *iustitia* or justice, the third virtue that appeared on the *clipeus virtutis*, is a cardinal virtue. For Augustus, justice means first and foremost a return to legality after the years of civil war. Augustus fighting against Mark Antony and the factions was in fact fighting against injustice, as Mark Antony was a *dominus* and a *tyrannus*. His leadership was thus arbitrary and not based on legal consensus, as that of Augustus. Thus, Augustus' war, like that of Aeneas against Turnus, is *"iustum et pium"* (*Res Gestae* 26, 3). Moreover Augustus' concept of justice is total. Thus, in his internal policy Augustus as ruler both enacts just laws, and rules according to just laws. A just law is a law sanctioned by tradition. Also his clientelar relationship is determined by *iustitia*. Augustus established a cult of *iustitia Augusta* at the end of his rule. *Pietas* was the time-honored ideal of social responsibility towards the gods, *deos*, and country, *patria*. *Pietas* was a quality that did not demand reciprocity, and extended beyond legal bounds. Moreover, *pietas* was also a private virtue, as it was generally considered the quality proper to

tradition rather than in the Hellenistic world. There were Roman warlords who shared Herod's Hellenistic ideology of rule rooted in the figure of Alexander the Great, including Scipio Africanus; Sulla; Pompey; Iulius Caesar, the patron of Herod's father, Antipater; and Mark Antony, Herod's first patron. But all of them ultimately failed, because they refused the basic values of their political and social environment and exchanged them for alien values, devoid of any meaning and dangerous for the political system they wished to dominate.[154]

Could the concept of Herodian kingship – inspired by the Israelite kings, and primarily by Solomon – which underlined peace, have influenced, in any way, or been influenced by the tone of Augustan propaganda? Schalit, for one, has discussed the similarity between Herod's ideology and that of Augustus. There is indeed a certain similarity between Jewish kingship, with its emphasis on peace, clearly expressed in the figure of King Solomon, and the ideals expressed by Virgil in the Bucolics' *Fourth Eclogue*. Moreover, the *Eclogue* was dedicated to Asinius Pollio, in whose household the sons of Herod, Alexander and Aristobulus, stayed when Herod sent them to Rome to be educated.[155] It seems to me, however, quite unlikely, if not impossible, that Virgil could have adopted the ideal mysticism of the *Fourth Eclogue* from the entourage of the two Judaean princes. Moreover the *Fourth Eclogue*, though partially expressing Augustan ideals, was a private composition, not intended to be read in public, composed for the consulship of Asinius Pollio.[156]

---

the Roman chief of family, *paterfamilias*. Thus, as a father's affection for his son goes beyond the legal and social relationship between a father and a son, so Augustus' love and care for his country made him the Father of his Country, *pater patriae*. Aeneas relationship to his father Anchises, to his son Ascanius-Julus, and to the gods, is the perfect example of *pietas*. Augustus' *pietas* towards the gods was realized with his restoration and building of temples. See Galinsky, *Augustan Culture*, pp. 80–88.

[154] Augustus, contrary to Mark Antony or Sextus Pompeius, never had himself depicted on his coins as a god. The coins minted from 42 BCE to 27 BCE depicted Octavian as *Divi Filius*. Coins minted in 31 BCE indeed depict Octavian like Neptune, but not as Neptune. However, in coins from 27 BCE onward, when the Principate was established, unambiguous imitation of divinities ceased altogether on state coinage. See J. Pollini, "Divine Assimilation in the Late Republic and Early Principate," in K. A. Raaflaub and M. Toher (eds.), *Between Republic and Empire, Interpretations of Augustus and His Principate*, Berkeley 1993, pp. 334–357.

[155] See Josephus, *AJ* XV, 343.

[156] According to Schalit, Augustus' Messianism was ecumenical and was thus directed to all the peoples ruled by Rome; however this was not the case. The Greeks and the various oriental peoples had no problem worshipping Augustus as a god, sometimes alone, sometimes together with the personification of Rome. The problem was only for the Romans and the Italics. Only Latin writers, such as Livy, Virgil and Horace, celebrated Augustus' Messianism. See Schalit, *King Herod*, p. 235. See also Schalit, *König Herodes*, pp. 477–478. It seems, however, quite strange if not impossible that Virgil could have picked up the ideal mysticism of the *Fourth Eclogue* from the entourage of the two Judaean princes. The *Fourth Eclogue*, though it partially expresses Augustan ideals, was a private matter as it was composed for the consulship of Asinius Pollio. On the *Fourth Eclogue* see Galinsky, *Augustan Culture*, pp. 91–93. Galinsky underscores that although this composition evokes the return to the Golden Age of Saturn, the lack of effort

6. Conclusions

The truth is that both Herod and Augustus faced the same problem regarding their respective subjects. The Romans and the various Italic populations rejected the idea of a god-king as firmly as did the Jews. The Hellenistic ruler's ideology, in this case, cannot be applied to Judaea or to Rome. Herod therefore took as his model the House of David and presented himself as the new Solomon, a credible claim, since he rebuilt the Temple to its full splendor and brought his subjects a long period of peace. Augustus, on the other hand, could not claim to be an actual god, but could claim to be the son of a god, *Divus Caesar*, his adopted father, deified after his ghastly murder. Through his adoption into the Julian family, Augustus could likewise claim to be the offspring of Aeneas, son of the goddess Venus and forefather of Rome. Clearly, the claim is similar, since both rulers greatly feared being identified as actual gods by their own native subjects and were thus forced to seek similar solutions. Thus Herod's and Augustus' ruling ideologies, though stemming from different contexts, are good examples of successfully coping with Hellenistic ideas, which were alien in both Jerusalem and Rome.

---

and pursuit, so typical of the Augustan ethos, is absent. Galinsky also notes the variety of traditions, eastern and western, upon which Virgil draws. Were these traditions inspired by Jewish Messianism? Probably not. It is noteworthy that Virgil could have had the opportunity to meet Herod's sons at Pollio's house. Herod's sons arrived in Rome in 23 BCE Virgil died only in 19 BCE. It is known that he frequented Pollios' house and thus surely met Herod's sons. However the *Fourth Eclogue* couldn't have been influenced in any way by Virgil's meeting with Herod's sons, as it was composed many years before, around 40 BCE. See A. La Penna, "Introduzione in Virgilio," *Bucoliche*, Milano 1983, pp. xlix–li.

II. The Court of King Herod

1. The Origins of the Court of King Herod

In this chapter we shall analyze the composition, responsibilities, and inner workings of the Herodian royal court, as well as its setting – the palaces scattered throughout every corner of Herod's kingdom. As stated in the previous chapter, Herod liked to present himself as the heir of King Solomon and thus wanted his court to recreate the legendary splendors and fabulous wealth of the royal court of the son of David, which had been rooted in the traditions of the ancient Near East.[1] On the other hand, however, Herod was anchored in the reality of his own times, and thus the courts of the Seleucids and Ptolemies influenced his court as well. Those courts, in turn, were heirs to both the Argaead Macedonian court, best exemplified by the court of Philip II, and to the older Achaemenid court that greatly influenced the further development of the great Near Eastern Hellenistic courts.[2] Herod's court was thus modeled on the Seleucid and Ptolemaic courts, as well as those of the Hasmoneans.

Herod's royal court may be regarded as one of the greatest centers of intrigue in the Classical world and one of the best known fleshpots of antiquity. As such, it scarcely differed from other earlier and contemporary Hellenistic royal courts, or from the household of Augustus and the later Imperial court in Rome. Herod's court, in fact, was the last Hellenistic court, and thanks to Josephus, we know much about everyday life there. Unfortunately, the same cannot be said for other Hellenistic courts: our knowledge of them is much more fragmentary and has been culled from literary, epigraphic, and archaeological sources. The general knowledge that we have of the Hellenistic courts spans a period of approximately two to three hundred years. We can thus basically reconstruct the general atmosphere, composition, and daily routine of the courts of the Antigonids, the Ptolemies, the Seleucids, and the Hasmoneans, but, with the exception of

---

[1] On the organization and composition of the royal court of ancient Israel see R. de Vaux, *Ancient Israel* I, New York 1965, pp. 115–132.

[2] On the Achaemenid court and its organization see A. T. Olmstead, *History of the Persian Empire*, Chicago 1948, p. 108 on the "seven princes," pp. 272–288 on daily life at Persepolis. On the Achaemenid palatial architecture which much influenced the architecture of the Hellenistic palaces of the Ptolemies and the Seleucids, see I. Nielsen, *Hellenistic Palaces, Tradition and Renewal*, Studies in Hellenistic Civilisation V, Aarhus 1995, pp. 35–51.

Alexander the Great, it is impossible to reconstruct the ambience of the court of any another specific ruler.

There were, however, some differences between Herod's court and those of other Hellenistic rulers, as well as the household of Augustus and the court of Imperial Rome, differences probably determined by Herod's personal position. It is important to underscore from the outset that Herod's court differed from Augustus' households in most respects. Herod's court, for example, originated in the Hellenistic Near East, where the king's power was absolute, and his court was thus a reflection of his power. In contrast, as head of the Roman state and *primus inter pares* of the Roman Senate, Augustus knew all too well that his household must not be too luxurious, which would have been antithetical to the conservative traditions of Republican Rome.

As in the case of every other Hellenistic ruler, Herod's maintenance of a royal court served a very important function, for the court was the primary context and medium for the transmission of the king's ideological message and his wishes to his subjects. One of the key functions of the royal court was to serve as the main governing and administrative center of the kingdom and to show both Herod's subjects and allies his kingly power in all its opulence.

As noted above, the Hellenistic royal courts were the primary model for Herod's royal court and thus all of the elements characterizing Hellenistic courts were to be found in Herod's court as well. According to Nielsen, the Hellenistic court developed at the beginning of the third century BCE as an amalgamation of older Near Estern traditions, such as those of Achaemenid Persia and of Pharaonic Egypt, with those of Argaead Macedonia. The court of Philip II, or more precisely, the military household of the king, was the primary model for the early Hellenistic courts.[3] Various institutions, such as the *philoi* or the king's friends, the royal pages, the royal guard, and of course social activities such as the symposium and hunting, became the paradigm for the most important institutions of the later Hellenistic courts.

As previously mentioned, the Seleucids united Macedonian elements with Achaemenid court tradition, and the Ptolemies did the same, albeit with very ancient Pharaonic traditions. Thus, various eastern elements were merged into the militaristic, severe, and rough Macedonian atmosphere of the court. For example, the Greek and Macedonian subjects, as well as the natives, had to prostrate themselves before the king, the *proskynesis*. The Macedonian king was polygamous, Philip II being the perfect example, recalling the courts of the Hellenistic East, where the king was expected to have an entire harem of concubines,

---

[3] On the Macedonian palace of Aegae see Nielsen, *Hellenistic Palaces*, pp. 15, 81–99. See also N. Sekunda, *The Army of Alexander the Great*, London 1984, pp. 6–8. See also Preaux, *monde hellenistique I*, p. 209.

guarded by eunuchs. In addition, the court life was intended to display luxury, or *tryphe*.

We do not know much about the Seleucid court because epigraphic or archaeological evidence, the most important data for the study of court life, is entirely lacking. There is, however, enough literary evidence to reconstruct a general image.[4] In contrast to the Seleucid court, there is ample information about the Ptolemaic court, derived from both epigraphic evidence and literary sources which have been analyzed by Mooren and Peremans, in particular.[5] According to Nielsen, the Attalid court at Pergamum also followed an eastern model of personal monarchy.[6]

Nonetheless, according to Nielsen, the Macedonian "national" model continued in various Hellenistic courts, mainly in the small states where eastern *tryphe* or luxury could hardly be imitated. Thus, the court of Antigonid Macedonia closely followed the Argaead model. The same may presumably be said of the Hasmonean court of Jerusalem. The common element, as stressed by Nielsen, is that the Antigonids and the Hasmoneans each ruled over a single, homogeneous ethnic element. Since, in these two cases, the simple Macedonian national model was conserved, the court was, in effect, no more than the military retinue of the king.

---

[4] The Seleucid court was mainly studied by Bickerman. On the Seleucid Court see Bickerman, *Institutions des Seleucides*, pp. 6–8, 13–14, 22–27, 37–38, 40–42, 48–50. See also Preaux, *monde hellenistique*, p. 215. See also A. Kuhrt, "The Seleucid Kings and Babylonia: New Perspectives on the Seleucid Realm in the East", in *Aspects of Hellenistic Kingship, Studies in Hellenistic Civilisation VII*, Aarhus 1996, pp. 41–55, 112–115.

[5] The main characteristic of the Ptolemaic court was that, with the exception of the most important positions as *epitropoi* or chamberlains, all the other positions were in fact nominal, and were, in fact, honorific titles. Thus, according to Ballet, these titles do not define tasks as such but must be seen as marks of retribution for high ranking officials of the kingdom. A person could have an honorific title at the court and a real position in the administration or the army at the same time. On the position of the Ptolemaic king see G. Hölbl, *A History of the Ptolemaic Empire*, London 2001, pp. 77–112, Appendix, and Stemmas I–III. On the organization of the Ptolemaic court see P. Ballet, *La vie quotidienne à Alexandrie, 331–30 avant J.-C. La Vie Quotidienne*, Paris, 1999, pp. 57, 76–77. See also L. Mooren, "Über die Ptolemaischen Hofrangtitel", *Studia Hellenistica 16* (1968), *Antidorum W. Peremans Sexagenario Ab Alumnis Oblatum*, Louvain 1968, pp. 162, 178. See also W. Peremans and E. Van't Dack, "Prosopographia Ptolemaica VI, La cour, les relations internationales et les possessions exterieures, la vie culturelle, nos. 14479–17250", *Studia Hellenistica 17*, pp. xv, xxi–xxiv. See also Preaux, *monde hellenistique*, pp. 220–226. On the palace of Alexandria see Nielsen, *Hellenistic Palaces*, pp. 130–138 and pp. 282–284. Various authors describe Alexandria's palace, the most important being Strabo, *Geographia* XVII, 1. 8 (793–794), Theocritus, *Idillia* XV, 8, and the *Letter of Aristeas*, 81 and 172–186. On the Pavilion of Ptolemy II see pp. 134–135, and on the similar floating Thalamegos, p. 136. On the cultic aspect of the Ptolemaic palace see Preaux, *monde hellenistique*, pp. 238–271.

[6] The Attalids ruled over different ethnic elements such as Ionian Greeks, Iranians, ethnic Anatolians, Phrygians, Lydians, and Galatians, although the Greek element was dominant. The model that the Attalids chose was personal monarchy, as among the Seleucids and Ptolemies. See Nielsen, *Hellenistic Palaces*, p. 101. However, it seems to me that in the Attalid court, the Greek ethnic element dominated, making it much more similar to the "national" model.

As already noted, the Hasmonean royal court exercised a strong influence upon the Herodian court. For Herod, this court was of great importance because he grew up in its midst and, from childhood on, had had the opportunity to observe everyday life there, replete with all its internecine intrigues. The Macedonian model appears to have been imitated by the late Hasmoneans, such as Alexander Jannaeus, who clearly wished to pose as a legitimate Greek ruler with respect to the other Greek powers, and the most legitimate model for this was the Argaead monarchy. The military character of the Hasmonean monarchy, in fact, had much in common with that of the Argaead monarchy.

We have attempted to reconstruct the Hasmonean court on the basis of Josephus, comparing it to those of the surrounding monarchies. Judas Aristobulus I was the first Hasmonean to be crowned king, but since he reigned for only one year, it was his brother Alexander Jannaeus who actually created the atmosphere of the Hasmonean royal court. Alexander Jannaeus' court lasted for an extended period of time – at least until the king's death in 76 BCE and the dismissal of most of his friends by the Pharisees, who were then in power. Unfortunately, the information provided by Josephus about Alexander Jannaeus' court is scant, but we can attempt a reconstruction based upon the meager evidence that he provides. In fact, due to the small size of Alexander Jannaeus' court, Josephus had little to write about it.

As mentioned in Chapter I, Alexander Jannaeus was, for the vast majority of his subjects, only the high priest. He could not, out of respect for his subjects, afford the ostentation of a truly luxurious royal court, and thus the royal court was probably quite small, comprising no more than one hundred individuals – members of the royal family, courtiers and servants – and in fact, the court of Philip II of Macedon was not much larger. The royal family was dominated not only by the king, Alexander Jannaeus, but also by his wife and queen, Salome Alexandra.[7] There is no mention of any other wives, and it is quite plausible that such a strong personality as the queen would have not permitted the king to take other wives. We do know, however, that Alexander Jannaeus had various concubines.[8]

Alexander Jannaeus' two surviving brothers never became part of the royal court.[9] The royal family also included the two sons of King Alexander Jannaeus and Queen Salome Alexandra, Hyrcanus II and Aristobulus II,[10] with their families, including their wives, sons, and daughters.[11] The most important person after the king and the queen was Diogenes, whom Josephus describes as a "friend,

---

[7] Salome Alexandra, as she had previously been the wife of Aristobulus, Alexander Jannaeus' brother, and helped Jannaeus greatly in reaching the throne, she undoubtedly had much authority. See Josephus, *AJ* XIII, 320.

[8] See Josephus, *AJ* XIII, 380.

[9] One brother was killed soon after Jannaeus ascended the throne, while the other was forced to retire to private life. See Josephus, *AJ* XIII, 323.

[10] See Josephus, *AJ* XIII, 407.

[11] In the case of Hyrcanus II, the family included his wife and his daughter Alexandra, and

philos of Alexander and a person of importance." He was probably the *epitropos*, or prime minister.¹² After Diogenes, the most important man at the court of Alexander Jannaeus, was Antipater, the father of Herod. His title was *strategos* of Idumaea. He was probably also a *philos* of Alexander Jannaeus and later continued to be a *philos* of Hyrcanus II.¹³ Another person described by Josephus is Galestes, "one of the powerful men," and after Alexander Jannaeus' death, he was exiled from court to command the Agaba garrison.¹⁴ There were other *philoi*, but Queen Salome exiled all of these, under the instigation of the Pharisees.¹⁵ A certain Pitholaus and Malichus probably commanded the royal bodyguard,¹⁶ and Antipater and Nicodemus dominated the diplomatic services. It is likely that they began their diplomatic careers at the court of Alexander Jannaeus, both as ambassadors and as *philoi* of the princes.¹⁷ Two categories of *philoi* that were hierarchically connected may be distinguished here: the first included the friends of the king, and the second, the friends of the two princes, who probably began their careers at the court as royal pages.

How did Alexander Jannaeus spend his leisure time? He appears not to have been a great intellectual and probably spent his time hunting and drinking hard with his friends and concubines. His symposia, for example, were not intellectual in character.¹⁸ His court was based in the royal palace in Jerusalem during the summer months. The outward appearance of this palace was probably fortress-like, as were many other Hellenistic royal palaces, including those in Macedonia and Pergamum.¹⁹ During the winter, the royal court moved to Jericho, where Alexander Jannaeus enlarged a small palace built by John Hyrcanus I, to in-

in the case of Aristobulus II, the family included his two sons, Antigonus and Alexander and two daughters. See Josephus, *AJ* XIV, 79 and 82.

¹² Diogenes was killed due to the instigation of the Pharisees when Salome Alexandra ascended the throne. It is difficult to imagine that he was a Gentile; he was probably a Hellenized Jew, perhaps a foreigner. See Josephus, *BJ* I, 113.

¹³ Contrary to Diogenes, Antipater relationship with the Pharisees was favorable. See Josephus, *AJ* XIV, 10 as *philos* of Hyrcanus II, 8.

¹⁴ Galestes was probably an important courtier at the court of Alexander Jannaeus, but the Pharisees apparently exiled him to the distant fortress of Agaba after the king's death. See Josephus, *AJ* XIII, 424.

¹⁵ See Josephus, *BJ* I, 113.

¹⁶ Later on, Pitholaus and Malichus are found commanding the army of Hyrcanus II, fighting under Roman command. They had probably been the commanders of the royal bodyguard of Alexander Jannaeus earlier on. See Josephus, *AJ* XIV, 84. Later, Pitholaus deserted to Aristobulus. See Josephus, *AJ* XIV, 93.

¹⁷ The former became Hyrcanus II's ambassador to Pompey and the latter, Aristobulus II's ambassador to Pompey. See Josephus, *AJ* XIV, 37.

¹⁸ Josephus writes that Alexander Jannaeus fell ill from hard drinking. See Josephus, *AJ* XIII, 398. The fact that he was nicknamed "Thracian" tells a great deal about his barbarous taste. See Josephus, *AJ* XIII, 383. See also M. Stern, "Thrakides, on the epithet of Alexander Jannaeus in Josephus and Syncellus", in Amit, M., Gafni, I., and Herr, D.M. (eds.), *Studies in Jewish History, The Second Temple Period*, Jerusalem 1991, pp. 125–128 (Hebrew).

¹⁹ On the Attalid palaces at Pergamum, see Nielsen, *Hellenistic Palaces*, pp. 102–111.

clude a pavilion, various pools, and a huge peristyle garden. Further additions were made when Alexander Jannaeus or his wife Salome Alexandra added two further palaces, the so-called Twin Palace, for their two sons, Hyrcanus II and Aristobulus II.

Before examining the Herodian court in detail, we shall attempt to reconstruct the everyday life and standard routine shared by most Hellenistic kings and their courts, whether Seleucids, Ptolemies, Hasmoneans, or Herodian.[20] First, all of the Hellenistic kings dressed in similar fashion. The king generally wore the garments of a Macedonian ruler, including the *kausia* hat and a simple *chlamys* over his tunic, probably intricately embroidered. For special ceremonies, while seated on the throne, he would wear the golden *diadema* was upon his head, rather than the *kausia*, and he would don the purple *chlamys*, a symbol of royalty. The king always wore the signet ring bearing his heraldic symbol.[21] The parents and the friends of the king also wore the purple *chlamys* as a symbol of their status. During a public ceremony the king personally conferred this dress upon them.[22]

With respect to daily routine, the king's morning began with the "lever." As soon as the king awoke, the chamberlain directed the servants, sometimes handsome eunuchs, to open the doors. The bodyguards then exchanged their tour of duty with the next set of guards. At that point the most important *philoi* came to salute the king, together with the prime minister, the most important official, who then announced the latest news to the king. The king then dressed with the assistance of slaves or servants.

The early part of the morning was occupied by "affairs of state." The king visited the archives, or more often, sat in the audience hall. There, assisted by his personal secretary and by various slaves responsible for the archives, he attended to letters of state and any correspondence requiring his personal intervention. The king thus issued directives for the administration of his kingdom. Audiences occupied the second part of the morning. Wearing the *diadema* on his head, the king sat on the throne in the huge audience hall, always one of the most impressive rooms of the palace, and received his subjects, acting as supreme judge, or else received ambassadors. On such occasions the king would have been surrounded by all of the officials of the kingdom and by his most important friends, whose counsel he sometimes requested. The protocol was quite rigid. On such occasions, the king enacted new laws that required his approval or signed treaties with other powers. The morning would probably have been ended with

---

[20] Our imaginary king's day is based mainly on Bickerman, *Institutions des Seleucides*, pp. 31–50.

[21] See Bickerman, *Institutions des Seleucides*, pp. 32–33. On the iconography of the Hellenistic kings, as reflected in their coinage see R. Fleischer, "Hellenistic Royal Iconography on Coins", in *Aspects of Hellenistic Kingship, Studies in Hellenistic Civilisation VII*, Aarhus 1996, pp. 28–41.

[22] See Bickerman, *Institutions des Seleucides*, p. 44.

a visit to the closest members of his family, such as the first born or the heir to the throne – who not always the same person – providing an opportunity for the king to consult the heir's educators, pedagogues, tutors, and philosophers and rhetors, who were responsible for his education. The king would also have visited the queen, if she did not sit together with him in the audience hall, as was the case at the Seleucid court.

The afternoon was generally consecrated to activities aimed at relaxing the king. Most important was hunting deer, boars, and lions. Here too, the king was accompanied by his friends, or *philoi*, this time all the way down to the lower levels of the hierarchy, together with slaves and servants who were responsible for the horses and collecting the game, skinning it, etc. The evening was devoted to symposia or banquets. Various servants were required to seat the hosts on the *kline*, to bring food, clear the tables, wash the hands of the hosts, pour wine for the guests, and to sweep the pavement during and after the symposium. In connection with the symposium, the chef was an important personality. At the Seleucid and Ptolemaic courts, pouring wine for the king and bringing him food was not a task for servants, at least in theory, but for his friends, and was seen as a special mark of royal favor.

The symposium was an important, cohesive element in court life. The Macedonian king could hold a symposium for his entire army in order to reinforce his ties with it. Often, however, the king dined with his most intimate *philoi* and various philosophers. The population of the city could also be invited to take part, in some fashion, in the king's symposium. A symposium also provided the king with the opportunity to discuss matters with the court philosophers, take pleasure from courtesans, or watch theater plays or mimes. Thus, philosophers, courtesans – or *hetairai* – actors, and mimes were a fixed presence at the king's court and came from the Greek populace and world.

The symposium also provided an occasion for the king to display the luxury and magnificence of his court. Sometimes the symposium took place inside the palace, where the guests could admire the frescoes on the walls, the mosaics on the floors, and the various bronze statues. More often, however, symposia took place in the palace courtyard or in gardens or *paradeisoi*, with luxuriant vegetation that could be admired by the king's guests. Here and there, golden or silver vases, bowls, and cups were used for the king, the royal family, and his most intimate friends.[23] After the end of the symposium, if the king was not completely

---

[23] On the *symposium* see O. Murray, "Hellenistic Royal Symposia", in *Aspects of Hellenistic Kingship, Studies in Hellenistic Civilisation VII*, Aarhus 1996, pp. 15–28. Murray suggests three models, the Greek, the Macedonian, and the Near Eastern symposia, each with its own characteristics that influenced the Hellenistic royal symposia. He then describes the setting and the ideal development, as described in the *Letter of Aristeas*, with all the intellectual trappings. Last but not least, Murray analyzes the ideal behavior of the king at the *symposium*, or his misbehavior.

inebriated, he would retire with one of his concubines, male or female, to his inner apartments.

2. The Royal Court of Herodian Judaea

A. The Composition of the Herodian Court

My main source here for reconstructing Herod's court is Josephus, who based himself on Nicolaus of Damascus. Not all members of Herod's court were recorded in Josephus' annals – only the most important or those involved in intrigues. Following Josephus in reconstructing the organization of Herod's court, we may surmise that it would appear to have strictly followed the model of the courts of the Seleucids and the Ptolemies. Thus, as much as the Hasmonean Court greatly influenced the Herodian Court, the primary model for the Herodian Court was that of the two rival Near Eastern Hellenistic courts of the Seleucids and the Ptolemies. For Herod, the model was thus the personal monarchy, in which the ruler presents himself as the overlord of the Greeks and Macedonians, as well as of the native populations.

According to Kokkinos, the origin of Herod's court must be traced back to Antipater's retinue[24] and to the court of Hyrcanus II. Herod, son of Antipater, probably grew up in the court of Jannaeus, which was probably the most important source of inspiration in creating the atmosphere of his own royal court. Herod, however, created an entirely different court from that of his Hasmonean predecessors, larger and far more luxurious.

There were two main reasons for the display of *tryphe* at Herod's court. In contrast to the Hasmoneans, Herod headed a multinational state, like the Ptolemies and the Seleucids, and, like them, he was the ruler of a personal monarchy with an idealized tie to a distant, glorious past, at least as far as the native subjects were concerned. Thus he modeled his court on those of the Ptolemies and the Seleucids. Herod was a king not merely in name, but also in fact, and presented himself as such to foreign ambassadors as well as to his subjects, Jew and Gentile alike. According to Kokkinos, at the time of his death the court of King Herod included 500 people who were mostly responsible for the administration of his palaces, and no fewer than 10,000 associates throughout the kingdom at large. It seems to

---

[24] Kokkinos in his lecture on the Herodian Court at the British Museum argued that the first Herodian court was established by Antipater, father of Herod at the time of Pompey in 63 BCE. There were earlier Herodian households in Idumaea, at Marissa and Ascalon, where a palace continued to belong to the family. Even so, it is better to argue for a household rather than a royal court. As I wrote in Chapter III, the character of Herod's household till his ascension to the throne was relatively military.

me, however, that Kokkinos's estimate is too great and that no more than 3,000 people could be associated with Herod's court throughout his kingdom[25].

Among the various groups at Herod's court were Herod and his extended family, which included his father's family, which held a privileged position, followed by Herod's own wives and sons. Then, in strict accordance with the hierarchic order of Seleucid and Ptolemaic courts, were the *philoi* – including Herod's friends, a group that included some of the most important dignitaries of the kingdom and members of Herod's family – and the friends of Herod's sons. Foreign dignitaries, as in every Hellenistic court, constituted an important, but separate group, and were not part of the strict hierarchical order of the court. Domestic servants, freedmen, and slaves who were responsible for various menial tasks completed the civil household. The military household group included Herod's personal bodyguard and the general military staff.[26] Two other distinct groups included members of the court who undertook cultural responsibilities, probably creating a cultural circle around the figure of Herod, as well as individuals from the lower social strata, such as prostitutes and catamites, who were closely connected with Herod's court.

B. Herod's Family (Syngenes)

Herod had a large family, far more extensive than that of his Hasmonean predecessors. His blood relatives consisted of one uncle, one brother, one sister, ten wives, fifteen children, twenty grandchildren, thirteen great-grandchildren, eight great-great-grandchildren, and two great-great-great-grandchildren.[27]

i. Herod's Brother and Sisters

This group, well researched by Kokkinos, must be set apart from the rest of Herod's family. Since his blood relatives from his father side, they were the most important members of Herod's family and included his uncle Joseph, his brother Pheroras, his sister Salome, and his nephew Achiab. All of them enjoyed the most important positions at Herod's court and were considered to be potential successors to the throne.

---

[25] Kokkinos bases himself on an estimate of Nicolaus of Damascus. My calculations are based on each palace's space and particular needs. Thus it seems to me that no more than 1,000 people resided in Herod's palaces in Jerusalem, with 700 in Jericho, 400 in Herodium, 300 in Caesarea Maritima, 200 in Masada, and another 500 scattered in the remaining palaces. Moreover, Herod's court followed its sovereign whenever he moved to a different residence.

[26] As this subject is more directly connected to Chapter III, only specific members with a hand in the court's intrigues will be considered.

[27] As primary source see Josephus, *AJ* XVIII, 130–141.

Herod's surviving paternal uncle,[28] Joseph (95 BCE–34 BCE), the brother of Antipater, was an important individual and was held for a while in great esteem by Herod. Between the years 35–34 BCE he acted as regent of the kingdom, residing at the Herodian court until 34 BCE, when he was executed. He was first married to the sister of Dositheus, and then to Salome, Herod's sister.[29]

Herod's surviving brother[30] Pheroras (65 BCE–5 BCE), also played an important role at Herod's court. Like Herod's uncle, Pheroras was a candidate for the succession and married a Hasmonean princess, perhaps the sister of Mariamme, in 37 BCE Pheroras' important position as a potential heir to the throne was underscored when, for a short period around 32–30 BCE, he served as regent, as did his uncle previously. When he married a maidservant, probably between 29 BCE and 20 BCE, Herod was forced to eliminate him from the succession, and he was sent to be governor of Peraea, a position he held until his death.[31]

Salome (50 BCE–10 CE) was Herod's only sister, and he appears to have enjoyed a particularly good relationship with her, enjoying her counsel on more than one occasion. She was first married to Joseph I in 45/44 BCE; then to an Idumaean, Costobar, not before 34 BCE; and finally to a Judaean, Hilkiya -Alexas in 20 BCE. All of her husbands enjoyed important positions at Herod's court, probably through her influence. Costobar was governor of Idumaea, and Hilkiya was one of the most intimate *philoi* of Herod. Salome survived Herod and was generously mentioned in his testament.[32]

The last member of Herod's father's family was the young Achiab (60–4 BCE). He was the son of Joseph I by the sister of Dositheus. Achiab also held an important position at Herod's court, as one of the commanders of the royal guard.[33]

---

[28] Herod had another uncle, Phallion, who died in the civil war between Hyrcanus II and Aristobulus II. On Phallion see N. Kokkinos, *The Herodian Dynasty, Origins, Role in Society, Eclipse, JSPSup. 30,* Sheffield 1998, pp. 147–150.

[29] On Joseph see Kokkinos, *Herodian Dynasty,* pp. 150–155.

[30] Herod's two older brothers, Phasael and Joseph II, died before Herod set up a court. Phasael I (77 BCE–40 BCE) died dramatically at the hands of Antigonus. See Kokkinos, *Herodian Dynasty,* pp. 156–160. His son Phasael II (47 BCE?–?) was married to Salampsio in around 20 BCE. He was the father of Antipater IV, Alexander III, Herod VI, Alexandra (married to Mentimius of Cyprus), and Cyprus III, married to Agrippa I.
Joseph II (70 BCE–38 BCE), died during the war against Antigonus. His son Joseph III (40 BCE–?) was married to Olympias, daughter of Herod in 8/7 BCE. Their sons were Mariamme IV, who married Herod IV of Chalcis. Their son was Aristobulus III of Lesser Armenia. See Kokkinos, *Herodian Dynasty,* pp. 162–164.

[31] On Pheroras see Kokkinos, *Herodian Dynasty,* pp. 164–177. Pheroras had two sons from his first wife and one daughter. As Herod had many sons of his own, Pheroras' sons were never candidates for the succcession.

[32] On Salome see Kokkinos, *Herodian Dynasty,* pp. 177–205. Salome had a son from Costobar, Antipatrus III, and a daughter, Berenices I, who married Aristobulus I. Salome probably had a son from Alexas, Alexas Hilkiya.

[33] On Achiab see Kokkinos, *Herodian Dynasty,* pp. 154–155.

ii. Herod's Wives

This part of King Herod's family has been previously researched by Kokkinos. How many wives did Herod have, and in what chronological order did he marry them? Josephus provides two lists of Herod's wives. The earlier list is found in *War*,[34] where Josephus reports in detail that Herod had nine wives, listing seven by name, together with their offspring by Herod. Mariamme the Hasmonean does not appear in the list. Josephus then adds two more wives, who were childless, bringing the total of Herod's wives to ten! The other list, found in *Antiquities*,[35] follows a slightly different order. There is no doubt regarding the chronological order of the first three wives, Doris, Mariamme the Hasmonean, and Mariamme II of Jerusalem. But a question arises concerning the other wives. Did Herod marry two members of his family, a niece and a cousin, and then Malthace, Cleopatra, Pallas, Phaedra, and Elpis, or did Herod marry the latter five women and then his unnamed niece and cousin? Hoehner prefers the list in *Antiquities*, while Kokkinos proposes dating Herod's marriage to his niece and cousin prior to the marriage to Mariamme II, or alternatively, according to the list in *War*.[36] I believe that Kokkinos is probably correct, for, as we shall see, following the execution of Mariamme I, Herod decided to marry other members of the royal family, who were his own family members. Since no offspring were produced, he then opted for marriage outside the royal family, marrying Mariamme II. Neither Kokkinos nor Hohner clarifies the legal position of Herod's wives.

In the following paragraphs, I shall attempt to explain the legal position of these consorts as well as the evolution of Herod's various marriages, including a chronological list of Herod's wives. First of all, however, it is important to note

---

[34] See Josephus, *BJ* I, 562–563. Josephus presents Herod's wives in the following order: Doris, Mariamme II, Malthace, Cleopatra, Pallas, Phaedra, Elpis, X cousin, X niece. Mariamme I is not named.

[35] See Josephus, *AJ* XVII, 19–22. The list's order is Doris, Mariamme II, X niece, X cousin, Malthace, Cleopatra, Pallas, Phaedra, Elpis. Mariamme I is not named in this list either.

[36] See both Hoehner and Kokkinos' chronologies in Kokkinos, *Herodian Dynasty*, pp. 243 and 244.

According to Kokkinos Herod's first wife was Doris, married in 47 BCE, divorced at least before 38 BCE. She was again called at court in 14 BCE. The second wife was Mariamme the Hasmonean. Herod married Mariamme in 38 BCE. She was executed in 29 BCE. The third and fourth wives were an unknown cousin and an unknown niece who Herod married around 29 BCE, or following the chronology given in *BJ*, in 10 BCE. According to Roller the unknown niece was possibly the daughter of Pheroras. The fifth wife was Mariamme II, daughter of the High Priest Boethus, who came from Alexandria. Herod married Mariamme II after 29 BCE. She was divorced no later than 6 BCE.

The sixth wife was Malthace of Samaria. Herod married Malthace around 28 BCE Malthace survived Herod. The seventh wife was Cleopatra of Jerusalem. Herod married Cleopatra in 28/27 BCE. The eighth wife was Pallas. Herod married Pallas around 16 BCE. The ninth wife was Phaedra. Herod married Phaedra around 16 BCE. The tenth wife was Elpis. Herod married Elpis around 16 BCE.

that Josephus always refers to Herod's wives as *gynaikes*, or women, rather than as queens – or *basilissai*. Thus, Herod's wives did not enjoy the title of queen, even though some of them were the mothers of Herod's heirs.[37] Did Herodian Judaea actually lack a queen? The question may be answered by a consideration of the chronological list of Herod's wives, according to Josephus, and by an explanation of the motives that brought Herod to marry so many women, one after the other.

Herod's first wife was Doris, whom he married in 47 BCE and divorced at least prior to 38 BCE, when she was sent away far from the court. She was recalled to the court in 14 BCE.[38] I believe that she never received the royal title of queen, even after she was recalled to Herod's court. Herod's second wife was Mariamme the Hasmonean, whom Herod married in 38 BCE and executed in 29 BCE.[39] The only Herodian queen would appear to have been Mariamme I, the Hasmonean, though that is not corroborated by Josephus. Since the Hasmonean Hyrcanus II understood quite well that Herod's position would improve significantly through this match, part of the arrangement between Hyrcanus II and Herod probably involved making Mariamme I queen. The result was that, when Herod was faced with divorcing her for adultery, he could not do so and had to sentence her to death. A similar situation arose at the Julio-Claudian court, in the case of Messalina.[40] A king or an emperor cannot divorce a queen, but must eliminate her according to the rules of the game. Thus Mariamme I paid with her life for the privileged position of queen.

The subsequent eight consorts were wives, not queens, as evidenced by Josephus' reference to them as *gynaikes*. Was Herod married to more than one wife at a given time? This seems to be an absurd notion, to say the least, and would have made Herod an exception among the Hellenistic and Roman rulers. As previously stated, Philip II was married to two wives simultaneously, but paid with his life for his second wedding, an important lesson for future rulers that was probably not lost on Herod. In addition, each of the Seleucids and Ptolemies, the quintessence of eastern rulers, had only one wife.

Josephus is quite specific in stating that the last Hasmonean rulers each had only one wife. The same also applies to all of Herod's sons. Antipas, for example, divorced a Nabataean princess in order to marry the beautiful and sensuous Herodias. The same can be said of Agrippa I and Agrippa II. The history of the

---

[37] In Josephus only Salome Alexandra appears as *basilissa* in *AJ* XIV, 1 and in *BJ* I, 76. Not even Mariamme I appears in Josephus with the attribute *basilissa*.

[38] On Doris see Josephus, *AJ* XIV, 300, XVII, 68 and *BJ* I, 241, 432–433, 448, 562, 590. See also Kokkinos, *Herodian Dynasty*, pp. 208–211. See also B. Bar Kochba, "Doris, the First Wife of Herod", *Cathedra 110*, 2003, pp. 5–19. According to Bar Kochba, Herod married Doris again, when he called her back to the court.

[39] On Mariamme see Josephus, *AJ* XIV, 300, 353, 467, XV, 23, 232–236 and *BJ* I, 241, 262, 432, 433. See also Kokkinos, *Herodian Dynasty*, pp. 211–216.

[40] On Messalina see B. Levick, *Claudius*, London, 1993, pp. 55–69, 118–119.

Julio-Claudian dynasty is dominated by divorces, it is true, but no member of the Imperial dynasty was married to more than one woman at a time. A hypothetical Herodian harem would not only have been unique, but would have made a terrible impression upon his subjects. If Herod desired numerous women, he could have taken concubines or prostitutes, both widely available in the Classical world. His third and fourth wives were, respectively, an unknown cousin and an unknown niece whom Herod married around 29 BCE, or, following the chronology given in *War*, in 10 BCE. According to Roller, the unknown niece was possibly the daughter of Pheroras.[41] These women were Herod's wives between the years 29–28 BCE.

In need of a possible heir, Herod would marry a wife, and as soon as she had produced an heir or heirs to the throne, he would divorce her, even if she was allowed to remain at court, as was the case with Mariamme II. In this fashion, he married and divorced Mariamme II, Malthace, and Cleopatra between the years 28 and 20 BCE.[42] Since Herod's women were wives and not queens, he could marry and divorce them at will. His wives were mere pawns in a series of political alliances between him and other noble families. This is reflected, for example, in the lesser status of Herod's surviving sons, as compared to that of Alexander and Aristobulus, who had been candidates for the throne. Archelaus was an *ethnarch*, while Antipas and Philip were *tetrarchs*, not kings, because their mothers were merely wives and not queens. Herod's fifth wife was Mariamme II, daughter of the High Priest Boethus from Alexandria. Herod married her some time after 29 BCE and divorced her no later than 6 BCE.[43] His sixth wife was Malthace of Samaria, whom he married around 28 BCE.[44] Malthace survived Herod. His seventh wife was Cleopatra of Jerusalem, whom he married in 28–27 BCE.[45] In the last years of his life, Herod probably no longer needed to produce another heir, but he still needed a beautiful young woman. This could certainly explain his last three weddings, weddings motivated by lust rather than by politics, probably during the years 16–6 BCE.[46] Thus his eighth wife was Pallas, whom he married around 16 BCE, his ninth wife was Phaedra, whom he married around 16 BCE, and the tenth was Elpis, whom Herod married also around 16 BCE.[47]

---

[41] See Kokkinos, *Herodian Dynasty*, p. 217. See also Roller, *Building Program of Herod the Great*, Berkeley 1998, p. 288.

[42] On Mariamme II see Josephus, *AJ* XV, 320, XVIII, 136 and *BJ* I, 562, 573, 588, 599. On Malthace see Josephus, *AJ* XVII, 250 and *BJ* I, 562. On Cleopatra see Josephus, *AJ* XVII, 21 and *BJ* I, 562.

[43] On Mariamme II see Kokkinos, *Herodian Dynasty*, pp. 217–223. See also Richardson, *Herod, King of the Jews*, p. 235.

[44] On Malthace see Kokkinos, *The Herodian Dynasty*, pp. 223–235. See also Richardson, *Herod, King of the Jews*, p. 235.

[45] On Cleopatra see Kokkinos, *Herodian Dynasty*, pp. 235–240.

[46] On Pallas see Josephus *AJ* XVII, 21 and *BJ* I, 562, on Phaedra and Elpis see Josephus, *AJ* XVII, 21 and *BJ* I, 563.

[47] On Pallas, Phaedra and Elpis see Kokkinos, *Herodian Dynasty*, pp. 240–246.

iii. Herod's Offspring and Heirs

Like other absolute rulers, from the moment Herod became king he needed to ensure the continuity of his rule, and continuity meant a viable dynastic policy. Before Herod, an established dynastic tradition of rule had been in place. Both the Oniad and Hasmonean rulers of Judaea had passed the rule from father to son, though on more than one occasion, it passed to a brother or to a more distant family relation.[48] A clear dynastic policy existed: rulership remains inside the family, with a clear tendency to pass it along from father to son. The main difference between Herod and the earlier Oniad and Hasmonean rulers was that Herod was king, while the latter were mainly high priests. Among the later Hasmoneans, rule passed from father to son as high priests, not as kings. Thus, though Salome Alexandra was queen, her legal status was probably due to her son Hyrcanus' position as high priest.

I believe that Herod needed to create a new dynastic policy based upon a new conception of kingship, though it was superficially similar to the dynastic policy of his immediate predecessors. As noted in Chapter I, as king of the Jews and the idealized successor of David and Solomon, Herod was bound to the Biblical conception of dynastic succession.[49] Later Jewish law also recognized the dynastic principle. Thus, according to the Sages, a son succeeds his father. It would be of interest to know the position of the contemporary Pharisees on this issue.[50] Herod would have needed to choose an heir from his own flesh and blood, as the previous rulers of Judaea had done, but for slightly different reasons, because Herod was a Jewish king. Thus, from the outset, it would have been problematic or impossible for Herod to choose one of his brothers to succeed him to the throne, or, even worse, to bring in or adopt a foreigner. In this respect, Augustus had an easier time. In the surrounding Hellenistic world, the dynastic principle that a son succeeded his father was recognized, though not always applied.[51]

Kokkinos presents a comprehensive list of Herod's sons and daughters. Herod had eleven sons, eight of whom he chose, at some point, as potential heirs. Three of his sons were never appointed as co-regents or designated as heirs, and

---

[48] There were notable exceptions: Jason in 174 BCE took the place of his brother Onias III, but through violence and the connivance of the Seleucid overlord Antiochus IV. At the beginning of the Maccabean struggle leadership passed though brothers, from Judas to Jonathan, and from Jonathan to Simon. But it is possible to argue that neither Judas nor Jonathan had a son. The same happened later on when Alexander Jannaeus I succeeded his brother Judas Aristobulus I. Once more, however, Judas Aristobulus I was compelled to marry his widow Salome Alexandra.

[49] On the dynastic policy of the Kings of Judah see de Vaux, *Institutions of the Old Testament I*, pp. 100–113.

[50] See Sipre Deut 162.

[51] Thus, Alexander succeeded his father Philip. Philip, however succeeded his half-witted brother. More than once in both the Ptolemaic and Seleucid dynasties a brother was successor rather than a son, but this was mainly a consequence of intra-dynastic strife.

2. The Royal Court of Herodian Judaea

Herod's daughters never played any important role at the royal court. Using Kokkinos' list,[52] I shall try to explain Herod's motives in his choice of an heir, as well as his reasons for eliminating previous candidates. Richardson's chronological framework for a listing of successors to Herod's throne has been selected as the most satisfactory. Antipater (46–4 BCE), Herod's first son, was born before Herod ascended the throne, and though he was the firstborn, his right to the succession was probably revoked when Herod married Mariamme I[53] and because Antipater's mother was a commoner. Once married to a Hasmonean, Herod may have toyed with the possibility of restoring the Hasmonean dynasty, which was still popular among certain segments of the population. The first possible heir may have been Aristobulus, the brother of Herod's second wife, the Hasmonean Mariamme, who was the grandson of the last Hasmonean ruler, Hyrcanus II. Was Herod ready to recognize Aristobulus as his heir? It seems that Herod had no choice, since his wedding to Mariamme was conditional upon recognition of Aristobulus as heir, and Herod in fact named Aristobulus high priest.[54] To appoint a Hasmonean high priest was an act replete with political meaning that would not have escaped Herod. Thus Herod was aware of the significance of the

---

[52] Antipater (46–4 BCE) was Herod's firstborn from Doris. He married the daughter of Antigonus II the Hasmonean. He was Crown Prince from 14–13 BCE till 5–4 BCE, when he was disinherited. In 4 BCE he was executed. Alexander (36–8 BCE) and Aristobulus (36–8 BCE), were the sons of Mariamme I, the Hasmonean. They were the heirs from 23–22 till 12 BCE. Both were executed 8 BCE. Alexander was married to Glaphyra, daughter of the King of Cappadocia. Aristobulus was married to Berenice I, the daughter of Salome and Costobar. Their sons were Herod IV, King of Chalcis, Aristobulus II, Agrippa I who married Cypros III, the daughter of Phasael II and Salampsio, Herodias who married Antipas the Tetrarch and Mariamme V.
– Mariamme I had another son (31 BCE–15 CE), whose name is not known.
– Herod III (28 BCE–probably after 33 CE) was the son of Mariamme II. He was appointed co-regent to the throne from 7 BCE till 6 BCE. He was married to Herodias, daughter of Aristobulus and Berenice I.
– Herod IV (27 BCE–after 33 CE) was the first son of Cleopatra. He was never on the succession list.
– Archelaus I (27 BCE–after 20 CE) was the first son of Malthace the Samaritan. He was associated to the throne in 5–4 BCE together with Antipas and Philip II. He was married to Mariamme III.
– Philip (26 BCE–33 CE) was the second son of Cleopatra. He was associated to the throne in 5–4 BCE together with Antipas and Archelaus.
– Antipas I (25 BCE–39 CE) was the son of Malthace the Samaritan. He was associated to the throne in 5–4 BCE together with Archelaus and Philip II, Tetrarch of Galilee, he was married first to the daughter of Aretas IV of Nabatea. After he divorced her, he married Herodias, daughter of Aristobulus and Berenice I, who divorced Philip to marry Antipas.
– Phasael III (15 BCE–post 33 CE) the son of Pallas, was never associated to the throne.
Herod had also five daughters. Two of them, Salampsio (33 BCE–?) and Cypros II (29 BCE–?) were the daughters of Mariamme the Hasmonean. Olympias (22 BCE–?) was the daughter of Malthace. Roxane (15 BCE–?), the daughter of Phaedra, married one of the sons of Pheroras. Salome II (15 BCE–?), the daughter of Elpis also married one of the sons of Pheroras.
On Herod's offspring see Kokkinos, *Herodian Dynasty*, pp. 206–208.
[53] See Josephus, *BJ* I, 433.
[54] See Josephus, *AJ*, XV 31, 34, 41 and XX 247–248.

step that he was taking. The only possible motive for such a dangerous move was to make Aristobulus his heir, and this could have been the first step in associating Aristobulus with his rule. As a genuine Hasmonean, Aristobulus could have been the perfect choice as the heir to Herod. His youth gave the promise of hope, and he was loved by the people.

Soon, however, Herod had Aristobulus drowned in one of the pools of the Jericho royal palace.[55] It is not difficult to understand Herod's motives. Aristobulus would have continued the Hasmonean dynasty rather than Herod's, since he was not a blood relative of Herod. He might also have represented a dangerous focus for sedition on the part of Sadducee nationalists, and his rule could have challenged Rome. Finally, the neighboring Cleopatra could have utilized Alexander to topple Herod from his throne.

Between 23–22 BCE Augustus granted Herod the right to name a successor. The obvious choices were the sons of Mariamme the Hasmonean, Alexander and Aristobulus (36–8 BCE), who were probably heirs to the throne of Judaea from birth.[56] Like Aristobulus, brother of Mariamme, they had Hasmonean and priestly bloodlines through their mother, and were the legitimate sons of King Herod. The two princes appear to have been the best choice. It is noteworthy that Mariamme the Hasmonean had another son (31 BCE–15 CE), whose name is unknown and who was never associated with the throne. According to Richardson, only Alexander was heir to the throne. However Herod carefully trained both princes. Like Hellenistic rulers before him, Herod's heirs were instructed by good Greek tutors, and Herod sent his two sons to Rome to complete their education as soon as Augustus gave his sanction to Herod's choice.[57] In Rome, they would have been presented to Augustus, who would thus become acquainted with the future rulers of Judaea. The two princes would have learned much from their presence in the political center of the *oikoumene*, enabling them to become good client kings to Rome. Herod came to Rome in 18–17 BCE to bring his sons back to Judaea after no less than a stay of five full years in Rome. The next step was to arrange marriages for the future rulers of Judaea with suitable royal matches. Alexander was married to Glaphyra, the daughter of the king of Cappadocia, another faithful client king of Rome, thereby strengthening Herod's position in the East and in the eyes of Rome. Aristobulus, his brother, was married to Berenice I, the daughter of Herod's sister, Salome,[58] a member of the Judaean royal family, thus further cementing the tie between Herod and his second heir to the throne, and between Herod's family, that had sprung from commoners, and the

---

[55] See Josephus, *AJ* XV, 51–56, 64.
[56] See Josephus, *AJ* XVI, 133.
[57] See Josephus, *AJ* XV, 342.
[58] See Josephus, *AJ* XVI, 11, 97.

Hasmonean aristocracy.⁵⁹ Aristobulus' offspring were Herod IV, King of Chalcis; Aristobulus II; Agrippa I, who married Cypros III, the daughter of Phasael II and Salampsio; Herodias, who married Antipas the *tetrarch*, and Mariamme V. According to Josephus, in 14–13 BCE, ten years after Alexander and Aristobulus were chosen as heirs, they had become very unpopular due to the intrigues of Salome. In order to avoid their being badly received by the population, Herod restored Doris and Antipater to favor,⁶⁰ deciding that Antipater should succeed him, and he excluded the sons of Mariamme as his heirs.⁶¹ Antipater was then sent to Rome to bring Herod's will to Augustus, to become known to Augustus, and to continue his neglected education as heir in Rome.⁶² In 12 BCE Herod brought the sons of Mariamme to Rome and accused them of insubordination before Augustus. Augustus sat at Aquileia in judgment, insisting upon reconciliation between Herod and the sons of Mariamme.⁶³ Though Herod consequently confirmed Antipater as heir, he placed Alexander and Aristobulus in subordinate positions,⁶⁴ and Augustus confirmed Herod's right to choose and name his own successors.⁶⁵ Finally, after a long series of intrigues, the sons of Mariamme were sentenced to death and executed. According to Josephus the intrigues of Salome, Herod's sister, and of Antipater, Herod's eldest son, were the main factors that brought this terrible fate upon the two young former heirs, making Herod infamous for generations to come as the murderer of his two sons. Even the good offices of Archelaus, King of Cappadocia and Herod's father-in-law, were to no avail. In 10 BCE, with the assent of Augustus, the two brothers were brought to Sebaste and executed.⁶⁶ Herod possibly had a more rational motive or *raison d'état* for having his two sons executed, above and beyond the fact of their hatred for him after the execution of their mother and their concomitant rebellious spirit. As King of Judaea, Herod was, first and foremost, the father of his nation. His sons' welfare and lives were relevant only insofar as they might serve as suitable heirs without challenging the future of the state. If Herod had truly loved his sons, he would never have chosen them as heirs. One need not evoke Freud's Oedipus complex to understand that for the two children, their mother's execution would have been an insurmountable shock and would have

---

⁵⁹ It is interesting that in that Herod and Augustus acted in a similar way. Herod married a Hasmonean princess, and then he had his sons married to royalty and aristocracy. Caesar Octavian, a mere commoner in the eyes of the patrician ruling class, married Livia, a Claudian, to strengthen his position vis-avis the Patrician ruling class. His last heir was Tiberius, also a Claudian.

⁶⁰ See Josephus, *BJ* I, 448, 450, 452, 453, 455 and *AJ* XVI 133, 190–191.
⁶¹ See Josephus, *AJ* XVI, 86 and *BJ* I, 151.
⁶² See Josephus, *AJ* XVI, 273.
⁶³ See Josephus, *AJ*, XVI, 104–122, 131 and *BJ* I, 452–454, 456.
⁶⁴ See Josephus, *AJ* XVI, 132–135 and *BJ* I, 457–466.
⁶⁵ See Josephus, *AJ* XVI, 127–129 and *BJ* I, 454.
⁶⁶ See Josephus, *AJ* XVI 394, 401.

prevented them from becoming as close to Herod as he might have wished. There was, however, probably another motive for the executions. Though both Alexander and Aristobulus enjoyed good brotherly relations as heirs to the throne, what would happen after Herod's death? The terrible example set by Hyrcanus II and Aristobulus II was still fresh in everyone's memory, and certainly in Herod's. Sibling co-heirs would only have meant Civil War. Though both princes were of Hasmonean lineage, since their father was not from a priestly family, they could not aspire to the position of high priest. Had their father been eligible to be high priest, as in the case of Hyrcanus II and Aristobulus II, at least one of the two princes could have been high priest and the other king. At any rate, this solution had proved to be infeasible between Hyrcanus II and Aristobulus II. Moreover, Alexander and Aristobulus, as heirs to the Hasmoneans, could have begun a policy hostile to Rome, even though they had been educated there. The fact that both were much beloved by the army can only corroborate this possibility. It is interesting to note that one of Herod's courtiers who had intrigued against the two princes was Eurycles of Sparta, also a friend of Augustus,[67] and that Augustus did nothing to save the two princes from their fate. On the contrary, this time he confirmed the death sentence.

Herod apparently did not contemplate leaving the kingdom to Antipater alone. In 7 BCE, Antipater was appointed as co-regent together with Herod II (28 BCE – probably after 33 CE), the son of Mariamme II. The motivation for this was clear. Herod II was the son of Mariamme II and grandson of the High Priest Simon. To strengthen his position, Herod II was married off to Herodias, daughter of Aristobulus and Berenice I.[68] Once again, it was important for Herod to appoint as co-regent to the throne an heir with priestly blood. In this case, given the Hasmonean's anti-Roman tendencies, there was a clear advantage in that the priestly blood was not Hasmonean, but belonged to a high priest chosen by and subservient to Herod. Herod probably still felt that Antipater, son of a commoner, would not have been the right choice.

Richardson sees in this choice Herod's tendency to leave his kingdom to more than one heir and to divide it. According to Richardson, though, Augustus would have preferred a single heir. The truth is that Herod would have also probably have preferred to leave the kingdom to a single individual, rather than to divide it. However, there was no suitable heir, and Herod was a practical ruler. In 6 BCE, after the intrigues involving Mariamme II, Herod divorced her, removed Herod II's grandfather, the high priest, and disinherited his son Herod II. Antipater remained Herod's sole heir.[69]

---

[67] See Josephus, *AJ* XVI 302–309 and *BJ* I, 513–533, 535.
[68] See Josephus, *AJ* XVII, 53 and *BJ* I, 557, 562, 573.
[69] See Josephus, *AJ* XVII, 78 and *BJ* I, 599–600.

In 5-4 BCE, it was Antipater's turn to be disinherited, and it is easy to understand why. His character and lineage – as the son of a commoner who had, moreover, been born before Herod ascended to the throne – made him unfit to be king since he was therefore not *porphyrogenitus*. Herod chose as new heirs the sons of Malthace, a Samaritan. Herod's marriage to Malthace was probably a love match, since he would have had no political interest in a union with a Samaritan. The two sons of Malthace, Archelaus (27 BCE–after 20 CE) and Antipas (25 BCE–39 CE), were associated with the throne. With them, Herod associated Philip (26 BCE–33 CE), the son of Cleopatra, who belonged to a noble, though probably not priestly, family of Jerusalem.[70] Herod hated both Archelaus and Philip as much as he loved Antipas, and so we may well ask why Herod would have associated both Archelaus and Philip with Antipas. The answer may be that Herod was possibly already mentally unstable by this time, which could explain his mistake. Augustus would certainly not have asked that Herod's kingdom be divided after his death. Possibly, because Archelaus and Antipas were the sons of a Samaritan, Herod had to associate them with the son of a noblewoman, hence the choice of Philip II. But why would Herod have chosen Archelaus, whom he so hated? In 4 BCE Archelaus, Antipas, and Philip indeed inherited the kingdom. Antipater had been killed in prison some days before the king's death. As *ethnarch*, Archelaus, married to Mariamme III, received Judaea, Samaria, and Idumaea. As *tetrarch*, Antipas inherited the Galilee and Peraea. He first married the daughter of Aretas IV of Nabataea, and after divorcing her, he married Herodias, daughter of Aristobulus and Berenice I, who divorced Philip II in order to marry Antipas. As *tetrarch*, Philip II obtained Gaulanitis, Trachonitis, and Paneas. To his sister Salome, Herod bequeathed Jamnia, Ashdod, and Phasaelis. A large sum of money was left to Augustus, his overlord.[71] One is left to wonder if Herod, by then mentally disturbed, chose Archelaus so that the people of Judaea would greatly regret his death, and in fact, that is what happened. While both Antipas and Philip proved to be decent rulers, Augustus was forced to depose Archelaus in 6 CE.[72]

---

[70] See Josephus, *AJ* XVII, 146–147 and *BJ* I, 646.

[71] See Josephus, *AJ* XVII, 188–190 and *BJ* I, 664.

[72] Richardson attempted to reconstruct a series of wills to underline the development of Herod's dynastic policy:
– Will I: Dated to 23–22 BCE. Herod was given the right by Augustus to name a successor. Herod chose Alexander and Aristobulus. Richardson underlines that the heir was Alexander, and that Aristobulus was provided for.
– Will II: Dated to 14–13 BCE. As Alexander and Aristobulus became unpopular, Herod restored Doris and Antipater to favor. Antipater should have thus succeeded Herod, excluding the sons of Mariamme. Antipater was then sent to Rome to bring Herod's will to Augustus.
– Will III: Dated to 12 BCE Augustus insisted upon reconciliation between Herod and the sons of Mariamme. Herod thus named Antipater heir and Alexander and Aristobulus as subordinate kings. Augustus confirmed the right of Herod to name his own successors.

C. Herod's Friends (philoi) and the Rest of His Court

As in the Ptolemaic and Seleucid courts, Herod's court also had both a civil and a military household. The most important members of the civil household were Herod's chosen friends, or *philoi*, who were essentially divided into a hierarchy comprised of three levels. The upper level, the inner circle of friends, consisted of those of Herod's friends who held the most important positions in the kingdom, or who were in close contact with the king. Members of this inner circle included Ptolemy, who was *epitropos* and minister of the interior, and Nicolaus of Damascus, who was both "minister of foreign affairs" and Herod's ambassador to Augustus. These two individuals held the most important managerial positions in the kingdom, after Herod, and functioned at the same level of power as Herod's uncle and brother. It is important to emphasize that most of Nicolaus' and Ptolemy' activity should be dated to the last years of Herod's reign. It is probable that at the beginning of Herod's reign, the most important tasks in the management of the kingdom – which had been a prerogative of Herod's family – passed into the hands of individuals who were not members of Herod's family, after Pheroras' exile.

The second level of the hierarchy included intimate friends of Herod with less important responsibilities. These were orators or ambassadors, some of whom held no specific position, other than that of counselor to Herod. To this circle belonged Olympus, Herod's ambassador to Augustus; Archelaus of Cappadocia; Alexas, Salome's husband; and three individuals without any specific task, Antipatrus Gadiad, Dositheus, son of Cleopatrides, and Lysimachus.

The third and lowest level of the hierarchy included the *philoi* of Herod's sons, and hence, people not directly connected with Herod. Their positions were linked to those of Herod's sons. When a son of Herod fell from favor or was executed, these *philoi* were in danger of sharing his fate. Only three such *philoi* are known by name: Antiphilus, Demetrius, and Sappinas. For the biographic details of most of Herod's courtiers, Roller's book provides a wealth of information, though he presents only lists and makes no attempt to understand the positions they held in Herod's court or their levels of influence.

– Will IV: Dated to 7 BCE. After the execution of the sons of Mariamme, Antipater was named heir together with Philip I, son of Mariamme II. The children of Malthace were still considered unsuitable as Samaritans.
– Will V: Dated to 6 BCE. Antipater was still heir, but Philip I had been disinherited.
– Will VI: Dated to 5–4 BCE. As Antipater was discredited, Herod fell back on the children of Malthace, Antipas and Archelaus, together with Philip II.
– Will VII: Dated to 4 BCE. The last will was confirmed at Herod's death.
See Richardson, *Herod King of the Jews*, pp. 34–35.

i. The Inner Circle of Friends: Ministers and Advisors (Ptolemy and Nicolaus)

Ptolemy knew Herod as early as 40 BCE, before Herod became king,[73] and followed him to Rome.[74] He was the royal treasurer, or in today's terminology, the finance minister.[75] As the most important person in the kingdom, Ptolemy received huge tracts of land from Herod as gifts.[76] He also served as minister of the interior, directing the quelling of civil disturbances.[77] For a certain period of time, Ptolemy fell out of favor.[78] After Herod's death, Ptolemy, like Nicolaus, continued to play a prominent role in Judaean affairs. He announced Herod's death to the people[79] and, together with Nicolaus, supported Archelaus' bid to the succession.[80] His origins are unknown. Roller[81] has suggested that he was from Alexandria because of his name. However I believe that he was in fact a Hellenized Jew from Judaea rather than an Alexandrian. His duties as treasurer and minister of the interior would have obliged him to have prior knowledge of the socio-political and economic situation of Judaea, and more significantly, his very early connection with Herod and the fact that Herod endowed him with lands, clearly attests to his Jewish origin.

Nicolaus of Damascus was the best known of all of Herod's courtiers. He played an important role in Herod's court, both as advisor, as ambassador to Augustus, and as intellectual. Today he would have been called a foreign minister. A Greek – or perhaps a native Hellenized Aramean from Damascus, which had been a Nabataean city at the time of his birth – Nicolaus began his career as the tutor of Mark Antony and Cleopatra's children. Herod had probably met Nicolaus in Rome in 40 BCE, and after 31 BCE he arrived at Herod's court, like many other members of the now defunct Ptolemaic court. His position as tutor at the Ptolemaic court would have been more than enough to ensure him a place in Herod's court, among Herod's most intimate friends. Nicolaus filled the role of Herod's advisor. He followed Herod when the latter joined Agrippa's expedition on the Bosporus, and he represented the king in the Ionian cities, where he successfully defended the rights of the Jews.[82] In the last years of Herod's reign he was sent as ambassador to Augustus.[83] He played a key role in bringing Antipater's downfall, exaggerating the accusations against him,[84] and after Herod's

---

[73] See Josephus, *BJ* I, 473.
[74] See Josephus, *AJ* XIV, 377 and *BJ* I, 280.
[75] See Josephus, *AJ* XVI, 191.
[76] See Josephus, *AJ* XVII, 289, and *BJ* II, 69.
[77] See Josephus, *AJ* XVI, 321.
[78] See Josephus, *AJ* XVI, 257.
[79] See Josephus, *AJ* XVII, 195 and *BJ* I, 667–669.
[80] See Josephus, *AJ* XVII, 219–228 and *BJ* II, 14–24.
[81] See Roller, *Building Program of Herod the Great*, p. 63.
[82] See Josephus, *AJ* XII, 126 and XVI 29–31 and 32–57 (Nicolaus' speech).
[83] See Josephus, *AJ* XVI, 299.
[84] See Josephus, *AJ* XVII, 99, and *BJ* I, 637–638.

death, he briefly supported Archelaus' bid to the succession.[85] Afterwards, he retired from politics and lived in Jerusalem or, more probably, in Rome. His intellectual output will be discussed later.[86]

ii. The Inner Circle of Friends: Orators, Ambassadors, and those without Formal Positions

Olympus was Herod's ambassador both to Augustus and to Archelaus of Cappadocia. He was sent to Rome to report the arrest of Alexander and Aristobulus,[87] and then to Archelaus, Alexander's father-in-law.[88] Roller has identified him as Cleopatra's personal physician,[89] though it seems quite improbable that a physician would have held such an important position at Herod's court.[90]

Another figure was Alexas, whom Roller believes was perhaps the son of Alexas of Laodicea, an intimate of Anthony and one of Cleopatra's courtiers.[91] Kokkinos suggests that he was a Judaean Jew by the name of Hilkiya. I believe that evidence points to Alexas being a Jew. If not, Herod would never have allowed his sister Salome to marry him.[92] He appears to have held an important position at Herod's court, and received large tracts of land around Gazara from Herod.[93]

Roller suggests that he may have been the military chief of staff, since he was the one to announce Herod's death to the army.[94] I believe, however, that this is unlikely since Herod's army was commanded by officers of Roman or Italic origin.

Antipater Gadia, another important figure, was probably also a Jew and was one of Herod's closest friends,[95] until he took the side of Costobar, then governor of Idumaea.[96] As a result, Antipater was executed. Another very close friend of Herod, Dositheus son of Cleopatrides, was, according to Roller, probably a Jew[97] from Alexandria. He too was executed, because of his involvement in Costobar's

---

[85] See Josephus, *AJ* XVII, 219, 240–248 and 315–316, and *BJ* II, 14, 34–37.
[86] On Nicolaus see also Roller, *Building Program of Herod the Great*, pp. 61–62.
[87] See Josephus, *AJ* XVI, 354 and *BJ* I, 535.
[88] See Josephus, *AJ* XVI, 332.
[89] See Plutarch, *Mark Antony*, 82.
[90] On Olympus see Roller, *Building Program of Herod the Great*, p. 62.
[91] On Alexas' origin see both Roller, *Building Program of Herod the Great*, pp. 57–58, and Kokkinos, *Herodian Dynasty*, p. 185.
[92] See Josephus, *AJ* XVII, 10 and *BJ* I, 566.
[93] There are also epigraphic sources such as a boundary stone from Gezer with an inscription in Greek naming Alexias and Hilkiya. See B. Rosenfeld, "The Boundary of Gezer Inscriptions and the History of Gezer at the End of the Second Temple Period", *IEJ* 38, 1988, pp. 235–245.
[94] See Josephus, *AJ* XVII, 193–194 and *BJ* I, 666.
[95] See Josephus, *AJ* XV, 252.
[96] See Josephus, *AJ* XV, 252–266. See also Roller, *Building Program of Herod the Great*, p. 58.
[97] A Jew with the same name is mentioned in 4 Macc. xii, 19–24, 35 and in Josephus, *Apion*, 2, 49.

plot.⁹⁸ Yet another Jew and close personal friend of Herod, Lysimachus, was royal ambassador to the Roman proconsul of Asia, L. Cornelius Lentulus Crus, and petitioned the latter to exempt the Jews of Asia from military service.⁹⁹ He too was involved in Costobar's revolt and was subsequently executed.¹⁰⁰

iii. The Outer Circle of Friends: Friends of Herod's Sons

This group is mentioned by Josephus in connection with Herod's sons. Antiphilus, for instance, a friend of Antipater, probably came from Alexandria and is mentioned in connection with Pheroras' plot. Accordingly, he was responsible for bringing the poison for Herod from Egypt.¹⁰¹ Demetrius was a close friend of Herod's son Alexander.¹⁰² Ptolemy, the brother of Nicolaus of Damascus, was a minor figure at the Herodian court and probably a friend of Antipas, who supported Antipas' bid for the succession.¹⁰³ Sappinus or Sappinas was probably a protégé of Ptolemy, and followed Herod to Rhodes¹⁰⁴ with Ptolemy. He was later accused of having conspired with Ptolemy in the plot in favor of Pheroras¹⁰⁵ and was probably a Hellenized Jew from Judaea.

iv. Visitors (Xenoi): Intellectuals, Dynasts, and Political Envoys

An important category of courtiers was comprised of foreigners who lived either permanently or temporarily at the Herodian court. There is no doubt that the most important of these figures was Eurycles of Sparta.¹⁰⁶ Another key personality was Melas, the ambassador of Archelaus King of Cappadocia, who kept his master informed of the fate of Glaphyra, Archelaus' beloved daughter and the wife of Alexander. Evaratus, the ambassador of Coos, and Crinagoras,

---

⁹⁸ See Josephus, *AJ* XV, 252–260.
⁹⁹ See Josephus, *AJ* XV, 236–237. See also Roller, *Building Program of Herod the Great*, pp. 58–59.
¹⁰⁰ See Josephus, *AJ* XV, 252 and 260. See also Roller, *Building Program of Herod the Great*, p. 61.
¹⁰¹ See Josephus, *AJ* XVII, 70–77 and *BJ* I, 592. See also Roller, *Building Program of Herod the Great*, p. 58.
¹⁰² See Josephus, *AJ* XVI, 243. See Roller, *Building Program of Herod the Great*, p. 58.
¹⁰³ See Josephus, *AJ* XVII, 225 and *BJ* II, 21. See Roller, *Building Program of Herod the Great*, p. 64.
¹⁰⁴ See Josephus, *AJ* XIV, 377.
¹⁰⁵ See Josephus, *AJ* XVI, 257. See Roller, *Building Program of Herod the Great*, p. 64.
¹⁰⁶ Eurycles of Sparta, took the side of Octavian during the battle of Actium. Together with Herod, he was one of the evergetai of the city of Nicopolis. He visited Herod's court in 28 BCE, when he was involved in the intrigues surrounding Mariamme's sons Alexander and Aristobulus. Later, he left Judaea for Cappadocia, where he visited Archelaus, father in law of Alexander. He visited Judaea once more in 8 BCE. See Josephus, *AJ* XVI, 301–310 and *BJ* I, 513–531. On Eurycles see also G. W. Bowesock, "Eurykles of Sparta", *JRS* 51, 1961, pp. 112–118. See also Roller, *Building Program of Herod the Great*, pp. 59–60.

the ambassador of Mytilene, were less important, but were nonetheless involved in court intrigues.

There was no ambassador from Rome at the court of Herod. If or when necessary, Herod would probably have consulted the Roman governor of Syria or Augustus himself. There were also other ambassadors from other city-states and kingdoms, but Josephus does not name these. All of these individuals can be identified as *presbytes* and *proxenes*, but not as *theoroi*, and as a Jewish king, Herod would not have received representatives of heathen gods in Jerusalem. However, when Herod's court resided at Caesarea Maritima, he could have received them without any difficulty. As noted in Chapter I, Herod certainly acted as *evergetes* of pagan temples outside his own state and probably received their *theoroi*.

Among those figures whose names are known to us, Melas was ambassador of Cappadocia at Herod's court and tried without success to help Alexander and Aristobulus to flee to Rome.[107] Evaratus of Coos, who befriended Herod's son Alexander,[108] is identified by Roller as C. Julius Euaratus, the priest of Apollo at Halasarna in 12 BCE.[109] Josephus does not mention Crinagoras of Mytilene, who was a Greek writer and a prominent citizen of Mytilene and who, according to Roller, may have traveled to Judaea in 26–25 BCE from Rome as a representative of the city of Mytilene.[110]

v. Herod's Military Household

Herod's military household is discussed in the context of his army in Chapter III. His personal bodyguard included the *doryphoroi*, and Thracian, German and Galatian contingents.[111] I would like to mention, at this juncture, four members of Herod's bodyguard and army, who were connected with intrigues at his court. Corinthus, a Nabataean who was one of Herod's bodyguards, and was corrupted by Syllaeus in an attempt to assasinate Herod, but was caught thanks to Phabatus.[112] Jucundus, another member of Herod's bodyguard, was clearly of Italic origin and was a friend of Alexander. He was accused by Eurycles of attempted murder of the king during a hunt.[113] Tyrannus was another of Herod's bodyguards and a friend of Alexander. He too was accused by Eurycles of attempting to murder the king during a hunt.[114] Soemus of Ituraea was the commander

---

[107] See Josephus, *AJ* XVI, 325.
[108] See Josephus, *AJ* XVI, 312 and *BJ* I, 532.
[109] See Roller, *Building Program of Herod the Great*, p. 59.
[110] See Roller, *Building Program of Herod the Great*, p. 62.
[111] See Josephus, *AJ* XVII, 198, and *BJ* I, 672.
[112] See Josephus, *BJ* I, 576–577.
[113] See Josephus, *AJ* XVII, 313–316.
[114] See Josephus, *AJ* XVII, 313–316.

of Alexandrium in 31 BCE, and Herod entrusted his wife Mariamme and his mother-in-law Alexandra[115] to his care.

vi. The Domestic Staff

Unlike the Seleucid and the Ptolemaic courts, which followed Macedonian custom, the officials at Herod's court – such as the steward, the cup bearer, and the chamberlains – were not young pages or individuals from noble families, and hence part of the circle of *philoi*, but, instead, were mere commoners. We may infer this based upon the fact that these people were tortured, which would have been unthinkable with respect to members of the upper echelons of society. The domestic staff was comprised of were free men, but their position in society was still far from being that of the upper crust. In that respect, the position of the domestic staff at Herod's court was similar to that of the domestic staff of Augustus and to that of the imperial court in Rome, and it set Herod's court apart, not only from other Hellenistic courts, but probably from the Hasmonean court as well. Herod's domestic staff, however, fulfilled many of the same tasks found in the other Hellenistic courts.

The domestic staff may be divided into three different categories. First were those responsible for the king, such as his steward, his cup-bearer, his secretary, and his treasurer. Second was the domestic staff attached to Herod's family, such as the personal servants of Herod's brother and sisters, the eunuchs who guarded Herod's wives and concubines, and the various individuals attached to Herod's sons as servants and tutors. Finally, there was the general domestic staff attached to the court – including butlers, servers, grooms, barbers – as well as those who held more important positions, such as chief cook and physicians. In addition, there were more lowly positions held by attendants, porters, and sweepers.

Most of the servants came from lower class backgrounds and were probably from among the local populace. Jews worked in Jerusalem and Judaea, and Gentiles worked at Caesarea Maritima and Sebaste. Some of the domestic staff came from a more respectable social position and were of Greek origin (with the exception of the Latin tutor), such as Herod's personal secretary and treasurer, the physicians and the tutors of Herod's sons.

The royal eunuchs deserve some attention here. Eunuchs were found at Herod's court, as well as at other Hellenistic courts and at the Imperial court of Rome. Eunuchs at Herod's court engaged in a variety of tasks, serving as Herod's personal attendants and in the more traditional roles of personal servants to Herod's women. Since eunuchs had no offspring, they were, in fact, the perfect civil servants or courtiers, fully devoted to their master.[116] It is not surprising,

---

[115] See Josephus, *AJ* XV, 184.
[116] On eunuchs see C. Grottanelli, "Faithful Bodies: Ancient Greek Sources on Oriental

therefore, that the best known of Herod's personal servants was a eunuch called Bagoas, who was perhaps of Iranian origin.

The domestic staff attached to the king included Phabatus, Herod's personal steward, who was probably a Jew. Syllaeus tried to play him against Herod, and bribed him to accuse Herod before Augustus. However, Phabatus either played one side against the other or eventually chose the side of Herod, who offered him a larger bribe.[117] Herod also had a personal cupbearer, who remains anonymous[118] and who was persuaded by Salome to falsely accuse Mariamme of having persuaded him into giving the king a love potion, which had probably been poisoned. Three of the most intimate of Herod's personal servants were eunuchs: his cup bearer, his servant during the symposia, and the servant responsible for his bedroom.[119] Bagoas, the best known eunuch, was involved in the Pharisee conspiracy to bring Pheroras to the throne and was promised that he would beget offspring.[120] Diophantus, probably of Greek origin,[121] was one of Herod's personal secretaries. Alexander accused him of forging documents in connection with Eurycles' slanders. Upon being discovered, he was executed. A certain Joseph, a Jew, was Herod's personal accountant and economic secretary.[122]

The domestic staff attached to Herod's family was also numerous. Mariamme had a personal servant, a eunuch,[123] who remains anonymous. Antipater of Samaria, the personal steward of Antipater, accused him of poisoning Herod.[124] The only known freedman was a certain Bathyllus, a former servant of Antipater, who denounced his master.[125] It is important to emphasize the fact that the term freedman as used by Josephus indicates a slave who was freed according to Hellenistic custom, and thus not a Roman *libertus*. His position was that of a commoner, not different from that of other servants of the Herodian court.[126] Bathyllus' position is far from that enjoyed by Claudius' *liberti*. Andromachus was probably the Greek tutor of Herod's sons, Alexander and Aristobulus, and perhaps an advisor to the King. He was dismissed from his position because of

---

Eunuchs", in A. I. Baumgarten (ed.), *Self, Soul & Body in Religious Experience, Studies in the History of Religions LXXVIII*, Leiden 1998, pp. 404–417. Grottanelli stresses that Greek authors such as Herodotus and Xenophon stressed the eunuch's faithfulness. On the other side Grottanelli emphasizes that the Greeks did not view the eunuchs as men, as they could not beget children.

[117] See Josephus, *BJ* I, 574–576.
[118] See Josephus, *AJ* XV, 223–226.
[119] See Josephus, *AJ* XV, 229–234 and *BJ* I, 488–492.
[120] See Josephus, *AJ* XVII, 44–45.
[121] See Josephus, *AJ* XVI, 319 and *BJ* I, 529. See also Roller, *Building Program of Herod the Great*, p. 58.
[122] See Josephus, *AJ* XV, 184.
[123] See Josephus, *AJ* XV, 226–227.
[124] See Josephus, *AJ* XVII, 69.
[125] See Josephus, *AJ* XVII, 79.
[126] Thus, in Athens, a freed slave become a metic, not a citizen, as in Rome. See S.C. Todd, *The Shape of Athenian Law*, Oxford 1993, pp. 174, 190–192. Moreover, in Athens, a freedman, if he behaved badly towards his former master, could once more become a slave.

his involvement in an alleged plot of Herod's sons, Alexander and Aristobulus.[127] According to Roller, he may have come from the court of the Ptolemies in Alexandria.[128] Gemellus, judging by the name, was of Roman origin. Together with Andromachus, he was tutor to Herod's children. He accompanied Herod's son, Alexander, to Rome and was dismissed for his involvement in an alleged plot by Herod's sons Alexander and Aristobulus.[129] It is believed that he was probably the Latin tutor of Herod's children.

The final category is that of the known members of the domestic staff who were attached to the court. The only known physician at the court of Herod was the brother of Antiphilus.[130] One of Herod's cooks is not mentioned by Josephus, but appears in an inscription from Rome. After Herod's death, his personal cook was ceded, most likely willed, to Augustus, and became the chief chef for Augustus' household, later dying in Rome.[131] Though Augustus was known for his frugality, it is probable that Herod's cook brought to his table the finest food in the Hellenistic and Roman world.[132] A barber by the name of Tryphon is also known. He was involved in a palace intrigue connected to Alexander and told the king that he had been persuaded by a certain Tero to cut the king's throat on Alexander's behalf.[133]

vii. The Herodian Cultural Circle

The Herodian court at Jerusalem became a cultural center, as did the Seleucid court[134] and other Hellenistic courts, at least for a period of time. The most

---

[127] See Josephus, *AJ* XVI, 241–245.

[128] See Roller, *Building Program of Herod the Great*, p. 58.

[129] See Josephus, *AJ* XVI, 242–243. See also Roller, *Building Program of Herod the Great*, pp. 60–61.

[130] See Josephus, *AJ* XVII, 73.

[131] The inscription in Latin comes from Rome. It is registered in CIL VI 9005 – Inscriptiones Latinae Selectae 1795. The inscription goes:
Genio/ Coeti Herodian. Praegustator./ divii Augusti,/idem postea vilicus in/hortis Sallustianis,/decessit non. Augustis/M. Cocceio Nerva/ C. Vibio Rufino/cos. (consulibus), Iulia Prima patrono suo.).

[132] Herod's court could undoubtedly stand its own against the most serious scrutiny of ritual purity, no less than a high priest's house. Wine was imported from both Greece and Italy, as the amphorae from Masada attest. The notation "for Herod" on Italic amphorae probably attest that this wine was prepared according to the prescriptions of contemporary Jewish halacha. On food in the Classical world see A. Dalby and S. Grainger, *The Classical Cookbook*, London 1996, pp. 56–114 on Late Classical, Hellenistic, Late Republican and Early Imperial food. These chapters describe food probably served at Herod's court. See also F. Salza Prina Ricotti, *Ricette della cucina romana a Pompei*, Roma 1993. On the diet in the Land of Israel in the Hellenistic-Roman period see M. Broshi, "The Diet of Palestine in the Roman Period", *IMJ* V, 1986, pp. 41–56.

[133] See Josephus, *AJ* XVI, 387 and *BJ* I, 547.

[134] At the Seleucid courts lived philosophers, historians and poets. Antiochus II tried to have Lycon at his court, head of the Aristotelian lyceum. Philonides, an Epicurean philosopher, lived at the court of Antiochus IV, Demetrius I and Alexander Balas. Mnesiptolemus was a historian,

significant cultural center was the library of Alexandria, which was part of the royal palace and became the model for similar institutions in the Hellenistic world, including at the Herodian court. The library was not a cultural institution of the city as such, but rather, an institution closely associated with the court, that worked for the court, and that existed for the king's pleasure only. The library served as a repository of books and as a cultural center where intellectuals of all types could write.[135] Another library, rival to the one in Alexandria, was that of Pergamum.[136] Libraries emerged quite late in Rome, around the time of Sulla's dictatorship.[137] Later, various patricians, including Lucullus, Cicero and Varro,

---

who lived at the Seleucid court. Antiochus III had various poets under his wings, including Aratus, Euphorion, who was the chief of the library of Antiochus III, and Simonides, an epic poet who glorified the same king.

[135] Strabo provides a description of the library, part of the Museum. See Strabo, *Geography* XVII, I, 8. The library was created in 317 BCE by Demetrius Phalerus. See Pliny, *NH* XXX, 4. See on Demetrius Phalerus and Ptolemy I, Plutarch, *Short Sayings of Kings and Commanders*, 189 d, *On Exile* 601 f, and Epiphanius, *De Mensuris et ponderibus* in Migne, *Patrologia Graeca* XLIII, p. 252. Well-known *hommes de lettres* directed this institution on the king's behalf. During the reign of Ptolemy II, Zenodotus of Ephesus was the first librarian of the Museum who edited an edition of the Iliad and Odyssey. He was followed by Apollonius of Rhodes, author of the *Argonautica*. Ptolemy III first chose Callimachus, who had praised his wife Berenice and later, the philosopher Eratosthenes. The staff of the library included scholars who researched the natural sciences (*physis*, the study of the nature): geometry, physics and biology. In those days disciplines were not clearly distinguished from one another. Callimachus compiled a catalogue of the Greek authors comprising no less than 120 volumes. The collection of the library was further enriched when Theophrastus left his collection to Neleus son of Coriscus. On Neleus son of Coriscus see Diogenes Laertius, *Life of the Philosophers* V, 52. But then Neleus was not elected head of the Lycaeum, but Strato, one of the tutors of the Ptolemies' heir, Ptolemy II. On Strato as tutor see Diogenes Laertius, *Life of the Philosophers* V, 58. This collection of books was no less than the *opera omnia* of the philosopher Aristotle. According to Canfora, in 48 BCE, besieged in Alexandria, Iulius Caesar did not burn the library in the Museum, but new book scrolls from the shipyard. See Dio Cassius, *Roman History* XLII, 38, 2 and Orosius, VI, 15, 31. When in 31 BCE Octavian entered Alexandria, the library lost its importance as cultural center, as there was no longer a court in Alexandria. It remained merely a collection of books. The library was visited by Strabo, who arrived in 26 BCE with the new prefect of Egypt, Cornelius Gallus. Strabo, *Geography* XVII, I, 46. A contemporary native Alexandrian who wrote in the library was Didymus, who composed a huge book of commentaries on Greek authors. See Seneca, *Epistulae ad Lucilium*, 88, 37. See L. Canfora, *The Vanished Library, A Wonder of the Ancient World*, Berkeley Los Angeles 1989.

[136] Eumenes began this library with the purchase of the collection of books of the well known orator Demosthenes. According to legend, when Egypt halted the export of papyrus, parchment production began at Pergamum. On the Pergamum library see Canfora, *Vanished Library*, pp. 45–48.

[137] During the rue of Sulla, the grammarian Tyrannius arrived from Athens as a prisoner. He assembled a library devoted primarily to Aristotle. He was probably patronized by Sulla, as the largest library in Rome at the beginning of the first century BCE belonged to him. See Plutarch, *Sulla*, 26. Cicero, *Ad Atticum* IV, 10, also praises Sulla's library. At the beginning of the Imperial period, there were two private libraries on the Palatine, the Latin library and the Greek library, which from the time of Augustus and onward were connected to the Temple of Apollo on the Palatine. During the early Imperial period, these libraries were probably public, only later becoming the private libraries of the Caesars.

created libraries that began to collect Latin books.[138] In Late Republican Rome, however, there was no court library, though many of the wealthiest members of the ruling class had their own personal collections.

Thus, since Herod wished to establish an impressive court, he needed to create a Greek cultural center at his court in Jerusalem and hence the need for a library. This situation was probably facilitated by the fact that after 31 BCE Alexandria had lost its attraction as a cultural center for Greek intellectuals searching for a patron. In Rome, the cultural output sponsored by Augustus was primarily Latin. Thus, various personalities abandoned Alexandria for Judaea, including Irenaeus, Philostratus, and Nicolaus. After Herod's death, some of them, such as Nicolaus, left for Rome. During the last years of Augustus' reign, Rome was already the undisputed center of both Latin and Greek culture. It is safe to say that most of the intellectuals at Herod's court arrived there as exiles from Ptolemaic Alexandria. For many Greek intellectuals, Jerusalem was the last station before the Imperial court in Rome.

Which Greek literary genres were most appreciated at Herod's court? Herod himself wrote his memoirs,[139] and it comes as no surprise that he was very interested in history. Nicolaus, the most important member of the literary circle of Herod's court, was a historian, and presumably there were also rhetors and poets.

Nicolaus' main work, the *Universal History*, was perhaps the longest history compendium written in Greek during that period. It was comprised of 144 books and focused upon the figure of Herod. A variety of topics were covered, including the history of the ancient Near East, Assyria, Babylonia and Media, Greece and the Trojan War, the history of Syria and Judaea, and early Roman history. Nicolaus' book ended with the death of Herod.[140] Just as Livius concluded his history of Rome with the "glorious" figure of Augustus, so Nicolaus ended his *Universal History* with the no less "glorious" kingdom of Herod.

Nicolaus was not the only man of culture in Herodian Jerusalem, however. Roller has listed various names of men of culture who resided for a period of time at Herod's court. Among the most prominent of these was Philostratus, who was active in Alexandria at the Ptolemaic court,[141] and whom Octavian had pardoned after his conquest of Egypt. Josephus does not mention him, but according to Crinagoras, "he [Philostratus] left the Nile for Judaea." He was in Herod's service only after 31 BCE, and ended his life far away from Herod, in Ostrakina in Egypt. He was the author of *Indika*, which was probably a history of India, and of the

---

[138] See Canfora, *Vanished Library*, p. 62.
[139] See Josephus, *AJ* XV, 174.
[140] See D. Dueck, *Strabo of Amasia, A Greek Man of Letters in Augustan Rome*, London 2000, pp. 133–134.
[141] Plutarch, *Mark Antony* 80. On Crinagoras see Greek Anthology 7. 645. See also Roller, *Building Program of Herod the Great*, p. 62–63.

Phoinikika, which was probably a history of the Phoenicians. Yet another figure, Ptolemy, also not mentioned by Josephus, probably wrote at Herod's court and composed a work about Herod.[142]

Is it possible to establish Herod's historical taste? The works of Nicolaus and of Philostratus show a predilection for Near Eastern history, since Herod's Judaea was part of that area. Yet another figure, Irenaeus, also came from Alexandria and was a rhetor, according to Roller. After Herod's death he joined Antipas' retinue, and supported his bid for the throne.[143]

The presence at Jerusalem of so many Greek men of culture probably did not pass unnoticed in rabbinic literature.[144] During the Herodian period, Jerusalem remained a center of Jewish culture.

As the Ptolemaic court, the Herodian court was not only a center for the output of culture, both Greek and Jewish, but was probably also a center where books were collected.[145] Even if we do not accept all the books listed by Wacholder, since Nicolaus' sources for his universal history came from many sources in addition to Herod's library, it is probable that various Greek authors, from Homer[146] to Hellenistic historians such as Polybius, were collected there. Moreover, it seems to me that Herod's library probably included various books on Alexander the Great, one of Herod's models, as well as books penned by Jewish authors who wrote in Greek, in addition to most of the Jewish literary output of the Land of Israel. Hebrew religious books, mainly Pentateuch scrolls, were also owned by the Temple in Jerusalem, by synagogues all over the country, and by wealthy priests as well.[147]

---

[142] See Roller, *Building Program of Herod the Great*, p. 64.

[143] See Josephus, *AJ* XVII, 226 and *BJ* II, 21. See also Roller, *Building Program of Herod the Great*, p. 59.

[144] The well-known conversations of Hillel and Shammai with Gentiles who, after their conversation with Hillel became proselytes, are perhaps a reflection of the intellectual atmosphere prevailing in Herodian Jerusalem. See BT, *Šabb.* 31 a. See also M. D. Herr, "The Historical Significance of the Dialogues between Sages and Roman Dignitaries", *SH* 22, 1971, pp. 123–150.

[145] According to Wacholder, at least 44 Greek authors were present in Herod's library. See B. Z. Wacholder, "Greek Authors in Herod's Library", *Studies in Bibliography and Booklore* 5, 1960, pp. 104–109. Wacholder reconstructs Herod's library by listing everything that Nicolaus can be shown to have read. I agree with T. Rajak that Nicolaus' sources for his universal history did not come only from Herod's library. Still, the cultural level of Herod's court was probably quite high. See T. Rajak, *Josephus, the Historian and His Society*, London 1983, p. 61.

[146] No doubt both the Iliad and Odyssey were very well known by the upper class in Herodian Jerusalem. See Amiran – Homer in m. *Yad.* 1. Rav Yehochanan ben Zakkai as well as the Sadducees priests knew it very well. See also S. Lieberman, *Hellenism in Jewish Palestine*, New York 1994.

[147] See Millard, *Reading and Writing* pp. 158–164. See also S. Schwartz, *Imperialism and Jewish Society, 200 BCE to 640 CE*, Princeton (N. J.) 2001, p. 63.

viii. *Those Who Were Different: Concubines, Prostitutes and Catamites*

Despite the cultural features of Herod's court, like all the other Hellenistic courts, it was also a center of attraction for the dregs of society. Members of Herod's court, mainly Greeks, frequented and perhaps introduced prostitutes and catamites to the court. These individuals lived in Jerusalem, where they probably earned a prosperous livelihood from other clients who were not members of Herod's court. According to Josephus, who complains of corruption, Herod's immoral court life influenced the mores of the entire city, or at least that of the upper classes not directly connected to Herod's court.[148]

There were undoubtedly prostitutes in Jerusalem, and they appear to have frequented the more fashionable ritual baths or *mikwaoth*.[149] Clearly, those who could meet members of the upper class of Jerusalem were also members of the upper class.[150] Prostitutes may have also served wealthy pilgrims during the feasts of pilgrimage, as well as rich foreigners living in Jerusalem. These prostitutes, who may correctly be called *hetairai*, were connected to the court and worked for affluent clients. One wonders if the hippodrome of Jerusalem was a meeting place for prostitutes, as it was in Rome. On the other hand, poor men's prostitutes, *pornai*, possibly did not have much work in a city renowned for the Temple and the piety of its inhabitants.

Like most of the male elite of the Classical world, Herod was probably bisexual. According to Kokkinos, Herod had one male lover, Hippicus, in whose honor Herod erected the Tower of Hippicus. Who was Hippicus? A friend, a bodyguard, or just a lover? In the Classical world, both in Greece and Rome, a homoerotic couple generally consisted of an older partner, the *erastos*, and a youth, the *eromenos*. Hippicus is called a friend, meaning a person of roughly the same age as Herod. This would seemingly rule out a homoerotic relationship between Herod and Hippicus. There were well-known relationships between partners of the same age in the Classical world, such as Alexander and Hephaestion, but that particular case was also regarded as friendship, despite its homoerotic overtones. Josephus is silent concerning the true nature of the relationship between Herod and Hippicus, though he does clearly state that Herod was fond of eunuchs and selected them in consideration of their beauty. This indicates that Herod had a highly developed aesthetic sense, but does not mean that Herod necessarily en-

---

[148] Josephus, *AJ* XV, 267.

[149] In a fragment found at Oxyrhynchus (Papyrus 840), an Apocrypha Gospel of the New Testament, Jesus argues with the "chief priest Levi, a Pharisee on purification rules. The Priest has been in a *mikweh* frequented by prostitutes and flute-girls. Levi thinks that he is pure because he plunged in the *mikweh*, from a different entrance than the prostitutes. See J. Jeremias and W. Schneemelcher, "Oxyrhynchus Papyrus 840", in W. Schneemelcher (ed.), *New Testament Apocrypha I, Gospels and Related Writings*, Louisville (Kent.) 1991, pp. 94–95.

[150] Still in the Pentateuch, Deut 23, 19 it is written than prostitutes could not bring sacrifices.

gaged in homoerotic relations. That there were homosexuals among the members of the upper class of Herodian Judaea is attested to by the Warren Cup from the British Museum.[151]

3. The setting of the Herodian Court: the Herodian Palace

A. *The Herodian Palace: Origins and Structure*

Much can be learned about the everyday functioning of Herod's royal court from his royal palaces and residences – the physical settings of the court. Only a close analysis of the plan and function of Herod's palaces can help us in researching the workings of Herod's court. Herod's palaces serve to emphasize the similarity of his court and those of other Hellenistic rulers, in particular those of the Seleucids and Ptolemies.

The palaces were therefore the spatial and temporal setting of Herod's court, and each member of the court fit spatially inside the palace and its surroundings. Like the other Hellenistic royal palaces, the Herodian Palace accommodated the court while fulfilling various tasks which each member of the court needed to play. Nielsen has clearly defined nine different functions of the Hellenistic Palace in relation to the court.[152] These functions are official and ceremonial, social, religious, administrative, service, residential, "public," and defensive. Here we shall consider all of these functions, with the exception of the religious function – since there were no chapels to heathen gods in the Herodian palaces – and the defensive one, which will be analyzed in Chapter III.

The first function is official and ceremonial. The king would often, though not always, receive his subjects or foreign dignitaries in state inside the palace. All of these rooms – audience halls, council halls, court rooms, and reception halls – were generally characterized by the presence of the throne, where the king symbolically sat, granting audience. The throne was the center of the room, and everything else evolved around it. The king did not stand alone, but was surrounded by the more important members of his family, such as the heirs, ministers and advisors, the most important *philoi*, servants, and of course the bodyguards. The main purpose of this room was to impress the visitor and make

---

[151] The original owner acquired the Warren Cup somewhere in the Land of Israel. The cup was produced between the years 30 BCE and 30 CE. It is quite probable that it was the property of a member of Herod's court. The possibility that this cup was owned by a member of the entourage of one of the early Roman governors of Judaea cannot be ruled out. On the Warren Cup, which depicts a homoerotic subject, see J. R. Clarke, *Looking at Lovemaking, Constructions of Sexuality in Roman Art*, Berkeley 1998, pp. 61–78.

[152] See Nielsen, *Hellenistic Palaces*, p. 14 Nielsen distinguishes nine different functions, official and ceremonial, social, religious, defensive, administrative, service, residential (a – for the king/governor and his family, b – for court or guests), "public", and defensive.

him feel the power and might of the hosting king. Therefore these rooms were generally the largest and most lavishly decorated spaces in the palace.

The throne was set between mosaic or *opus sectile* pavements, which were walls decorated with frescoes. Often, rows of columns fulfilled an architectural, as well as a decorative, task. In the most important Herodian palaces, this room was shaped as a basilical hall. Good examples are the First Winter Palace and the Third Winter Palace in Jericho and the Upper Terrace of the Promontory Palace in Caesarea Maritima. Another example, which, however, lacked rows of columns, comes from the Second Winter Palace at Jericho. This basilical hall was probably present as well in Jerusalem, as well as at Lower Herodium, although it did not survive. Smaller audience halls, characterized by a broad square-shaped room preceded by a *dystilos in antis* and sometimes followed by a further room, characterized other Herodian palaces such as the Western Palace in Masada, the Lower Terrace of the Promontory Palace in Caesarea, the Upper Herodium fortified palace, and probably also the Antonia Fortress. Clearly, in all of these palaces the king's need to impress visitors, as well as the need for *tryphe*, were somehow reduced, since these palaces were situated in less important surroundings than were the other main palaces.[153]

As noted above, the second function of the palace was social. The most important in Hellenistic palaces was the banqueting hall, which could host the king together with hundreds of his courtiers, guests, or subjects, as well as just the king and a few select guests. The main element of the banqueting hall was the *kline* or reclining bed, where the guests were accommodated and were served food by the servants. This was also the occasion to display *tryphe*, since drinks were frequently served in silver vessels. Banqueting halls also had to accommodate the king's bodyguards, who weeded out unwelcome individuals, and to impress guests with the king's might. Often there were hundreds of servants on hand, whose main task was to wait on the guests.

The main characteristic of these surrounding is space, and hence during the Hellenistic period the palace courtyard was considered to be the best setting for the banqueting hall. Courtyards that could fulfill this function were present in most of the Herodian palaces, though sometimes in reduced dimensions. The palaces in Jericho are good examples of various huge courtyards that could be used as banqueting halls. These include the courtyard of the First Winter Palace, as well as the upper and lower terraces of the Second Winter Palace, the latter surrounding a swimming pool, and the two courtyards of the Northern Wing of the Third Winter Palace, which faced a sunken garden and could together serve the needs and pleasures of hundreds if not thousands of guests. Other good

---

[153] On the official and ceremonial functions of the Herodian palaces see Nielsen, *Hellenistic Palaces*, on Masada Western Palace see pp. 295, Jericho First Winter Palace see p. 299, Jericho Third Winter Palace see p. 303, Lower Herodium p. 306. See also Netzer, *Palaces of the Hasmoneans and Herod the Great*, pp. 121–122 on the Promontory Palace of Caesarea Maritima.

examples are the pool complex in Lower Herodium, which was surrounded by a portico, as well as the two courtyards in the palace itself. Once more, all of these courtyards could accommodate hundreds of guests. Another example of a great courtyard comes from the palace of Caesarea Maritima, whose two courtyards were located in the Lower Terrace, around a swimming pool, and in the Upper Terrace's courtyard.

It would be interesting to speculate about what happened in Jerusalem, since the palace had more than one courtyard. Were these courtyards surrounded by porticoes large enough to host the king's various guests in this, the most important palace in the kingdom? Or did King Herod hold his banquets in other public spaces? Greatly reduced courtyards which could also be used as banqueting halls are present in the Western Palace in Masada, as well in Upper Herodium and the Antonia *tetrapyrgia*. But then in the first case, in Masada, the people who could have been hosted, coming from the surrounding areas, would have been among the "happy few." As for the other two examples, in Upper Herodium and Antonia, the nearby palaces of Lower Herodium and the Royal Palace of Jerusalem fulfilled these tasks in any case.[154]

The third function of the palace was administrative. Various offices such as the archives and the treasury were located there. There are two main reasons for this. First, the king, who was the most important resident of the palace, stood at the head of the immense bureaucracy which characterized the Hellenistic state, and it was important for him to have immediate access to various civil servants whenever necessary. The various government ministers were found in the palace more often than not, and on a daily basis these rooms were the privileged space of civil servants. While these courtiers worked in these rooms every day, all year round, they often lived far away, probably in the surrounding city or villages, together with their families. In fact, the social standing of these courtiers was probably distinguished enough to permit them to live their own lives far away from the palace, each in his own house, with one exception. In Masada there were various smaller palaces which could host the various military and civil members of the permanent staff living in Masada, and all of these rooms required a very large staff in order to keep them running smoothly. Although these rooms can hardly be identified now, they existed in every palace. In some of the palaces, such as the First and Third Winter Palaces in Jericho, where the private space is not so clearly separated from the private space, it is difficult to determine precisely where these rooms stood. It seems to me that these would have been situated not far from the

---

[154] On the social functions of the Herodian palaces see Nielsen, *Hellenistic Palaces*, on Masada Western Palace see p. 298, on Masada Northern Palace see p. 298, on Jericho First Winter Palace see p. 299, Jericho Second Winter Palace see p. 301, Jericho Third Winter Palace see p. 304, Lower Herodium p. 306. See also Netzer, *Palaces of the Hasmoneans and Herod the Great*, pp. 125–128 on the Royal Palace at Jerusalem.

audience hall. However, in other palaces, as the Palace in Caesarea Maritima, it is clear that these rooms stood somewhere in the Upper Terrace, since that was the public wing of the complex. In Jerusalem, where the palace space was congested, and hence precious, it is possible that these rooms stood in one of the three towers of the citadel, which dominated, horizontally, the palace complex. In Lower Herodium, which was also the capital of a *toparchia*, it seems that these rooms were situated north of the Pool Complex, far away from the palace. In Masada these chambers clearly stood somewhere in the Western Palace.[155]

Service rooms were a significant part of the Hellenistic Palace and consisted primarily of storerooms, kitchens, and servants' quarters. The main feature of these rooms was that they were never entered by the king or by any of the most important courtiers. These rooms were in fact the realm of the servants who worked at the court. Storerooms were mainly used for food – for dry food such as wheat, barley, dried figs or dates – as well as liquids stored in amphorae, such as wine and oil. The storerooms contained such implements as vessels, cleaning tools, and various materials for upkeep of the palaces, while the kitchens served to provide food for the king and his courtiers. A common characteristic of all of these rooms was that the smell emanating from it was probably less than inviting, and thus the servant's quarters and those of courtiers who had the lowest standing were probably located nearby. With the exception of the fortified palaces such as Masada and Upper Herodium, none of these structures, such as storerooms, kitchens, and servant quarters, can be identified in the main Herodian palaces in Jericho and Caesarea Maritima. According to an oral communication I received from Professor Netzer, there were no actual servants' quarters, since servants slept in the rooms in which they worked. But then we may ask why the storerooms have not been identified. I think that the only answer to this must be that each day fresh food was brought into the palace from outside, which was not a difficult task since the palaces in Jerusalem, Caesarea Maritima, and Lower Herodium stood in an urban space. On the other hand, the various storage rooms found in Masada in the Northern Palace and Western Palace areas did not serve Herod and his court on a daily basis, and any food stored there would have been used only during a siege.[156]

A characteristic feature of Hellenistic palaces is the residential area. Nielsen divides the spaces that were part of the residential area of the palaces in two: the

---

[155] On the administrative functions of the Herodian palaces see Nielsen, *Hellenistic Palaces*, on Masada Western Palace see p. 296, on Jericho First Winter Palace see p. 299, Jericho Third Winter Palace see p. 304, Lower Herodium p. 306. See also Netzer, *Palaces of the Hasmoneans and Herod the Great*, pp. 121–122 on the Promontory Palace at Caesarea Maritima and pp. 125–128 on the main palace at Jerusalem.

[156] On the service rooms in the Herodian palaces see Nielsen, *Hellenistic Palaces* on Masada Western Palace see p. 296, on Masada Northern Palace see p. 298, on Jericho First Winter Palace see p. 299, Jericho Third Winter Palace see p. 304, Lower Herodium p. 306.

spaces reserved for the king and his family, and the space reserved for the court and guests. In the Herodian palaces there is no hint of a residential space used by court members, and thus I have considered here only the residential space shared by the king and his family. Probably anyone caught in this area, who could not justify his unwelcome presence, would have risked serious punishment. The residential area included bedrooms, bathrooms, private dining rooms, and the harem. Yet the king was never alone, even in these areas. His bodyguards, as well as his personal servants, would always stand at the side of the king. Moreover, specialized servants, such as eunuchs, would have taken care of the bath houses or the harem. Bedrooms have not survived, since these probably stood on the upper floor. The royal bedchambers, unlike all of the other bedrooms, would have been decorated with mosaic pavements, wall paintings, and a stucco ceiling. These rooms would not have been much bigger than other bedrooms and would have been distinguished from other bedrooms only by virtue of their decorations and furnishings. The main features of the residential areas of the Herodian palaces that survived and that can be easily recognized are the bathrooms, which are Hellenistic in style, and the bathhouses, which are in Roman style. More or less, each Herodian palace that has been excavated is characterized by a bathroom or a bathhouse. Thus the three Winter Palaces in Jericho are characterized by Roman bathhouses, as is the Lower Terrace of the Promontory Palace at Caesarea Maritima. Upper and Lower Herodium are also characterized by Roman bathhouses. In Masada, the Northern Hanging Palace is characterized by a huge bathhouse with a courtyard in Roman Style and a smaller bathroom in the lower terrace. The Western Palace is also characterized by a set of two Hellenistic bathrooms. Although the main palace and the Antonia have not been excavated, according to Josephus they were furnished with various bathhouses. It is possible to suggest the presence of a Roman bathhouse in the Antonia, similar to that found in Upper Herodium.

Another feature that is often found in the Herodian Palaces is the existence of private dining rooms. There the king dined alone or with a few select guests, assisted by his servants and bodyguards. Private dining rooms can be found in Jericho on the veranda of the Second Winter Palace and in the Third Winter Palace in the wing south of Wadi Kelt. Here the dining room occupies an entire building, identified by Netzer as the Agrippeum. In Caesarea Maritima the area near the veranda on the west of the Promontory Palace, situated on the lower terrace, could have served as a private dining room. In Masada the lower and upper terraces of the Northern Hanging Palace probably served as private dining rooms. No room has been identified as a harem in the Herodian palaces, and I believe that this is not accidental. Herod, as I have noted earlier, had only one wife at a time. Divorced wives did not live at court, while concubines, because of their lower standing, did not need as much space as a queen or a king's wife. Moreover, I presume that when King Herod visited various areas of his kingdom, he did not bring all of his concubines with him, and most of them needed to wait in Jerusalem for the king's return.[157]

The public space of the Hellenistic Palace often included the *gymnasium*, the *palaestra*, the library, the theatre, and the hippodrome. The main function of these spaces was not only for the king's entertainment, but also to show off the king to his subjects. These structures, such as the hippodrome and the theatre, are usually open spaces, and there the king appears not merely in front of his courtiers, who numbered no more than a few hundred people in the audience hall, for example, but in front of the masses, sometimes numbering tens of thousands of people. Therefore even in these public spaces, and not merely in the audience hall, the king had to display himself, as it were, in all the splendor of his *tryphe* in order to impress not merely his courtiers, but all of his subjects as well. Although the king was surrounded by his bodyguards, by his heirs and wife, as well as by the most important courtiers, here in fact the king stood alone in front of his subjects. Therefore the king had to, in effect, put on a show twice, first in organizing entertainments that could satisfy the basest instincts of his subjects, the mob, and second in his role as king, who put a "supernatural barrier," as it were, between himself and his subjects. Otherwise nothing could stop the mob from rioting and endangering the security of the king.

These buildings or public spaces can be found only in the most important palaces, in Jerusalem, Jericho, and Caesarea Maritima. It is interesting that the theatre and hippodrome of Caesarea Maritima were integrated into the palace complex itself, and somehow separated from the city. However, in the Jewish areas of the kingdom, these buildings were separated from the palace. Thus, in Jerusalem, the hippodrome and the theatre were situated in an area far away from the main palace. In Jericho the hippodrome was not far from the palaces, but not in the same actual area. The reason for this is probably that King Herod felt more at ease among his Jewish subjects than he did among his Gentile subjects. Therefore, for security reasons, the theatre and the hippodrome in Caesarea Maritima were near the palace and separated from the city grid. In Jerusalem, the public space of Herod's palace became simply a public space shared by the king and his subjects.[158]

Recreational spaces were also an important element of the Hellenistic palace. These elements consisted of gardens, parks, pavilions, and swimming pools. Here the king relaxed – alone, or with his most intimate courtiers, a wife, a chosen con-

---

[157] On the residential area of the Herodian palaces see Nielsen, *Hellenistic Palaces*, on Masada Western Palace see p. 296, on Masada Northern Palace see p. 298, on Jericho First Winter Palace see p. 299, Jericho Second Winter Palace see p. 302, Jericho Third Winter Palace see p. 304, Lower Herodium p. 307. See also Netzer, *Palaces of the Hasmoneans and Herod the Great*, p. 134, fig. 172 on the Herodian Roman bathouses.

[158] On the public space in the Herodian palaces see Nielsen, *Hellenistic Palaces*, on Jericho Third Winter Palace see pp. 304–305. See also Netzer, *Palaces of the Hasmoneans and Herod the Great*, pp. 121–122 on the Promontory Palace at Caesarea Maritima.

cubine, his heir, or the most important *philoi*. These recreational spaces, whose main purpose was to guarantee a private area for the king, despite the presence of servants and body guards, can be found in all of the Herodian palaces. Only the dimensions of these areas change according to the available space and the main function of the particular palace. The three Winter Palaces of Jericho, for example, were set in a huge garden. More specifically, the second Winter Palace was erected over two pools, and the third Winter Palace included a huge sunken garden. The lower terrace of the Promontory Palace of Caesarea Maritima was built around a swimming pool. Lower Herodium possessed a huge pool, with a pavilion in the middle. Here the king could even use small boats for recreation. Even Upper Herodium possessed a courtyard that was also used as a garden.[159]

As noted above, the defensive spaces of some of the Herodian palaces will be discussed in Chapter III.

Like that of the Hasmoneans, Herod's court was centered in Jerusalem. However, Herod had two palaces in his capital. The three towers, Hippicus, Mariamme, and Phasael, surrounded the main palace, which was much larger than the Hasmonean palace that was still used at the beginning of Herod's reign. The other palace was the tetrapyrgion of the Antonia, which could be used in the event of war, though it appears that Herod never used the Antonia. At Jericho, where the Hasmoneans erected their winter palaces, Herod erected a small palace at the beginning of his reign, not far from the Hasmonean palaces. Only after 32 BCE did he erect an edifice on the ruins of the earlier Hasmonean palatial complex, which had been irreparably damaged by an earthquake. Later, he built another, larger palace, and finally, in 15 BCE, upon the visit of Agrippa, a third huge palace. All of the palaces, which included a theater-hippodrome, were used simultaneously. Moreover, since Herod liked to travel around the kingdom, there were other royal palaces scattered around Judaea, such as the Herodium complex, and Masada, far away, near the Dead Sea. In contrast to the Hasmonean tradition, Herod's court sometimes resided in Gentile areas, and, for example, Herod erected palaces at Caesarea Maritima, Sebaste, and Paneas. The Herodian court later developed its own offshoots, such as Amatha-Betharamatha in Peraea, where Herod's brother Pheroras had a court of his own.

After Herod's death, Archelaus resided in Jerusalem, Jericho, and Caesarea Maritima – maintaining a court, albeit in reduced form – while his brother Antipas shifted his court first to Sepphoris and then to Tiberias. Philip, half-brother of Archelaus, held court at Paneas. None of the reigning sons of Herod, however, were actually kings. Archelaus was an *ethnarch*, while Antipas and Philip were *tetrarchs*, since they ruled smaller territories than did a king, and hence their

---

[159] On the recreational space in the Herodian palaces see Nielsen, *Hellenistic Palaces*, on Jericho First Winter Palace see p. 299, Jericho Second Winter Palace see pp. 302–303, Lower Herodium pp. 306–307. See also Netzer, *Palaces of the Hasmoneans and Herod the Great*, pp. 121–122 on the Promontory Palace at Caesarea Maritima.

courts were also smaller. Agrippa I's court was located in Paneas and Tiberias, and then, when he became king, it was located in Jerusalem, Jericho, and Caesarea Maritima. The court of Agrippa II, the last Herodian ruler, was ensconced at Paneas and Tiberias.

When Herod erected his palaces across his kingdom, Hellenistic palaces were hardly a new item in the landscape of urban and rural Judaea. These Hellenistic palaces, particularly those erected by the Hasmoneans in Jericho, had an important influence upon Herod's palatial architecture. These included the palaces of Hyrcanus the Tobiad[160] and the palace at Tel Anafa.[161] However, the most important palaces were those built by the Hasmoneans in Jerusalem and Jericho. John Hyrcanus I erected the first palatial structure. Although built following native tradition, it had several characteristics in common with other Hellenistic palaces, such as the *oikos* decorated with mosaic pavements, walls painted in the First Eastern Style, and a bathhouse with a bathtub. The palace acquired its main Hellenistic elements during the reign of Alexander Jannaeus, around 100 BCE, as the Doric pavillon and a huge garden enclosed by stoas, and later during the civil wars, the *tetrapyrgion*. The Twin Palace, built for Hyrcanus II and Aristobulus II, once more reflected local trends. The influence of native traditions and the lack of basic "Hellenistic" elements are noteworthy. Thus, the Hasmoneans' winter palaces lack a peristyle. However other elements are present, such as *paradeisoi*, which are of Eastern origin, but mediated by the palatial architecture of Antioch and Alexandria. It is interesting to note that although the shape and style of the Doric pavilion is Greek, its plan and execution are Achaemenid (cfr. figure II, 1).[162]

Towards the end of the Hasmonean period Roman influence apparently also began to permeate local architectural trends. Thus, the governor's residence at Tell Judeideh presents elements coming from the Roman *domus*, such as its elongated shape and the small peristyle garden surrounding a swimming pool.[163]

Herod's palaces, as well as his other building projects, are probably some of the most impressive architectural creations of the Classical world. It is therefore worthwhile to try to understand Herod's involvement in them. Both Netzer and Levine have dealt with this topic. According to Netzer, Herod's building projects were an expression of the king's desire and ability to build extensively. These

---

[160] The earliest Hellenistic palace known in the Land of Israel is that of Hyrcanus the Tobiad. On Hyrcanus the Tobiad's palace, see Nielsen, *Hellenistic Palaces*, pp. 138–146.

[161] See S. C. Herbert, "Tel Anafa, Final Report on Ten Years of Excavation at a Hellenistic and Roman Settlement in Northern Israel, Pt. I", *JRA Supp. Series no. 10*, Ann Arbor, 1994. See also S. Weinberg, "Tel Anafa, the Hellenistic Town", *IEJ* 21, 1971, pp. 86–109.

[162] On the Hasmonean winter palaces at Jericho, see E. Netzer, *The Palaces of the Hasmoneans and Herod the Great*, Jerusalem 2001, pp. 14–39. See also Nielsen, *Hellenistic Palaces*, pp. 155–159. As a written source see Josephus, *AJ* XV, 53–56, 121–122 and *BJ* I, 138–140. See also Pliny, *NH* XII, 115–118, XIII, 44–46, and Strabo, *Geography* XVI, 763.

[163] See Nielsen, *Hellenistic Palaces*, pp. 160–163.

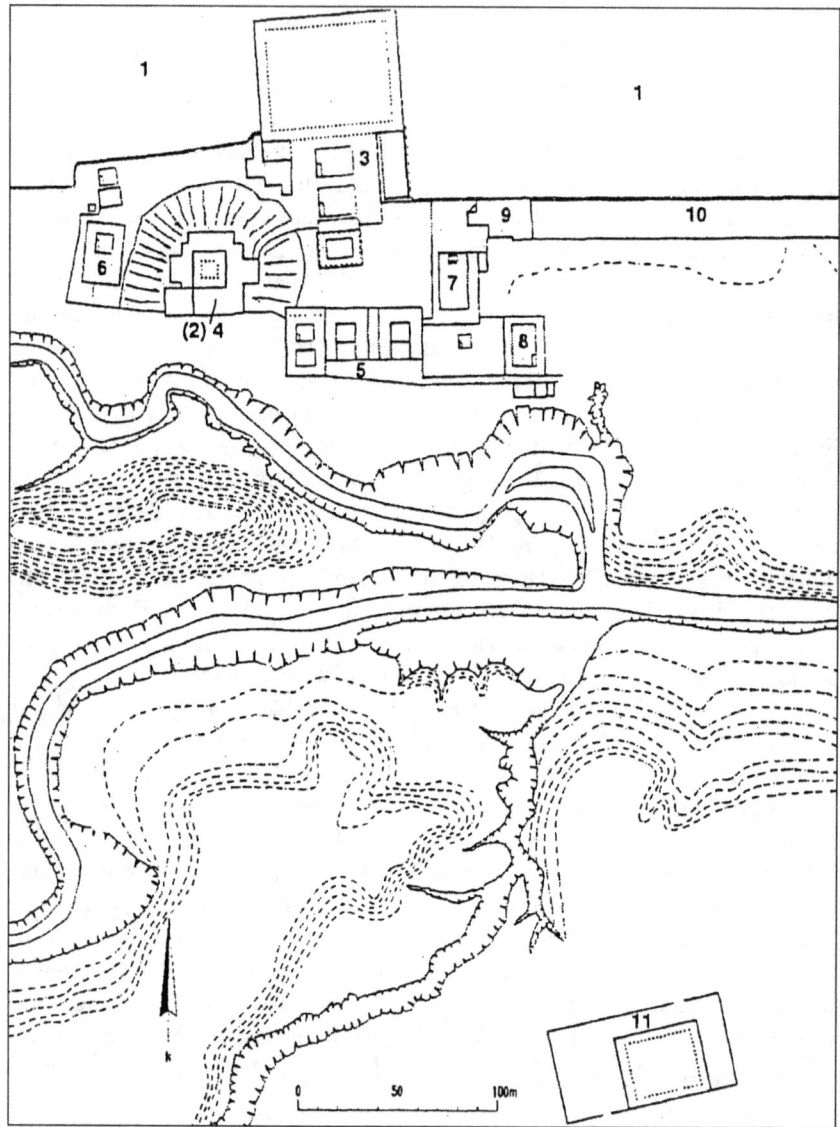

Figure II, 1 – The Hasmonaean Palaces in Jericho, from E. Netzer, *Hasmonean and Herodian Palaces at Jericho I, Final Report of the 1973–1987 Excavations, Stratigraphy and Architecture*, Jerusalem 2001, plan 8, p. 6, Courtesy of Professor Emeritus Ehud Netzer, The Hebrew University of Jerusalem.

3. The setting of the Herodian Court: the Herodian Palace

projects involved innovative and original planning by King Herod himself, as well as a grandiose approach, indicated by the proportions of the huge podium and the monumental stones of the Temple Mount and its Royal Stoa, and by the size of the Herodium palace fortress, which was a monumental structure of 50 acres. Structures such as the towers in Jerusalem, in the harbor in Caesarea, and in Herodium were the creation of Herod's building genius alone. Thus, Herod followed the path of the Hellenistic monarchs who were personally involved in all of their construction projects. According to Levine, King Herod was involved in and followed the work while it was underway, but did not play an active role. A gifted architect or perhaps even a team of experts determined the sites, designed the plans, and made the basic development decisions. Herod's involvement in all of this would have been similar to that of Augustus in his own building projects. I believe that Netzer's view is probably more accurate. Becoming entirely involved in relatively minor details is the characteristic of the absolute ruler, who needs to control and micro-manage everything. In contrast, when Augustus constructed the framework of Republican Rome, he could not appear to be adopting one of the most obvious features of the absolute Hellenistic ruler.

But even according to Netzer, there were architects. If so, who were they and where did they come from? Some probably came from the Hellenistic East, among the many Greeks who sought their fortune in Herod's court. A good example of a Greek at Herod's court was the historian Nicolaus of Damascus, who has been mentioned earlier. Architects also came from the Roman West, and according to Netzer, some of them accompanied Agrippa during his visit to the East in 15 BCE and helped in the building of the third palace at Jericho. Moreover, since most of the Herodian buildings share features found in other buildings in Judaea dating back to the Hasmonean period – such as the Western Palace at Masada – it may be surmised that some architects were probably Jewish natives.[164]

Native building traditions greatly influenced Herodian palace architecture. The palaces erected at Jericho, for instance, were constructed using local mud brick covered with stucco, on stone foundations, a traditional construction technique in the Land of Israel from the earliest periods. Characteristic Hasmonean features, such as the shape of the Twin Palace, influenced the earlier Herodian palaces. This square shaped, two-storied building with a central courtyard had the main reception room situated south of the courtyard, and it was entered through a *distylos in antis*. Thus the earlier Herodian structures at Masada, such as the core of the Western Palace and Buildings VII, VIII, IX, XI, and XII, were strongly influenced by the plan of the Twin Palace.[165]

---

[164] See E. Netzer, "Herod's Building Projects: Personal or State Necessity?", *Cathedra* 15 1980, pp. 38–67.
[165] See G. Foerster, "Hellenistic and Roman Trends in the Herodian Architecture of Masada", *Judaea and the Greco-Roman World in the Time of Herod in the Light of Archaeological Evidence*, *Abhandlungen der Akademie der Wissenschaften in Göttingen 215*, Göttingen 1996, pp. 56–57.

There are also some Hellenistic features that were appropriated in the Herodian palaces through the mediation of Hasmonean architecture, including the bathhouse with the bathtub[166] and the *oikos* decorated with mosaic pavements and wall paintings. Once more, the Core Palace of Masada is the best example. Hellenistic palatial architecture was one of the main influences on the Herodian palaces. Thus Late Ptolemaic palatial architecture strongly influenced the general layout of the Herodian palaces, as well as the Roman *domus* of the Late Republican period. Thus, the built-up area of the palaces was considerably extended and included the creation of complexes containing buildings, open spaces, and pools and gardens, which integrated residence, administrative, leisure, and entertainment structures within it. There were various wings, ceremonial and residential, for the king and his court and for administrative and service personnel, including storerooms and recreational areas that included gardens, pavilions, and swimming pools.[167] Another fundamental concept that originated in Hellenistic architecture and that was reflected in the Herodian palaces was the use of impressive natural landscapes as settings for the buildings, as seen in the Jericho Palace III, which was erected on both sides of Wadi Qelt; Masada's Northern Palace, which was built on a high rock cliff in the desert; and Caesarea Maritima's palace, which stands by the seashore.[168]

The absorption of Roman elements, however, was the main characteristic of Herod's palaces. Herod adopted new Roman building techniques from contemporary Italy, such as the use of *opus reticulatum* and *opus quadratum*, mainly for the building of bathhouses. Thus, *opus reticulatum* and *opus quadratum* are found in several Herodian structures, including the Third Winter Palace at Jericho, a building at Paneas, and a circular building near the present day Damascus Gate in Jerusalem. According to Netzer, only builders who came from Italy could have executed these features.[169] Another Roman technological innovation, the use of concrete vaults in bathhouses, is also present in Herodian buildings.

According to Föertsch, one of the most interesting features that originated in Roman Italy was the use of landscapes as settings for architectural creations. The placement of the palatial building within the landscape, melding both into a unique composition, is one of the characteristic features of the architectural lexicon of Late Republican and Early Imperial Roman villas. Thus, the Hero-

---

[166] See Nielsen, *Hellenistic Palaces*, p. 187.
[167] See Nielsen, *Hellenistic Palaces*, p. 14.
[168] See R. Förtsch, "The Residences of King Herod and their Relations to Roman Villa Architecture", in *Judaea and the Greco-Roman World in the Time of Herod in the Light of Archaeological Evidence, Abhandlungen der Akademie der Wissenschaften in Göttingen 215*, Göttingen 1996, pp. 76–77. According to Förtsch this concept, however, was probably borrowed from the architectural lexicon of the Roman villa.
[169] See Netzer, "Herod's Building Projects: State Necessity or Personal Need? A Symposium", p. 60 and E. Netzer, *The Winter Palaces and the King's Estate in Jericho, Jericho (Kardom)*, 1983, p. 108.

dium complex shares many features with the Villas of Settefinestre and the Villa of Vedio Pollio. I believe that this conjunction of landscape and architecture originated in Eastern Hellenistic influences, though, clearly, the shaping of the landscape is a feature that derives from Roman Italy. Both Herodium and the palatial complex of Jericho Palace III have features in common with the Villa of Tiberius at Sperlonga. The Northern Palace at Masada shares certain features with the Villa Gregoriana in Tivoli and Villa Jovis in Capri. The Promontory Palace at Caesarea has features in common with the Villa at Punta Campanella, the Villa of Torre Astura, and the Villa of Capo di Sorrento.

Various wings of the Herodian palaces originated in single structures of the Roman urban *domus* and villas of the Late Republic and Early Empire in Roman Italy. R. Förtsch has distinguished five main architectural forms – the *atrium*, the *vestibulum*, the *triclinium cum procoetone*, the *specus estivus*, and the Corinthian *oecus*, the prototype of the Roman palatial basilica – features used by Herod in almost every palace.[170] The atrium is found in Upper Herodium, the *vestibulum* in the Northern Palace of Masada, the *triclinium cum procoetone* at Jericho Palace III, the *triclinium* with front windows at Upper Herodium, and the *specus aestivus* and the *nymphaeum* in the Monumental Building in Lower Herodium. The Corinthian *oecus* is found at Jericho Palace III.

Herod also incorporated various features from contemporary Roman private architecture in his palaces, including bathhouses and other rooms with a strong Roman influence. The bathhouses found in his palaces closely imitated the new bathhouses developed in Pompeii and in other parts of Roman Campania during the first century BCE. These include a side courtyard, used as *palaestra*, and a bathing complex that consisted of an *apodyterium*, a *frigidarium* or cold room, a *tepidarium*, or warm room, and a *caldarium* or hot room.[171] The bath-buildings of the Herodian palaces of Jericho, the Masada Western Palace, and the Herodium complex were probably similar to those in Herod's palaces in Jerusalem.

Last but not least, Roman art was also a source of inspiration. Most of the Herodian wall paintings follow the Roman-Italic model rather than the Eastern prototype in the Second Style.[172]

The typology of Herodian palaces follows that of earlier or contemporary palaces of the Hellenistic kings, including the Hasmoneans. Herodian palaces included:[173]

---

[170] See Förtsch, *Residences of King Herod and their Relations to Roman Villa*, pp. 78–87.

[171] See F. Yeguel, *Bath and Bathing in Classical Antiquity*, Cambridge (Mass.) 1995, p. 64. On the bathhouses of Pompeii and Herculanum as prototypes for the Herodian bath-buildings, see Yeguel, pp. 57–66. See also Roller, *Building Program of Herod the Great*, p. 64.

[172] See K. Fittschen, "Wall Decorations in Herod's Kingdom: Their Relationship with Wall Decoration in Greece and Italy", *Judaea and the Greco-Roman World in the Time of Herod in the Light of Archaeological Evidence*, Abhandlungen der Akademie der Wissenschaften in Göttingen 215, Göttingen 1996, pp. 139–163.

[173] On the typology of the Herodian palaces see: Nielsen, *Hellenistic Palaces*, pp. 181–182.

- City palaces erected in an urban context, such as the main Jerusalem palace, the Caesarea palace, the Acropolis Palace of Sebaste, capital of Samaria, and the Lower Herodium palace, capital of a *toparchia*.
- Winter palaces, or palaces used by Herod's court during the cold winter months, such as the palatial complex in Jericho.
- Fortified palaces, most of them constructed in fortresses that Herod took over from the Hasmoneans. These palaces were used in the event of war or rebellion and included the Antonia in Jerusalem and the various desert fortresses such as Masada, Upper Herodium, Machaerus, and Cypros. Their defensive features are analyzed in the Chapter III.

The plethora of palaces built by Herod throughout his kingdom was probably influenced by the Hellenistic heritage of Antigonus Monopthalmos. Herod certainly realized that in times of peace, the capital and center of the kingdom would be where the king and his court were settled. Since Herod dominated a vast kingdom, composed of diverse ethnic elements that included Jews, Greeks, Samaritans and Ituraeans, it was necessary that the king be seen everywhere together with his court, and by every segment of the kingdom's population. Thus, King Herod needed to display his *tryphe* everywhere and to erect palaces, most notably in Jerusalem, in Caesarea Maritima, and even in such faraway places as Masada on the Dead Sea. The Herodian palaces are thus a clear expression of what C. Geertz terms "the ceremonial forms by which kings take symbolic possession of their realms." Geertz adds that "in particular royal progresses locate the society's Center and affirm its connection with transcendent things by stamping a territory with ritual signs of dominance," which, in the case of Herod, were the palaces.[174]

B. *City Palaces*

In this section I shall analyze the palaces erected in an urban context, such as the main Jerusalem palace, the Caesarea palace, the Acropolis Palace of Sebaste, capital of Samaria, and the Lower palace of Herodium, capital of a *toparchia*.

Jerusalem was the capital of Herod's kingdom, as well as the political and religious capital of the Jews. Jerusalem, like Jericho, was the traditional center of the Hasmonean dynasty, which Herod had usurped. It was difficult, but essential to Herod's political success, to erase the memory of the glorious Hasmonean dynasty. Thus, in Jerusalem, Herod's palaces were built on new sites, far from the Hasmonean palace, which Herod probably left intact. Herod's palace in Jerusa-

---

[174] See C. Geertz, *Local Knowledge, Further Essays in Interpretative Anthropology*, New York (NY) 1983, p. 125.

lem was the main symbol of his status as Hellenistic king, similar to those of the Ptolemies and the Seleucids. All of the Hellenistic kings had a main urban palace in the most important city of their kingdom, such as the fortress palaces of the Macedonian kings,[175] the Promontory Palace of the Ptolemies in Alexandria,[176] the Seleucid palace in Antioch,[177] and the Attalid palace at the Acropolis of Pergamum.[178] City walls separated these palaces, including the Herodian urban palaces, from the city.

Although Herod's main palace in Jerusalem has not survived, Josephus provides a general description that enables us to visualize it.[179] The palace was entirely enclosed by a wall with towers that separated the structure from the Upper City. The only information that archaeology has provided aids in establishing the its enormous dimensions. The palace was built on a raised platform which extended over 300–350 m. north-south and at least 60 m. east-west, under today's Armenian Quarter.[180] Josephus' description clarifies the structures inside the Herodian palace, including large *triclinia* and peristyle courtyards, garden courts, and bathhouses in Roman style. Other Herodian palaces are useful in enabling us to reconstruct the structure of Herod's main palace in Jerusalem.[181] Like the palace in Jericho, the Jerusalem palace contained two richly appointed reception halls. According to Josephus, one hall was named after Augustus, the *Augusteum*, and the other after Agrippa, the *Agrippeum*. Josephus' descriptions leave no doubt that the Jerusalem palace included large peristyle courtyards, used as small pools and as gardens. The Jerusalem palace probably included a combination of gardens and pools, bathhouses, probably in the Roman style, and storage and service rooms.

---

[175] See Nielsen, *Hellenistic Palaces*, pp. 81–99.

[176] See A. Bernard, *Alexandrie des Ptolemées*, Paris 1995, pp. 90–93, see also Nielsen, *Hellenistic Palaces*, pp. 130–138.

[177] See J. J. Pollitt, *Art in the Hellenistic Age*, Cambridge 1986, pp. 277–279, see also Nielsen, *Hellenistic Palaces*, pp. 112–115.

[178] See Pollitt, *Art in the Hellenistic Age*, pp. 233–234; see also Nielsen, *Hellenistic Palaces*, pp. 102–112.

[179] See Josephus, *BJ* V, 177–182.

[180] See D. Bahat, *The Illustrated Atlas of Jerusalem*, Jerusalem 1990, p. 47.

[181] The northern wing of the Third Winter Palace in Jericho, on the northern bank of Wadi Kelt, was perhaps the most similar of all the Herodian palaces to the main palace in Jerusalem. On Jericho see E. Netzer, "The Palaces Built by Herod – A Research Update", *Judaea and the Graeco-Roman World in the Time of Herod in the Light of Archaeological Evidence, Abhandlungen der Akademie der Wissenschaften in Göttingen* 215, Göttingen 1996, pp. 28–29. Another interesting comparison can be made with the similar Herodium Lower Palace. On Herodium see Netzer, "Palaces Built by Herod – A Research Update", pp. 29–34. It may also be compared to the two city palaces in the Gentile areas: the Promontory Palace at Caesarea Maritima and the Acropolis Palace at Sebaste. On Caesarea Maritima see E. Netzer, "The Promontory Palace", in A. Raban, and K. Holum, (eds.), *Caesarea Maritima, a Retrospective after Two Millennia*, *DMOA XXI*, Leiden 1996, pp. 201–207. On Sebaste see D. Barag, "King Herod's Royal Castle at Samaria-Sebaste", *PEF 125*, 1993, pp. 14–17.

Herod's palace at Caesarea, described by Josephus and mentioned in the New Testament,[182] was part of a large complex that included a hippodrome and a theater (cfr. figure II, 2). Herod began the erection of a palace at Caesarea Maritima between the years 19–10 BCE. The palace was built on two terraces – a lower terrace, the Promontory Palace, which was private in character; and an upper terrace, which had an official ceremonial function. The Promontory Palace, built on a cliff, included a peristyle courtyard with a swimming pool, and a semicircular veranda facing the sea.[183] The upper terrace included a peristyle courtyard, and its public character was emphasized by the presence of a bema or the tribunal of justice in the courtyard, and an audience hall.[184] According to Burrell, the upper terrace is quite similar to Roman *praetorium* in the East, such as Gortyn in Crete, and in the West, in locations such as Aquincum in Pannonia and Colonia Agrippiniensis in Germania Superior. The structure most similar to the Herodian palace at Caesarea Maritima is the Palace of *dux ripae* at Dura Europus.[185] After Archelaus was sent into exile, this became the main residence of the Roman *praefectus*, and after the death of Agrippa I in 44 CE, it became the residence of the Roman procurator. Herod's palace included an amphitheater and a theater as well.[186] The source of inspiration here is clear. As in the overall planning of Caesarea and its harbor, Herod took Ptolemaic Alexandria as his model. Herod's palace, erected on the seaside, was clearly inspired by the *basileia* of Alexandria. The Ptolemaic palace also included such features as a theater and a hippodrome. According to Gleason, another source of inspiration for the Caesarea Maritima palatial complex, i.e., the palace itself, the theater and the hippodrome, was in Rome. It is possible that during Herod's first visits to Rome

---

[182] See Josephus, *AJ* XV, 331–341, and Acts 23: 35.

[183] On the Promontory Palace see Netzer, *Palaces of the Hasmoneans and Herod the Great*, pp. 117–122. See also Netzer, "Promontory Palace", pp. 201–207. See also Nielsen, *Hellenistic Palaces*, pp. 183–185, fig. 95.

[184] On the upper wing of Herod's palace at Caesarea Maritima see B. Burrell, "Palace to Praetorium: The Romanization of Caesarea", in A. Raban, and K. Holum, (eds.), *Caesarea Maritima, a Retrospective after Two Millennia, DMOA XXI*, Leiden 1996, pp. 228–232 and 240–245.

[185] See Burrell, "Palace to Praetorium", pp. 233–238. The Praetorium of Gortyn was a squared structure that measured 150 by 140 m. The Praetorium of Aquincum measured 150 by 140 m. The Praetorium of Colonia measured around 180 sq. m. However, this palace was erected along the city wall, and not in the camp-city Center. The Palace of the *dux ripae* at Dura Europus included, like the Herodian palace at Caesarea Maritima, two wings, one public facing the city, and one private, facing the cliff over the Euphrates. The main characteristic of the plan of the Praetorium is a central courtyard and an aisled hall on one of its sides.

[186] Herod's amphitheater was built on a sandy plain north of the palace. The amphitheater followed a north-south axis. The southern side was semicircular. The theater, situated near the southernmost part of the city wall, not very far from the seaside, is of Hellenistic type, built on a slope. The theater's original *cavea* could accommodate about 3,500 spectators. On the upper terrace of the palace, the hippodrome, still under excavation see Y. Porath, "The Caesarea Excavation Project – March 1992–June 1994, Expedition of the Israel Antiquities Authority", *Excavations and Surveys in Israel 17*, Jerusalem 1998, pp. 39–41.

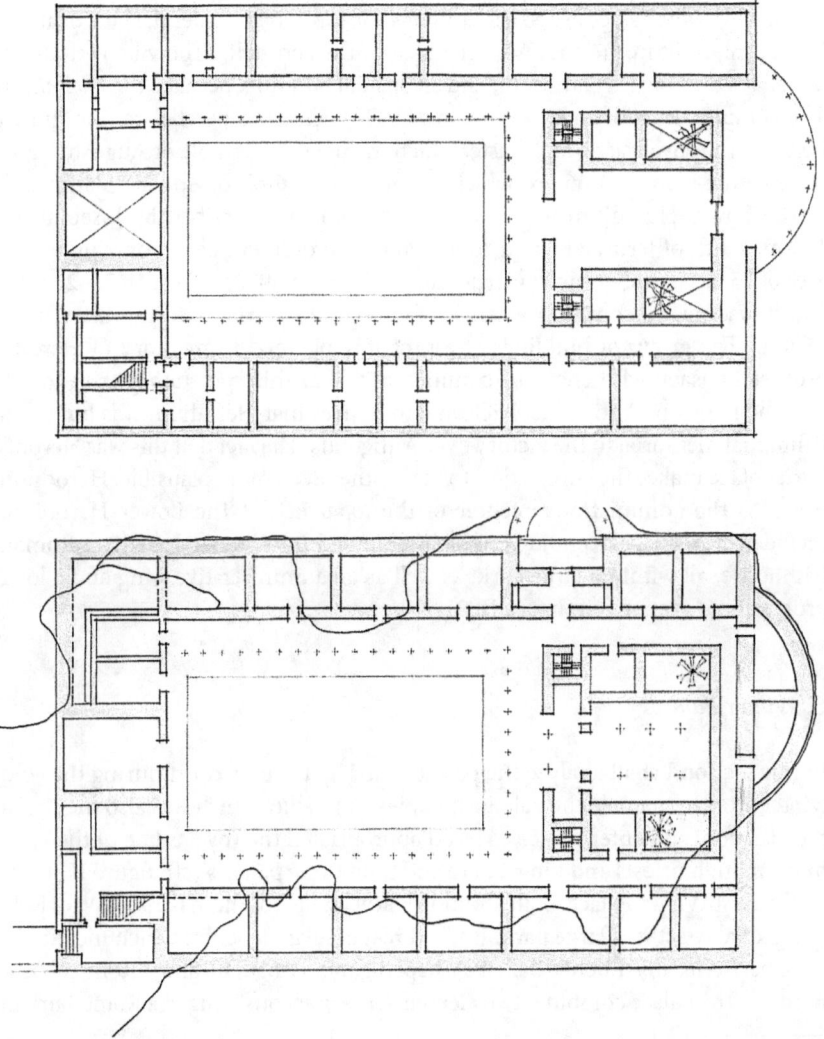

Figure II, 2 – Plan of the Promontory Palace from E. Netzer, *The Palaces of the Hasmonaeans and Herod the Great*, Jerusalem 2001, p. 122, fig. 62, Courtesy of Professor Emeritus Ehud Netzer, The Hebrew University of Jerusalem.

in 40 BCE he was inspired by the Theater and Domus of Pompey in the Campus Martius. Herod's second visit to Rome in 22 BCE could have provided another source of influence in the planning of the palatial complex of Caesarea Maritima: the Palatine Domus of Augustus and the Circus Maximus.[187]

---

[187] See K. Gleason, "Ruler and Spectacle: The Promontory Palace", in A. Raban, and K.

The Acropolis Palace at Sebaste consisted of a spacious residential villa of about 750 sq.m., built in the southwestern area of the acropolis. The villa included a peristyle courtyard, a bathroom, and an apsidal building, perhaps the *triclinium*. The complex was fortified. According to G. Foerster, a parallel can be drawn between the royal castle at Sebaste, which included the temple of Augustus, and the Palatine Domus complex, which included the temple of Apollo Palatinus.[188]

The Lower Herodium is part of a huge complex described by Josephus,[189] 15 km. south of Jerusalem, and consisted of two different parts covering a total area of 15 ha. Herod began constructing this huge palatial complex in 23–20 BCE, and it was nearly complete when he showed it to Agrippa during his visit in 15 BCE. The group of buildings was probably planned in memory of Herod's brother Phasael, who chose to commit suicide at this spot rather than to fall into the hands of Antigonus. Nielsen emphasizes that Herodium was built as a triumphal memorial to the victory over Antigonus. The fact that this was Herod's burial place makes the connection to his brother even more plausible. Herodium was also the administrative center of the *toparchia*.[190] The Lower Herodium included a main palace and a pool surrounded by a peristyle with a Roman bathhouse, all within a large park, as well as an administrative wing and a long processional avenue (cfr. figure II, 3).[191]

C. Winter Palaces

In this section I shall analyze the palaces used by Herod's court during the cold winter months, namely the palatial complex in Jericho, which was also the site of the Hasmonean winter palaces. Herod appropriated the royal estate of the Hasmonean high priests and kings there and built three palaces (cfr. figure II, 4).

The First Winter Palace, built around 35 BCE on the southern bank of Wadi Kelt, was probably set in a large park. It was a rectangular structure which included a huge peristyle, an audience hall, a T-shaped banqueting hall, and a Roman bathroom.[192] The palace combines two elements, the first consisting of a Roman urban

---

Holum, (eds.), *Caesarea Maritima, a Retrospective after Two Millennia*, DMOA XXI, Leiden 1996, pp. 208–227.

[188] On the Acropolis Palace at Sebaste see Barag, "King Herod's Royal Castle at Samaria-Sebaste", pp. 3–17.

[189] See Josephus, *AJ* XVI, 12–14, *BJ* I, 418–421 and 670–673.

[190] On Herodium see Nielsen, *Hellenistic Palaces*, pp. 201–203 and 305–307, figs. 111–113 and pls. 41–44.

[191] On Lower Herodium see Netzer, *Palaces of the Hasmoneans and Herod the Great*, pp. 107–116.

[192] Jericho's First Winter Palace appears to have been set in a large park. South of the palace was a large swimming pool (Birket Mousa). See Netzer, *Palaces of the Hasmoneans and Herod the Great*, pp. 40–42. See also Nielsen, *Hellenistic Palaces*, pp. 193–196, 299–301, figs. 104–105, pl. 37. The palace is mentioned by Strabo, *Geography*, XVI, 2. 40.

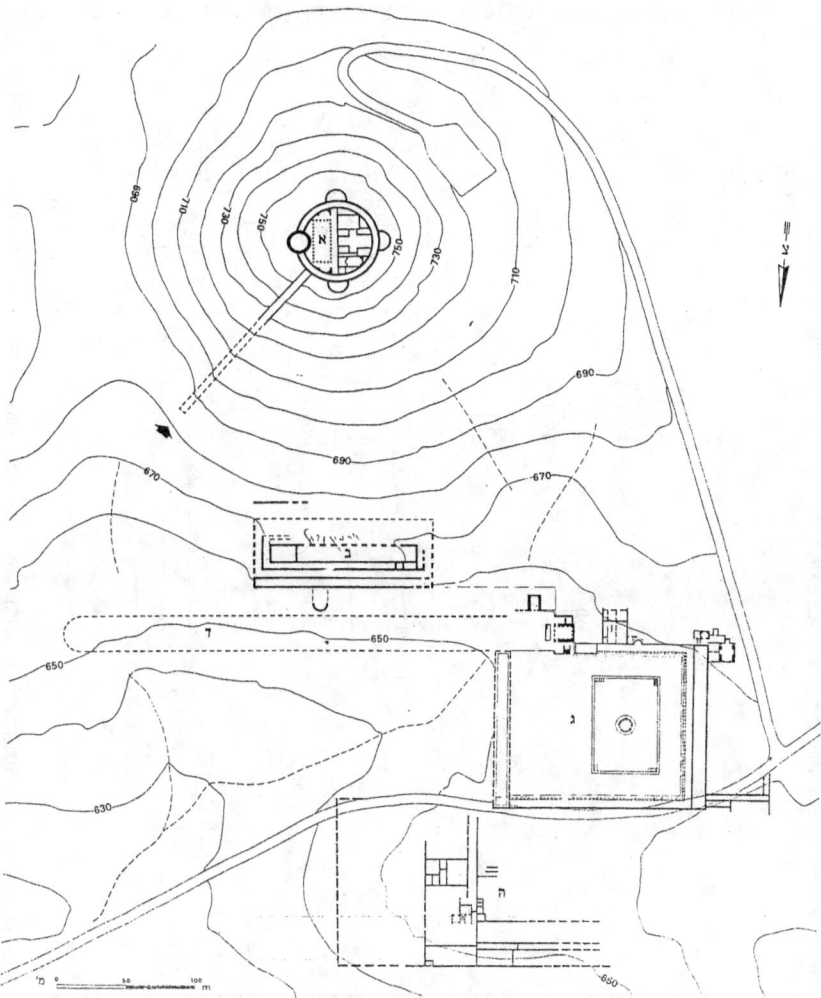

Figure II, 3 – Plan of the Herodium Complex from E. Netzer, *The Palaces of the Hasmonaeans and Herod the Great*, Jerusalem 2001, p. 108, fig. 138, Courtesy of Professor Emeritus Ehud Netzer, The Hebrew University of Jerusalem.

domus, and the second consisting of the surrounding garden and a swimming pool, clearly inspired by Eastern traditions. The Hasmonean palace gardens are a good example of this, not far from Herod's Palace. The source of Herod's inspiration is clear. When he visited Rome in 40 BCE he had the opportunity to visit more than one Roman *domus*. Mark Antony's huge urban mansion would most likely have been similar in plan and concept. The best contemporary example is

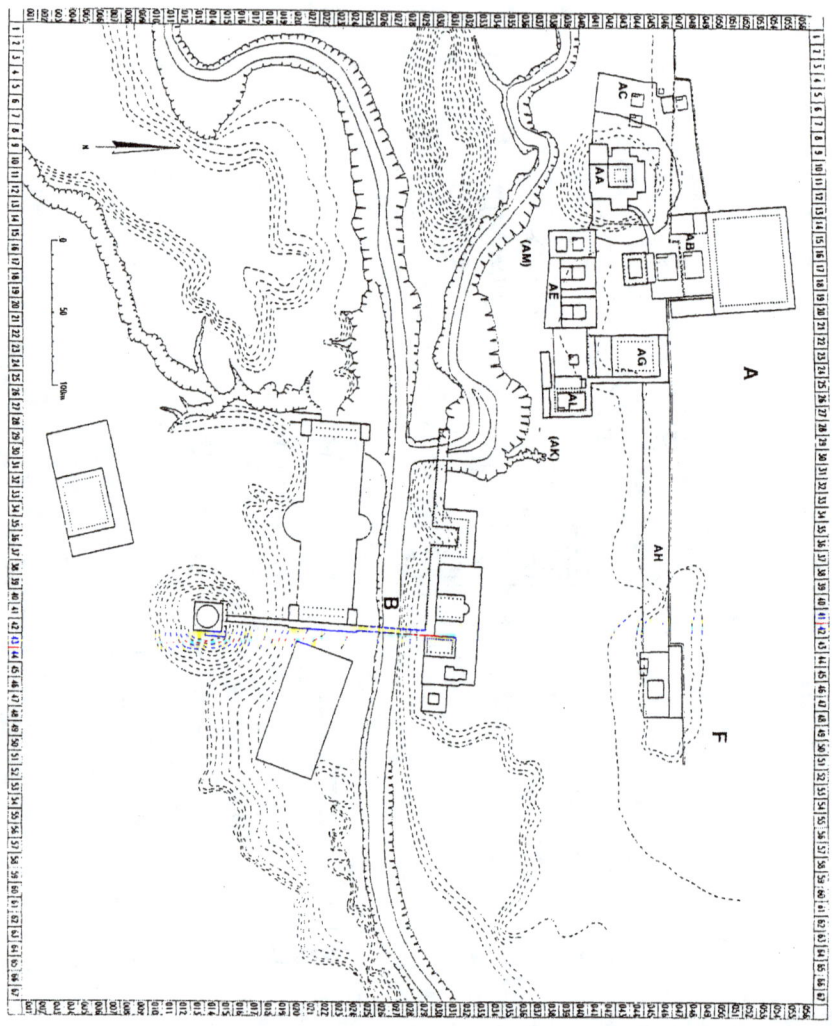

Figure II, 4 – The Herodian Palaces at Jericho from E. Netzer, *The Palaces of the Hasmonaeans and Herod the Great*, Jerusalem 2001, p. 17, fig. 6, Courtesy of Professor Emeritus Ehud Netzer, The Hebrew University of Jerusalem.

the House of the Faun in Pompeii.[193] If we compare the First Winter Palace to the House of the Faun, it may be inferred that Doric columns were used for the peristyle courtyard, though for the Egyptian *oecus* Ionic or Corinthian columns

---

[193] This private residence of a wealthy Pompeian was built around 180 BCE and restored in 100 BCE. It is slightly smaller than the Herodian palace. Its plan reflected that of the Roman urban *domus*. See Nielsen, *Hellenistic Palaces*, pp. 166–168, 291–292, fig. 87.

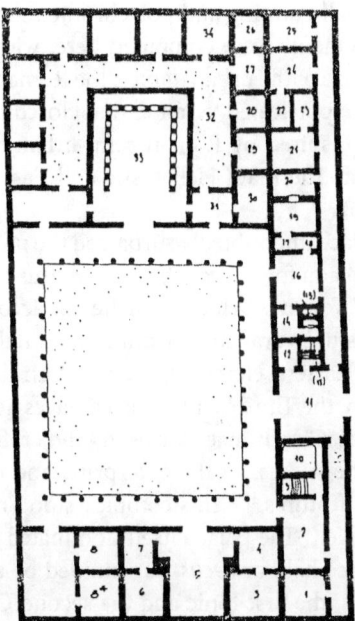

Figure II, 5 – Plan of Jericho First Winter Palace from E. Netzer, *The Palaces of the Hasmonaeans and Herod the Great*, Jerusalem 2001, p. 41, fig. 43, Courtesy of Professor Emeritus Ehud Netzer, The Hebrew University of Jerusalem.

were probably used. First Style wall paintings and perhaps polychrome mosaics decorated, at the very least, the audience and banqueting halls (cfr. figure II, 5).

The Second Winter Palace was built around 25 BCE, above the ruins of the Hasmonean palaces. Two events enabled Herod to construct this palace, the first being an earthquake that destroyed the Hasmonean palaces in 33 BCE, and the second being the victory of Augustus over Cleopatra, since the latter had been regarded as protector of the last Hasmoneans. It should be emphasized that this palace was built after the execution of Hyrcanus II who was, in fact, the owner of the palatial environs. Herod could thus completely erase the memory of the Hasmoneans, at least in Jericho. Alexander Jannaeus' fortified palace was transformed into an artificial mound, probably covered by vegetation. The Twin Palace met the same fate. For obvious reasons of economy, other elements of the Hasmonean palaces, such as the huge pools and the eastern Twin Palace garden, were included in the Herodian palace. As indicated by the swimming pools and gardens, the main purpose of this palace was recreational. The complex was built on two terraces. The upper terrace included a pool and a rectangular building with a peristyle courtyard, a *triclinium*, and a monumental veranda. The lower terrace included similar elements, such as a pool surrounded by a peristyle, yet another pool, and a Roman bathhouse. The most important rooms were decorated with First Style Wall Painting and polychrome mosaics. Once again, both Roman and Eastern elements were combined here, with the Roman elements including the main feature of the urban *domus*: the Roman bathhouse, combined with a new element, the porticated veranda that closed the upper terrace. This element was probably inspired by Roman semi-urban and rural architecture, namely that of the villa. The main Hellenistic and Eastern elements were the gardens (cfr. figure II, 6).[194]

The Third Winter Palace undoubtedly surpassed the previous palatial complex in its splendor. The occasion for the construction of this complex was the visit of Agrippa to Judaea in 15 BCE. It is believed that he was accompanied by architects, as well as painters and stucco craftsmen from Roman Italy. If the earlier palaces combined Roman and Eastern elements, even though they were built by local architects and craftsmen, the Third Winter Palace leaves no doubt that it was built with direct Roman input. Clearly, native artisans and craftsmen still contributed an important part to the success of the enterprise, and the end result displays both local and Roman features.[195] This complex stood at the center of a park on both sides of Wadi Kelt. The palace itself dominated the northern side and included a huge audience hall, or *oecus*, surrounded by a Corinthian peristyle; two peristyle courtyards, the first Ionic and the second Corinthian; a reception room; and a Roman bathhouse. Frescoes of the Second and Third Style, as well as *opus sectile* marble pavements and polychrome mosaics decorated the palace. Netzer identifies the huge audience hall as the *Augusteum*. A bridge connected it to the sunken garden, a huge swimming pool, and a building erected on top of an artificial slope, all situated south of Wadi Kelt. This building, similar to the Temple of Mercurius at Baiae, is identified by Netzer as the *Agrippeum*. A complex including a theater, a hippodrome, and a *gymnasium* – a *palaestra* – was situated 2 km. north of the palace.[196] This combination of palace, hippodrome, and theater is also present in Caesarea and at the royal palace of Seleucid Antioch (cfr. figure II, 7).[197]

---

[194] On Jericho's Second Winter Palace see Netzer, *Palaces of the Hasmoneans and Herod the Great*, pp. 43–47. See also Nielsen, *Hellenistic Palaces*, pp. 196–197, 301–303, fig. 106.

[195] The use of sun-dried bricks covered by stucco on rubble and stone foundations clearly indicates a native tradition. However the use of stronger clay bricks combined in *opus reticulatum*, *opus mixtum*, and *opus quadratum* in the Roman bathhouse, and in the sunken garden originated in Rome. Also mortar was used to build the vaults and the domes of the bathhouse as well as the dome like ceiling of the huge structure south of Wadi Kelt.

[196] On Jericho's Third Winter Palace see Netzer, *Palaces of the Hasmoneans and Herod the Great*, pp. 48–63. See also Nielsen, *Hellenistic Palaces*, pp. 196–200, 303–305, figs. 107–110, pls. 37–40. See also S. Rozemberg, "The Wall Paintings of the Herodian Palaces at Jericho", in *Judaea and the Greco-Roman World in the Time of Herod in the Light of Archaeological Evidence, Abhandlungen der Akademie der Wissenschaften in Göttingen N. 215*, Göttingen 1996, pp. 121–139. See also Josephus, *AJ* XVII, 115–162, 174–179, 193–195.

[197] See Netzer, *Palaces of the Hasmoneans and Herod the Great*, pp. 64–67. See also Netzer, "Promontory Palace", p. 201.

3. The setting of the Herodian Court: the Herodian Palace

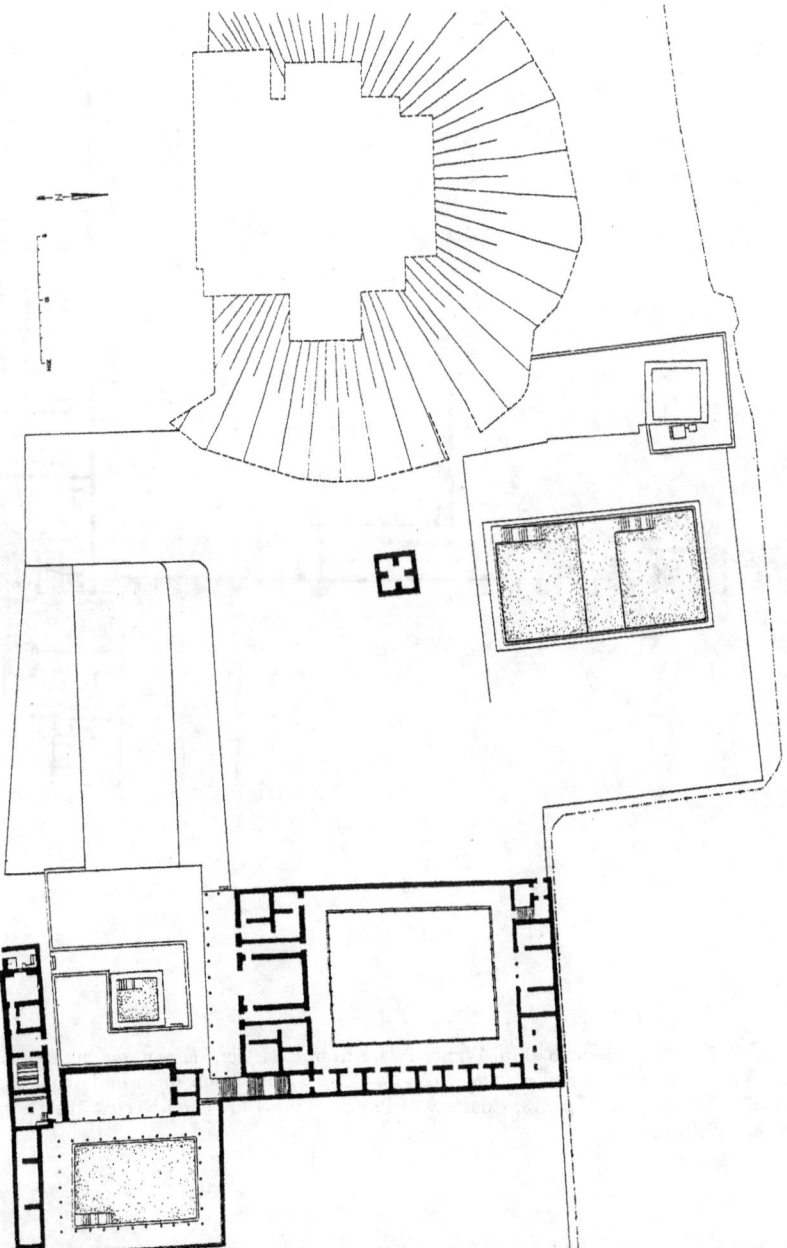

Figure II, 6 – Plan of Jericho Second Winter Palace from E. Netzer, *The Palaces of the Hasmonaeans and Herod the Great*, Jerusalem 2001, p. 44, fig. 47, Courtesy of Professor Emeritus Ehud Netzer, The Hebrew University of Jerusalem.

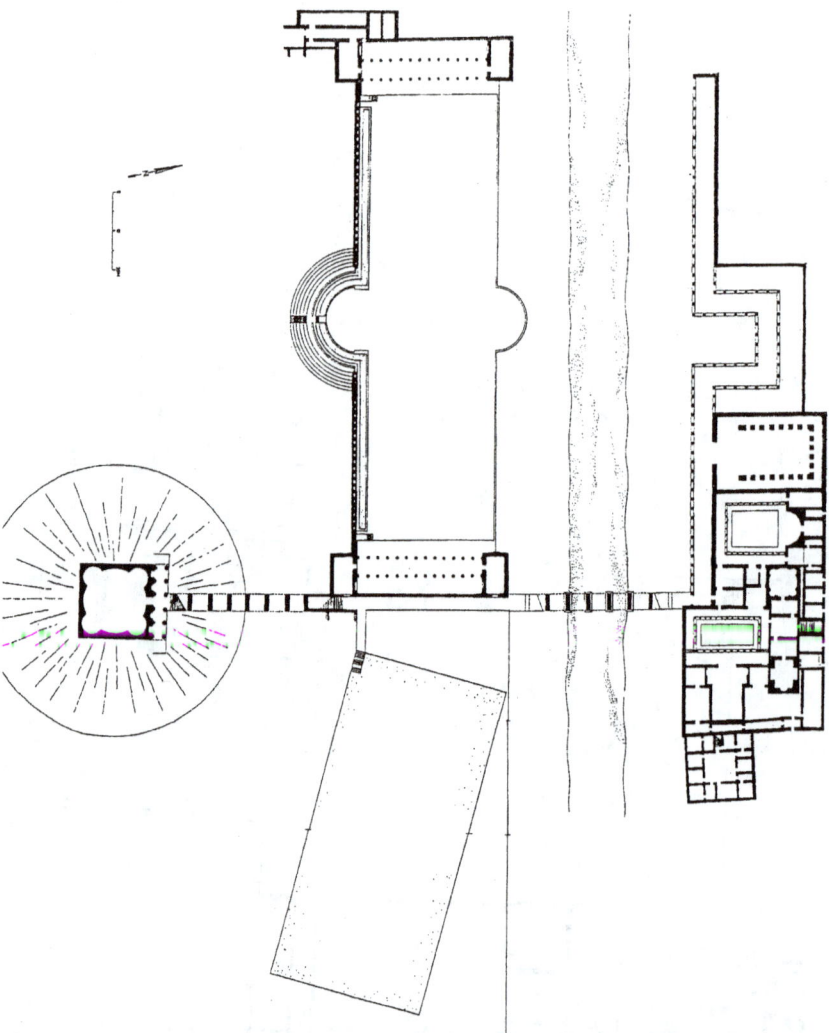

Figure II, 7 – Plan of Jericho Third Winter Palace from E. Netzer, *Hasmonean and Herodian Palaces at Jericho I, Final Report of the 1973-1987 Excavations, Stratigraphy and Architecture*, Jerusalem 2001, plan 48, p. 318, Courtesy of Professor Emeritus Ehud Netzer, The Hebrew University of Jerusalem.

D. Fortified Palaces

In this section I shall analyze the fortified palaces, most of them constructed in fortresses that Herod took over from the Hasmoneans. As already noted above, these palaces were used in the event of war or rebellion and included the Towers and the Antonia in Jerusalem, as well as the various desert fortresses such as Masada, Upper Herodium, Machaerus, and Cypros. Their defensive features are analyzed in the Chapter III.

A citadel with three huge towers (see also Chapter III) was built north of Herod's palace at the northwest corner of the city wall. The towers were named Hippicus, Phasael, and Mariamme, for Herod's friend, brother, and wife, respectively, and Josephus provides a vivid description of them.[198] The interiors of these towers were used as palaces. The Hippicus Tower contained a two-storey high palace situated at the top of the tower. The Tower of Phasael, similar to the Pharos of Alexandria, consisted of two main towers. The upper one, which was smaller than its lower counterpart, was utilized as a palace and included bathing facilities, probably in the form of a Roman bath. This palace tower was topped by a further smaller tower. The Tower of Mariamme was similar to the other two, but even more richly decorated and furnished.

Josephus describes the Antonia Fortress in detail (see also Chapter III).[199] Rebuilt by Herod before 31 BCE and named after Mark Antony, it was situated close to the northwestern corner of the Temple Mount. The interior of the fortress was designed and furnished as a palace, and including bathing facilities similar to the Roman baths at Herodium, as described by Josephus.

At Masada, a natural plateau on a cliff facing the Dead Sea, there stood a palace-fortress described in detail by Josephus.[200] In fact, Herod built two main palaces there. The older, Western Palace or Core Palace had an official and ceremonial task and its layout was rooted in earlier Hasmonean buildings. This palace consisted of a rectangular structure with various courtyards and included an audience hall preceded by a *distylos in antis*, a reception rooms, a throne room, and service rooms which included a Hellenistic bathroom and storehouses.[201] Some of the palace rooms were decorated with mosaics. Masada was thus a small palace where the king resided to judge the thinly populated local area. According to Foerster, the models for the plan of the Western Palace were the Seleucid palaces of Dura Europus, Seleucia, and Vouni (cfr. figure II, 8).[202]

---

[198] See Josephus, *BJ* V, 156–176.
[199] See Josephus, *BJ* V, 238–246; see also Josephus, *AJ* XVIII, 91–95.
[200] See Josephus, *BJ* VII, 280–300.
[201] On the Western Palace see Netzer, *Palaces of the Hasmoneans and Herod the Great*, pp. 80–87.
[202] See Foerster, "Hellenistic and Roman Trends", pp. 55–73.

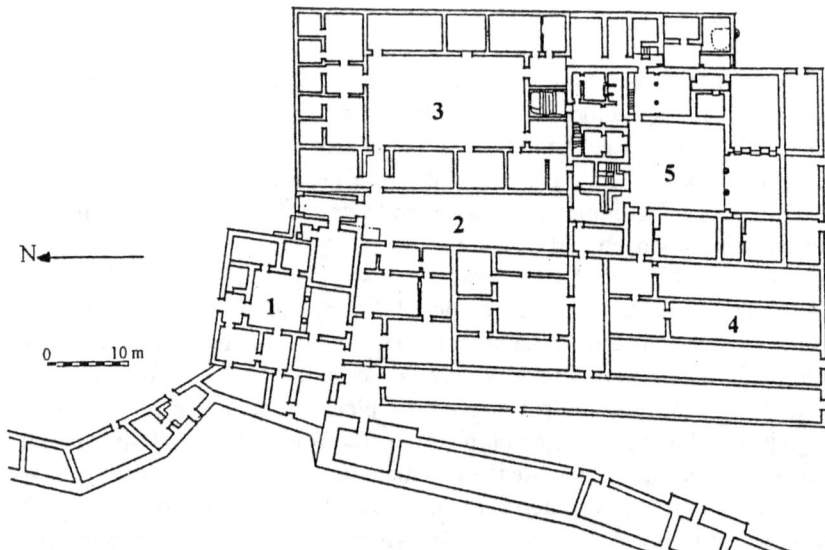

Figure II, 8 – The Core Palace (Western Palace) from E. Netzer, *The Palaces of the Hasmonaeans and Herod the Great*, Jerusalem 2001, p. 96, fig. 129. Courtesy of Professor Emeritus Ehud Netzer, The Hebrew University of Jerusalem.

The more private Northern Palace, hanging on a cliff, was built around 25 BCE. Decorated with a monumental façade, it included three terraces. The lower terrace included a hypostyle square enclosed by a peristyle, as well as a Roman bath complex. Frescoes of the Second Style decorated this building, identified by Netzer as the *Agrippeum*. The middle terrace consisted of a circular pavilion structure, perhaps a private dining room. The upper terrace consisted of a semi-circular peristyle veranda. Netzer identifies the upper terrace as the *Augusteum*. A forecourt separated the palace from a Roman bathhouse, which included a peristyle courtyard.[203] The Northern Palace's architecture was probably inspired by Hellenistic palaces and by Roman *domus* and villas.[204] The façade of the Northern Palace is clearly inspired by Alexandrian tradition. Similar effects can be seen on the façade of the garden peristyle of the Palace of Ptolemais, and on the façades of the Khazne, the Corinthian Tomb, and the Deir at Petra. Each terrace reflects a distinct source of inspiration. The upper terrace resembles the same elements found at the Villa dei Misteri and the Villa of Diomedes at Pompeii. The *tholos* – or middle terrace – was perhaps inspired by elements of the Thalamegos

---

[203] On the Northern Palace see Netzer, *Palaces of the Hasmoneans and Herod the Great*, pp. 88–97.

[204] On Masada and its sources of inspiration see Nielsen, *Hellenistic Palaces*, pp. 186–191, 295–299, figs. 96, 100–102, pls. 33–36.

3. The setting of the Herodian Court: the Herodian Palace

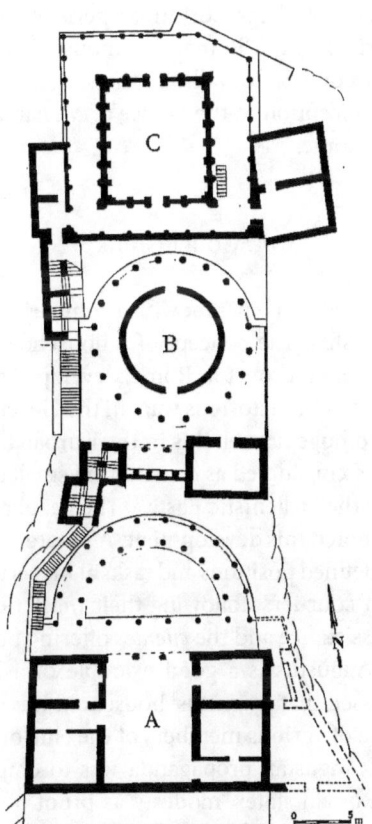

Figure II, 9 – Plan of the Hanging Palace (Northern Palace) from E. Netzer, *The Palaces of the Hasmonaeans and Herod the Great*, Jerusalem 2001, p. 90, fig. 113, Courtesy of Professor Emeritus Ehud Netzer, The Hebrew University of Jerusalem.

of Ptolemy IV, as well as by the illusionist effects of Second Style painting and Petra tomb façades. The lower platform's cubicula and bath are similar to those of the Roman Villa below the Farnesina (cfr. figure II, 9).[205]

The Upper Herodium was a palace fortress built on top of an artificial mound south of the main complex and was very similar in both its inner and outer conception to the Antonia Fortress in Jerusalem. Herod probably used the Upper Herodium for private purposes, to host his family and close friends, though it could have also been used for minor receptions. The Mountain Palace Fortress situated on the summit of Herodium was a circular structure, also called the cylinder, and was partially buried within an artificial, cone-shaped mountain.

---

[205] See Foerster, "Hellenistic and Roman Trends", pp. 55–73.

The palace itself consisted of a large Corinthian peristyle courtyard, a rectangular *triclinium*, living quarters, and a Roman bathhouse. The palace was decorated with First Style and Second Style wall paintings, as well as mosaic floors. The court was similar in conception to the House of Menander in Pompeii and the Forum of Augustus at Rome.[206]

4. Conclusions

It is appropriate to conclude this chapter with a comparison of Herod's court and the household of Augustus. The concept of a household, the preliminary step toward the establishment of a court in Rome, developed at the beginning of the second century BCE, after the victorious wars in the Hellenistic East. The Roman ruling class maintained huge households in their urban *domus* and country villas that could rightly be considered as constituting small courts, quite similar in conception to those of the Hellenistic East.[207] The peculiar social characteristics of Roman society promoted this development. A senator always had two types of individuals with well-defined positions and tasks at his service: *liberti* and *clientes*. Both formed a core of courtiers, following their master everywhere, the *liberti* providing economic assistance and the *clientes* offering political backing.[208]

The household of Augustus is a good example of a Late Republic "court," though it must be stressed that Augustus' household was certainly a modest one in comparison to those of various members of the elite of the Late Republic. An important element of Augustan propaganda was to emphasize the simple life of the master of the Roman state: "modesty as proof of honesty."[209] Augustus' *domus*, though not, *de iure*, a royal court, functioned like one *de facto*, as did the households of contemporary Roman senators, such as V. Messalla. What was different in the eyes of the Romans was that Augustus was the *princeps senatus*, the most important senator, and thus, his household was more important and more representative than others. Moreover Maecenas, Augustus' secretary, en-

---

[206] On Upper Herodium see Netzer, *Palaces of the Hasmoneans and Herod the Great*, pp. 98–107.

[207] Thus, a wealthy senatorial household consisted of slaves, mostly of Greek origin, each with his own specific housekeeping duty, as butler or cook, as described by Plautus in his comedies. For certain families the domus became a center of Greek culture and art similar to the Hellenistic courts. The best-known example is the Circle of the Scipiones. Thus, various Greek philosophers, mainly Stoics, arrived in Rome to live as guests at the "court" of one Roman senator or another. As a cultural center the *domus* was also the focus of the private art collection of Greek art, mainly statues and paintings, sometimes original, sometimes copies. However art, as we shall see, was generally displayed in temples dedicated by the warlord.

[208] On the *clientes* and *liberti* in Republican Rome see F. Dupont, *La vie quotidienne du citoyen romain sous la République*, Paris 1989, on the *clientes*, pp. 30–32, on the *liberti*, pp. 73–90.

[209] According to Suetonius, Livia spun her husband's togas herself. See Suetonius, *Augustus*, 73. 2.

sured that his master was always surrounded by intellectuals to celebrate the new regime, though they were now mainly Romans rather than Greeks. Augustus' *liberti* and *clientes* also surrounded him.

The new concept of an Imperial family introduced by Augustus made the difference between Augustus' household and those of the members of the Late Republican elite quite clear. Augustus' heir would emerge from among the members of this family. The importance attributed to the Imperial family was something new. Augustus was concerned from the beginning about an heir to his huge enterprise that would be his own flesh and blood, or at least, legally adopted. The importance of the Imperial family, or more correctly, the family of the *princeps senatus*, is underlined in the Ara Pacis. In the sacrificial procession, the senators are depicted alone. Augustus and Agrippa, on the other hand, are depicted with their families – their women, sons, daughters – and in the case of Augustus, even with his private secretary, the *eques* Maecenas.[210] There was thus a considerable difference and distinction between Augustus' household and Herod's court. Augustus attempted to minimize the importance of his household, while Herod flaunted it. And yet there was a common element in both "courts." Augustus, like Herod, continued a pattern inherited from the immediate past. In the case of Augustus, the model was the Late Republican patrician household, while, in the case of Herod, it was the Hasmonean royal court. Another point of commonality between Augustus and Herod was that a strong bond tied both Augustus and Herod to their own large families. In the case of Augustus, this included the sons of his second wife, Livia, from her previous marriage; in the case of Herod, the concept of heir included only his own flesh and blood, the sons borne by his various wives, with the possible exception of Aristobulus III, the high priest. In each case, the source of the strong family bond was distinct. In Augustus' case it originated in the concept of "adoption" and in the tradition of the ideals of the Roman Republican senatorial families. In Herod's case, it was simply a custom shared with other Hellenistic rulers, such as the Seleucids.[211]

After Augustus, the Roman court developed and evolved during the reigns of two emperors, Claudius and Domitian. The Imperial court was a development of the household of Late Republican nobility, and though it was also modeled on Hellenistic examples, there was a clear-cut difference. Slaves performed most of the menial tasks, as in the homes of the Late Republican nobility, while more important duties were carried out by the emperor's *liberti*. In the Hellenistic courts, with the exception of Herod's court, as we have seen, all of the personnel, or most of it, consisted of free individuals. Some of the tasks, such as that of chamberlain or cup bearer, were allotted to members of noble families. In Imperial Rome,

---

[210] On the Ara Pacis see Galinsky, *Augustan Culture*, pp. 141–155 and Zanker, *Augusto e il potere delle immagini*, pp. 131–135.

[211] See E. Will, *Histoire politique du monde hellénistique, 323-30 av. J.-C.*, Paris 2003, passim.

heir to Republican Rome, all of these tasks were thought to be demeaning and beneath the dignity of free-born Romans, although suitable for *liberti*. The only exception was the teaching of Latin rhetoric, the language of free, proud men, while slaves taught Greek, traditionally the language of servants. Turcan provides a clear and detailed description of the Imperial court.[212] The presence at the Imperial court of slaves and *liberti* is similar to the presence of commoners at Herod court and differs from the earlier Hellenistic courts where important tasks were confided to noblemen.

As in the case of the court's organization, a comparison of the Mansion of Augustus on the Palatine with the more impressive Herodian palaces is instructive in enabling us to understand the difference between Augustus as *primus inter pares*, whose *de facto* power was based only on his *auctoritas* and *potestas*, and Herod as a supreme ruler, recognized *de iure* and *de facto*. The only literary source describing the private dwellings of Augustus prior to the construction of his Palatine mansion is Suetonius.[213] His first houses were clearly *domus*, the Roman patrician house, not unlike the contemporary dwellings in Rome or Pompeii. The House of Augustus, his dwelling complex on the Palatine, was built between 36 and 28 BCE. According to Suetonius, it included the House of Hortensius – or the House of Livia, as it was called by the excavators – and the House of Catulus, which was annexed and incorporated into it. This complex was destroyed by fire in 3 CE.[214] The later palatial mansion[215] was erected on two terraces with a difference in height of 9 m. The complex covered an area of 12,000 sq. m. and consisted of two parts, the main mansion, with official and residential quarters, and religious and public buildings.

Was Augustus' palatial mansion a *domus* – a palatial mansion of the *princeps senatus*, the first among the Romans – or was it a Hellenistic palace? According to I. Nielsen, although Augustus was still a *triumvir*, he nevertheless built his new house on the Palatine according to models found in the palaces of Hellenistic kings. The size of his house, 12,000 sq. m., was not particularly small, and its decoration was lavish. Augustus built his palace beside the Hut of Romulus, the legendary first king of Rome and ancestor of Augustus, and constructed his mausoleum next to the tomb of Romulus. Like the Hellenistic palaces, the Palatine complex included a temple, the Temple of Apollo Palatinus, aimed at promoting the tutelary *numen* of Augustus.   Nielsen identifies the model for Augustus'

---

[212] See R. Turcan, *Vivere alla corte dei Cesari*, Firenze, 1991, pp. 51–59, 60–61. See also Levick, *Claudius*, pp. 47, 57, 53, 83, 93–103.

[213] See Suetonius, *Augustus* II (72).

[214] See Richardson, *Herod King of the Jews*, p. 118. See as original source Suetonius, *De Grammaticis* (17).

[215] See Nielsen, *Hellenistic Palaces*, pp. 174–178. See also See Zanker, *Augusto e il potere delle immagini*, pp. 72–73. The mansion included a tower-room that served as a private study, which Augustus called his Syracuse and Technyphion (Suetonius, *Augustus* II, (72, 2), and a private shrine to Vesta.

4. Conclusions

palatial mansion as a Hellenistic palace.[216] But was it? And how did it reflect Augustus' image? According to Zanker and Galinsky,[217] the mansion on the Palatine is not a palace, but a "modest dwelling." First, Augustus' mansion follows the plan of a *domus*, with the combined use of atrium and peristyle courtyard. Augustus therefore uses the Republican tradition, and his dwelling repeats the plan of the patrician elite city house.[218] We do not know if the contemporary houses of Marcus Antony, Agrippa, and Asinius Pollio were much smaller. Later Imperial palaces, such as the Domus Tiberiana, Nero's Domus Aurea[219], and Domitian's Domus Augustana[220], are much larger in size and distinct in plan, and much more closely resemble Hellenistic palaces. Another difference between the *domus* that Augustus built on the Palatine and the later Roman palaces built on the Palatine or elsewhere, such as the Domus Aurea, is the lack of a garden area or *hortus* incorporated into the palace. The gardens in Augustus' *domus* were the Portico of the Danaids, built near the palace, and were part of the palace, as in the Hellenistic palaces or in the later Domus Aurea. An element common to Augustus' *domus* and the later Imperial palaces is the Corinthian *oechus* prototype of the basilical hall, used as the main audience hall in later palaces.

According to Zanker, what really distinguished the *domus* of Augustus from other patrician dwellings were not its dimensions, but the sacral character of the complex. The Temple of Apollo Palatinus gave the house this character, as did the sanctuaries in the Hellenistic palaces.[221] The Palatine mansion of Augustus, however, was not the only private dwelling connected to a shrine in Late Republican Rome. The mansions of Pompey and of Iulius Caesar present similar features, but both followed models found in Hellenistic royal palaces. Pompey' palatial mansion was a huge complex that included a theater with a temple and a great portico; the sacral structure was connected to the palace through the theater, but was not part of it. Iulius Caesar's palatial mansion itself, although relatively small, had a holy quality as Domus of the Vestal Virgins and as Temple of Vesta.[222]

---

[216] See Nielsen, *Hellenistic Palaces*, p. 179.
[217] See Galinsky, *Augustan Culture*, p. 146.
[218] See Zanker, *Augusto e il potere delle immagini*, pp. 56–57.
[219] The Domus Aurea was erected in 64 CE by the architects Severus and Celer for the emperor Nero. See Tacitus, *Annales* XV, 42. Suetonius gives a short description. See Suetonius, *Nero*, 31. See E. Segala and I. Sciortino, *Domus Aurea, Soprintendenza archeologica di Roma*, Milano 1999.
[220] The Domus Augustana was the new Imperial palace erected by Domitian on the Palatine. Its architect was Rabirius. It stood side by side with the House of Augustus, the House of Livia, and the Domus Tiberiana. The palace was praised by Statius and by Martial. See J. B. Ward-Perkins, *Roman Imperial Architecture*, Harmondsworth 1981, p. 63. See Statius, *Silvae* IV, 2, 18 and Martialis, *Epigrammata* VIII, 36. See also W. L. MacDonald, *The Architecture of the Roman Empire* I, New Haven (Con.) 1986, pp. 47–74.
[221] See Zanker, *Augusto e il potere delle immagini*, pp. 55–56.
[222] See Nielsen, *Hellenistic Palaces*, p. 173.

Augustus' palatial mansion reflected his political position of *primus inter pares*. It was a compromise between the contemporary patrician *domus* and the palatial mansions of the Late Republican warlords, directly inspired by Hellenistic royal palaces. It was relatively large, but its plan was similar in most of its details to a contemporary *domus*, and it lacked both the huge peristyles and gardens of a Hellenistic royal palace or the palatial mansion of Pompey. Like the Hellenistic palaces, it had a temple that was connected to the palatial mansion, but not part of its actual, integral structure, as was the case with Julius Caesar's Regia, which gave the palatial mansion its sacred character. The Portico of the Danaids, built near the palatial mansion, gave it a monumental character, and, in fact, Augustus' political supremacy was reflected in the inscription at the entrance, which underlined the most important of Augustus' attributes – *pater patriae* – and in the civic crown atop the entrance pediment. Both Pompey and Iulius Caesar had private mansions that echoed and mirrored their ambitions as Hellenistic rulers. Thus, Augustus' *domus* reflected his position as *primus inter pares*, emphasized his achievements, and strengthened his position through proximity with the Temple of Apollo, both an Etruscan-Italic god and Augustus' patron.

Did the Herodian palace architecture influence the development of Roman Imperial architecture? Although it is difficult to substantiate this claim, there are two examples of later Roman Imperial and private villae that present elements in common with the Herodian palaces and are chronologically later. The first example, Villa Jovis, is situated outside Rome and is an Imperial villa.[223] Various elements of the Northern Palace of Masada are found there, such as the Veranda of the Villa Jovis, which recalls the same plan as the Upper Terrace of Masada's Northern Palace. Other common elements include cisterns and a bathhouse. Herod probably invented the idea of erecting a palace on a cliff at Masada. Was this repeated at Capri? Did the Northern Palace of Masada influence the plan and setting of Villa Jovis? Another Roman villa, whose architectonic layout is similar to Herod's palace architecture, was the Grotte di Catullo at Sirmione. Here, obviously, it was the private outer wing of the Promontory Palace at Caesarea Maritima that presents similarities to the Roman villa at Sirmione. However, the relationship between the two buildings is unclear. According to the recent excavations, the building is no longer dated to the Early Imperial period, but rather to the Late Republican period, the early and middle first century BCE. Thus the Promontory Palace could not have influenced this distant villa, since

---

[223] Villa Jovis, together with Sperlonga, was one of Tiberius' palaces situated outside Rome that has been amply excavated. Tacitus wrote that Tiberius had twelve villas on Capri. See Tacitus, *Ann.* IV, 67, 5. See also Suetonius, *Tiberius* III, 65, 6. This impressive, albeit "small" villa was erected on a rock cliff. On Villa Jovis see H. Mielsch, *Die Römische Villa, Architectur und Lebensdform*, München 1987, p. 142. See also C. Krause, *Villa Jovis, Die Residenz des Tiberius auf Capri*, Mainz 2003. Krause shows Masada's Northern Palace, together with the Villa dei Misteri at Pompeii and the Villa della Farnesina at Rome, and the Villa di Damecuta at Capri, pp. 85–91.

the villa was built a bit earlier. In this case we have to search for a common Hellenistic denominator which influenced both buildings. If, however, the building can be dated to the Early Imperial period, to the first century BCE, it is much more probable that Herod's Promontory Palace at Caesarea Maritima influenced the location of the villa on a rock cliff above the lake, as well as the layout of the Grotte di Catullo. In any case, the similarity between the two buildings is quite striking.[224]

Appendix I.
Herod's Portrait

Since this entire dissertation centers on Herod, I would now like to consider his physical appearance. First of all, we do not have any verifiable portrait of Herod, since he did not mint any coins with his own bust on the obverse, as did his son Philip, his grandson Agrippa I, and, later, his great-grandson Agrippa II.

Kokkinos has suggested that there were portraits of Herod on the obverse of coins dated to the years 63 (41 BCE) and 74 (30 BCE), from Ascalon, a city possibly connected with Herod's family and certainly one that enjoyed a good relationship with Herod's kingdom. However, the year 41 BCE was prior to Herod's rule, when he was still a mere courtier of Hyrcanus II, and in the year 30 BCE, Herod's rule was still insecure, as far as the Ascalonites were concerned, and thus this possibility must be rejected.

We know that outside Judaea various statues were erected to honor Herod. Bases had been found at Syah in the Hauran, at Coos, on the Acropolis, and possibly in the Agora of Athens. Sadly, the statues themselves have not survived. In any case, it is clear that statues of Herod existed outside Judaea. In the 1960s, a bust depicting a bearded man was found near Memphis in Egypt. Dated to the Late Hellenistic period, it had been remodeled in the third century CE to represent Alexander Severus. Some scholars, most notably Vermeule, identify the subject as Herod. This is entirely possible since it was found in an Idumaean context in Egypt, though other scholars identify it as Ptolemy IX or X. Other remaining portraits of the two Ptolemaic rulers depict a chin beard. However, the Memphis statue had features far more pleasant and noble than those found in other known portraits of Ptolemy IX or X (cfr. figure II, 10).

Another bust, from Byblos, depicting a man without beard, has also been taken as a possible depiction of Herod.[225] It is probable that the Jewish king mod-

---

[224] See P. Gros, *L'architecture romaine, II. Maisons, palais villas, et tombeaux*, Paris 2001, p. 312, figs. 340–342.

[225] See Kokkinos, *Herodian Dynasty*, pp. 134–138. On the Memphis bust see also R. R. R. Smith, *Hellenistic Sculpture*, London 1991, fig. 244. The bust is conserved at Boston, Museum of Fine Arts, Cat. No. 5951.

Figure II, 10 – Portrait attributed to King Herod (BMFA.59.51., Courtesy of Boston Museum of Fine Arts).

eled his portraits on those of other contemporary Hellenistic rulers, and hence the similarity to the bust of Ptolemy IX or X. The chin beard is of interest since it is unlikely that Herod would have grown a beard for religious reasons, and even his "saintly" grandson Agrippa I was clean-shaven. The chin beard was in fact a Late Hellenistic fashion and may have been an attribute of royalty.

A word on Herod's dress. At his court, Herod was probably dressed like other Hellenistic kings. The *kausia*, the *diadema*, and the purple *clamys* were essential elements of royal garb. But when Herod was crowned as a Jewish king, he probably wore a more Eastern type of robe. As a Roman citizen of senatorial rank, when visiting Agrippa or Augustus, Herod would probably have worn the Roman toga rather than the trappings of a Hellenistic ruler, which would have been inappropriate in the eyes of the rulers of the known world.

Appendix II.
The *Gymnasium* of Jerusalem

In concluding, it seems to me that it is important to deal with the possible existence of a *gymnasium* in Jerusalem in the Herodian period. This *gymnasium*, established by the High Priest Jason, according to scholars such as Levine,[226] probably continued to exist well into the Hasmonean and, most likely into the Herodian period as well. It seems to me that during the Herodian period, with such a huge royal court residing in Jerusalem, a *gymnasium* was even more of a necessity than during the earlier Hasmonean period. Thus, while the priestly aristocracy that made up the Hasmonean court in the days of Alexander Jannaeus hardly needed a *gymnasium*, since most of them could afford a personal trainer, this was not the situation in the Herodian court, where many of the courtiers came from a lower class background and could hardly afford private personal trainers. Therefore the existence of a *gymnasium* would suit the needs of some of Herod's courtiers who came from a lower socio-economic background, rather than those of the courtiers who lived in the Hasmonean period, as well as reflecting King Herod's policy of pushing the country towards Hellenisation. Last but not least, as we shall see, Josephus mentions the existence, in his own time, of a *xistos* in Jerusalem, which was part of a *gymnasium*.

Thus there appears to be a cultural framework in Jerusalem in which Greek education could be learned, outside the court, and it seems to me that in Hasmonean and Herodian Jerusalem, the ruling class of Judaea could enjoy Greek edu-

---

[226] See L.I. Levine, *Judaism and Hellenism, Conflict or Confluence?*, Seattle 1998, p. 91 and L.I. Levine, *Jerusalem, Portrait of the City in the Second Temple Period (538 BCE–70 CE)*, Philadelphia 2002, p. 324.

cation, side by side with Jewish education.[227] Jason the High Priest, for example, established a *gymnasium* in Jerusalem.[228] Doran suggests that the *gymnasium* of Jerusalem was somehow different from the other Greek *gymnasia*, as indicated in the Greek translation of the Pentateuch and Pentateuch exegesis referring to the "Greek way," i.e., in Greek, following Hellenistic Jewish authors such as Demetrius, Aristobulus and Ezekiel the Tragedian.[229] It seems to me, however, that in the Jerusalem *gymnasium* the same disciplines were taught as in the Greek *gymnasia*, including rhetoric, so much important for success, yet without, of course, any emphasis on Pagan worship, which was an essential part of the Greek educational institution. Levine has argued that the *gymnasium* in Jerusalem was not destroyed when the Maccabees took over, and Hengel likewise argues that in Hasmonean Judaea it was still possible to enjoy Greek education.[230] Probably after the Maccabean liberation of Jerusalem this *gymnasium* continued without the Pagan cultic ceremonies that consisted of sacrifices to Heracles. The Late Hasmonean and Herodian *gymnasium* would probably have presented a curriculum similar to that of a Greek *gymnasium*, with some important differences – thus the *epheboi* who did not obliterate their circumcision with the *epispasmos*, or of course did not sacrifice to the gods of Greece. Since the *gymnasium* was an institution to educate the well-to-do in the ways of the surrounding Greco-Roman world, this institution would have been necessary in Hasmonean and Herodian Jerusalem, to prepare future generals, or at least ambassadors, for their careers. There is no motivation to believe that this institution did not continue to operate in Herodian Jerusalem and afterwards. Thus, although Josephus he does not mention the *gymnasium* in his description of Jerusalem, he does mention the *xistos*, which was a building connected to the *gymnasium*, used for sports[231] The

---

[227] See R. Doran, "High Cost of a Good Education," in Collins, J. J., and Sterling, G. E., (eds.), *Hellenism in the Land of Israel*, Notre Dame (Ind.), 2001, pp. 95–97. See also Hengel, *Judaism and Hellenism* I, pp. 65–70 on Greek education and its development. See also pp. 70–78 on the development of *gymnasia* in the Greek Near East and at Jerusalem.

[228] See 2 Macc., 4.

[229] See Doran, "High Cost of a Good Education," pp. 102–105.

[230] Yet Hengel does not specifically mention the *gymnasium*. See Hengel, *Judaism and Hellenism*, pp. 76–77. Yet the examples of Eupolemus, one of the leaders of one of the Jewish embassies to Rome, who was perhaps the same Eupolemus who wrote a treatise in Greek on the Jewish king, had indeed received the practical rudiments of Greek culture. Eupolemus son of Joannes, and Jason son of Eleazar the ambassadors of Judas Maccabaeus to Rome, had probably an average Greek education. See 1 Macc., VIII, 23–29, Josephus, *AJ* XII, 417–419 and *BJ* I, 38. Did they learn at the Oniad *gymnasium*? Jonathan, as well, sent two envoys to Rome, Numenius son of Antiochus and Antipater son of Jason, to renew the treaty with Rome. See 1 Macc. 12: 1–23 and Josephus, *AJ* XIII, 164–170. Simon sent another embassy, perhpas headed by the same Numenius, envoy of Jonathan. See 1 Macc. 14: 24 and Josephus, *AJ* XIII, 227. It seems to me that Jonathan and Simon's ambassadors to Rome were too young to have studied in the Oniad *gymnasium*. Thus it is possible that their received a Greek education at the Jerusalem *gymnasium*, which continued in use after the Hasmonean domination of the city.

[231] See Josephus, *BJ* IV, 144.

Appendix II. The Gymnasium of Jerusalem

xistos, according to Josephus, was situated on the Western Hill, encompassed by the First Wall, in the same spot where Jason had earlier erected the *gymnasium* earlier.[232] Thus it seems to me that when Josephus mentions the *xistos*, he is in fact referring to the *gymnasium*. It would be strange for the *xistos* to stand alone, and not together with the *gymnasium*.

---

[232] In 4 Macc., 12 it is written that the *gymnasium* was built under the Acropolis, or the Akra. B. Bar Kochba argued that the Akra was situated on the South-Eastern hill of Jerusalem. Thus the *gymnasium* should be situated on the Western hill, outside the walls and unpopulated in the period. This is exactly in the same spot where the *xistos* mentioned by Josephus stood. One therefore wonders if this last building is not really Jason's *gymnasium*. It is important to emphasize that Josephus describes it as a structure still existing in 70 CE.

III. The Army of King Herod

1. Herod and his Army

This chapter is dedicated to an analysis of King Herod's army, which played a key role in Herod's career from the outset of his reign. An examination of the Herodian army is therefore critical to an understanding of the internal mechanisms upon which Herod's political power was based, as well as of his extraterritorial policies. My examination of the function of the army will encompass the following issues. Was the main task of Herod's army to control his "disaffected" Jewish subjects, as Josephus states,[1] or did it play various roles in the consolidation and maintenance of Herod's power? In fact, we find Herod's army fighting against the king's foreign enemies, the Nabataeans, in two wars, and units from Herod's army also took part in at least one campaign, Cornelius Gallus's expedition to Arabia, as auxiliary forces of the Roman army. Thus, the Herodian army clearly had a multifaceted function.

The first two primary functions, to safeguard Herod within the kingdom and to wage wars against foreign enemies, are shared by other Hellenistic armies, including the Hasmonean army. Yet, since Herod was *socius et amicus populi romani*, it was only natural that his army was likewise intended to serve as an auxiliary force for Rome.[2] In this chapter I shall first analyze the structure of King Herod's army – its ethnic makeup, its strength, and its various units – and then examine the campaigns waged by Herod's army in order to better understand its purpose. In the second part of this chapter I shall analyze the development of the fortifications of Herod's kingdom, which constituted its static defense, as well as the military colonies.[3]

---

[1] See Josephus, *AJ* XV, 365–369.
[2] During this period Augustus organized the auxiliary forces of the Roman army. See G. L. Cheesman, *The Auxilia of the Roman Imperial Army*, Chicago 1975.
[3] My discussion of Herod's army will take into account Shatzman's book about the armies of the Hasmoneans and Herod. See I. Shatzman, *The Armies of the Hasmoneans and Herod*, TSAJ 25, Tübingen 1991. Before the publication of this book, Herod's army was not a major topic of research. However, even Shatzman's book is not entirely dedicated to an analysis of Herod's army. The first half of the book is dedicated to the Hasmonean army. Contrary to Herod's armed forces, the Hasmonean army had been widely researched. Bar-Kochba's book dedicated to the early Hasmonean army is a good example. See B. Bar-Kochva, *Judah Maccabaeus, The Jewish Struggle against the Seleucids*, Cambridge 1989. In this analysis we shall follow Shatzman's

The strong bond between Herod and his army was probably the earliest feature of Herod's rule. The best example of this is Herod's role as governor of Galilee, a role assigned to him by his father Antipater.[4] Back in Jerusalem, Herod had to face the *synedrion* to justify his actions, appearing before them surrounded by his bodyguard, and he was immediately acquitted.[5] Thus, backed by his army, Herod successfully placed himself in opposition to the legitimate authority of the state, thereby becoming an alternative source of authority, more powerful than the state itself. When Herod became king, the army continued to maintain its privileged position and became the pillar of the Herodian state, precisely because its oath of allegiance was to the king himself and not to the population.

Like his model Alexander the Great, and like the other Hellenistic kings before him, including the Hasmonean rulers, Herod was the commander-in-chief of his army. This point should be stressed for yet another reason, since Herod's army was probably the most important cohesive element in his kingdom, uniting disparate groups that came from the various populations comprising the mosaic of Herod's kingdom. Thus, it gathered together Jews, Greeks from various cities of the kingdom, Ituraeans, and even Nabataean mercenaries.[6] Herod's royal bodyguard included Gauls, Germans, and Thracians. Herod's highly charismatic personality was the common bond between all of these groups of soldiers, who would otherwise have had differing and perhaps conflicting allegiances. This explains why, upon Herod's death, both his armed forces and his state disintegrated – part of the army swore an oath of allegiance to his son Archelaus and his Roman overlords, while part of it rebelled against them, plunging Judaea into a vicious civil war.[7] Archelaus' personality was simply not strong enough to keep his father's army intact. The idea of an army intimately bound and loyal to the ruler, rather than to the state's population, was part of a heritage common to the Hellenistic world.

A. The Ethnic Composition and the Strength of Herod's Army

Both Jews and Gentiles served in Herod's army. Shatzman has demonstrated, successfully in my opinion, that the most important element in King Herod's army was Jewish, as had been the case in the Hasmonean army before it. Shatz-

---

scholarship, albeit not always that closely, and many of our conclusions differ from his. On the Herodian armies see also H. M. Gracey, "The Armies of the Judaean Client Kings," in *The Defence of the Roman and Byzantine East*, Oxford, BAR, 1986.

[4] See Josephus, *AJ* XIV, 156–184, and *BJ* I, 203–216.
[5] See Josephus, *AJ* XIV, 177–184.
[6] On Greeks see Josephus, *BJ* II, 52 et alia, on the Ituraeans see Josephus, *AJ* XIV, 452–453 et alia, on Nabataeans see Josephus, *BJ* I, 576. On Germans and Thracians see Josephus, *AJ* XVII, 198–199.
[7] See Josephus, *AJ* XVII, 206–298.

man shows quite clearly that during the conquest of the kingdom in 39–37 BCE, during the First Nabataean War in 32 BCE later on, and during the revolt that broke out in 4 BCE, most of Herod's soldiers were Jews. Thus, during the war between Herod and Antigonus, Josephus writes that many countrymen joined Herod's army after he landed at Ptolemais. After the conquest of Joppa, the "local population" again joined his army, including Jews as well as Idumaeans. Likewise, Jews from Jerusalem and Jericho also joined Herod's army. During the First Nabataean War, it seems that the vast majority of soldiers were Jews. Herod's speech to his Jewish soldiers makes it more than probable that the vast majority of soldiers were Jews. Last, when describing the revolt of 4 BCE, after Herod's death, Josephus states that most of the royal troops joined the rebels.[8] Clearly these soldiers were Jews, as the Gentiles mercenaries had no interest in joining the Jewish rebels.

Although it is not clear if Jews were the vast majority, or simply a small majority among Herod's soldiers, this clearly points to the fact that Herod clearly enjoyed a measure of support from the Jewish population, and, of course, from its Idumaean element. A large number of foreign mercenaries also served in Herod's army, including Greeks, Gauls, Ituraeans, and Thracians, among others. Is this an indication that Herod's army was mainly composed of Gentile mercenaries? Kasher, for example, argues that Herod's army was composed primarily of Gentile mercenaries,[9] but Gentile mercenaries had already fought in the armies of the Hasmoneans, probably in specific units, and were not the most important element in these armed forces. The Hasmonean armies were overwhelmingly Jewish,[10] and it seems to me that in the Herodian army, with the exception of the units composed of Ituraeans, all of the foreign mercenaries were concentrated in Herod's personal Guard, which represented a small percentage of the army, rather than the army as a whole.

The second question we must ask is whether it is possible to determine the total strength of King Herod's army. Basing his data on a careful reading of Josephus, Shatzman has shown that Herod's army numbered approximately 20,000 men at the beginning of his rule and approximately 16,000 men toward the final years of his reign.[11] Although I essentially agree with Shatzman's read-

---

[8] See Josephus *AJ* XIV, 394, 396–397, 400, 458, *AJ* XVII, 266 and *BJ* I, 290, 292–294, 366, 371, 373–379, 382, 384, *BJ* II, 52. See also Shatzman, *Armies of the Hasmoneans and Herod*, p. 186 on the Jewish ethnic element preponderance in Herod's army.

[9] See A. Kasher, *Jews and Hellenistic Cities in Eretz-Israel, Relations of the Jews with the Hellenistic Cities during the Second Temple Period*, TSAJ 21, Tübingen 1990, pp. 209–214.

[10] Already John Hyrcanus I recruited foreign mercenaries. See Josephus *AJ* XIII, 249 and *BJ* I, 61. Alexander Jannaeus employed Pisidian, Cilician, Greek and probably Thracian mercenaries. See Josephus, *AJ* XIII 374 and 378 and *BJ* I, 88. See also Shatzman, *Armies of the Hasmoneans and Herod*, pp. 31–32.

[11] See Shatzman, *Armies of the Hasmoneans and Herod*, pp. 193–195 on the number of soldiers in Herod's army.

ing of Josephus data, I have reached slightly different conclusions, using the data given by Josephus on the tactical structure of Herod's army in a different way in order to reconstruct the total strength of Herod's army. The problem in reconstructing the total strength of this army is that Josephus does not often mention specific numbers, providing instead the Greek names of different types of tactical military units. It is possible to count Herod's soldiers according to the tactical units indicated by Josephus. Thus, Josephus mentions *ilai* to indicate units of cavalry and *telos* or *meros* to indicate units of infantry. These terms are used by Hellenistic writers such as Asclepiodotus, Aelianus, and Polybius to indicate different types of Hellenistic military units – or Hellenistic military units modeled on their Roman counterparts – or Roman military units. One can legitimately ask if Josephus, writing about the Herodian *ile*,[12] had in mind Asclepiodotus' or Aelianus' definition of the term, or the translation of the Roman term *ala*. It seems to me that the *ile* of the Herodian army, as described by Josephus, was probably the *ile* of Aelianus that numbered 200 men, commanded by an *ilarch*[13]. The same difficulty arises regarding Josephus' use of the term *telos* or *lochos*, sometimes used interchangeably. It seems to me that this term in Josephus, referring to the Herodian army, indicates, more often than not, a unit of light infantry numbering 2,000 men, although sometimes the term *telos* is used instead of *lochos* to indicate an infantry unit of 512 men[14]. Josephus used the word *lochagos* to refer to the commander of a *telos* or light infantry unit.[15] Josephus also uses the word

---

[12] On the *ila* in the Herodian and the Roman army see Josephus, *AJ* XVII, 286; *AJ* XIX, 365; *AJ* XX, 98, 122; *BJ* II, 67, 236, 500, 544; *BJ* III, 66, 97; *BJ* VI, 68, 172; *BJ* VII, 5, 225; *Vita* 121, 214. See also Shatzman, *Armies of the Hasmoneans and Herod*, p. 208. Josephus wrote of *ilai* and of the *hipparchos* as the commander of the Herodian cavalry. The *ile* related to the Herodian army, as described by Josephus, was probably the *ile* of Aelianus that numbered 200 men, commanded by an *ilarch*. According to Aelianus 2–3 *ilai* formed a *hipparchia*, which was around 400–600 men strong and was commanded by the *hipparchos*. On the other hand, the *ile* described by Asclepiodotus, which numbered 64 men, is highly unlikely. Also the Roman auxiliary *ala* is quite improbable. The Greek term for the Roman *ala* is *ile*. The Greek term for *praefectus* is *hipparchos*. Both terms are used by Josephus in his description of the Roman army. See Le Bohec, *esercito Romano*, pp. 34–39.

[13] See Josephus, *AJ* XIV, 413. The number 400 cavalrymen can refer only to two Aelianus's *ilai*.

[14] See Josephus, *AJ* XIV, 413.

[15] In Greek the term *telos* has various meanings. It can be a unit of cavalry as well as infantry. The *telos* appears in Asclepiodotus as a unit of cavalry composed of 24 *ilai*, around 2,000 men. See Sekunda, *Seleucid Army*, p. 25. However more often *telos* can be used to indicate a unit of light or heavy infantry, which numbered around 2,000 men and was divided in two *chiliarchiai*. See Shatzman, *Armies of the Hasmoneans and Herod*, p. 158. See also Sekunda, *Seleucid Army*, p. 9. In the Seleucid army, *telos* indicates a infantry unit, modeled after the Roman legion. On the other side *telos* is used by Aelianus instead of *lochos* to indicate a unit of 512 men. On Aelianus' *lochos* see Sekunda, *Army of Alexander the Great*, p. 25. According to Asclepiodotus the *lochos* included around 8 men. See Sekunda, *Seleucid Army*, p. 29. However, following the context, it seems to me that Josephus used the term *telos* to indicate the basic unit of light infantry and not of heavy infantry. See Josephus, *AJ* XIV, 415, 472 and *BJ* I, 305. Josephus used the world

1. Herod and his Army

meros,[16] a term used by several Greek authors, including Polybius, to indicate the Roman legion. As in Josephus, the term is used to indicate the *sebastenoi*, a heavy infantry unit probably modeled on the Roman legions, which numbered approximately 3,000 men.

It is thus possible to reconstruct the total strength of Herod's army on three occasions: during the civil war against Antigonus, during the First Nabataean War, and at the time of Herod's death.

It is difficult to extrapolate from Josephus the exact number of Herod's soldiers during the time of the conquest of the kingdom. It seems that at the beginning of the civil war Herod's army numbered 3,000–5000 men, although before the siege of Jerusalem, it probably reached a strength of 10,000–12,000 soldiers. Thus, Josephus wrote that Herod appointed Joseph to govern Idumaea, aided by 2,400 soldiers. Josephus later wrote that the force sent by Herod against the robbers residing in Arbel in Galilee consisted of an *ile* of cavalry and three *tele* of infantry. In this case, *telos* probably means *lochos*, Thus, on this specific occasion, Herod's army amounted to 200 horsemen and approximately 1500 light infantrymen, and not 6000 infantrymen. Forty days later, Herod marched to Galilee with his entire army, which, according to Shatzman, numbered around 3,000–5,000 men. Since Herod later marched to Samaria with 3,600 soldiers, probably an equal number must have remained in Galilee. Herod also had other soldiers garrisoned in still other places, including Samaria, Joppa and Jericho. Thus, before the siege of Jerusalem, Herod's entire force probably amounted to 10,000–12,000 soldiers. It was probably only after Gindarus, that Ventidius could send Herod two legions, numbering approximately 8,000 men, and 1,000 cavalrymen under the command of Machaeras. Later, Mark Antony himself sent another reinforcement commanded by Sosius and consisting of two legions and other forces to help him in the final stages of the operations and the siege of Jerusalem. During the same period Herod, with two more Roman legions, recruited 800 mercenaries from Ituraea at Mount Lebanon.[17]

Writing about the siege of Jerusalem in *Antiquities*, Josephus puts the total strength of Herod's army at 30,000 men.[18] Does this number indicate both the ar-

---

lochagos to refer to the commander of a *telos* or light infantry unit, whether of the Herodian or the Roman army. This term is found twice, to indicate an officer commanding a Herodian light infantry unit in *AJ* XVII, 199 and an officer commanding the Roman *auxilia* in *BJ* III. Maybe, as seen on parallel passages in Josephus' *BJ*, the meaning of *telos* is *lochos*. See Josephus, *BJ* I, 349. I would suggest that in this case according to Josephus, *lochos* indicates a unit of 512 men, following Aelianus rather than Asclepiodotus.

[16] Josephus calls the Sebastenoi units *meros*. See Josephus, *AJ* XVII, 266, 275–276, 283, 294 and *BJ* II, 52, 58, 63, 74. See also Shatzman, *Armies of the Hasmoneans and Herod*, p. 194.

[17] See Josephus, *AJ* XIV, 411, 413–414, 415, 416, 431–432, 434, 447, 452 and *BJ* I, 302, 303, 305, 314–316, 317, 327, 329. See also Shatzman, *Armies of the Hasmoneans and Herod*, pp. 154–155.

[18] See Josephus, *AJ* XIV, 468.

mies of Sosius and Herod? In *War* Josephus writes that Herod's army consisted of eleven infantry units (*tele*) and 6,000 cavalrymen.[19] It is difficult to imagine that here Josephus would have used the world *telos* synonymously with his previous use of the word *lochos*. Thus, the entire Herodian infantry would have amounted to no more than 5,500 soldiers. It appears that in this case, as I have mentioned earlier, the term *telos* indicates an infantry unit numbering approximately 2,000 men. Thus, the infantry numbered around 12,000 men. Despite this, it seems to me that this number indicates Herod's soldiers, as well as the units of the Roman army that were present at the siege of Jerusalem and who were detached from their legions. If we add the 6,000 men in the cavalry, of which half the soldiers were, once more, Roman, we arrive at a total of 9,000 circa. Thus, the number given by Josephus probably represents only the army that Herod actually utilized in the siege. However Herod would have probably left many soldiers behind in Galilee, Samaria, and Idumaea to garrison these regions, and, in all probability, his army must have consisted of approximately 15,000 men. At the beginning of the campaign, Herod sent Joseph with 2,400 soldiers to Idumaea. This number can be useful in determining the number of soldiers left behind to garrison Galilee, Samaria, and Idumaea at around 7,500–10,000. The Roman army that participated in the final phase of the civil war, including the siege of Jerusalem, numbered around 35,000 men.[20]

The second occasion that enables us to calculate the evolving number of Herod's soldiers is the First Nabataean War. In 32 BCE Herod was sent by Mark Antony to fight against the Nabataeans. Josephus does not report the number of soldiers in the Herodian army during the war, but relates that the Nabataean losses in the final phase of the war were 4,000 prisoners, 5,000 dead, and another 7,000 dead.[21] The total losses of the Nabataean army thus amounted to 16,000 casualties. If we accept Josephus' numbers, we must arrive at the conclusion that

---

[19] See Josephus, *AJ* XIV, 468 and *BJ* I, 346. If Josephus had intended Roman soldiers, he would have used the term *meros* or legion. Therefore it seems to me that the Roman soldiers present at the siege of Jerusalem were detachments from the legions, but that no full legion was present at the siege.

[20] The Roman army besieging Jerusalem consisted of the two armies of Machaeras and Sosius, which included the two legions of Machaeras. Around five *cohortes* of Machaeras army were posted around Jericho sometime before the beginning of the siege. See Josephus, *AJ* XIV, 449–450 and *BJ* I, 323. Moreover there were probably another four legions of Sosius. Thus the Roman army numbered around 24,000 men, including provincial auxiliary troops from Syria, 8,000 according to Shatzman, a total of more than 30,000 men. See Shatzman, *Armies of the Hasmoneans and Herod*, p. 161. It seems probable that half of the besieging force of Jerusalem consisted of Roman soldiers. For Mark Antony it involved a great deal of expense to send his friend Herod some six legions out of a total of 30 at his disposal to control the entire East. Shatzman gives the following numbers, 24,000 Roman soldiers (6 legions), 15,000 Herodian soldiers, 6000 cavalrymen and 8000 Syrian *auxilia*. In comparison Titus had an army of 21,000 or 23,000 Roman legionaries, 25,000–30,000 *auxilia* and 15,000–20,000 soldiers furnished by the client kings. See Shatzman, *Armies of the Hasmoneans and Herod*, pp. 161–162.

[21] See Josephus, *AJ* XV, 157–158, and *BJ* I, 383–384.

the Nabataean army could have numbered approximately 20,000 men, a huge army for a kingdom without a centralized system of administration. Thus, if Herod's army had comprised more or less the same number of soldiers as the Nabataean army, we arrive at the figure of 15,000–20,000 men.

The third instance that provides information enabling an evaluation of the strength of Herod's army is the rebellion after Herod's death. What was the strength of the army at Herod's death in 4 BCE? This may be calculated on the basis of Josephus' description of the disturbances that followed Herod's death and Archelaus' succession. The leaderless army was divided among two camps, one following Archelaus, Herod's legitimate but deeply disliked heir, and the other joining the rebels. The forces that took the side of Archelaus totaled 3,000 soldiers who followed the Roman army commanders of Herod, Rufus, and Gratus, probably the Sebastenoi, together with an *ile* of cavalrymen of the same unit.[22] The royal Guard, which numbered around 3,000, probably also took the side of the Romans.[23] There was also an indeterminate group under the command of Achiab, Herod's cousin, probably consisting of 1,500 soldiers.[24] Thus, most of the soldiers faithful to Archelaus were from the Gentile component of the army, including its Roman commanders. The rebel forces included most of the army and were probably comprised entirely of Jews. According to Josephus, the rebel army included no fewer than 10,000 men who had served in the Herodian army.[25] Thus, in the final year of his reign, Herod's army probably numbered no more than 18,000 soldiers in the standing army including 13,000 men, the military colonists, whom Josephus does not mention as taking part in the rebellion.[26] We thus reach a total of approximately 20,000 soldiers. However, even if the military colonists did take part in the rebellion, although Josephus does not mention this, Herod's army would not have numbered more than 18,000 soldiers.

After Herod's death his army was, for the most part, dispersed. Part of it, mostly Gentiles, continued to serve Archelaus and could later be found as the provincial *auxilia* of Judaea. A small part of Herod's army probably continued to serve Archelaus' brothers, Antipas and Philip. The lack of Herod's army was soon felt by Augustus and later by Tiberius, and both rulers continued to send reinforcements to the East both to replace Herod's army and to have units ready to quell any Jewish uprisings, since Herod's death was a major destabilizing influ-

---

[22] See Josephus, *AJ* XVII, 266.
[23] See Shatzman, *Armies of the Hasmoneans and Herod*, p. 193.
[24] See Josephus, *AJ* XVII, 270. See also Shatzman, *Armies of the Hasmoneans and Herod*, p. 193.
[25] See Josephus, *AJ* XVII, 270, 297 and *BJ* II, 55, 76–77.
[26] Josephus reports that Herod settled 3,000 Idumaeans in Trachonitis (Josephus, *AJ* XVI, 285), 600 men of Zamaris in Batanaea (Josephus, *AJ* XVII, 24), an unnumbered quantity of horsemen in Heshbon (Josephus, *AJ* XV, 293–296) and Gabae (Josephus, *AJ* XV, 294 and *BJ* III, 36), probably no more than 1,000 men, 6,000 colonists in Samaria (Josephus, *AJ* XV, 296, and *BJ* I, 403), and 2,000 Idumaeans in Idumaea (Josephus, *BJ* II, 55).

ence. Describing the civil war that followed Herod's death, Josephus reports that in 4 BCE one more legion was sent to garrison Syria.[27] Under Tiberius there were already four legions that garrisoned Syria.[28]

In comparison to other Hellenistic armies, or the armies of other client kings of Rome, Herod's army was smaller than that of the later Hasmonean armies and significantly smaller than the huge Ptolemaic and Seleucid armies. And yet, it was probably bigger than the armies of Rome's other client kings.[29]

B. The Structure of Herod's Army

Schalit first raised the issue of whether Herod's army was organized according to a Hellenistic or a Roman model[30]. As we shall see, the question is irrelevant. It appears possible to define the Herodian army as a Hellenistic army with many

---

[27] See Josephus, *AJ* XVII, 251, 286 and *BJ* II 40, 66.

[28] Under Tiberius there were already four legions that were garrisoned in Syria, three of them permanently; the Legio III Gallica at Emesa, the Legio VI Ferrata at Laodicea, the Legio X Fretensis at Cyrrhus, and for the time being, the Legio XII Fulminata at Raphaneae. See Paulys, *Real-Encyclopaëdie der Classischen Alterturmswissenschaft* XXIV, Stuttgard 1925, pp. 11589, 1672, 1700. See also G. Webster, *The Roman Imperial Army*, London 1985, p. 413. See also L. Keppie, *The Making of the Roman Army, from Republic to Empire*, London 1998, pp. 206, 207, 209. See also Y. Le Bohec, *L' esercito Romano*, Roma 1993, pp. 228-230 on the Roman army in the East during the Empire, and p. 271-272 on the various Roman legions and their permanent garrisons.

[29] On the strength of the army of Alexander the Great and the later Hellenistic armies see is D. Head, *Armies of the Macedonian and Punic Wars, 359 BC to 146 BC*, Goring-by-Sea 1982, pp. 13, 18-19, 20-26, 76-77, 81, 83. See also Bar-Kochva, *Seleucid Army*, chapter 10; Alexander the Great army numbered 35.000 men. At Raphia in 217 BCE Ptolemy IV could muster an army of 70,000 infantrymen. Antiochus III had 62,000 infantrymen, 6,000 cavalrymen and 102 Indian elephants. See also E. Galili, "Raphia 217 BCE, Revisited," *SCI III* 1976-77, p. 52. The army of the Hasmoneans began in 168 BCE as a group of guerrilla fighters under the leadership of Judas Maccabaeus. In 165 BCE at the battle of Emmaus, Judas could muster 3,000 fighters against Gorgias. See I *Macc.* 4. 6 and Josephus, *AJ* XII, 307. In the campaign of Bethsur in 164 BCE, Judas could already muster 10,000 men. I *Macc.* 4. 30 and Josephus, *AJ* XII, 313-314. In 137 BCE Simon the Hasmonean could muster an army of 20,000 men against Caendebeus. See I *Macc.* 16. 4. The Hasmonean king Alexander Jannaeus fought against Ptolemy X Latyrus with 50,000 soldiers, however, later on against Demetrius III Eucareus his army numbered only 19,000 men. See Josephus, *AJ* XIII, 337. Josephus reports that Timagenes wrote that Jannaeus' army numbered 80,000 men! This number has to be rejected as inflated. See Josephus, *AJ* XIII, 378. Josephus wrote that the Hasmonean army numbered 1,000 cavalrymen, 8,000 mercenaries and 10,000 Jews. His widow, Salome Alexandra could face Tigranes II, King of Armenia with 30,000 men. See Shatzman, *Armies of the Hasmoneans and Herod*, p. 34. In 14 CE Augustus' army numbered between 23 and 25 legions, around 120,000 men. Doubled by the various *auxilia*, the Roman army included around 240,000 men. See Le Bohec, *esercito Romano*, p. 43. The Roman army under Tiberius, however still numbered the same 25 legions of the final years of Augustus' reign and, together with the *auxilia* numbered around 240,000 men. See Tacitus, *Annales* IV, 5, see also Le Bohec, *esercito Romano*, p. 43.

[30] See Schalit, *König Herodes*, p. 169.

Roman features, a situation which is not exceptional, since by the middle of the second century BCE, as Sekunda has shown, the Seleucid army of Antiochus III and the Ptolemaic army of Ptolemy IV exemplified Roman characteristics in terms of the organization and the weaponry used by part of the heavy infantry.[31] Like the armies of the Seleucids and the Ptolemies – and perhaps that of the Hasmoneans before him – Herod's army showed a strong Roman influence in many ways. As will be shown, the command was made up of Romans or Italic mercenary officers, and the heavy infantry was organized according to a Roman model. The Herodian soldiers were apparently accustomed to build *castra*, like those constructed by the Roman soldiers, and the military engineers were Roman trained. The Guard, the light infantry, and the cavalry probably followed a Hellenistic model. Moreover the ratio between cavalry and infantry, as we shall see, reflects that of the Hellenistic armies. Finally, the Herodian military colonies also originated in Hellenistic models, as did most of the fortifications built by Herod.

Although Josephus does not provide much data on the subject, it is possible to reconstruct the supreme command of Herod's army. The hierarchy was obviously headed by Herod himself, who was the commander of the army. His position was not an honorary one, since he actually directed field operations personally during both the conquest of the kingdom and the First Nabataean War, rather than delegating command. It should be clear that, in this respect, Herod's position was no different than that of Alexander the Great and the Hellenistic kings. Alexander the Great was supreme commander of his army, present at every battle. When describing the conquest of the kingdom and the First Nabataean War, Josephus depicts Herod as a remarkably professional field commander. In that respect, Herod had the real touch of the *condottiero*. Moreover, according to Josephus, Herod not only knew how to handle campaign strategy and logistics very well, but also had the ability to communicate with his soldiers and encourage them to fight, as his speech to the army during the First Nabataean War clearly shows. That speech was probably copied from Nicolaus of Damascus, and indeed, the warlord's speech before a battle was a common *topos* among Classical writers.[32]

The superior officers mentioned by Josephus were either members of Herod's family or came from Roman Italy. Like the Hellenistic kings and Augustus, some of the military commanders were members of Herod's family – Herod's brother Joseph, sent to re-conquer Idumaea from Antigonus' partisans, and Achiab, during the civil war that followed Herod's death, are good examples. It would be interesting to know if the various commands assigned to members of Herod's family or to Idumaeans such as Costobar, Herod's kinsman, were reflections

---

[31] See Sekunda, *Seleucid Army*, and *The Ptolemaic Army*, Stockport 1994, passim.

[32] On Herod's leadership see Josephus, *AJ* XIV 452–455, 465–467, 483–484, XV, 127–146, 148–154 and *BJ* I, 304–308, 329–330, 343–344, 354–356, 373–379, 381–385.

of a natural talent for command or sheer nepotism.[33] And yet, Herod's real lieutenants appear to have been commanders of Italic, perhaps even Roman, background. A certain Volumnius appears as *stratopedarch*.[34] A certain Rufus was in charge of the infantry of the Sebastenoi, and Gratus was in charge of the Sebastenoi cavalry.[35] Perhaps they were also the commanders of Herod's Guard. These Romans could have had a double task: to organize the Herodian army on a more solid ground and to serve as a link between the armies of Herod and of Augustus. It is not impossible that they acted on behalf of Augustus, or that Augustus, following an expressed wish of Herod, sent them to please him, as "military advisers." It is also possible that these three Italics or Romans were political exiles from Italy, without any connection to Augustus; perhaps they were Mark Antony's veterans to whom Herod granted refuge inside his kingdom in order to utilize their military talents.[36]

Josephus indicates the senior officers of the Herodian army by the vague term of *hegemones*[37] and *strategoi*.[38] Their exact duties are difficult to identify. In the Hellenistic world these two terms have both a civil-administrative and a military resonance. Both were also utilized in relation to the Roman army, with reference to various duties at every level or echelon. The only senior officer with a specific task in the Herodian army was the *stratopedarch*. This is a Greek translation of the Roman legion's *praefectus castrorum*.[39] In the Herodian army these officers of Roman origin probably always played an active role. In times of peace, as well as in times of war, their main duty was to direct the *poliorcetica*, the construction of siege machinery and artillery, while during military campaigns, they were also responsible for the erection of the temporary camps.

The strong Roman influence on the Herodian *poliorcetica* is suggested by Josephus' description of the siege of Jerusalem in 37 BCE,[40] which was directly supervised by Herod and was reminiscent of the siege of Alesia by Julius Caesar in 52 BCE.[41] Like Caesar, Herod enclosed the city with a ring of fortifications,

---

[33] See Josephus, *AJ* XIV, 413, 438, 448–450 and *BJ* I, 323–325 on Joseph; *AJ* XV, 253–255 on Costobar; and *AJ* XV, 250, XVII, 184, 270, 297 and *BJ* I, 662, II, 55, 77 on Achiab.

[34] See Josephus, *AJ* XVI, 332 and *BJ* I, 535.

[35] See Josephus, *AJ* XVII, 275–276, 283, 294 and *BJ* II, 52, 58, 63, 74.

[36] See Josephus, *AJ* XVII, 266 and *BJ* II, 52. See also Gracey, "Armies of the Judaean Client Kings," p. 314 and Shatzman, *Armies of the Hasmoneans and Herod*, p. 209.

[37] On the *hegemon* in Josephus see Shatzman, *Armies of the Hasmoneans and Herod*, p. 208.

[38] On the *strategos* in Josephus see Shatzman, *Armies of the Hasmoneans and Herod*, p. 208.

[39] On the *praefectus castrorum* see P. Connolly, *The Roman Army*, London 1976, p. 47. See also Le Bohec, *esercito Romano*, p. 52. Josephus reports on the *stratopedarch* in the Herodian army in the following passages: *BJ* I, 535; *BJ* II, 556. *Vita*, 407. The *praefectus castrorum* of the Roman army appears in *BJ* II, 531; *BJ* VI, 238. See Shatzman, *Armies of the Hasmoneans and Herod*, p. 208.

[40] See Josephus, *AJ* XIV, 466.

[41] See L. Keppie, "The Roman Army of the Later Republic," in J. Hackett (ed.), *Warfare in the Ancient World*, New York 1989, p. 181. See also Iulius Caesar, *Gallic War* VII, 69–74.

erected towers, and cut down all the trees around the enclave. Herod's engineers, under the direction of the *stratopedarch,* clearly followed a Roman method of deployment rather than a Hellenistic one. Thus, following the textual and archaeological evidence, we may surmise that Herod's army possessed artillery to protect fortifications, including both arrow-thrower and stone-thrower machines.[42] Moreover Herod's army not only prepared a siege with equipment such as siege towers and catapults, as used by Hellenistic armies, but also constructed a real line of fortifications with towers around the city as the Roman army.[43] The catapults and the other artillery machines used by Herod already had a long history.[44]

Another of the most important responsibilities of the *stratopedarch* that reflects Roman influence on the Herodian army was probably the introduction of the Roman temporary camp, or *castra,* built at the end of each day after the Roman army marched during a military campaign. Two pieces of evidence supporting this are Josephus' description of the First Nabataean War[45] and the fact that

---

[42] See Josephus, *BJ* VII, 177. The Jewish patriots in the 66–70 CE war operated artillery machines from the fortifications of Jerusalem. Josephus, *BJ* V, 267, 347, 358–359. These machines were probably mounted on the walls of Jerusalem at the time of Herod and reinforced at the time of Agrippa I. It seems quite unlikely that all these machines were mounted either by the Roman administration, which would have had no interest in doing so, or by the Jewish patriots, who probably lacked the necessary know-how. Therefore these probably go back to Herodian times.

[43] The purpose of these bulwarks was dual: to prevent any of the defenders from fleeing the city, while keeping any auxiliary force from coming to the aid of the besieged city. To this end, Iulius Caesar built two rings of fortifications during the siege of Alesia, an outer and an inner ring. See L. Keppie, "The Roman Army of the Later Republic," p. 183. Herod, however, probably built only one ring of fortification, since the possibility of a relieving army arriving was remote.

[44] See E. W. Marsden, *Greek and Roman Artillery, Historical Development,* Oxford 1969. See also P. Connolly, *The Greek Armies,* London 1977, pp. 64–66. See also N. Sekunda, "Hellenistic Warfare," in J. Hackett (ed.), *Warfare in the Ancient World,* New York 1989, p. 131. See also Connolly, *Roman Army,* pp. 47, 66. See also Le Bohec, *esercito Romano,* p. 182. See also Vitruvius, *The Ten Books on Architecture X,* 10–15.

[45] See Josephus, *AJ* XV, 112 and *BJ* I, 367 as evidence for Herod's army *castra.* Herod's order to build a *castra* was not obeyed by the soldiers who wanted to continue to fight.

Herod's army had the know-how to build such camps.[46] The temporary camp built by the Herodian army was probably the one described by Polybius.[47]

Herod's Guard was the most colorful of all of his army units, most of the information about Herod's Guards derives from Josephus' description of its various units, which had taken part in the royal funeral procession. The personal bodyguard included the *doryphoroi*, as well as a Thracian, a German, and a Galatian contingent.[48] It is very difficult to establish the strength of the *doryphoroi*. It might simply have been a bodyguard that numbered several hundred men, or a Guard unit of several thousand men. We do not know if this unit was an infantry or cavalry unit, or if perhaps it served as an infantry unit while on guard duty at Herod's palaces and as a cavalry unit when in the field. The composition of the *doryphoroi* had no specific ethnic connotation. Whatever its size, this unit probably consisted of young men coming from the best families in the kingdom, as well as distinguished veteran soldiers who had served for a period as the king's bodyguard. Thracian[49] and Galatian soldiers could be found not only in the Herodian army, but in other Hellenistic armies as well. No less interesting were the Galatian soldiers in the Herodian Guard. The Galatians were originally part of Cleopatra's bodyguard, and Augustus gave this small contingent of 400 soldiers to Herod after Actium as a present.[50]

---

[46] Herod had very good reason to have his military engineers erect military camps similar to those built by the Roman army rather than ones of the type erected by the Hellenistic armies. The military camps of the Hellenistic armies presented several serious disadvantages not present in the Roman *castra*. First, the erection of a camp was not routine as in the Roman army; it was a rare occurrence, probably only undertaken while facing an enemy. The main inconveniences of the Hellenistic encampments were that the outer perimeter was not well defended. Nor were trenches excavated or stockades erected as in the Roman camp. Moreover at night, guard duties were probably less efficient than in the Roman camp. The result was that a surprise night attack could have fatal results. Thus, the Nabataeans during Demetrius Poliorcetes' expedition on Petra in 312 BCE surprised his encampment with an army of 4,000 infantry and 600 cavalry. Only 50 cavalrymen escaped. See Diodorus, *History* XIX, 85. Also Hasdrubal and Syphax encampments were damaged during a night surprise attack by Scipio's army in 204 BCE, two years before his final victory at Zama. See Polybius, *History* XIV, 5 and Titus Livius, *History of Rome* XXX, 5.

[47] See Polybius, *History* VI, 41–42 and Connolly, *Roman Army*, pp. 12–15. It is noteworthy that in the Augustan period, temporary *castra* developed into a permanent fortification. See P. Connolly, *The Roman Fort*, Oxford 1991, p. 5. See also A. Johnson, *Roman Forts of the 1st and 2nd centuries AD in Britain and the German Provinces*, London 1983. In the second century CE, these Augustan wooden forts became impressive forts built in stone such as the one at Saalburg. On Saalburg see E. Schallmayer, *Hundert Jahre Saalburg, Vom Römischen Grenzposten zum Europäischen Museum*, Mainz 1997.

[48] See Josephus, *AJ* XVII, 198, and *BJ* I, 672.

[49] Thracians fought as auxiliaries in nearly every Hellenistic army and later in the Roman army. See Head, *Armies of the Macedonian and Punic Wars*, pp. 12, 17–18. See also Bar-Kochva, *Seleucid Army*, pp. 33–34, 42, 50–51 and II *Macc.* 12, 35. On Thracian mercenaries in the Seleucid Army see also Bar-Kochva, *Judas Maccabaeus*, pp. 76–77.

[50] See Josephus, *AJ* XV, 217.

Where did they originally come from, Galatia or Gaul?[51] Josephus' information on the Galatians serving in the Herodian Guard is helpful in enabling us to estimate the numbers of the various units that served in the Guard. Together with the 400 Galatians, the Thracians, and the Germans, each unit would have numbered between 400 and 500 men. German tribesmen also served in Herod's Guard.[52] Herod's Guard, according to Shatzman, numbered no fewer than 2000 soldiers.[53] Herod's bodyguard was no exception in the Hellenistic world, where bodyguards and guard units were common in the army of Alexander the Great, and in Ptolemaic and the Seleucid armies as well. It should be recalled that Augustus created the Praetorian Guard.[54]

Before considering the bulk of Herod's army, or the cavalry and infantry units, I shall attempt to establish the proportional relationship between the various units of the Herodian army, and in particular, between the infantry and the cavalry. A close reading of Josephus makes it clear that during the civil war Herod always deployed a ratio of 1 to 5 between cavalry and infantry. This ratio undoubtedly reflects the total cavalry/infantry ratio in the Herodian army, and the high proportion of cavalry to infantry is typical of Hellenistic armies, but not of the Roman army.[55] Thus, during the conquest of the kingdom in 38 BCE, Herod's brother Joseph went to battle against Idumaea with 2,000 infantrymen and 400 horsemen. Here the cavalry's strength was 1/5 of that of the infantry. Later, Herod's force at Arbela consisted of 1,500 infantrymen and 200 cavalrymen. The proportion of infantry to cavalry was 7, 5 to 1. Later, Herod proceeded to Samaria with 3,000 infantrymen and 600 horsemen. Once more, the cavalry was 1/5 the

---

[51] On Galatians see Head, *Armies of the Macedonian and Punic Wars*, pp. 37–38. Galatians or Celts from Asia Minor, or from military colonies in the kingdom east of the Taurus, served in the army of the Seleucid overlords. A unit of 5,000 Galatian soldiers is recorded in the army of Antiochus IV. See Sekunda, *Seleucid Army*, pp. 12, 18–19. It seems, however, that the Celts that served in the Ptolemaic army, and then in Herod's army came from Gallia.

[52] Augustus also introduced a German bodyguard (*germani corporis custodes*) in the Praetorian Guard. See B. Rankov, *The Praetorian Guard*, London 1994, pp. 11–12.

[53] See Shatzman, *Armies of the Hasmoneans and Herod*, p. 185.

[54] On Alexander the Great bodyguard, the *somatophylakes*, see Sekunda, *Army of Alexander the Great*, pp. 8–10, 17–18, 29–30. See also Head, *Armies of the Macedonian and Punic Wars*, p. 12. In the Hellenistic period both the Seleucids and the Ptolemies had guard regiments. See Head, *Armies of the Macedonian and Punic Wars*, pp. 20, 23–24. See also Sekunda, *Seleucid Army*, pp. 12, 22–24. There were no guard units in the Roman Republic. The Praetorian Guard was a creation of Augustus in 26–25 BCE. See Rankov, *Praetorian Guard*, p. 4.

[55] See Josephus, *AJ* XIV, 413, 415, 431–432, XVII, 266 and *BJ* I, 303, 314–316. See also Shatzman, *Armies of the Hasmoneans and Herod*, p. 193. The Romans, contrary to the Hellenistic practice, had a lesser percentage of cavalry. Thus, Ventidius sent Machaeras to help Herod with two legions (8,000–10,000 men) and 1,000 cavalrymen. See Josephus, *AJ* XIV, 434 and *BJ* I, 317. Here the cavalry was only 1/8 the size of the infantry. This data reflects the very low proportion between cavalry and infantry in the Roman army. The Roman manipular legion had 4,200 effectives, 3,900 infantrymen and 300 cavalrymen. A contingent of allies, also numbered around 4,200 men, included 900 cavalrymen. During the Empire a Roman legion of 5,500 included 120 cavalrymen. See Connolly, *Roman Army*, pp. 11 and 41.

size of the infantry. During the disturbances that followed the death of Herod, Rufus had at his disposition 3,000 infantrymen, and according to Shatzman, 500 cavalrymen. Here too, the cavalry was about 1/5 the size of the infantry.

The only known unit of Herod's cavalry is that of the 500 Babylonian horsemen of Zamaris, which formed the military colonies and settled in Batanea.[56] The most interesting feature about Zamaris' horsemen is that we do not know of any auxiliary unit of the Roman army armed as Parthians, that is, cavalrymen probably armed with the composite bow[57]. This was a unique unit not only in terms of Herod's army, but also among the armies of Rome and Rome's allies. Another cavalry unit probably consisted of mounted Ituraean archers. In this case, epigraphic material related to Ituraean units in the Roman army can be a useful source of information.[58]

Herod's infantry included both light infantry, referred to by Josephus as *telos* or *lochos*, and heavy infantry, referred to by Josephus as *meros*. The only known units of light infantry were the 800 Ituraean archers from Mount Lebanon,[59] though there were probably also some other light troops from Ituraea.[60] Since these units served later as *auxilia* in the Roman army, epigraphic data can be useful in reconstructing the strength of these units.[61] The Ituraean archers are the only known example of foreign mercenaries who did not serve in the Guard

---

[56] On Zamaris see Josephus, *AJ* XVII, 24. See also Shatzman, *Armies of the Hasmoneans and Herod*, pp. 175–180. It is possible that Jews living in Babylonia performed military service for their Parthian overlords. Babylonian Jews already served in the Achaemenid and Seleucid armies. Thus Zamaris could have been a local aristocrat who, for motives unknown to Josephus, decided to emigrate to the Roman Empire with all his retainers. According to Shatzman, these soldiers were light-armed cavalry archers, bows being the most spectacular and traditional Parthian arm. These horse-archers had several forms of attack. One method was to release their bows at a distance of 45 m. from the enemy in a frontal attack. Another method was to bring the mount to a half-turn and release their bows on the enemy while turning to ride away. Arrows were shot over the horse's rump, the well-known Parthian shot. Thus, the main weapons of Zamaris' unit were the composite bow and a short sword. See P. Wilcox, *Rome's Enemies 3, Parthians and Sassanid Persians*, London 1986, pp. 6, 12–13.

[57] Professor Shatzman in a oral conversation told me that it is much more plausible that Zamaris cavalrymen were light cavalrymen armed with the composite bow that than heavy armed *cataphracti*.

[58] It is known that in the first century CE the *Ala I Augusta Ituraeorum* that served in Pannonia Inferior appeared as an auxiliary unit of the Roman army. Its predecessor was probably a light cavalry unit in the Herodian army. This unit numbered around 500 troopers. See Cheesmann, *Auxilia*, p. 182.

[59] See Josephus, *AJ* XIV, 452 and *BJ* I, 329.

[60] See Josephus, *AJ* XIV, 468 and *BJ* I, 346.

[61] Various Ituraean light infantry units serving as *auxilia* in the Roman Imperial army are known from epigraphical sources. All these units were probably *cohortes miliariae*, and their total number was about 7,000 soldiers. These units appear to have continued after Herod's death, serving as *auxilia* in the Roman army, the ones appearing in the epigraphic record. These are the *Cohors I Augusta Ituraeorum* S. that served in Pannonia and Dacia, the *Cohors I Ituraeorum* that served in Germania Superior and Dacia, the *Cohors II Ituraeorum* E. that served in Egypt. The *Cohors III Ituraeorum* that served in Egypt, the *Cohortes IV, V, VI Ituraeorum* that are supposed

units. It is probable that there were other light infantry units composed of Jews and perhaps including Idumaeans.[62] The best known units of heavy infantry in the Herodian army were the *sebastenoi*, a unit that took the side of Archelaus in the civil war following Herod's death. According to Josephus, who calls it *meros* or a legion, it consisted of 3,000 men, comprised of both infantry and cavalry, and it was commanded by Rufus and Gratus, both officers of Italic origin.[63] Josephus mentions that after Herod's death the various *sebastenoi* units became *auxilia* in the Roman Imperial army. Epigraphic data confirm Josephus account.[64] It is probable that there were other heavy infantry units, organized along the lines of a Roman model. Thus, Josephus utilizes various terms in describing Herod's infantry that could imply that it was organized along Roman lines.[65] These terms are likewise utilized by Polybius, by Asclepiodotus, and in Ptolemaic papyri to indicate units of heavy infantry that were organized and equipped like the Roman legions.[66]

2. The Campaigns of Herod's Army

We may now ask how applicable to Herod's army is Clausewitz's axiom that war is simply the continuation of diplomacy by other means (*On War*, 1, i, 24) or whether we may apply another of Clausewitz's axioms – that war is an act of violence intended to compel our opponent to fulfill our will (*On War* I, i, 2) – to the wars fought by the Herodian army. Were the classical ends and means in war, as proposed by Clausewitz – namely the destruction of the enemy's military

---

to have existed on behalf of the *Cohors VII Ituraeorum* that served in Egypt. See Cheesmann, *Auxilia*, p. 182.

[62] According to Shatzman, the Idumaeans settled in Trachonitis served as archers. See Josephus *AJ* XVI, 292 and *BJ* II, 58. See Shatzman, *Armies of the Hasmoneans and Herod*, p. 175.

[63] Josephus calls the Sebastenoi units *meros*. During the civil war that followed Herod's death, these units included infantry, ca. 3,000 men, and cavalry, ca. 500 men. See Josephus, *AJ* XVII, 266, 275–276, 283, 294 and *BJ* II, 52, 58, 63, 74.

[64] See Josephus, *AJ* XX, 122, and *BJ* II, 236. See also *Acts* 27, 1.Thus there was an *Ala Sebastenorum* that served in Mauretania Caesarensis, and a *Cohors I Sebastenorum M(iliaria)* that continued to serve in the Land of Israel. The fact that Cohors I is mentioned means that Cohors II also existed, thus 3,000 soldiers, the same number mentioned by Josephus. See also Shatzman, *Armies of the Hasmoneans and Herod*, pp. 185, 194.

[65] For the Herodian army Josephus utilized the terms *chilarchos* for *tribunus militum*, *taxiarchos* for *centurio*, and *speira* for *cohors*. For the use of the terms in Josephus see Shatzman, *Armies of the Hasmoneans and Herod*, pp. 206–208.

[66] Polybius translates *tribunus* as *chiliarches*, legion as *meros*, cohors as *speira*, manipulum as *semaia*, centurio as *taxiarchos*, and centuria as *taxis*. Asclepiodotus translates *tribunus* as *chiliarches*, legion as *phalangarchia*, cohors as *chiliarchia*, manipulum as *syntagma*, centurio as *taxiarchos* or *hekatontarches*, and centuria as *taxis*. Ptolemaic papyri translate legion as *phalanx*, cohors as *syntaxis*, manipulum as *semeia*, centurio as *hekatontarches*, and centuria as *hekatontarchia*. See Sekunda, *Seleucid Army*, pp. 29–30. See also Sekunda, *Ptolemaic Army*, p. 9.

power, the conquest of the enemy country, and the subjugation of the will of the enemy (*On War* I, ii) – realized by Herod in the wars he conducted against his enemies, as detailed by Josephus in *Antiquities* and *War*? Here, I shall attempt to adumbrate several key points by analyzing the most important campaigns waged by Herod's army: the civil war between Herod and Antigonus; the First Nabataean War, or Cornelius Gallus' campaign in Arabia, where a small contingent of Herod's army served as *auxilia*; and finally the Second Nabataean War.

The conquest of the kingdom and siege of Jerusalem (40–37 BCE) comprised the first military campaign undertaken by the Herodian army, whose purpose was to re-conquer Judaea and Jerusalem from the hands of Antigonus, the Hasmonean puppet-ruler of the Parthians. The war is described in detail by Josephus.[67] Herod could count on the military assistance of Mark Antony, but until the final phase of this military operation – the siege of Jerusalem – the Roman army and its commanders were in fact more of a hindrance than a help to Herod.

The first campaign in Galilee shows the basic long-term strategy of the two opponents, Antigonus and Herod. Antigonus' forces closed themselves into strongholds and prepared for siege. The Hasmonean ruler tried, with varying degrees of success, to profit from proverbial Roman greed by attempting to corrupt all of the Roman officers sent by Mark Antony to help Herod. Antigonus' bribery of Silo, Machaeras, and the Roman army delayed the conquest.[68] Thus, Antigonus' strategy was quite similar to that of Jugurtha sixty years earlier, when the latter secretly attempted to corrupt Roman officials, while seeking, through unofficial channels, to be recognized as king of Judaea by Rome. As in the case of Jugurtha, Antigonus' strategy was doomed to failure. Only Silo and, later, Machaeras accepted bribes from the Hasmoneans, while Ventidius, governor of Syria, remained immune to the inducements offered by Antigonus.[69] Herod's solution, which brought him success, was to offer Machaeras an even larger bribe. His strategy was based on the support of the Jewish population, and all of Galilee joined him.

Galilean Jews had good reason to support Herod. They remembered how, some years before, the young Herod had eliminated the bandits that infested the region and achieved a certain measure of peace. The fact that Sepphoris still had a garrison faithful to Antigonus[70] and that he had organized guerrilla bands to impede Herod's army did not change the final results, even though the fighting in Galilee continued for three years. Since Herod had the support of the local population, he could counterpoise the Hasmonean guerrillas with equally vicious

---

[67] On the conquest of the kingdom and the siege of Jerusalem see Josephus, *AJ* XIV, 394–491 and *BJ* I, 290–360.

[68] See Josephus, *AJ* XV 115–119 and *BJ* I 367–369.

[69] See Josephus, *AJ* XIV, 406–408, *BJ* I, 291, 297–299 on Silo. See Josephus, *AJ* XIV 435–436, 438, *BJ* I, 317–320.

[70] See Josephus, *AJ* XIV, 414 and *BJ* I, 304.

counter-guerrillas, as in the episode of the caves,[71] and he offered pardons to any partisans of Antigonus who surrendered. The only difficulty with this strategy was that his Roman allies frequently behaved quite brutally with the local population, most notably at Jericho and during the conquest of Jerusalem. The conquest of other regions of the kingdom, including Samaria and Idumaea, was much easier, especially since the Idumaeans were Herod's kinsmen.[72] In contrast, the conquest of Judaea, an area where much of the populace supported Antigonus, presented the same pattern of warfare as in Galilee – Hasmonean guerrilla and Herodian counter-guerrilla warfare. Josephus reports that Herod enlisted 800 Ituraean archers from Mount Lebanon, soldiers much better suited for guerrilla activity than heavily armed troops, to aid in the conquest of Judaea.[73]

The main objective of the entire war, however, was the conquest of Jerusalem. Although at the end of the first year Herod could pitch his camp in front of Jerusalem, Antigonus' bribery of Silo, Machaeras, and the Roman army delayed the conquest of Jerusalem for three years. With the arrival of spring (37 BCE), Herod began to construct his siege-works. Three siege walls with towers were erected around the city, following Roman tactics. In less than two months Jerusalem fell to Herod, and Antigonus, prisoner of Sosius, was sent to Mark Antony and subsequently beheaded.[74] Herod had achieved his primary objective, the conquest of Judaea and Jerusalem.

In conclusion, Herod had faced two main obstacles during the war, bribery and guerrilla warfare. The first was easily overcome through the only possible solution – paying higher bribes. The second was dealt with effectively though the creation of counter-guerrilla forces and, particularly, through a policy of promoting friendship with the local population, as Josephus states on several occasions. Thus, the locals did not shelter the guerrillas and the conflict against them was limited to areas outside the villages and urban areas. Moreover, with his firm stand in relation to his Roman allies, Herod not only conquered the kingdom, but also the hearts of most of his subjects.

The First Nabataean War (32–31 BCE),[75] which resulted from Herod's obligations to Mark Antony, was the first time that Herod's army fought as an auxiliary force of Mark Antony's Roman army. The First Nabataean War was, in fact, a local offshoot of the global war between Mark Antony and Cleopatra and Caesar Octavian. For Mark Antony and Cleopatra, the war would end in defeat at Actium. For Herod, the war would end in a splendid military and diplomatic

---

[71] See Josephus, *AJ* XIV 421–430, *BJ* I, 307, 309–314.

[72] Josephus wrote in *BJ* I, 303 that Herod himself conquered Idumaea and then surrendered it to Joseph, as the new governor. According to *AJ* XIV, 413 however, Herod sent his brother Joseph to conquer Idumaea.

[73] See Josephus, *AJ* XIV, 452, *BJ* I, 329.

[74] See Josephus, *AJ* XIV 489–490 and XV 6–9 and *BJ* I 357–358, 364–365.

[75] On the First Nabataean War see Josephus, *AJ* XV, 108–160 and *BJ* I, 364–385. See also A. Kasher, *Jews, Idumaeans and Ancient Arabs*, TSAJ 18, Tübingen 1988, pp. 135–152.

victory. In this war Herod's army had to cope with two differently constituted armies – the Nabataean army, which was quite numerous, but composed mainly of light infantry and cavalry; and the Ptolemaic army, similar in its composition to the Herodian army, but much larger. The main purpose of the war was to subdue the Nabataeans. Cleopatra, queen of Ptolemaic Egypt, was disturbed that the Nabataeans had stopped paying tribute[76] and that they had dominated the Spice Route. She had a further motive, however, since by sending Herod's army away from the main theater of war, she could preclude any claim on his part to participation in the final victory against Caesar Octavian.

According to Josephus, the First Nabataean War was quite popular among the Jewish population, since it would appear that they wished to take revenge for Nabataean meddling in the quarrel between Hyrcanus II and Aristobulus that had caused 20 years of civil war and unrest. Herod, however, was probably interested in something else, namely sharing the benefits of Nabataean domination of the Spice Route with Cleopatra and Mark Antony. The Nabataean army, no match for Herod's well trained and highly organized army, was defeated at Diospolis (Dium) and at Canatha.[77] The war, however, was complicated by the intervention of Cleopatra, who was jealous of Herod's success and viewed it as a threat to her dream of dominating the Spice Route, sending a Ptolemaic army under the command of Athenion to hinder Herod. Herod's tired troops were defeated by this modern and bigger army, and the defeated Nabataeans joined the Ptolemaic army in the battle. However, as soon as Cleopatra recalled Athenion and his army, Herod reorganized his own army for a final clash with the Nabataeans. When an earthquake struck Judaea, Herod opted for making peace. His ambassadors probably proposed the status quo ante bellum to the Nabataeans, but the Nabataeans killed the Jewish ambassadors, making peace impossible. Herod was thus forced to continue the war, and his army attacked the enemy on the west bank of the Jordan and then at Philadelphia,[78] where a much larger Nabataean force was again soundly defeated.

Herod's army achieved all of its objectives. The Nabataean army was completely annihilated, and the Nabataeans had to concede various territories to Herod, as well as control of part of the Spice Route and probably the tribute that they were supposed to pay Cleopatra.[79] But Herod enjoyed an even more important victory.[80] Though fighting against the Nabataeans and Cleopatra as an ally of Mark Antony, Herod did not directly confront Caesar Octavian (as was his

---

[76] According to Kasher the Nabataeans did not want to pay any tribute to Cleopatra. See A. Kasher, "The War of Herod against the Nabataeans," *Proceedings of the National Academies of Sciences*, Vol. VII, 4, 1986, pp. 109–142.
[77] See Josephus, *AJ* XV, 111–112 and *BJ* I 366–367.
[78] Philadelphia is only mentioned by Josephus in *BJ* I, 380.
[79] See Josephus, *AJ* XV 148–160 and *BJ* 381–385.
[80] See also Z. Yavetz, *Augustus, The Victory of Moderation*, Tel Aviv 1994, p. 322.

2. The Campaigns of Herod's Army

duty as Mark Antony's ally and *cliens*) and could thus appear in a more positive light vis-à-vis the victor of Actium. In the end, this diplomatic victory would have more far-reaching consequences than the war itself, for as an ally of Augustus' Rome, Herod would receive more territory than he had ever conquered in battle, without needing to employ a military option.

Cornelius Gallus' expedition to Arabia (25 BCE) was the other occasion on which Herod's army fought as an auxiliary force of the Roman army. This time, however, the Roman army took orders from Augustus, who was now the undisputed ruler of the Roman world. The expedition is described by Strabo.[81] Josephus mentions only that Herod sent 500 chosen men to Cornelius Gallus as an auxiliary force.[82] The purpose of the expedition was economic – to dominate the Spice Route and Arabia, which was the land-bridge between Egypt and India. The Nabataeans, who dominated access to the Spice Lands of Arabia, were greatly alarmed by Rome's plans. Syllaeus, the Nabataean *epitropos,* promised to guide Cornelius Gallus' army on the march and to furnish him with supplies, although his real purpose was to trap the Roman army and keep it from reaching the Spice Lands. The Nabataeans clearly had no interest in the Romans' domination of the spice trade, which would have been the final blow to their control of the Spice Route after Herod's victory in 32–31 BCE. Moreover, according to Strabo, Syllaeus wished to dominate Arabia himself.

Herod had good reason to send an auxiliary corps. First, as client king of Rome he had no choice, and second, doing so had the potential to provide him with the opportunity to share the Spice Route with Rome. The expedition proved to be a failure for Rome. Duped by Syllaeus, and with his logistical lines overextended, Gallus found that the effectiveness of his army had been reduced, perhaps by half. Strabo, for instance, was convinced that Gallus would have subjugated all of Arabia but for the treason of Syllaeus.[83] Cornelius Gallus' reputation was now ruined. The Arabian petty kings, however, preferred a treaty of friendship with Rome to a new Roman expedition. Herod's soldiers behaved very well, proving themselves to be invaluable allies of Augustus, and it would appear that Herod's army enjoyed yet another diplomatic victory since his army "intelligence" collected proof of Syllaeus' treason. This evidence would become very useful 15 years later, during the Second Nabataean War.

The Second Nabataean War (9 BCE)[84] stands out as one of those wars that contradicts Clausewitz's principle that war is the continuation of diplomacy by

---

[81] See Strabo, *Geography* XVI, 4, 22–24.
[82] See Josephus, *AJ* XV, 317.
[83] See Strabo, *Geography* XVII, 1, 53.
[84] On the Second Nabataean War see Josephus, *AJ* XVI, 271–299, 333–355 and *BJ* I, 574–577 (Syllaeus voyage to Rome). Only the *AJ* recounts in detail the Second Nabataean War. In *BJ*, only Syllaeus' voyage to Rome is described. Once more, in *BJ* Josephus did not want to wound Roman pride by showing Augustus' position on the war. Moreover, there is no indication that

other means. Herod won or lost the Second Nabataean War on the diplomatic table, not on the battlefield, where his army clearly achieved a degree of success. Although most of this war was fought on the diplomatic front, it may be considered a "limited war," because there were some limited military activities. It all began because Syllaeus, the Nabataean *epitropos*, wished to regain the territories conquered by the Jewish king in the First Nabataean War and to regain complete control of the Spice Route. Since Syllaeus knew that the Nabataean army was no match for the Herodian army, his only means of achieving success was to destabilize Herod's power, and thus he provided financial support to a native rebellion in Trachonitis.

Herod's army easily defeated the rebels. The native ringleaders succeeded in fleeing to Nabataea and, from there, raided both Herod's kingdom and Syria. Herod decided to organize a retaliatory expedition, with the approval of Saturninus, governor of Syria (10–6 BCE). The Romans clearly understood the nature of the problem and that only serious punitive action could bring quiet to Syria and Trachonitis. Since Herod had also a claim of sixty talents from the Nabataean king Obadas, he requested that the money, as well as the ringleaders, be handed over to him. When the Nabataeans refused, Herod called up his army and invaded Nabataea. The only true military action was the siege of Raepta, the headquarters of the robbers, which was successfully stormed by Herod's army. Herod's military action was in fact limited to a small retaliatory raid, with a locally limited effect, and there was no clash with the Nabataean army.

Following the raid, Syllaeus complained to Augustus in Rome about Herod's unjustified aggression. Augustus did not consult Saturninus. Had he done so, he would have been informed that the representative of Rome had given his sanction for the operation to Rome's ally. In fact, Augustus' anger was directed at Herod for another, more significant reason. In declaring war and in mustering his army without Augustus' permission, Herod had shown disrespect to the *maiestas* of Rome. Herod's "crime" was no less than *maiestas*. Augustus felt that as a client king, Herod had defied his authority. Thus Augustus was compelled to chastise Herod, threatening to withdraw his title of *socius et amicus* of Rome and to treat Judaea as a subject rather than an ally. Augustus' reaction tied Herod's hands and led to a further destabilization of Herod's rule. However, Herod's diplomatic efforts brought the war to a successful conclusion. Herod was aided by the jealousy of Aretas, pretender to the Nabataean crown, who was suspicious of the all-powerful Syllaeus and therefore sent ambassadors to Augustus to accuse Syllaeus of poisoning Obadas. Apparently Augustus was not impressed. Only the oratorical talents of Nicolaus of Damascus apparently brought an end to Herod's humiliating situation, since Nicolaus reported that Saturninus had sanctioned

---

the Nabataeans were a formal ally of Rome as Judaea was. On the Second Nabataean War see also Kasher, *Jews, Idumaeans and Ancient Arabs*, pp. 164–174.

the raid and therefore Herod's action had been legal. Furthermore, it appears that Nicolaus produced other incriminating documents as well as proof of Syllaeus' treason against Gallus' army. For Herod at least, the story had a happy end, since Syllaeus was beheaded for treason.

But did Syllaeus succeed in ruining Herod's standing with Augustus? According to Sartre,[85] Augustus was so impressed by Herod's standing that he toyed with the idea of giving him the Nabataean kingdom, but was dissuaded from doing so because of Herod's old age and his family troubles. Moreover, Augustus' stepson Tiberius, who closely continued the policies of Augustus, favored Herod's son, Herod Antipas, *tetrarch* of Galilee, in another war against the Nabataeans.[86] While it is true that the Nabataeans were the aggressors and that Antipas' Gentile army deserted him, it is also true that it was probably unnecessary to send Vitellius, the Governor of Syria, to conquer Petra, the Nabataean political center. Moreover, some years later, Claudius gave all of the territories that once formed part of his grandfather's kingdom to Agrippa I, Herod's grandson. In conclusion, it seems to me that Herod did not fall from Augustus' favor as consequence of the Second Nabataean War.

3. The Fortifications

A. *The Sources of Herodian Fortifications*

In this section I shall analyze the various types of fortifications erected by Herod (cfr. figure III, 1). My analysis of the typology and function of Herod's fortifications is not, in general, based upon Shatzman's study, but rather, it relies, in part, upon Netzer's books and articles, particularly regarding the major fortifications, and upon Dar's survey of Samaria, as well as upon other specialized studies.[87]

---

[85] See M. Sartre, *D'Alexandre à Zénobie, Histoire du Levant Antique, IVe siècle av. J.-C.–IIIe siècle ap. J.-C.*, Paris 2001, pp. 518–519. See also Josephus, *AJ* XVI, 355.

[86] The roots of this Third Nabataean War were in the diplomatic treaty of peace between Herod and Aretas. One of the provisions was that the young Antipas was to marry Aretas' daughter. As soon as he was on the throne as tetrarch of Galilee, he divorced the Nabataean princess and sent her back to his father to marry Herodias. Some year later Aretas attacked him with the excuse of a border dispute in Gamalitis. Some of Antipas' soldiers, in fact, lent by his half brother Philip the Tetrarch, deserted to the side of the Nabataeans. Antipas was thus defeated. Antipas wrote to Tiberius. The Roman emperor immediately had Vitellius, governor of Syria, march against Aretas to bring him back in chains, dead or alive. Vitellius certainly prepared to go to war with two legions, but his departure to Rome and the death of Tiberius and the succession of Gaius brought an end to this war. See Josephus, *AJ* XVIII, 109–126.

[87] See for example S. Dar, *Landscape and Pattern. An Archaeological Survey of Samaria, 800 BCE–636 CE*, Debevoise (N.C.) 1986 and S. Dar, *Landscape and Pattern*, BAR International Series, Oxford 1986. See also E. Netzer, "Cypros," *Qadmoniot* 8, 1975, pp. 54–61; E. Netzer, *Greater Herodium*, Qedem 13, Jerusalem 1981 and E., Netzer, *Masada 3, The Yigael Yadin*

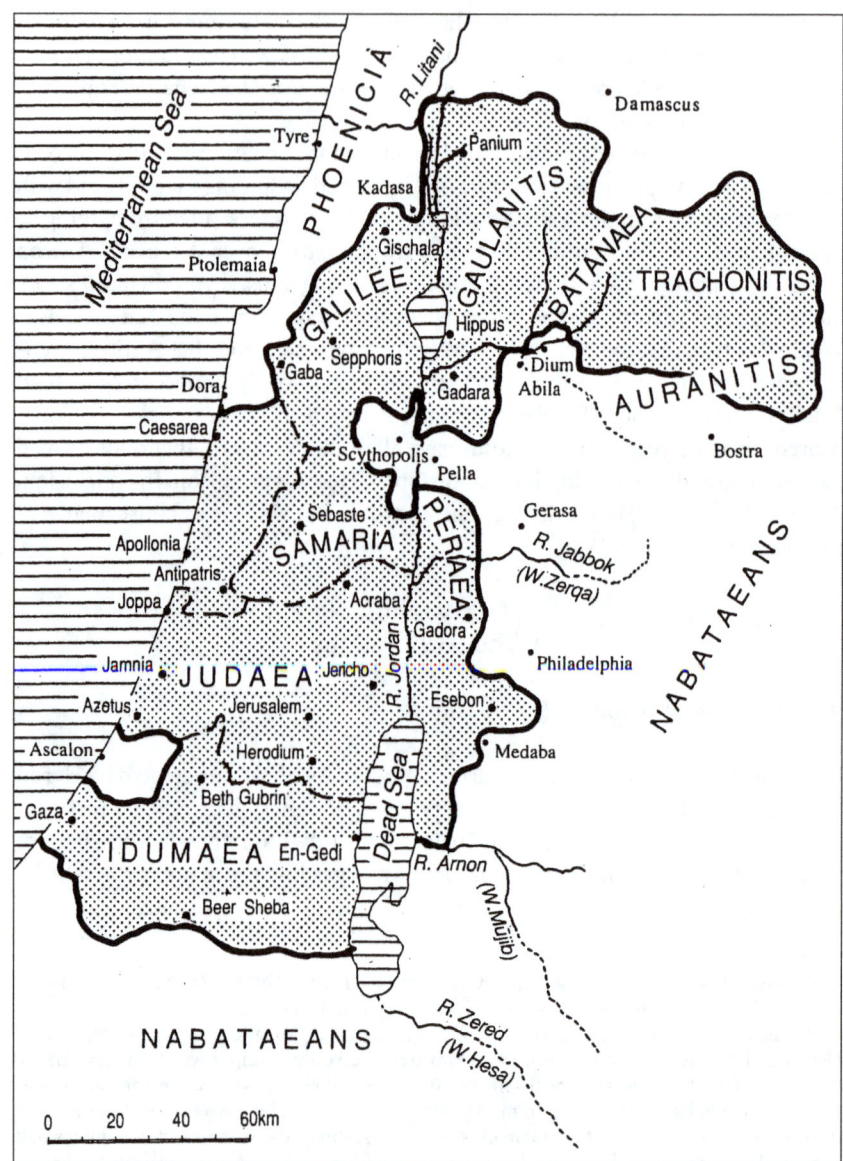

Figure III, 1 – Herod's Kingdom after 20 BCE from I. Shatzman, *The Armies of the Hasmonaeans and Herod*, Tübingen 1991, p. 192, map 14, Courtesy of Mohr Siebeck, Tübingen.

The Herodian fortifications may be subdivided into three main types: urban fortifications, which included city walls; the city acropolis and castles or *tetrapyrgia;* and smaller fortifications, or fortlets and towers, whose purpose was to defend crossroads and the countryside. Most of Herod's defense structures, such as the city walls, royal fortresses, and main forts, were not built as protection against internal enemies. In fact, Herod's fortifications were too powerful to have been intended to serve either against a local rabble or against an improbable mutiny of the army. Most of the fortifications were probably erected as protection against an external enemy, a regular army, which could have been only that of the last Ptolemies, the Parthians, or the Nabataeans. The final examples of static defense analyzed here are the military colonies, an important characteristic of Herod's army. These colonies were neither new nor innovative, but were a common element in the Classical world, as exemplified by the military colonies founded and maintained by the Hellenistic armies, as well as by the Roman Republican and Imperial armies.

Herodian fortifications were influenced by various sources. City walls and towers, as well as bigger fortifications such as *tetrapyrgia*, followed a Hellenistic trend, while some of the city gates appear to have followed a Roman prototype. On the other hand, the smaller fortifications followed a local trend, albeit improved during the Hellenistic period. Thus, in this study of the Herodian fortifications, I shall first analyze the origins of Herodian city wall structures, followed by other types of fortifications such as *tetrapyrgia* and smaller fortifications.

During the Hellenistic and Herodian periods, the entire city wall was built using ashlars, the Phoenician stone-dressing tradition of the Iron Age remained unchanged.[88] The main inspiration, however, was Hellenistic. Thus the city walls, as well as most of the towers, some of the gates, were all constructed according to Hellenistic prototypes[89]. The most outstanding feature introduced into the defensive system of the Hellenistic period and continuing in the Herodian period

---

Excavations 1963–1965, Final Reports, The Buildings, Stratigraphy and Architecture, Jerusalem 1991, pp. 615–623.

[88] See E. Stern, "The Phoenician Architectural Elements in Palestine during the Late Iron Age and the Persian Period," *The Architecture of Ancient Israel, from the Prehistoric to the Persian Period,* Jerusalem 1992, pp. 302–304. See also Z. Herzog, "Settlement and Fortification Planning in the Iron Age," *The Architecture of Ancient Israel, from the Prehistoric to the Persian Period,* Jerusalem 1992, pp. 269–271.

[89] See generally A. W. McNicoll, *Hellenistic Fortifications, From the Aegean to the Euphrates,* Oxford Monographs on Classical Archaeology, Oxford 1997. See R. Arav, *Settlement Patterns and City Planning, 337–301 BCE* British Archaeological Reports, International Series 485, Oxford 1989, passim. On the city walls of Philoteria, built in brick, locally available, see P. Bar-Adon, "Philoteria," *IEJ* 4, 1954, pp. 128–129. On the stone city walls of Ptolemais see R. Arav, Settlement Patterns. On the stone city walls of Dor see E. Stern, "The Walls of Dor," *IEJ* 38, 1988, pp. 6–14 and E. Stern, *Dor Ruler of the Seas,* Jerusalem 1994, pp. 204–206. On the stone city walls of Samaria see J. W. Crowfoot, *The Buildings at Samaria,* London 1942, pp. 24–31, 117–120. On the stone city walls of Marissa see J. Horowitz, "Town Planning of Hellenistic Marisa," *PEQ* 112, 1980, pp. 93–111. On the artillery development see A. W. Lawrence, *Greek Architecture,*

were the round and square tower as well as the bastion. A major problem for the scholar is that Hellenistic city gates are not well known in the Land of Israel.[90] However, during the Herodian period, gates appeared which followed a Roman prototype. This type of Roman gate, which greatly influenced the Herodian gates, generally had three entrances that were covered by arches, with the middle one larger than those on the sides. Two flanking towers protected the gate and could be circular, octagonal, or square shaped. Like the Hellenistic city gates, this type of gate also had a direct axial passage. This inner court can be reinforced with two additional sets of inner gates, also with three entrances. Some Herodian gates and towers closely reflect Roman prototypes.[91] Herod was very successful in combining these essentially unrelated elements, adopting the best elements from each source to build city walls.

However, Herod also built various citadels and fortified palaces or *tetrapyrgia*, in addition to fortresses, following, on the whole, Hellenistic prototypes. As his main model for the first two types of fortifications Herod selected the *tetrapyrgion*,[92] which originated in the Hellenistic world, and was a fortress with

---

Harmondsworth 1957, pls. 128, 129A, and Marsden, *Greek and Roman Artillery*, pp. 122–155, diagram 2, pp. 151 ff. 163, diagram 14.

[90] The first type of gate, adopted in the third century, is the "courtyard city gate." Later, a second type of gate was developed in the later half of the second century BCE. On the "courtyard city gate" see Connolly, *Greek Armies*, p. 69. Good examples are the Dipylon and the Sacred Gate at Athens. See P. Connolly, *The Ancient City, Life in Classical Athens and Rome*, Oxford 1998, p. 18. On the Dypilon Gate in the early Hellenistic period see U. Knigge, *The Athenian Kerameikos, History – Monuments – Excavations*, Athens 1991, pp. 70–72. The Arcadian Gate at Messene is another good example. See N. Kaltsas, *Ancient Messene*, Athens 1989, p. 15. Also the Epipolae Gate of the Euryalus Fort at Syracuse is a good example. See Connolly, *Greek Armies*, pp. 68–69. The second type of gate type consisted of an entrance between two overlapping stretches of wall. Only two city gates, at Dor, and Samaria, have been excavated.

[91] On the fortifications of the Roman Republic see P. Gros, *L'architecture romaine I, Les monuments publics*, Paris 1996, pp. 26–43 and P. Connolly, *Hannibal and the Enemies of Rome*, London 1978, pp. 30–31. See also S. Nappo, *Pompeii, Guide to the Lost City*, London 1998, pp. 11, 22–23. Only with Augustus did the new cities that he founded, such as Augusta Taurinorum, Augusta Praetoria and Nemausus, or cities whose walls were restructured, such as Verona, exhibit new characteristics that cannot be labeled Hellenistic, as the gates. Good examples are the Porta Venere at Spello, the Porta dei Leoni at Verona, the Porta Palatina at Turin, and the Porta Pretoria at Aosta. See Gros, *Architecture romaine*, pp. 37–41. On the ideal city walls, see Vitruvius, *The Ten Books on Architecture* I, 5. Towers of various shapes, sometimes multi-storied, were part of the city walls, as a huge multi-story octagonal tower called the Tour Magne at Nemausus. See Gros, *Architecture romaine I*, pp. 48–49.

[92] This building probably originated in Asia Minor in the fourth century BCE. The earliest example is probably the palace of Mausolus at Halicarnassus. The Macedonian kings built *tetrapyrgia* in the northern part of the kingdom, as a contribution to the defense of the kingdom against the invading Scythian nomads. The best example is the Macedonian palace-fortress of Demetrias. The city of Seuthas also had a citadel built as a *tetrapyrgion*. The Seleucid king Antiochus II erected a *tetrapyrgion* that served as royal palace near Antioch. On the *tetrapyrgion* in the Hellenistic world and its origins see Nielsen, *Hellenistic Palaces*, pp. 65, 67, 98, 115, 142, 157, 168, 182. See also Förtsch, "Residences of King Herod and their Relations to Roman Villa Architecture," pp. 88–89.

four towers on the outside, erected on the corners, built on the highest hill of the area. The inside was furnished with luxurious elements of domestic architecture. Good examples are the Antonia and Herodium.

The main source for smaller fortresses in the Herodian period was Hasmonean, although the main features stemmed from a tradition that had begun in the Iron Age. The Ptolemies had already improved these fortifications.[93] Later on, the Seleucid needed to build a series of fortification in an attempt to contain the Maccabaean armies, and still other fortifications were erected during the Hasmonean Period.[94] From the beginning of their struggle, the Hasmoneans made good use of the existing fortifications,[95] and in the first century BCE they introduced a new type of fortress, in addition to the extant Hellenistic fortifications. All of these fortresses were constructed with stone walls, and since these fortresses contained no natural springs, sophisticated cisterns were built to supply water within them. Convenience was eschewed in favor of an inaccessible and impregnable location. Sometimes this was overemphasized, as in Alexandrium, Hyrcania, and Machaerus. At times quite far from strategic roads, or in locations which did not afford a commanding view of the environment, these fortifications were unable to prevent an impending threat. Josephus is a good source for these fortresses.[96] In the regional fortifications built in Judaea, military concerns were addressed to a greater degree than ever before, so as to include better defense systems against artillery, battering rams, and missiles. Since Herod adopted and improved most of the Hasmonean fortifications, these will be discussed together with the Herodian fortifications. Even during the Herodian period, all of the smaller fortifications followed an established architectural tradition that dated back to the Iron Age. However, even in these, some Hellenistic elements were present, such as the *proteichisma*.

---

[93] In the Ptolemaic and early Seleucid periods fortresses, often situated on a well-protected hillock and at an important road junction, were still built with mud brick walls. Good examples are Bethsur, Beersheba, Arad, and En Gedi.

[94] Thus the Seleucid general Bacchides built in 162 BCE in Judaea various strongholds at Jericho, Emmaus, Bethhoron, Bethel, Thamnatha, Pharathon and Tephon, the fortified village of Bethsur, the citadel of Gazara, and the well known Akra in Jerusalem (already begun by Antiochus III some years before. He placed troops and stores of food in them. See I *Macc.* 9.50–2, and Josephus, *AJ* XIII, 15–17.

[95] Thus, in 165 BCE, after the conquest of Jerusalem, Judas Maccabaeus had walls with towers erected around Mount Zion, the Temple Mount was fortified, and outside Jerusalem, the citadel of Bethsur was once more fortified. See I *Macc.* 4. 60, and Josephus, *AJ* XII, 326.After Judas's death, Jonathan, his brother and heir, continued the struggle. One of his first acts was to fortify Bethbatzi. See I *Macc.* 9. 62, and Josephus, *AJ* XIII, 26.

[96] See Josephus, *AJ* XIII, 422. He gives us a list of twenty-two fortifications that played a prominent role in the civil war between Hyrcanus II and Aristobulus II. It seems that the Hasmonean state in its last years possessed around thirty fortifications, mainly in Judaea.

B. The Evolution of Herodian Fortifications

During Herod's rule the conception of static defense evolved over three main periods. In the first period, from 37 till 31 BCE, Herod mainly repaired existing fortifications that had been destroyed by years of civil war. Thus, in 37 BCE, after the conquest of Jerusalem, when Herod could truly consider himself "master in his own home," he probably also began to attend to the standing defense system of the kingdom. The example of Jerusalem is striking. In 63 BCE, Pompey conquered the city after a bloody siege. The fortifications, or parts of them, were dismantled. Later, Hyrcanus II rebuilt these fortifications, at least in part, and they were used in 40 BCE by the last Hasmonean ruler, Antigonus. Thus, in 37 BCE, the fortifications of Jerusalem had to be repaired, if not rebuilt. The same could be said for other village or city walls and fortresses that had been damaged by the endless civil war and by years of neglect.

Herod had good reason to rebuild these fortifications. In the period from 37 to 31 BCE, he faced three main external dangers: a potential Parthian invasion, albeit only a remote possibility; Cleopatra, his powerful southern neighbor; and the Nabataeans, always ready to profit from the internal discord in Herod's kingdom. During this period Herod probably repaired most of the Hasmonean fortifications without adding anything new. An interesting example is the fortification of Masada at this time. The Hasmoneans did not, apparently, fortify the top of the mountain, but kept a garrison living in tents,[97] so Herod probably built a series of dwellings to house the soldiers who were scattered around the top of the mountain and organized a water supply. In Jerusalem, Herod appears to have only repaired the existing fortifications.

In the second period, from 31 BCE till 10 BCE, Herod not only improved, but in some cases dramatically modified, existing standing defense systems. He expanded the static defenses of his kingdom with the erection of two huge urban centers and various palace-fortresses, the renovation of existing fortifications, and the establishment of colonies. In 31 BCE, after Actium, the internal situation dramatically changed, and the international situation was likewise altered. The Parthians remained a constant threat, at least until late in Augustus' rule. Cleopatra, however, was no longer a threat. With the Nabataeans, however, the situation probably worsened. Thus Herod's static defenses had to meet new needs. As an important client kingdom, Herod had all the city fortifications of Jerusalem improved though the building of the Citadel, the Temple Mount, and the Antonia. During this period two new cities were built – Sebaste and Caesarea Maritima – both with huge city walls, and the former with a fortified acropolis as well. These urban centers clearly served the kingdom's strategic interests, with

---

[97] See E. Netzer, *Masada III, The Yigael Yadin Excavations 1963–1965, Final Reports, The Buildings, Stratigraphy and Architecture*, Jerusalem 1991, pp. 615–623.

Caesarea Maritima functioning as the main military harbor of the kingdom and Sebaste as a huge garrison city.

Several changes were made in the administration of the burgeoning kingdom, even within its core, Judaea. Instead of Bethsur, Herodium, created ex nihilo, now became the new capital of the *toparchia,* and a huge castle of the *tetrapyrgion* type was erected there. The various fortresses facing the King's Highway and protecting Herod's palaces at Jericho were partially rebuilt, or completely fortified, such as Masada. Military colonies were also a feature of this period. The border between Idumaea and Nabataea was fortified with the creation of various colonies. Most of the military colonies were scattered, mainly in the unruly north among the Ituraean brigands, and in the south, in Idumaea, facing the Nabataeans.[98] Herod's building enterprises included the reshaping of Judea's desert fortresses that had once served the Hasmoneans. These fortresses controlled Judaea and in times of peace served as prisons and garrisons. In times of war, Herod could escape to them and await relief, in the comfort of a royal palace. In Transjordan, the Decapolis area, inhabited by Greeks, was fortified. In the new territories in the north – Batanaea, Trachonitis, Auranitis, and Gaulanitis – the small settlement of Paneas was transformed into a city, though no archaeological evidence for this has been found. Soldiers were settled as colonists at various sites.

The third period, which included the final years of Herod's reign, from 10 BCE to 4 BCE, was characterized by a slow completion of all the building projects. The difficult but victorious Nabataean War of 8 BCE was not characterized by any modification of the static defenses of the kingdom.

After Herod's death, his descendants continued to implement his defensive policies. His son Antipas founded Tiberias, the new capital, and probably fortified it with a city wall. His grandson Agrippa I erected the Third Wall of Jerusalem, doubling the area of the city protected by walls.

C. *The Types and Distribution of Fortifications of the Herodian Kingdom*

I shall now examine the existing factual evidence for the standing defenses of Herod's kingdom. We must exercise due caution in considering material evidence, even if it appears to be confirmed by literary sources, in this case Josephus and Strabo. Material evidence cannot provide a complete and total image of the situation, and, it should be emphasized, the data is sometimes easily misinterpreted. A good example is as follows. The area of Judaea proper has been

---

[98] Kasher argues that Herod's kingdom static defenses were mainly created to face and contain the Nabataeans. Thus the fortifications of Samaria, Judaea, Transjordan as well as the fortifications and colonies in Idumaea were part of a unique defense system, whose main task was to defend Herod's kingdom from the Nabataeans. See Kasher, *Jews, Idumaeans and Ancient Arabs,* pp. 153–157.

thoroughly excavated, and numerous surveys have provided equally valuable material. Galilee and Idumaea, today the northern half of the Negev region, have also been carefully studied. Other regions of Herod's kingdom, mainly the regions in the north that were not originally part of the Herodian kingdom, have not been as thoroughly excavated and surveyed as has been the core area of Herod's kingdom. Moreover, since some of these regions today lie in Syria, Lebanon, and Jordan, for current political reasons certain data are unavailable or may have been misinterpreted. Moreover, it is difficult to compare the material from Israel with similar material from other regions in the Mediterranean basin and from farther away in the Near East.[99] The first part of this section is devoted to cities; the second to fortified royal residences. The third part covers fortifications as such, according to region. I have tried to analyze each region with its own peculiarities, while attempting to present a generalized view of the situation.

i. The Herodian Cities

A study of the fortifications of the urban centers in the Herodian kingdom is essential to an understanding of the location of the urban settlements. As I have noted above, the Herodian city walls and towers followed a Hellenistic plan, while some of the city gates followed a Roman prototype. Herod inherited the city of Jerusalem from the Hasmoneans as the capital city of the kingdom. During the Hasmonean period, Jerusalem was probably the only real city of the kingdom. The status of Jerusalem during the Herodian period is less obvious. Clearly it continued to be both the capital of the kingdom and royal residence, as well as the administrative capital of Judaea. Jerusalem was also the only totally Jewish city of the kingdom. The growth of Jerusalem was clearly reflected in the development of its defenses: as the city grew in importance and in population, new walls were added. An analysis of this period clearly shows not only the primary importance of Jerusalem, but the fact that it was no longer the only city of the kingdom, since Herod added new cities.

The other two major urban entities of the kingdom were both established by Herod – Sebaste, founded in 25 BCE, and Caesarea Maritima, founded in 23 BCE. Both cities had a mixed population of Jews and Greeks and, like Jerusalem, enjoyed the status of royal city from the outset. Herod built Sebaste on the growing Greek settlement of Samaria. The city had been freed by Pompey and refounded by Gabinius,[100] and despite its clearly Gentile character, it was actually a huge garrison, a mature settlement of army veterans. The defenses of the city protected

---

[99] No less problematic is the fact that very much interesting comparative material coming from the Crimea, where the Greek settlers built numerous fortifications against the dangerous Scythian nomads, has been published only in Russian and is available only with difficulty in the West. See Nielsen, *Hellenistic Palaces*, pp. 99–101.

[100] See Josephus, *BJ* I, 156 and 166.

3. The Fortifications

the royal residence, but also served as a warning to the surrounding Samaritans. As for Caesarea Maritima, from Herod's reign and onward it became the main harbor of the kingdom, playing an increasingly more important role.[101] Another royal city erected by Herod with status similar to that of Caesarea Maritima and Sebaste was Paneas in Gaulanitis; however there is not enough data available about Paneas during this period of time.

Herod was a founder of cities, but not a sympathizer of *poleis*, or city-states. All of the walled cities were royal cities, or cities where the king resided and ruled. These cities enjoyed a reduced municipal autonomy, but no more than that, and it is no coincidence that none of these cities had an autonomous mint. The other Gentile cities of the kingdom, or more correctly, the urban centers, such as Gaza and the cities of the Decapolis, were garrisoned by Herod's soldiers, who probably resided in the acropolis or in a fortress bordering the town. However, these cities showed no trace of fortifications, such as city walls, to protect their entire population. The Herodian dynastic rulers continued the policy of urbanization of their respective enclaves in Herod's kingdom. Thus, Antipas made Sepphoris, a small walled settlement, the capital of his kingdom, probably adding public buildings and a royal palace on the acropolis, and he later built the city of Tiberias. Both cities were mixed Jewish cities, with a strong Gentile minority.[102]

The city walls of Herod's cities were not dissimilar to the earlier Hellenistic city fortifications.[103] In some particulars, however, it seems that the Herodian city fortifications show a certain Roman influence, mainly in the towers and the city gate.

Josephus describes in detail the topography of the city of Jerusalem. His description is extremely valuable for us because he records the various alterations made to the terrain from the Iron Age through the time of the Jewish War, reconstructing the original layout of the city and its evolution.[104] Herodian Jerusalem included two city walls, with Agrippa I later adding another wall, the Third Wall (cfr. figure III, 2). The First Wall was the greatest building project during the Hasmonean period. The wall's circumference included the Upper City, the Lower City separated from the Upper City by a scarp, and the City of

---

[101] Thus, after the deposition of Archelaus, the Roman governor made this city his chief residence. Agrippa I also made it the second city of the kingdom. After the destruction of Jerusalem, Caesarea Maritima became the undisputed seat of the Roman governor.

[102] See Josephus, *AJ* XVIII, 27 on Sepphoris and *AJ* XVIII, 36–38 and *BJ* II, 168 on Tiberias.

[103] Herod continued the traditional Phoenician technique of employing rectangular ashlars stones with margins on all sides, laid as headers and stretchers. In such details the Herodian city walls continued the earlier fortifications so that in both Jerusalem and Caesarea Maritima it is impossible to distinguish between the Hellenistic and the Herodian Early Roman phases of construction.

[104] See Josephus, *BJ* V, 136–141.

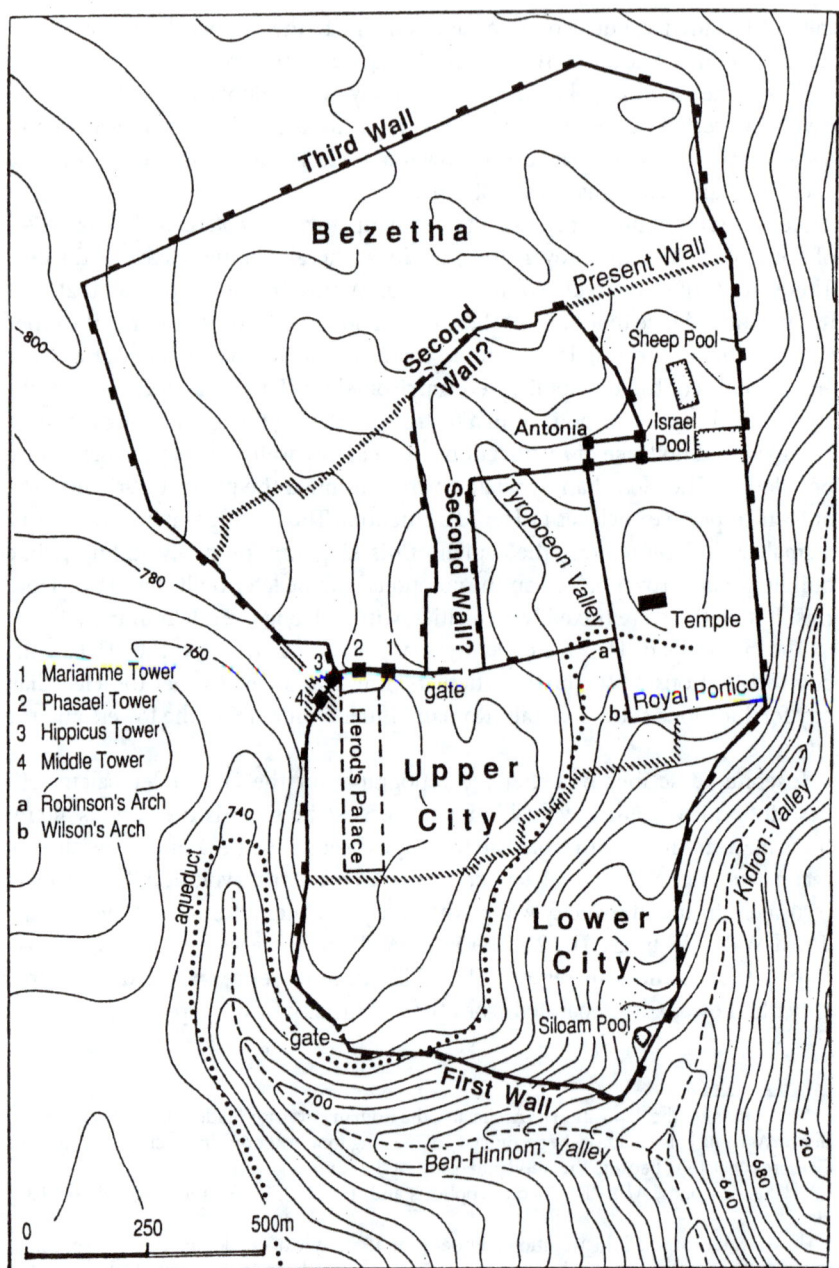

Figure III, 2 – Jerusalem Walls from I. Shatzman, *The Armies of the Hasmonaeans and Herod*, Tübingen 1991, p. 219, map 15, Courtesy of Mohr Siebeck, Tübingen.

3. The Fortifications 163

David, separated from the Lower City by the Tyropoeon Valley.[105] Archaeological excavations have confirmed Josephus' data.[106] It is still unclear who built the Second Wall, although Josephus claims that the last Hasmoneans built it,[107] since Herod was faced by two city walls, the First and Second Walls, in 37 BCE. Like the First Wall, however, it appears that Herod repaired it and built the gate beneath today's Damascus' Gate. Josephus also describes the Second Wall in detail.[108] Most archaeologists today agree that the Second Wall followed a line north of the First Wall, in the area today occupied by the Christian and Muslim Quarters in the northern part of the Old City.[109] The main features of the Second Wall are the foundations of a gate, situated under Damascus Gate. The gate underlying the present day Damascus Gate was erected by the Romans, who built the colony of Aelia Capitolina (a finding proved beyond any doubt by M. Magen). Its foundations, however, consisted of three openings between two projecting towers.[110] Thus it seems that the Herodian city gate, which certainly followed a Roman prototype, probably lies under the Roman gate of Aelia Capitolina. The Third Wall was built by Agrippa I and is described by Josephus.[111] Archaeological excavations confirm Josephus' data.[112] The northern part of the city stood on a plateau and was difficult to defend. The Tower of Psephinus[113] was the outstanding tower of the Third Wall and probably of all the city walls of Jerusalem. Josephus describes it as a high, octagonal tower. The Tour Magne, built as part of the fortifications of the city wall of Roman Nemausus (Nîmes), is probably a similar structure.[114]

After Jerusalem, Caesarea Maritima was the most important royal city (cfr. figure III, 3). It is noteworthy that when describing the foundation of the city in

---

[105] See Josephus, *BJ* V, 142–145, 159.
[106] On the First Wall see D. Bahat, *The Illustrated Atlas of Jerusalem*, Jerusalem 1990, pp. 37–38, 41. See also N. Avigad, *Discovering Jerusalem*, Jerusalem 1983, pp. 65–74.
[107] See Josephus, *AJ* XIV, 476.
[108] See Josephus, *BJ* V, 146, 158–159.
[109] On the Second Wall see Bahat, *Atlas of Jerusalem*, pp. 41–43.
[110] See M. Magen, "Excavations at the Damascus Gate," *Ancient Jerusalem Revealed, Expanded Edition 2000*, Jerusalem 2,000, pp. 281–287. Magen dates the gate after the destruction of the Second Temple. The Herodian ashlar stones are recognized as coming from previous Herodian gates and the city-wall. See also C. Arnould, *Les arcs romains de Jérusalem, Architecture, décor et urbanisme, Novum Testamentum et Orbis Antiquus 35*, Göttingen 1997, pp. 150–248. Arnaud dates the arch to the Herodian period. The similar gate of Tiberias, built during the reign of Antipas, and the contemporary gates of Augusta Praetoria, Augusta Taurinorum, and Verona seem to confirm this date.
[111] See Josephus, *BJ* V, 147–150, 156–159.
[112] On the Third Wall see Bahat, *Atlas of Jerusalem*, p. 43. See also E. L. Sukenik and L. A. Mayer, *The Third Wall of Jerusalem, An Account of Excavations*, Jerusalem 1930. See also S. Ben-Arieh, "The "Third Wall" of Jerusalem," *Ancient Jerusalem Revealed, Archaeology in the Holy City 1968-1974*, Jerusalem 1976, pp. 60–63.
[113] See Josephus, *BJ* V, 160.
[114] On Jerusalem city walls see also McNicoll, *Hellenistic Fortifications*, pp. 199–206.

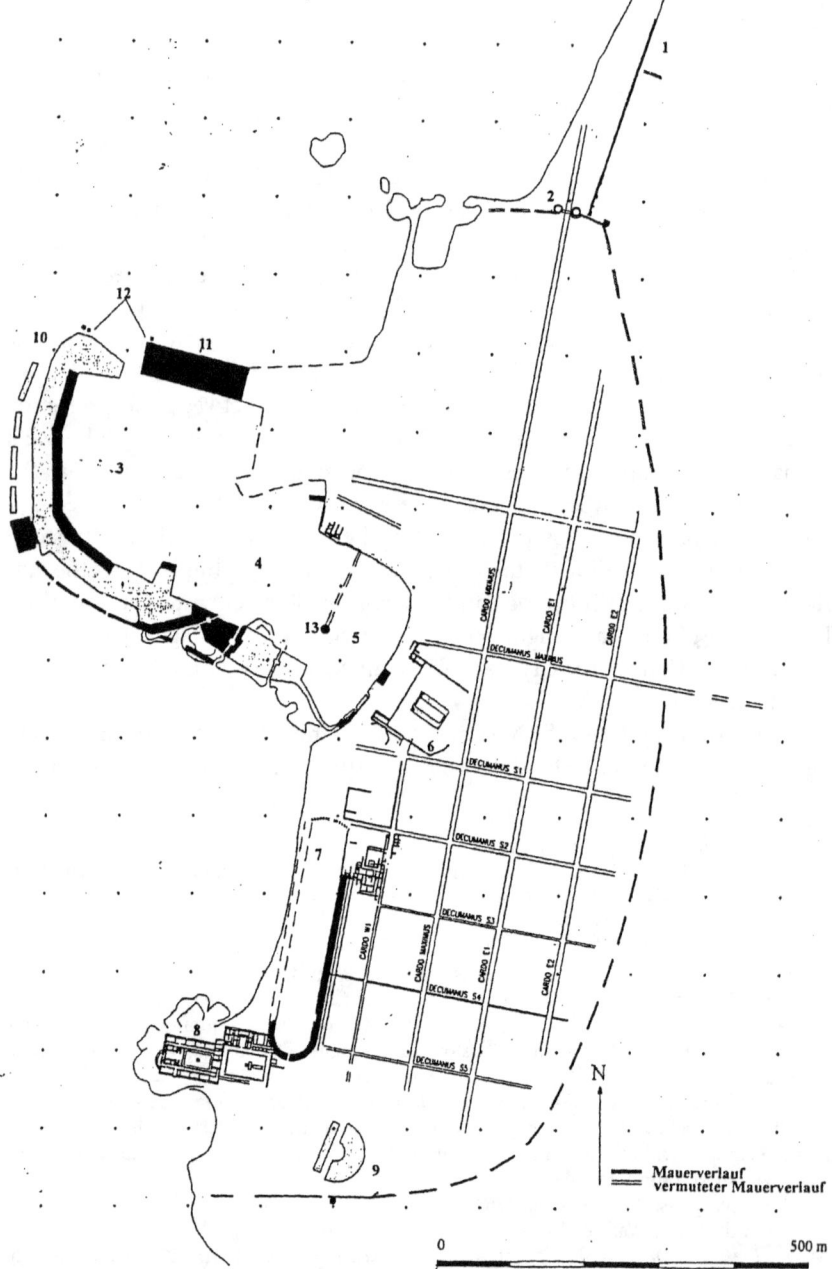

Figure III, 3 – Caesarea Maritima City Plan from E. Netzer, *The Palaces of the Hasmonaeans and Herod the Great*, Jerusalem 2001, p. 117, fig. 155, Courtesy of Professor Emeritus Ehud Netzer, The Hebrew University of Jerusalem.

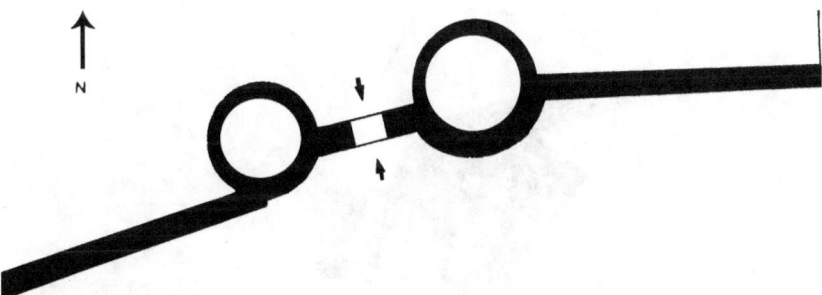

Figure III, 4 – Plan of the Northern Gate of Caesarea Maritima, Courtesy of Dahlit Weinblatt – Krausz.

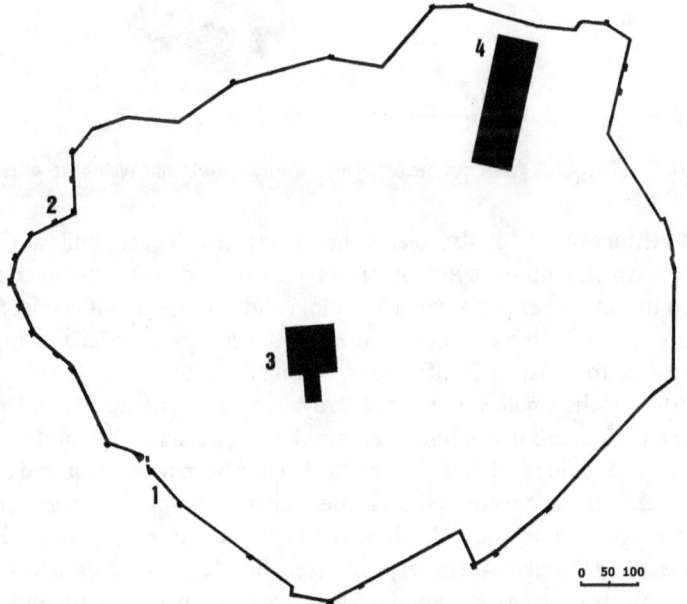

Figure III, 5 – Sebaste City Plan, Courtesy of Dahlit Weinblatt – Krausz.

23 BCE,[115] Josephus does not mention the construction of any encircling wall.[116] Did Herod erect any city wall around the most important city in the kingdom after Jerusalem? It seems, in fact, that Herod both repaired and extended the Hellenistic city wall of the earlier settlement of Straton's Tower, erected in the

---

[115] See Josephus, *AJ* XV, 331–341.
[116] For a general discussion see Shatzman, *Armies of the Hasmoneans and Herod*, p. 247.

Figure III, 6 – Plan of the Western Gate of Sebaste, Courtesy of Dahlit Weinblatt – Krausz.

second century BCE.[117] It also seems that he erected the gate built at Caesarea Maritima, which followed a Roman prototype, since a certain resemblance exists between the city-gates of Caesarea Maritima and Sebaste, and it is thus possible that the city wall is Herodian (cfr. figure III, 4). Perhaps, as in Jerusalem, Herod only repaired the existing fortifications, adding the gate.

Sebaste was the smallest of the three royal cities (cfr. figure III, 5). Up to the Herodian period, this urban settlement was known as Samaria,[118] and from 40 to 37 BCE Herod subjugated the kingdom, which had been newly acquired from Samaria. In 25 BCE he transformed the settlement, which was once more part of the Judaean kingdom, into one of the three royal cities mentioned above.[119] The Gentile character of the city was conserved.[120] Josephus describes its establishment,[121] and it seems that the city extended over an irregular area larger than that of the Hellenistic city. The impressive encircling city wall was constructed beyond the old lines, and the Western Gate, which followed a Roman prototype, was flanked by two round towers (cfr. figure III, 6). On the acropolis, Herod constructed a

---

[117] On the fortifications of Caesarea Maritima see A. Frova, *Scavi di Caesarea Maritima*, Milan 1965. See also K. G. Holum, *King Herod's Dream, Caesarea on the Sea*, New York 1988, pp. 44–53.
[118] See Crowfoot, Kenyon, and Sukenik, *The Buildings at Samaria*, pp. 39–41, 121–129.
[119] See Josephus, *AJ* XV, 292–298; also *BJ* I, 403.
[120] For a general discussion see Shatzman, *Armies of the Hasmoneans and Herod*, p. 255.
[121] See Josephus, *AJ* XV, 292–298 and *BJ* I, 403.

Figure III, 7, Plan of the Southern Gate of Tiberias, Courtesy of Dahlit Weinblatt - Krausz.

fortified castle, identified by Barag, which included a palace with a storeroom complex and the Temple of Augustus.[122]

At Sepphoris in Galilee, Herod appears to have constructed a royal palace-fortress[123] that was used as an arsenal. The city probably had a wall around the acropolis, where the palace was likely situated. Antipas extended the earlier Herodian building, erecting a city wall. Josephus calls the city *Metropolis*.[124]

The city of Tiberias was founded by Antipas during the reign of Tiberius. Although Josephus does not mention the erection of any city wall, archaeological

---

[122] See Crowfoot, Kenyon, and Sukenik, *The Buildings at Samaria*, pp. 39–41, 121–129. See also Barag, "King Herod's Royal Castle at Samaria-Sebaste," pp. 3–17.

[123] For a general treatment see Shatzman, *Armies of the Hasmoneans and Herod*, p. 259. Josephus mentions that the rebels attacked the city in 4 BCE. See Josephus, *AJ* XVII, 271 and *BJ* II, 56.

[124] See Josephus, *AJ* XVIII, 36.

excavations have confirmed its existence. The city southern gate follows a Roman prototype (cfr. figure III, 7).[125]

ii. The City Acropolis and the Tetrapyrgia

After 31 BCE, Herod erected various fortified palaces, which can be divided in two types.[126] The first consists of citadels that were situated in the cities, such as the citadel towers and the Antonia in Jerusalem, or the acropolis of Sebaste. The purpose of these citadels was to defend the king during a siege of the city by an external enemy, or to protect the king against possible rebellion by his subjects. In the Classical world, *stasis* or social unrest always began in the cities rather than in the countryside. Thus Herod's main palace at Jerusalem was fortified. However Herod's palaces at Jericho and at Caesarea Maritima, were unfortified. The second type of fortified palaces or castles were scattered all around the kingdom. Some of them were situated in important administrative centers, such as Herodium, at the site of the new capital of a *toparchia*. Other fortifications, such as Masada, were situated in inaccessible locations, far from any population center or urban concentration. The common purpose of these fortifications was to protect the king, his family, and his retinue. Because they were protected by strong ramparts, these fortifications could serve the king in time of war, allowing him to await relief and rescue by his own army or by Roman forces.

These fortifications, however, served the king not only in times of war, but in times of peace as well. Often, the king had to be away from the city, visiting the farthest reaches of his kingdom, and generally his family – and always his courtiers, counselors or friends, and the most important civil and military administrative officials – would follow him on his journeys around the realm. Thus, within the kingdom's borders, there was a real need for places that were fortified against all odds and could host not only the King, but his family and the main officials of the kingdom.

These fortifications were shaped as multi-storied towers[127] and as *tetrapyrgya*. The fortified palaces in Jerusalem were built in the same locations as early Has-

---

[125] See Josephus, *AJ* XVIII, 36–38. See G. Foerster, "Studies in the history of Caesarea Maritima," in Fritsch, C. T. (ed.), *The Joint Expedition to Caesarea Maritima I, Bulletin of the American Schools of Oriental Research Supplemental Studies* No. 19, (1975).

[126] On Hellenistic castles in Asia Minor see McNicoll, *Hellenistic Fortifications*, pp. 171–181.

[127] Towers constitute an important part of the Herodian architectural assemblage. The Pharos of Alexandria and the huge siege tower of Demetrius Poliorcetes are the Hellenistic architectural models. These two structures were multi-storied towers with functional purposes. The former was a lighthouse and the latter, a siege tower. The concept of multi-storied towers was adapted by Herod as palatial dwellings. The fortresses of Antonia and Herodium included even larger multi-storied towers with a residential function. The main difference between the three towers of the Citadel and the Antonia and Herodium is the architectural setting: the towers around Herod's palace in Jerusalem were independent units. The Herodium and Antonia towers were parts of

3. The Fortifications

monean fortifications that did not originally serve as royal residences. Thus, the citadel in Jerusalem was rebuilt completely by Herod, on Hasmonean fortifications, as part of the First Wall.[128] Josephus provides a vivid description of these towers,[129] of which only one base has survived.[130]

The well-known Antonia was probably built at the same location as the Baris Fortress.[131] Josephus describes the Antonia Fortress in detail, as a rectangular building with four protruding towers.[132] Clearly, the purpose of the Antonia was to withstand a siege by a hostile army rather than by rebellious subjects.

Herodium replaced Bethsur as the administrative capital of the *toparchia*.[133] A description of the fortress is found in Josephus (cfr. figure III, 8).[134] Upper Herodium was a circular building with four protruding round towers (cfr. figure III, 9). The construction of such a *chef d'oeuvre* of Hellenistic fortification can be rationalized only in terms of an external threat from a conventional army, and not as a means of defense against an armed rabble.[135] Upper Herodium and the Antonia in Jerusalem have the same features of the Hellenistic *tetrapyrgion*. The main difference between them is that while Herodium followed a circular plan, the Antonia was rectangular. According to Netzer, the Antonia Fortress was the prototype for the palace-fortress of Herodium, which differs only in its circular plan.[136]

---

architectural complexes. Multi-storied towers in Herodian architecture can be also serve their original function, such as the Drusion tower in the Caesarea harbor, which was a lighthouse. See Netzer, *Greater Herodium*, pp. 28-29.

[128] See Bahat, *Atlas of Jerusalem*, pp. 38-39.

[129] The Herodian citadel had three towers, much larger than its Hasmonean predecessors. These three massive multi-storied towers were built north of Herod's palace, at the northwestern corner of the city wall. The towers were named Hippicus, Phasael and Mariamme, for Herod's friend, brother and wife respectively. See Josephus, *BJ* V, 156-176.

[130] This was a multi-storied tower and is identified as either Hippicus or Phasael. See R. Hachlili, *Ancient Jewish Art and Archaeology in the Land of Israel*, Handbuch der Orientalistik, Leiden 1988, pp. 49-50.

[131] The Baris served only a defensive purpose, serving as royal residence only during sieges, as the Hasmoneans had erected a fortified palace in Jerusalem. On the Hasmonean palace and the Baris see Nielsen, *Hellenistic Palaces*, p. 155. See also Josephus, *AJ* XX, 189-192, *BJ* II, 344.

[132] The Antonia was situated close to the northwestern corner of the Temple Mount and dominated the Temple Mount. See Josephus, *AJ* XVIII, 91-95 and *BJ* V, 238-246.

[133] See Josephus, *BJ* III, 55. See also Shatzman, *Armies of the Hasmoneans and Herod*, p. 231. Were all the *toparchiai* capitals of Judaea (Jerusalem, Jericho, Herodium, Bethleptenpha, Emmaus, Lydda, Thamna, Gophna, Acrabatene) fortified? There is no clear answer to this question. It seems that some *toparchiai* capitals, such as Herodium and Jericho, had a fortress. See Shatzman, *Armies of the Hasmoneans and Herod*, pp. 232-233.

[134] See Josephus, *AJ* XV, 324.

[135] The fortress probably served two main functions. It was the main administrative center of the *toparchia* and also defended the huge palace built by Herod below the fortress. On Herodium see Netzer, *Greater Herodium*, pp. 79-110.

[136] See E. Netzer, "The Palaces built by Herod – A Research Update," *Judaea and the Graeco Roman World in the Time of Herod in the Light of Archaeological Evidence*, Abhandlungen der

Figure III, 8 – View of Upper Herodium, Courtesy of Albatross.

3. The Fortifications

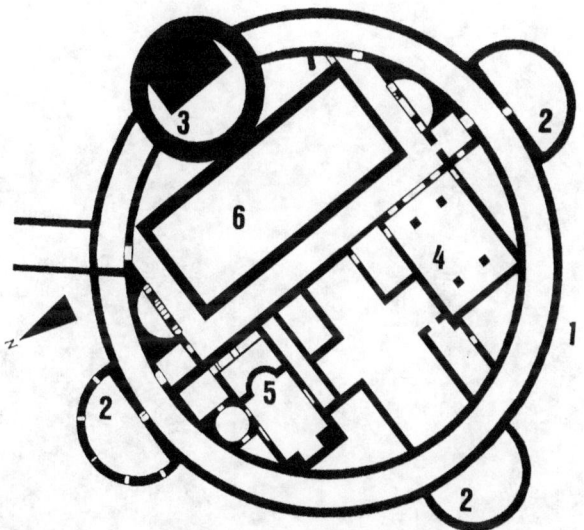

Figure III, 9 – Plan of the Upper Herodium, Courtesy of Dahlit Weinblatt-Krausz.

Masada is the largest and the best known among the desert fortresses, built on a rock cliff about 25 km. south of 'En Gedi (cfr. figure III, 10). Josephus' description of it is well known.[137] The fortress was surrounded by an impressive casemate wall with thirty towers (cfr. figure III, 11) and was characterized by a sophisticated water system and storerooms (cfr. figure III, 12).[138]

Machaerus was situated east of the Dead Sea on the summit of Qal'at al-Mishnaqa, atop a 700 m. high hill, on its northeastern slope. Strabo[139] mentions this Hasmonean fortification together with the others destroyed by Pompey, and archaeological excavations have yielded further information and evidence. A small city was situated below the fortress. Josephus provides a description of

---

Akademie der Wissenschaften in Göttingen, Göttingen 1996, p. 31. See Netzer, *Greater Herodium*, p. 100.

[137] See Josephus, *BJ* VII, 8.

[138] Three construction stages may be discerned at Masada. Three Herodian building phases have been detected at Masada. The first is dated from 37 to 30 BCE, the second from 30 to 20 BCE, and the third from 20 to 4 BCE. See Netzer, *Masada III, Buildings, Stratigraphy and Architecture*, pp. 388–541, 604–607, 619–623, 640–646. See also G. Foerster, *Masada V, The Yigael Yadin Excavations 1963–1965, Final Reports, Art and Architecture*, Jerusalem 1996, pp. 209–213.

[139] See Strabo, *Geography* XVI, 2, 400.

Figure III, 10, View of Masada from the North, Courtesy of Albatross.

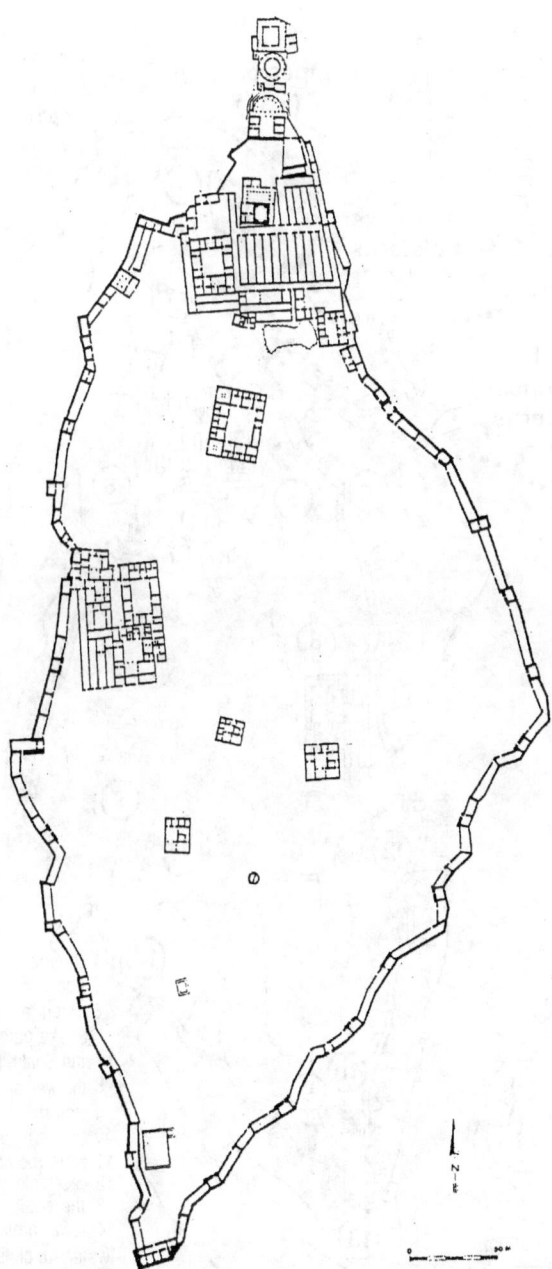

Figure III, 11 – Plan of Masada Fortifications (E. Netzer, *Masada 3, The Yigael Yadin Excavations 1963-1965, Final Reports, The Buildings, Stratigraphy and Architecture*, Jerusalem 1991, plan 75, p. 652, Courtesy of Professor Emeritus Ehud Netzer, The Hebrew University of Jerusalem.

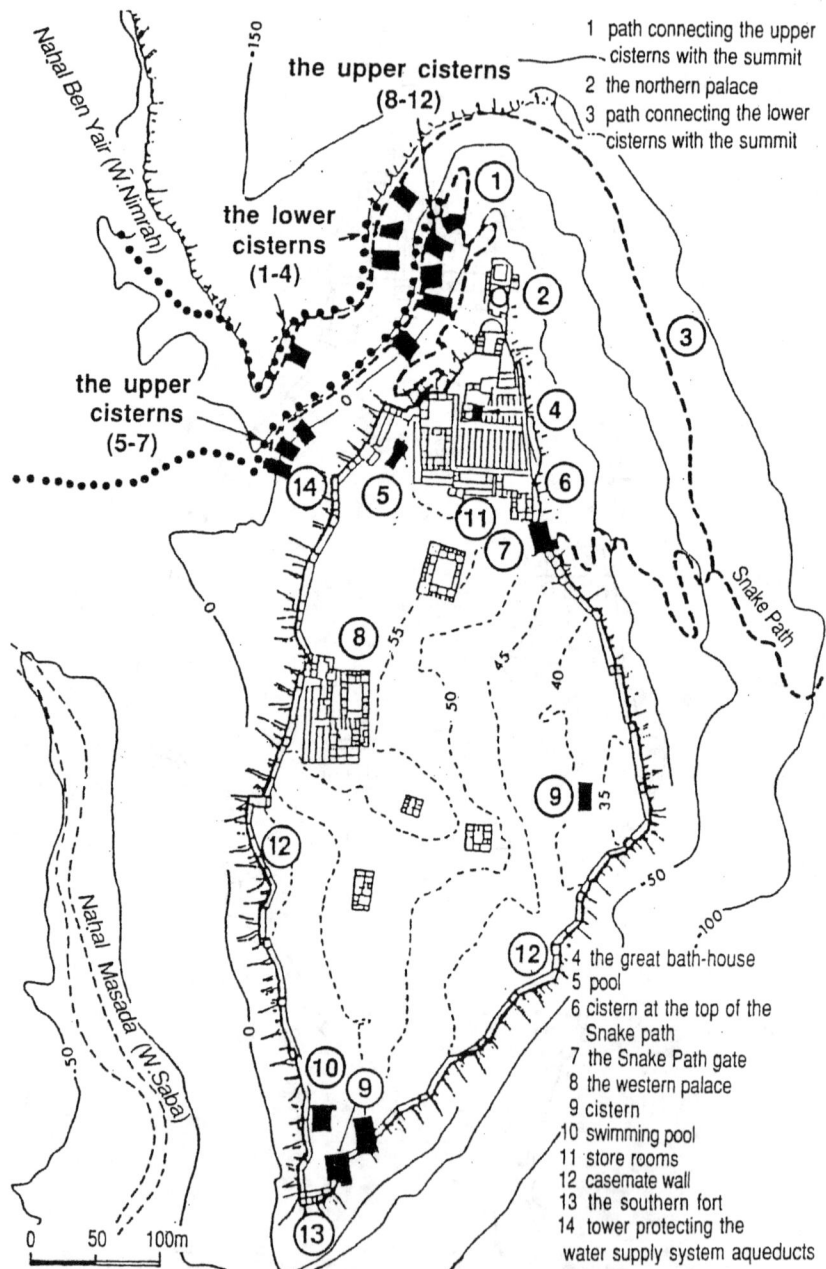

Figure III, 12 – Plan of Masada Fortifications and water supply from I. Shatzman, *The Armies of the Hasmonaeans and Herod*, Tübingen 1991, p. 235, map 18, Courtesy of Mohr Siebeck, Tübingen.

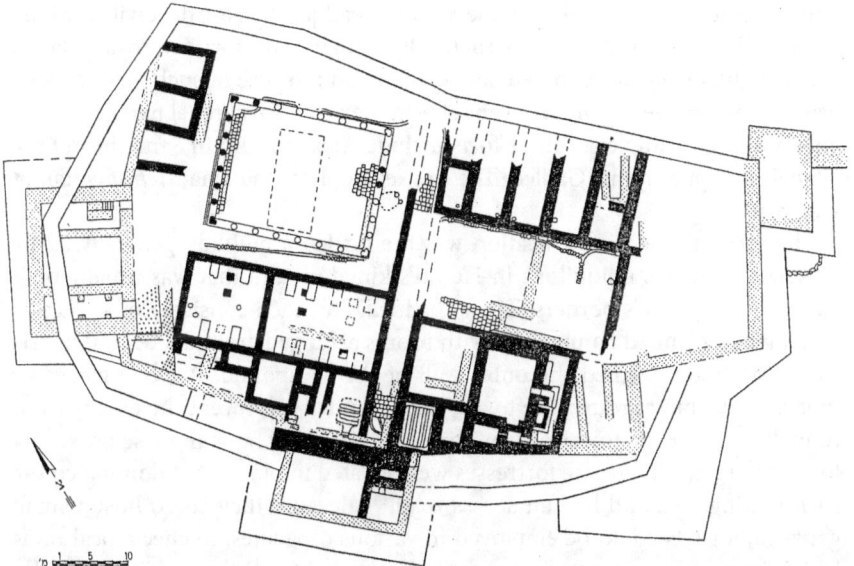

Figure III, 13 - Plan of Machaerous from E. Netzer, *The Palaces of the Hasmonaeans and Herod the Great*, Jerusalem 2001, p. 76, fig. 94, Courtesy of Professor Emeritus Ehud Netzer, The Hebrew University of Jerusalem.

the Herodian fortress,[140] which was probably of the *tetrapyrgion* type, like the Antonia and Herodium (cfr. figure III, 13).[141]

iii. The Regional Distribution of the Static Defenses in the Herodian Kingdom

Different regions of the Herodian kingdom had their own particular type of administration, and each faced different defense challenges. Herod restored most of the existing Hasmonean fortifications in the parts of the kingdom once ruled by the Hasmoneans, and probably built new fortifications, or restored old Seleucid fortifications in the newly acquired northern parts of his kingdom. These fortifications served a dual purpose: to protect the surrounding area from the enemy or from enemies specific to that region, and to serve as part of the general defenses of the kingdom against foreign invasion.

Three types of fortifications can be clearly discerned. First were the forts that were situated throughout Herod's kingdom. These buildings contained the residence of a *strategos*, or military governor, and were occasionally located in

---

[140] See Josephus, *BJ* VII, 171–177.
[141] On the excavations see V. Corbo, "Macheronte, La regia fortezza erodiana," *LA* 29, 1979, pp. 315–326.

dangerous and untamed regions, serving as headquarters for the civil administration. These fortifications are structurally similar to the fortified royal palaces, albeit slightly smaller. As noted above, the main purpose of such fortifications was administrative, but in the event of war, they could also repel parts of a large enemy army. Examples of these forts include Alexandrium in Samaria and the citadel of Sepphoris in Galilee. The best example is the small *tetrapyrgion* at Horvath ʿEleq.

The second type of fortification was the fortlet, a building generally 22 by 22 sq. m., that was ubiquitous in Herod's kingdom and that was usually built along the kingdom's borders. These fortified sites each consisted of a roughly rectangular, planned compound, with rooms arranged around a central courtyard. The tower formed the outer wall of the compound. A stone glacis, or *proteichisma*, built around the tower, was intended to prevent the enemy from tunneling under the tower or from bringing battering rams in close proximity to the fortress. All of these fortresses were located in places that dominated the surrounding area and had an access road.[142] Because they could host a small garrison, fortlets could be employed in various capacities, to check local raids by foreign forces, to control major crossroads, and to protect the local population against bandits. Finally, fortlets were also built along vulnerable coastlines, where they served both as the primary defense against hostile landing parties, as well as primary points for communication with major forces of Herod's standing army that were located nearby and that could be called upon to ward off invaders from the sea.

Finally there were the towers, the smallest of the fortifications in the Herodian kingdom. The few examples of these that have been excavated indicate that their primary function was that of observation towers along communication routes. These fortifications can be classed according to region – Judaea, Idumaea, and Galilee, where a friendly population of Jews and Idumaeans were the majority; and Samaria, Transjordan, the Coastal Plain, and the Decapolis, where the majority of the population consisted of Gentiles who were sometimes hostile.

---

[142] According to Y. Baruch these were roadside fortresses; however Hirschfeld maintains that these were fortified villas. Hirschfeld argues that around this type of "manor" villages developed, as was the case at Horvath Salit, ʿAroer, and Nahal Yattir. However it may be argued that fortresses are not built in the middle of nowhere. Thus, villages develop around the various fortresses. Soldiers need to have a surrounding population. Thus, around the fort of Bethsur a village developed in the Achaemenid and Hellenistic periods. The fortress was erected before the village. The village's development was a consequence of the presence of the fortress. Other examples are the *cannabae* outside the Roman legionary and auxiliary fortresses along the Rhine-Danube line. See B. Zissu, *Rural Settlements in the Judaean Hills and Foothills From the Late Second Temple Period to the Bar Kokhba Revolt*, Thesis submitted for the Doctor of Philosophy degree, The Hebrew University, Jerusalem, 2001.

3. The Fortifications

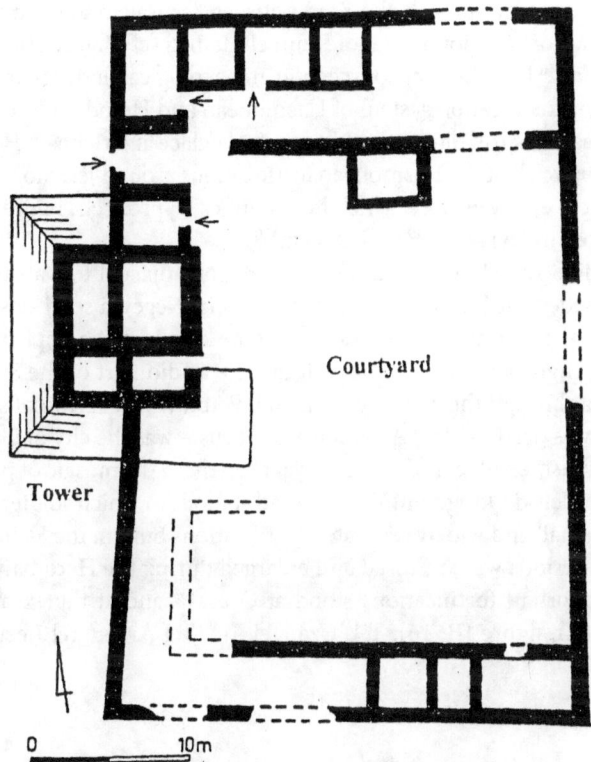

Figure III, 14 – Plan of Rujum el-Hamiri from Y. Hirschfeld, *Ramat Hanadiv Excavations, Final Report of the 1984–1998 Seasons, General Discussion, Ramat Hanadiv in Context*, Jerusalem 2000, p. 715, fig. 31, Courtesy of the Israel Exploration Society, Jerusalem.

Judaea was the core of the Herodian kingdom, with Jerusalem as its capital. The defenses of other urban centers, such as Gazara and Bethsur,[143] were probably repaired, but were not central to the Herodian static defense system. The smaller fortifications of Herodian Judaea were concentrated in two main areas, in central Judaea, as well as in the area of the Winter Palaces of Jericho, where the Royal Highway passed by.

In the area of central Judaea there was a group of roadside fortresses in the form of fortified towers. Along the fortified route from Jerusalem to Joppa, two towers have been investigated. The first, a tower at Giv'at Sha'ul[144] dominated the route from Jerusalem to Joppa. The second, a fortress at Horvath Mesad, situated

---

[143] On the fort of Bethsur see O. R. Sellers, *The Citadel of Bethsur*, Philadelphia, 1933. See also R. W. Funk, "The 1957 Campaign at Beth-Zur," *BASOR 150*, 1958, pp. 8–20.

[144] On Giv'at Sha'ul see Shatzman, *Armies of the Hasmoneans and Herod*, p. 54.

west of Jerusalem, dominated the road between Jerusalem and Emmaus.[145] A further similar fortification is that of Rujm el-Hamiri (cfr. figure III, 14), southeast of Hebron.[146] Both literary sources and archaeological findings are helpful in identifying the fortification system of Hasmonean and Herodian Jericho. Unlike the Hasmoneans, Herod did not build a fortified palace at Jericho.[147] Herod, however, did improve all of the Hasmonean fortifications around Jericho, particularly those at Nuseib el-Aweishiret, which he rebuilt as Cypros (cfr. figure III, 15),[148] as well as those in Hyrcania[149] and Dagon.[150]

Idumaea, like Transjordan, was a frontier region adjacent to Nabataean territory and included the border areas of the northern Negev, a semi-desert region. Idumaea was also an important crossroads of the kingdom. An important stretch of the Royal Highway passed through Idumaea, as did part of the Spice Route, which passed through the Nabataean capital, Petra, whose terminal station – at least until it was destroyed by Alexander Jannaeus – was the city of Gaza.[151] The Idumaeans, kinsmen of Herod, were a loyal element in the mosaic of populations that made up Herod's kingdom. Various road stations in which soldiers were garrisoned and small and widely separated fortifications built in the Hellenistic and Hasmonean periods were restored and enlarged during the Herodian period.[152] The most important fortifications stood at Oresa[153] and at the excavated sites of Tel Arad (cfr. figure III, 16), Tel 'Uza, Tel 'Ira, Tel Aroer, Tel Beersheba, Tel

---

[145] On Horvath Mesad see Shatzman, *Armies of the Hasmoneans and Herod*, pp. 54, 226. See M. Fisher, "Horvat Mesad," *ESI 2*, 1983, pp. 67–68. Fisher has suggested that this was a way station. See also M. Fisher, "The Jerusalem-Emmaus Road in the Light of the Excavations of Horvat Mesad," in A. Kasher, G. Fuks and U. Rappaport (eds.), *Greece and Rome in Eretz-Israel*, Jerusalem 1989, pp. 198–200.

[146] On Rujm el-Hamiri see Y. Barouch, "The Roman Castles in the Hills of Hebron" (Hebrew), *Researches on Judaea and Samaria 4*, 1995, pp. 137–143 and see also Y. Barouch, "Road Stations in Judaea during the Second Temple Period," *Researches on Judaea and Samaria 6*, 1997, pp. 125–135.

[147] See E. Netzer, "The Hasmonean Palaces in Palaestine," *Basileia - Die Palaeste der Hellenistischen Könige*, Mainz, 1996, pp. 203 208.

[148] On Cypros see E. Netzer, "Cypros," *Qadmoniot 8*, 1975, pp. 54–61.

[149] On Hyrcania (Khirbet el-Mird) see G. R. H. Wright, "The Archaeological Remains at El-Mird in the Wilderness of Judaea," *Biblica 42*, 1961, pp. 1–21. See also Shatzman, *Armies of the Hasmoneans and Herod*, p. 229.

[150] See I *Macc.* 16. 15. See also Josephus, *AJ* XIII, 230, *BJ* I, 56 and Strabo, *Geography* XVI, 2. 40. On the excavations at Dagon and the various fortresses in the Judaean Desert see Y. Tsafrir and Y. Magen, "The Desert Fortresses of Judaea in the Second Temple Period," *The Jerusalem Cathedra 2*, 1982, pp. 120–145.

[151] See B. Isaac, "Trade Routes to Arabia and the Roman Army," *Roman Frontier Studies XII*, III, *BAR International Series 71*, 1979, Oxford 1979, pp. 889–901.

[152] See Gracey, "Armies of the Judaean Client Kings," p. 319.

[153] See Josephus, *AJ* XIV, 361, *BJ* I, 266, 294.

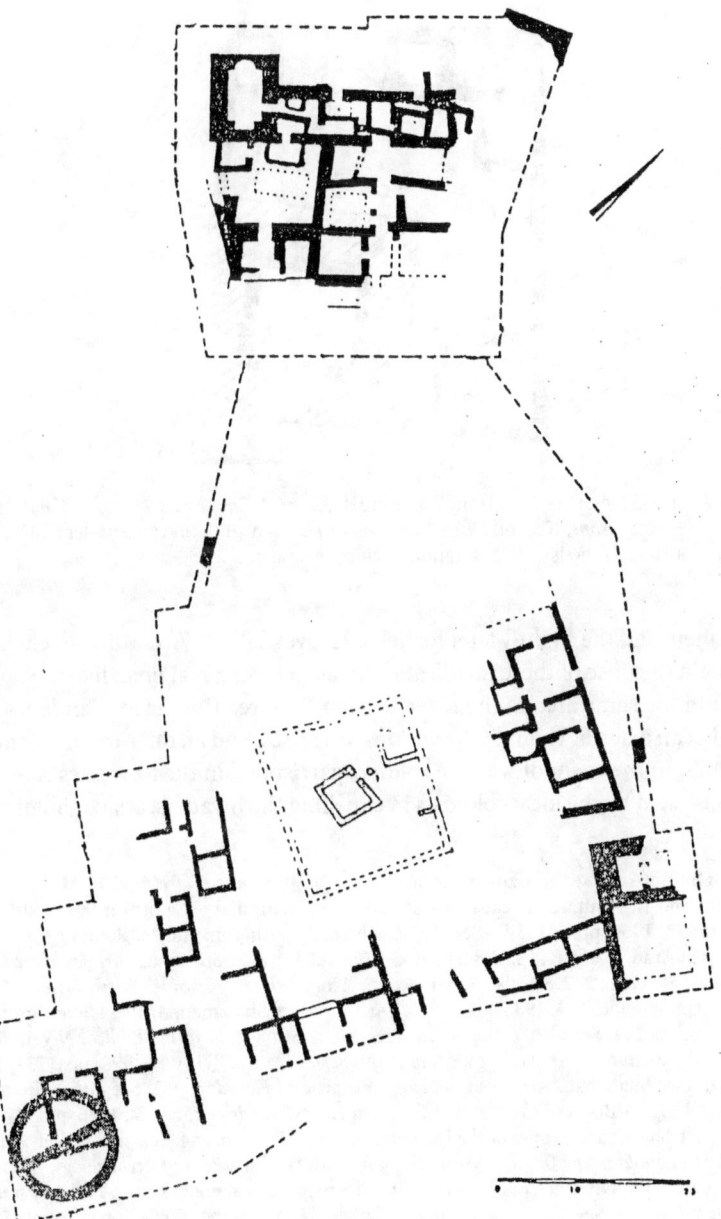

Figure III, 15 – Plan of Cypros from E. Netzer, *The Palaces of the Hasmonaeans and Herod the Great*, Jerusalem 2001, p. 71, fig. 85, Courtesy of Professor Emeritus Ehud Netzer, The Hebrew University of Jerusalem.

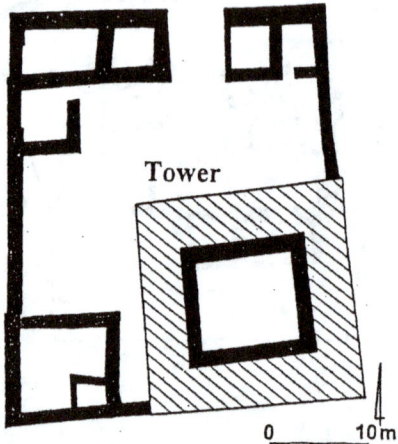

Figure III, 16 – Plan of Tel Arad from Y. Hirschfeld, *Ramat Hanadiv Excavations, Final Report of the 1984–1998 Seasons, General Discussion, Ramat Hanadiv in Context,* Jerusalem 2000, p. 719, fig. 40, Courtesy of the Israel Exploration Society, Jerusalem.

Sharuhen, and the slightly later fortlet at Horvat Salit[154]. According to Gichon,[155] the main purpose of these fortifications was to form a real *limes* like the one that stood in the same area in the Later Roman Empire. This "Herodian *limes*" consisted of an exterior chain of the various fortresses, and an interior one of military colonies. In the event of war, the soldiers garrisoned in the fortresses could have been assisted by the local colonists in expelling the invaders. Shatzman disagrees

---

[154] On Tel Arad see Shatzman, *Armies of the Hasmoneans and Herod,* p. 242. See also Y. Aharoni and R. Amiran, "Excavations at Tel Arad, Preliminary Report on the First Season," 1962, *IEJ 14,* 1964, pp. 131–147. See also Z. Herzog, M. Aharoni and M. Rainey, "The Israelite Fortress at Arad," *BASOR 254,* 1984, pp. 1–34. On Tel ʿUzza see Shatzman, *Armies of the Hasmoneans and Herod,* p. 242. See also Y. Beit-Arieh, "Horvat ʿUzza, A Border Fortress in the Eastern Negev," *Qadmoniot 73–4,* 1986, pp. 31–40. On Tel ʿIra see Shatzman, *Armies of the Hasmoneans and Herod,* p. 244. See also Y. Beit-Arieh, *Tel ʿIra, A Stronghold in the Biblical Negev,* Tel Aviv University, Institute of Archaeology, Monograph Series No. 15, Tel Aviv 1999, pp. 173–174. On Tel ʿUzza see Shatzman, *Armies of the Hasmoneans and Herod,* p. 242. See also Y. Beit-Arieh, "Horvat ʿUzza, A Border Fortress in the Eastern Negev," *Qadmoniot 73–4,* 1986, pp. 31–40. On Tel ʿIra see Shatzman, *Armies of the Hasmoneans and Herod,* p. 244. See also Y. Beit-Arieh, *Tel ʿIra, A Stronghold in the Biblical Negev,* Tel Aviv University, Institute of Archaeology, Monograph Series No. 15, Tel Aviv 1999, pp. 173–174. On Tel Aroer see Shatzman, *Armies of the Hasmoneans and Herod,* p. 244. See also A. Biran and A. Cohen, "Aroer in the Negev," *Eretz-Israel 15,* 1981, pp. 250–273. See also A. Biran, "Aroer in Judaea," *NEAEHL* 4, 1993, pp. 89–92. On Tel Beersheba see Shatzman, *Armies of the Hasmoneans and Herod,* p. 56. The Hasmonean fort was built on a Hellenistic fort and a temple. See also Y. Aharoni, "Tel Beersheba," *IEJ 24,* 1974, p. 271. On Tel Sharuhen see See Shatzman, *Armies of the Hasmoneans and Herod,* p. 246. On Horvat Salit see D. Alon, "Horvat Salit (Kh. Salentah)," *ESI 5,* 1986, pp. 94–96.

[155] See M. Gichon, "Idumaea and the Herodian Limes," *IEJ 17,* pp. 27–42.

with this view, believing that the main purpose of the various fortifications in Idumaea was to safeguard traffic along the Royal Highway and the Spice Route and that it is improbable that such a line of defense would have been effective against any regular army.[156] I believe that there is a certain validity to each of the aforementioned views. Herod clearly wished to form a military border against the Nabataeans. On the other hand, as Herod came to dominate the Spice Route against strong Nabataean opposition, these fortifications were also intended to defend the Spice Route, which was an important source of income for King Herod.

In Galilee, during the Hasmonean and Herodian periods, few cities appear to have been fortified, though several fortresses controlled the countryside and probably defended it from the scourge of banditry.[157] As in Judaea, the most important Jewish urban settlements situated in central and southern Galilee were fortified. Josephus mentions the Akra of Gush Halav and Jotopata.[158] The same cities are mentioned in Tannaitic sources[159] and are included under the category of walled cities. Most of our information comes from literary sources rather than from archaeological evidence. At the beginning of Herod's rule, Galilee was a border region, whose northern boundary was protected by at least four fortifications during the Hasmonean period. The location of three of these fortifications remains unknown;[160] the fourth was situated near Mount Lebanon.[161] What happened to these fortifications during the Herodian period? During the first part of Herod's reign, when the border passed though these fortifications, Herod probably renovated them. Later, as he received various territories from Augustus, north of the old border, he probably maintained these fortifications but did not invest heavily in their improvement. Another fortification that was probably renovated by Herod during the first part of his reign is that of Mount Tabor.[162] None of the Hasmonean fortifications excavated in the Galilee, such as Romema on the Carmel[163] and Khirbet el-Tufaniyeh,[164] were in use during the

---

[156] See Shatzman, *Armies of the Hasmoneans and Herod*, p. 246.

[157] See Shatzman, *Armies of the Hasmoneans and Herod*, p. 87.

[158] See Josephus, *AJ* XIII, 338, XIV, 414 an *BJ* I, 304. These cities are mentioned in connection with the war between Ptolemy Lathirus and Alexander Jannaeus.

[159] See m. 'Arak. 9, 6.

[160] Marion of Tyre conquered three Hasmonean fortresses in 41 BCE. But where these fortifications situated?

[161] Strabo (*Geography* XVI, 2, 40) mentions the fortress of Mount Lebanon, erected by Silas the Jew.

[162] This fortification on Mount Carmel is mentioned as having been built by Antiochus III and conquered and rebuilt by Alexander Jannaeus. See Josephus, *AJ* XIII, 396. See also Josephus, *BJ* II, 573. Probably the source of this precious information for Josephus was Polybius, *History* V, 70, 6–12.

[163] On Romema on the Carmel see Shatzman, *Armies of the Hasmoneans and Herod*, p. 86. It is possible that Jannaeus, trying to conquer Ptolemais, built the fortress.

[164] On Khirbet el-Tufaniyeh see Shatzman, *Armies of the Hasmoneans and Herod*, p. 86.

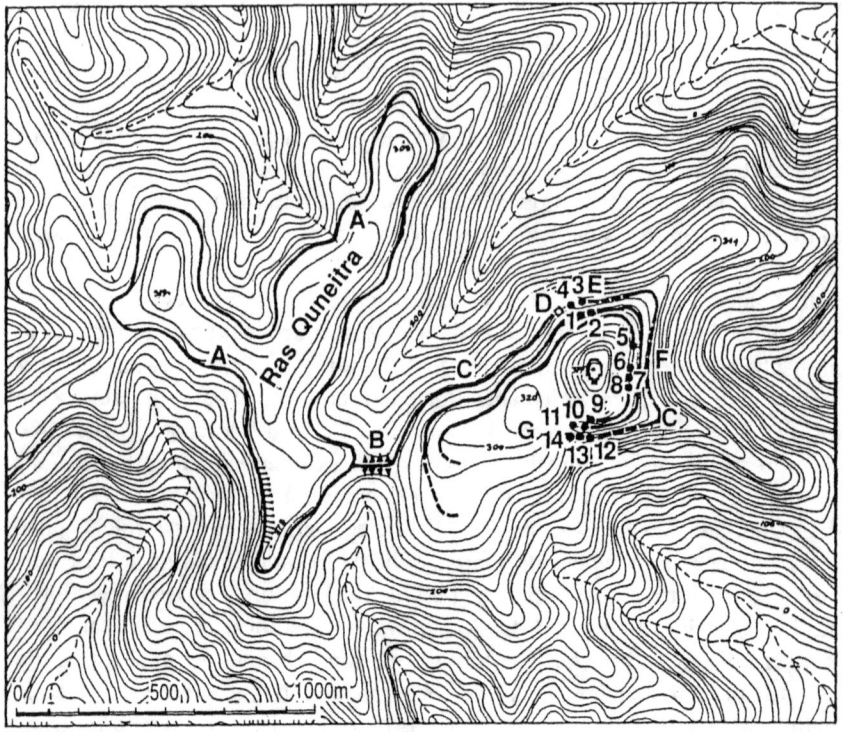

Figure III, 17 – The Water Supply System of Alexandrium from I. Shatzman, *The Armies of the Hasmonaeans and Herod*, Tübingen 1991, p. 70, map 8, Courtesy of Mohr Siebeck, Tübingen.

Herodian period. The internal political situation was thus apparently excellent. Herod did found the military colony of Gabae in the Galilee. Alexander Jannaeus had conquered Gabae, and Josephus mentions a Hasmonean fortress at a site called Agaba, which may be Gabae.[165] A small fort has been excavated at Sha'ar ha-'Amaqim. Dated to the end of the third century BCE, it remained in use until the early first century CE.[166] Herod established a colony there, but no fortifications dated to this period were found during the excavations.

In Samaria the main population was Samaritan. The Samaritans, whose settlements were concentrated in the area around Shechem, were generally hostile to the rulers of Judaea and to the Jews, and so the main task of the huge garrison at Sebaste and of the colonists living in Samaria was to keep the Samaritans in check. Various forts were built in the region, probably for the same purpose. Another motivation for the extensive fortification of Samaria was that the

---

[165] See Josephus, *AJ* XIII, 422–424.
[166] See Shatzman, *Armies of the Hasmoneans and Herod*, pp. 85, 258.

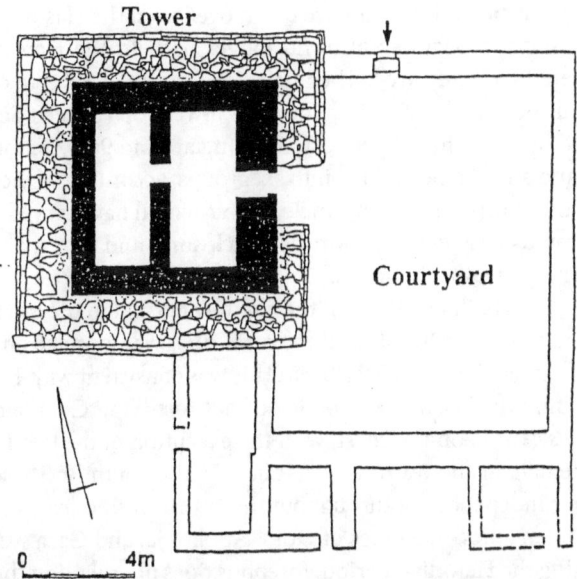

Figure III, 18 – Plan of Ofarim from Y. Hirschfeld, *Ramat Hanadiv Excavations, Final Report of the 1984–1998 Seasons, General Discussion, Ramat Hanadiv in Context*, Jerusalem 2000, p. 714, fig. 28, Courtesy of the Israel Exploration Society, Jerusalem.

King's Highway passed through eastern Samaria. The fortress of Alexandrium (cfr. figure III, 17)[167], which probably controlled that highway, also fulfilled an important role as an administrative center and as a state prison. It was also the most impressive of Herod's fortresses.

Various small fortresses were built in Samaria, including Kafr Sur, er-Rass, Khirbet Firdusi, Khirbet et-Tell, Kafr Haris, Kafr Laqif, Khirbet el 'Urmeh, Qasr e-Leja, and 'Ofarim (cfr. figure III, 18)[168]. Most of them were first constructed

---

[167] Alexandrium-Sartaba was probably the most important fortification in this region. Josephus notes that it was built by the Hasmoneans. See Josephus, *AJ* XIII, 417. This fort in the *toparchia* of Acrabatene, which commanded the route along the Jordan Valley, was the first major Hasmonean fortress to be restored by Herod, an undertaking assigned to his brother Pheroras in 38 BCE. See Josephus, *AJ* XIV, 419, *BJ* I, 308. During the Herodian period the Alexandrium fortress was used as state prison for members of the royal family. Herod had Mariamme and her mother, Alexandra, kept there in 30 BCE. See Josephus, *AJ* XV, 185–186. Later, he had his sons Alexander and Aristobulus executed at Sebastia and buried there. See Josephus, *AJ* XVI, 394. He showed the fortification to Agrippa during Agrippa's tour of 15 BCE. See Josephus, *AJ* XVI, 13. See Shatzman, *Armies of the Hasmoneans and Herod*, pp. 70–71, 257. On the excavations proper see Y. Tsafrir and Y. Magen, "Two Seasons of Excavations at the Sartaba-Alexandrium Fortress," *Qadmoniot 17*, 1984, pp. 26–32.

[168] In the area of Kafr Sur stood a fort surrounded by a stone wall. Dar has suggested that there was another fortress, at er-Rass, however this view is rejected by Shatzman. See Dar,

during the Hellenistic period and were taken over from the Hasmoneans. Some of the Hellenistic fortifications were no longer used in the Herodian period, and others were lightly repaired. The huge city-fortress of Sebaste obviated the need for small forts in the vicinity. The field towers of Western Samaria have been surveyed by Dar. These towers, numbering around 962, are found only in western Samaria and can be divided into six groups, according to their measurements. Their true purpose remains unclear. They could have served as elements of a privately built complement to fortified enclosures and farms, or as posts for signaling warnings against brigands.[169]

The fortifications built by Herod in the coastal area and in the Decapolis comprise a different category. One of the three royal cities was founded on the *paralia*, or the coast – namely Caesarea Maritima. This was consistent with Herod's practice of continuing the Hasmonean policy of not fortifying Gentile cities. Thus, no Greek *poleis* existed on the coast, with the exception of the two independent *poleis* of Ptolemais in the north and Ascalon in the south.[170] These two cities preserved their independence throughout the entire Hasmonean and Herodian periods as Roman allies. The cities of Dora, Apollonia, and Gaza were probably unwalled during the Herodian period. Josephus does not mention the two urban centers of Jamnia and Azotus.[171] The Greek cities on the coast dominated several positions along the Via Maris, and Herod rebuilt or constructed several forts

---

Landscape and Pattern, p. 217. On Khirbet Firdusi see Dar, *Landscape and Pattern*, pp. 218–220. This fortress may have formed part of the estates of Ptolemy, Herod's prime minister. On Khirbet et-Tell see Shatzman, Armies of the Hasmoneans and Herod, pp. 67–69 on the various forts erected in Samaria. Nearby is Kafr Haris and the village of Arous, also recorded as belonging to Ptolemy. See Josephus, *AJ* XVII, 289; also *BJ* II, 69. See Dar, *Landscape and Pattern*, pp. 221–223. Dar considers the site of Kafr Laqif to have been a fortress, but there is no conclusive evidence attesting to this. See Dar, *Landscape and Pattern*, p. 223. On Khirbet el ʿUrmeh see E. Eshel and Z. E. Erlich, "The Fortress of Acraba in Kh. Urmeh," *Cathedra* 47, 1988, pp. 17–24. On Qasr e-Leja see Dar, *Landscape and Pattern*, pp. 10–12. On ʿOfarim see S. Riklin, "The Courtyard Towers in the Light of Finds from ʿOfarim," *ʿAtiqot* 32, pp. 95–98, 1997.

[169] These towers were originally built in the third-second centuries BCE, during the Hellenistic period. They remained in use until the end of the first century CE in most cases, and until the second century CE in others. A possible non-military explanation of their character is that they were used in the production of wine, as storage rooms for grapes before marketing. They could also have been associated with oil production and may have served as storage rooms for oil jars. Another possible explanation is that each field tower protected the vineyard (cleros) of an individual landowner. Could they be an indication of a colonization program started by the Ptolemies or Seleucids overlords, continued by the Hasmoneans and perhaps by Herod? Shatzman emphasizes the non-military character of these installations. They were probably related to the farms of the military settlers, though they did not serve a military function. See Dar, *Landscape and Pattern*, pp. 12–15, 93–121, 217–260. See also Shatzman, *Armies of the Hasmoneans and Herod*, pp. 64–66.

[170] In 30 BCE Augustus returned to Herod the cities of Gadara, Hippos, Samaria, Gaza, Anthedon, Joppa, and Straton's Tower. See Josephus, *AJ* XV, 215–217, and *BJ* I, 396–397.

[171] See Shatzman, *Armies of the Hasmoneans and Herod*, pp. 251–252. Jamnia had a relatively important harbor.

along the entire Via Maris. Some, such as Tel Michal, were renovated during the Herodian period, while others, such as Horvat 'Eleq, were built anew. The *archon* of Idumaea was also the governor of the city of Gaza. Gaza had previously belonged to the Nabataeans as one of the terminal harbors of the Spice Route until it was destroyed by Jannaeus. Briefly independent under Pompey and Gabinius, Gaza once more became an important commercial center. Herod's wars with the Nabataeans and the opening of Sebastos harbor at Caesarea Maritima, however, ended Gaza's commercial ambitions for an extended period. No fortifications have been excavated there.[172] Herod rebuilt the settlement of Anthedon in honor of Agrippa as Agrippium, and no fortifications have been excavated there either.[173] The city of Joppa probably maintained its old Hasmonean fortifications and is not mentioned as having been rebuilt by Herod. Once Caesarea took its place, Joppa clearly declined in importance as a harbor.[174] The city of Antipatris, located at Tel Afeq, on the former site of Hellenistic Pegae, was founded by Herod in about 9 BCE. It was situated in the plain of Capharsaba, a region abundant in water and plants, on the main north-south coastal road, the Via Maris, between Caesarea and Lydda. No Herodian period fortifications are known to have existed there.[175] Tel Michal is situated in the southern Sharon Plain, north of Joppa.[176]

The complex of Horvat 'Eleq is situated in the southern part of the Carmel ridge, not far from the coast (cfr. figure III, 19). The fortress dominated Caesarea Maritima's water sources, as well as the roads leading from the city to the interior of the kingdom.[177] Excavators regard the fortress as the center of an agricultural estate, perhaps one that was used as a palace. In my opinion, however, the presence of such a massive tower and the absence of decorative elements points to the existence of a small fortress.

The fact that Herod built various fortifications to control the potentially hostile Greek settlements on the coast is paralleled by the fortifications he built to control the cities of the Decapolis. We know that Gadara, for instance, was extremely hostile to Herod. The other cities of the Decapolis would have also been a disaffected group. The excavations conducted at Scythopolis, Gadara, Pella, Gerasa, and Philadelphia did not reveal any city wall dating to this period,

---

[172] See also Shatzman, *Armies of the Hasmoneans and Herod*, p. 252.
[173] See Josephus, *AJ* XIII, 357, and *BJ* I, 416. See also Shatzman, *Armies of the Hasmoneans and Herod*, p. 252.
[174] See Shatzman, *Armies of the Hasmoneans and Herod*, p. 251.
[175] See Shatzman, *Armies of the Hasmoneans and Herod*, p. 251.
[176] On Tel Michal see Shatzman, *Armies of the Hasmoneans and Herod*, pp. 81–82.
[177] The complex of Horvat 'Eleq comprised a large fortified building erected at the top of a hill and hydraulic and agricultural installations including a Roman style bath house, a pool, an aqueduct, a columbarium and an oil press. See Y. Hirschfeld, *Ramat Hanadiv Excavations, Final Report of the 1984–1998 Seasons, General Discussion, Ramat Hanadiv in Context*, Jerusalem 2000, pp. 685–709. The excavator sees the fortress as the center of an agricultural estate, perhaps used as palace.

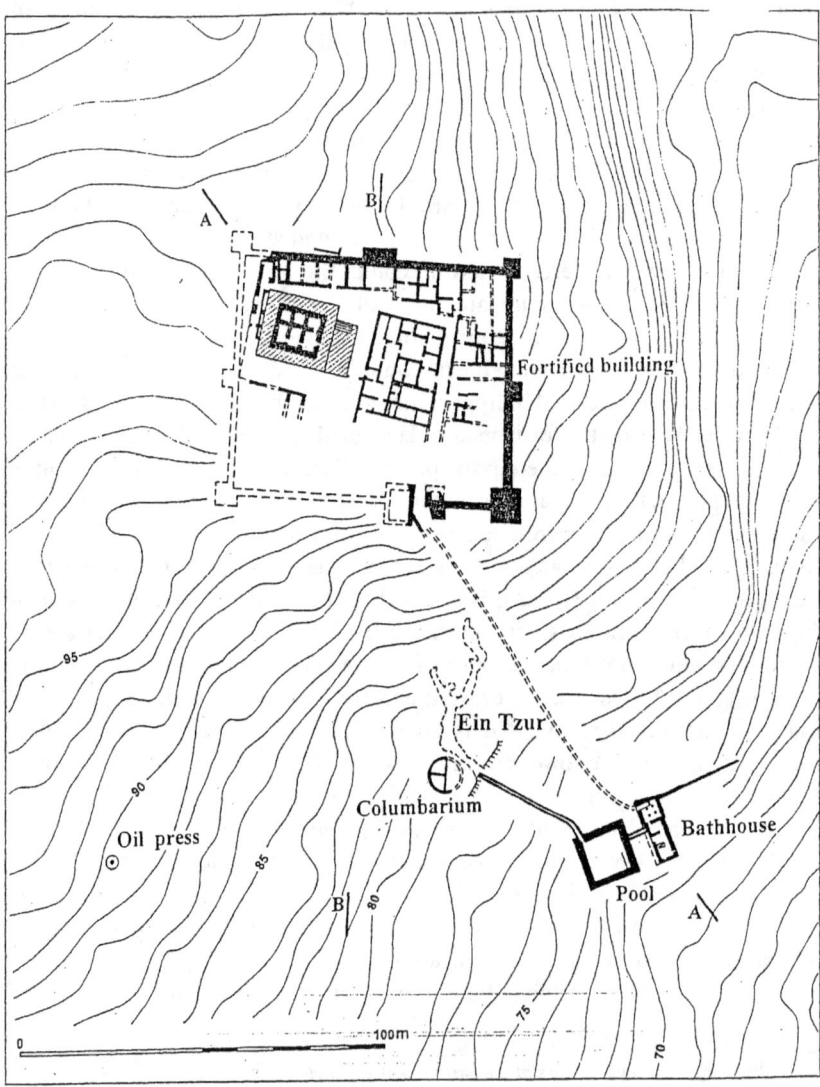

Figure III, 19 – Plan of Horvat 'Eleq from Y. Hirschfeld, *Ramat Hanadiv Excavations, Final Report of the 1984–1998 Seasons, General Discussion, Ramat Hanadiv in Context,* Jerusalem 2000, p. 686, fig. 3, Courtesy of the Israel Exploration Society, Jerusalem.

and hence we can probably conclude that none of the Greek cities – either on the coast and or in the Decapolis, whose legal status was identical – was fortified during the Herodian period. Herod was a Jewish king. As open as he was to Hellenistic culture, he knew very well that fortified Greek cities inside the kingdom, with independent political institutions, were not in his best interest. He would, however, have maintained citadels or forts heavily garrisoned in the cities themselves, or in close proximity to them.[178] Strabo mentions a Hasmonean fortress at Scythopolis destroyed by Pompey.[179] The recently excavated Tel Istaba settlement shows evidence of fortification in the Hellenistic period, but whether or not this is Hasmonean is difficult to establish.[180] The city of Scythopolis was refounded by Pompey in 63 BCE, and rebuilt at the time of Gabinius,[181] far from Tel Istaba, at the foot of Tel Beth Shean.[182]

During Herod's reign the different regions of Transjordan formed a very sensitive frontier territory. As previously described, the Greek inhabitants of the Decapolis could be a source of danger in both in times of peace and war. The major source of trouble was the Nabataean population over the border, and the two Nabataean Wars were fought in this region. The region of Transjordan may be divided into three parts. First is the northern region, which includes Gaulanitis, Batanea, Trachonitis, and Auranitis. There is, unfortunately, no data on the static defenses of these regions, except for the information that Herod established military colonies in Trachonitis and Batanea. Next is the central region, which includes the cities of the Decapolis – Hippos, Gadara, Pella, Abila, Dium, Gerasa, and Philadelphia. We have already dealt with the Decapolis in general terms, together with the other Gentile cities within Herod's kingdom. As previously stated, Herod may have placed garrisons in the cities of the Decapolis. Last is the southern region, comprising Peraea and Esebonitis. In Peraea we know of at least two major fortifications, one of which may even be considered a fortified royal palace. The most important site was Betharamatha, east of Jericho, where Herod

---

[178] Alexander Jannaeus began the conquest of Transjordan. See Josephus, *AJ* XIII, 382, 395–397, and *BJ* I, 104–105. See also Syncellus I (558–559). Thus, around twenty cities were conquered by Alexander Jannaeus, most of them part of the Decapolis. Alexander Jannaeus probably fortified all of the new cities with small forts. Thus Strabo, *Geography* XVI, 2, 40, mentions a fortification near Philadelphia destroyed by Pompey. Under Pompey and Gabinius, all these cities may have rebuilt their city walls. But did these cities have the financial resources to rebuild their city-walls between 63 and 37 BCE? This seems improbable. Pompey' and Gabinius' act was symbolic in essence. All of these cities really begin to develop in the second half of the first century CE, under direct Roman rule, mainly after the Jewish War, during which most of the Decapolis cities were damaged. See also Richardson, *Herod King of the Jews*, pp. 88–91.

[179] See Strabo, *Geography* XVI, 2. 40.

[180] See Shatzman, *Armies of the Hasmoneans and Herod*, p. 87. Applebaum reports a fortress with casemate walls on Mt. Gilboa, but this site is too far from Scythopolis.

[181] See Josephus, *BJ* I, 156 and 166.

[182] It is noteworthy that the new city included a huge temple on the tell and two small temples facing the tell. Clearly, a Herodian fortification would have been built in the surrounding area, and not on Tell Istaba. See D. T. Ariel, "Tell Istaba," *IEJ* 38, 1988, pp. 30–35.

had a palace that burned down in 4 BCE.[183] Antipas later rebuilt the settlement as the city of Livias.[184] Another Herodian fortress was located somewhere in southern Peraea. The residence of Pheroras, tetrarch of Peraea, was at Esebonitis.[185] That urban center had a major fortification and was heavily garrisoned. Where was this fort located? One possibility is at Machaerus, which has been excavated. The archaeological data that have emerged from Machaerus are similar to what is reported by Josephus. Other possible locations are Amathus or Gadora (Tell Jadur near es-Salt).[186]

4. Military Colonies and Their Role in Defending the Herodian Kingdom

The various military colonies established by Herod in the less secure parts of his kingdom may have played an important role in the static defense of the kingdom. In most cases, their function was to suppress rebellion among the local population groups. The only exceptions appear to have been the colonies founded in Idumaea. According to Josephus, Herod settled more than 12,000 military colonists.[187]

In the northern regions of his kingdom, Herod founded colonies in Trachonitis in Batanaea. In the central part of the kingdom, he established colonies in Galilee and Samaria, and in the south he founded colonies in Esebonitis and in Idumaea. It is noteworthy that, to the best of our knowledge, no colony was ever founded in Judaea proper. The colony founded in the northeastern part of Trachonitis[188] was made up of 3,000 Idumaeans and was established after a rebellion of local Ituraeans.[189] The colony had been destroyed in 10–9 BCE, during a later rebellion, and was probably reestablished by Herod.[190] The primary purpose of the colony is quite clear – to have a group of loyal soldiers on the spot, who could quell any local attempt at rebellion. For this task, Herod chose his kinsmen, the Idumaeans, who were clearly loyal to him. Another possible purpose of the colony may have been to foster the integration and mixing of the Idumaeans with

---

[183] See Josephus, *AJ* XVII, 277 and *BJ* II, 59. See also Shatzman, *Armies of the Hasmoneans and Herod*, p. 261.

[184] See Josephus, *AJ* XVIII, 36–38.

[185] See Josephus, *AJ* XV, 294.

[186] See Shatzman, *Armies of the Hasmoneans and Herod*, p. 261.

[187] Josephus reports that Herod settled 3,000 Idumaeans in Trachonitis (Josephus, *AJ* XVI, 285), 600 men of Zamaris in Batanea (Josephus, *AJ* XVII, 24), an unnumbered quantity of horsemen in Heshbon (Josephus, *AJ* XV, 293–296) and Gabaee (Josephus, *AJ* XV, 294 and *BJ* III, 36), probably no more than 1,000 men, 6,000 colonists in Samaria (Josephus, *AJ* XV, 296, and *BJ* I, 403), and 2,000 Idumaeans in Idumaea (Josephus, *BJ* II, 55).

[188] See Josephus, *AJ* XVI, 285 ff.

[189] See Josephus, *AJ* XVI, 271 ff.

[190] See Josephus, *AJ* XVI, 292.

4. Military Colonies and Their Role in Defending the Herodian Kingdom 189

the local population, bringing it closer to the fold of Judaism, in the long term, and making the area more secure through peaceful means. These settled colonists would also have provided an example of sedentary living to their still nomadic fellow Idumaeans, thus getting to the source of the aforementioned problem.

Another colony in the northern territories was set up in Batanaea and was made up of 500 horsemen. All of the colonists were Babylonian Jews who had settled in the Herodian kingdom under their leader, Zamaris. The colony was named Bathyra.[191] This colony probably had a dual purpose, like the other colony discussed above. One objective was to keep the local population in check, and, as in the case of Trachonitis, the colonists belonged to a group that was loyal to Herod, namely Babylonian Jews. Another goal was probably to guard the border against nomadic incursions.

In Galilee Herod founded the well-known colony of Gabae.[192] According to Gracey,[193] the colony was established to suppress possible insurrection on the part of the Jewish population. The colonists themselves may have been Jews. In Galilee a considerable part of the population was Gentile. Galilee was a region in which brigands were always a serious problem, and it is possible that the main purpose of the colony was to keep brigands and outlaws, Jew and Gentile alike, in check.

In Samaria, Herod distributed plots of land to 6,000 men.[194] According to Gracey, the main purpose of these colonies would have been to protect Jerusalem[195] and Judaea. However, Samaria was a separate region and one might have expected that Herod would have founded colonies in Judaea instead. We may surmise that Herod probably had the unruly Samaritans in mind, rather than the Jews. He selected Gentile colonists, rather than Jews, since settling Jews here would have certainly aggravated the existing religious tensions between Jews and Samaritans.[196] The purpose of the colony of horsemen founded in Esebonitis was probably to keep the local population in check, to protect the Jewish settlers, and to contribute to the defense of the region against the Nabataeans.[197]

Various colonies were founded in Idumaea. It is striking that the colonists there were of the same stock as the local population: approximately 2,000 Idumaean veterans were settled there by Herod. Their revolt upon his death can be interpreted in various ways.[198] As already stated, the only possible purpose of a

---

[191] See Josephus, *AJ* XVII, 24–26.
[192] See Josephus, *AJ* XV, 294, Josephus, *BJ* III, 36.
[193] See Gracey, "Armies of the Judaean Client Kings," p. 314.
[194] See Josephus, *AJ* XV, 296 and *BJ* I, 403.
[195] See Gracey, "Armies of the Judaean Client Kings," p. 314.
[196] Herod, probably also attempting to appease the Samaritans, married a Samaritan woman, Malthace.
[197] See Josephus, *AJ* XV, 294. See also Gracey, "Armies of the Judaean Client Kings," p. 313.
[198] See Josephus, *BJ* II, 55. As I will write elsewhere, the fact that most of Herod's army rebelled after his death not only indicates their deep loyalty to him (Herod was the state) but also

colony in Idumaea would have been to keep the Nabataeans at bay, as it is unlikely that soldiers coming from the same stock as the local population would quell any attempted rebellion by the locals.

Several questions concerning the Herodian military colonies remain open.

Were these infantry or cavalry colonies? They would appear to have included both: Idumaeans were known during the Classical period as light infantrymen, while other elements among the colonists were cavalrymen, as were, for instance, the colonists of Bathyra. Did these colonies follow a Hellenistic or a Roman model? Based upon the data at our disposal, the model for the Herodian colonies was Hellenistic rather than Roman.[199] The Herodian pattern everywhere was similar to the Hellenistic one. Colonists settled in the royal domain, with the possible exception of Sebaste, which was not a *polis*, but rather, a royal city, erected in the royal domain. The Herodian colonies appear to have followed a clear Seleucid precedent of settling army veterans together in villages.

5. Herod's Navy

Shatzman has suggested that Herod constructed and maintained a navy, and he provides three pieces of evidence in support of this view. The first is that Herod received ships from Cassius and Murcus to operate on the Sea of Galilee.[200] Second, according to Shatzman, Sebastos, the harbor of Caesarea Maritima, could serve as the base for Herod's navy. Third, when Herod sailed to join M. Agrippa's expedition to the Black Sea, his military contribution must have been substantial, and this would have been possible only if he was able to deploy a naval fleet.[201]

To this data, I would like to add Herod's and Archelaus' coins depicting warships. If these rulers did not possess warships, they would not have depicted them on their coins. Moreover, Herod's and Archelaus' coins also depict anchors, which symbolize the domination of the sea littoral.[202] It is likely that the Hasmo-

---

that Herod was the only pillar of the state. Without him everything could collapse. See Gracey, "Armies of the Judaean Client Kings," p. 317.

[199] On the patterns of Hellenistic colonization in Asia Minor see M. Sartre, *L'Asie Mineure et l'Anatolie d'Alexandre à Dioclétien, IVe siècle av. J.-C. – IIIe siècle ap. J.-C.*, Paris 1995, pp. 9, 26, 47–48, 50–51, 91. On the patterns of Hellenistic colonization in Syria see Sartre, *D'Alexandre à Zénobie*, pp. 29, 58, 114, 120–151, 168, 210–225, 269–286, 309, 514, 544. On Roman colonization under Augustus see R. MacMullen, *Romanization in the Time of Augustus*, New Haven (Conn.) 2000, pp. 8–9, 13, 16–17 on colonies founded in the East, 32–33 in Africa, 52–53, Spain, 94–95 in Gaul.

[200] See Josephus, *AJ* XIV, 280.

[201] See Josephus, *AJ* VI, 17–23. See also Strabo, *Geography* XI, 2–3, Dio, *Roman History* 54, 24, 4–7. See also Shatzman, *Armies of the Hasmoneans and Herod*, pp. 186–187.

[202] See Meshorer, *Treasury of Jewish Coins*, pp. 70–71 and pls. 45, nos. 59–59i, 46, nos. 65–65b on Herod's coins depicting an anchor and a warship and p. 79, and plate 47, nos. 67–70h and plate 48, nos. 71–72i on Archelaus coins depicting an anchor and a warship, and warship's

neans had previously built a war fleet. The Hasmoneans took interest in creating a fleet and probably developed an interest in the sea following the conquest of Joppa, during the reign of John Hyrcanus I. However, it is quite probable that the Hasmonean state had a navy only from the reign of Alexander Jannaeus onward. In 95 BCE this king conquered most of the coast, thus adding to Joppa the cities of Dora and of Straton's Tower, dominated by the petty tyrant Zoilus. Thus, he had at his disposition not only the harbor of Joppa, but also the two harbors of Straton's Tower and Dora. The main harbor of the Hasmonean kingdom was probably located at Joppa.[203] Josephus reports that Hyrcanus accused his brother Aristobulus in front of Pompey during their hearing in Damascus, of being responsible for piracy. It must be said that during the civil war between Hyrcanus and Aristobulus the sailors of the Hasmonean fleet were probably unpaid for long periods. It is possible that in order to survive, these sailors had to engage in piracy[204].

The most important evidence for Herod's navy is of course, Sebastos, the harbor of Caesarea Maritima. Caesarea Maritima holds an important strategic position, in the middle of the coast of the Land of Israel, between Joppa to the south and Dora to the north.[205] Until 22 BCE, Herod's kingdom had no other harbors, with the exception of Joppa – already used by the Hasmoneans – as well as Dora and Straton's Tower. However, in 22 BCE, Herod decided to expand the two harbors already existing at Straton's Tower and to create a huge, modern, artificial harbor, with both civil and military functions. Herod chose the South Harbor, which already possessed a lighthouse, as the starting point for his enterprise. The harbor was called Sebastos, in honor of Augustus, and its construction was a huge project.

I would like to summarize the structure of Sebastos, as described by Josephus.[206] The archeological data confirm Josephus' description. The excavated harbor consisted of two stone breakwaters. The southern breakwater was 200 m. in length, extending westward before turning northward for an additional 300 m. The entire southern breakwater was 480 m. in length and measured 40 to 60 m. in

---

prows. See also a coin of Herod from Sebaste, the smallest of the four denominations minted there, that depicts an *aphlaston*, pp. 64–65.

[203] The assumption that Alexander Jannaeus developed a fleet is based upon coins depicting the anchor, in the Hellenstic period a symbol of maritime power, and on graffiti from the Tomb of Jason in Jerusalem depicting a naval battle. See Meshorer, *Ancient Jewish Coinage I*, pp. 61–62, pls. 5–7. See also L. Y. Rahmani, "Jason's Tomb," *IEJ* 17, 1967, pp. 69–73.

[204] Among the Greeks, the border line between a regular sailor in the fleet of a city-state and a pirate was very thin. See Josephus, *AJ* XIV, 43. According to Uriel Rappaport, the accusations of Pompey were justified, see U. Rappaport, "La Judée et Rome pendant le règne d'Alexandre Jannée," *Revue des études juives, Historia Judaica LXXVIII* 1968, pp. 329–342.

[205] Josephus emphasizes Herod's strategic choice of location. See Josephus, *BJ* III, 408. With the exception of Dora, both Ptolemais and Ascalon were outside the borders of Herod's kingdom, as they were during the rule of the last Hasmoneans.

[206] See Josephus, *AJ* XV, 334–338 and *BJ* I, 411–413.

width. The northern breakwater, which was shorter, was 200 m. long, extending westward, and was more or less as wide as the southern breakwater. The distance between the two breakwaters was 18 m.[207] The use of a fortification to encircle the harbor would appear to emphasize the primarily military character of the harbor. The entrance was marked on the southern breakwater by a lighthouse, the Drusion tower mentioned by Josephus. The position of the tower, at the entrance to the harbor, as well as the dimensions of the stones found underwater, suggest a lighthouse 80 to 90 m. tall.[208] The total area of the harbor was 20 ha. (200,000 sq. m.). The Southern Harbor of Straton's Tower was incorporated into Sebastos as an inner harbor basin, directly facing the platform of the huge Temple of Roma and Augustus that measured approximately 100 sq. m. The quay line, running east-west, measured around 300 m.[209] The Northern Harbor remained in use. Sebastos may be compared to other military harbors of classical antiquity, such as Piraeus, also mentioned by Josephus, as well as the harbor of Carthage and the harbor of Alexandria.[210] This comparison is helpful in enabling us to deduce the military function of Sebastos. In Classical Antiquity, when a harbor was divided into two or more harbors, each had a different function, and one of these was always military. The military function of Sebastos can also be deduced from the fact that it had different harbors, each with its own function. Thus, like all the other harbors – Piraeus, Carthage, and Alexandria – Sebastos most likely had two or more harbors with different functions, to accommodate both warships and mercantile vessels.[211] If the warships were moored at Sebastos, the mercantile vessels could have been anchored at the Northern Harbor, constructed in the Hellenistic period, or else in the Southern Harbor, which had become the inner

---

[207] See Vitruvius, *Architecture* V, 12. See K. G. Holum, *King's Herod's Dream, Caesarea on the Sea*, New York 1988, pp. 100–105.

[208] See A. Raban and R. L. Hohlfelder, "The Ancient Harbors of Caesarea Maritima," *Archaeology* 34, 1981, pp. 56–60. See also Holum, *Caesarea on the Sea*, pp. 90–105.

[209] See Holum, *Caesarea on the Sea*, p. 100.

[210] Josephus compares it to the harbor of Piraeus, built in the fourth century BCE. On the Piraeus harbor see D. Blackman, "Naval Installations," in *The Age of the Galley, Mediterranean Oared Vessels since Pre-classical Times*, London 1995, pp. 227–228. See also V. Gabrielsen, "The Athenian Navy in the Fourth Century BC," in *The Age of the Galley, Mediterranean Oared Vessels since Pre-classical Times*, London 1995, pp. 234–235. Another similar harbor, with a clear military purpose was that of Carthage, built in the third century BCE and described by Appian. See Appian, *Roman History* VIII, xiv, 96. See also Connolly, *Hannibal*, p. 37. On the Carthage harbor see also Blackman, *Naval Installations*, pp. 225–226. The Hellenistic harbors of Alexandria, described by Strabo, also present similarities with Sebastos. See Strabo, *Geography* VIII, 6. See also A. Bernard, *Alexandrie des Ptolémées*, Paris 1995, pp. 46–47. On the Alexandria's harbors see also B. Rankov, "Fleets of the Early Roman Empire, 31 BC–AD 324," in *The Age of the Galley, Mediterranean Oared Vessels since Pre-classical Times*, London 1995, p. 80.

[211] This problem of a harbor with two basins is also addressed by Redde, who opts for the possibility that when there were two harbors, one had a military purpose while the other was civilian. See M. Redde, *Mare Nostrum, Les infrastructures, le dispositif, et l'histoire de la marine militaire sous l'Empire Romain*, BEFAR 260, Rome 1986, pp. 151–152.

5. Herod's Navy

basin of Sebastos, or possibly in both of these harbors. Sebastos was an obvious choice as military harbor because it was fortified and had a huge lighthouse. How many ships could Sebastos accommodate? Levine has noted that Sebastos could accommodate at least 100 warships, and if these were small warships, then it could accommodate no fewer than 166. Obviously, only a small number of these ships were warships. During this period, Augustus also developed the military harbors of Italy, Misenum and Ravenna.[212]

It is impossible to establish which type of ship was used by Herod's navy. As I have written earlier, the only sources for our knowledge of Herod's warships are the coins minted by Herod and Archelaus depicting small warships.[213] It seems to me that these small warships could have been similar to the Roman *liburna*.[214]

As Shatzman points out, Herod also possessed a small military fleet on the Sea of Galilee.[215] Cassius and Murcus gave him these ships as early as 43 BCE, and he probably had boats on the Dead Sea, like his Hasmonean predecessors.[216]

---

[212] See P. A. Gianfrotta, "Harbor Structures of the Augustan Age in Italy," ," in Raban, A. and Holum, K. (eds.), *Caesarea Maritima, A Retrospective after Two Millennia, DMOA XXI*, pp. 65-77. In this article the breakwaters of the harbors, both civil and military, of Puteoli, Nisida, Misenum are compared to the ones of Sebastos. On Roman military harbors see also Rankov, "Fleets of the Early Roman Empire," p. 79 on Misenum, p. 80 on Ravenna and Alexandria. Artificial harbors with a military purpose, similar to Sebastos, were later erected at Ostia, at Portus by Trajan, and at Leptis Magna. In conclusion, Sebastos, the harbor of Caesarea Maritima was similar to the other great harbors of Classical antiquity and shared their characteristics.

[213] See Meshorer, *Treasury of Jewish Coins*, pp. 70-71 and 79, pl. 46, nos. 65-65 b on Herod's coins depicting warships and plate 47, nos. 70-70 h and plate 48, nos. 71-72 i on Archelaus coins depicting warships, and warship's prows. Herod was not the only ruler who depicted warships on his coins. During the civil wars all the warlords depicted various types of warships on their coins. The warships are generally accurately portrayed, clearly indicating if a big or a small warship was intended. See J. S. Morrison, *Greek and Roman Oared Warships, 399-30 BC. Oxbow Monograph 62*, Oxford 1996, pp. 230-233.

[214] Most of the iconographic sources that depict *liburnae* are later and generally dated to the Trajanic period. See Morrison, *Greek and Roman Oared Warships*, pp. 247-253, pls. 44-49, and pp. 263-264, and 317. See also J. Warry, *Warfare in the Classical World*, London 1980, pp. 182-183.

[215] See Josephus, *AJ* XIV, 280. What type of craft were these? The boat excavated by Shelley Wachsmann in 1986 may provide an answer to this question. According to the excavators, this ship could have been a small fishing vessel, later used in 67 CE at the battle of Migdal. See S. Wachsmann, *The Sea of Galilee Boat, An Extraordinary 2,000 Year Old Discovery*, New York 1995, pp. 135, 179-181, 193, 302, 305. Similar river boats are depicted on the Trajan column. A boat of this type, used to patrol the Rhine, was excavated at Obestimm in Germany. Both a sail and oars propelled this ship dated from 90 CE to 112 CE, armed with a ram, its flanks covered with shields, and with a crew of around twenty-five men. The size is similar to the ship excavated in the Sea of Galilee. See O. Höckmann, *Schiffhart Zwischen Alpen und Nordsee*, in *Römer Zwischen Alpen und Nordmeer* Mainz 2,000, pp. 264-268, pl. 22, p. 438 (catalogue).

[216] It seems that the Hasmoneans also had a small fleet of at least four boats that patrolled the Dead Sea. At Khirbet el-Yahud, a spot situated on the northern shore of the Dead Sea, not far from Masada a building was excavated that could have been used as a ship shed. See Netzer, *Palaces of the Hasmoneans and Herod the Great*, pp. 77-78. There are, however, scholars who suggest that the main function of the building was as a fortress providing defense to the areas of

Since Josephus does not name any other Herodian dignitary who could have commanded the fleet, the *strategos* of Caesarea Maritima would appear to be the most likely candidate for this position.[217]

What was the purpose of such a fleet? As with the army, we can say that the purpose of Herod's fleet was to control his kingdom's littoral and to serve as an auxiliary force to Rome. However, in contrast to the function of the army, the function of Herod's fleet was not to face external enemies. As a ruler whose state included a long strip of territory along the sea, Herod needed to control it. Herod required ships to effectively control smuggling along the coast. The primary use of his fleet, both on the sea and on the Sea of Galilee, was in the realm of "revenue service." Another important task would have been to police the coast against possible pirates, who were one of the scourges of the ancient world.

Herod's fleet served also as an auxiliary force to Rome. The only record of the possible use of Herod's military fleet as a Roman auxiliary concerns the naval war in Pontus. Herod sent an auxiliary contingent of his fleet to Agrippa when the latter was governor of Asia.[218] Herod's fleet followed Agrippa to Sinope, on the Pontus, where it was employed to crush a revolt that had arisen over a disputed claim to the crown of the Cimmerian Bosporus, which a usurper, a certain Scribonius, had seized.[219]

There is yet another motivation that can explain the need for Herod's ships. Augustus had no fleet in the East. He reorganized the Roman fleet, but it was based in the western Mediterranean and was moored at Forum Iulii, Misenum, and Ravenna. The waters of the eastern Mediterranean were defended by Rome's allies. Only during the reign of Hadrian was a *classis syriaca* organized, more than one hundred years after Herod's death.[220] After Herod's death, Archelaus appar-

---

'Ain Feshkha and Jericho. The main problem with this view is that these areas are too far away from one another.

[217] See Josephus, *AJ* XIX, 356. Josephus reports that Agrippa I named a *strategos* to administer the city of Caesarea Maritima. It is probable that there was a *strategos* of Caesarea Maritima during Herod the Great's rule. Who were the sailors of Herod's navy? Probably the native Greek populations of the coastal cities ruled by Herod, such as Dora, Caesarea Maritima, and Joppa were the main components of Herod's navy. It seems logical to suppose that the Gentile coastal cities of the kingdom, with a lengthy tradition of seafaring, would have contributed in such a way to the kingdom's defense. Joppa had a mixed population of Jews and Greeks, and more than a handful of Jews must have served in the navy. Sailors from the local Jewish population probably manned the fleet on the Sea of Galilee.

[218] See Josephus, *AJ* XVI, 16–22.

[219] See E. S. Shuckburgh, *Augustus Caesar,* New York (N.Y.) 1995, p. 182.

[220] Following Herod's death it appears that only the coastal cities of the Land of Israel, such as Gaza, Ascalon, Dora, and Ptolemais continued to contribute ships to the Roman overlord. It's curious that both Ascalon and Dora continued to depict ships on their city-coins until the reign of Hadrian and even after, when an Imperial fleet probably took over their task. See Y. Meshorer, *City-Coins of Eretz-Israel and the Decapolis in the Roman Period,* Jerusalem 1985, p. 16, nos. 20–23 (Dora); p. 26, n. 41. (Ascalon). It is possible that part of the *classis syriaca* was at Caesarea Maritima. Late coins depict a *liburna* with the inscription *portus augusti,* and

ently continued to employ the war fleet as before. A coin minted by Archelaus depicts a warship on the obverse and the ship's prow with the ram on the reverse. This coin emphasizes Archelaus' possession of a war fleet, and thus, his superior position. This was important because neither Antipas nor Philip, Archelaus' co-heirs to the kingdom of Herod the Great, had any coastal territory.[221] However, there is no mention in Josephus or any other sources of what happened to Herod's fleet after Archelaus.

6. Conclusions

Herod was a supremely capable military commander whose talents in planning, organization, and logistics were, without any doubt, impressive. Although it is still possible to define Herod's army as a Hellenistic army – the last Hellenistic army, as it were – his was also a modern army that fully integrated Late Hellenistic and Roman military technology, and he followed the latest developments in military technology closely. On the one hand, like most of the Hellenistic armies, Herod's army had a very strong cavalry, well equipped to face those of the Nabataeans or the Parthians, while, on the other hand, his heavy infantry was equipped and probably maneuvered like those of contemporary Roman legions. Moreover, Herod's army had the know-how to build siege machines, artillery, and temporary military camps.

Herod's army was an instrument of cohesion in the kingdom. In his army Jews and Gentile served side by side. However, like that of the Hasmoneans before him, Herod's army was a Jewish army, since the Jews were its most important element. Is this an indication that most of the Jewish subjects supported Herod's rule? This is arguable, and in fact Josephus states that Herod's Jewish subjects were often rebellious and hostile to Herod's policy.[222] However, if that were the case, it seems strange that Herod would maintain an army of mostly Jewish soldiers. Perhaps, for Herod's Jewish subjects, his army was the most tangible symbol of their independence.[223] Herod's death brought an end to the institution of

---

the inscription *Colonia Prima Flavia Augusta Caesarea, Metropolis Syria Palaestina*, see p. 21, no. 33. On the *classis syriaca* see Redde, *Mare Nostrum*, pp. 236–237. According to Redde the *classis syriaca* was organized only in the second century CE. See also Shatzman, *Armies of the Hasmoneans and Herod*, p. 187. See also Rankov, "Fleets of the Early Roman Empire," pp. 81 and 83. On the number of ships in a fleet in the Classic period see L. Casson, *Ships and Seafaring in Ancient Times*, London 1994, p. 78. See also Morrison, *Greek and Roman Oared Warships*, p. 115, 117, 118, 127–130, 132, 137, 140, p. 146 and 164. See also Warry, *Warfare in Classical World*, pp. 116, 185.

[221] See Meshorer, *Treasury of Jewish Coins*, pp. 79–80. However, according to Meshorer, the coin was minted to celebrate Archelaus' trip to Rome.

[222] See Josephus, *AJ* XV, 365 ff.

[223] We must emphasize that this is our own view. On the contrary, for Mendels "the effect of an army that, even if Jewish, operated against the Jews themselves, was destructive. Those

a primarily Jewish army, as such. Without Herod's charisma, the cracks in Jewish society once more appeared on the surface, with the result that the Romans eliminated most of Herod's Jewish soldiers. The armies of Herod's sons – Archelaus, Antipas, and Philip – were probably very small, a far cry from the size of their father's armed forces. Herod Agrippa I appears to have had no time to rebuild his grandfather's Jewish army,[224] and the small army of Agrippa II,[225] though partly composed of Jews, was negligible in numbers.

As in the case of the standing army, Herod's static defenses represent the last stage in the evolution of a Hellenistic model. It should be stressed that the Herodian fortifications, as well as the military colonies, were planned as a defense against Herod's enemies – the Ptolemies, the Nabataeans, and the Parthians – and none of these, including the Ptolemies, had the engineering capacity to successfully besiege the Herodian royal cities or *tetrapyrgia*. Not so the Romans, whose military engineers, albeit with some difficulty, had the capability of razing any of Herod's walled cities and fortifications. But the Herodian fortifications were, after all, built to contribute to the military effort of the Roman Empire, not to hinder it. That was probably Augustus' main motivation in allowing his faithful ally to build so many fortifications. In defending Herod's kingdom, these fortifications also defended Rome. The Jewish commanders in 66–70 CE had probably forgotten this, but not, apparently, Josephus. Thus, between 67 and 73 CE, the Jewish War against Rome was transformed from a war of pitched battles into a war of siege that the Roman army was exceedingly well equipped to win. The most obvious consequence of Herod's strategy and the organization of his internal static defenses – a clear demonstration of the success of his strategic thinking – is that they were never put to a real test during his reign.

Jews who were still hoping for an independent sovereign Jewish State could not view this force as their true national army. For them it was rather a threat and a false symbol of nationalism." See D. Mendels, *The Rise and Fall of Jewish Nationalism,* New York 1992, p. 341. However, I wonder what the Jews thought of the foreign mercenaries in the armies of John Hyrcanus I and of the Cilicians and Pisidians in Alexander Jannaeus' army. Or what they felt about Alexander Jannaeus' revenge against his opponents in Jerusalem, and the thousands executed by his army. On the contrary, Herod always restrained his army.

[224] On Herod's sons and Agrippa I's army see Mendels, *Rise and Fall of Jewish Nationalism,* pp. 342–345.

[225] On Agrippa II's small army see Josephus, *BJ* III, 68. Agrippa II's army included 1,000 archers, light infantry, probably Ituraeans, and 1,000 cavalrymen, probably Jews. See also Gracey, "Armies of the Judaean Client Kings," pp. 319–321.

IV. The Administration and Economy of the Herodian Kingdom

1. The Administration of the Herodian Kingdom

A. *The Sources of the Administrative Division of Herodian Judaea*

In the first section of this chapter we shall analyze the interrelated topics of the administration and economy of the Herodian kingdom. The administration of the Herodian Kingdom was rooted in the past and continued a tradition that stretched back to the Persian period. Thus it seems reasonable to posit that two administrative traditions coexisted in Herodian Judaea.

The first was the "greater" traditional administrative division of the Land of Israel as part of the satrapy of Abr Naharain that also begun during Achaemenid rule. During the Hellenistic period, the Ptolemies and later the Seleucids established an administrative division of Coile Syria that continued more or less unchanged under the Hasmoneans and the Herodians. This division did not originate in the local needs of the populations, but in the central establishment of the Ptolemies, and particularly the Seleucids, and answered the monarch's needs rather than local requirements.[1] Thus the division of the Hasmonean and Herodian Judaea into administrative units was clearly rooted in the Hellenistic period.

This division consisted of *komai* or villages, which were the basic administrative unit, administered by a *kommogrammateus*, who was appointed by the government, and assisted, at least in the Jewish areas of the kingdom, by seven local magistrates. The *komai* were grouped in a *toparchia*, or administrative district, which was controlled by a *strategos* or a *toparch* who ran the administration from

---

[1] On the administration of Ptolemaic Coile Syria see M. Sartre, *D'Alexandre à Zénobie, histoire du Levant Antique, IVe siècle av. J.-C. – IIIe siècle ap. J.-C.* Paris 2001, pp. 154–155. See also E. J. Bickerman, *The Jews in the Greek Age*, Cambridge (Mass.) 1988, pp. 73–123. For the Seleucid period see Arrian quoted in Appianus, *Syriake*, 62. See also See Strabo, *Geography* XVI, 2, 4. See also Sartre, *Alexandre à Zénobie*, pp. 165–168. See also Bickerman, *Jews in the Greek Age*, pp. 123–124. A common characteristic of Ptolemaic and especially Seleucid rule was the importance of the Graeco-Phoenician cities as quasi-independent administrative units. See also on the administration of Coile Syria in the Early Hellenistic Period M. Hengel, *Judaism and Hellenism, Studies in the Encounter in Palestine during the Early Hellenistic Period I*, Philadelphia 1974, pp. 18–20 and 23–29.

one of the villages or from a city designated as the *metropolis* or district capital. The *meridarchiai*, which were larger administrative units, generally including one or more regions, were administrated by a *meridarch*.

The second administrative tradition, which was called *ma'amad*, was the basic administrative division of post-exilic Judaea and still existed in Herodian Judaea. It basically referred to post-exilic Judaea and dated back to the Persian period. Based on the *ma'amadoth*, it had distinctly cultic roots. The division of the entire community of Israel – priests, Levites, and Israelites – into *ma'amadoth* corresponded to the *mishmaroth* or "watches" of the priests and the Levites in the Temple. Thus, an administrative district consisted of the *ma'amad* and the corresponding priestly *mishmereth*[2]. After the Hasmonean conquests and during the Herodian period, this division extended outside Judaea proper to Idumaea, Galilee, and the Transjordanian region, wherever Jews lived. During the Herodian period the priests, as well as the Levites, were divided into twenty-four groups, or *mishmaroth*. The whole of Judaea was thus divided into the corresponding twenty-four groups of the *ma'amadoth*.[3]

According to Schalit, the Hasmoneans found an original solution for the administration of Judaea proper, basing the administrative division of their kingdom on two elements: a secular element, the *toparchiai*, inherited from the previous Hellenistic rulers, and a religious element, derived from the Jewish *ma'amadoth* tradition. The Hasmoneans merely superimposed the secular division into *toparchiai* onto the religious division of *ma'amadoth*. Jonathan probably initiated this process, and by the time of Alexander Jannaeus there were twenty-four *toparchiai* as the *ma'amadoth* in the Temple.[4] Thus in the Hasmonean Period the *ma'amadoth* were an institution interchangeable with the *toparchiai*. As high priests and secular rulers, the Hasmoneans headed both the religious and civil administration of Judaea. However, as I have indicated above, this system of superimposing the *ma'amad* upon a secular *toparchia* probably began much earlier.

---

[2] See S. Safrai, "The Temple and the Divine Service", in *The World History of the Jewish People, The Herodian Period*, New Brunswick 1975, p. 291. See E. and H. Eshel, "4Q471 Fragment 1 and Ma'amadot in the War Scroll", in J. Trebolle Barrea and L. Vegas Montaner (eds.), *The Madrid Qumran Congress III, Proceedings of the International Congress on the Dead Sea Scrolls, Madrid 18–21 March 1991*, Leiden 1991, pp. 617–618. The *ma'amad* appears in 1 Chr 23–28 and in 2 Chr 35: 65 in connection with priests and Levites. In Rabbinic literature it refers to priests, Levites and laymen who attended when the public offering or *tamid* was being sacrificed. See TJ, *Ta'an.* 4:2, p. 67:4 and TJ, *Pesh.* 4: 1, p. 30: 2. See Eshel, "4Q471 Fragment 1 and Ma'amadot in the War Scroll", pp. 617–618.

[3] See m. *Šeb.*1, 2, t. *Šeb.* 7, 10–15, m. *Ta'an.* 4, 2. See also M. Avi-Yona, *Carta's Atlas of the Period of the Second Temple, the Mishnah and the Talmud*, Jerusalem 1974, p. 58, no. 85. It is possible to show that that division in *ma'amadoth* mirrored the contemporary division of the Greek city states and *ethne* as well as tribes or *phylai*, which were the basic administrative unit of the Greek world. A clear parallel may thus be drawn with the Greek world and Rome, where the tribe, like the *ma'amad* in Judaea, had both an administrative and religious function.

[4] See A. Schalit, "Domestic Politics and Political Institutions", in *The World History of the Jewish People VI, The Hellenistic Period*, New Brunswick 1972, pp. 266–267.

The innovation here is that the secular and religious ruler was one and the same individual. Thus, the *toparchiai* were no longer under the control of Macedonian *toparch* and *meridarch*, and the *ma'amadoth* were no longer under the control of the native high priest. Instead, both came under the control of the Hasmonean ruler, who was simultaneously *strategos* of Judaea, as well as high priest.

It seems that Jonathan was the first Hasmonean ruler to create a new Hasmonean administration towards the end of his rule. It is clear, however, that his administration did not change anything from the previous Seleucid rule, to which Jonathan was still bound. During the first years of his reign Jonathan succeeded, *de facto*, in dominating the central part of Judaea. This included the *toparchiai* of Jerusalem, also the capital, Jericho, Bethsur, Keilah, Beth ha-Keren and Mizpah, already administrative centers during the Achaemenid period.[5] During the rule of John Hyrcanus I, the true administrative challenge began for the Hasmonean rulers, since he conquered Gentile areas, and new *toparchiai* were annexed. Thus the *toparchiai* of Acrabata, Narbata, eastern Idumaea (Marissa), western Idumaea ('En Gedi), and Jamnia were annexed.[6]

It is extremely difficult and challenging to reconstruct the administrative division of the country in 76 BCE at the end of Alexander Jannaeus' rule, when the Hasmonean kingdom was at its peak, because data for that period is scant. Several complementary sources are, however, available. The firsts of these are the *First Book of Maccabees* and Josephus' *Antiquities* and *War*, which describe the administrative division of Judaea proper at the time of Jonathan in 142 BCE, with changes that may be dated to the rule of John Hyrcanus I, such as the conquest of Idumaea. For the rest of the kingdom, the later administrative divisions at the time of Herod are well documented in Josephus' *War*.[7] There is also the list of the cities of the priests appearing in the Mishna, which may be consulted with caution. Thus, using all of these sources – both earlier and later – as well as Rabbinic literature, it is possible to reconstruct the situation towards the end of Alexander Jannaeus' rule.

The entire Hasmonean kingdom was divided into seven *meridarchiai*: Judaea, Idumaea, Galilee, Peraea, Moabitis, Samaria, and Giladitis. We know the capitals of some of the *meridarchiai*, such as Jerusalem, Adora, Sepphoris, Gadora or Amathus, Heshbon, and Gamala.[8] Judaea probably conserved the division

---

[5] See Avi-Yona, *Atlas of Second Temple, Mishnah and Talmud*, p. 33, n. 47. See also Schalit, *König Herodes*, p. 205. See 1 Macc. 11, 33 and Josephus, *AJ* XIII, 102 (Akkaron), 127 (Apherims, Lydda, and Ramathain). See also Avi-Yona, *Atlas of Second Temple, Mishnah and Talmud*, p. 33, n. 47. Under Simon the *toparchiai* of Joppa and Gazara were annexed to the Hasmonean state. See Schalit, *König Herodes*, p. 205.

[6] See Schalit, *König Herodes*, p. 205.

[7] See 1 *Macc.* 11, 33, Josephus, *AJ* XIII, 102, 127 and *BJ* I, 63, and III, 54–55.

[8] Sepphoris was the traditional capital of the Galilee before the founding of Tiberias. Gadora is attested at the time of Jonathan. Heshbon was the capital of a *toparchia* in the Herodian period. Samaria was chosen as the capital of the *meridarchia* by the Hasmonean ruler. Josephus includes

into *toparchiai* that dated from the time of Jonathan. Thus, the capitals of the *toparchiai* were Jerusalem, Jericho, Bethsur, Keilah, Beth ha-Kerem, Mizpah, Akkaron, Lydda, Ramathain, and Apherims, Gazara, Jamnia and Joppa, probably Ashdod, Acrabata and Narbata, and Betharamatha. In Idumaea the *toparchiai* were probably those of Marissa – Beth Govrin and 'En Gedi. In Moabitis-Peraea the *toparchiai* were probably those of Gadora, Amathus, and Machaerus. In Galilea the *toparchiai* were probably those of Arbela, Sepphoris, Tarichaeae, Gabara, and of Upper Galilee. In Giladitis the only known *toparchiai* are those of Gamala and Abila.[9] On the borders of the Hasmonean kingdom there were also Greek cities such as Pegae in Judaea; Anthedon, Gaza, Raphia, and Rhinocorura in Idumaea; Scythopolis, Dora, Straton Tower, and Apollonia in Samaria; Philoteria in Galilee; Antioch Seleucia, Hippos, Dium, Abila, Gadara, Pella, and Gerasa, in Giladitis.[10] All these cities lacked a definite administrative framework.

B. The Administrative Division of the Herodian Kingdom

Herod's kingdom included diverse ethnic elements: Jews living in Judaea, Galilee, and Idumaea; Samaritans; Greeks living in various urban centers on the coast and in the interior; and various nomadic populations scattered throughout the

---

Gamala in the list of cities conquered by Alexander Jannaeus, and it was probably the capital of the *meridarchia* of Giladitis. Adora is well documented for the earlier periods. See Josephus, *BJ* I, 63 Adora also was the location of Gabinius' *synedrion* for Idumaea. See Josephus, *AJ* XV, 91 and *BJ* I, 170. Following Gabinius' reforms, Amathus appeared as the site of the local *synedrion* of Peraea. See Josephus *AJ* XV, 91 and *BJ* I, 170. Sepphoris also was the site of Gabinius' *synedrion* for Galilee. See Josephus, *AJ* XV, 91 and *BJ* I, 170. On Gamala see Josephus, *AJ* XIII, 397.

[9] On Judaea see Josephus, *AJ* XIII, 215. Ashdod is mentioned in the Mishna as one of the cities of the twenty-four *ma'amadoth*. As it appears in connection with Jonathan, the city was probably the capital of a *toparchia* in the Late Hasmonean period. In Idumaea on Marissa – Beth Govrin see Josephus, *AJ* XIII, 396. The importance of 'En Gedi in the Late Hasmonean period has been demonstrated through archaeological excavations, as Josephus does not mention it in this connection. Moreover, 'En Gedi, like Beth Govrin, is mentioned as the site of one of the cities of the twenty-four *mishmaroth*. In Moabitis – Peraea, Gadora and Machaerus are mentioned in the Mishna as cities of the twenty-four *mishmaroth*. Amathus was a *toparchia* capital in the Herodian period. In Galilee, Sepphoris and Tarichaeae, the last mentioned as Migdol, are also mentioned in the Mishna as cities of the twenty-four *ma'amadoth*. All four cities appear as *toparchia* capitals in the Herodian period. In Giladitis, Abila was also one of the cities of the twenty-four *ma'amadoth*. See Schalit, *König Herodes*, p. 205.

[10] Although Josephus mentions some of them as having been conquered by Alexander Jannaeus, their status is not clear to us. The Greek cities, with the exception of Samaria, did not become capitals of *toparchiai*. After the Hasmonean conquest it is probable that these cities survived as mere *komai* or villages. Josephus, *AJ* XIII, 396 mention Straton's Tower, Apollonia, Gaza, Anthedon, Raphia, and Rhinocolura, Scythopolis, Seleucia, Gadara and Pella. Josephus, *AJ* XIII, 397 also reports various cities or villages that were not administrative capitals, such as Mount Carmel and Mount Tabor in the middle of the country, and Medeba, Lemba, Oronaim, Gelithon and Zoara in Moabitis. See Avi-Yona, *Atlas of Second Temple, Mishnah and Talmud*, p. 46, no. 68.

1. The Administration of the Herodian Kingdom

northern regions of the kingdom. Despite this ethnic diversity, however, there was a uniform system of administration that, in fact, exemplifies the iron will of King Herod.[11] Herod's administrative division of his territory largely followed that of the Hasmoneans in Judaea proper, albeit with several changes, including the establishment of new *toparchiai*, which is indicative of prosperity.[12]

The *meridarchiai* in Herod's kingdom in the final years of his reign were Judaea (which, at a certain point, included Idumaea as well), Peraea, Galilee and Samaria, Batanaea, Trachonitis and Auranitis. Judaea- Idumaea, Peraea, Samaria and Galilee were the remains of the mutilated Hasmonean kingdom after division by Pompey and Gabinius. Later, in 23 BCE, Augustus gave Herod Gaulanitis, and in 20 BCE, Batanaea, Trachonitis and Auranitis. The latter *meridarchiai* were administrative districts of the province of Syria ceded by Augustus in 23 and 20 BCE, respectively.[13] Thus the most important changes were the unification of Judaea and Idumaea into a single *meridarchia*[14] and the establishment of the new *meridarchiai* of Batanea, Trachonitis, and Auranitis, which took the place of the Hasmonean *meridarchia* of Giladitis. Herod appointed *meridarches* to govern these units,[15] and it is clear that the position of *meridarch* was an important one in Herod's kingdom, since he conferred it upon his relatives. Of the three *meridarches* whose identities are known – Costobar in Idumaea, at the beginning of Herod's reign; Pheroras in Peraea; and Achiab in Judaea – all are members of Herod's family.[16]

---

[11] As a source on Herod's administration, see Schalit, *König Herodes*, pp. 183–223, on pp. 208–211 there are lists of *toparchiai*.

[12] Avi-Yona suggested that under Herod the Great the *toparchiai* were grouped in *merides*, each under a *meridarch*. See Josephus, *AJ* XII, 261–264 and XV, 217. See also 1 Macc. 10, 65. See Schürer, *History of the Jewish People II*, p. 186.

[13] See Josephus, *AJ* XV, 217, 343, 344, 360 and *BJ* I, 396, 398, 400. See also Appian, *Civil War* V, 75.

[14] After Costobar's execution, Herod probably annexed Idumaea to Judaea, creating one *meridarchia* from two. The purpose of the reform is clear. During the Herodian period, Idumaeans were identical to Jews for all practical purposes. Thus, the Mishna's list of the cities of the twenty-four *ma'amadoth* includes cities in Idumaea. Furthermore, as Herod was of Idumaean stock, he probably wished in this administrative reform to obliterate his origins.

[15] See Josephus, *AJ* XV, 216.

[16] Costobar was *meridarch* of Idumaea and Gaza. See Josephus, *AJ* XV, 254. Knowing the treacherous character of the latter, Herod either convinced himself that his sister Salome, Costobar's wife, would keep an eye upon his brother-in-law, or that the Idumaeans would be more loyal to their Jewish king than to the husband of the king's sister. In any case, Herod's judgment proved sound. Pheroras, exiled from the court, was appointed *meridarch* of Peraea, a position that he held until his death. See Josephus, *AJ* XV, 362, and XVII, 58–59, 61. In Peraea were the urban agglomerations of the Decapolis, once, under Ptolemaic and Seleucid rule, as under Pompey and Gabinius, proud Greek *poleis*, but now, with the exception of Gadara, lacking any will to rebel. Herod's brother could deal well with the Greeks. In the last years of Herod's rule the young Achiab served as *meridarch* of Judaea. See Josephus, *AJ* XVII, 270 and *BJ* II, 55.

The *meridarchiai* were divided into *toparchiai*, but Herod introduced various changes.[17] It is possible to reconstruct the list of the Herodian *toparchiai* of Judaea following Josephus and Pliny.[18] New *toparchiai* were added to Judaea-Idumaea in 40 and 30 BCE. Thus, Jerusalem was in the center and to the north were Gophna and Acrabata. To the northwest were Thamna, Lydda, and Joppa; to the west Emmaus and probably Jamnia; to the southwest Bethleptenpha; to the south Idumaea, whose capital was probably Beth-Govrin; to the southeast 'En Gedi and Herodium; and to the east Jericho.[19] Herodium took the place of Hasmonean Bethsur.

Peraea was divided into at least five *toparchiai*: Amathus, Abila, Gadara, Livias, and Machaerus.[20] Galilee was divided into upper and lower Galilee, and, minimally, into four *toparchiai*, Arbela, Tarichaeae, Sepphoris, and perhaps Gabara.[21] We know very little about the administrative division of the other *meridarchiai* and can only speculate. For example, Samaria-Cuthea included the cities of Sebaste, Caesarea Maritima, and the Jewish city of Narbata. But how many *toparchiai* were there in Samaritis? Were those *toparchiai* centered around Sebaste, Caesarea Maritima, and Gabae? This seems quite possible, since the three urban centers were Herodian foundations. It is probable that Gaulanitis was divided into at least two *toparchiai*, the first centered around Gamala, as in the Hasmonean period, the second around Caesareum-Paneas, the best candidate for *metropolis*. Nothing is known of the administrative organization of Batanaea, Trachonitis, or Auranitis.

---

[17] See Stern, "The Reign of Herod", in *The World History of the Jewish People VII, The Herodian Period*, New Brunswick 1975, pp. 92–93.

[18] See Josephus, *BJ* III, 54–55 and Pliny in *NH* V, 14, 70.

[19] Josephus, *BJ* III, 54–55, provides a combined list of the *toparchiai* of Judaea and Idumaea.

Josephus reports as *toparchiai* Jerusalem, Gophna, Acrabata, Thamna, Lydda, Emmaus, Pella, Idumaea, 'En Gedi, Herodium and Jericho. At the end of the list, Josephus mentions Jamnia and Joppa as cities "having jurisdiction over their surrounding districts." Josephus also refers in *AJ* XVII, 31 to Jamnia, given by Herod in his testament to his sister Salome as a *toparchia*. Pliny in *NH* V, 14, 70 also provide a list of Judaean *toparchiai*: Orine, Gophanitica, Acrabatena, Thamnitica, Lydda, Emmaus, Betholethephene, Herodium and Hiericus. To Josephus' list Pliny adds Betholethepene or Bethleptenphta. Iopicas is Joppa and Orine stands for Jerusalem.

[20] Josephus, *BJ* II, 252 mention only Julias, once Herodian Livias, and Abila. Amathus is mentioned in *AJ* XVII, 277, as the site of government buildings, burnt down in the wake of the rebellion that followed Herod's death. In *BJ* IV, 413 Josephus mentions Gadara as the capital of Peraea. Abila is mentioned as Abel one of the cities of the twenty-four *mishmaroth*. Machaerus is not mentioned by Josephus as capital of a *toparchia*, but the archeological remains, similar to those of Herodium, point in that direction.

[21] On Upper and Lower Galilee see Josephus, *BJ* III, 35–43. Josephus, *BJ* II, 252, mentions Tarichaeae and Tiberias. But Tiberias was founded by Antipas. Till then the capital of the *meridarchia* was Sepphoris. Gabara is mentioned by Josephus in *BJ* II, 629 and *Vita* 40, 203 as an important Galilean town. Eusebius, however, mentions it as a *kome* or village. See also Avi-Yona, *Atlas of the Second Temple, Mishnah and Talmud*, pp. 56–57, nos. 83–84.

In conclusion, Herod's administration continued the Hellenistic-Hasmonean local administrative tradition, but differed significantly from the Hellenistic administrative tradition of Coile Syria, which continued to be implemented in the administration of the eastern Roman provinces, and as in the latter, the cities had a far greater importance. In other words, in Herod's kingdom the city had much less importance in the administrative system than in Coile Syria and in the administration of the eastern Roman provinces.

In the Herodian kingdom only Jerusalem could play the role of "autonomous city." Thus, when Rome annexed Judaea in 6 CE, the cities of Caesarea Maritima and Sebaste became autonomous, a status, as noted in Chapter V, not enjoyed under Herodian rule. Under Roman administration, these cities had a clear-cut Greek character. In fact, the Eastern Greek cities were not only centers of the provincial administration, whether senatorial or imperial, or of the imperial cult, but enjoyed relative autonomy. Moreover they were reinforced by the creation of *coloniae* and *municipia* and the foundation of new Greek cities.

2. Taxation and Revenues in the Herodian Kingdom

A. *The Taxation System of Herodian Judaea*

The Hasmoneans and Herod inherited a taxation system that originated in the Land of Israel and Coile Syria during the Ptolemaic and Seleucid periods. There were two types of taxation, direct and indirect. The most important direct taxes collected by the Hellenistic rulers were the *phoros*, or tribute of the soil, paid by the community, and the *epikephalion*, the capitation or poll tax, a tribute that was paid by each individual. Priests were exempted from the poll tax, at least during the Seleucid period. Indirect taxes included the registration tax, mutation duties, a tax on the sale and purchase of goods, customs duties, and toll duties. Taxes were generally collected by a tax farmer.[22]

Although the system of taxation did not change significantly during the Hasmonean and Herodian periods, the percentage rate of taxation and the number of different taxes most certainly did. While the Ptolemies, the Seleucids, and the Romans were powers that dominated Judaea and the Land of Israel from an external vantage point, both the Hasmoneans and Herod dominated its internal taxation system. Thus, although Herod and his Hasmonean predecessors needed

---

[22] On taxation in Ptolemaic Coile Syria see the Sartre, *Alexandre à Zénobie*, pp. 163–164. On Joseph the Tobiad as tax farmer see Josephus, *AJ* XII, 169–184. Modern literature on the subject is immensely vast. On the various types of taxes in the Seleucid kingdom see Sartre, *Alexandre à Zénobie*, pp. 179–180. For the taxes collected in Seleucid Judaea and the various exemptions, see the edict of Antiochus III in Josephus, *AJ* XII, 142–144. See also on the taxation of Coile Syria in the early Hellenistic period, Period Hengel, *Judaism and Hellenism*, pp. 18–23.

to collect taxes, they were also interested in the welfare of their subjects, even if their good intentions frequently clashed with the reality of current affairs. Tax collection under the last Hasmonean rulers was probably similar to that under the Seleucids, albeit with certain differences. According to Schalit, Alexander Jannaeus adopted the efficient Seleucid taxation methods. The Jewish subjects continued to pay the capitation, or head tax, while the priests remained exempt. The Gentiles had to pay both the capitation and the tribute.[23] It seems that the crown tax was never levied by the Hasmonean rulers. Other indirect taxes probably remained as before. What probably changed dramatically with the Hasmoneans was the actual method of tax collection. There appear to have been no tax farmers in the Jewish areas of the kingdom, and so the *komogrammateus*, assisted by seven elected magistrates, collected the taxes. In the Gentile areas, however, it is probable that the king's officials, either tax farmers or tax collectors, were responsible for this. Josephus does not report any complaints from Jewish subjects regarding the Hasmonean rulers' taxation practices.

In contrast to the positive opinions that Josephus expresses with respect to the Hasmoneans, he is very negative regarding Herod's taxation of his subjects.[24] His views, though extremely biased, in my opinion, still influence modern historiography. Pastor, for instance, emphasizes that even according to most modern scholars, the Jews suffered terribly from economic oppression under Herod.[25] King Herod thus came to be known as a ruler who drained the lifeblood of his subjects through high taxation rates. The rival perception is that Herod's policies were no more severe than those of his predecessors. Sanders is a good example of this more cautious view, expressing the belief that Herod's economic policy contributed to prosperity and progress.[26] In contrast, a third group of scholars, exemplified by Gabba and Pastor, has reevaluated Herod's taxation policy, pre-

---

[23] See Schalit, "Domestic Politics and Political Institutions", pp. 267–268. It is probable that the position of the Gentile subjects living in the Hasmonean kingdom was similar or identical to that of the Helots in the Lacedaemonian state.

[24] See Josephus, *AJ* XVII, 154–155.

[25] According to these scholars, this was the result of the concentration of land in the hands of the king. The average Jewish cultivator, a tenant paying excessive rent, a poor freeholder on marginal soil or a landless farm laborer, suffered most from this situation. According to most scholars, exorbitant taxes impoverished the population as lavish spending and grandiose building programs drained the wealth of the people. A good example of a scholar with a negative approach is Klausner. See J. Klausner, "The Economy of Judaea in the Period of the Second Temple", in *The World History of the Jewish People VII, The Herodian Period*, New Brunswick 1972, pp. 180–205. An historian ahead of his time, with a positive vision of Herod's demands, was A. H. M. Jones. See A. H. M. Jones, *The Herods of Judaea*, Oxford 1938, pp. 86–88. See also T. Rajak, *Josephus, The Historian and His Society*, London 2002, p. 122.

[26] Sanders clearly states that the Herodians wished for as much tax revenue as they could get without provoking a revolt. See E. P. Sanders, *The Historical Figure of Jesus*, London 1993, pp. 15–18, 20–22, 27–28, 31–32.

senting it in a more positive light.[27] It seems to me that although Herod's subjects certainly paid relatively high taxes for a short period of time at the beginning of Herod's rule, as we shall see, most of Herod's revenues came from sources other than his own subjects' taxes.

It is therefore important distinguish between two periods during Herod's rule. The first period began in 37 BCE and ended in 31 BCE, when Herod was under the sway of Mark Antony. During this period, Herod was forced to transfer various territories to Cleopatra that were parts of the royal lands that had been important sources of income for him. He also needed to maintain a very strong army. His territory was not extensive, and Gentile subjects who could be taxed constituted a small minority. During this period, tax collection was therefore harsh, and Herod's subjects paid relatively high taxation rates. During the last years of Marcus Antony's rule, the situation appears to have improved considerably. Herod was in dire straits in 37 BCE. He had to pay off Mark Antony and the conquering troops, so he sheared the kingdom's population, including the wealthy. Costobar was given the job of arresting people who owed money to the king. With his funds gone, Herod converted his valuables into cash to pay Mark Antony. Moreover, since it was the Sabbatical Year, the Jews, then the absolute majority of Herod's subjects, had no means to pay taxes. However, in 31 BCE, Josephus wrote that Herod, whose country had been yielding rich crops for a long time, having procured revenues and sources, could enroll an auxiliary force for Mark Antony. This despite the fact that between 37 and 31 BCE, Cleopatra dominated vast resources of the kingdom, including harbors and balsam plantations. Herod had also received a lease from Cleopatra on the collection of the Nabataean tribute. The Ptolemaic queen clearly gave this asset to Herod since she was unable to collect the tribute from these nomadic tribes herself.[28]

The second period began in 31 BCE and continued until Herod's death. After the victory of Octavian in 31 BCE, the situation changed dramatically. The royal lands that were a source of great income were returned to Herod. Octavian added to the kingdom of his *socius* and *amicus* all of the Gentile cities whose territory had once been part of the Hasmonean kingdom. The financial pressure on the Jewish subjects was thereby lightened immediately and significantly. This process continued when Augustus gave Herod more territories. According to both Gabba and Pastor, after 31 BCE Herod did not exploit his kingdom excessively. On two

---

[27] According to Gabba the taxes were collected by brutal methods, unchanged from Iulius Caesar's death. Because of such methods and not the rate of taxation, the population complained to Rome after Herod's death (Josephus, *BJ* II, 4, 86 and *AJ* XVII, 204–205 and 308). See E. Gabba, "The Social and Economic History of Palestine 63 BCE–70 CE", in *Cambridge History of Judaism* III, *The Early Roman Period*, pp. 118–121. For Pastor's view, see J. Pastor, *Land and Economy in Ancient Palestine*, London 1997, p. 98.

[28] See Josephus, *AJ* XV, 5, 107, 109, 264, and *BJ* I, 359. See also Pastor, *Land and Economy*, pp. 105–106.

occasions, in fact, in 20 BCE and 14 BCE, the king remitted the taxes due.[29] Military colonists, such as the Jewish colonists of Batanaea, were totally exempt from any tax,[30] as were the Hellenistic *cleruchs* and Roman colonists.

As mentioned earlier, Herod continued the policy of his Hellenistic and Hasmonean predecessors, levying both direct and indirect taxes from his subjects. Josephus mentions a specific tax only once, the "tribute he [Herod] used to have from the fruits of the ground," clearly the "*phoros*" or tribute.[31] In contrast to the situation during the Hasmonean period, Jews – at least at the beginning of Herod's rule – were required to pay the tribute, which until then had been an obligation solely associated with the Gentile population. It seems to me that in the last years of his rule, Herod, like the Hasmoneans before him, probably exempted the Jews from the payment of the tribute, since the economic situation was stable enough. All of Herod's subjects had to pay the *epikephaleion*, the capitation or poll tax. In the early years of his reign, the rate of the poll tax, like the tribute, was probably much higher than in Herod's later years and was probably reduced after 31 BCE. Like the Seleucids, Herod also levied indirect taxes on sales and purchases, mutation duties, and on certain trades, in particular the transit trade (which was generally in the hands of Greeks and Nabataeans), through excise duties and tolls, customs duties, and toll duties on commercial activities. There were other taxes such as the registration tax, which was paid on all goods before export or import. The *halike*, the tax paid on Dead Sea salt, was also probably levied, though now it was Herod who directly controlled the salt mines along the Dead Sea.

Jews did not pay taxes to the king alone. During the Second Temple period in Judaea, the entire Jewish population – with the exception of those of priestly lineage and less those of Levitical lineage – had to pay special taxes for the maintenance of the Temple and its priests, such as the *terumah*, the *ma'aseroth*, and the annual half-shekel. However, these taxes, which constituted a very small percentage of the annual earnings of the peasantry, are irrelevant in the present context.[32]

---

[29] In 20 BCE Herod remitted a third of the taxes, according to Josephus, to help people recover from years of low yields. See Josephus, *AJ* XV, 365. In 14 BCE Herod once more remitted a third of the previous year's taxes. See Josephus, *AJ* XVI, 65.

[30] See Josephus, *AJ* XVII, 25. See Gabba, "Social, Economic and Political History", pp. 118–121.

[31] See Josephus, *AJ* XV, 303. Josephus clearly mentions a type of tax that was levied directly on the produce of the soil through payment of a proportional or fixed quota. Pastor underlines Josephus' anti-Herod bias. As, according to Pastor, in the Herodian reign the Roman system of taxation was in effect and the Roman tax on the field produce was 12.5 percent, Herod charged the average tax. See Pastor, *Land and Economy*, p. 106.

[32] On the "taxes" paid to the priests and Levites, not relevant here, see m. *Ter., Ma'aŬ.,* and *Ma'aŬ. Š.* See also Schürer, *History of the Jewish People II*, pp. 262–265. See also Josephus, *AJ* IV, 68–73. See Sanders, *Judaism, Practice and Belief*, pp. 147–153.

Pastor, discussing taxation during Herod's reign, highlights two points – that taxation under Herod was no lower or higher than that of the successive Roman administration, and that Herod, at least twice, resorted to punitive taxation of his subjects, which caused resentment.[33] It should be emphasized that punitive taxation cannot in any way be regarded as a permanent source of income. The purpose of such measures was not to collect more money from "exceptional taxation" which, even on a yearly basis constituted a negligible portion of all revenues, but to have potentially rebellious subjects feel the iron hand of the king where it hurt them the most, in their pockets.

I would like to highlight yet a third point, that taxation under Herod was probably directed primarily toward the ruling class, since it would seem that Herod also taxed priests and *bouleutes*, contrary to Seleucid and Hasmonean practice. This might help to explain, at least in part, why Josephus, a priest, had such a negative attitude toward Herod's taxation policies – not because Herod levied taxes that were too high, but because Herod forced the upper classes to pay them. Prior to Herod's reign, the upper classes of Judaea were exempt from most of the taxes. The upper classes in the classical world paid their dues through voluntary *euergetism*. In the early years of his rule, Herod could not tax the severely impoverished, middle, and lower classes of the peasantry too excessively. He therefore began to tax the upper classes, not because of a specific social policy, but out of dire need. It is quite probable that Herod continued to tax the upper class until the end of his reign in order to keep them under economic control and reduce their independence. By then he understood the advantage of taxing those with the means to pay and lightening the burden of those who could not.

It is interesting to note that Josephus does not mention the use of the Hellenistic and Roman practice of tax farmers in connection with Herod or the Hasmoneans. Like the Hasmonean rulers, Herod probably used state functionaries to perform this activity, and these officials probably received a regular salary. Thus the profit of the tax farmers was eliminated from the system. In this way, the population paid a smaller amount, since the pockets of the tax farmers did not have to be lined.

Finally, it is interesting to compare the taxation system of Herod's subjects with the taxation of citizens in classical Athens and Late Republican and Early Imperial Rome. There was an enormous ideological gap between Herodian Judaea and

---

[33] See Pastor, *Land and Economy*, p. 106. Pastor argues that "if Herod's taxation was much lower than Roman taxes there would have been no point in complaining to Augustus, after Herod's death, about the oppressive level of taxation under Herod. Moreover, if the taxes were really much higher than Roman taxes, then the Roman taxation under the provincial administration would have seemed a blessing, and not a cause for complaint." In 37 BCE Herod punished towns in Galilee for renewing the revolt (Josephus, *AJ* XIV, 433 and *BJ* I, 314), and fined the Pharisees, who refused to take an oath of allegiance (Josephus, *AJ* XVII, 42). The former case was an exceptional measure, in the wake of the war against Antigonus. In the latter, the Pharisees did not pay and Pheroras' second wife paid on their behalf. See Pastor, *Land and Economy*, p. 107.

the classical world. The ideal situation in the classical Greek city was that citizens did not have to pay any taxes at all. If a tax needed to be paid, it fell upon the wealthier elements of the society. In either case, whether or not the state imposed taxes, the wealthy elements were supposed to give only a voluntary contribution. In Republican Rome citizens who were owners of property paid taxes and not the proletariat.[34]

It is also important to compare the administration and the taxes in Herodian Judaea with those of Judaea under the procurators and those of other Roman provinces in the East. There are several important differences between Herod's administration and taxation and those of the Roman provincial administration that ensued.[35] In conclusion, it may be stated that in Herodian Judaea all of the social classes paid taxes in one way or another, although the main burden fell upon the ruling class, as it did elsewhere in the classical world. The taxes, as elsewhere in the classical world, were unequally distributed: the ruling class paid a far greater share than did the peasant majority. Under the Seleucids and the Hasmoneans, the priests were probably exempted from paying taxes; Herod, however, did not ignore this important internal source of revenues, which would explain the vicious comments made by our main source, Josephus, who was himself a priest. Moreover, Herod favored his Jewish subjects. Jewish subjects paid only a tribute, while the Gentile subjects probably had to pay both a tribute and a poll tax.

B. *The Income of King Herod*

The income of Herod's kingdom was legendary. Its annual income was probably between 1,050 and 2,000 talents. Sartre points out that only with difficulty was such a fabulous sum of money collected from all of the Roman provinces of Asia Minor during the second century CE. Moreover, it would appear that only about 900 talents were collected from direct taxation of Herod's subjects. We can easily reconstruct the annual tax revenues of the Herodian state. In *Antiquities* Josephus presents what appears to have been the amount of income derived from direct taxes collected by Herod's sons. From Batanaea, Trachonitis, and Auranitis, Philip obtained an annual income of 100 talents. From Peraea and Galilee Antipas obtained an annual income of 200 talents, while from Judaea,

---

[34] On taxation in Classic Athens see S. C. Todd, *The Shape of Athenian Law*, Oxford 1993, pp. 184, 197–198, 239. On *liturgiai* see pp. 120, 184, 197, 305, 328. On taxation in Late Republican and Augustan Rome see W. Eck, *The Age of Augustus*, Oxford 2003, pp. 89–90.

[35] On Roman provincial administration see A. Lintott, *Imperium Romanum, Politics and Administration*, London 1993, pp. 79–80 on the *publicani* and Judaea; pp. 156–157 on the discussion of Roman and Jewish Law in provincial administration. Sartre writes on the taxation of the province of Asia and on the *publicani*'s abuses till Marcus Aurelius. Judaea was not alone. See Sartre, *Asie Mineure et l'Anatolie d'Alexandre à Dioclétien*, pp. 117, 201.

Idumaea, and Samaria, Archelaus received an annual income of 600 talents.[36] Clearly, direct taxation of Herod's subjects played a minimal role in his annual revenues. His revenues were based less on the taxation of his subjects and more on the exploitation of royal lands,[37] protectionist customs duties that in no way damaged his subjects, and various tax-farming contracts in the eastern half of the Roman Empire. These constituted the bulk of the income of Herod's kingdom.

Before reviewing Herod's sources of income in detail, with the exception of taxation, which has been analyzed above, it is important to emphasize once more an important fact. As stated in Chapter I, after 30 BCE Herod, as *socius* and *amicus* of Rome, did not pay any tribute to Rome.[38] Herod's revenues consisted first and foremost of income from the royal lands. The king was the largest owner of fertile lands, some of which were his personal property, but most of which were former royal lands of the Ptolemies, Seleucids, and Hasmoneans, as well as lands confiscated from enemies of the state.[39] Herod thus owned the area in the Esdraelon Valley, where there was a large agricultural output of cereal.[40] The royal gardens of Jericho and 'En Gedi produced balsam. These were rented for 200 talents a year to Cleopatra,[41] and were clearly of greater value than the sum of the annual rent. As previously stated, during the first years of his rule Herod collected tribute from the Nabataeans and continued to do so after his victory in the war against them in 32–31 BCE. There is no reason to suppose that this tribute ceased with the Second Nabataean War in 9 BCE. Moreover, since Herod then dominated Gaza, the key station of the Spice Route, after 31 BCE the Nabataeans probably had to pay enormous sums to the Herodian customs officials in order to sell their spices to the rest of the *oikoumene*. These were not the only revenues

---

[36] See also Gabba, "Social, Economic and Political History of Palestine", p. 118. See also Sartre, *Asie Mineure et Anatolie d'Alexandre à Dioclétien*, p. 202. See Josephus, *AJ* XVII, 318–320. In *BJ* II, 94–98 the income from Archelaus is slightly inferior, 400 talents. The disproportion between the income from Philip's or Antipas' territories and those of Archelaus is probably due to the fact that Judaea's lands were more heavily exploited. Josephus does not include indirect taxes such as customs duties from Caesarea Maritima, nor the income from royal lands. Further information useful in estimating Herod's wealth: in his testament he bequeathed 1,550 talents to his sister, Augustus and others. In comparison, to achieve senatorial rank in Rome one needed a "mere" 1,000,000 *sestertii* – 50 talents. See Pastor, *Land and Economy*, pp. 105–109.

[37] See Josephus, *AJ* XVII, 221–2 and 253 and *BJ* II, 16–18, 41. See also Gabba, "Social, Economic and Political History of Palestine", p. 118.

[38] See Gabba, "Social, Economic and Political History of Palestine", p. 121.

[39] For the confiscation see Josephus, *AJ* XV, 5 and XVII 305–307.

[40] See Josephus, *AJ* XVI, 207 and *Vita* 119.

[41] See Josephus, *AJ* XV, 96, 106 and 132 and *BJ* I, 361–362. Herod was in an unfavorable position vis-à-vis Cleopatra's whims. The balsam plantations were worth much more than the sum Herod received from Cleopatra for the lease. According to Pliny, *NH* XII, 118, the cuttings and shoots of the balsam alone were worth 800,000 *sestertii* – 30 talents. See Pastor, *Land and Economy*, p. 108.

from the Nabataeans, since Herod also lent money at interest to Obadas[42] and rented grazing lands to the Nabataeans.[43] After Herod's diplomatic victory in the Second Nabataean War, the Nabataeans probably hurried to pay the loan and the interest, as well as the arrears in rent on grazing lands.

Herod levied customs duties not only at Gaza, but also at Joppa, Caesarea Maritima, and Jamnia. Pastor proposes a 2% custom rate, using as examples classical Athens and the Roman province of Asia.[44] Obviously Caesarea Maritima's harbor was a major source of income, being one of the largest harbors in the East after Alexandria.[45] Gabba emphasizes that Herod also obtained various contracts for land revenues from the Roman government. The Roman government also leased Phasaelis in Lycia-Pamphylia and some cities of Cilicia and Batanaea to Herod for revenues, before Augustus ceded it to Herod. In these areas Herod probably collected *vectigalia*, or indirect taxes, and *stipendia*, or direct taxes. In 20 BCE Augustus either designated Herod *epitropos* of all of Syria or associated Herod with the procurator of Syria for the purpose of tax collecting. According to Gabba, this meant that Herod had a huge tax collecting-farming contract in Roman Syria. Herod also paid Augustus 300 talents for half of the output of the copper mines in eastern Cyprus, and Augustus entrusted Herod with the management of the other half.[46] The revenues from Cyprus, one of the richer copper-producing regions of the eastern Mediterranean, must have been much larger.

C. Herod's Social Program

Herod more than once remitted the taxes to the Jewish population in years of drought, thereby providing them with significant relief. This action did not follow any Hellenistic precedent of *euergetism*, but rather Augustus' *annona*'s policy in Rome. Moreover, like the Roman emperors from Augustus and on-

---

[42] According to Josephus, Obadas avoided repaying 60 talents as interest on a loan of 500 talents. Moreover, the Nabataean king did not hurry to pay back the latter sum. See Josephus, *AJ* XVI, 279 and 343. See also Pastor, *Land and Economy*, p. 108.

[43] Josephus reports that the Nabataeans did not pay for the grazing lands that they rented and used. See Josephus, *AJ* XVI, 291. See also Pastor, *Land and Economy*, p. 108.

[44] In classical Athens, the customs duties were indeed 2%. In the province of Asia between the first century BCE and first century CE the rate was 2.5% on both imports and exports. See Pastor, *Land and Economy*, p. 107.

[45] As examples Pastor gives Rhodes. Before 170 BCE Rhodes brought in 1,000,000 drachmas from harbor duties. After 170 BCE and the creation of Delos, it brought in only 150,000 drachmas per year. (10,000 drachmas correspond to 1 talent). See Polybius, *History* XXX, 31, 10–12. Another example: Hyrcanus paid 6 talents (20,675 *modii*) at Joppa for harbor duties. This once more shows how much money can be raised by a customs office. See Pastor, *Land and Economy*, p. 107.

[46] See Josephus, *AJ* XV, 360 and XVI, 128 and *BJ* I, 399, 428. See also Gabba, "Social, Economic and Political History of Palestine", pp. 118–121.

wards, Herod not only demonstrated much concern for his subjects in cases of famine, but acted to prevent hunger. Josephus reports that during the famine of 25–24 BCE,[47] Herod directly asked Petronius, *praefectus* of Egypt and then the main provider of wheat to the city of Rome, for food to alleviate the famine. Petronius complied and Herod was able to relieve the famine with a huge quantity of imported wheat.[48] This action could not have been taken without the agreement of Augustus, since Egypt was his private domain. Moreover, Augustus needed Egypt's grain no less than Herod did, since famine was also an occurrence in Rome, where it could seriously endanger the ruler's stability. In 28 BCE Augustus quadrupled the allowance of grain to Rome's population.[49] Herod needed to be rather forceful on behalf of his subjects in this unprecedented act, asking the Roman ruler for wheat that was also needed in Rome, for the welfare of Augustus' own subjects. This probably earned Herod the well-deserved title *euergetes*.[50] Herod then, according to Josephus, had the Egyptian grain distributed to the strong, and provided bakers to bake bread for the weak. He also distributed clothes to the needy. Although, according to Pastor, such behavior was typical of Hellenistic rulers who, as *euergetes*, helped their subjects in times of need, Herod probably imitated Augustus, who acted in typical Roman, rather than Hellenistic, fashion.[51]

Did Herod have also a well-defined economic or social program? According to Pastor, Herod's policies were initiatives in a few practical areas and not true innovations. Therefore, according to Pastor, Herod thus followed Hellenistic as well as Hasmonean tradition. Herod's policy of granting estates to loyal subjects or founding military colonies continued a Hellenistic tradition. Moreover, Herod's colonies provided a solution for the landless population that had been expelled by Pompey's settlers. Through a rational use of his administrative system, Herod maximized his political and social power, incidentally providing solutions to some of the economic and social ills of Judaean society.[52] In contrast to Pastor, I feel that Herod probably had a long-range, far-reaching social program in mind which, though not revolutionary, provided work and income for his Jewish subjects, many of whom had been ruined and impoverished after years of civil

---

[47] See Josephus, *AJ* XV, 299–316.
[48] Josephus, *AJ* XV, 314 claims that 80,000 kor were distributed to the inhabitants of the kingdom, and 10,000 more to people outside the kingdom. According to Pastor, Herod brought 33,550,000–41,850,000 liters of grain or 28,000–33,000 tons of wheat from Egypt, 180 to 220 shiploads. That the quantity imported by Herod was considerable is clear in comparison to the 135,000 annual tons of grain imported from Egypt to Rome. See Pastor, *Land and Economy*, p. 122.
[49] See Dio, *Roman History* LIII, 2, 1–2.
[50] This title is found on a stone weight dated to Herod's thirty-second year of rule (8 BCE). See Y. Meshorer, "A Stone Weight from the Reign of Herod", *IEJ* 20, 1970, p. 97.
[51] On the famine, see Pastor, *Land and Economy*, pp. 115–127.
[52] See Pastor, *Land and Economy*, p. 98.

wars. This program consisted of the creation of military colonies and the erection of public buildings everywhere in the kingdom, but mainly in Jerusalem. The result of this social program was a process of urbanization. Herod was no revolutionary. As an ally of Rome, Herod did not distribute confiscated lands to those in need, but instead, annexed them to his own estates. He thus needed to find other methods to subsidize and assist the population of his kingdom. As such, Herod settled many of the ruined peasantry in military colonies, on lands that were part of his royal estates. The massive building activity of King Herod is dated between 25 BCE and the last years of his rule, around 8 BCE, and at least 50,000 people worked on his building projects.[53] These workers were not slaves, but free citizens, as was common in classical Greece and in the Hellenistic world. Zissu clearly shows that at the end of the first century BCE there was a clear improvement in the economic condition of the villages in rural Judaea after some fifty years of neglect and decline. The beginning of the decline is explained by the beginning of the civil wars that followed years of growth under the Hasmoneans. The renewed growth can be explained by the fact that the workers involved in Herodian building projects, after the cessation of most of the state-sponsored building activities, returned to the countryside, purchasing back from the state or from individuals properties that they had lost during the civil war, or purchasing new properties. This also explains the growth of Jerusalem during the first half of the first century CE.

According to Geiger, Herod's social policies emulated Augustus' own social program in Rome.[54] Thus it seems to me that, in contrast to Rome and the Greek cities, Herod assisted the lower classes not only in a passive way, with distribution of food as in Greece and Rome, but also actively, like Augustus. The foundation of military colonies was well known in the classical state as a way to assist impoverished citizens. Thus Herod did not create anything new in this context, but, like Augustus, his building program enabled the poorest citizens to obtain work – and thus money – from the king and hence from the state. The Herodian state took care of the poorest elements of society, gave them paid work and, later, the possibility of owning land.

---

[53] Josephus wrote that there were 18,000 left without work in 64 CE. See Gabba, "Social, Economic and Political History of Palestine", pp. 118–121. See also Pastor, *Land and Economy*, pp. 113–115. That means that during Herod's reign there were at least 50,000 working in his building projects.

[54] See J. Geiger, "Rome and Jerusalem: Public Building and the Economy", in D. Jacobson and N. Kokkinos (orgs.), *Herod and Augustus International Conference – 21st, 22nd & 23rd June 2005*, The Institute of Jewish Studies, University College London 2005. According to Brunt, Augustus not only gave grain doles to the indigent free population of Rome, but also provided public employment in his building projects. Brunt stresses that free labor was much cheaper than slave labor. Thus, slaves were the main manpower in mines and in the countryside, where non-professional labor could be utilized, but not in building projects, where specialized labor was needed. See Suetonius, *Augustus* 40, 2 on doles. See P. A. Brunt, "Free Labor and Public Works at Rome", *JRS* LXX 1980, pp. 81–100. Brunt's main source is Suetonius, *Vespasianus* 18.

Herod's social program, directed towards the poorest elements of society, is critical to an understanding of the role of slavery in the Herodian economy. Slavery certainly existed in Herodian Judaea, and although it was an everyday reality in Late Second Temple Judaea, as well as in late Republican and early Imperial Rome, it seems that slavery had a much more minor role in Judaea's economy that in that of Rome.[55] In fact, it is possible to say that slavery was not an important component of the labor force. The presence of slaves was thus felt much less in Herodian Judaea than in Augustan Italy. But then slavery was less common in the Greek East as a whole than in the Latin West. Asia Minor is a good example.[56]

3. The Division of the Land in the Herodian Kingdom

A. Royal Land and Royal Estates

The lands of the Herodian kingdom can be roughly divided into two types: royal land, or *basilike ge*, and private land. Private land, situated mainly in the Jewish areas of the kingdom, belonged to priests,[57] secular aristocrats, and small freeholders. The aristocracy and the gentry lived in manors, while freeholders were concentrated in villages.

There are various sources, such as Josephus, Talmudic literature, and contemporary and later inscriptions, in addition to archaeological surveys and excavations, which enable us to establish the extent of King Herod's royal estates. Some of these royal estates had previously formed part of the royal domain of the Ptolemies, Seleucids, and the Hasmoneans. After Herod's death they either passed to his heirs, until the time of Agrippa II, and then, or perhaps already at Herod's death, to the imperial domains or *saltus*. The royal land spread over vast estates throughout the country and came from various sources, including Herod's personal inheritance, such as the lands around Marissa. In fact, the majority of Herod's estates came from his personal inheritance, such as his father Antipater's property, probably around Marissa, and the inheritance or

---

[55] Slave economy was in fact a much important facet of the economy of Roman Italy in the period considered, and it is emblematic of the Roman World. On slavery at Rome see K. Bradley, *Slavery and Society at Rome, Key Themes in Ancient History*, Cambridge 1994. See also on Roman slavery K. Hopkins, *Conquerors and Slaves: Sociological Studies in Roman History* I, Cambridge 1978. For a collection of primary sources on Graeco and Roman slavery see T. Wiedemann, *Greek and Roman Slavery*, Baltimore 1981. On buildings and artifacts connected to slavery see F. H. Thomson, *Archaeology of Greek and Roman Slavery*, London 2003.

[56] See Sartre, *Asie Mineure et l'Anatolie d'Alexandre à Dioclétien*, pp. 92, 205–206, 261, and 283–284.

[57] Priests owned land in Judaea and in Galilee. That was not exceptional in the Hellenistic east. In Ptolemaic Egypt, the Egyptian temples and their priests were the owners of considerable tracts of land. See M. Chaveau, *L'Egypte au temps de Cléopâtre - 180-30 av. J.-C., La Vie Quotidienne*, Paris 1997, pp. 151-153.

dowry of his wife Mariamme, as well as estates that he acquired prior to his rise to power.[58] Another source included Herod's personal properties, comprising portions of the Jordan Valley, such as Phasaelis and 'En Boqeq; the surroundings of Antipatris; various estates in Peraea; and lands in Galilee, such as Gabae[59]. No less important were the royal lands of Herod's predecessors, the Hasmoneans, as well as the Seleucids and the Ptolemies. These properties consisted of Akkaron, Gazara, Har ha-Melech, Jericho, and 'En Gedi in Judaea, as well as the Esdraelon Valley in Galilee.[60] Herod also owned vast tracts of land in the Gentile areas of the kingdom. Thus, after Augustus bestowed territories upon Herod in 31 BCE, Herod probably expropriated vast properties for himself in these Gentile areas, probably around the Gentile cities of Gaza, Anthedon, Straton's Tower, Samaria, Gadara and Hippos and the rest of the Decapolis, as well as Joppa. Herod probably made all the *chora* of the Gentile cities royal domains.[61] Last but not least,

---

[58] On Herod's grandfather fortune see Josephus, *AJ* XIV, 8, 10. Antipater distributed Herod's grandfather's property to Herod's brothers as well. Thus, Herod's brother Pheroras enjoyed an income of no less than 100 talents from his private possessions. See Josephus, *BJ* I, 483. Schalit proposed that Marissa was Antipater's property. This explains why the Parthians sacked it in 40 BCE. See Schalit, *König Herodes,* pp. 257–258, n. 382. This property provided his father Antipater with rental income. See Josephus, *AJ* XIV, 372, and *BJ* I, 276. Josephus also writes that before 40 BCE Antipater and his sons, probably as high officials of the Hasmonean state, received revenues from Judaea from Hyrcanus II. See Josephus, *AJ* XIV, 163. Regarding the dowry of Mariamme, women in Second Temple period could inherit land, as shown in the Book of Judith. Mariamme was probably given landed property as a dowry by her grandfather, Hyrcanus II. See Pastor, *Land and Economy,* pp. 99–100.

[59] On Phasaelis see Josephus, *AJ* XVI, 145, and *BJ* I, 418 and II, 167. On 'En Boqeq see M. Gichon, "En Boqeq", *NEAEHL* 2, pp. 395–396. On Antipatris see Josephus, *AJ*, XVI, 142–143. On Peraea see Josephus, *AJ* XVII, 277 and *BJ* II, 57, 59. On Gabae see Josephus, *AJ* XV, 294 and *BJ* III, 36. Josephus called the land *"chorion"* meaning a royal estate according to Z. Safrai and M. Lin, "Geva in the Hasmonean Period", *Cathedra* 69, 1993, p. 25.

[60] Josephus states that the lands in the Land of Israel owned by the Hasmoneans were leased to Jewish colonists (Josephus, *AJ* XIII, 273). In Judaea, on the Akkaron region see I Macc 10: 88–9 and B. Bar Kochva, "Manpower, Economics, and Internal Strife in the Hasmonean State", in H. Van Effentere (ed.), *Armées et fiscalité dans le monde antique, Colloque National du CNRS No. 936,* Paris 1977, pp. 167–195. It seems that the Akkaron region included Jamnia; see I Macc. 12: 8–9. On 'En Gedi see Josephus, *AJ* XV, 96, 106 and 132 and *BJ* I, 361–362. On Gazara see I Macc. 14: 7 and the Pampras inscription published in CIJ I, p. 225 nos. 1, 183, 1, 184. Har ha-Melech was originally a Hasmonean domain, see Siphri Deut X, 41, 85. This royal domain became part of the imperial domains after 70 CE; see Josephus, *BJ* VII, 216–217. An imperial superintendent resided at Lydda in the first half of second century CE. On the estates of Jericho see Netzer's publications on the Hasmonean and Herodian palaces built on the palm-date estates as E. Netzer, *Hasmonean and Herodian Palaces at Jericho 1-2, Final Reports of the 1973-1987 Excavations,* Jerusalem 2001–2004. See also Horace, *Epist.* II, 184. On 'En Gedi, a royal estate since Hasmonean times, see Josephus, *AJ* XV, 96, 106 and 132 and *BJ* I, 361–362. See also N. Lewis, *The Documents from the Bar-Kochba Period in the Cave of Letters Vol. 2, Greek Papyri,* Jerusalem 1989, p. 42. On the Esdraelon Valley see Josephus, *AJ* XVI, 207 and *Vita* 119.

[61] See Josephus, *AJ* XV, 217 and *BJ* I, 396. Herod probably had royal domains at Samaria see Josephus, *AJ* XV, 296 and *BJ* I, 403. See also Barag, "King Herod's Royal Castle at Samaria-Sebaste", pp. 3–18.

3. The Division of the Land in the Herodian Kingdom

Herod owned the lands granted to him by Augustus in the northern territories of Batanaea, Gaulanitis, Trachonitis, and Ituraea.[62] In addition, Herod may have annexed various properties to the crown in the years 40–37 BCE, properties deriving mainly from lands confiscated from Antigonus' supporters, who were Herod's political enemies.[63]

Most of the royal land was exploited directly by the crown.[64] Royal lands were also given, temporarily or permanently, as gifts to certain individuals and groups. Herod, for instance, gave lands to his courtiers, such as Ptolemy, to urban settlements that he founded on his own land, and to military colonists.[65]

Most scholars presume that the best lands of the Jewish areas of settlement became royal land. Some of these were given as gift land. Applebaum suggests that Greek civil servants, administrators, and soldiers were rewarded with properties farmed by Jewish tenants. Pastor argues that there is no evidence for Gentile settlements in Jewish areas, through there is evidence for the opposite situation.[66] Moreover these lands were probably gift lands that they had received from the Hasmoneans. Thus no Jewish farmer suffered as a result of Herod's confiscations, and, moreover, Herod's gift lands and colonies were situated outside the Jewish areas.

The division of the land in the Herodian kingdom recalls that of Hellenistic Asia Minor and Syria. There, as in Herodian Judaea, most of the land was royal land, which was worked by peasants. Moreover, part of this land was also given

---

[62] It seems that the Herodian domains in Batanaea, which passed to Agrippa II, later became imperial domains or *saltus*. This inference may be reconstructed from various inscriptions, see J. P. Rey-Coquais, "Une inscription du Liban-Nord", *MUSJ* 47, 1972, pp. 96–97 and J. P. Rey-Coquais, "Syrie Romaine de Pompée à Dioclétien", *JRS* 68, 1978, pp. 44–73. For a second inscription, see M. Sartre, "Les metrokomiai de Syrie du Sud", *Syria* 76, 1999, pp. 197–222. According to Sartre, *metrokomiai* indicates the presence of the imperial *saltus*. See also a Latin inscription in *IGLS* XIV, 565. Also see the Byzantine writer, George of Cyprus, 1076, edited by H. Gelzer, Leipzig 1890, who mentions a *Saltus Bataneus*. Talmudic literature (TJ, *Šeb.* VI, 1) mentions that Yehuda ha-Nasi was given lands in the Auranitis by Caracalla. Later, Herod granted part of these lands to colonists, Idumaeans and Zamaris.

[63] In 37 BCE, after the conquest of Jerusalem, Herod confiscated the estates of forty-five opponents, supporters of Antigonus and probably priests. And yet Josephus does not mention that explicitly. See Josephus, *AJ* XV, 5–7. Herod, however, most certainly confiscated estates of his enemies. See Josephus, *AJ* XV, 5 and XVII, 307. See Pastor, *Land and Economy*, p. 100.

[64] The best example is the Jordan Valley estate. Other royal estates existed in the Golan, the Jezreel and the Sharon Valleys, the Shephela and the Samaritan and Judaean Mountains. See Josephus, *AJ* XV, 96, 106 and 132 and *BJ* I, 361–362. See Pastor, *Land and Economy*, p. 108. See also S. Dar, "The Agrarian Economy in the Herodian Period", *The World of the Herods and the Nabataeans, An International Conference at the British Museum*, London 2001, pp. 17–18.

[65] Thus, Ptolemy, Herod's senior minister, was given an estate in Samaria (not in a Jewish region), that Dar identifies with Aris. See Josephus, *AJ* XVII, 289 and *BJ* II, 69. See S. Dar, "The Estate of Ptolemy, Senior Minister of Herod", in M. Stern (ed.), *Jews and Judaism in Second Temple, Mishna, and Talmud Period*, Jerusalem 1993, pp. 38–50.

[66] Pastor gives Gabae as an example. See Pastor, *Land and Economy*, pp. 101–103.

to officials as gifts, and there were domains which belonged to sanctuaries.[67] However, the main difference between the Herodian kingdom and the Hellenistic monarchies, as well as the Roman Republic and early Empire, was land ownership by cities. In the Graeco-Roman world each city, whether *polis*, *municipium*, or *colonia*, owned its own hinterland, the *chora*. In the Herodian kingdom, with the exception of Jerusalem, it appears that no city owned the *chora*.

B. Private Owned Lands

It is difficult to generalize concerning private lands throughout the Herodian kingdom. Privately owned lands fell into two categories, the first populated by small, freehold farmers who tilled family lands and lived mostly in villages in Judaea and Galilee, while the second included manor estates. What was the percentage of each class? Ancient sources are very problematic for this period. The New Testament is filled with examples of a few rich landowners and many poor people, tenants of the former who were not even freeholders. On the other hand, the Mishna deals with religious obligations, such as the bringing of the first fruits to the Temple, an obligation that can be fulfilled only by a freeholder. Both sources, however, probably reflect a much later situation: the New Testament probably reflected the situation during the last years of the Roman procurators, when the economic situation worsened, while the Mishna probably reflected a theoretical, ideal situation. The situation in the Gentile areas remains unclear. Were there privately owned lands in the Gentile areas? Archaeological data can be useful in enabling us to obtain a more precise picture of the situation. Surveys conduced in Judaea, for example, as well the archaeological excavations of village dwellings and various manors, can be very helpful. Still, it is difficult to determine what the exact situation of the peasants, freeholders, and tenants was, as well as the probable situation of the manor owners during the Herodian period proper. It seems that although at the outset of the Herodian period the situation was quite difficult, towards the end of the Herodian period there was a certain amount of prosperity that continued well into the First Century CE. Thus the economic situation of the peasants reflects the evolution of taxation, which has been analyzed above, as well as the efficacy and consequences of Herod's social programs.

i. The Village

There were villages that were part of the royal estates, and villages that were surrounded by privately owned lands. Jewish peasants – freeholders as well as

---

[67] On Asia Minor see Sartre, *Asie Mineure et Anatolie d'Alexandre à Dioclétien*, pp. 84–85, 90–91, 92–93, 275–283. On Syria see Sartre, *Alexandre à Zénobie*, pp. 204–213, 736–750.

3. The Division of the Land in the Herodian Kingdom

tenants – lived in various types of settlements, along the periphery of cities, in villages, and in smaller settlements between them. Both Josephus and the New Testament distinguish between a city (*polis*)[68] and a village (*kome*). Josephus also mentions the *polichnion*, a settlement somewhere between a village and a city in size and institutions.[69] The Mishna, on the other hand, draws the distinction between *kerach*, *ir*, and *kefar*.[70] The large Gentile or mixed Jewish-Gentile cities are referred to as *kerachim*. These controlled large localities, known as *ayaroth*,[71] with organized community services, as noted in Talmudic literature.[72] These *ayaroth* can, in turn, be identified as district capitals of *toparchiai*.[73] The *kome* or *kefar* was the standard, most widespread form of settlement.[74] In archaeological contexts, Jewish settlements present certain specific characteristics – the presence of *mikwaoth*, stone vessels, and synagogues – and outside these settlements burial sites with ossuaries have been found, dating from the very end of the Herodian period or slightly later.[75] The villages occupied an area of 1–1.5 hectares. The

---

[68] Safrai, for the period after 135 CE, divides the *poleis* of Roman Palaestina into *metropolis* or capital of a province, major cities, and smaller cities. See Z. Safrai, *The Economy of Roman Palestine*, London 1994, p. 18.

[69] Thus, 'En Gedi, a chief of *toparchia*, is referred to by Josephus once as a *polis* and once as a *polichnion*. In *Mark* 1: 38, a legal term is utilized to denote extended urban settlements with the legal status of a village, *komopolis*, perhaps equivalent to *polichnion*.

[70] See m. *Meg.* 1: 1, 2: 3; m. *Ketub.*13: 10; m. *Qidd.* 2: 3; m. *B. Meṣiʿa* 4: 6, 8: 6; m. ʿ*Arak.* 6: 5, 9: 3; and m. *Kelim* 1: 7.

[71] Safrai suggests a much similar hierarchy of settlements for the period after 135 CE. Following the Mishna, Safrai, for the period after 135 CE, divides the towns of the Galilee and the Golan into large towns or capitals of an area, "medium size towns", or large villages or local centers, and "small towns", or small village towns. In Hebrew the town is called *ir*, in Aramaic *kiriah*. The population and size of the town are not fixed. Josephus in *BJ* III, 43 writes that in Galilee every village had at least 15,000 inhabitants. Moreover, according to the Talmud, BT, *Taʿan.* 21 a large city had the capacity to send forth 1,500 men of military age, while a small town could send 500. See Safrai, *Economy of Roman Palestine*, pp. 18–19, 39, 41–42.

[72] See TB, *Sanh.* 17 b.

[73] Bethar, Gophna, Thamna, Acrabata, Emmaus, Bethleptenpha, Herodium, Lydda, and perhaps 'En Gedi are good examples.

[74] Another form of village were fortified settlements built on earlier cities such as Tel ʿAzeqa, Tel Gezer, Tel ʿIra, Tel ʿAroʿer, Tel Shilo, Horvath Jibʾit, Khirbet el-Khafira, Horvath Turas, Khirbet el-'Aqed, Sokho, Bethar, Tibneh, Khirbet Abu Shawam, and Tel ʿArad. The Mishna differentiates between a city whose roofs form its walls, such as the settlements described above, and walled cities from the time of Joshua Ben Nun. See m. ʿ*Arak.* 9: 3 and m. *Kelim* 1: 7. See also B. Zissu, *Rural Settlements in the Judaean Hills and Foothills From the Late Second Temple Period to the Bar Kokhba Revolt*, Thesis submitted for the Degree "Doctor of Philosophy," The Hebrew University, Jerusalem.

[75] *Mikwaoth* were used from the Hasmonean period, onward (see TB, *Šabb.* 13 a). In Jewish settlements, one to seven ritual baths have been found per village. There were also ritual baths outside settlements, near roads, perhaps for the use of Jewish pilgrims, near olive and winepresses so that wine and oil could be produced in purity, and near cemeteries. The stone vessels found in the survey consist of tableware (bowls and cups) and storage vessels. Public buildings present in Jewish rural settlements, have been found at Kiriath Sefer, Horvath 'Ethri, and Khirbet Umm el-'Amdan. Ossuaries appear slightly

construction was well planned; the exterior walls of the buildings, as in the early First Temple period Israelite settlements, formed a continuous line that resembled a defensive wall. At the center of the village was a public area, sometimes containing a rock-cut ritual bath and cisterns. Residential quarters, or *insulae*, were built around inner courtyards that were closed to the outside,[76] and ritual baths and cisterns were hewn inside them. Alleys separated houses. Kiriath Sefer (cfr. figure IV, 1), Horbath 'Ethri, and Khirbet Umm el-'Amdan had a central public building, a *bouleterion*-synagogue. Construction was modest and rural in style, based on local materials, particularly unhewn stones. The floors were made of compressed earth or dressed stones. Industrial facilities such as olive presses, storage caves, and cisterns were sometimes carved into the bedrock. Burials took place outside the village in family caves containing a room with shelves and *kochim*, and were used for both primary and secondary burial.

The archaeological survey by Zissu of various areas of Judaea can be helpful in illustrating the situation of Herodian Judaea.[77] The villages surveyed have a similar "life story." All were founded in the Late Achaemenid and Early Hellenistic, Ptolemaic period. There was energetic construction, a good indicator of economic growth, during the Hasmonean period, followed by stagnation during the years of civil war and the early Herodian period. This was followed by a marked increase in the size of the villages, a sign of prosperity, during the last years of Herod's rule and the early years of Roman rule, in the first half of the first century CE. The settlements were damaged during the Great Revolt and were destroyed during the Bar Kochba War. According to Zissu, the survey cannot provide us with any information on the percentage of small freeholders versus

---

later than most of the period considered, at the end of the Herodian period at the beginning of the late first century BCE. Until then, sarcophagi in stone, such as those found in Jerusalem, and in wood, such as those found at 'En Gedi, were used through the Hasmonean and most of the Herodian period. See Zissu, *Rural Settlements in the Judaean Hills and Foothills*.

[76] According to Safrai there are two types of villages after 135 CE in Galilee and in the Golan. The first group includes villages composed of a small number of private houses and the second group includes the *ir* or "Roman villa," usually a house or a number of houses belonging to a wealthy landowner. The village is a settlement of less than 10 dunams, with 80–100 families. The Talmudic village, like the Late Second Temple period village, was characterized by the presence of a synagogue and *mikwaoth*. See Safrai, *Economy of Roman Palestine*, pp. 64–66.

[77] See Zissu, *Rural Settlements in the Judaean Hills and Foothills*. The region analyzed is the area of Hadom ha-Shomron, or the Footstool of the Samarian hills, pp. 17–25; northeastern Benjamin and the hill country of Ephraim, pp. 26–37; the Modi'in area and western Benjamin, pp. 38–50; central Benjamin, pp. 51–76; the Jerusalem area, pp. 77–102; the northern Hebron hills, pp. 103–128; the southern Hebron hills pp. 129–140; the northern Judaean Shephela pp. 141–150; the central Judaean Shephela, pp. 158–185; the southern Judaean Shephela, pp. 158–185; and the Beersheba and Arad valleys, pp. 220–228. The corpus includes approximately 320 sites. The data for the whole of Judaea reported by Dio Cassius, *Historia Romana* LXIX, 14: 1, indicates that there were in Judaea proper around 50 fortresses and 985 Jewish villages, destroyed during the Bar Kochba revolt, confirms Zissu's data collected in the survey. The Jewish settlements are identified as such on the basis of the presence of ritual baths, stone vessels, ossuaries, and in some settlements, a public building or synagogue.

3. The Division of the Land in the Herodian Kingdom

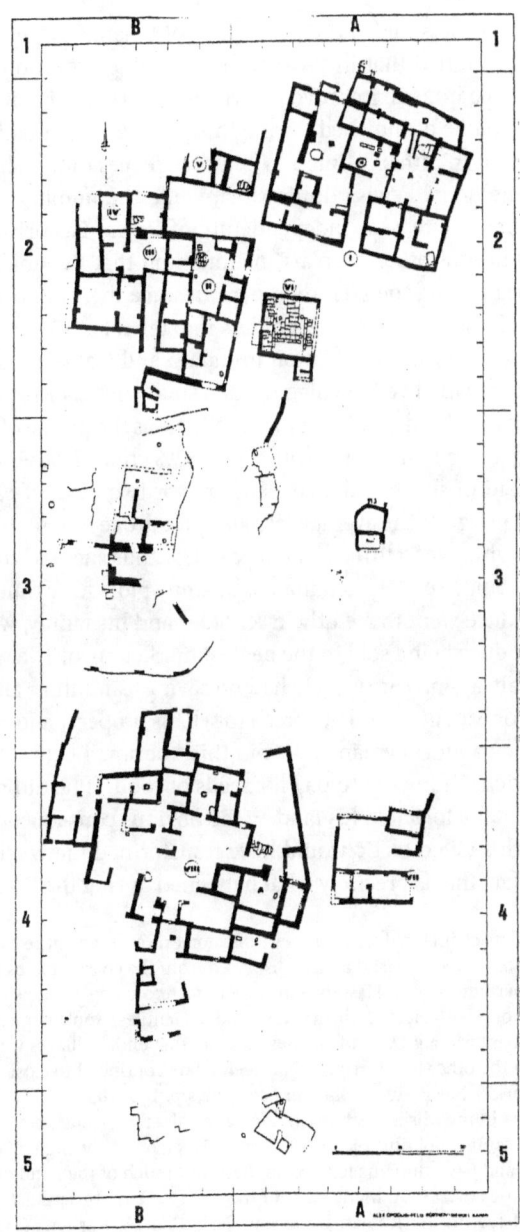

Figure IV, 1 – Plan of the Village of Kiryat Sefer from Y., Magen, Y., Zionit, and E., Sirkis, "A Jewish Village and Synagogue of the Second Temple Period", *Qadmoniot* XXXII, 1 (117) 1999, p. 26, in B. Zissu, *Rural Settlements in the Judaean Hills and Foothills From the Late Second Temple Period to the Bar Kokhba Revolt*, Thesis submitted for the Degree "Doctor of Philosophy", The Hebrew University, Jerusalem, 2001 (Hebrew), fig. 14. Courtesy of Dr. B. Zissu.

wealthier manor owners, or on the percentage of tenants and hired laborers. It may, however, be argued that in prosperous times the position of freeholders, who lived in village houses, improved as villages increased in size. Conversely, the number of tenants diminished during this period. This situation appears to have been reversed in difficult times. When the villages diminished in size, the number of freeholders likewise diminished, while the number of tenants and evicted freeholders increased. Independently of Zissu, Pastor likewise argues against the position of other scholars, maintaining that freeholders continued to exist in Judaea during the Herodian period, since there is no written source indicating that Herod converted freeholders into tenants.[78]

The majority of the rural population in Judaea and Galilee was composed of small freeholders,[79] who lived in villages, often small towns surrounded by fields, vegetable gardens, orchards, and vineyards. What was the profile of the ideal freeholder? Dar suggests a family farm with about 52% grain, 22% vines, 25% olives, ten to fifteen head of sheep and goats, and one or two head of cattle. Later, he believes, the small size of the average farmer's plot drove him to develop intensified agriculture with two to three yields a year. Dar thus suggests that the average family holding comprised 39–45 dunams.[80] Family plots were thus quite small.[81] Most of the produce went to feed the freeholder and his family, with only small quantities of produce being sold in the nearest market town. The situation of the freeholder was always precarious. He had no savings, and thus, after a short period of draught or war, he would be forced to sell his property and work as a hired laborer or even as a journeyman. To avoid this, the small landholder borrowed money from a rich landowner to pay for seeds or food. If he did not succeed in repaying the debt, he forfeited his land.[82] The obvious consequence is that, over the long term, this failed tactic would have transformed many freeholders into tenants, and in fact that is precisely what happened during the Roman period, in

---

[78] Various scholars claim that from Pompey's division onwards, an entire class of Jewish tenants was created. These were Jewish farmers displaced from the coastal plains and Transjordan after the dismemberment of the Hasmonean kingdom. According to the same scholars, the situation became worse with Herod, who granted land to Gentiles. Applebaum argues that in the first century BCE there was a growth of large estates and that entire villages were assimilated in tenancy. Pastor, on the other hand, argues that freeholders continued to exist in Judaea proper in the Herodian period. See Pastor, *Land and Economy*, pp. 103–105.

[79] The term used in the Mishna is householder, equivalent to *oikodespotes* in the Gospels.

[80] The average family holding of 39–45 dunam is surprisingly high if compared to 40 dunams for Attica and 5–25 dunams for Roman Italy. But much of the Land of Israel was drier than Attica, and Attica drier than many parts of Italy. See S. Dar, "Agriculture and Agricultural Produce in Eretz-Israel in the Roman-Byzantine Period", in A. Kasher, A, Oppenheimer, U. Rappaport, *Man and Land in Eretz-Israel in Antiquity*, Jerusalem 1986, pp. 81, 144–148. Other data proposed are 25 dunams according to Applebaum and 31.3 dunams by Ben-David, based upon the Mishna. See also Pastor, *Land and Economy*, pp. 10–11.

[81] See M. Goodman, *The Ruling Class of Judaea, The Origins of the Jewish Revolt against Rome AD 66–70*, Cambridge 1987, pp. 61–62. See also Klausner, "Economy of Judaea", p. 189.

[82] See Klausner, "Economy of Judaea", p. 189.

the second half of the first century CE, according to the Gospels. Zissu's survey confirms that situation. The situation, however, was probably not so dramatic in the period we are considering, since Herod's social program could have reduced the severity of the problem.

Tenants probably had plots that were the same size as those of the freeholders, though the land was not theirs and belonged to rich landowners or the king. According to the Mishna, there were four types of tenants: the *kablan*, the *aris*, the *choker*, and the *socher*. The *kablan* was a contractor, who undertook to tend the fields and pay all expenses in exchange for half, a third, or a quarter of the harvest. The *aris*, or lessee, was a poor freeholder, whose landhold was not enough for his needs. In order to survive, he had to lease a small parcel from the nearest landowner. The *aris* received seeds, implements, and farm animals from the landowner, as well as an agreed-upon portion of the produce. The leaseholder or *choker* differed from the contractor and lessee in that he bore the loss if the land produced less than the amount agreed upon. As in the case of the lessee, the rent was paid in produce. The *socher* or tenant, like the leaseholder, was responsible for the profit or loss. However, he paid his rent in cash rather than products.[83]

Hired laborers were impoverished peasants from neighboring villages, freeholders who had been forced to relinquish their own land and worked it as hired labor, and younger sons who had sold their inheritance because it was not enough to support them and their families. These laborers were employed by owners of large estates and worked at a fixed rate, whether for a year, a month, by the day, or even by the hour. No single contract between laborers and owners could be signed for a period of more than six years,[84] and hence, after a six year period, laborers would need to search for new work and another house.

The best example of a typical rural freeholder house comes from Capernaum (cfr. figure IV, 2). This is the so-called Triple Courtyard House, a complex that was built between the first and third centuries CE and represents a wealthy village house of the period. Another Late Second Temple village with many private dwellings is Kiryath Sefer.[85]

Village communities similar to those in Judaea were found elsewhere in the Hellenistic East, in Asia Minor and northwestern Syria.[86]

---

[83] See Klausner, "Economy of Judaea", pp. 191–192.

[84] See TB, *Yoma* 35b. The work day lasted from sunrise to sunset, with an hour's rest in the heat of the day. The wage probably averaged one drachma, as in Tobit 5: 4, or, later on, one *denarius*, as in Matt 20: 2, 9–10, 13, or the equivalent in food or goods. The wage could be as high as one *tetradrachm* or one as. See Klausner, "Economy of Judaea", pp. 190–191.

[85] On Capernaum see Y. Hirschfeld, *The Palestinian Dwelling in the Roman-Byzantine Period, Studium Biblicum Franciscanum, Collectio Minor 34*, Jerusalem 1995, pp. 68–69, fig. 43. On Kiryath Sefer see Y. Magen, Y. Zionit, and E. Sirkis, "A Jewish Village and Synagogue of the Second Temple Period", *Qadmoniot XXXII*, 1 (117) 1999, pp. 25–32.

[86] On Asia Minor see Sartre, *Asie Mineure et l'Anatolie d'Alexandre à Dioclétien*, pp. 99–101. On northwestern Syria see M. Sartre, *Alexandre à Zénobie*, pp. 213–216.

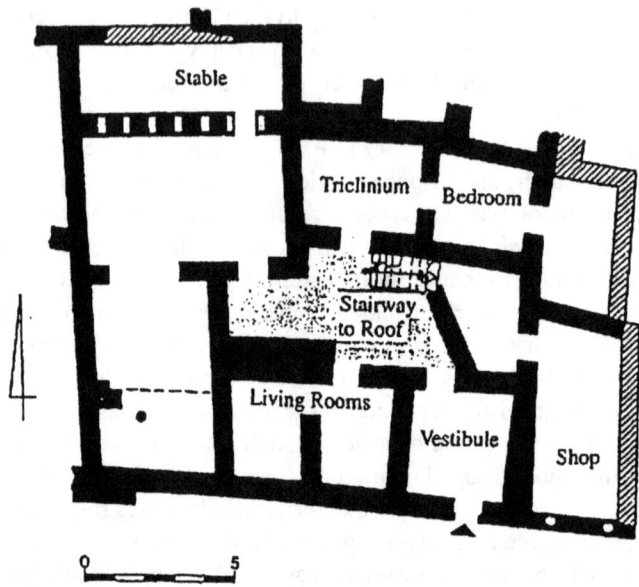

Figure IV, 2 – Capernaum Village House from Y. Hirschfeld, *The Palestinian Dwelling in the Roman-Byzantine Period*, Studium Biblicum Franciscanum, Collectio Minor 34, Jerusalem 1995, pp. 68–69, fig. 43, Courtesy of the Israel Exploration Society, Jerusalem.

ii. The Manor

The wealthier landowner's houses were scattered throughout Herodian Judaea, together with freeholder's village houses.[87] According to Fiensy, during the Herodian period, landowners' estates varied in size from 80 to 500 *iugera*.[88] Thus, it is possible to divide the landowners into at least two classes, large landowners and small landowners. The large landowners, called *ba'alei nechasim* in Talmudic literature, were relatively few. During the period under consideration, this class included members of the royal family, courtiers, and officials, but also the families of the various indigenous high priests and the surviving members of the Sadducee aristocracy. All of these Jewish manor owners – like their counterparts in the Greek East, who were members of the *bouleutic* class, or like their counterparts in the Roman West, who were members of the senatorial and equestrian

---

[87] Safrai defines the villas of Roman Galilee and Golan after 135 CE. According to Safrai the *villa* or *oikos*, fulfilled three basic purposes. It was the residence of the laborers or slaves. It served as the central storage area for implements necessary for farm work or for the processing of the crops (olive presses, winepresses, etc.). It was also the permanent residence of the *epitropos*, or sometimes of the owner, Safrai, *Economy of Roman Palestine*, p. 83.

[88] See D. A. Fiensy, "The Social History of Palestine in the Herodian Period", in *The Land is Mine, Studies in the Bible and Early Christianity 20*, Lewiston, Queenston, Lampeter 1991, pp. 23–24. See also Pastor, *Land and Economy*, p. 9.

class – generally lived in the city, visiting their domains infrequently. For all of them, entrenched in their urban residences, the rural manor was a temporary residence in case of trouble. Thus, the members of the Herodian upper class generally appointed a steward, the *oikonomos* or *epitropos*, to survey and oversee their estates, which were the main source of their wealth.[89] Throughout the entire period considered, those who tilled the manor field were freemen rather than slaves. Thus the landowners often sold their harvest for cash to freeholders and then used this cash to purchase goods and services from the same freeholders. However, during the Herodian Period we must envisage a situation in which most of the freeholders sold or mortgaged their estates, not to private landowners, but to the king, who returned the property to the poor freeholder in exchange for military or other service. Herod thus protected the freeholders as much as he could. According to Klausner, later in the late Second Temple period, there were many freeholders who worked the land of great landowners, and not that of the king.[90]

Most of the landowners who owned smaller estates lived in their manor houses, which thus maintained a certain standard of comfort. The Herodian manor was firmly rooted in the Hellenistic East and was a far cry from the Roman villas of the Latin West. Zissu defines the manor as a closed compound on agricultural land in which farm workers lived and did some of the work. The primary purpose of this small unit was residential. The manor owner and his family lived there together with tenant farmers and laborers. Manors were characterized by storerooms and facilities for processing agricultural produce. It is possible to distinguish between two types of manors, ordinary farmhouses without a tower and protected farmhouses with a corner tower and a *proteichisma*, or an outwork, sometimes sloped, that surrounded the base of the tower. These are considered to be fortresses in this study. The plan could vary, but a corner tower always protected these buildings. The manor was erected in the center of the property, usually in a dominant location.[91] In the center of the farmhouse stood a courtyard surrounded by residential rooms, storerooms, workrooms, industrial facilities, ritual baths, cisterns, and other facilities.[92] The owner used the tower as a residence. Another obvious function of the tower was to provide security against unwelcome guests, such as bandits. Rural houses in the Chersonese and in Asia Minor share similarities with their Judaean counterparts. Both were built around

---

[89] The *oikonomos* or *epitropos* is mentioned in the Gospels, see Matt 20, 8 and Luke 16: 1–8. Rabban Gamaliel II of Yavneh, when he was in the city, also had need of a steward, though he lived in a much later period. See Klausner, "Economy of Judaea", pp. 189–190.

[90] Rabban Gamaliel II of Yavneh employed workers to till his fields, see m. *Demai* 3, 1. He also leased his fields for a share in the production, see m. *B. Meṣiʿa* 5, 8. See Klausner, "Economy of Judaea", pp. 189–190.

[91] This was probably the *ir* having a single owner mentioned in m. *ʿErub.* 5: 6, and TJ, *Yebam.* 8, 8 d. See Zissu, *Rural Settlements in the Judaean Hills and Foothills.*

[92] See m. *B. Bat.* 4: 7.

a courtyard and had a fortified tower. The owner lived in an *oikos*, or building that shared characteristics with Greek and Hellenistic country houses and Roman villas. The *oikos* was as well the central reception room, sometimes decorated with mosaic pavements, painted walls, and carved architectural decorations. It also had a peristyle and a bath complex that included a *mikveh*.[93]

The best example is Khirbet el-Murak or the House of Hilkiya excavated in the Hebron area (cfr. figure IV, 3). This country manor is a rectangular building whose total area exceeded 1,600 sq.m. The fortified manor was defended by a tower, but presented at the interior a peristyle courtyard and a Roman bathhouse.[94]

Another similar building is the manor of Ramat ha-Nadiv, Horvat 'Aqav, which was founded in the last quarter of the first century BCE and continued to exist until the Great Revolt (cfr. figure IV, 4). The manor is located not far from Caesarea Maritima. It consists of a large L-shaped structure covering an area of 2,800 sq.m. The manor is surrounded by a wall and is situated in the highest part of Ramat ha-Nadiv. Inside the manor was characterized by a central courtyard probably surrounded by a peristyle, and living quarters two stories high, storehouses, and a tower three stories high.[95] Viticulture was apparently the main economic asset of the owner. The fact that the owners were Jews and that the manor was quite close to Caesarea Maritima further emphasizes the pre-eminence of Jews over Gentiles in the Herodian kingdom. Other structures that Hirschfeld classifies as fortified manors were excavated in Samaria, Judaea, and Idumaea. These structures – Qasr e-Leja, 'Ofarim, Horvat Mezad, Tel Goded, Rujm el-Hamiri, Horvat Salit, Tel Aro'er, Tel Arad, and En-Boqeq – are treated as fortresses rather than fortified manors (see Chapter III on Herod's army).[96]

Some of the manors, such as the Palace of Hilkiya and the manor of Horvath 'Aqav at Ramat ha-Nadiv, in addition to various others, incorporate characteristics similar to the late Republican and early Imperial rural villas in Roman Italy, such as Settefinestre. There is, however, a huge difference between the more extended manors of rural Judaea and the villas of Roman Italy and Spain, and not only in terms of size. In the manor, laborers, tenants, and even freeholders performed the agricultural work. In the Roman West, the agricultural work was

---

[93] The components of the *ir* or the *birta* are mentioned in the m. *B. Batra* 4: 7. "If a man sold an *ir*, he had sold the houses, cisterns, trenches, vaults, bathhouses, dovecotes, olive presses and irrigated fields, but not the movable property". See Zissu, *Rural Settlements in the Judaean Hills and Foothills*.

[94] On the manor of Hilkiya see E. Damati, "The Palace of Hilkiya", *Qadmoniot 15*, pp. 117–121, 1982. See also Hirschfeld, *Palestinian Dwelling in the Roman-Byzantine Period*, pp. 88–89, fig. 63.

[95] On Horvath 'Aqav see Y. Hirschfeld, *Ramat Hanadiv Excavations, Final Report of the 1984–1998 Seasons*, Jerusalem 2000, pp. 709–712.

[96] Tel Goded is the only exception. See F.J. Bliss and R.A.S. Macallister, *Excavations in Palestine during the Years 1898–1900*, London 1902, pp. 44–51; See also Hirschfeld, *Ramat Hanadiv*, pp. 712–720.

3. The Division of the Land in the Herodian Kingdom

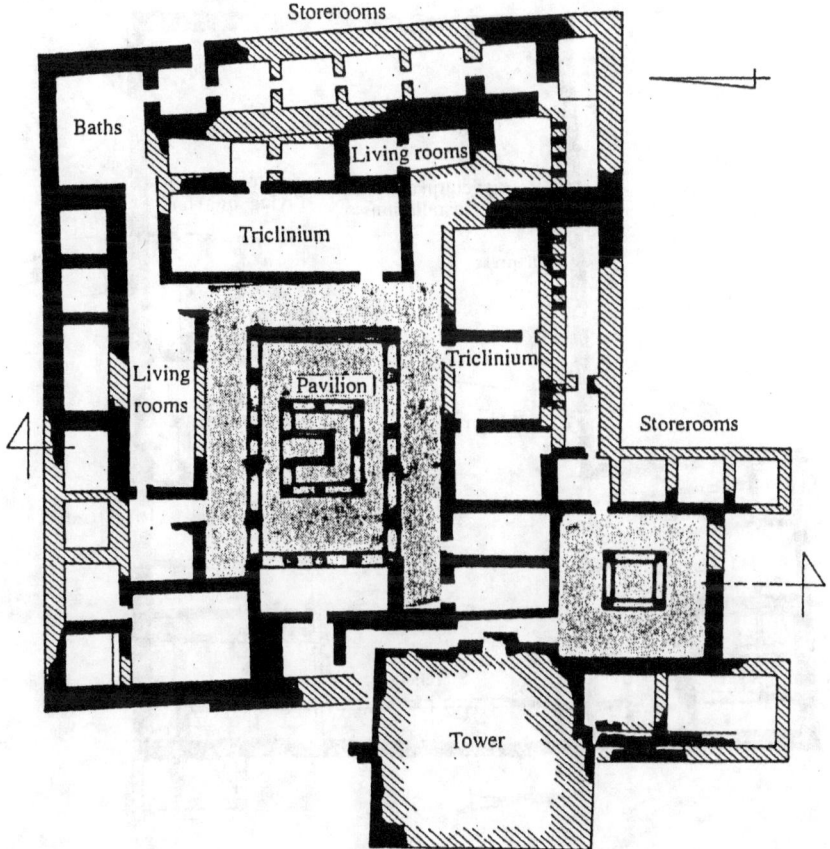

Figure IV, 3 – Plan of Hilkiah Palace from Y. Hirschfeld, *The Palestinian Dwelling in the Roman-Byzantine Period, Studium Biblicum Franciscanum, Collectio Minor 34*, Jerusalem 1995, pp. 88–89, fig. 63, Courtesy of the Israel Exploration Society, Jerusalem.

done by slave labor, while there is no evidence for slave labor in the Herodian kingdom.[97] If there was no slave labor, then the Herodian manors cannot be characterized as villas. In fact the rich landowners of the Herodian kingdom participated in a still-Hellenistic agrarian economy, as did Syria and Asia Minor, where slave labor did not exist.[98]

---

[97] On the Roman villa, see H. Mielsch, *La villa romana*, Firenze 1987, published originally in German as *Die Römische Villa, Architectur und Lebensform*, München 1987. The Italian edition also includes a short guide of the villas excavated in Italy, G. Tagliamonte, *Guida archeologica*, pp. 170–205. See also R. MacMullen, *Romanization in the Time of Augustus*, New Haven (Conn.) 2000, p. 58.

[98] On Roman Asia Minor see Sartre, *Asie Mineure et Anatolie d'Alexandre à Dioclétien*, pp. 283–288. On rural Syria see Sartre, *Alexandre à Zénobie*, pp. 767–770.

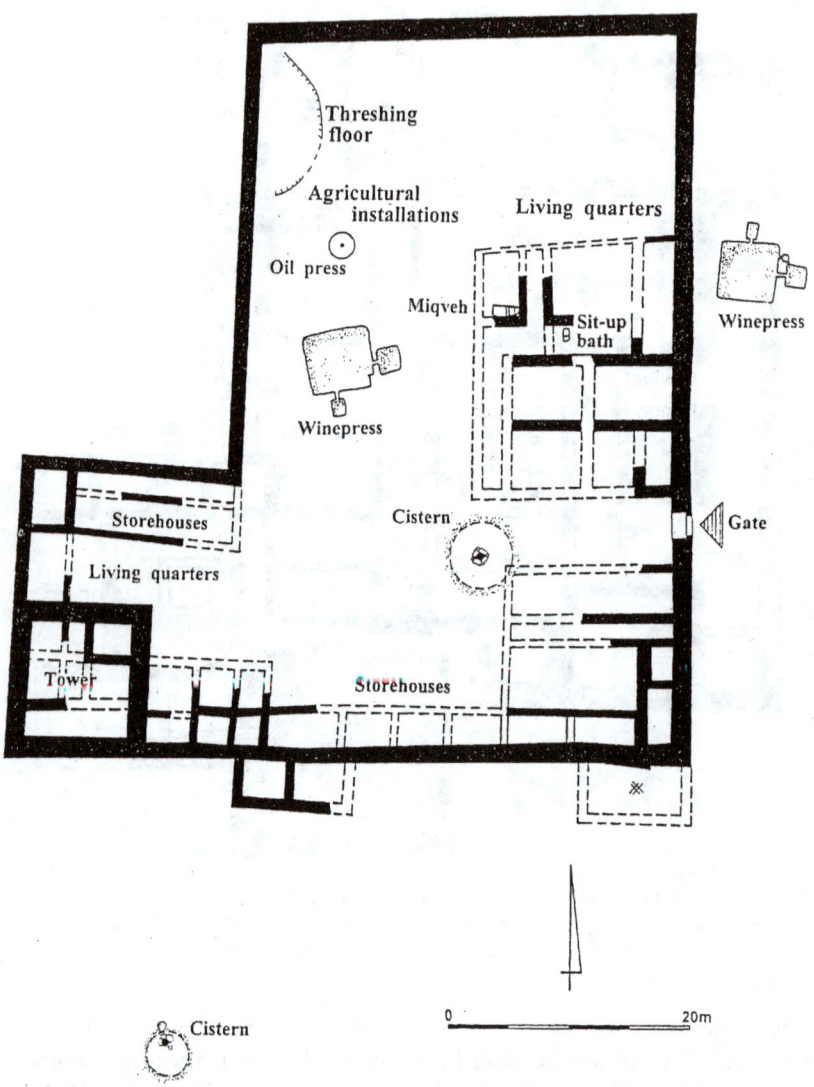

Figure IV, 4 – Plan of Horvat ʿAqav (from Y. Hirschfeld, *Ramat Hanadiv Excavations, Final Report of the 1984–1998 Seasons, General Discussion, Ramat Hanadiv in Context,* Jerusalem 2000, p. 710, fig. 24, Courtesy of the Israel Exploration Society, Jerusalem.

4. The Economic Resources

The agricultural output of Herodian Judaea did not differ on the whole from that of other Mediterranean lands and was based upon grain, such as wheat and barley, and on olive and vine cultivation. Animal husbandry consisted primarily of goats and sheep, with bovines far less common. The countryside of Herodian Judaea mirrored that of other Mediterranean lands as far away as Hispania and Africa in the West or Achaea and Asia in the East. There were, however, local crops, such as balsam and date palms, concentrated in a specific region, as well as the raising of turtledoves. Wool and pottery production, like agricultural production, followed quite closely that of other Mediterranean countries. Local manufactures, such as purple dye, glass, and stone, were typical of Herodian Judaea, though not atypical of other Mediterranean countries, most notably neighboring Phoenicia. Herod's control of the economy was felt and brought unprecedented prosperity to Judaea, prosperity that was reflected in the development of international trade at levels never before achieved. As I will detail below, excellent examples include the export of balsam from royal estates and spices arriving via the Spice Route that Herod marketed throughout the Mediterranean.

A. The Agriculture Products

Judaea, the core of the Herodian kingdom, was primarily an agricultural area. Josephus correctly states that Judaea lived mainly from agriculture.[99] According to Klausner, trade began only in the period of Alexander Jannaeus, after the conquest of the coastal strip.[100] Trade will be analyzed in the last part of this chapter; here I shall deal mainly with agriculture, which, in the Herodian kingdom, as it was everywhere else in the classical world, was the most important economic resource. The situation of Judaea, on the whole, reflects that of other parts of the Land of Israel, such as the coastal strip, Galilee, Samaria, and northwestern Idumaea. The crops were roughly the same, although the percentage of arable soil was variable. A great part of the Land of Israel did not have arable soil. According to calculations based on the surface of modern Israel, 26,318 sq. km. – only 44% of the area – are Mediterranean soils (11,725 sq. km.), and dry farming was prevalent in Herodian times. The situation in the Land of Israel was probably not different from that in other Mediterranean countries, such as Greece and Asia Minor, where dry farming was also prevalent. It is estimated that 65–70% of the regions with Mediterranean soil were cultivated in antiquity. Of these, at least 50% would have been required to feed the population. Thus,

---

[99] See Josephus, *Apion* I, 2.
[100] See Klausner, "Economy of Judaea", p. 179.

according to Dar, no fewer than 500,000 hectares (5,000,000 dunams in Judaea, Samaria, and Idumaea) were probably cultivated during the Herodian period. To this we must add the 300,000 hectares (3,000,000 dunams) of the northeastern lands of Gaulanitis, Batanaea, Trachonitis, and Auranitis, as well as the pasture lands in the south (Idumaea) and the semi-arid areas of Judaea. Accordingly, it appears that the agricultural resources of the Herodian kingdom could support a population of 1,500,000 persons. According to Dar, farming was thus much more important than grazing was.[101] The same phenomenon may be observed in late Republican Italy and early Imperial Italy, where, because of the dramatic changes in the socioeconomic structure, the ratio between farming and grazing also changed, though the types of products remained the same.[102]

Because agricultural products were the main economic assets of the Herodian kingdom, it is important to define the various products and their importance in the local economy. Only the agricultural production of Judaea proper can be studied in depth, since data for most of the other regions is currently lacking. Some of the data is later and must be used cautiously.[103] According to Pastor, the "typical" Jewish farmer of Late Second Temple period Judaea limited himself to a small range of products that were common throughout most of the Mediter-

---

[101] A careful estimation of wheat production in the Herodian period also leads to the conclusion that the land could support a population of 1,500,000 persons. See Dar, "Agrarian Economy in the Herodian Period", pp. 17–18. The data of Dar are, however, contradicted by the research of Safrai on the economy of Roman Judaea after 70 CE. Basing himself on Talmudic literature, Safrai claims that the land devoted to grazing before the destruction of the Temple was considerably greater than after the catastrophe in 70 CE. According to Pastor, however, Safrai's data do not necessarily conflict with those of Dar. Based upon the socio-economic situation of Judaea during the Second Temple period, the ratio of farming to grazing lands probably changed only slightly in one direction or in another. See Z. Safrai, "The influence of Demographic Stratification on the Agricultural and Economic Structure during the Mishnaic and Talmudic Periods", in Kasher, A. Oppenheimer, A. Rappaport, U. *Man and Land in Eretz-Israel in Antiquity*, Jerusalem 1986, p. 33. See also Pastor, *Land and Economy*, p. 10.

[102] See Cary and Scullard, *History of Rome*, pp. 187–188. Augustus tried to change the situation with his colonization in northern Italy, see pp. 299–300, 327.

[103] Thus, Talmudic literature mentions over 500 types of produce. Of these, about 150 types of cultivated crops, 8 types of grain, 20 types of legumes, 24 types of vegetables, 30 types of fruit, and about 20 types of spice plants. Which products were introduced after the catastrophes of 70 CE and 135 CE? For example, rice and flax, the latter mainly in Galilee, were cultivated only after 70 CE and thus, in this case Talmudic literature is not helpful. On the other hand, the importance of dove breeding in the economy of Judaea in the late Second Temple period can be reconstructed mainly from archaeological excavations, and in a lesser measure from Talmudic literature. See Safrai, *Economy of Roman Palestine*, p. 104. Safrai also provides useful comparisons with other Mediterranean countries.

See also M. Broshi, "The Diet of Palestine in the Roman Period", *IMJ* 5, 1986, pp. 41–56. Broshi catalogues the types of food eaten by the lower class of Judaea. This obviously reflects the produces cultivated as well as the animal that were breed. Broshi emphasizes that although the diet was basically Mediterranean, sea fish was not part of it.

ranean region. He grew grain, olives, and grapes, raised a small herd of sheep and goats, and kept several head of cattle.[104]

The grains grown in the Land of Israel during the Hellenistic-Roman period, as in other Mediterranean countries such as Greece, Asia Minor, and Italy, were mainly wheat and barley. Talmudic literature mentions no fewer than eight types of grain. Five are described as the "five major species of grain." Along with wheat and barley, spelt, oats, rye, and millet were cultivated, but in much smaller quantities.[105] Wheat and barley were cultivated with both dry farming and irrigation. Well and spring water was conveyed to the fields by pipes, aqueducts, and man-made channels. Grain was grown throughout the Land of Israel, but mainly in Judaea, Samaria, and Galilee.[106] Grapes were more profitable than wheat and olives,[107] and winepresses that have been found on archaeological sites offer tangible evidence that grapes were cultivated in a given area. The cultivation of grapes was widespread only in parts of Judaea, such as in the Lydda region (probably only after 70 CE) and the Sharon Valley, Carmel, and Kefar Signa. The latter supplied the wine for the Temple offerings. In the Gentile areas of the kingdom, grapes were also grown. Not all of the grapes were utilized for wine, however. Dried raisins, as well as vinegar, were also obtained from grapes.[108] Olives were grown mainly for the production of oil. They was cultivated in both Judaea and Galilee throughout the entire period in question and exported to Tyre, Sidon, Syria (from Galilee), and Egypt (from Judaea). According to Talmudic sources, the production of olive oil was centered in Jerusalem.[109]

---

[104] The villages in Samaria surveyed by Dar, including Kefar Buraq, can help us to evaluate the percentage of each product from a typical farm also in neighboring Judaea. Grain constituted 26.4% of cultivated crops; grapes followed with 20.2%, and olives with 12.9 %. However the situation in the nearby Karawat Beni Hasan was probably much more typical. There, no less than 52% of the cultivated area was for grain, 22.2% was for grapes, and 24.8% for olives. See J. Pastor, *Landscape and Pattern*, BAR International Series, Oxford 1986, pp. 245 ff. See also Pastor, *Land and Economy*, p. 10.

[105] Wheat was, according to Safrai, the most important grain in the Land of Israel. Wheat was expensive to produce with the limited resources of the Judaean farmer. Wheat was associated with the city while barley was associated with the poor and with the *chora*. In fact, barley requires less water and it ripens earlier than wheat. See D. Rathbone, "The Grain Trade and Grain Shortages in the Hellenistic East", in Garnsey, P. and Whittaker, C. R. *Trade and Famine in Classical Antiquity*, Cambridge 1983, pp. 46–48. See also Safrai, *Economy of Roman Palestine*, pp. 108, 110, 117–118.

[106] See Klausner, "Economy of Judaea", pp. 180–181.

[107] See Safrai, *Economy of Roman Palestine*, pp. 107, 126, 132–133. The grape truly developed in Judaea only during the Hellenistic period. The percentage of grape cultivation increased not only in Hellenistic Judaea but also in Late Republican Rome, where most of the villa owners preferred to grow vines rather than grain. On the wine of Sharon and Carmel, see m. *Nidd*. 2, 7. On Kefar Signa as a center of production see m. *Menaḥ*. 8, 6. On Lydda, Ascalon and Gaza see m., *Menaḥ*. 8, 6. See also Klausner, "Economy of Judaea", p. 183.

[108] On dried raisins see Klausner, "Economy of Judaea", p. 183.

[109] See Safrai, *Economy of Roman Palestine*, p. 119. Oil was produced in Samaria at Shifkon and Beth-Shean, in Jordan Valley at Ragaba, in Galilee at Tekoa, and Gush-Halav, but also at

Figs were less common than grain, olives, and grapes, but were nonetheless a popular product of Late Second Temple period Judaea. It is important to underline that figs were the main source of sugar in that period. Figs were sold fresh, but mainly as pressed and dried figs for export. They were considered to be a rather profitable crop, though much effort had to be invested in their cultivation. The Land of Israel was usually self-sufficient in fig production.[110]

There were also crops that were not part of the traditional Mediterranean agricultural economy, such as dates and balsam. Dates were grown in the Dead Sea region, probably by landowners with large plots, but also in the Jordan Valley and in Jericho in the royal orchards that surrounded the palaces of the Hasmoneans and Herod. Dates were considered a luxury product and were consumed locally and also exported as dried fruit and wine. Judaean dates were greatly appreciated in the classical world. Together with Egypt, Judaea was the only center of date cultivation in the Roman Empire.[111] Some vegetables had been cultivated since the time of the Bible, such as cabbage, beetroot, radishes, turnips, lettuce, horseradish, lentils, beans and pulses. During the Hellenistic period, probably as early as the Ptolemaic period, cucumbers (*melafefon*), artichokes (*kinres*), aspargus (*aspargus*), Egyptian beans, and Egyptian and Greek pumpkins were introduced. Still, vegetables comprised a very small percentage of the cultivation. Fruits were also cultivated in the Land of Israel, but their economic importance was limited.[112] The only exception was the carob, which was grown on trees scattered through the fields of different crops, and its seeds often complemented the diet of the Jewish farmers and especially of the poor.[113] Balsam was grown only in the royal estates of 'En Gedi and Jericho and fetched twice its weight in gold. It was used as a spice-perfume and for medicinal purposes. The balsam of 'En Gedi was one of the most important exports of Judaea. Strabo relates that the Jews grew balsam only in a limited area so as to maintain the scarcity of the product and hence its high price.[114] Together with balsam, myrrh, henna, and roses were also cultivated.[115]

Meron and Netofah. See Klausner, "Economy of Judaea", p. 183. On the oil economy of the Hellenistic city of Marissa see A. Kloner, "The Economy of Hellenistic Maresha", in Archibald, Z. H. Davis, J. Gabrielsen, V. Oliver, G. J. (eds.), *Hellenistic Economies*, London and New York 2001, pp. 103–131.

[110] See Safrai, *Economy of Roman Palestine*, pp. 136–137. Figs were sold abroad, even to Rome, and Judaean figs appeared upon the imperial table. Augustus thus favored a type of Judaean fig called Nicolaite. See TJ, *Ma'aÛ.* 4, 1. See also Klausner, "Economy of Judaea", p. 183.

[111] See Pastor, *Land and Economy*, p. 11. Pliny reports that Judaea was as famous for its dates as Egypt was for its perfumes. More important, he mentions five different kinds of Judaean dates. Tacitus likewise praises Judaean dates. See Pliny, *NH* XIII, 44. See Tacitus, *Hist.* V, 6. See also Klausner, "Economy of Judaea", pp. 181–183.

[112] See Safrai, *Economy of Roman Palestine*, p. 143. See also Klausner, "Economy of Judaea", pp. 181–182.

[113] See Safrai, *Economy of Roman Palestine*, p. 141.

[114] According to Pompeius Trogus, the area cultivated was 200 iugera. On the other side Josephus mentions that the area cultivated was 100–120 stadia – about 52 sq. km. See Pom-

Sheep and goats were the most common livestock and were raised for meat, milk, and wool, with cattle being far less common and playing a much less important role. Sheep were raised mainly in Judaea and were of minor economic importance in Galilee.[116] Wool was used for weaving, and Judaea was a center of wool production.[117] Turtledoves were also a very important economic resource of Late Hellenistic – Early Roman Judaea. The Jews raised turtledoves and pigeons for sacrificial use in the Temple and for fertilizer, though dove raising declined sharply after 70 CE.[118] Doves of various types were raised in *columbaria*. The *columbarium* or dovecote was a structure built as a round tower. The diameter of the tower in Judaea was around 9 m. The interior part of the tower was divided into three spaces by partition walls. The walls served both to help support the roof and to hold niches for the doves. These towers stood near water and fields for agriculture. *Columbaria* were found in Judaea proper at Masada, Jericho, Cypros, Herodium, inside Herod's royal estates at Jerusalem and Mazor and at Horvat Abu Haf and Horvat 'Aleq.[119] Turtledoves, however, were by no means the only fowl raised by Jews, and poultry appeared by the beginning of the Second Temple period. As the Akkadian names for fowl indicate, they arrived with the

---

peius Trogus, *Historiae Philippicae* 36, 31. See also Tacitus, *Hist.* 5, 6, who mentions it. See also Josephus, *BJ* IV, 469. See also Pliny, *NH* XII, 54, 11–124. See also Strabo, *Geog.* XVI, 2, 41.

[115] Henna was used in the production of a bluish dye with which women painted their faces. Roses were also cultivated in special flower gardens for the sake of their costly rose oil. See Safrai, *Economy of Roman Palestine*, pp.147–148 on both balsam and myrrh. See also Pastor, *Land and Economy*, pp. 10–11 and Klausner, "Economy of Judaea", p. 184. On the roses see m. *Šabb.* 14, 4.

[116] Sheep were raised for wool, milk and much less for meat, which was considered expensive. It was consumed only in the Temple. See Safrai, *Economy of Roman Palestine*, pp. 165–171.

[117] In Galilee after 70 CE flax was cultivated for weaving; thus, its production is not relevant here. Flax all through the Second Temple period was imported mainly from Egypt. See Klausner, "Economy of Judaea", p.185. See also Safrai, *Economy of Roman Palestine*, p. 155.

[118] The terms used in Hebrew are *yona* for pigeon, *tur* for turtledove, *gozal* for fledgling, *prida* for dovelet, *yonat shovach* for the domestic pigeon, and *yonat bar* for the wild pigeon. There was also a Herodian pigeon, the *yona hordasith*. See Klausner, "Economy of Judaea", p.185. See also Safrai, *Economy of Roman Palestine*, pp. 174–179, 185. Sanders argues for a massive consumption of fowls, i.e. doves, for sacrifices. See Sanders, *Judaism, Practice and Belief*, pp. 88–89.

[119] Varro describes *columbaria* in his tractate on agriculture, *De Re Rustica* 3.7. 1–7, 11 methods of raising pigeons inside large towers with a vaulted roof, containing up to 5,000 pigeons. Columella, in his tractate on agriculture *De Re Rustica* II, VII, VIII, 3–5 describes a similar building. Jewish sources inform us that pigeons were raised in dovecotes (see m. *B. Bat.* 5, 3), and that they were built in the fields (see t. *Ber.* 4, 14). The dovecote might be built inside the tower (see t. *'Arak.* 4, 13 5, 14) and its shape may be round (see t. *Neg.* 6.3). The dovecote was one of the standard installations of a typical manor (see m. *B. Bat.* 4.7, 9). Obviously the dovecote must be built as far away as possible from the settlement, no less than 50 cubits (see m. *B. Bat.* 2, 5, 9) because of the awful smell: "just like corpses, graves and tanneries!" The *columbarium* probably originated in Ptolemaic Egypt, where pigeons were raised. See B. Zissu, "Two Herodian dovecotes: Horvat Abu Haf and Horvat 'Aleq", in *The Roman and Byzantine Near East: Some Recent Archaeological Research*, *JRA* Supp. Series 14, 1995, pp. 56–69. On columbaria in Jerusalem see A. Kloner, "Columbaria in Jerusalem", in J. Schwartz, Z. Amar, and I. Ziffer (eds.), *Jerusalem and Eretz Israel*, Tel Aviv 2000, pp. 61–66.

Jews returning from Babylonia. Fowl were raised in coops in courtyards.[120] Fishing, another food source, was widely practiced only in the Sea of Galilee, which abounded in fresh water fish.[121] It provided both fresh fish for local consumption and salted fish for export. One of the most important cities was Tarichaeae, "salted," a fact confirmed by Strabo.[122]

Salt and bitumen from the Dead Sea were the most important natural resource in Judaea. They were used for tarring ships and in medicinal preparations. According to Pliny, Judaean bitumen was considered to be the finest in the world.[123]

It is possible to define the products and the agrarian economy of Hellenistic Judaea as being typically Mediterranean. There was a similar agrarian output in Hellenistic Asia Minor, where grain, cattle, grapes, and olives were cultivated, but these constituted the backbone of the economy to a lesser extent.[124]

B. Industry: Glass, Purple-Dye, Pottery and Stone

As elsewhere in the classical world, artisans supplemented the basic agrarian economy. Peasants exchanged agrarian products for a range of items manufactured mainly in the villages themselves, such as pottery and agricultural implements. The peasant arrived in Jerusalem three times a year and bought products unavailable in village markets, such as table ware, glass, or stone vessels. Some of the artisans – such as the potters,[125] blacksmiths, and carpenters, who were some of the best known artisans of Herodian Judaea – could be found in villages and small cities. There were entire towns or settlements connected with a certain

---

[120] See Klausner, "Economy of Judaea", p.185. See also Safrai, *Economy of Roman Palestine*, pp. 181, 185.

[121] See Josephus, *BJ* III, 509.

[122] Strabo praises the local specialty, a pickle or conserve of salted fish called *muries*. See Strabo, *Geog.* XVI, 1. Tacitus mentions fishponds near Jerusalem. See Tacitus, *Hist.* 5, 12. See Klausner, "Economy of Judaea", p.185. See also Safrai, *Economy of Roman Palestine*, pp. 163–164.

[123] According to Josephus large lumps of pitch were found floating on the surface of the lake. See Josephus, *BJ* IV, 481. See Pliny, *Nat. Hist.* XVI, 25. See also Klausner, "Economy of Judaea", p. 186. See Safrai, *Economy of Roman Palestine*, pp. 185–187 on salt, p. 188 on asphalt.

[124] On the economy of Asia Minor in the Roman period see Sartre, *Alexandre à Zénobie*, pp. 95, 222, 271–275.

[125] *Tituli picti* – jar inscriptions in both Jewish and Greek characters found in the excavations of Masada reflect the prominence of Jews in pottery trade. The *tituli picti* include the term *kalon keramion*, perhaps the translation of a Hebrew expression indicating the high quality of jars. The term in Greek indicates that trading pottery, for example jars, were sold in the Greek world, outside the area where Aramaic was spoken. In fact this pottery was sold not far away, but in cities like Caesarea Maritima or even Jerusalem. See H. M. Cotton and J. Geiger, *Masada, The Yigael Yadin Excavations 1963-1965: Final Reports, III, The Latin and Greek Documents*, Jerusalem 1989, p. 180. See also Pastor, *Land and Economy*, p. 115.

trade. Thus, Migdal Zeboaya, east of the Jordan – Magdala of the dyers – was connected with dyers; Beth Saida took its name from the fishing industry; and Kefar Hanania and Kefar Shihim were well known centers of pottery production, albeit in later periods.[126]

Crafts houses or guilds are mentioned in the Talmud. It is probable that artisans were organized into guilds during in Late Second Temple period in Jerusalem, as they had been during the First Temple period. Professional guilds were a characteristic of the classical world, examples being the *thyasoi* in the Greek East and the *collegia* in Roman Italy.[127] Skills passed from father to son, though it was probably necessary for a future guild member to spend a certain amount of time as an apprentice.[128] Some crafts were organized in the form of cottage industries in which entire families were employed.[129] Klausner furnishes a long list of artisans who worked in the city, both for the urban proletariat and in particular for the upper class. These included millers, bakers, cheese makers, tanners, cobblers, mat-makers, barbers, surgeons, stone artisans, weavers, dyers, embroiders, workers in gold thread, tailors, laundry men, goldsmiths, silversmiths, and perfumers.[130] Most of the artisans could therefore be found only in the great cities of the region, such as Jerusalem and Caesarea Maritima. If most of the artisans in Jerusalem were Jews, it is probable that most of them were Gentiles in Caesarea Maritima.

There were various products typical of the Jerusalem workshops that deserve to be treated in greater depth, such as the Jerusalem painted pottery and stone vessels. The so-called Jerusalem painted pottery, dated to the Herodian period and the first century CE to 70 CE, was produced in Jerusalem. It was similar to the Nabataean tableware, but was heavier and was crafted of coarser clay. This type of pottery, called Pseudo-Nabataean, is represented by painted bowls decorated with floral motifs in red paint.[131] It is possible that the beginning of this pottery production was a consequence of Herod's Nabataean wars, since Jerusalem pottery competed with the similar, but more expensive, Nabataean pottery, which was probably of better quality. Jerusalem pottery, however, was apparently not exported outside Judaea and its production met only local needs. Could this perhaps be considered local protectionism?

---

[126] On Migdal Zeboaya see Klausner, "Economy of Judaea", p. 188.

[127] In the Talmud the *beth zagag, beth kaddar* and *beth zabba* are terms, which indicate guilds. See TB, *Môed Qaṭ*.13b, and TB, *Pesaḥ.* 55b. See also Klausner, "Economy of Judaea", p. 188.

[128] In the Talmud one finds "a carpenter and the son of a carpenter", TB, *'Abod. Zar.* 50b. The example of Jesus and his father, who were both carpenters, indicates that this situation also prevailed in the Late Second Temple period. See also Klausner, "Economy of Judaea", p. 188.

[129] An inscription from Bethfage near Jerusalem includes a list of names of men employed in a local manufacture. See Klausner, "Economy of Judaea", p. 188.

[130] Ben Sira gives a list of artisans that lived in the city as carpenters, work masters, smiths and potters see Sir XXXVIII, 27–28. See also Klausner, "Economy of Judaea", pp. 186–188.

[131] See N. Avigad, *Discovering Jerusalem*, Jerusalem 1980, pp. 117–118, fig. 115, fig. 201, p. 185. See also J. Gunneweg, I. Perlman, J. Yellin, "Pseudo-Nabataean Ware and Pottery of Jerusalem", *BASOR* 262, 1986, pp. 77–82.

Stone vessels were also produced in Jerusalem. The main reason for the establishment of this industry was purely religious. Stone does not transmit or absorb ritual impurity, according to Jewish tradition, and thus stone vessels helped preserve the ritual purity of the products stored inside the Jewish house. These vessels appeared at the end of first century BCE and were produced until 70 CE. There were simple measuring cups, found everywhere in Judaea, in addition to ossuaries. There were also vessels that reproduced Eastern Terra Sigillata shapes, as well as *kraters*, single-legged tables (*monopodia*), and three-legged tripods (*tripodium*) that imitated and were decorated like similar objects produced in stone, wood, and metal in the Hellenistic and Roman world.[132]

In summation, the artisan production of Herodian Judaea was quite similar to that of Late Hellenistic Asia Minor and Phoenicia[133].

C. Markets and Internal Trade

Herodian Judaea could boast a monetary output of its own. When the Tyrian mint stopped producing silver *shekels* in 19 BCE, Herod bought the right to mint coins from the Phoenician city and transferred it to the Temple of Jerusalem. Tyrian *shekels* were used only for the Temple.[134] With the exception of Tyrian *shekels*, Herodian Judaea did not mint any silver denominations, and foreign silver denominations were used. Thus, at the beginning of the Herod's reign, Seleucid and Ptolemaic silver *tetradrachms* were in use. By the end of Herod's reign, Augustan *cistophori* and *denarii* were already commonly used. On the other hand, bronze coins were minted at Sebaste in 37 BCE in various denominations.[135] Small *dileptons-prutoth* were minted in Jerusalem throughout Herod's reign, for

---

[132] See Y. Magen, *The Industry of Stone Vessels in Jerusalem in the Second Temple Period*, Jerusalem 1988. Stone vessels originated in the Hellenistic East and spread throughout the Roman world. Livy and Varro mention them. Similar objects have been found in Pompeii. See Avigad, *Discovering Jerusalem*, pp. 172–173.

[133] On the main crafts of the cities of Hellenistic and Roman Asia Minor see Sartre, *Asie Mineure et l'Anatolie d'Alexandre à Dioclétien*, pp. 71–75, 295–299. On the industrial production of Phoenicia, in the Hellenistic Roman period see Sartre, *Alexandre à Zénobie*, pp. 223–224, 728, 792–799, 806–808. See also Pliny, *Nat. Hist.* IX, 60–62.

[134] The Tyrian silver *shekels* were produced in Tyre from 126–125 BCE, when Tyre became independent from the Seleucid kingdom, until 19 BCE, when Augustus closed the mint. The obverse depicts the head of Herakles-Melqart, the reverse the eagle. According to Meshorer Herod "bought" the mint's rights and transferred it to the Jerusalem Temple, where Tyrian shekels were minted until 66 CE. The Herodian coins bear the Greek letters KR (*kratos*) or government as the symbol of the new mint. Meshorer quotes the t. *Ketub.* 13, 20 in support of his thesis: "Silver, whenever it is mentioned in the Pentateuch, is Tyrian silver. What is Tyrian silver (coin)? It is a Jerusalemite". See Meshorer, *Ancient Jewish Coinage* II, pp. 7–9.

[135] The bronze coins were minted in 37 BCE in Samaria in four denominations. These were the Talmudic *hadris* (8 *perutoth*), the *hanzin* (4 *prutoth*), the *shamin* (2 *prutoth*), and the lowest, the *prutah*. See Meshorer, *Ancient Jewish Coinage* II, p. 14.

local needs. Like the Hasmonean coinage, the Herodian bronze coins followed a Hellenistic system rather than the Roman monetary system. The Roman system was introduced only in 6 CE with the first procurator, Coponius.[136]

The main purpose of the internal commerce of the Herodian kingdom was to bring the city and town products to the countryside and villages, and vice-versa. It is probable that by the Late Second Temple period the *rochel* or traveling salesman represented the most important commercial link between town and village. It is clear that this institution represented a rather undeveloped trade network.[137] The market day (*yom ha knisa*) was an established practice in Late Second Temple period Judaea. Every Monday, Thursday, and sometimes Friday as well, the peasants came to the nearest town or to the city of Jerusalem to sell their own products.[138] Every city, town, and village had its own market. The market, as everywhere in the classical world, was in fact an area of the city where some of the artisans came to sell their merchandise, and the peasants could bring their own products. In the Hellenistic world, the city agora remained the principal market, as in classical Greece. In the Roman cities the forum played the same role, though a particular site, always adjacent to the forum, the *macellum*, was always designated for this purpose. In Hasmonean and Herodian Judaea the situation was not different. In Jerusalem, the shops facing of the western side of the Temple Mount *temenos* provide a good reference. Although Jerusalem was the main market, it was not the only one in Judaea. Each chief city of a *toparchia* probably had its own market area, and some of the towns had a market devoted to a specific product or type of merchandise.[139] Not all of the markets were fixed. The *atliz katalysis* was a temporary market, where cattle, meat, and wine were sold. The meat was sold in the *macellum*, in a later period called *makuli*. As stated in Chapter IV above, the *agoranomos* was responsible for the market police.[140] Pilgrimages to Jerusalem were the main stimulus to internal trade. Jews from Judaea and from the Diaspora brought a huge quantity of money to Jerusalem three times a year. Each Passover some 300,000 people made a pilgrimage to Jerusalem. This would have enriched not only sheep and cattle-dealers, but other artisans as well.[141]

---

[136] The bronze coins minted in Jerusalem were no less than seventeen different types. The *perutoth* coined under the Roman procurators were equal in weight to the Roman *quadrans*, rather than the Greek *dilepton*. See Meshorer, *Ancient Jewish Coinage* II, pp. 13, 15–16.

[137] See Safrai, *Economy of Roman Palestine*, p. 77.

[138] See t. B. Meṣi'a 3, 20 and m. Meg. 1, 1–2; 3, 6.

[139] After 70 CE a cattle market is attested at Emmaus. This market probably antedated the destruction of the Second Temple. See m. Ker. 3, 7 and TB, Ḥul. 91 b.

[140] The *agoranomos* was responsible for supervising the levy of taxes on all goods and produce in the market and was in charge of market police and traffic. To help the *agoranomos* there were also appraisers or *shammaim*, who assessed the values of the goods for taxation, and market and commissioners or *mesharim beshuk*, who would check the price of goods. See *Gen. Rabba* 99. See also Klausner, "Economy of Judaea", pp. 202–203.

[141] Thus Josephus estimates 2,700,000, see Josephus, *BJ* VI, 421 and 3,000,000, see Josephus, *BJ* II, 280. See also Klausner, "Economy of Judaea", p. 199.

In the Gentile cities and urban centers of the Herodian kingdom, the equivalent of the Jewish markets were held – the Gentile fairs, a characteristic of Gentile cities – which were established in connection with pagan festivals. Outside the kingdom fairs were held in the neighboring independent cities of Ascalon and Ptolemais.[142]

D. International Trade: Maritime Trade and the Spice Route

Already from the early Hellenistic period, Judaea shared in the international trade of the Eastern Mediterranean[143]. International trade in the Herodian kingdom consisted of products that were both exported and imported. The spice trade, under Herod's control during those years, is worthy of special attention. Most of the products sold outside the kingdom were agricultural products exported to neighboring lands, including the Roman provinces of Syria and Egypt. The Sharon Valley had a surplus of wine and cattle; Jericho and the Valley of Gennesareth had a surplus of fruit; and the lowlands of Judaea had large quantities of wine and oil. Galilee produced surpluses of oil and vegetables and supplied the country with grain. Judaean wine was sold to Egypt and Syria. Galilean oil and grain were well known.[144] There were also luxury products that were exported, such as the figs and dates of Judaea, and balsam. Industrial products, such as glass and purple dye, were also exported, albeit in a smaller quantities.

An important product that has to be mentioned is the Eastern Terra Sigillata I, and perhaps Eastern Terra Sigillata II. Eastern Terra Sigillata I was produced, according to archaeometric analysis, in eastern Cyprus, not far from the copper mines owned by Herod. It is possible that Herod purchased the ateliers for the production of this type of tableware. The most common forms of Eastern Terra Sigillata I were bowls and plates. This ware strongly represented Roman taste. On the other hand, Eastern Terra Sigillata II was produced on the southern coast of Anatolia from a type of clay different from that of Cyprus. It is interesting that Cilicia, as stated above, was also connected to Herod, and he had the tax-farming rights to the region. The most common Eastern Terra Sigillata II forms are *kraters* and bowls. Eastern Terra Sigillata II has been found at Athens, Tarsus, Paphos, and Petra. It is important to note that the Herodian kingdom was one of the most important marketing centers for this ware. Most of the vessels found, though by no means all, have vegetal rather than animal or human figurative motifs, indicating that this ceramic may have been produced in Herodian workshops for a Jewish market, as well as for the entire eastern Mediterranean. The Western Terra

---

[142] See Klausner, "Economy of Judaea", pp. 198–199.
[143] See Hengel, *Judaism and Hellenism*, pp. 32–55.
[144] See m. *Pesḥ*. 3, 1; m. *Ma'as'*. 5, 8; m. *Kelim* 17, 12 and m. *Neg.* 6, 1. See also Klausner, "Economy of Judaea", pp. 199–200.

Sigillata, produced mainly in Aretium during this period, was made in ateliers owned by Augustus' *liberti*. Herod might have controlled similar production.[145]

The products imported to the Herodian kingdom were, however, of a more varied quality and quantity than those that were exported. Some – such as the Babylonian and Median beers, Egyptian zythum, or barley beer, together with smoked fish, lentils, and grits from Cilicia – were agricultural products mainly consumed by the lower classes. Other products, such as cheese from Bithynia, mackerel from Spain, and wines produced in the Greek East and in Roman Italy,[146] were agricultural products connected with the upper class. Other luxury items imported from outside the kingdom included silk from Miletus, purple dye

---

[145] On Eastern Terra Sigillata see J. Gunneweg, I. Perlman, J. Yellin, *The Provenance, Typology and Chronology of Eastern Terra Sigillata*, Qedem 17, Jerusalem 1983. According to Gunneweg the provenance of ETS I is certainly Cyprus, pp. 11–14. The provenance of Eastern Terra Sigillata II, on the other hand, was probably the southern coast of Anatolia. The Eastern Terra Sigillata I was found at Anafa in layers dated to 150–80 BCE. At Jerusalem it was found in layers dated to 30 BCE–70 CE. At Masada it was found in layers dated to 20 BCE–73 CE. At Jericho it was found in layers dated to 20 BCE–53/100 CE, and at Avdat it was found in layers dated to 20 BCE–40 CE (p. 11). On the other hand only twelve shards of Western Terra Sigillata were found. This pottery appears during Augustus' reign, not before (pp. 16–17). Two shards were found at Avdat in layers dated to 25 BCE–40 CE. Five shards were found at Caesarea Maritima in layers dated to 20 BCE. One shard was found in Jerusalem in layers dated to 30 BCE–70 CE. Four shards were found at Cypros in layers dated to the years BCE–70 CE. Most of the Jews probably did not use Western Terra Sigillata, as only one shard was found in Jerusalem, but it was used at the royal court, as shards were found at Cypros, and by the Roman soldiers quartered at Jerusalem after 6 CE. Eastern Terra Sigillata I was also found at Tarsus and Samaria (pp. 100–101). A characteristic of Eastern Terra Sigillata I is its Roman forms, introduced around 50 BCE and different from the previous Late Hellenistic forms of Eastern Terra Sigillata I (p. 33). The most common forms of Eastern Terra Sigillata I are cups and plates. On Eastern Terra Sigillata I forms, see p. 106, fig. 23, nos. 1–5. Eastern Terra Sigillata II has also been found at sites inside the Herodian kingdom, in layers connected with the period of rule of the great king. Eastern Terra Sigillata II was found at Jerusalem in layers dated pre-30 BCE. Eastern Terra Sigillata II was also found at Masada, in layers dated between 20 BCE–73 CE. At Cypros it was found in layers dated between 14 BCE–70 CE. At Anafa it was found in layers dated between 10 BCE–80 CE. At Samaria it was found in layers dated between 50 BCE–37 CE (p. 102). The most common ETS II forms are kraters, and bowls (p. 107, fig. 23, nos. 1–5). Eastern Terra Sigillata II has also been found at Athens, Tarsus, Paphos, and Petra.

[146] There is ample evidence that Jews of the upper class enjoyed Gentile wine. Wine amphorae from Italy were found in the Jewish Quarter. These amphorae were inscribed in Latin with various trademarks. See Avigad, *Discovering Jerusalem*, pp. 87–88, n. 69. Herod himself much enjoyed alimentary products from Roman Italy. H. Cotton and J. Geiger show that Herod imported more luxury goods from Italy than the Hellenistic East. Amphorae found at Masada were scratched with the words "*herodes rex iudaeorum*" followed by the year in which the wine was shipped, the type of wine, and sometimes, the name of the vineyard. Most of the amphorae were sent in the years 26–25 BCE, however the greatest group belongs to the year 19 BCE, and the last to the year 14 BCE. Various types of Italic wine could be found at the table of King Herod. AM – Amineum, Philonianum, produced by the vineyard of Lucius Lavinus, Tarantinum, and MAS – Massicum, from Campania. Together with wine amphorae, amphorae indicating for crème of apples, *garum*, MU – *mulsum* or honey wine (or *muria* – vinegar sauce) were also found at Masada. See J. Geiger, "Herod and Rome: New Aspects", *The Jews in the Hellenistic-Roman World, Studies in Memory of Menahem Stern*, Jerusalem 1996, pp. 134–137.

from Tyre, glass from Sidon,[147] jewelry from Alexandria, and of course linen, also from Egypt. The Pelusian linen was used to make the vestment of the high priest. Animals used for agricultural purposes were imported from rich landowners, such as camels and asses from Arabia, as well as Libyan asses from Cyrenaica. From Egypt came papyrus, the most important tool of any bureaucracy.[148]

The spice trade was one of the most lucrative branches of commerce in antiquity and in the Middle Ages. It is quite probable that from 31 BCE to the end of his reign Herod controlled most of this trade. In assessing Herod's primary role in the spice trade, it is important to provide a brief overview. Spices came to the eastern centers of the Roman Empire from as far away as China and southeastern Asia, India, Persia, Arabia, and East Africa. From China and Southeast Asia came spices such as aloe wood, amomum, benzoin, camphor, cassia, cinnamon, cloves, galanga, ginger, lakawood, nutmeg, sandal, and turmeric. From India came many of the same spices as from the Far East, such as aloe wood, amomum, cinnamon, turmeric, and sandal wood, but also bdellium, cardamom, pepper, putchuck, sesame, spike lavender, and ginger. From Persia came assafoetida and sacopoenium. From Arabia came balsam, incense, and myrrh, and from Eastern Africa came ammi or royal cumin, balsam, incense, ginger, and myrrh.[149]

International trade in the Herodian kingdom clearly displayed Roman rather than Hellenistic features. Although Herod's kingdom was still independent from Rome, it was closely linked to Rome by strong diplomatic ties. Moreover, most of its exchanges were with areas that had become provinces of the Roman Empire, namely the eastern provinces of Asia and Syria, though such exchanges in fact continued an earlier pattern dating back to the Hellenistic period. Thus, the international trade of the Herodian kingdom was mainly concentrated in areas under the direct authority of Rome. Another factor that emphasizes the Roman character of this trade is the direct trade with Italy. This trade flourished, particularly in exports from Judaea. Luxury products such as balsam and exotic

---

[147] A glass pitcher of mold-blown glass, made by Ennion, a glassmaker working in the first century CE, apparently in Sidon, was excavated in the Jewish Quarter. Three other vessels from the same mould are known. See Avigad, *Discovering Jerusalem*, pp. 107–108, figs. 95–96.

[148] On imported agricultural products see m. *Pesḥ.* 3, 1 and m. *Ma'as´.* 5, 8 and m. *Kelim* 17, 12 and m. *Neg.* 6, 1. On cheese from Bithynia see m. *'Abod. Zar.*2, 4. On mackerel from Spain see m. *Šabb.* 22, 2 and m. *Makš.* 7, 3. On camels and asses from Arabia, as well as Libyan asses from Cyrenaica; purple dye from Tyre and jewelry from Alexandria; and papyrus from Egypt see m. *Soṭah* 2, 1. On woolen cloth as fine as silk from Miletus see TB, *Šabb.* 30 b and TB, *Ker.* 111 b. See also Klausner, "Economy of Judaea", pp. 199–200.

[149] On the spice trade see J. Innes Miller, *The Spice Trade of the Roman Empire, 29 BC to AD 641*, Oxford 1969. On spices from the Far East see pp. 40–48; from India see pp. 69–99; from Persia see p. 100; from Arabia see pp. 100–107; from Eastern Africa see pp. 107–110. Spices were also grown in the Roman Empire, such as balsam from Judaea, ascalonia from Ascalon, and sylphium from Cyrenaica. See list on pp. 114–119. See also appendix with importation taxes for spices from Alexandria pp. 120–153. On customs duties collected for spices at Alexandria see Justinian, *Digesta* XXXIX 4. 16 [7], pp. 275–278.

products, particularly spices, arrived at various ports of Roman Italy, such as Brundisium and Puteoli. From Italy, wines were imported for the cellars of King Herod and the Judaean aristocracy. The trade with Italy consisted only of luxury products for a very small circle of individuals, the upper class of Roman Italy and Judaea, and involved enormous amounts of money.

5. Conclusions

In this chapter I have surveyed and analyzed the administration and the economy of the Herodian kingdom. The administrative segment of the Herodian kingdom, a heritage from the Seleucids and Hasmoneans, presents a division into *kome*, *toparchia*, and *meridarchia*, found in the Hellenistic East. The Hasmoneans had already merged the native element, the *ma'amad*, with the wider Mediterranean tradition. In addition, the tax system of Herodian Judaea continued a Seleucid and Hasmonean tradition and was thus part of the Hellenistic East, with some differences. On the other hand, the taxation system of Hellenistic Judaea was quite different from that of Republican and Imperial Rome, although once the Romans began to rule Judaea as a province, they did not change the taxation system much. The main problem is that Herodian Judaea, like the entire Mediterranean, was exhausted after years of civil wars. Thus the early years of Herod's rule, when taxation was high, were greatly resented, and yet Herod developed a social program, similar to that of Augustus in Rome. This program consisted of the creation of military colonies and a vast building program throughout in the kingdom, especially Jerusalem, resulting in the growth of urbanization. Herodian Judaea was characterized by the much reduced importance of slavery in the local economy. This was common in the Hellenistic East, but not in the Roman West, where slavery was probably one of the most important sources of manpower.

The territory of Herodian Judaea was divided into royal land and private land. Royal land, which was the direct property of the king, was generally worked by tenants and was given as territory to military colonies, or it could be given as a gift to Herod's supporters. Private lands were owned by free owners, living in villages together with tenants, and by manor owners. Once more, the situation was very similar to that of the Hellenistic East, especially that of Hellenistic Syria and Asia Minor. It is important to stress that the manors of rural Judaea as institution were quite different from the *villae* of late Republican and early Imperial Italy. Manors employed tenants as manpower, while *villae* in the Roman West utilized slaves as manpower.

The economy of Herodian Judaea was Mediterranean, and thus the main crops were wheat, barley, olive, and wine. Sheep were also raised. However, as in every corner of the Mediterranean, the economy of Herodian Judaea was characterized by its own distinct agricultural activities, such as the cultivation of balsam and palm trees. *Columbaria* were also an important element in the local economy. Once more, there are parallels with Hellenistic Syria and Asia Minor. Herod, victorious in the Nabataean wars, probably dominated the Spice Route. However, most of the international trade took place within the Roman Empire, especially Italy.

In conclusion, all of this clearly points to Herodian Judaea as a typically Mediterranean country and economy.

Appendix I.
The Languages of Herodian Judaea

Herod's territories included various and different populations. His administration therefore had to cope with various peoples and ethnic groups who spoke and wrote in different languages, such as Aramaic, Hebrew, and of course Greek. Therefore, in the words of Millard, Herodian Judaea was a polyglot society. Did Herod's process of Hellenization initiate a shift towards the use of Greek language to the detriment of other spoken and written languages such as Aramaic and Hebrew? It is worth asking as well if the close tie between Herod and Rome was also cemented with the introduction of Latin. As we shall see, it seems to me that during the Herodian Period there is a major shift towards the use of Greek. Yet this shift had already begun during the late Hellenistic Period and continued under the Hasmoneans. Herod therefore continued earlier trends, simply strengthening them.

It is possible to reconstruct the languages spoken and written by the populations of Herod's kingdom through a variety of sources, literary, epigraphic and archaeological. First of all, literary sources can enlighten us as to the languages used by the ruling class of Judaea, though to a lesser degree regarding the everyday languages used by the lower classes. Thus Josephus, our main source for the period, who wrote in Greek, describes more than once his knowledge of Hebrew and he is a useful source regarding the various languages spoken and written in the surrounding world, namely Hebrew, Aramaic, Greek, and Latin.[150] Other literary sources such as the Bible's Apocrypha and Pseudepigrapha can be useful, although they were conserved in the Greek or in translation into other languages, and not in the original language in which these texts were written, which more often than not was Hebrew.[151] Through various fragments left by the Dead Sea sectarians, it is possible to reconstruct in part the original text of some of these books.[152] However, these books are helpful in reconstructing the literary

---

[150] See T. Rajak, *Josephus, The Historian and His Society*, London 2002, pp.

[151] See J. Charlesworth, J., *The Old Testament Pseudepigrapha*, Garden City (N.Y.), 1983.

[152] The various texts found at Qumran include Bible Manuscripts. All of the Books of the Hebrew Bible, with the exception of Esther, have been found in fragmentary form. See L. H. Schiff-

language written by the ruling class of Judaea, though not in reconstructing the language spoken and written by most of the population. Last but not least, the New Testament books that relate to Judaea during the time of Jesus are no less useful as sources for knowledge of the language spoken by the vast majority of the population, and not merely by the ruling class.

On the other hand, various papyrological, epigraphic, and numismatic sources can be useful in reconstructing the languages spoken by the vast majority of the population, and not merely the ruling class. The papyrological material postdates, on the whole, the Herodian Period. These papyri consist of legal deeds which deal with gifts and sales of property, loans and receipts, marriage and divorce. Although these documents were written after 70 CE, they probably continued earlier traditions.[153] Together with papyri, *ostraca* can also be an important source for the language written by most of the population. Monumental inscriptions, as well as inscriptions carved on *ossuaria* and on objects for everyday use, as well as legends on coins and weights, are also useful in understanding the everyday language of the various population groups living in Herod's kingdom.[154]

---

mann, *Reclaiming the Dead Sea Scrolls, The History of Judaism, the Background of Christianity, the Lost Library of Qumran*, Philadelphia 1994, pp. 163-164. The only exception is the Isaiah Scroll, see pp. 173-174. Five percent of the Texts were of the Septuaginta type. Re. Apocryphal literature see pp. 181-195. The fragments found included the Books of Enoch, Jubilees, Genesis Apocryphon, Tobit, the Testaments of Levi and Naphtali, as well as the Testament of Kohath. For Wisdom literature, see pp. 197-210. The fragments found included the Book of Ben Sira and the Book of Mysteries.

[153] The most important papyrological collections consist of the papyri found on the top of Masada. These, however, were literary in nature, like those in the caves of Wadi Murabba'at, dated as well at the end of the First Revolt, and the various papyri related to the Bar Kochba Rebellion that were found in the caves of Nahal Hever and in the surrounding archaeological sites. See H. M. Cotton and J. Geiger, *Masada II, The Yigael Yadin Excavations 1963-1965, The Latin and Greek Documents*, Jerusalem 1989 and S. Talmon and Y. Yadin, *Madada VI, The Yigael Yadin Excavations 1963-1965, Final Reports, Hebrew Fragments, The Ben Sira Scroll from Masada*, Jerusalem 1999, P. Benoit, J. T. Milik and R. de Vaux, *Les grottes de Muraba'at, Discoveries in the Judaean Desert 2*, Oxford 1962, H. M. Cotton and A. Yardeni, *Aramaic, Hebrew and Greek Documentary Texts from Nahal Hever and Other Sites, Discoveries in the Judaean Desert 27*, Oxford 1997. See also N. Lewis, *Documents from the Bar Kochba Period in the Cave of Letters, Greek Papyri, Judaean Desert Series*, Jerusalem 1989, and Y. Yadin, J. C. Greenfeld, A. Yardeni, B. A. Levine, *Documents from the Bar Kochba Period in the Cave of Letters, Hebrew, Aramaic, and Nabatean Aramaic Papyri, Judaean Desert Series*, Jerusalem 2002. Re. the archives of Babatha, see also N. Lewis and J. C. Greenfield (eds.), *The Documents from the Bar Kochba Period in the Cave of Letters. I. Greek Papyri*, Jerusalem 1989, H. M. Cotton, "The Archive of Salome Komiase, Daughter of Levi: Another Archive from the "Cave of Letters," *ZPE* 105, 1995, pp. 171-208.

[154] On the *ostraca* from Khirbet el – Kôm see L. T. Geraty, "The Khirbet el – Kôm Ostracon", *BASOR* 220, 1975, pp. 55-61. See also L. T. Geraty, "The Historical Linguistic, and Biblical Significance of the Khirbet el – Kôm Ostraca," in C. L. Meyers and M. O'Connor (eds.), *The World of the Lord Shall Go Forth: Essays in Honor of David Noel Freedman*, Winona Lake (In.), 1983, pp. 545-548. Re. an *ostracon* from Maresha, see E. Eshel and A. Kloner, "An Aramaic *Ostracon* of an Edomite Marriage from Maresha, Dated 176 BCE, *IEJ* 46, 1996, pp. 1-22. Re. three *ostraca* from Gezer, see J. Rosenbaum and J. D. Seger, "Three Unpublished *Ostraca* from Gezer," *BASOR* 264, 1986, pp. 51-60. For the well known ostraca from Masada, see Y. Yadin, J. Naveh, and Y.

The most widespread language with various regional differentiations was probably Aramaic, which was the spoken and written language of most of Herod's subjects. Various papyri, *ostraca*, monumental inscriptions, and coin legends testify that Jews, as well as Gentiles living in Galilee, Idumaeans, Samaritans, and probably the northern nomadic populations such as the Ituraeans, spoke and wrote in Aramaic as well. It seems that the Jews living in Judaea utilized Hebrew as well as Aramaic, although it seems that the latter was used more in everyday life. It is possible that part of the lower classes of the Gentile populations residing in the coastal and the Decapolis region spoke Aramaic as well.[155] Nabataean, a variant of Aramaic, was mainly written and spoken outside the borders of the kingdom.[156]

On the other hand, Hebrew was still spoken and written by the lower classes in Jerusalem and in Judaea. According to the Mishna, marriage contracts in Judaea were written in Hebrew.[157] Various papyri, including deeds of marriages and some of the Bar Kochba letters, were written in Hebrew. Various *ostraca* written in a mixture of Hebrew and Aramaic come from Masada, and a further *ostracon* in Hebrew comes from Qumran. The Hasmonean rulers John Hyrcanus I, Alex-

---

Meshorer, *Masada I, The Yigael Yadin Excavations 1963-1965, Final Reports, The Aramaic and Hebrew Ostraca and Jar Inscriptions. The Coins of Masada*, Jerusalem 1989.

[155] See Millard, *Reading and Writing in the Time of Jesus*, pp. 87-88, 96-98, 105. A group of coins minted by Alexander Jannaeus bear an Aramaic legend. See J. Naveh, "Dated Coins of Alexander Jannaeus," *IEJ* 18, 1968, pp. 20-26. The Gentile population of Galilee spoke and wrote in Aramaic. A monumental dedicatory inscription from Dan is written in Greek and Aramaic. See A. Biran, *Biblical Dan*, Jerusalem 1994, pp. 221-224. The Idumaeans spoke and wrote Aramaic at least from the third century BCE. The *ostraca* discovered near Hebron, one in Greek and one in Aramaic, are dated to the third century BCE. See Geraty, "The Khirbet el - Kôm Ostracon," pp. 55-61. See also Geraty, "The Historical Linguistic, and Biblical Significance of the Khirbet el - Kôm Ostraca," pp. 545-548. An ostracon from Maresha, a text of a wedding contract in Aramaic, is dated to 176 BCE. See Eshel and Kloner, "An Aramaic Ostracon of an Edomite Marriage from Maresha," pp. 1-22. It seems that the Samaritans spoke and wrote in Aramaic, as the various dedications in Aramaic found on Mount Gerizim clearly testify. See J. Naveh and Y. Magen, "Aramaic and Hebrew Inscriptions of the second century BCE at Mount Gerizim," *'Atiqot* 32, 1997, pp. 9*-17*. Three monumental inscriptions from Judaea testify to the use of Aramaic. See R. A. S. Macalister, *The Excavations of Gezer 1902-1905 and 1907-1909*, London 1912, p. 137. See J. A. Fitzmyer and D. J. Harrington, *Palestinian Aramaic Texts, Biblica et Orientalia* 34, Rome 1978, no. 37 and 70. Some of the names scratched on the ossuaria are indeed Aramaic. See L. Y. Rachmani, *A Catalogue of Jewish Ossuaries, in the Collections of the State of Israel*, Jerusalem 1994, p. 11. Most of the papyri were written in Aramaic. The *ostraca* found at Masada are in a language, which according to Naveh, is more often than not undefined, either Hebrew or Aramaic. According to Naveh, Aramaic was the main written language in the period, although Hebrew was spoken some of the Jews.

[156] Re. Nabataean, see Millard, *Reading and Writing in the Time of Jesus*, pp. 100-102.

[157] See Millard, *Reading and Writing in the Time of Jesus*, p. 87. According to m. *Ket.* 4.12 marriage contracts were generally composed in Aramaic in Galilee and in Jerusalem, whereas in Judaea they were written in Hebrew. See F. M. Cross and E. Eshel, "*Ostraca* from Khirbet Qumrân, *IEJ* 47, 1997, pp. 17-28. See also A. Yardeni, "A Draft of a Deed on an *Ostracon* from Khirbet Qumran," *IEJ* 47, 1997, pp. 233-237.

Appendix I. The Languages of Herodian Judaea

ander Jannaeus, Hyrcanus II, as well as the rebels during the First Revolt, minted coins bearing Hebrew legends.[158] Hebrew was used by the priestly ruling class of Judaea to write the epitaphs that decorated their monumental tombs. Thus the ruling priestly class of pre-Herodian Judaea was still proficient in Hebrew, which was the ethnic language of the Jews, before the Babylonian captivity.[159] Yet we must keep in mind that the attachment of the priestly ruling class of Judaea to Hebrew was nothing out of the ordinary. The Hellenized aristocracy of nearby Phoenicia was still proficient in the cognate Phoenician language, as in Roman Africa, and its old ruling class, and not the Italian colonists, still spoke and write in Punic.[160] Likewise, the lower strata of the population used Hebrew no less than Aramaic in their more modest burial inscriptions, which consisted of names scratched on the ossuaries. Moreover, Hebrew was still the language used in the Temple. Two inscriptions from the Temple Mount area, one of these monumental, attest to the use of Hebrew. The liturgical language of the Temple was Hebrew,[161] which was also the language in which the Torah was read in the synagogues on the Shabbath. However, it was often translated after the Torah reading into Aramaic and in Greek, depending on to the main language spoken by the public.[162]

Together with Aramaic and Hebrew, Greek was also the dominant language of Judaea from the Hellenistic Period and onwards.[163] Greek was spoken and writ-

---

[158] See N. Avigad, "A Bulla of King Jonathan," *IEJ* 25, 1975, pp. 245–246. Re. the coins minted by the Hasmoneans and by the rebels during the First Revolt, which bore a Hebrew legend, see Y. Meshorer, *A Treasury of Jewish Coins, From the Persian Period to Bar Kokhba*, Jerusalem 2001.

[159] A good example is the inscription of the Bene Hezir Tomb. See R. Hestrin, *Inscription Reveal: Documents from the Time of the Bible, the Mishna, and the Talmud*, Israel Museum Catalogue, Jerusalem 1973, no. 173. Re. the Hebrew alphabet in the First Temple Period, see J. Naveh, *Early History of the Alphabet*, Jerusalem 1987, pp. 65–78.

[160] See on Neo-Punic Naveh, *Early History of the Alphabet*, p. 62.

[161] Re. the ossuaries' inscriptions see Rachmani, *A Catalogue of Jewish Ossuaries, in the Collections of the State of Israel*, p. 11. Fifty per cent of the inscriptions were in Hebrew. From the Temple excavations come a stone vessel with inscription "Korban" and two birds engraved upside down. Is the inscription in Hebrew or in Aramaic? See B. Mazar, "The Excavations in the Old City of Jerusalem", *Eretz-Israel* 9, 1969, pp. 168–170. See also Millard, p. 89. On the Temple Mount an inscription in Hebrew was found that indicated the place where trumpets were sounded. See B. Mazar, "The Archaeological Excavations near the Temple Mount," in Y. Yadin (ed.), *Jerusalem Revealed*, Jerusalem 1976, pp. 25–40.

[162] See Millard, *Reading and Writing in the Time of Jesus*, pp. 85–86. See also Naveh, Early History of the Alphabet, p. 78.

[163] See Millard, *Reading and Writing in the Time of Jesus*, pp. 36, 105–106. For the development of Greek language in the early Hellenistic period, see M. Hengel, *Judaism and Hellenism, Studies in the Encounter in Palestine during the Early Hellenistic Period* I–II, Philadelphia 1974, pp. 58–65. Hengel emphasizes the frequency of Greek names. The earlier Greek inscriptions in the Land of Israel date from the Hellenistic Period. This consists of the monumental inscription from Hefziba, dated to the rule of Antiochus III. This monumental inscription brings together two letters of Ptolemy son of Thraseas governor of Syria and Phoenicia. See Y. H. Landau, "A Greek Inscription Found Near Hefzibah," *IEJ* 16, 1966, pp. 54–70. A further monumental inscription is a Seleucid inscription from Jamnia. See B. Isaac, "A Seleucid Inscription from Jamnia

ten side by side with Aramaic and Hebrew. The use of Greek is thus attested to in various papyri and *ostraca*,[164] together with Aramaic or Hebrew, and sometimes alone. The Greek *ostraca* and papyri used by the population of Masada during the Great Revolt is a clear indication of the importance that Greek assumed even among the lower class as a written and spoken language. The importance of Greek is also attested to on ossuaries. According to Rachmani, if the inscription on these objects was bilingual, that is, in Aramaic and Greek or in Hebrew and Greek, the main text itself was always in Greek.[165] The growing importance of Greek is seen on the legends on the coins minted by the Hasmoneans and the Herodian rulers. The Hasmonean rulers minted bilingual coins in Hebrew and Greek, with a certain shift towards Greek under the later Hasmonean rulers. John Hyrcanus I minted coins with legends in Hebrew only, but Alexander Jannaeus had begun to mint coins bearing bilingual legends, in Hebrew as well as in Greek. His coins are thus characterized by a Greek legend on the obverse and a Hebrew or Aramaic legend on the reverse. It is important to point to the fact that Mattathias Antigonus likewise minted bilingual coins in Greek and Hebrew.[166] This of course does not indicate the languages written and spoken by the population, but merely the attitude of the rulers towards the languages in questions and a trend towards linguistic "Hellenization." Comparing Herod with the Hasmoneans, it is possible to see a clear cut shift towards the Greek language on his coins.

It seems to me that from the time of King Herod and onwards, Greek slowly became much more important than before. Thus Herod minted coins with legends only in Greek. Neither Hebrew nor Aramaic is used on his coins. It is important to emphasize that this policy must have been deliberate, and in fact, not only his earlier coins minted at Samaria, but his later coins minted at Jerusalem bear only Greek legends. This is significant because these small bronze coins were used only in the interior of the kingdom, and thus the vast majority of those who used these coins were Herod's subjects. Therefore the use of Greek on coins minted for internal use only presupposes that most of Herod's subjects could deal with the use of the Greek language. This shift towards Greek did not

---

on Sea: Antiochus V Eupator and the Sidonians," *IEJ* 41, 1991, pp. 132–144. Various burial inscriptions, some of these in verse, come from the necropolis of Marissa. See J. P. Peters and H. Thiersch, *Painted Tombs in the Necropolis of Marissa*, London 1905. See also E. D. Oren and U. Rappaport, "The Necropolis of Maresha – Beth-Govrin," *IEJ* 34, 1984, pp. 114–153. The most important group of papyri dealing with the Land of Israel during the Hellenistic Period are the Papyri of Zenon. See P. W. Pestman, *A Guide to the Zenon Archive*, Leiden 1981. See also C. Orrieux, *Les papyrus de Zenon: L'horizon d'un grec en Egypte au IIIième siècle avant J. C.*, Paris 1983. See also W. Clarysse and K. Vandorpe, *Zenon, un home d'affaires grecs à l'ombre des pyramides*, Louvain 1995. See also Millard, *Reading and Writing in the Time of Jesus*, pp. 36, 106.

[164] See also Millard, *Reading and Writing in the Time of Jesus*, pp. 105, 115.

[165] See Rachmani, *A Catalogue of Jewish Ossuaries, in the Collections of the State of Israel*, p. 11. See also Millard, *Reading and Writing in the Time of Jesus*, pp. 113–114.

[166] See U. Rappaport, "The Hasmonean State and Hellenism," *Tarbiz* 60, 1991, pp. 481–490 (Hebrew).

Appendix I. The Languages of Herodian Judaea

end with Herod, but continued after his death. Thus his sons, Archelaus, Antipas and Philip, continued the same trend, as did the various Roman *praefecti* and *procuratores*, as well as Agrippa I and Agrippa II.[167] Moreover, from Herod's onwards, coins are not the only objects bearing the ruler's mark used in everyday life bearing Greek legends. Thus two weights, which were used in the city markets, one bearing the name of King Herod himself, the other bearing the name of Agrippa I, or Agrippa II, have Greek inscriptions as well.[168]

From Herod's rule and onwards, the presence of Jewish Greek-speaking groups, not attested to before, is felt at least in Jerusalem. Thus Greek also made its appearance on the Temple Mount, as exemplified by two monumental inscriptions that are dated to the Herodian Period from the Temple Mount, in Greek. The first, also mentioned by Josephus, is the well known warning inscription. However, this inscription is directed to Gentiles, not to Jews. The second inscription is a donation from Rhodes to restore one of the Temple Mount pavements.[169] However, once more it is quite clear that the spoken and written language of the Jewish community of Rhodes was Greek, and not Hebrew or Aramaic. This can probably attest to the increasing importance of pilgrims coming from the Greek Diaspora and Gentile visitors who wished to visit the Temple in Jerusalem. The use of Greek is also attested to in the synagogues' inscriptions. Thus the well known Theodotus inscription in Greek points to the presence of a Jewish group coming from the Diaspora, living in Jerusalem, whose first language was Greek.[170] It is important, however, to emphasize that these Greek speaking groups were a negligible element of the kingdom's population.

It seems to me that it is possible to justify Herod's shift towards Greek for two reasons, one ideological, and one practical. First, as ruler of Judaea and ally of

---

[167] Re. the coins of the Hasmoneans, Herod, Archelaus, Antipas, Philip, and the Roman governors, Agrippa I and Agrippa II, that bore Greek legends, see Meshorer, *A Treasury of Jewish Coins,* passim. See also Millard, *Reading and Writing in the Time of Jesus,* p. 107. It is interesting that the independent government during the First Revolt, as well as Bar Kochba, minted coins with Hebrew legends, not Aramaic. This indicates a certain ideology, but not an a priori negative attitude towards the use of Greek. Three of Bar Kochba' letters were written in Greek.

[168] The weight bearing the name of Herod is dated to 9 BCE. The inscription reads, "Year 32 of Herod the king, pious and loyal to Caesar. Inspector of markets, 3 minas." See Y. Meshorer, "A Stone Weight from the Reign of Herod, 20, 1970, pp. 97–98. The other weight is dated to year five of Agrippa. See B. Mazar, "The Excavations in the Old City of Jerusalem," *Eretz-Israel* 9, 1969, pp. 161–176, pl. 46. See also B. Mazar, "The Excavations in the Old City of Jerusalem near the Temple Mount, Preliminary Report of the Second and Third Seasons, 1969–1970," *Eretz-Israel* 10, 1971, pp. 1–33, pl. 23.

[169] Re. the Temple Mount warning inscription, see Josephus, *AJ* XV, 417–418. See also Geva, "Jerusalem, the Second Temple Period," p. 344. See Millard, pp. 108–109. The other inscription of a resident of Rhodes laying a pavement on Temple Mount is dated to Herod's twentieth year. See B. Isaac, "A Donation for Herod's Temple," *SEG* 33, 1983, no. 1277, pp. 86–92.

[170] The synagogue of Theodotus' inscription is dated to the first century CE. See R. Weill, *La cité de David,* Paris 1920, pl. xxv. See also J. S. Kloppenborg, "Dating Theodotos ("CIJ" II 1404)," *JJS* 51,2, 2000, pp. 243–280.

Rome, Herod wished to draw Judaea's populations closer to the surrounding Hellenistic-Roman world by strengthening the use of Greek, a language that symbolized a common feature, or "*koiné diálektos.*" The growing importance of Greek was reflected in the languages used by the ruling class of Judaea, which was, to a certain degree, also polyglot. Although Aramaic was mainly used in their contact with the lower strata of the population, the languages spoken and written by the upper priestly class was Hebrew and Greek, and indeed, Greek was widely known. Thus the Letter of Aristeas, although not to be taken literally, shows the wishful thinking of the priestly ruling class of Judaea regarding bilingualism in Hebrew and Greek. This may be reflected in the fact that around 130 BCE, the grandson of Ben Sira translated his grandfather's book, written in around 180 BCE, from Hebrew to Greek. Eupolemus likewise wrote in Greek. The ambassadors of Judas Maccabaeus, of Jonathan, and of John Hyrcanus all knew Greek well enough to function as ambassadors. Moreover, it seems that the Septuagint was widely known.[171] Yet there is a further shift with Herod towards the use of Greek as the main language used by the ruling class of Judaea. Herod's creation of a new ruling class somehow heightened the importance of Greek, not merely as one of the languages of the ruling class of Judaea, but as its main language. This is indicated by the fact that most of the high priests appointed by Herod came from the Greek Alexandrian Diaspora, and that most of the well known courtiers of Herod, such as Nicolaus of Damascus, were Greek intellectuals The fact that Herod's army was commanded by officers of Italic or Roman origin may also be a further indication of a shift towards Greek. Thus it is no surprise that after the First Revolt, Josephus, as well as Justus of Tiberias, wrote in Greek. Although this process began much earlier, it seems to me that Herod greatly influenced it.[172]

---

[171] See Schiffmann, *Reclaiming the Dead Sea Scrolls*, pp. 212–214.

[172] The spoken and written languages of the ruling class of Judaea can be assumed by their literary production. Aramaic was known. Thus some of the books of the Bible were translated in Aramaic as the Pentateuch itself, the Book of Job. Some other were written in Aramaic as the Genesis Apocryphon and maybe the Book of Tobit. The language of the Temple cult used by the priests and the high priest was Hebrew. This was also the written language of the Pentateuch as well as most of the apocrypha as the Wisdom of Ben Sira, and the First Book of the Maccabees. Moreover the ruling class wrote and read Greek from the Late Hellenistic Period onwards. Thus the Septuaginta, coming from Alexandria, as well as local translations of the Pentateuch, were widely known. Also there were books written in Greek in Judaea as the works of Eupolemus and the Second Book of Maccabees, composed by Jason of Cyrene. Greek was also the main language of the court in the Hasmonean and Herodian Period. See J. Barr, Hebrew, "Aramaic and Greek in the Hellenistic Age", in *CHJ* II, Cambridge 1989, pp. 79–114; J. A. Fitzmyer, The Languages of Palestine in the First Century AD.", in J. A. Fitzmyer, *A Wandering Aramean: Collected Aramaic Essays*, Missoula (Mt.), 1979, pp. 29–56; J. C. Greenfield, "Languages of Palestine, 200 BCE–200 CE", in H. H., Paper (ed.), *Jewish Languages, Theme and Variations*, New York 1978, pp. 143–154; M. O. Wise, "Languages of Palestine", in J. B. Green, S. McKnight and I. H. Marshall (eds.), *Dictionary of Jesus and the Gospels*, Downers Grove (Ill.) 1992, pp. 434–444.

I would like to add a word on the use of Latin. First of all, it is important to emphasize that, in contrast to Greek, Latin was not widely used in the Greek East after the Roman conquest, and Judaea was not an exception. Thus the use of Latin can be dated after the Roman annexation of Judaea in 6 CE. Moreover, Latin was written and spoken only by and among the Roman administrators, and not with the local population. Furthermore, most of the soldiers that garrisoned Judaea after 6 CE were locals, and thus, although they were proficient in Latin, they spoke Greek. Latin was thus a language written and spoken by a minority, not comparable to use of Aramaic, Hebrew, and Greek[173].

---

[173] On the use of Latin, see Millard, pp. 125-131. The Temple Mount enclosure warning inscription was also in Latin. See Josephus, *AJ* XV, 417-418. On the Tiberieum inscription found at Caesarea Maritima see Hestrin, *Inscription Reveal*, no. 216.

V. The Ruling Bodies of Herodian Judaea

Herod was the supreme ruler of Judaea, though he did not rule alone and needed the collaboration of a ruling class to implement his policies. In this chapter I shall first discuss who comprised the ruling class of Judaea during this period, as well as the relationship of the various parties and sects – Sadducees, Essenes, Pharisees, and Herodians – with Herod the king. After that I shall analyze the various corporate bodies through which the ruling class of Judaea could cooperate with or oppose Herod's policies, such as the *boulē*, a kind of limited senate, and the *synedrion-Sanhedrin*, a small court that dealt mainly with religious offenses. In Herodian Judaea, it should be noted, not only the ruler and the ruling class had representation, but the People's Assembly, or *ekklesia*, also had a say in public affairs. Each of these bodies reflected the main elements that strengthened the power of the Herodian ruler. Thus, the *ekklesia* reflected the people, the *plethos*; the *boulē* reflected the new Herodian lay aristocracy; and the *synedrion-Sanhedrin* during this period probably reflected the new Herodian priestly aristocracy and the Pharisees. Obviously, these bodies had only an auxiliary role and no decision-making power, which rested in the hands of Herod alone. Last but not least, there were the various law courts of the Herodian kingdom.

1. The Legal Position of the Ruler in Herodian Judaea

First, I shall analyze the legal position of Herod, since, despite the auxiliary groups that ostensibly helped him reign, he was in fact the supreme ruler. During the Herodian period there is a clear movement toward the strengthening of the monarchic authority of the ruler. Although Herod was not the first king of the Second Temple period, he was definitely the first real absolute ruler, fully embodying the monarchic principle.[1] Herod inherited two main sources of monarchic authority: that of the Hellenistic king in the tradition of Alexander the Great and the Hasmoneans, as well as that of the First Temple Period' kings

---

[1] Goodblatt was essentially correct in stating that the institutions of Second Temple period Judaea were basically monarchic, whether the chief of state was the Oniad or Hasmonean high priest or the Herodian king. See D. M. Goodblatt, *The Monarchic Principle*, TSAJ 38, Tübingen 1994.

of Jehuda. In that latter respect, for Jews, Herod's absolute rule marked a break with the recent past, since Herod was not high priest.

Following the Hellenistic tradition of kingship, the Herodian King was not only the warlord, but also the supreme judge and supreme legal authority. According to Isocrates' theory concerning the legislative power of the Hellenistic king, the will of the king makes the law. Aristotle also wrote that those who are elevated above their fellow man to the point of being regarded as "gods among men" do not require laws, but embody the law itself, and according to Diotogenes, "the king is the living law."[2] The Hellenistic rulers, however, and Herod among them, did not shoulder this burden exclusively. In an act of *philanthropia*, the Hellenistic king delegated the right of legislation to the various legislative bodies of the kingdom. Therefore, as Hellenistic king, Herod was also the supreme head of the various secular bodies of Jerusalem, such as the *ekklesia* and the *boulē*. As Hellenistic ruler, he was also the supreme ruler of the Greek royal cities of his kingdom as well, including Caesarea Maritima and Sebaste, though he ruled these cities though appointed governors and magistrates. These cities lacked the *boulē*, which had not been authorized in their founding constitutions.

The Hellenistic tradition of kingship was not new to the Jews. Before Herod, the Hasmonean kings had ruled the kingdom both as Hellenistic rulers and as high priests. The powers conferred by the title of king lay only in the secular domain – with the king as army commander in the military sphere and supreme legislator in the socio-economic spheres – but did not extend to religious affairs. However, as high priests, the Hasmoneans were also the supreme religious authority. As I have explained earlier, like the Hasmoneans, the roots of Herod's authority derived from the wide Hellenistic conception of kingship. However, since Herod could not be high priest, he therefore searched for alternative sources of Jewish kingship and authority in the distant Jewish past. As I have already noted, Herod presented himself to his Jewish subjects as the heir to First Temple Jewish kingship, and as we shall see, as Jewish king, Herod was also the head of the Jewish religious court, the *synedrion-Sanhedrin*. Indeed Jewish law recognizes the king's right to establish his own courts to maintain public order,[3] and the king had the right to put to death whoever disobeyed his directives. For his Jewish subjects, Herod was not only the king, but also the supreme judge. His new situation in Judaea as the source of law and as supreme judge is paralleled in Augustan Rome.[4]

---

[2] See Isocrates, *To Demonicus* 36, Aristotle, *Politics* III, 8. 2, Stobaeus, *Florilegium* VII, 61, 10. See also Preaux, *monde hellenistique* I, p. 271.

[3] See m. *Sanh.* II, 4. See also BT, *Sanh.* 49 a; BT, *Šabb.* 56 a; Sifre, Deut 157–162; and m. Ker. I.

[4] See O. Tellegen-Couperus, *A Short History of Roman Law*, London 1993, pp. 38–43 and 75–81, and 86–87 on imperial legislation. See also M. Cary and H. H. Scullard, *A History of Rome*, London 1986, pp. 235–237 on Sulla reforms as dictator, pp. 239–244 on the slow abolition of Sulla reforms. On Iulius Caesar reforms as dictator see pp. 279–282. See also E. S. Gruen, *The Last Generation of the Roman Republic*, Berkeley (Ca.), 1974, pp. 6–46.

2. Herod and the Judaean Ruling Class

I shall now analyze Herod's relationship with the ruling class of Judaea, the Sadducees, who had been the ruling class of Hasmonean Judaea, as well as the various other sects, including the burgeoning Pharisees, the Essenes, and the "New Testament *Herodians*." Herod attempted to consolidate a new ruling class that would be entirely loyal to him. Regarding the social standing of the Sadducees and the Pharisees, there is no doubt that the ruling class of Hasmonean and Herodian Judaea included both the Sadducees and the Pharisees, the latter, at least, during the reign of Salome Alexandra. It is possible to identify a "revolution" in Herodian Judaea in terms of the composition of the ruling class. Just as Augustus carried out what has been defined by Syme as the Roman Revolution,[5] through the proscriptions of 43–42 BCE, Herod enacted a similar revolution in the creation of a new ruling class in Judaea. This new class was composed of the nobility constituted by high priests coming from outside Judaea, and by also elevating the social standing of the Pharisees and of some members of his entourage, he created a new secular nobility, in opposition to the Sadducees, who had been identified with the old Hasmonean order.

Levine represents the Sadducees as the defenders of the priestly landed aristocracy.[6] Herod probably had a bad relationship with the Sadducees from the very start. The Sadducees were obviously pro-Hasmonean, and it is probable that when Herod conquered Jerusalem in 37 BCE, the Sadducees were those who suffered the most.[7] The Sadducees, as such, reemerged only under direct Roman rule after Herod's death. The Roman procurators presumed that the Sadducees, as the landed upper class of the Greek East, would have supported the rule of Rome, but as Goodman has demonstrated, they proved to be sadly mistaken.[8] Herod checked the power of the remaining Sadducees, controlling the nomination of the high priest, the most important magistrature to which the Sadducees could aspire and appointed high priests from outside Judaea, such as Anael from Babylonia, who was high priest between the years 37–36 and 35–30 BCE; Boethus, who was high priest between the years 24–5 BCE; as well as his son, Simon son of Boethus, from Alexandria, who was high priest in the year 5 BCE. It would have

---

[5] The Augustan revolution consisted of eliminating the old senatorial nobility consisting of a few Roman patrician and plebeian families. Instead, Augustus created a new ruling class composed of the leftovers of the old nobility that identified with the Caesarean-Augustan ideological platform, together with a new main force of *homines novi*, knights and the rising Italic nobility that stood behind Augustus. See R. Syme, *The Roman Revolution*, London 1939, passim.

[6] See L. I. Levine, "The Political Struggle between Pharisees and Sadducees in the Hasmonean Period", in A. Oppenheimer, U. Rappaport and M. Stern (eds.), *Jerusalem in the Second Temple Period, Abraham Schalit Memorial Volume*, Jerusalem 1980, pp. 61–83.

[7] See Josephus, *AJ* XV, 5 and XVII, 307 on Herod's confiscation from the aristocracy.

[8] See M. Goodman, *The Ruling Class of Judaea, The Origins of the Jewish Revolt against Rome AD 66–70*, Cambridge 1987, pp. 36, 42–44, 249.

been easy to keep high priests coming from outside Judaea, far removed from politics, and thus the position of high priest, charged with political significance and once dominated by the Hasmoneans, became a symbolic position, devoid of any real influence.[9] Not all scholars, however, see the relationship between the Sadducees and Herod in such a negative light. The best example is Regev, who argues that during the Herodian Period the Sadducees maintained a certain influence, and that the high priests appointed by Herod could be defined as Sadducees.[10] The main motivation for Herod to do away with the Sadducees was that he probably feared – with some justification – Sadducee nationalism. The Sadducees probably supported the last Hasmonean's struggle, not only against Herod, but also against Rome as well, taking the side of Antigonus. But what was the attitude of the Sadducees toward Herod? The Sadducees probably saw only the Hasmoneans as the legitimate kings of Judaea, regarding Herod as a usurper or, at best, a parvenu. Moreover, as priests, the Sadducees could not accept the legitimacy of a ruler who was not of priestly lineage.[11]

According to Josephus, the attitude of the Essenes toward Herod's rule was probably positive. Herod freed the Essenes from the oath of loyalty to the king, required in 20 BCE.[12] A certain Maenemus, identified by some scholars with the Menahem who appears in Talmudic literature,[13] prophesied to Herod that he would be king of the Jews. He also instructed Herod "to love justice and piety, because if he would not, God's wrath would be shown at the end."[14] This prophecy

---

[9] Richardson stresses that Josephus never mentioned the Sadducees as such in the account of Herod's reign, neither in *AJ*, nor in *BJ*. According to Richardson, the Sadducees indeed faded away during Herod's reign. See Richardson, *Herod King of the Jews*, p. 254. On Herod and the Sadducees see also Sanders, *Judaism, Practice and Belief*, pp. 320–321, where he deals only with the high priests.

[10] See A. Regev, *The Sadducees and their Halakhah, Religion and Society in the Second Temple Period*, Jerusalem 2005, pp. 293–347.

[11] On Herod and the political parties see Richardson, *Herod, King of the Jews*, pp. 249–260. On the Sadducees see A. Baumgarten, "On the Legitimacy of Herod and his Sons as Kings of Israel", in *Jews and Judaism in the Second Temple, Mishna and Talmud Period, Studies in Honor of Shmuel Safrai*, Jerusalem 1993, pp. 33–34. See also M. Stern, *The Kingdom of Herod*, Tel Aviv 1992, pp. 89–92.

[12] Josephus, *AJ* XV, 368–370.

[13] See TB, *Ḥag*. 16 b. According to the passage, Menahem left the Sanhedrin with 160 disciples for the royal service. Could this perhaps be Josephus' Maenemus?

[14] See Josephus, *AJ* XV, 373–379. In two articles, Daniel argued that it is possible to identify the Herodians of the New Testament with the Essenes. See C. Daniel, "Les 'Hérodiens' du Nouveau Testament sont-ils Esséniens", *Revue de Qumran* 6, 1967–1969, pp. 31–53 and "Nouveaux arguments en faveur de l'identification des Hérodiens et des Ésseniens", *Revue de Qumran* 7, 1969–1971, pp. 397–402. Josephus reports Herod's positive opinion of the Essenes. Accordingly, Herod held the Essenes in honor and had a higher opinion of them than was consistent with their human nature. See Josephus, *AJ* XV, 372. On Herod's positive attitude towards the Essenes, and their own towards Herod in the early years of his reign, see Sanders, *Judaism, Practice and Belief*, pp. 345–347.

only enhanced Herod's positive attitude towards the Essenes.[15] Were the Essenes a marginal element in the politics of Herodian Judaea? If so, even had they not accepted Herod's rule, they would never have become a real source of danger, since their secluded life in rural communities and in close-knitted urban quarters made them an element that did not take an active role in political struggles. On the other hand, the Essenes may have already been active and politically relevant during Herod's reign. If so, then Herod's achievement in bringing the Essenes over to his side would have been of great significance.

We do not know what the Qumran sect, identified by some scholars as Essenes, thought of Herod, nor vice-versa.[16] Knohl presumes that the Qumran sectarians, identified as Essenes, regarded the aforementioned Menahem, who was active in the Herodian court, as the Messiah.[17] The sectarians of Qumran were a politically marginal group. What is certain is that the settlement at Qumran, probably destroyed in 40 BCE, was rebuilt and that the sectarians continued to dwell there undisturbed until the Great Revolt, when the settlement was destroyed. Herod was clearly not disturbed by this group.

The Pharisees did not represent the bourgeoisie or the poorer classes, but were probably part of the landed gentry, as Neusner recognizes. What was Herod's policy towards the Pharisees, and how did they react to it? It is difficult to provide a definitive answer to these questions on the basis of Josephus.[18] First of all, most contemporary historiographers do see in the Pharisees a group that was, in the main, hostile to Herod. Alon, Richardson, Schwartz, and Ben Shammai are probably the best example of this trend.[19] On the other hand, the sources provide a mixed answer, both positive and negative, and it is also important to consider the attitude of the sources toward the Pharisees – in particular, Josephus – which

---

[15] See Josephus, *AJ* XV, 378.

[16] Fritsch, for example, identifies the Qumran sect with the Essenes, and argues that this group was pushed to the Dead Sea shore because of Herod's enmity. See G. T. Fritsch, "Herod the Great and the Qumran Community", *JBL* 74, 1955, pp. 173–181. On the other hand, Richardson argues that Herod does not appear in any of the Dead Sea Scrolls. See Richardson, *Herod King of the Jews*, p. 259.

[17] See I. Knohl, *The Messiah before Jesus*, Jerusalem 2000. Broshi and Eshel, in their review of Knohl's book, entirely reject his arguments. See M. Broshi and H. Eshel, "A Messiah before Jesus Christ", *Tarbiz* 60, 1 2002, pp. 1–33.

[18] See Josephus, *AJ* XVII, 172–176 on Sameas and Pollio, and *AJ* XV, 3–4, 370 and *AJ* XVII, 42 on Pollio and Sameas and the Pharisees refusal to take the oath of allegiance, *AJ* XV 260–263 on the Sons of Baba, *BJ* I 648–650 on the eagle affair, and *AJ* XVII, 41–46 and *BJ* I, 571 on the Pharisees at Herod's court.

[19] See for a classic treatment of the subject G. Allon, "The Attitude of the Pharisees toward Roman Rule and the Herodian Dynasty", *Scripta Hierosolymitana* 7, 1961, pp. 53–78. Both Schalit and Alon emphasize that as Herod was of Idumaean stock, thus, a descendant of converts to Judaism, he could not be recognized as a legitimate king of Israel. Sanders sees the relationship between Herod and the Pharisees as positive only in the first years of his reign. See Sanders, *Judaism, Practice and Belief*, pp. 383–394.

are still a source of argument.[20] In my analysis I would like to stress that the Pharisees should not be regarded as a united group with a common political ideology and way of life, although a mainstream faction can be recognized among them. Talmudic literature underscores the fact that the Pharisees were not a monolithic movement and that there were various subgroups among them. In Rabbinic literature, the two schools of Hillel and of Shammai provide the best example of the lack of a cohesive viewpoint among the Pharisees, and that they were not united, either internally or, most likely, even superficially. Moreover, if the schools of Hillel and of Shammai comprised the mainstream segments of the movement, independent views, such as of those of the Rabbis who tore the eagle off of the Temple façade, subsisted peripherally. Thus I suggest here that the relationship between King Herod and the Pharisees is intended to refer only to the mainstream segment of the Pharisaic movement, and hence would like to consider the relationship between King Herod and the Pharisees on two levels – first the relationship between Herod and the Pharisees as a political party, exemplified by the relationship between Herod and the Pharisee leaders Pollio and Sameas, and then the position of the Pharisees, not as a political party, but as holy men at Herod's court.

Josephus speaks of two Pharisean leaders: Pollio and Sameas.[21] As Schwartz successfully argues, during the Herodian period the Pharisees were a political force to be reckoned with.[22] It is probable that when Herod became king, he endeavored to win the friendship of the Pharisee mainstream, since, like the Pharisees, he shared a political enmity towards the Hasmoneans. According to Josephus, after Herod conquered Jerusalem he enjoyed a positive relationship with Pollio the Pharisee, who had opposed him years earlier in the episode of Ezechias,[23] and with Sameas, his disciple, whom Herod had always held in great regard, according to Josephus.[24] In 20 BCE, more than fifteen years later, both Pollio and Sameas were excused from taking an oath in support of Herod, just as the Essenes had been.[25] Some years later, Herod once more asked the Pharisees for an

---

[20] I think that Mason, who states that Josephus was quite hostile to the Pharisees throughout his works, is quite right. This negative attitude does influence modern scholars' analyses of the relationship between Herod and the Pharisees. See on Josephus and the Pharisees S. Mason, *Flavius Josephus on the Pharisees, A Composition – Critical Study*, Studia Post Biblica, Leiden 1991.

[21] See Josephus, *AJ* XIV, 172–176, *AJ* XV, 3–4, 370, and *AJ* XVII, 172–176 on Sameas and Pollio.

[22] See D. R. Schwartz, "Josephus and Nicolaus on the Pharisees", *JSJ* 14, 1983, pp. 151–171.

[23] See Josephus, *AJ* XIV, 172–174.

[24] See Josephus, *AJ* XIV, 175–176.

[25] See Josephus, *AJ* XV, 368–370. According to Schwartz this passage was written by Josephus. The later passage regarding the Pharisees' refusal to take the oath, Josephus, *AJ* XVII, 41–45, on the other hand, comes from Nicolaus. Schwartz argues that the first passage by Josephus presents the Pharisees in a positive light and Herod in a negative light. Josephus' purpose was to show the Pharisees' positive attitude towards Herod and Augustus. The second passage by Nicolaus presents the Pharisees in a negative light and Herod in a positive light. See Schwartz,

oath of loyalty to himself and to Augustus. Six thousand Pharisees refused, and the wife of Pheroras, Herod's brother, paid their fine for non-compliance. Was it the same oath as before or another oath? In the first case, only the Pharisees leaders were concerned, and the oath was to Herod alone. The second time, all of the Pharisees were involved, and the oath was to both Herod and Augustus. I presume that these are two separate oaths.[26] According to various scholars, the number six thousand is exaggerated, and only six hundred refused to take the oath. The number, however, is not particularly relevant. If Herod excused his supporters Pollio and Sameas from taking the oath for any reason whatsoever, there could be no rationale not to excuse the other Pharisees. The oath was probably a mere formality, and the fact that the Pharisees specifically refused to take the oath does not mean that they had a negative attitude toward Herod or toward the Romans. Had that been the case, a member of the Herodian family would not have paid the fine. It is possible that only a minority refused the oath and that the vast majority accepted, though that seems doubtful. And yet Herod absolved the Essenes, as an entire group, from taking the oath, while he absolved only the Pharisee leaders Pollio and Sameas, forcing, or attempting to force, the oath upon the Pharisees as a whole. Perhaps the possible opposition of the Essenes as a group was irrelevant to the stability of Herod's rule, though it is impossible to say the same thing about the Pharisees, who were far more powerful. One possibility is that the oath of loyalty was intended to be administered to the Gentile population of the kingdom and not to the Jews, since Herod respected Jewish Law and to demand such an oath would have been a severe infringement of the Law of the Fathers. If Herod wished to be sure of the loyalty of his Jewish subjects, he could have used other methods. Augustus, for instance, reports in the *Res Gestae* that the Italic population swore an oath of allegiance before the confrontation with Mark Antony,[27] and it is possible that Herod took this oath as a model. This would confirm that the original purpose of the oath was to test the loyalty of the Gentile population of the kingdom.

"Josephus and Nicolaus on the Pharisees", pp. 151–171. Schalit's proposal to identify Josephus' Pollio and Sameas with the rabbinic Hillel and Shammai is appealing. Josephus does not mention Hillel or Shammai. According to Rabbinic sources, m. 'Abot 10–11 there were two pairs of Sages, leaders of the Pharisean movement, who lived during this period. Shemaya and Avtalion, two converts, followed by their disciples, Hillel and Shammai. On the Pharisean leadership of Hillel and Shammai see I. Ben Shalom, *The School of Shammai and the Zealot's Struggle against Rome*, Jerusalem 1993, pp. 99–100. See M. Hadas-Lebel, *Hillel, Un sage au temps de Jésus*, Paris 1999, pp. 41–43. See also J. Lehmann, "Le procès d'Hérode, Saméas et Pollion", *REJ* 24, 1892. See also A. Kaminka, "Hillel's Life and Work", in *Jewish Quarterly Review* 30, 1939–40, pp. 107–122. Kaminka also argues for the identification of Pollio with Hillel. Schalit also identifies Pollio as Hillel. See Schalit, *King Herod*, p. 234. See also Schalit, *König Herodes*, p. 474. On the other side Feldman identified Josephus's Pollio with Avtallion. See L. H. Feldman, "The Identity of Pollio, the Pharisee, in Josephus", *JQR* 49, 1958–59, pp. 53–62.

[26] See Josephus, *AJ* XVII, 41–45.
[27] See *Res Gestae* 25. 2. See also Southern, *Augustus*, p. 96.

Were the Pharisees hostile to Rome during the Herodian period? We have no clear-cut answer.[28] Most scholars who point to a negative relationship between Herod and the Pharisees regard the tie between Herod and the Pharisee leaders Pollio and Sameas as merely a sign of mutual respect.[29] An interesting case is that of the sons of Baba, who were protected by Costobar, the first husband of Salome.[30] These persons "of great dignity and power among the multitude" greatly favored the Hasmonean Antigonus. After the conquest of Jerusalem by Herod, Costobar sheltered them for a long period of time after Herod's rise to power. Were they Pharisees? It appears unlikely that any Pharisee would have supported Antigonus, and in fact, Josephus does not mention any tie between them and the Pharisees.[31] The example generally reported by the scholars to illustrate Pharisee hostility toward Herod is the Eagle affair,[32] when two young masters, Judas and Matthias, tore down the golden eagle from the facade of the Temple.[33] Josephus does not mention that they were Pharisees, though it is quite possible that they were, albeit a marginal element.

As already stated, the Pharisees were not a monolithic movement. Were they connected to the nationalist School of Shammai as Ben Shalom hints? This does not appear likely, since their act was not motivated by any negative feeling towards Rome – symbolized by the eagle – but by religious fanaticism, since the eagle was a graven image and such images are forbidden to Jews. Another

---

[28] It is possible that the Pharisees were an important component of the delegation sent to Rome to invite Augustus to take the rule of Judaea from the hands of Archelaus. Clearly the delegation did not have a hostile attitude toward Rome. See Josephus, *AJ* XVII, 299–314 and *BJ* II, 80–92. The delegation of fifty ambassadors came to Rome with the permission of Varus, the governor of Syria. Josephus stresses that the 8,000 Jews living then in Rome supported this delegation.

[29] See Richardson, *Herod King of the Jews*, p. 256. I. Ben Shalom also sees Sameas' and Pollio's attitude towards Herod as basically negative, although they were not actively opposed to Herod's rule. This means, according to Ben Shalom, that there were Pharisees actively opposed to Herod. See Ben Shalom, *School of Shammai*, pp. 289–292.

[30] See Josephus, *AJ* XV, 260–263.

[31] Kasher argues that not all the Idumaeans supported Herod. Thus Costobar and the sons of Baba conspired against him. Kasher argues for an Idumaean origin of the Sons of Baba and of Baba Ben Butha. This would explain why most of the Idumaeans took the side of the rebels in 66 CE. See Kasher, *Jews, Idumaeans and Ancient Arabs*, pp. 214–220, "Appendix B – The Costobar Conspiracy and the Sons of Baba".

[32] On the Eagle affair, see Ben Shalom, *School of Shammai*, pp. 108–109. I. Ben Shalom does identify Judas and Matthias as Pharisees. Ben Shalom stresses, however, that the names of the two hotheads were not recorded in Talmudic sources. Also very important is Baumgarten's intervention on the Pharisees in the series of lectures dedicated to "Common Judaism, or a Plurality of 'Judaisms' in Late Antiquity, the State of Debate", *The Thirteenth School in Jewish Studies*, Jerusalem May 13–16 2003. Baumgarten sees the episode of the eagle as a typical case of hidden transcripts, as defined by J.C. Scott. See J.C. Scott, *Domination and the Arts of Resistance – Hidden Transcripts*, New Haven 1990, p. 223. Thus, according to Baumgarten, the episode of the eagle was not really marginal; the two Pharisee leaders were not, in fact, isolated, but represented a wider popular resistance to Herod's regime.

[33] See Josephus, *BJ* I, 648–650.

example is the description of Herod that appears in the Assumption of Moses,[34] which presents Herod as a negative figure, rash and perverse, determined to exterminate the Sadducees and therefore greatly feared.[35] Even if the text is Pharisee, it was written after Herod's death, at least ten years later. The attitude that underlies the Assumption of Moses does not reflect a contemporary view of Herod's rule, but, rather, a later one. Moreover, it may reflect the view of the author alone and not of the Pharisees as a group. The two last years of Herod's rule were harsh and provoked enough fear to erase the previous years from the public memory and to engender a negative view of his entire reign. Archelaus' harsh rule probably contributed to influencing the author's negative view.[36] Later Rabbinic sources present a much more balanced view. Herod appears both as the "Slayer of the Sages" and as the builder of the Temple, in reparation for his sins.[37] D. Schwartz stresses that the Sages regarded Herod in a more positive light than they did the Hasmoneans.[38] According to Baumgarten, the negative view of Herod among the Sages began at the time of Gamaliel II of Yavne, when the Patriarch indeed offered an alternative to the leadership of Agrippa II.[39] Rabbinic sources thus sully the name of Herod, the ancestor of Agrippa II, but that does not reflect the real relationship between the Pharisees and Herod during the period under consideration. Thus we may conclude that the Pharisees were still far from making a transition from politics to piety, and that they were a political group to be reckoned with. Herod was politically adept enough to search for a positive relationship with the mainstream Pharisee group, though it was a relationship that was not entirely free of a certain degree of friction.

The Pharisees, however, were not just a political group; they were also holy men, with prophetic gifts. Josephus reports in both *Antiquities* and *War* that the Pharisees had great influence at court as holy men.[40] This does not seem to be

---

[34] On the assumption of Moses, see J. H. Charlesworth, *Old Testament Pseudepigrapha*, 1, pp. 919–931. See also I. Zeitlin, "The Assumption of Moses and the Bar Kokhba Revolt", *JQR* 38, 1947–48, pp. 1–45. Most scholars, however, date the text to the first century CE, most likely between 1 and 30 CE, but certainly before 70 CE, as the Temple was apparently standing when it was written. The book was composed in Judaea, according to Charles, by a Pharisee who was resisting growing nationalism in his party.

[35] See T. Mos. 6, 2–9, in Charlesworth, *Old Testament Pseudepigrapha* 1, p. 929.

[36] Baumgarten underscores that although Herod is depicted as rash and perverse, the legitimacy of Herod's claim to the throne is not disputed. See Baumgarten, "Legitimacy of Herod and his Sons as Kings of Israel", pp. 32–33.

[37] See the dialogue between Herod and Baba ben Buta. TB, *B. Bat.* 3 b.

[38] See D. Schwartz, "Jewish Sources on the Herods", in *International Conference at the British Museum*, "The World of the Herods and the Nabataeans," held between 17–19 April 2001.

[39] Baumgarten stresses that only during Agrippa I's reign, the legitimacy of Herod's royal house was disputed, but then by a very small group. Only after the destruction of the Second Temple and the beginning of a new Jewish leadership, the legitimacy of the House of Herod was put in doubt, because of his origins. See Baumgarten, "Legitimacy of Herod and his Sons as Kings of Israel", pp. 36–37.

[40] See Josephus, *AJ* XVII, 41–45 and *BJ* I, 571. Also in the New Testament the Pharisees

particularly strange if one compares the Pharisees' standing at Herod's court as soothsayers, seers, or prophets to that of Trasyllus at Tiberius's court.[41] According to Josephus, the Pharisees – grateful that Pheroras's wife had paid the fine that Herod had imposed on them when they refused to take the oath of allegiance to Augustus – predicted to Pheroras and his wife that the throne would fall from Herod's hands and pass to them. As soon as Salome learned of this, she told King Herod, who swiftly executed all of the culprits, including the Pharisees who had been accused and a eunuch named Bagoas. According to Mason, Josephus stresses that although the Pharisees prided themselves greatly on their exegetical powers, and although they were perfectly able to make predictions, they chose instead to employ their talents to the king's detriment, thus betraying his trust.[42] As Baumgarten highlights, according to Josephus, the Pharisees behaved as common sorcerers who consorted with women and eunuchs, and not as holy men. I believe that Mason is correct in seeing Josephus as the author of this episode, and thus correct in attributing to Josephus the negative attitude and antipathy towards the Pharisees, rather than to his original source, which Josephus elaborated upon and which was probably neutral, or perhaps even favorable, toward the Pharisees.[43] It is quite possible that the original source for both *Antiquities* and *War*, whoever he was, only stressed the important position achieved by the Pharisees at Herod's court and did not forcefully present a negative relationship between them and Herod. It is interesting that Josephus has to admit that Herod's reaction was rather moderate and that only the guilty Pharisees were punished. There is no hint that the Pharisees, on the whole, suffered as a result of this episode.

---

appear as men of magic. See Matt 12: 22–29. Also the Sectarians of Qumran denunciated the Pharisees use of magic in Pesher Nahum (4QpNah). See A. I. Baumgarten, "Pharisaic Authority: Prophecy and Power (Ant. 17. 41–45)", pp. 10–11.

[41] The Greek astrologer was much prized and honored as future teller by Tiberius. See Suetonius, *Tiberius* III, XIV. Vespasian consulted a certain Seleucus of Syria (Tacitus, *Historiae* 2, 78, 1) and the famous Tiberius Claudius Balbillus (Dio, *Roman History* 65, 9, 2). See also B. Levick, *Vespasian*, London 1999, p. 70

[42] Mason argues that the depiction of the Pharisees in this episode does not differ from Josephus's depiction of the Pharisees thought his works, which is on the main quite negative. Thus, according to Mason, Josephus highlights in *AJ* XVII, 41 the topic that the Pharisees had real prophetic power, but, as usual, they rather misbehaved. Then Josephus elaborates the story itself in *AJ* XVII, 42–45. See S. Mason, *Flavius Josephus on the Pharisees, A Composition – Critical Study*, Studia Post Biblica, Leiden 1991, pp. 261–272. For the analysis of the parallel passage in *BJ* see Mason, *Flavius Josephus on the Pharisees*, pp. 116–119.

[43] Mason writes in the analysis of the passage in *AJ* that most scholars, as Hölscher and Rivkin, see Nicolaus of Damascus, not just as the main source of this episode, but also that the negative attitude towards the Pharisees exemplified in this sordid episode originated in Nicolaus, and not in Josephus. However Mason shows quite convincingly that Josephus, even if he is not the main source, is however, responsible for the negative image of the Pharisees. Mason stress that in *BJ* Josephus depicts once more in a negative way the Pharisee, while Herod, positively depicted, is shown as their victim. For the analysis of the parallel passage in *BJ* I, 571 see Mason, *Flavius Josephus on the Pharisees*, pp. 116–119, 272–280.

2. Herod and the Judaean Ruling Class

The conclusions, then, are striking. First of all, the Pharisees were not just a political party to be reckoned with, but they were powerful enough to be present at Herod's court as holy men. In that respect, they were not different, as Baumgarten stresses, from other personalities in the Eastern Mediterranean, most notably Apollonius of Tyana, who were both philosophers and holy men. Second, it is obvious that the Pharisees had such a standing at the royal court only because Herod wished it or tolerated them there. Third, it is certainly possible that some Pharisee holy men would have preferred Herod's brother as king, instead of Herod, but it seems to me that these holy men did not represent the mainstream Pharisee movement. On the contrary, the episode merely shows that the Pharisees had no problem in recognizing the monarchical rule of Herod and his family. Baumgarten stresses that had the Pharisees not have recognized the legitimacy of Herod's claims to the crown, they would not have conspired to place Pheroras on Herod's throne.[44]

In conclusion, Herod had, in fact, many interests in common with the mainstream Pharisee group. Some of the Pharisees, such as the leaders Pollio and Sameas, collaborated with Herod and were courted by him. Moreover, Pharisees found a place at Herod's court and benefited from the elimination of the Sadducees as a political class.

Herod also tried to create a new ruling class unrelated to the sects. The individuals who received benefits from Herod and who were obviously faithful to him included courtiers, army officers, and officials of the royal administration. After Herod's death, the Roman attitude toward them was the same as the attitude toward the Sadducees, whom the Romans regarded as members of the same ruling class.

Among the ruling class of Judaea the most interesting, albeit puzzling, group is that of the *Herodians* mentioned in the New Testament. Josephus refers to the *herodeioi* as a group that, during the civil war between Herod and Antigonus, took the side of Herod. Thus, at the beginning of the war, some Galileans revolted against Herod and drowned a group of Herod's supporters, who are called *herodeioi*. Later, Machaeras takes revenge on the Jews, killing friends, called *herodeioi*, and foes, the latter obviously partisans of Antigonus. Later, when Herod conquered Jerusalem, he showed favor to his friends and supporters, the *herodeioi*, but Antigonus' partisans were slain. Richardson sees in these *herodeioi* a political group that supported Herod during his reign.[45]

---

[44] See also Baumgarten, "Legitimacy of Herod and his Sons as Kings of Israel", p. 34. Baumgarten stresses that if the Pharisees would not have recognized the legitimacy of Herod's claims to the crown, they would not had conspired to have Pheroras sit on Herod's throne.

[45] The episode of the drowning of Herod's partisans in the Sea of Galilee is reported in Josephus, *AJ* XIV, 450 and *BJ* I, 326. In both passages the term *herodeioi* is used. Also later describing the indiscriminate murder of friends and foes by Machaeras, Josephus uses the term *herodeioi* in both *AJ* XIV, 436 and *BJ* I, 319. However describing the conquest of Jerusalem and

The problem is that Josephus uses this term only in describing the opposing factions during the civil war. Thus I believe that Josephus does not really mention a political party as such, but only Herod's partisans, and, moreover, neither their social standing nor their origin is clear. I believe that once Herod became king, he banded together a group of supporters that identified so closely with him, that they can be defined as *Herodians*, or using the New Testament term, *herodianoi*, and, in that, Richardson is correct. The presence of this group was obviously felt only after Herod's death, during Roman rule, since earlier, during Herod's lifetime, the existence of such group as an organized "party" was not necessary under direct Herodian rule. It is noteworthy that if the New Testament term refers to a group active during Jesus' lifetime, it can indicate a pressure group tied to Antipas, and later to Agrippa I. On the other hand, if the term is a later denotation, it can refer to a group that was active when some of the New Testament texts were written and hence tied to Agrippa II.[46]

Thus I believe that after Herod's death, various groups, each connected to Herod for a particular reason, automatically banded together and formed a pressure group on the Roman government. These groups were probably comprised of those elements of the ruling class of Judaea who had been favored by Herod, often with grants of land, and thus included members of Herod's family; Jewish landowners who owed their estates to Herod's generosity; the family of Ptolemy; Herod's prime ministers; members of Herod's courts; Idumaeans, Herod's kinsmen; and the various High Priest families coming from Babylonia and Alexandria who felt alone after Herod's death. To this group, who were certainly part of the ruling class of Judaea, I would like to add the Babylonian Jews who came with Zamaris and settled in the north of the country. The feature common to all of these groups is that they owed everything to Herod, and it would have been advantageous for them to have had one of Herod's sons, such as Antipas, or one of his grandsons, such as Agrippa I, crowned King of Judaea.[47] Their ideology,

---

its aftermath Josephus uses the term *herodeioi* only in *BJ* I, 358, but not in *AJ* XV, 1, where he is also more generic. See also Richardson, *Herod King of the Jews*, p. 260.

[46] Richardson suggests three possibilities for the Herodian – *herodianoi*, mentioned in the New Testament (Matt 22:16 and Mark 3: 6; 12: 13). The first suggestion is that Herodians is a late term that appears in the New Testament's text because this group was still relevant at the time of writing. Thus the group is connected with Agrippa II. However, according to Richardson, this possibility is historically implausible. Agrippa II during the Great War fought on the side of the Romans, and thus most of the Jews could not accept him as a possible ruler. The second suggestion is that the term Herodians is refers to a group active during the lifetime of Jesus, and its members identify with Antipas first and then with Agrippa I. The third suggestion, proposed by Richardson is that the Herodians was a group tied directly to Herod. Thus Richardson supports his thesis using the passages of Josephus which refers to the *herodeioi*. See Richardson, *Herod King of the Jews*, p. 260. See also H. H. Rowley, "The Herodians in the Gospels", *JST* 41, 1940, pp. 14–27.

[47] Goodman gives the best definition of the groups favored by Herod, which would have composed the Herodians. These are Jewish landowners granted lands expropriated after 37 BCE,

according to Richardson, presented all of the same elements as Herod's had, such as the necessity of a King in order to maintain independence, as well as personal ties with Rome's ruling families.[48] The New Testament points to another group discussed below, close to the *Herodians*, and these are the Pharisees. When Mark and Matthew mention the *Herodians*, they always mention them together with the Pharisees. I think that this is hardly accidental. The Pharisees were interested in both peace and independence of the sort that only a Herodian ruler could provide. Clearly, this would explain the positive image of Agrippa I that is found in later Talmudic literature. Although the Pharisees had a political and social agenda that differed from that of the *Herodians*, they probably saw eye to eye on various issues. This association and cooperation, however, ended in 66 CE.[49]

3. The Ruling Bodies of the Herodian State

A. *The Political Constitution of Herodian Judaea*

Before Herod's rule, it is possible to distinguish four main phases in the evolution of the collective bodies of Hellenistic and Hasmonean Judaea. In the first phase, the beginning of the Hellenistic Period, the institutions of Judaea had hardly changed from those of the early Persian Period.[50] The high priest was assisted by an assembly formed by the elders. Two social classes – the *horin*, or free men, obviously the lower class, and the *sganim*, the priests and the other dignitaries, the upper class – formed this corporate body. In the second phase, the Ptolemaic and Seleucid periods, the corporate bodies of Judaea became more similar to those of the Greek city-states, at least in name. The Oniad high priest presided over a council of elders, the *gerousia*, and a popular assembly, or *ekklesia*, although it seems that the latter body had little influence. Thus, Hecataeus of Abdera, probably one of the earliest sources on the Hellenistic period, defined the government of the Jews as a theocracy ruled by a high priest, assisted by the *gerousia*, or council of elders, and by the *ekklesia*, or popular assembly. After the Seleucid

---

members of Herod's family, Idumaeans, and of course the families of the high priests appointed by Herod. See Goodman, *Ruling Class of Judaea*, pp. 40–43, 58–60.

[48] See Richardson, *Herod King of the Jews*, pp. 259–260.

[49] See Mark 12: 13–17 and Matt 22: 15–22 depicts the Herodians together with the Pharisees, when the two groups wish that Jesus declare himself on the taxes payable to Rome. However Luke 20: 20–26 mention scribes and chief priests. Once more Mark 3: 6 and 8: 15 depicts the Herodians associated with the Pharisees committed to Herod's destruction. See Richardson, *Herod King of the Jews*, pp. 309–310.

[50] See Schürer, *History of the Jewish People*, p. 201. See also Goodblatt, *Monarchic Principle*, pp. 78–83. See L. Finkelstein, "The Men of the Great Synagogue (circa 400–170 BCE)", in *CHJ*, *The Hellenistic Age*, Cambridge 1989, pp. 229–244.

conquest, the *gerousia* is also attested to in the Charter of Antiochus III[51]. In the third phase, the beginning of the Hasmonean period, the conservative political constitution of Jerusalem of the early Hellenistic Period had been replaced by a similar constitution, albeit a more democratic one, in which the popular assembly had more power.[52] As before, the *gerousia* and the *ekklesia* stood side by side. It appears, however, that during the early Hasmonean period the *gerousia* lost much of its power to the great assembly, *ekklesia megale*. The latter term, coined by Simon in 141 BCE, clearly reflects the democratization of society. The fourth and later phase dates from the reign of Alexander Jannaeus onwards. The only corporate body attested to for this period is the *hever ha-yehudim*, wider in its composition than a council.[53] The meaning of the world *hever* is unclear. Though scholars have tried to translate it as "council," its meanings are wide enough as to include the Greek words *koinon* ("commonwealth") and *ethnos* ("people"). Goodblatt states that the only certain thing about the *hever* is that it was a corporate body of wider composition than a council. The *Council of the Hasmoneans*, mentioned in Rabbinic sources, was probably no more than an advisory body composed of the king's *philoi*. Pompey's conquest brought an end to the political institutions of the Hasmonean state, and Gabinius later divided the country in five *synedria* or *synodoi*.[54] Later, Iulius Caesar once more unified the country

---

[51] See V. Tcherikover, "Hellenistic Palestine: The Political Situation from 332 to 175 BCE", in *The World History of the Jewish People VI, The Hellenistic Period*, New Brunswick 1972, pp. 106, 111. See also Schürer, *History of the Jewish People II*, pp. 202–203. See Bickerman, *Jews in the Greek Age*, pp. 110, 125, 143, 154. See also Goodblatt, *Monarchic Principle*, pp. 89–99.

[52] See Schürer, *History of the Jewish People II*, p. 203. See also A. Schalit, "Domestic Politics and Political Institutions", in *The World History of the Jewish People VI, The Hellenistic Period*, New Brunswick 1972, p. 258.

[53] See Meshorer, *Treasury of Jewish Coins*, pp. 23–53. On the *Council of the Hasmoneans* mentioned in Rabbinic sources see TB, *Sanh.* 82a and ʿ*Abod. Zar.* 36b. The *gerousia* is no longer mentioned in connection with later Hasmoneans, the only exception being Salome Alexandra. See Goodblatt, *Monarchic Principle*, pp. 99–103. Schalit differentiates between two bodies, the *Court of the Hasmoneans*, a permanent restricted council responsible for daily affairs, and a larger body, the *hever ha-yehudim*, convened only to confirm the rulings of the Hasmonean ruler. See Schalit, "Domestic Politics and Political Institutions", pp. 261–262.

[54] On *synedria* see Josephus, *AJ* XIV, 90–91. On *synodoi* see Josephus, *BJ* I, 170. See also H.D. Mantel, "The High Priesthood and the Sanhedrin in the Time of the Second Temple", in *The World History of the Jewish People VII, The Herodian Period*, New Brunswick 1975, p. 274. See also Schürer, *History of the Jewish People II*, pp. 205–206. The first council sat at Jerusalem, the others at Jericho in Judaea, Amathus in Idumaea and Sepphoris in Galilee. Josephus remarks that the Jews were freed from monarchy and were now ruled by the aristocracy. Two things are clear. The first is that only the upper members of the local society made up these bodies, and the second, that these bodies had only a juridical authority. This division of the Hasmonean state into five different and separate juridical entities, independent of one another, indeed mirrors the Roman treatment of rebel states such as Macedonia, divided in 166 BCE into four different republics. According to the jurist Rabello, the Romans did not make Judaea a *provincia*, or an allied state. Judaea shared the fate of Antigonid Macedonia. Gabinius thus divided the area of the much-reduced Hasmonean state into five regions, *synedria* or *synodoi*, each ruled by local elite. The jurisdiction of these bodies followed traditional Jewish law. Thus, the judicial autonomy of

under Hyrcanus II and his *epitropos*, Antipater.⁵⁵ The *hever ha-yehudim* is once more attested to on the coins of the latter ruler.

The political institutions of the Hasmonean state changed only slightly during the Herodian period. Thus, during the Herodian period we recognize the existence of three main collective bodies, the Municipal Council of Jerusalem or *boulē*, the popular assembly or *ekklesia*, and, we believe, a new body, the *synedrion/Sanhedrin*, which first appeared during Herod's reign. There are various problems related to this topic. First, the three literary sources – Josephus, Rabbinic sources, and the New Testament – can be interpreted in conflicting ways. Josephus, obviously our most important source, mentions the *boulē*, the *ekklesia*, and the *synedrion*.

i. The *boulē*

Did the *boulē*, attested to under Roman rule in Josephus, the New Testament, and Dio Cassius,⁵⁶ already exist during the Herodian period? I believe so, since

---

the Jews was not attacked, only their unity. See A. M. Rabello, "Civil Justice in Palestine from 63 BCE to 70 CE", in Katzoff, R. Petroff, Y. and Shaps, D. (eds.), *Classical Studies in Honor of David Sohlberg*, Ramat Gan 1996, pp. 293–306, in *The Jews in the Roman Empire: Legal Problems, from Herod to Justinian*, Variorum Collected Studies Series, Aldershot 2000.

⁵⁵ See Josephus, *AJ* XIV, 143–144, and *BJ* I, 199.

⁵⁶ For the period after Herod, the *boulē* of Jerusalem is mentioned by Josephus, the New Testament and Dio Cassius. All of Josephus' references portray the *boulē* as a corporate body that existed during and after the reign of Agrippa I. The most important reference is a letter addressed by Claudius to Agrippa I in which the *boulē* is mentioned. See Josephus, *AJ* XX, 11. If the document is authentic, the reference leaves no doubt that Jerusalem had a municipal council similar to that of the Greek cities. Moreover the letter mentions both the *boulē* and the *demos*. In our view, this leaves no doubt that the *boulē* mentioned is the municipal council. Josephus mentions the *boulē* in connection to the Roman governors of Judaea (Josephus, *BJ* II, 331). The procurator mentioned is Gessius Florus. Once more the *boulē* is mentioned on the eve of the Great War (Josephus, *BJ* II, 405.). Another very important references to the *boulē* is the reference to Aristeus of Emmaus, secretary of the *boulē*, murdered by Simon bar Giora (Josephus, *BJ* V, 532.). Dio Cassius mentions the *bouleutai* of Jerusalem as standing in the forecourt of the Temple when Titus stormed the place (Dio Cassius, *Historia* LXVI, 6. 2.). The New Testament reference to the *bouleutes* Joseph of Arimathea (Emmaus), if accurate, is important because it shows that there were members of the *boulē* who were not part of the priestly aristocracy. See Mark 15: 43, Luke 23: 50. Various scholars have tried to identify the *boulē* mentioned by Josephus and the New Testament with the *synedrion/Sanhedrin*. Both Josephus and the New Testaments mention the terms *boulē* and *synedrion*. Presumably, these ancient sources had two different corporate bodies in mind. It is important to separate their responsibilities. The *synedria* of Josephus, the New Testament, and Rabbinic literature, clearly points to various types of courts of law rather than to a city senate that deals with entertainment buildings. Josephus mentions not only the *boulē* of Jerusalem, but also the *boulē* of Tiberias as a corporate body composed of sixty members. On the *boulē* of Tiberias see mainly Josephus, *BJ* II, 639–641. Obviously the *boulē* of Tiberias cannot be confounded with a *synedrion/Sanhedrin*, and its decision-making responsibilities were precisely parallel to those of its Jerusalem counterpart. Like the Jerusalem *boulē*, the *boulē* of Tiberias did not act as a court of justice, rather, as a small city senate. Both the *boulē* and the *synedrion/Sanhedrin* were composed of members of the ruling class, includ-

Josephus mentions the existence of the *boulē* during the Herodian period at least once, when Herod summoned the "most eminent men" of the city to explain that the theatre and hippodrome were innocuous from a religious point of view.[57] I believe that Josephus had a corporate body in mind, rather than an *ad hoc concilium*, when describing this meeting. These men were presumably members of the *boulē*, since they are defined as "most eminent." Moreover, the subject, clearly of a civic nature, was without doubt one that was apt to be debated by the *boulē*.

It seems to me that the composition of the Herodian *boulē* did not differ much from the composition of the first century CE *boulē*. In the later period, the *boulē* was made up of the most important members of Jerusalem aristocracy, both laymen and priests, and there is no reason to think that the Herodian *boulē* was different in its composition. Compared to those of other Greek *poleis*, it is probable that the *boulē* of Jerusalem numbered some several hundred members, which was the standard size of these corporate bodies in the Greek East. This corporate body met frequently at predetermined times and discussed matters connected with the welfare, administration, and economy of the city.

Josephus mentions city magistrates in connection with the *boulē*. First were the *archontes*,[58] found in other Greek city-states, and second was the secretary of the *boulē*,[59] also found in the Greek cities. Other magistrates mentioned by Josephus are the *deka protoi*, or the ten most eminent members of the *boulē*,[60] found in the Greek cities and in Carthage.[61] Another magistrate, this time mentioned in an epigraphic source, is the *agoranomos*, responsible for the city markets.[62] Josephus does not mention all of the city magistrates. Since Jerusalem had a *gymnasium*, a theater, and a water system, there were obviously magistrates who were responsible for these institutions. These magistrates are known from literary and epigraphic sources to have existed in the other cities of the Greek East. Thus Jerusalem probably had a *gymnasiarch* as well, responsible for the *gymnasium*, and perhaps magistrates who were responsible for the theater, since Herod had erected such a structure. There were most likely also the *sitones* and *meledones*,

---

ing members of the priestly aristocracy and members of the lay aristocracy, which included the leading Pharisees. The same person could have simultaneously been a member of both the *boulē* and the *synedrion/Sanhedrin*. See also Goodblatt, *Monarchic Principle*, pp. 117–118.

[57] See Josephus, *AJ* XVI, 278.
[58] See Josephus, *AJ* XX, 11.
[59] See Josephus, *BJ* V, 532 and also Schürer, *History of the Jewish People II*, p. 214.
[60] Josephus mentions the *deka protoi* as envoys to Nero together with Ishmael, the high priest and the treasurer Helkias. See Josephus, *AJ* XX, 194.
[61] See also Schürer, *History of the Jewish People II*, p. 214.
[62] See Y. Meshorer, "A Stone Weight from the Reign of Herod", *IEJ* 20, 1970, pp. 97–98. The inscription in Greek reads "Year 32 of King Herod, Benefactor, Friend of Caesar, market inspector, 3 minas." The *agoranomos* appears also in Talmudic literature as *logistes*. Was he elected or were, as Safrai indicates, the sons of Herod involved in his appointment? The *agoranomos* was responsible for the supply of goods to the city, the setting of market prices, and he certified and provided weights and measures. See Safrai, *Economy of Roman Palestine*, pp. 37–38.

3. The Ruling Bodies of the Herodian State 265

magistrates responsible for the purchase of wheat, which was always lacking in the overpopulated cities. Other magistrates, in all probability, were responsible for public medicine, including urban hygiene and medical assistance to the poor, and for the water resources of the city.[63]

The *boulē* of Jerusalem, as in the other Greek cities, convened in the *bouleterion*, situated in the Upper City of Jerusalem. Josephus describes this building[64] as standing near the *xyston* or the *gymnasium*. Clearly the two most important buildings of the Hellenistic Greek city-state stood side by side in Jerusalem, as they did in other Greek cities all over the eastern Mediterranean.

The political constitution of Herodian Jerusalem served as model for the later tetrarchic capitals, such as Tiberias, founded by Antipas. Tiberias also had a *boulē* composed of sixty members, *deka protoi*, *archontes*, *uparchoi*, and an *agoranomos*.[65]

Thus, the city constitution of Herodian Jerusalem did not differ at all from those of the Classical cities, including Athens, Rome, and Carthage[66], all of which had magistrates, a permanent council, and an assembly, or in the case of Rome, assemblies, which were convened on certain occasions.[67] Herodian Jerusalem, though a royal city like Pergamum and Alexandria, functioned like any other Greek city-state, with all of the traditional trappings of Archaic and Classical Greek origin. It is possible to argue that the presence of a *boulē* in a royal city as Jerusalem is surprising, since Alexandria, the best example of royal city, had no *boulē*. Yet we must keep in mind that Herod closely controlled the ruling class of Judaea, from whence came the *boulē*'s members, and, moreover, it seems to me

---

[63] See Preaux, *monde hellenistique* II, pp. 442–448.

[64] See Josephus, *BJ* V, 154 and VI, 354.

[65] About the various city bodies of Tiberias, on the *boulē*, composed of 60 members, and on the *deka protoi*, see Josephus, *BJ* II, 639–641, on the *deka protoi*, see Josephus, *Vita* 69, 296, on the *archontes*, see Josephus, *BJ* II, 599, On the *uparchoi*, see Josephus, *BJ* II, 615, and on the *agoranomos*, see Josephus, *AJ* XVIII, 149. See also L. I. Levine, *The Ancient Synagogue, The First Thousand Years*, New York 2000, p. 50.

[66] See Aristotle, in the *Constitution of the Athenians*. See also J. B. Bury and R. Meiggs, *A History of Greece*, London 2001, pp. 161–180, 332–334. See also R. Flacelière, *La vita quotidiana in Grecia nel secolo di Pericle*, Milano 1983, pp. 58–60, 290–306 and O. Murray, *La Grecia delle origini*, Bologna 1983, pp. 209–232 on Athens before Solon and on Solon's reforms and 313–321 on Pisistratus and on Cleisthenes's reforms. On the constitution of Classic Athens see J. K. Davies, *La Grecia Classica*, Bologna 1983, pp. 104–138. The constitution of Rome is well described by Polybius, who much admired it. All the constitutional changes brought by Augustus are described by Dio Cassius in his *Roman History*. See also Cary and Scullard, *History of Rome*, pp. 62–69, 75–83, 97–99, 177–181, 235–237, 279–281, 315–321. The constitution of Punic Carthage was quite similar to those of the Greek city states and that of Rome. It is described by Aristotle, *Politica* II, xi, 1–14. See also A. Di Vita and G. Di Vita-Evrard, *Libya, The Lost Cities of the Roman Empire*, Cologne 1999, pp. 28–29 and D. Hoyos, *Hannibal's Dynasty, Power and Politics in the Western Mediterranean, 247–183 BC*, London 2003.

[67] On the civic institutions of Herodian Jerusalem see also L. I. Levine, *Judaism and Hellenism, Conflict or Confluence?*, Seattle 1998, pp. 84–85.

that Herod called the *boulē* to ratify his decisions less frequently than he did the *ekklesia*, leaving to the *boulē* only matters of civic legislation.

ii. The ekklesia

The popular assembly or Herodian *ekklesia*, mentioned by Josephus,[68] probably continued performing the tasks and functions of the *megale ekklesia* mentioned in the *First Book of Maccabees*. Though this corporate body in fact had no real decision-making power, it was of great importance to Herod, enabling him to sense the opinion of the Jewish masses and to learn if his policies were favorably received by the majority of his subjects or if there was discontent. Moreover, in giving the people the right to vote on a given proposal, Herod made the entire population a partner in his important decisions, rather than mere witnesses to them. This apparent incongruity was, in fact, common among Hellenistic rulers, who liked to demonstrate that their rule derived from the people.[69]

Josephus mentions the General Assembly at least three times. First, when Herod decided to begin work on the Temple, he convened the General Assembly to present his program and to receive their token assent.[70] Another occasion was the trial of Tero, his son, and the barber Tryphon, accused of plotting together with Alexander. Herod had the guilty parties accused in front of the Assembly and judged by them. The same Assembly subsequently executed the accused.[71] Last but not least, Herod convened the Assembly to judge those responsible for pulling down the eagle.[72] Herod presumably convened the Assembly for more trivial matters not mentioned by Josephus. In both instances, when the Assembly served in an advisory capacity and when it served a judicial function, it took on a role similar to those of the *ekklesia* of the Greek city-states and of the Roman *comitia*. The Herodian *ekklesia* was probably convened *ad hoc* and consisted entirely of free men of military age, perhaps divided between priests and laymen

---

[68] See Josephus, *AJ* XV, 381, on Herod calling the general assembly before the beginning of the works on the Temple Mount and *AJ* XVI, 393–394 and *BJ*, I, 150 when Herod called the general assembly in the occasion of the trial of Tero.

[69] The Ptolemies in Alexandria, who abolished the *boulē* but conserved the *ekklesia*, provide a good example. See Ballet, *VQ Alexandrie*, pp. 52–53. See also Will, *Histoire politique du monde hellénistique* II, pp. 440–445, 522–527, 537–539.

[70] See Josephus, *AJ* XV, 381. Josephus uses the word *to plethos*, the multitude, for the assembly. However, it is clear that this multitude came there because it was invited and played a public role.

[71] See Josephus, *AJ* XVI, 393–394 and *BJ*, I, 150. Josephus uses the word *to plethos*. On Herod and the Assembly convened by Herod, see also Sanders, *Judaism, Practice and Belief,* pp. 483–484. Sanders argues that this assembly was convened only when Herod wished to legalize an instance of capital punishment. But I presume that Herod convened this assembly on more trivial occasions not mentioned by Josephus. Goodblatt defines the *plethos* as *ekklesia*, see Goodblatt, *Monarchic Principle*, p. 115.

[72] See Josephus, *BJ* I, 648–650.

as in the *ekklesia megale* called by Simon. Women, minors, slaves, and Gentiles could not be part of the Assembly.

Josephus does not mention the activity of the popular assembly after Herod's death, though its existence is mentioned in Claudius' letter to both the *boulē* and the *demos* of Jerusalem. After Herod's death, once Judaea became a Roman province and the Romans governed though the Sadducee and Herodian upper classes, the *ekklesia* continued to exist legally, though it was no longer convened. It is probable that after Judaea became a Roman province, the General Assembly in Jerusalem shared the fate of the parallel *ekklesiai* of Greek city-states, which also disappeared silently in most cities between the end of the first century BCE and the beginning of the first century CE.[73] In Rome the situation differed – although towards the end of Augustus's rule and during Tiberius' reign the *comitia* met less and less,[74] they continued to maintain a certain power.

iii. The synedrion/Sanhedrin

During the Herodian period a new corporate body appeared, which was called the Sanhedrin in Rabbinic sources and *synedrion* by both Josephus and the New Testament. Josephus twice mentions the term *synedrion* in the Herodian period, though as a temporary court rather than a permanent one. The first time that the word *synedrion* appears in connection with Herod is in reference to the court that tried Herod. The second time that the word *synedrion* is mentioned by Josephus is in reference to a court convened by Herod to try Hyrcanus II. Josephus also refers to a court of justice convened in Berytus for the trial of his own sons as a *synedrion*. The Roman governor of Syria, the king of Cappadocia, and various other officials sat in judgment in this court, which clearly did not officiate in Jerusalem. These bodies, courts of justice that were convened *ad hoc*, were not the same as the Sanhedrin of Rabbinic sources.[75] Josephus twice mentions a *synedrion* similar to the Great Sanhedrin of Rabbinic tradition, on both occasions after Herod's death.[76] The first reference gives the impression that the

---

[73] See Josephus, *AJ* XX, 11. Here clearly *demos* does not mean the General Assembly, but it is the Greek translation of the Roman *senatus populusque*. See also Stern, *The Kingdom of Herod*, p. 101.

[74] On the position of the Roman *comitia* in the Early Imperial period, see F. Millar, "The Roman City State under the Emperors, 29 BC–AD 69", in *Rome, the Greek World and the East I, The Roman Republic and the Augustan Revolution*, London 2002, pp. 360-377.

[75] See Josephus, *AJ* XIV, 163-184 on the *synedrion* as the court that tried Herod. See Josephus, *AJ* XV, 173 on the *synedrion* as the court that tried Hyrcanus II. See also Mantel, "High Priesthood and the Sanhedrin", p. 275. See Josephus, *AJ* XVI, 357 and *BJ* I, 357 on the *synedrion* as the court of justice that tried Herod's sons at Berytus. See also Mantel, "High Priesthood and the Sanhedrin", p. 275. See also on Josephus Goodblatt, *Monarchic Principle*, pp. 108-119.

[76] In the first reference, Ananus, the Sadducee high priest, convened the judges of the *synedrion* to condemn James. See Josephus, *AJ* XX, 199-200. In the second reference, it was King Agrippa II who convened the *synedrion*. The king wished to permit the Levite singers to wear

high priest convened the *synedrion*. In the second reference, the king appears to have convened the *synedrion*.[77] It is not clear who served as members of this body. Josephus mentions judges, but one may infer from the offenses tried there that the judges were priests.

With many reservations, Rabbinic tradition can be helpful in trying to reconstruct the function, structure, and authority of the original Herodian *synedrion/ Sanhedrin*. Rabbinic sources mention two different Sanhedrins, the Great Sanhedrin and the Small Sanhedrin, and, in parallel, the *beth din*.[78] According to Rabbinic tradition, the Great Sanhedrin sat in the Chamber of Hewn Stone, inside the Temple Mount compound,[79] and was composed of 71 members, under the *nasi*, or president, and the *av beth-din*, or deputy.[80] It met for regular daily sessions between morning and evening. Obviously, there were no sessions on the Sabbath or during the Festivals.[81] The juridical competence of the Great Sanhedrin covered a variety of specific topics.[82] These were: to pass judgment on a tribe; to declare voluntary wars; to add territory to the city of Jerusalem; to appoint small "sanhedrins" for the "various tribes";[83] to judge rebellious elders;[84] to appoint a king or high priest;[85] to judge a false prophet or the high priest; to proclaim an apostate city; and to discuss questions concerning the sacrificial red heifer, the administration of the water of bitterness, and the breaking of the heifer's neck to atone for an anonymous murder.[86] The Mishna suggests that vacancies were filled by co-option. The ceremony in which new members were admitted consisted of the *semichat yadaim*, or the imposition of hands, a ceremony connected to Pharisean tradition.[87] Also, according to Rabbinic tradition, the high priest could judge and be judged by the Sanhedrin, while a non-Davidic

---

priestly garments; although the priests bitterly opposed the king wishes, the king succeeded in having his way. See Josephus, *AJ* XX, 216-218.

[77] See also Mantel, "High Priesthood and the Sanhedrin", p. 276.

[78] Rabbinic sources mention the Great Sanhedrin of 71 members who sat in the Chamber of Hewn Stone. This is the Sanhedrin that has parallels in Josephus and the New Testament. However, Rabbinic sources also mention a small Sanhedrin composed of 23 scholars that could be established in a town with no more than 120 inhabitants. This Sanhedrin was competent to try capital cases. Moreover Tannaitic sources often refer to the *beth din*, or court, as parallel to both the Great Sanhedrin and the Sanhedrin. The term *beth din* also refers to smaller courts of three members each, located on the Temple Mount. See Goodblatt, *Monarchic Principle*, pp. 105-106 for Rabbinic sources.

[79] See m. *Sanh.* 11, 2 and t. *Sanh.* 7, 1.

[80] See m. *Ḥag.*2, 2; BT, *Ḥag.* 16b, and TJ, *Ḥag.* 2, 2.

[81] See t. *Ḥag.* 2, 9 and t. *Sanh.* 7, 1.

[82] On the Sanhedrin in general, see Schürer, *History of the Jewish People II*; On the *nasi* and *av beth din*, see pp. 215-218. On the competence of the Sanhedrin, see pp. 218-223. On the times and places of sessions, see pp. 223-225. On the juridical procedure, see pp. 225-226.

[83] See m. *Sanh.* 1, 5.

[84] See m. *Sanh.* 11, 2.

[85] See t. *Sanh.* 7, 1.

[86] See m. *Soṭah* 9, 1.

[87] See m. *Sanh.* 4: 4.

king could neither judge nor be judged.[88] According to the Rabbis, the Sanhedrin appears to have been composed of learned Pharisee masters. If any of these points can be accepted, even with many reservations – as Goodblatt points out – there are many issues concerning the Sanhedrin described in Rabbinic sources that are anachronistic and can be immediately dismissed.[89] According to Safrai, the sectarians of the Dead Sea also adopted an institution similar to the Sanhedrin described in Rabbinic literature as their ruling council.[90] Thus, one cannot entirely dismiss the probability that the Rabbinic Sanhedrin was a corporate body that, at least in part, reflected a much earlier reality.

Finally, the New Testament also mentions the *synedrion*, and the term can also be interpreted as a meeting, a Jewish national council, or a council.[91] The members of the *synedrion* are widely described as chief priests, elders, scribes, and Pharisees.[92] Thus the *synedrion* described in Christian writings does present a different composition from the corporate body presented in Rabbinic sources, since, together with Pharisees, chief priests and elders also sit in judgment. The task of both corporate bodies as a supreme court, however, is roughly the same.

Several points in common between Josephus and the Rabbinic tradition are worth mentioning. Josephus' *synedrion* dealt with some of the same offenses described in Rabbinical sources on the Sanhedrin, such as the judgment of a false prophet and a matter that clearly refers to the Temple service, the wearing of priestly garments by the Levites. The New Testament also presents the judgment of a false prophet. Clearly, the city *boulē* could not have dealt with these matters, but other points are problematic. Thus, for example, Josephus' *synedrion* is made up of unspecified judges, probably priests. The Rabbinic Sanhedrin is composed of learned Pharisees, most of them laymen, while the New Testament *synedrion* is composed of former high priests, elders, scribes, and Pharisees. Another problem is that most of the material from the literary sources deals with a later period, after Judaea became a Roman province, rather than with the Herodian period proper.

---

[88] See m. *Sanh.* 2, 1–2.

[89] See Goodblatt, *Monarchic Principle*, p. 107. Goodblatt points to the tribal system and the Urim and Tummim.

[90] See Vermes, *Dead Sea Scrolls*, The Community Rule (1QS), V–VIII, pp. 67–73. This council was composed of priests and lay leaders. It dealt with administration, the dispensation of justice and the conduct of the final war. This body would have also acted as the legislative body of the nation as soon as the community would have gained the leadership of the nation. See also Schürer, *History of the Jewish People II*, pp. 208–209.

[91] See Goodblatt, *Monarchic Principle*, pp. 119–124.

[92] The passion story, as well as the accounts of the trials of the Apostles in Acts describes a supreme religious court invested with religious powers, similar to the *synedrion* of Josephus and the Rabbinic Sanhedrin. See Mark 14: 53, 55, 64, Matt 26: 57, 59, but neither Luke nor John appears to describe a supreme Jewish court. See also Acts 4, 5, 6: 12, 22: 5, 30. See Schürer, *History of the Jewish People*, p. 206. See also Goodblatt, *Monarchic Principle*, pp. 120–124, who, however, dismisses all these points as not indicative of a Jewish supreme court.

Most of the scholars dealing with the corporate institutions of the Late Second Temple period, such as Büchler, Mantel, Tcherikover, and Rivkin, have adopted an apologetic position regarding this topic. In an attempt to resolve the difference between the *Sanhedrin* as depicted in the Rabbinic sources and the term *synedrion* as used in both Josephus and the New Testament, these scholars pointed to the existence of two *synedria*, which, for the sake of convenience, I shall refer to as a *synedrion* and a *Sanhedrin*.[93] The first, the *synedrion*, was composed of aristocrats and chaired by the high priest, and it had competence in political matters. The other, the *Sanhedrin*, was composed of Torah scholars and chaired by the leading Pharisee. The *Sanhedrin* dealt only with religious matters. A clearly apologetic theory was put forth whose purpose was to show that it was a council composed of Sadducees and the high priest who judged Jesus, while the Pharisees, the forerunners of normative Judaism, were represented in another court that dealt only with religious matters. In the nineteenth century Büchler proposed his theory of three different bodies. The first body was called the *beth din ha-gadol*, the Great Tribunal, or Great Sanhedrin, the *Sanhedrin* with seventy-one members. This was an institution concerned with religious matters, such as Temple worship and the interpretation of the Law. Pharisees or Sadducees dominated this body. The second body is the *synedrion*, mentioned by Josephus and the New Testament, a body consisting essentially of priests. This council was involved in Temple matters as well as in politics. The third body, distinct from the other two was the *boulē*. Büchler thus proposed the existence of two Sanhedrins, the first, a Pharisaic institution that sat in the Chamber of Hewn Stone, and the other, a criminal court of political character. Mantel's theory was similar to that of Büchler. Thus, according to Mantel there were two corporate bodies, the *boulē* ruled by the high priest and composed of Sadducee aristocrats, and the *synedrion/Sanhedrin*, a court of Torah scholars. It was the *boulē* that judged Jesus. According to Tcherikover, the problem is linguistic in character. The Greek terminology used by Josephus and the New Testament misleads us. Thus, rather than revealing Greek style institutions in Jerusalem, this terminology conceals traditional ones. Tcherikover thus identified the *boulē* of Josephus with the *Sanhedrin*. Rivkin slightly differs from Tcherikover, stating that the *synedrion/Sanhedrin* was the *concilium* of the Sadducee political leadership, appointed by Rome. Rivkin, like Tcherikover, identified the *beth din* with the *boulē*, which was the religious Pharisaic corporate body of Torah scholars.

Other scholars, such as Sanders, prefer simply to indicate the problem, identifying the various terms appearing in Josephus, Rabbinic literature, and the New

---

[93] See Schürer, *History of the Jewish People II*, pp. 207–208, 280. See also H. Mantel, *Studies in the History of Sanhedrin*, Cambridge 1961. See also Mantel, "High Priesthood and the Sanhedrin", pp. 280–281. See V. Tcherikover, "Was Jerusalem a Polis", *IEJ* 14, 1965, pp. 67–72. See E. Rivkin, "Beth Din, Boule, Sanhedrin: A Tragedy of Errors", *HUCA* 46, 1975, pp. 181–199.

Testament without defining clear-cut institutions or corporate bodies.[94] Sanders differentiates between various terms. *Synedrion*, a common Greek noun, refers to a meeting of some sort. The *synedrion* was the assembly described by Josephus and the New Testament. *Sanhedrin*, a Hebrew word, means court of justice or council. The Sanhedrin was the Special Court described in Rabbinic literature. Sanders does identify the Sanhedrin with the *boulē*. McLaren, another New Testament scholar, stresses that in the New Testament the *synedrion* is often just a meeting of Jewish leadership, and not an institutionalized, formal council.[95] Finally, Goodblatt altogether denies the existence of the *synedrion/Sanhedrin*, and points to the monarchy, rather than to the corporate bodies, as the main institution of leadership in Jewish Classical antiquity.[96]

I suggest a new reading of the sources. The *synedrion/Sanhedrin* was created during the Herodian Period as a religious court and continued until the destruction of the Second Temple. It evolved, however, in its composition after the death of King Herod. It seems possible to reconstruct the original Herodian *synedrion/Sanhedrin* as a body similar to that which is described in Rabbinic sources: a council in which the Pharisees had a prominent role, but one that was strictly supervised by Herod. This would explain all of the material dealing with the legal position of the king in Rabbinic sources vis-à-vis the Sanhedrin. In exchange for Pharisee support, Herod gave them the legal right to sit in a corporate body whose function was that of supreme religious court, with the right to legislate on various issues of a religious nature. After Herod's death and the establishment of direct Roman domination over Judaea, the membership of the *synedrion/Sanhedrin* changed, at least in part, though its functions did not. After Herod's death, the Sadducees came to dominate Judaean politics and Jewish religion, and the *synedrion/Sanhedrin* was filled with aristocratic priests, favored by the Roman rulers.[97] The original Herodian *synedrion/Sanhedrin* had to include some non-Sadducees priests identified with the Herodian *weltanschauung*, for it would

---

[94] Sanders argues that Jerusalem was not, in fact, a *polis*. See Sanders, *Judaism, Practice and Belief*, pp. 473–475.

[95] McLaren adds that even if *synedrion* refers to an institution, the latter was not necessarily "a permanent body." It was the *boulē* that fulfilled administrative functions and acted "as the official representative of the Jews in Jerusalem on formal occasions." See J.S. McLaren, *Power and Politics in Palestine. The Jews and the Governing of their Land, 100 BC–AD 70*, JSNT Supplement Series 63, Sheffield 1991. The role of the *boulē* in the Gessius Florus affair is discussed on pp. 164–169. On the *synedrion* mentioned in Acts 4: 15, see p. 104. On a general discussion of possible Jewish councils or courts in Acts, see pp. 102–114, 139–145.

[96] See Goodblatt, *Monarchic Principle*, pp. 125–130.

[97] Thus the *synedrion/Sanhedrin* described by Josephus was composed of priests and was under the authority of the high priest or of the king. Moreover, in Rabbinic sources the high priest is given the same status as the Davidic king vis-à-vis the Sanhedrin. Here, Rabbinic sources somehow reflect a later development of the Sanhedrin. The *synedrion/Sanhedrin* described in the New Testament is also composed of ex-high priests, scribes, most of them probably priests, and Pharisees.

have been impossible for laymen unfamiliar with all the intricacies of the Temple Mount cult to create legislation on these matters. This does not mean that there were no Pharisees at all in the post-Herodian *synedrion/Sanhedrin*, but that they were the minority.

I believe that even a body like the *synedrion/Sanhedrin*, which appears to be so typical of first century Judaea, was not at all alien to the framework of the surrounding Classical world. Perhaps the Athenian *Areopagus*, a council composed of ex-*archontes*, was the indirect model for the Herodian *synedrion/Sanhedrin*.[98] Both the *synedrion/Sanhedrin* and the *Areopagus* were corporate bodies whose main task was that of a Supreme Court, and both had well-defined jurisdiction with respect to religious offenses. Moreover, another interesting common element is that both bodies chose their members through cooptation and not through election. However, there was a basic difference. The *synedrion/Sanhedrin* was created ex-nihilo during the Herodian period, while the *Areopagus* was an institution that can be traced back to the beginning of Athenian history.

iv. Outside Judaea: The Greek Cities and the Nomadic Tribes

Together with Jerusalem, Caesarea Maritima and Sebaste were royal cities. The situation of the latter two cities was, however, much more akin to that of Ptolemaic Alexandria than to Jerusalem. Caesarea Maritima presented all of the characteristics of a city, while Sebaste was in fact the pagan urban center of a huge military colony.[99] Both cities lacked not only a popular assembly, but a *boulē* as well. It is quite possible that Herod administered the city through a *strategos*, or governor, as his grandson Agrippa I later did.[100] These cities probably received a *boule* only after Archelaus' exile, when neither Caesarea Maritima nor Sebaste had the status of a royal city. A coin from Caesarea minted in the year 68 CE bears the inscription, "under the rule of Vespasian, the people of Caesarea Maritima,"

---

[98] On the *Areopagus* see OCD, under Areopagus. See also A. Lintott, *Imperium Romanum, Politics and Administration*, London 1993, 147–148. Lintott stress that during the last years of the Republic, Roman citizens were elected to the *Areopagus*. On the *Areopagus*, see also Cicero, *Pro Balbo* 28–30 and *Philippicae*, 5. 14 and 8. 27. See also Tacitus, *Annales* II, 55. For modern literature on the Athenian *Areopagus* in Roman times see D. G. Geagan, *The Athenian Constitution after Sulla*, Hesperia Supplements 12, Princeton (NJ) 1967, pp. 32–41 and 83 ff. See also J. H. Oliver, *Marcus Aurelius: Aspects of Civic and Cultural Policy in the East*, Hesperia Supplements 13, Princeton (NJ) 1970, pp. 44–65. On Sulla and the *Areopagus* see specifically, C. Habicht, *Athens from Alexander to Antony*, Cambridge (MA) 1999, pp. 315–316.

[99] On Caesarea Maritima and Sebaste see Schürer, *History of the Jewish People* II, pp. 115–118 and 160–164. See also Kasher, *Jews and Hellenistic Cities in Eretz-Israel*, pp. 199–203. Kasher sees Caesarea Maritima and Sebaste as cities with a different status from the other Gentile cities in the kingdom. Kasher stresses the loyalty of these cities to Herod, and that their main purpose was that of checking possible rebellions of the Jews. On the foundation of other cities see pp. 206–207 on Phasaelis, pp. 207–208 on Antipatris, and pp. 208–209 on Gabae.

[100] See Josephus, *AJ* XIX, 356. Josephus reports that Agrippa I named a *strategos* to administer the city of Caesarea Maritima.

on the reverse. The "people of Caesarea" clearly does not indicate a popular assembly, but, rather, a *boulē*.[101]

As stated in Chapter III, all of the other urban centers, such as Gaza on the coast and the Decapolis, were under military administration. Thus there was no self-government for the Greek cities once they were under Herod's rule.[102] Although, at first glance, it seems that Herod's rule was indeed harsh toward the Greek cities in his kingdom, the legal position of the Greek cities in Herodian Judaea was parallel to that of the Greek cities under the Antigonids, as well as under the Ptolemaic and Seleucid rulers.[103]

The situation of the nomadic peoples living in the northern part of the kingdom was similar to that of the urban centers of Gaza and the Decapolis, and they were under the rule of Herod's military or civil administration. It is possible that the Ituraeans enjoyed a certain autonomy at the beginning of Herodian rule under their elected or nominated tribal leaders, the *phylarches*.

B. The Courts of Herodian Judaea

As *socius* and *amicus populi romani*, Herod enjoyed virtually complete autonomy in the jurisdiction of his kingdom. Civil justice in Judaea was not much influenced by contemporary Roman laws or jurisprudence.[104] From Josephus and Rabbinic sources we know of various secular and religious courts in Herodian Judaea.

First, there was the Royal Court, or Herod's Court, which Josephus also calls the *synedrion* or *dykasterion*. Members of the royal family, *syngeneis*, and *philoi* made up this royal tribunal. To these Herod could add representatives of the

---

[101] See Y. Meshorer, *City-Coins of Eretz-Israel and the Decapolis in the Roman Period*, Jerusalem 1995, Fig. 24, p. 20.

[102] On these cities see A. Kasher, *Jews and Hellenistic Cities in Eretz-Israel, Relations of the Jews with the Hellenistic Cities during the Second Temple Period*, TSAJ 21, Tübingen 1990, pp. 195–197. Kasher rightly argues that Herod policy towards these cities, exemplified in the episode of Gadara, was not different from the policy of Alexander Jannaeus.

[103] See Preaux, *monde hellenistique* II, pp. 416–418 and 421–425. At Pergamum, Eumenes I named five *strategoi* (OGIS 267, ll. 20 folls.). At Athens, Cassander made Demetrius of Phalerus both lawgiver and *epimeletes* (Diodorus, *Hist.* XVIII, 74, 3). On the attitude of the Antigonids see Billows, *Antigonos the One-Eyed*. See also Habicht, *Athens from Alexander to Antony*, pp. 6–97. On Ptolemaic Alexandria see Fraser, *Ptolemaic Alexandria* I, pp. 94–95, II, pp. 173, note 3. See also Ballet, *VQ à Alexandrie*, pp. 52–53. see also Hölbl, *Ptolemaic Empire*, pp. 160–178 on the Ptolemaic ruler's position vis-à-vis the natives. On the attitude of the Seleucids see E. Bickerman, *Institutions des Seleucides*, Paris 1938. See also Sherwin-White and Kuhrt, *From Samarkhand to Sardis*, pp. 51–52 on Jerusalem; p. 162 on the civic institutions (Seleucia Pieria as an example). The authors stress that there we have little knowledge of civic life and politics anywhere in the Seleucid kingdom.

[104] See A.M. Rabello, , "Civil Justice in Palestine from 63 BCE to 70 CE", in R. Katzoff, Y. Petroff , and D. Shaps, (eds.), *Classical Studies in Honor of David Sohlberg*, Ramat Gan 1996, pp. 298–299.

Roman government. The only types of cases brought to this court were those involving the royal family. From what the sources tell us, no other kinds of cases were ever brought before this tribunal. Josephus reports that the trials of Mariamme,[105] Alexander, Aristobulus,[106] and Archelaus[107] were handled by this body, which operated in accordance with Hellenistic royal tradition. The previously discussed Popular assembly, or *ekklesia*, also functioned as a court, which could try common citizens. This situation mirrors the legal powers of the Greek *ekklesia* and of the Roman *comitia*. The Sanhedrin, which also functioned as the Supreme Court for specific offenses, has likewise been discussed above.

In Herodian Judaea local law courts also existed at lower levels. It is possible to distinguish two different levels. With respect to the first, Jewish cities such as Sepphoris or Jericho were ruled by the same *synedria*, probably the *batei din* mentioned in Tannaitic literature that were established by Gabinius. According to the Mishna, these were small councils of twenty-three members[108] whose function was to stand as the local courts. It is significant that, according to the Mishna, these bodies had the right to pass sentences for capital crimes.[109] With respect to the second, and lower, level, Josephus wrote that in chief of *toparchiai*, such as 'En Gedi, and the villages, the main authority was in the hands of seven appointed magistrates, the seven elders, who formed the lowest court, and they were found in towns and villages. Their main task was to settle legal cases. Moreover, Josephus asserts that two Levites had to be co-opted by the local courts, together with the seven judges.[110] This body appears in the Talmud as the *tovei ha-'ir*. However, the information supplied by Josephus and that provided by the Mishna are at odds in this regard.[111]

---

[105] Mariamme was tried by a court made up of *syngeneis*, and *philoi*. See Josephus, *AJ* XV, 228–231. See also A. M. Rabello, "Herod's Domestic Court? The Judgement of Death for Herod's Sons", *Jewish Law Annual 10*, Boston 1992; pp. 42–44 in *The Jews in the Roman Empire: Legal Problems, from Herod to Justinian*, Variorum Collected Studies Series, Aldershot 2000.

[106] Alexander and Aristobulus were tried in Berytus by a court consisting of *syngeneis*, and *philoi*, but also by Archelaus King of Cappadocia, and various Roman officials including Saturninus, the governor of the Province of Syria. See Josephus, *AJ* XVI, 356–357 and *BJ* I, 538. See also Rabello, "Herod's Domestic Court", pp. 48–54.

[107] Archelaus was tried in Berytus by a Court made up of *syngeneis*, and *philoi*, but also by Varus governor of Syria. See Josephus, *AJ* XVII, 89 ff. and *BJ* I, 564–589. See also Rabello, "Herod's Domestic Court", pp. 54–56.

[108] See m. *Sanh*. I, 6.

[109] See m. *Sanh*. I, 4.

[110] See Josephus, *AJ* IV, 214. Josephus obviously attributes to Moses the composition of the contemporary local courts of Judaea. According to Josephus, Moses decreed that "seven men should bear rule in every city... and that two men of the Tribe of Levi should be assigned to each court as subordinate officers." However this commandment does not appear in the Pentateuch. See also Josephus, *AJ* XVI, 203.

[111] Safrai notes for the Talmudic Jewish towns of Galilee the Seven Town Elders, or *tovei ha-ir*, found also in Josephus, and alongside it a smaller group of three *archontes* led by a mayor, *rosh ha-ir*. There was a local assembly that elected them, or *anashei ha-ir*. See JT, *Meg*. III, 74a

We do not know how justice worked in the Gentile areas of the kingdom.[112] In any case, justice was under the strict control of the crown through judges who were nominated by the king rather than elected.

As in Herodian Judaea, in Asia Minor and in north-western Syria some of the small cities and villages were entities independent from cities, with magistrates of their own. The inscriptions conserve their names; however the precise roles of the *pistoi*, the *pronoetai*, the *episkopoi*, the *dioikeitai*, and the *strategoi* are not known.[113]

4. Conclusions

In this chapter I have analyzed various issues. First, I have discussed Herod the ruler as the source of law in his kingdom, a role or task which has parallels in the

---

and BT, *Meg.* 26 a–b. In addition there were other functionaries, such as the Dispensers of Charity – *parnese ha-zedakah*, the head of the synagogue or *archisynagogos*, who could serve as mayor, the *hazanim* and the *parnesim*, whose roles are unclear. The elected representatives and the assembly together appointed these functionaries. See BT, *Bek.* 55 a, BT, *Šabb.* 104 a, t. *Ta'an.* 1: 7. See Safrai, *Economy of Roman Palestine*, pp. 47–48. The Mishna alludes to the Law Court or *beth din*. See m., *Soṭah* 1, 3 and m., *Sanh.* 11, 4. The Talmud also mentions the "seven foremost men of the town." See BT, *Meg.* 26 a. Safrai suggests the existence of two parallel legal systems during the Talmudic period. One was the municipal court where the seven elders served as judges, as described above. The other system, probably later than 70 CE, operated within the sphere of the sages. See Z. Safrai, *Economy of Roman Palestine*, London 1994, pp. 53–54. On the other hand, according to the Mishna, at the highest level was a court composed of three ordained judges, which dealt with indemnity law and with monetary cases. This court theoretically also had the right to pass capital punishment judgments. At a lower level was a court composed of three laymen chosen by the litigants or a court composed of one ordained judge. This court was responsible for civil and criminal cases. Thus, it could judge cases involving money, robbery and assault, award of damages, condemning a wrongdoer to be scourged, and also cases connected with *halitzah*. This court also dealt with religious issues such as the date of the new moon, intercalation of the year, and with some sacrifices such as sin-offerings, or the redemption of the second tithe. See m. *Sanh.* 1, 1–3. Not all the scholars agree with Safrai. According to other scholars the courts described by the Mishna, were, at least till Late Antiquity, voluntary and parallel to the municipal courts. See for example H., Lapin, "The Origins and the Development of the Rabbinic Movement in the Land of Israel", in S. T. Katz (ed.), *CHJ IV, The Late Roman-Rabbinic Period*, Cambridge 2006, pp. 206–229. According to Lapin, Rabbis remained a marginal group till the second half of the fourth century.

[112] It is possible that in the Greek areas of the kingdom, Greek courts or *dikasteria*, modeled after those of Classical Athens, probably handled cases of both criminal and civil law for Gentile subjects. The *dikasteria* are found as early as Classical Athens. Justice in the Gentile rural areas of the kingdom probably followed Ptolemaic precedents. In Ptolemaic Egypt three types of court can be distinguished: the *dykasterion*, a council, acted as arbitrator between two parties; the *laocrites*, native tribunals, where the judges were priests and where Egyptian Law was applied; and the *chrematistes*, courts that dealt with affairs both private and public, which had a fiscal character. See Preaux, *monde hellenistique* I, pp. 277–281.

[113] See Sartre, *Alexandre à Zénobie*, pp. 773–774.

wider Hellenistic context, beginning in Augustan Rome. Herod, however, acted as source of law, not merely as a Hellenistic king but as a Jewish king as well.

To the traditional ruling class of Judaea – local priests that made up the landed nobility – Herod added new members, priestly families coming from the Diaspora, as well as lay nobility. This situation is paralleled in Rome, where Augustus added to the traditional ruling class of Rome – which had been made up of Senators – new members coming from the equestrian order and from Italic municipal ruling class.

The ruling bodies of Herodian Judaea, the *boulē* and the *ekklesia*, find their parallels in the Greek East city. Thus the elite of the city sat in the Greek *boulē*. However, in contrast to Herodian Judaea, the *ekklesia* of the Greek city during the early Roman Period no longer appeared, and all of the power was concentrated in the hands of the *boulē*. However, in Augustan Rome both the *Senate* and the *comitia*, parallel to the *boulē* and *ekklesia*, were still active. Even the *Synedrion/Sanhedrin* finds its parallel in the Late Hellenistic – early Imperial Areopagus of Athens.

Last, I have analyzed the juridical system of Judaea and its various law courts. Although the Herodian ruler, as supreme judge, had a counterpart in the Hellenistic world and in Augustan Rome, the lower courts of Herodian Judaea stemmed from a Jewish source. That does not mean that we do not find similar parallels in the Hellenistic East.

Appendix I.
The Law on Thieves in Jerusalem and Rome

The Law on Thieves, enacted by King Herod, is the only example of a law which can be dated to the rule of King Herod with a certain degree of accuracy. Josephus reports that Herod issues a royal decree which banished burglars to slavery abroad.[114]

Josephus points out that Herod's Law on Thieves was a violation of the Laws of the Country, or in other words, of the Torah, as it was commonly interpreted in his own time. Thus, according to the Pentateuch,[115] a man who did not have the means to make restitution was sold into bondage to another Jew, but not to Gentiles outside Judaea. The main problem is that we do not have any contemporary sources for this, neither from the Apocrypha nor the Pseudepigrapha nor from the Sectarian community living in Qumran, which deals with this specific subject. The subject is discussed only in later Rabbinic legal literature, which

---

[114] See Josephus, *AJ* XVI, 1–5.
[115] See Exod 22, 2–3.

Appendix I. The Law on Thieves in Jerusalem and Rome

underlines, as does Josephus, the obligation to sell a Jew as a Hebrew indebted servant only to another Jew, and not to a Gentile.[116]

Thus, most scholars presume that Herod was influenced by Roman law in formulating his Law on the Thieves, therefore excluding Josephus, a contemporary Jewish source. According to Boaz Cohen,[117] Herod utilized a Roman law pertinent to housebreaking, reported in the *Digesta* (47.18.2), whereby burglars were sent to the mines or sold into slavery.[118] Rabello, however, points to a possible Hellenistic influence upon Herod's Law on Thieves.[119] There are two reasons for believing that Herod was inspired by Roman law when he enacted the Law on Thieves. First, at the beginning of his rule, Augustus faced the same problem in the form of bands of bandits in Italy. He repressed the bandits, killing most of them and sending those who remained to the amphitheaters.[120] Also, it is during this period that the Roman jurist Labeo gave the juridical definition of theft and the penalties incurred by law.[121]

Moreover, Josephus emphasizes that Herod's law, contrary to Biblical law, did not distinguish between a burglary committed at night or by day. Philo, like Josephus, distinguishes between burglars who commit their offense by night, which is punishable by death, or by day, in which case they are to be treated as common thieves. The subject is widely discussed in Rabbinic legal literature, but the difference between day and night is seen as merely metaphoric.[122]

---

[116] There is the obligation to sell a Hebrew only to another Hebrew. He can go free after six years, or after he pays the balance of his indebtedness. See Sifre, Deut, 118. See also D. Nakman, *The Halakhah in the Writings of Josephus*, Ph.D. Thesis submitted for the Degree "Doctor of Philosophy," Bar-Ilan University, Ramat Gan 2004 (Hebrew). See Appendix 1, p. 363, no. 80. See also Table III, note 69.

[117] See Cohen, *Jewish and Roman Law* I, pp. 164–165. See also B. Cohen, "Civil Bondage in Jewish and Roman Law", *Louis Ginzburg Jubilee Volume*, New York 1945, pp. 113–132.

[118] Various punishments are meted out to burglars; the more atrocious ones who break in at night are usually beaten and sent to the mines, whereas those who break in by day are condemned, after being clubbed, either to perpetual labor, or for a specific period of time. See Digest 47.18.2.

[119] See Rabello, "Civil Justice in Palestine," p. 298.

[120] On Augustus and bandits, see Southern, *Augustus*, p. 87 and note 5, p. 229.

[121] In Roman law the Twelve Tables distinguish between two definitions of thieves: the manifest thief who was caught in the act, and the non-manifest thief, *furtum nec manifestum*. See J. A. C. Thomas, *Textbook of Roman Law*, Amsterdam 1976, pp. 354–361 on theft and robbery. According to Gaius, it is Labeo, who lived in the Augustan period, who formulated the double definition of theft (manifest and non-manifest). Praetor's intervention and later penalty consisted in fourfold damages for manifest theft (189), and double damages for non-manifest theft (190). See Gaius, *Institutes* III, 183–188.

[122] See Exodus 22, 1. See B. Cohen, *Jewish and Roman Law* I, New York 1966, p. 165. Cohen points out that Roman law made the same distinction, as in Biblical Law, as did the author of the *Collatio* (VII, 1) as well. See Philo, *Spec. Leg.* iv, 7. Nakman points out that the Mekilta de Rabbi Yshmael, Mishpatim 13, p. 293 and BT, *Sanh*. 72 b. regard the difference between daytime and nighttime burglary as metaphoric. For other Rabbinic sources see JT, *Sanh*. 8, 8 (26, p. 3) and BT, *Qidd*. 18 a. See Nakman, *The Halakhah in the Writings of Josephus*, Appendix 1, p. 363,

Last but not least, Josephus states that the thief has to pay a fourfold fine. However, according to the Pentateuch, a thief must make fourfold compensation only in the case of the theft of a sheep, and not in every case, as Josephus writes. Philo, as well as other Jewish sources of law, contemporary and late, does not confirm Josephus' interpretation of the Biblical law.[123]

Did Herod's Law on Thieves indeed contrast with contemporary Jewish law? Certainly Josephus' interpretation of the law is problematic. Thus, although in any source of Jewish law it is stipulated that a Jew cannot by sold in slavery to Gentiles, it is not clear if the difference between daytime and nighttime burglary is dealt with in contemporary Jewish law, nor if Josephus' general statement that a thief has to pay a fourfold fine can be accepted as being representative of Jewish law. It is probable that here Josephus is simply being inexact.

I would like, however, to suggest a further possibility and propose that this law, which is incompatible with Jewish law, was applied mainly in Gentile areas, as a deterrent against banditry. I have arrived at this conclusion on chronological grounds. First of all, this law is reported only in the part of Antiquities dealing with Herod, dependant from Nicolaus of Damascus, and set in a chronological frame. Thus, according to a chronological reading of Josephus, this law was enacted around 20 BCE, slightly before Herod sailed to Italy to visit his sons Alexander and Aristobulus in 18–17 BCE. How it is possible that Herod, at the height of his rule, would enact a law that would clearly have provoked the hostility of the Jewish population of his kingdom? As king, Herod could have enacted other laws to curb the scourge of Jewish banditry, and one must ask if this law was applied to Judaea, Galilee, or Idumaea, where the vast majority of Jews lived. It seems strange that Herod would enact such a law only in 20 BCE. The Jewish parts of the kingdom were problematic only during the years after the civil wars terminated in 37 BCE. At that time, Judaea would have been filled with soldiers who had turned to banditry and brigandage. By around 20 BCE, however, the situation had completely changed, since Herod's building projects had brought a livelihood to most of the lower class population. It is, however, possible that Herod's Law on Thieves was in fact applied in the Gentile areas of the kingdom. In 20 BCE, Augustus presented Herod with Ituraea, the territory of Zenodorus. Herod's army had to purge it of bandits in the following years, and military colonies were founded to reinforce Herod's grip on this problematic area. I believe that this law was therefore applied only in Ituraea, as a deterrent against banditry.

---

no. 80. See also Table III, notes 66–68. We may ask if Josephus somehow simplified things or if he presented only the strictest law.

[123] See Exodus 22, 3. See also Philo, *Spec. Leg.* iv, 11–12, who speaks of repaying the value of the theft twofold. It seems that Josephus once more simplified Biblical law. In contrast to Josephus, Philo, as well as the Septuaginta, Samaritan, and Rabbinic Law, draw the distinction. Only Karaitic law accords with Josephus' interpretation. See Nakman, *The Halakhah in the Writings of Josephus*, Appendix 1, p. 363, no. 80. See also Table III, notes 64–65.

Herod wanted to get rid of them by any available means, and this law was one of them. Josephus, writing more than one hundred years after the enactment of this law, did not recognize that it was probably limited to the Gentile population of Herod's kingdom. Josephus most likely assumed that this law also applied to Herod's Jewish subjects either because of his erroneous interpretation of the sources or because he wished to further damage Herod's image.

VI. The Cults of the Herodian Kingdom

1. The High Priest and Temple Cult in the Herodian Period

This chapter is primarily dedicated to the religious cults in Herodian Judaea, and therefore to the most important and well known of all Herod's building enterprises, the Temple in Jerusalem. Herod was not a high priest, as were the Hasmonean rulers who had preceded him, and thus, in order to dominate both the Temple Mount and the Temple cult, Herod needed to control the nomination of the high priest. How Herod selected his high priests and who they were are discussed in the first part of this chapter, followed by a review of the Temple's bureaucracy of priests and Levites. The chapter will then dwell on some aspects of the cult during the Herodian period, focusing on the new holy days of Hanukka and Purim, particularly the former, which took its definitive form as the Feast of Lights during the Herodian Period.

The second part of the chapter will be dedicated to Herod's Temple Mount enterprise and will analyze its Jewish, Greek-Hellenistic, and Roman sources of inspiration, as well as the Herodian building itself, which was probably the greatest cultic *temenos* in the Classical World.

The third part of this chapter will discuss the development of the synagogue in Judaea during the Herodian Period, both according to Josephus and in light of archaeological evidence, focusing on the synagogue's dual function as a religious edifice – where the Torah was read publicly – and as an administrative center, the seat of the local assembly or court of law.

Last but not least, I shall survey the pagan cults in Herodian Judaea, since Herod erected three temples dedicated to the Imperial cult at Sebaste, Caesarea Maritima, and Paneas.

A. *The High Priest and the Temple Bureaucracy*

The high priests who dominated Judaea until the time of Herod's reign were figures who were not all that far removed from the Classical World. In Greece and Rome, the pagan hierarchy of priesthood depended upon one person. In Athens, for instance, the *archon basileus* was the chief priest and was elected every year. In the Hellenistic states, the king functioned as high priest, more often than not in both Greek and native religions. The Hellenistic king was the supreme priest for life, and his son and heir would succeed him at that task. In Rome, the *pontifex maximus* held an elected position, with an appointment for life, and he was high priest of the Roman religion. It is interesting to compare the fate of the Jewish high priest and that of the Roman *pontifex maximus* during the earlier Imperial Period. From Herod's time and on, the Jewish high priest was appointed and dismissed quite frequently. The Roman *pontifex maximus*, however, which was a position which became a prerogative of the Roman emperor from the time of Augustus and on, became a hereditary appointment.[1]

Herod's appropriation of the authority to appoint high priests may be regarded as constituting the real "Herodian revolution." Before Herod, the high priest was chosen from the Oniad family and later from the Hasmonean family. Until the time of the late Hasmoneans, the foreign overlord of Judaea was the authority who appointed the high priest.[2] Under Herod, all of this changed drastically and dramatically. True, Herod was not the first ruler to appoint the high priest, but he was the first native Jewish ruler to do so. Moreover, Herod's considerations differed greatly from those of the Seleucids or, after Herod's death, those of the Roman overlords. As a secular ruler, Herod was well aware that until he was proclaimed king in Rome, the real ruler of Judaea, and equally important, the only authority recognized by the Jews scattered in the Diaspora throughout the Roman Empire and Parthia, was the high priest. But the authority of a dynasty of high priests, backed by a four-hundred-year-old tradition, was far too dangerous for Herod. The new ruler perhaps toyed at first with the idea of an impossible diarchy with the Hasmoneans, a Herodian king and a Hasmonean high priest, to be succeeded by a Herodian-Hasmonean king and a Hasmonean high priest. Soon, however, Herod understood that the only way to avoid the potential threat to his own power, posed by the high priest, was to control the position himself. Thus Herod not only nominated high priests, but also chose them from the distant, less

---

[1] On the *pontifex maximus* see G. W. Bowersock, "The Pontificate of Augustus," in K. A. Raauflaub and M. Toher (eds.), *Between Republic and Empire, Interpretations of Augustus and His Principate*, Los Angeles (Ca.), 1990, pp. 380–394.

[2] The Ptolemies and later the Seleucids continued to select a high priest from the Oniad family. The main consideration of the foreign overlord was that the Oniads were part of the local elite and were better accepted by the other members of the elite as well as the population. Often the appointment passed from father to son. This could, however, change according to the foreign overlord's whims. When Jason bribed Antiochus IV with a huge sum of money, the foreign king appointed him instead of the legitimate high priest Onias III. Jason was nevertheless a member of the Oniad family. When Antiochus IV realized that Jason did not satisfy his expectations, a certain Menelaus, a priest and member of the elite, but not a member of the Oniad family, was appointed to replace him. Later, when the Hasmonean Jonathan was found to be the better candidate for the position of high priest, the Seleucid ruler Alexander Balas appointed him. Thus, also the first Hasmonean high priests, including John Hyrcanus I, were Seleucid appointments. See E. Bickerman, *The Jews in the Greek Age*, Cambridge (Mass.) 1988, pp. 144–145 and Schürer, *History of the Jewish people* I, pp. 149–150.

politicized, and more faithful Diaspora. High priests thus came from Babylonia and Alexandria, rather than from Judaea. In contrast to the early Seleucid rulers, it was in Herod's interest to appoint members of the Jewish Diaspora elite to the high priesthood, rather than from the local Jewish elite. Herod's "revolution" is comparable to the Augustan revolution, as defined by Syme.³ In the same way, Herod created a new high priesthood subservient to himself as the new secular ruler. From Herod and onward, there was no dynasty of high priests, but rather, individual high priests who were chosen and removed at will by Herod. Herod thus also created a new "nobility" of high priests, consisting of a few carefully chosen families. As in Rome, where the old nobility was no longer a source of power, so in Judaea the high priesthood no longer posed a political threat to the king. It is quite ironic, however, that, in this case, the positions of Herod and Augustus were for once reversed. Since Herod could not be elected high priest, he succeeded in controlling this key position by other means, notably with his own men, whom he appointed to the position, thus reducing the importance of the office in the eyes of the population and simultaneously elevating his own status as king. Augustus had no difficulty in being appointed *pontifex maximus* in Rome, since the office, though charged with symbolic meaning, was not only elective, but of lesser importance than it was in Judaea, where being the high priest was synonymous with being the ruler. After Herod's death, however, things did not proceed quite so smoothly. Once the figure of a strong-willed king vanished with the death of Agrippa I, the high priests could no longer be in control of the situation. In fact, the Roman procurators and the Herodian kings dismissed the high priests at will, though after Archelaus' fall, they once more represented the Jews, this time vis-à-vis Rome. However, the high priests had neither the power, the authority, nor the will to perform political duties as the Jewish supreme authority in Judaea with respect to the Romans. The result was a disaster: the First Revolt and the destruction of the Temple.⁴

---

³ See the two books of R. Syme, *Roman Revolution*, Oxford 1939 and *The Augustan Aristocracy*, Oxford 1986.

⁴ On the high priests after Herod's death and their role in bringing about, or at least not avoiding, the confrontation with Rome see Goodman, *The Ruling Class of Judaea*. See also L. I. Levine, *Jerusalem, Portrait of the City in the Second Temple Period (538 BCE–70 CE)*, Philadelphia 2002, pp. 352–358. Levine underlines the exiguous number of families from whom the high priest was chosen. He also emphasizes that these families were elevated to the priesthood by Herod. The chronology of first century CE high priests is quite a complicated subject. See for example H. Eshel, "Some Notes concerning High Priests in the First Century CE," *Zion* 64, 4, 1999, pp. 495–504. Eshel deals with two aspects of first century CE's high priests chronology. In 4Q348 a high priest is mentioned. Eshel identifies him as Joseph son of Camei (Camydus), who served between 46–47 CE. An inscription from Masada bears the name of Ananias the high priest. His name apparently appeared on a seal, which was used to assure the purity of vessel contents. In the same way, Eshel argues, the Paleo-Hebrew seal of Elionaeus son of Cantheras, who served as high priest in 44–46 CE was used as a guarantee of purity for the contents of sacred vessels. See also D. Schwartz, "Ishmael ben Phiabi and the Chronology of Provincia Judaea," in D. Schwartz (ed.), *Studies in the Jewish Background of Christianity*, WUNT 60, Tübingen 1992,

Richardson has compiled a list of high priests who served under Herod.[5] The first one who was appointed by Herod was the Babylonian Ananel,[6] who occupied this position for only two years, from 37–36/35 BCE, and then from 35 BCE to 30 BCE. Thus, even at the outset of his rule, Herod decided to promote a Diaspora Jew to this highest religious position. The choice was probably not a casual one, since at this time, Mark Antony, ruler of the East, was at war with Parthia, and a Babylonian high priest would most likely have ensured the sympathy of the powerful Parthian Jews for Rome, or at least guaranteed their neutrality in the event of war, and in fact, Josephus does not write that Parthian Jews actively opposed Mark Antony in his war with Parthia. Herod ultimately dismissed Ananel in favor of Aristobulus III,[7] Mariamme's younger brother, though Herod soon learned how dangerous it was to appoint a Hasmonean as high priest, no matter how good Herod's intentions had been, and Aristobulus III, the young Hasmonean, held the post for less than a year.

Jesus son of Phabes[8] succeeded Ananel and was high priest from 30 BCE to 24 BCE. Jesus was an Egyptian Jew, according to Richardson, probably from Leontopolis.[9] It is possible that just as Herod had toyed before with the idea of a Hasmonean restoration, now he considered the idea of an Oniad restoration. Things somehow went wrong, and after six years, Jesus was dismissed. It is possible that Herod may have chosen a Diaspora Jew once more, in order to please Rome, and more importantly, to support the new Roman rule over Egypt. In fact, after Augustus annexed Egypt and demoted Alexandria from its status as the capital of a kingdom to the rank of a provincial city, the Greeks living in the city were a source of potential rebellion.

---

pp. 218–242. Two high priests with the name of Ishmael son of Phabes are known. The first was appointed by the Roman governor Valerius Gratus in 15 CE. The second, probably his son or grandson was appointed as high priest by Agrippa II. The latter is mentioned in various different sources including Josephus, *AJ* XVIII, 34 and XX, 179, 189–196, BT, *Yoma* 9a and Acts 24: 10. Schwartz argues that Ishmael, the high priests, as well as Felix, the Governor of Judaea, were appointed in 49 CE, after their predecessors Ananias son of Nedebaeus and Cumanus were sent to Rome. This data can be helpful to accept as truthful the sources mentioned previously, Josephus, Rabbinic sources, as well as the New Testament at face value. Moreover, using the chronology proposed by Schwartz, these sources can be supplemented by Tacitus' information on Judaea between 49–52 CE.

[5] Richardson begins the list with Mattathias Antigonus, 40–37 BCE, Ananel – 37–36/35 BCE, Aristobulus III – 35 BCE, Ananel – 35–30 BCE, Jesus son of Phabes – 30–24 BCE, Boethus – 24–5 BCE, Simon son of Boethus – 5–4 BCE, Matthias son of Theophilus – 5–4 BCE, Joseph son of Ellemus, and Joazar son of Boethus – 4 BCE. See Richardson, *Herod King of the Jews*, pp. 243–247. See also Regev, *The Sadducees*, pp. 318–319. According to Regev, Ananel is called the "Egyptian," and his family is called Beth Zaddok.

[6] On Ananel see Josephus, *AJ* XV, 22, 34, 39–41, 56.

[7] On Aristobulus III see Josephus, *AJ* XV, 31–34, 41, 51–56, 64, XX, 247–248.

[8] On Jesus son of Phabes see Josephus, *AJ* XV, 322.

[9] Richardson argues that the plan of the Temple of Leontopolis influenced the building of the Temple Mount. Jesus was high priest when Herod began the Temple Mount projects. See also m, *Parah* 3, 5 and m, *Soṭah*, 9, 15. See Richardson, *Herod King of the Jews*, pp. 245–247.

The next high priest, Boethus,[10] who served from 24 BCE to 5 BCE, was another Egyptian Jew, this time from Alexandria. Why did Herod choose him? First, because the Egyptian Diaspora, now part of the Roman Empire, was the most powerful of the Jewish Diasporas, and, moreover, Boethus had a pretty daughter, Mariamme II, whose marriage to Herod enabled him to tie the Alexandrian high priest to him more closely as his father-in-law. Boethus was not the only member of the family to be appointed high priest. Boethus' sons, Herod's brothers-in-law Simon (who served from 5 to 4 BCE) and Joazar[11] (who served in the last months of Herod's rule), succeeded their father as high priests.

Not all of the high priests, however, were Diaspora Jews. Matthias son of Theophilus, who was high priest for a brief period in 5–4 BCE, was probably from Jerusalem. Joseph son of Ellemus,[12] who was high priest only for one day, the Day of Atonement, when Matthias was tainted by seminal impurity, was also probably from Jerusalem. It is not clear why Herod chose local Jews. One possibility is that in the last years of his rule, sometimes suffering from insanity, Herod dismissed Simon, son of Boethus, and appointed Matthias, son of Theophilus, in his stead. It is clear, however, that Herod soon regretted his choice and appointed the brother of Simon, Joazar, as high priest.

The high priest was not alone in managing the Temple and was assisted by a hierarchy of priests.[13] I believe that the establishment of this hierarchy may be safely dated to the Herodian period and not earlier. This hierarchy, known mainly from Talmudic sources, was probably established definitively only during this period, when the Temple answered not only the everyday needs of Judaea, but also those of the huge Jewish Diaspora. Thus, the Temple's team of priests and Levites was, from Herod onward, responsible for controlling and assisting the huge crowds of pilgrims. It was the Augustan *pax romana* that permitted safe movement throughout the entire Mediterranean basin, which greatly facilitated Jewish pilgrims. The high priest, or *archiereus*, was assisted by the *segan*, translated in Josephus as *strategos tou ierou*, or captain of the Temple.[14] The captain of the Temple may have been the son of the high priest, and this was the position he held before succeeding his father. During the earlier period, under the Oniads and the Hasmoneans, this was clearly the case. As captain of the Temple, the next high priest had adequate time to prepare himself for the burdensome task. During the Herodian period it is probable that Simon and Joazar occupied, perhaps in turn, the position of captain of the Temple during their father's long tenure.

---

[10] On Boethus see Josephus, *AJ* XV, 320, XVII 78, 339, XVIII, 3.
[11] On Simon son of Boethus see Josephus, *AJ* XV 320–322, XVII 78; On Joazar son of Boethus see Josephus, *AJ* XVII, 164, 339.
[12] On Matthias son of Theophilus see Josephus, AJ XX, 223. On Joseph son of Ellemus see Josephus, *AJ* XVII, 166.
[13] On the Temple officers see also S. Safrai, "The Temple and the Divine Service," in *The World History of the Jewish People, the Herodian Period*, pp. 297–300.
[14] See Josephus, *AJ* XX, 131, 208.

There were, however, exceptions to the rule. There is an interesting example of the captain of the Temple acting as high priest, when Joseph son of Ellemus took the place of Matthias, son of Theophilus, when the latter could not act as high priest, since he was ritually impure.

Various officials assisted the high priest and the captain of the Temple. First, there were the *seganim* or *strategoi*, the heads of Temple police. The administration of the Temple's huge treasury was an enormous task. The main individuals responsible were the *gizbarim* or *gazophylakes*, who were three in number. The Mishna also names two other financial officials, the seven *amarkalim* or officers of the treasury, and the two *katolikin* or *katholikoi*. The latter managed the public Temple funds, as well as funds deposited by private individuals. They were also responsible for the sacred vessels, the curtains, and Temple vestments. These fourteen officers formed the standing council of the Temple, which regulated everything connected with the affairs and services of the Temple. The Levites also performed administrative tasks, though these were police duties. In the Mishna the Temple captain is called *ish har ha-bayit*, or *ish ha-bayit*.[15] All of these officials held permanent posts. The non-permanent officials, both priests and Levites, were organized into twenty-four courses or *mishmaroth*. The priestly and Levitical courses lasted in the Temple for a week, from one Sabbath to another.[16] The weekly service was subdivided among the various families, the *batei avoth*. On Sabbath the entire course was on duty.[17]

During the Herodian period the priests had little real power, numbering some 20,000 priests and an unknown number of Levites.[18] It is difficult to classify the priests during the Hasmonean and Herodian periods as a holy order, as Schürer did – incorrectly in my opinion – more than one hundred years ago. It would be far more accurate to assert that the best definition or description of the priests as a group would be that they formed a hereditary aristocracy,[19] not unlike the

---

[15] See Schürer, *History of the Jewish People*, pp. 275–276 on the high priest. On the *segan* see pp. 277–278. On the *seganim* see pp. 278–279. On the administration of Temple treasure and its officials, the *gizbarim*, the *amarkalim*, and the *katolikin* see pp. 279–283. On the Levites responsibilities see pp. 284–287. See also A. Edersheim, *The Temple, Its Ministry and Services As They Were at the Time of Jesus Christ*, Grand Rapids (Mi.), 1997, p. 73.

[16] See Safrai, "Temple and the Divine Service," on the priestly courses, pp. 291–293. On the Levites and their courses, see pp. 293–294.

[17] On Levites see Schürer, *History of the Jewish People II*, pp. 250–254, on the division into courses see p. 254. See also Edersheim, *Temple*, pp. 63–67. It seems that the priests who did not serve in the Temple had to meet in the synagogues of their districts to pray and fast every day with the exception of the Sabbath, the day preceding it and the day following it.

[18] See Sanders, *Judaism, Practice and Belief*, p. 78.

[19] On the priestly caste as aristocracy, see Levine, *Jerusalem*, pp. 115–119. See also J. Jeremias, *Jerusalem in the Time of Jesus: An Investigation into Economic & Social Conditions during the New Testament Period*, Philadelphia 1979, pp. 181–198. Jeremias argues for a priestly aristocracy from which came the high priests. This aristocracy was composed of the Zadokites at the beginning of the Hellenistic period, the Hasmonean family, and the Diaspora families invited by Herod the Great to Jerusalem in the last years of the Second Temple period. Jeremias differentiates between

Greek *kaloikagathoi* or the Roman Senate. In Greece and in Rome, priesthood was on the main the prerogative of the aristocracy, though it was not hereditary. The priest in ancient Greece, as in Rome, was a magistrate of aristocratic stock.[20] Levine rightly argues that in Hasmonean Judaea the priests fulfilled the role of the aristocracy perfectly. Since they had a Greek education, they were utilized as diplomats and dominated the upper ranks of the Hasmonean army. However, throughout the Herodian period proper, the Herodian revolution deprived the high priest of any political power – which was assumed by the king – or religious power, which was probably shared with the Pharisees, with the priestly aristocracy relegated to the sidelines. With the exception of the new high priestly families, there is no record of any courtier or military officer of priestly origin at Herod's court, with the possible exception of the members of the new families of high priests who were appointed by Herod. In fact, most of Herod's courtiers were new men who owed everything to the king rather than to their social status. Only after Herod's death, with the beginning of direct Roman rule, did priests once more take part in politics as well as in religious life. At that juncture, they were not alone, as they had been during the Hasmonean period, since a new secular Herodian aristocracy shared the burden of ruling Judaea with them under Roman rule.

B. The Temple Cult in the Herodian Period

As in any other civic temple in the Hellenistic Roman world, the Temple of Jerusalem was characterized by the sacrifices performed daily in the Temple.[21] These sacrifices followed a strict routine. The Temple's cultic calendar was punctuated by the Sabbath. The most important Jewish holidays were the three pilgrimages, on Passover, Pentecost, and Tabernacles. During these feasts, pilgrims from

---

the high priestly aristocracy and the common priests, who had no share in the aristocracy. The problem is evident. Josephus was a common priest and an aristocrat as well. On the contrary, it seems to me that the term priest and aristocrat are interchangeable in Second Temple Judaea.

[20] See on Greek priesthood P. Connolly, *The Ancient City, Life in Classical Athens and Rome*, Oxford 1998, pp. 60–61. See W. Burkert, *Greek Religion*, Cambridge (Mass.) 1998, pp. 95–99. See on Roman priesthood R. Del Ponte, *La religione dei romani*, Milano 1992, pp. 96–187 on the most important Roman priesthoods. See also Connolly, *Classical Athens and Rome*, pp. 172–173.

[21] However, there were two main differences between the Jewish and pagan sacrifices. The main difference was that sacrifices by Jews could be offered only in the Jerusalem Temple. The second difference was in the type of sacrifices. The *olah*, the most common sacrifice, where the animal was entirely burnt, and its meat not shared by the priests or those who brought the sacrifice, was unique in Judaism and it had no parallel in the pagan world. Sanders argues for this difference. See Sanders, *Judaism, Practice and Belief*, p. 49. See also Burkert, *Greek Religion*, p. 63. However Burkert points out that the sacrifices to the chthonic gods were also completely burned on the altar.

Judaea flocked to Jerusalem, and from Herod's reign and onward, pilgrims arrived from the entire *oikoumene*. A no less important occasion was the Day of Atonement. All of these cultic celebrations were prescribed in the Pentateuch. However, from the late Hellenistic period onward, Greek influence was felt even in the precincts of the Temple. On the whole, this Hellenistic influence was aesthetic, and thus in Jerusalem of the late Second Temple period, floral garlands decorated the Temple, and the horns of the ox to be sacrificed on Pentecost were gilded. Last but not least, a clear sign that the Jerusalem Temple was becoming a cosmopolitan entity, an integral part of the Graeco-Roman Word, were the sacrifices offered there by Gentiles.[22]

During the Second Temple period, from the Hasmoneans onward, new holidays were introduced, such as Hanukkah, Nicanor Day, and Purim. The Hasmoneans introduced new holidays that were not prescribed in the Pentateuch: Hanukkah and Nicanor Day. Hanukkah celebrated the purification and rededication of the Temple on the 25th of Kislev in 165 BCE, and its first celebration is described in both the *First Books of Maccabees* and *Second Books of Maccabees*. The *First Book of Maccabees* also describes how during the Hasmonean period Hanukkah was celebrated in the Temple for eight days. Sacrifices were offered on the new altar of burnt offerings. Songs, harps, and cymbals and the singing of *Hallel*, as during the pilgrimage feasts, accompanied the sacrifices.[23] Hanukkah could also have symbolized the consecration of the Hasmonean dynasty, which was celebrated with sacrifices, stressing the sacral character of the occasion under the leadership of the Hasmonean high priest. It is important to underline that, initially, Hanukkah was a deferred celebration of Tabernacles, which could not

---

[22] See Levine, *Jerusalem*, p. 257 on the garlands and the gilding of the horns of the ox. On sacrifices offered by the Gentiles see D. Schwartz, "On Sacrifices by Gentiles in the Temple of Jerusalem," *Studies in the Jewish Background of Christianity*, WUNT 60, Tübingen 1992, pp. 102–116. According to Schürer, the Jerusalem Temple in the period under consideration had become cosmopolitan. Therefore, although Gentiles had no need to sacrifice in Jerusalem, as they could offer sacrifices everywhere, yet the Hebrew Bible, Josephus, and the Rabbis are positive that Gentiles can bring sacrifices to the Temple. Thus Gentile's sacrifices were accepted in both theory and practice. Schwartz argues, however, that the reality was slightly different. First, in the Hebrew Bible Gentile's sacrifices are not contemplated. Second, the Rabbis are positive on the subject, albeit in a much more restrictive form than Schürer would admit. Last but not least, Josephus is apologetic, as he wished to present Judaism as universalistic. Schwartz thus states that the acceptance of votive offerings from Gentiles must be seen not as evidence that the Temple was cosmopolitan; rather, it was a compromise that reflected the reality of first century Judaea, a small province in a huge empire.

[23] The first Hanukkah is described in the 1 Macc 4: 36–61. Also 2 Macc 10, 3–9 reports the purification of the Temple on the 25th of Kislev. 2 Macc emphasizes the tie between Hanukkah and the Feast of Booths. The inauguration of the altar was celebrated for eight days as the Feast of Tabernacles. The 13th of Adar was established as Nicanor Day. On Hanukkah see also BT, *Šabb.* 21 a. In the following years, as the Hasmoneans became the undisputed rulers of Judaea, Hanukkah became a Festival with the recital of *hallel*. See also M. Benovitz, "Herod and Hanukkah," *Zion* LXVIII, 1, 2003, pp. 6–15. See also Levine, *Jerusalem*, pp. 82–84.

be celebrated before the restoration of the Temple. It was also inspired by the inauguration of the First Temple by Solomon, celebrated on Tabernacles, which lasted for eight days.[24]

The second holiday introduced by the Hasmoneans, Nicanor Day, had a more secular character and celebrated Judas Maccabaeus's victory over Nicanor in 161 BCE. Nicanor Day, in fact, celebrated the Hasmonean Dynasty. Since the sources do not point to an annual celebration of the Hasmonean Dynasty, we can assume that the purpose of Nicanor Day was not only to celebrate the Maccabee's victory, but also to celebrate the later achievements of the Hasmonean dynasty. Nicanor Day fell on the 13th of Adar.[25]

The development of Hanukkah and Nicanor Day during the Herodian period and in the final years of the Second Temple is noteworthy. Both holidays were a source of embarrassment for both Herod and the Pharisees. For Herod, these holidays were problematic since they celebrated the dynasty he had supplanted, whose past military glory remained much alive among the Jews. For the Pharisees, these two holidays were a bitter reminder of the Hasmoneans, who often supported the Sadducees. According to Krauss and Benovitz, it seems that during the Herodian period Hanukkah was no longer celebrated in the Temple and became a home celebration, as it is today, taking its present form as the Feast of Lights. Thus, according to Benovitz, the new Pharisaic celebration of Hanukkah with lights can be connected to Roman solstice festivals, such as the Saturnalia, celebrated in the East with the adoption of the Julian solar calendar. The Saturnalia, held on the 17th of December, developed in the Roman world into a feast of lights in the first century BCE Candles were sent as gifts and were lit on the altar of Saturnus in Rome. Benovitz points to the fact that the Saturnalia is also linked to the winter solstice in Rabbinic sources. Therefore, both the ritual of increasing the number of lights, according to Beth Hillel, and the affinity of the language used to describe both Hanukkah and the Saturnalia suggest that the Hanukkah lights marked the solstice. Hence, a cosmopolitan king like Herod chose lamp lighting to mark the Hanukkah festival, clearly a Roman influence. According to Benovitz, Herod, moreover, transformed Hanukkah from a celebration of the Hasmonean dynasty and of the Temple dedication into the festival of his own reign, *dies herodis*, and of the dedication of his own Temple. I do not find this last argument convincing. As already stated, like Solomon before him, Herod celebrated the inauguration of the Temple during the feast of Tabernacles, not during Hanukkah. Moreover, *dies herodis* could have been the commemoration of Herod's birthday and it may have celebrated, as well, his recognition by Rome as

---

[24] See 1 Kgs 8, 1.
[25] On Nicanor Day see 1 Macc. 7: 5–50 and 2 Macc.14: 1–15, 36. See also Levine, *Jerusalem*, p. 85. See also V. Noam, *Megillat Ta'anit, Versions, Interpretation, History*, Jerusalem 2003, pp. 298–302.

king of Judaea, though not his conquest of Jerusalem. Another possibility is that *dies herodis* was the synonym used by pagan writers to indicate the Sabbath.[26]

Purim is another celebration that can be dated to the pre-Herodian period. Although the Scroll of Esther does not appear in the Qumran library, in the Second Book of Maccabees, the 14th of Adar is already mentioned as "Mordechai's Day."[27] Thus, Purim was already celebrated during the Hasmonean period. In Herod's day, Purim was probably celebrated on the 14th and 15th of Adar and not only on the 14th of Adar.[28]

Finally, the 15th of Ab, towards the end of the summer, was a feast day. It was the day when the tax for the Wood Offering was paid. The Mishna describes this day in detail as an occasion for merry celebrations of another kind, giving us the rabbis' version. The daughters of Jerusalem, i.e., young maidens dressed in white garments, a symbol of purity, danced in the vineyards in front of young lads and sang verses from Proverbs and the Song of Songs.[29]

I would like to conclude this section by arguing, as Mendels, that one of the tragic results of the Herodian revolution was the diminishing of the Temple's holy status within Jewish consciousness, a situation engendered primarily by the loss of the political power and prestige of the high priest and the priestly aristocracy, who were responsible for the Temple cult. After Herod's death the priestly class was not sufficiently strong, nor did it have enough prestige, to mediate success-

---

[26] S. Krauss proposed that this change took place during Herod's reign. Krauss' proposal is based on the two following points. First, the *dies herodis* in Persius Flaccus' Fifth Satire, is perhaps Hanukkah. Second, Hanukkah lights are dated to Hillel and Shammai, contemporaries of Herod, in Talmudic literature. Krauss believed that Hanukkah lights in a homier setting took the place of the original celebration, which consisted of jubilation and palm branches, in the wake of Herodian and Roman opposition. Benovitz argues that the Festival evolved into the Festival of Lights not because of Herod's opposition, but with his active encouragement. According to Benovitz, this holiday was co-opted by Herod to celebrate his nomination as king in 40 BCE, and later, as the Festival of the Dedication of the Temple in 21 BCE (Josephus, *AJ* XV, 421–423). Herod only transformed Hanukka from a celebration of the Hasmonean dynasty and the Temple dedication into the festival of his own reign and of the dedication of his Temple. Both Hillel and Shammai set rules for the celebration of Hanukkah. According to Beth Shammai, the lights decreased from the first to the eighth day. According to Beth Hillel, the lights increased from the first to the eighth day. See BT, *Šabbath* 21 a. See also Benovitz, "Herod and Hanukkah," pp. 24–32. Hanukka in post-Herodian times came to be associated with the Hasmonean dedication of the Temple. There are references to Hanukka in Josephus, *Apion* II, 118, 282, in Seneca, *Epistula Moralia* 95, 47, and in Persius Flaccus, *Saturae* 5, 176–184 and the holiday is thus known as *luchnokaia*. See Benovitz, "Herod and Hanukkah," pp. 16–24, 32–40.

[27] See 2 Macc 15, 36.

[28] See Esth 9, 19–20, m, *Meg*. See also Noam, *Megillat Ta'anit*, pp. 303–304. According to most scholars, the Fast of Esther dates from the Gaonic period. See also Noam, *Megillat Ta'anit*, p. 302. On Purim see also m, *Meg*. See also Levine, *Jerusalem*, p. 117. Alexandrian Jewry celebrated a similar holiday, described in the Fourth Book of Maccabees.

[29] See m, *Ta'an.* IV, 8. See Prov 31, 30 and Song III, 11. In *Megillath Ta'anith* the 15th of Ab is first remembered as the Day of the Wood Offering for the altar of burnt offering. It was a day when the dead could not be eulogized. See Noam, *Megillat Ta'anit*, pp. 217–222.

fully between Rome and Judaea, leading to its reduced status in the eyes of most Jews. In tandem with this, the Temple also lost some of its eminence and standing among Jews, since it was administered by the selfsame priests and high priest whose status had changed for the worse.

Similar though not identical arguments are presented by Mendels, who contends that, beginning with Pompey's conquest, the Temple lost its national symbolism and became only a religious symbol. Thus the Temple was divested of its political significance, and most of the Jews began to regard it as a religious, cultural, and spiritual symbol, rather than a symbol of political independence. While the Temple lost its political symbolism as a result of Pompey's conquest, Herod was in fact the main catalyst. Following the wishes of his Roman overlords, Herod rebuilt a new and bigger Temple only as a religious and spiritual center, at the same time lowering its political profile. Moreover, according to Mendels, in rebuilding the Temple, Herod wished to elevate his own personal stature, like any other Hellenistic king, and wished to court favor with Diaspora Jews. Mendels also stresses that another element responsible for the diminishing of the Temple's status was the support that the priests, as part of the aristocratic elite, gave to Rome. This support for a foreign power weakened the status of the Jewish priests as result of the political tensions.[30] Although Mendels' arguments are quite persuasive, it seems to me that the Temple remained a political symbol for all the Jews until the catastrophe of 70 CE, with the only possible exception of the Qumran Sect and Christians.

2. Herod and the Rebuilding of the Temple

A. Sources of Inspiration and Parallels for Herod's Temple

Before analyzing all of the elements of the Herodian Temple, I would like to discuss its sources of inspiration. Herod appropriated as source of inspiration for his Temple elements that derived from the Jewish past of the Temple Mount, as well as Hellenistic and Roman elements coming from the surrounding Mediterranean world. Thus the Herodian Temple was the natural outgrowth of the previous

---

[30] According to Mendels, the Roman purpose, from Pompey onwards, was to divest the Temple of its political significance. Mendels stresses that the Romans wished native temples to be religious and spiritual centers, rather than political and nationalistic symbols. Herod succeeded well in following Rome's wishes. Thus, for example, in Josephus the Temple is mentioned only in religious contexts from 6 till 66 CE. In fact, in this period the priesthood had already lost its political, albeit not its economic, preeminence. Only with the war in 66–70 CE would the Temple once again become a political symbol, while the priesthood would regain its political power. See D. Mendels, *The Rise and Fall of Jewish Nationalism, Jewish and Christian Ethnicity in Ancient Palestine*, New York 1992, pp. 277–332.

cultic buildings erected on the Temple Mount for the purposes of the Israelite and – following the destruction of the First Temple – Jewish cult.

The Temple of Solomon described in the First Book of Kings[31] was an ideal model for the Herodian Temple Mount, as King Solomon was the legendary model for King Herod. Speaking in front of the *ekklesia* before beginning construction on the Temple Mount, Herod compared himself to Solomon as a ruler, proclaiming that he would erect an even more magnificent edifice, surpassing that which had been built in the glorious days of Solomon,[32] and in fact he did rebuild the Temple into a true "House for all Nations," more splendid than that which had been constructed by Solomon.

In addition to the Temple of Solomon, the Temple described in the Book of Ezekiel[33] also had a deep influence on Herod's Temple. In his project, Herod celebrated the confluence of all the Jews living within the borders of the Roman Empire, i. e., *oikoumene*, as well as outside it, in the most holy and unique cultic location. As the rebuilder of the Temple, Herod thus wished to celebrate an ideal ingathering of the Twelve Tribes and therefore required a large and magnificent structure to celebrate the ingathering of exiles. Ezekiel's dream was probably reflected in the shape of the Herodian Temple Mount itself, with the various concentric courts of the Herodian Temple possibly inspired by the Temple of Ezekiel's vision. The function of these courts was to host hundreds of thousands of Jews annually, arriving from the four corners of the world, corresponding to the structure of the Temple dreamed of by Ezekiel to host the Twelve Tribes.

If Herod was inspired by both the Temple of Solomon and that of Ezekiel, he was obviously critical of the Temple that stood, since he wished to rebuild it. Indeed in his speech, Herod referred to the Temple rebuilt by the Babylonian exiles,[34] stating that they did not construct as beautiful a Temple as that erected by King Solomon, although the Persian overlords were actually responsible for that situation, since they had been the ones to dictate the dimensions of the new Temple. Herod thus disparaged the standing structure.[35] It seems to me, however, that Herod probably had in mind the Late Hellenistic-Hasmonean Temple, still extant in his time, and not the earlier structure erected during the Persian Period by Zerubabel.

The development of the Temple is described in various sources. The Hellenistic Jewish writer Pseudo-Hecataeus provides a description of the Temple during the

---

[31] See 1 Kgs 6, 1–7, 2, and 7, 13–7, 51.

[32] See Josephus, *AJ* XV, 385.

[33] See Ezek 40, 5–43, 2. The plan of Ezekiel's Temple courts clearly influenced both the Temple envisioned by the Dead Sea Sectarians and the Temple built by Herod. As the rebuilder of the Temple, Herod thus wished to celebrate an ideal gathering of the Twelve Tribes.

[34] Se Josephus, *AJ* XV, 385–386.

[35] See Ezra 1, 7–11; 3, 2–3, 8; 6, 1–2, 3–6. The Temple rebuilt at the beginning of the Second Temple period by Zerubabel was probably quite similar to Solomon's Temple, although much smaller.

2. Herod and the Rebuilding of the Temple

Early Hellenistic period. The Temple on Mount Moriah was then surrounded by monumental walls.[36] The situation changed during the Late Hellenistic period, and both Josephus and Ben Sira[37] report that in the last years of Ptolemaic rule, under the aegis of the high priest Simon (the Just), the Temple Mount was redesigned into a more agreeable Hellenistic structure. Josephus clearly notes a peristyle courtyard as the main characteristic of the Late Hellenistic and Hasmonean Temple. Only with the conquest of Antiochus III was the impressive, but small, structure terminated. With the possible exception of a column, there are no remains of this structure.[38] It seems that the Temple rebuilt by the Oniad Simon had a plan similar to that of the Temple and surrounding inner courtyard and peristyle described in the Temple Scroll.[39] The Hasmoneans, as Herod points out,[40] apparently did not significantly change the Late Hellenistic Temple. Archaeological excavations have shown that the Hasmoneans dug water cisterns.[41] The Letter of Aristeas is helpful in reconstructing the Late Hellenistic-Hasmonean Temple Mount, and although some elements are imaginary, other elements probably reflect the reality of the pre-Herodian Temple.[42]

---

[36] The description given by Pseudo-Hecataeus is reflected in the contemporary Phoenician sanctuary of Amrit in Lebanon. The only difference is that in the center of the court at Amrit stood an *aedicula* rather than a temple. See Hecataeus in Josephus, *Apion* 198-200 in M. Stern, *Greek and Roman Authors on Jews and Judaism I, From Herodotus to Plutarch*, Jerusalem 1976, p. 39. See also Sanders, *Judaism, Practice and Belief*, pp. 55-56.

[37] See Sir 50, 1-4. See also See Josephus, *AJ* XII, 141.

[38] It seems that the Late Hellenistic - Hasmonean Temple Mount was square shaped. This square Temple Mount probably measured 500 cubits (280 m.), the measurement given in the Mishna in Mid. The outer side of the Temple was walled. The Hellenistic construction is conserved in the so-called seam on the eastern outer wall of the Temple Mount, where the southern Herodian wall joins the earlier Hellenistic wall. See H. Shanks (ed.), *Jerusalem, An Archeological Biography*, New York 1995, pp. 62-69. According to Ritmeyer it is thus possible to identify m, Mid. Temple's Square. A peristyle, as Josephus writes, decorated the inner part of the walls. The remaining column is in the Ionic order. Avigad writes that the Ionic capital can be dated to the Hellenistic period, and that it presents various features similar to the capitals of the Ionic temples of Sardis and Dydima, as well as Zechariah's Tomb in the Kidron Valley. According to Avi-Yonah it could have come from the Temple rebuilt by Antiochus IV, and dedicated to Olympian Zeus. However, Avigad points out that on the column's drum the Roman numeral VIII is carved, thus dating the capital to the Herodian period. See N. Avigad, *Discovering Jerusalem*, Jerusalem 1983, pp. 161-165, figs. 177-182. See W. B. Dinsmoor, *The Architecture of Ancient Greece, An Account of Its Historic Development*, London 1985, pp. 280-281.

[39] The Sanctuary described in the Temple Scroll combined a temple built in the Eastern style inside a court surrounded by a peristyle, a structure typical of Late Hellenistic structures in the East.

[40] See Josephus, *AJ* XVII, 162.

[41] The Hasmoneans built a southern extension to the Temple Mount.

[42] This composition, in the form of a letter, related the history of the translation of the Pentateuch in Greek at the time of the Lagid king Ptolemy II, when Judaea was still part of the Ptolemaic kingdom. The king sends an embassy to the high priest in Jerusalem, so that he may send sages to Alexandria, the kingdom capital, to translate the Pentateuch. Most scholars, including Bickerman and Momigliano, date the composition to the second century BCE, at the beginning of Hasmonean rule. See *Let. Arist* 84-101. See also M. Hadas, "Introduction" in *Aristeas to*

It is thus possible to say that the pre-Herodian Temple, a Temple surrounded by a square peristyle on all its four sides, looked quite similar to a Hellenistic *agora*, and it is therefore possible that the Temple Mount served as the Late Hellenistic-Hasmonean *agora* of Jerusalem.[43] Therefore, if we compare the pre-Herodian Temple built by Simon the Just and enlarged by the Hasmoneans with that of Herod, it is clear that Herod did not build something truly revolutionary. The real revolution had already taken place under Simon the Just, who had transformed a Near Eastern sanctuary into the *agora* of Jerusalem, strengthening the civic meaning of the religious complex. As we shall see, Herod merely updated the project, transforming a Greek *agora* into a Roman *forum*. This was nothing new and also occurred elsewhere in the contemporary Mediterranean East and West. Thus, both the Late Hellenistic-Hasmonean "*agora*" and the Herodian "*forum*" most certainly belonged to the architectural tradition of the Classical World.

While rebuilding the Temple, Herod had also in mind the schismatic Temple of Onias III,[44] if not the Samaritan Temple on Mount Garizim.[45] The Temple of

---

Philokrates (Letter of Aristeas), New York 1973, pp. 9–10. See R. J. H. Shutt, "Letter of Aristeas, A New Translation and Introduction," in J. H. Charlesworth (ed.), *The Old Testament Pseudepigrapha*, Garden City (N. Y.), 1983, pp. 7–11. On the Temple Mount described in the Letter of Aristeas as a reflection of late second century BCE–early first century BCE reality, see M. Harari, "Un punto di vista archeologico sulla lettera di Aristea," *Studi Ellenistici II*, 1987, pp. 96–106. Harari argues that L. H. Vincent was the first scholar to analyze the composition in an architectural light. He accepted the description of Jerusalem as realistic, and dated the *ekphrais* to the Late Hellenistic period. The Italian scholar Harari also points out that the composition is an authentic description of Hasmonean Jerusalem. According to him, many elements, such as the list of the gifts given by Ptolemy Philadelphus to the Temple, the description of the city, the subterranean water system, and the Temple itself are not an idealized image of the Holy City of the Jews, but a first hand, personal account of a pilgrim in early Hasmonean Jerusalem. See also R. Bonfil, "On Judaea and Jerusalem in the Letter of Aristeas," *Beth-Mikra* 2 (49), pp. 131–142. Bonfil argues that the author's description of the Temple and the cult of Jerusalem and Judaea, as well as the priests, is not idealized but reflects an existing reality. Most of the scholars date the composition to the second half of the second century BCE. Certain elements in the description, such as the three encompassing walls, are imaginary. Other elements, such as the curtains of the Temple, the inner part of the Temple court, the underground water reservoirs, which clearly date the description to the Hasmonean period and not earlier, and the Baris fortification display authentic Hasmonean elements.

[43] On similar Hellenistic *agoras* see H. Lauter, *Die Architektur des Hellenismus*, Darmstadt 1986, pp. 92–99 and figs. 10, 11, 12 a, 12 b, 14, 18, 19 a. A further example is the Temple of Athena at Pergamum. See W. Radt, *Pergamon, Geschichte und Bauten einer antiken Metropole*, Darmstadt 1999, pp. 160–161, figs. 104–106.

[44] The Temple of Onias was erected at Leontopolis (Tell El Yahudiye) in Egypt by Onias IV, son of Onias III, murdered in Daphne, and brother of Menelaus in 172 BCE. Fleeing the persecution of Antiochus IV, he sought haven in Egypt. Ptolemy VI not only offered him a welcome sanctuary, but also presented him with Leontopolis, where, according to Isaiah, a Jewish Temple would be built. He erected a Temple there between the years 167–164 BCE, when the Temple in Jerusalem was in pagan hands. After the restoration of the Temple, the importance of Onias' temple decreased, but it still continued to function under its Oniad high priests until Vespasian closed it in 73 CE. It seems that at least some of the priests in Jerusalem and some of the Pharisees recognized the validity to this temple to some extent. Thus, a priest who of-

2. Herod and the Rebuilding of the Temple

Onias could have been relevant to Herod's decision to rebuild a huge Temple to serve as the focus of pilgrimages originating not only from the Land of Israel,

---

ficiated in Leontopolis could also officiate in Jerusalem. A sacrifice offered in Leontopolis was considered valid. The Temple itself was excavated by no less than Flinders Petrie. It consisted of a tower built inside a cultic precinct. If this is indeed the Oniad Temple, it clearly reflects a native character, without Hellenistic elements. Josephus, however, described the Leontopolis temple as a copy of the Temple of Jerusalem of modest dimensions. See Josephus, *AJ* XIII, 64–71, 73, 387–388 and *BJ* VII, 420–436. An interesting document dated to 164 BCE is a papyrus that preserves a letter by Herodes, *dioiketes* of Ptolemaic Egypt, to Onias IV. On the Temple of Onias see J. M. Mordrzejewski, *The Jews of Egypt, From Ramses II to Emperor Hadrian*, Philadelphia 1995, pp. 123–129. See also J. Frey, "Temple and Rival Temple – The Cases of Elephantine, Mt. Gerizim, and Leontopolis," in B. Ego, A. Lange and P. Pilhofer (eds.), *Gemeinde ohne Tempel: Community Without Temple*, WUNT 118, Tübingen 1999, pp. 186–198. On the early years of the Temple of Onias see E. S. Gruen, "The Origins and Objectives of Onias' Temple," *SCI* 16, 1997, pp. 47–70 on the foundation of the Temple. Gruen believes that the Jewish sanctuary in Egypt was a reinforcement and not a rival of the Jerusalem Temple. This Temple defied the enemies of the Jews, not Jerusalem. Gruen argues that the Temple of Onias was founded between 159 and 152 BCE when there was no high priest in Jerusalem. After 152 BCE Onias avoided the title of high priest in order to minimize conflict with Jerusalem. Moreover, Onias' dynasty was very helpful to the Hasmoneans in Alexander Jannaeus' time and actively helped Hyrcanus II's soldiers when they invaded Egypt together with Iulius Caesar's army. See also F. Parente, "Onias III's Death and the Founding of the Temple of Leontopolis," in F. Parente and J. Sievers (eds.), *Josephus and the History of the Greco-Roman Period, Essays in Memory of Morton Smith*, Studia Post Biblica 41, Leiden 1994, pp. 69–98. See also F. Parente, "Le témoignage de Théodore de Mopsueste sur le sort d'Onias III et la fondation du temple de Léontopolis," *REJ* 154, 3–4, 1995, pp. 429–436. On the Temple of Onias and the surrounding Egyptians, often hostile, see G. Bohak, "CPJ III, 520; the Egyptian Reaction to Onias' temple, *JSJ* 26, 1, 1995, pp. 32–41. Bohak argues that CPJ III, 520 was written in the second century BCE by a native Egyptian and its invective is addressed against Onias' Temple. Heliopolis, an Egyptian sanctuary, was turned into a military camp of Onias' army, always ready to quell a possible Egyptian rebellion. Moreover in Onias' Temple were sacrificed animals that were sacred to the Egyptians. Did Joseph and Asenath refer to the Temple of Onias? Bohak is positive. See G. Bohak, Asenath's Honeycomb and Onias' Temple; The Key to "Joseph and Asenath," *WCJS* 11, A, 1994, pp. 163–170. On the relationship between the Temple of Onias and the Qumran sectarians see D. J. Kaufman, "The Dead Sea Scrolls and the Oniad High Priesthood," *Qumran Chronicle* 7,1–2, 1997, pp. 51–63 and P. A. Rainbow, "The Last Oniad and the Teacher of Righteousness," *JJS* 48,1, 1997, pp. 30–52. See also J. E. Taylor, "A Second Temple in Egypt; The Evidence for the Zadokite Temple of Onias," *JSJ* 29,3, 1998, pp. 297–321. Taylor argues that the Zadokites mentioned in the Damascus Document were the Oniad priests. Moreover the Damascus Document mentions a solar calendar, but then, the Temple of Heliopolis was founded at Heliopolis, the city of the sun. Taylor thus argues for a tie with the sun and a possible solar calendar. See also P. Schäfer, "From Jerusalem the Great to Alexandria the Small"; The Relationship between Palestine and Egypt in the Graeco-Roman Period, in P. Schäfer (ed.), *The Talmud Yerushalmi and Graeco-Roman Culture I*, TSAJ 71, Tübingen 1998, pp. 129–140. See also A. Wasserstein, "Notes on the Temple of Onias at Leontopolis," *ICS* 18, 1993, pp. 119–129, C. T. R. Hayward, "The Jewish Temple at Leontopolis; A Reconsideration," *JJS* 33,1–2, 1982, pp. 429–443 and M. Delcor, "Le temple d'Onias en Egypte," *RB* 75, 1968, pp. 188–205.

[45] According to Josephus, the Samaritan Temple on Mount Gerizim was founded by Manasseh, brother of the high priest Jaddus, high priest at the time of Darius III, under the patronage of Sanaballetes the Cuthean, Persian satrap of Samaria. See Josephus, *AJ* XI, 304–312. Josephus' account is contradicted by archaeological evidence. Archaeologists indeed found a Samaritan Temple on Mount Garizim; however this is dated to the Late Hellenistic period. The Samaritan

but from the Diaspora as well. Although it seems that there was no relationship between most of the Jews living in Egypt and the Temple of Onias at Leontopolis, we may well wonder if Herod's magnificent Temple might have convinced Egyptian Jews connected to Onias' Temple to worship in Jerusalem rather than in Leontopolis. As I have mentioned earlier, Richardson argues that Jesus son of Phabes was from Leontopolis and that the plan of Herod's Temple was inspired by the Temple in Leontopolis.[46]

There is also another temple that might possibly have influenced Herod's Temple Mount – though it was never built – namely the Temple described in the sectarian Temple Scroll.[47] I do not believe that the edifice as described in

---

Sanctuary, excavated by Y. Magen, is dated to the period between Antiochus III and its destruction by John Hyrcanus I. The sanctuary presents many similar characteristics with the Temple described by Pseudo-Hecataeus, including the fortress build in the eastern area. The Temple itself, not excavated, was surrounded by a sacred precinct surrounded by a wall. A huge staircase was situated in its western part. To the east of the steps there is an open area paved with irregular stone slabs. A large public building was discovered north of the staircase. Opposite this structure there is another public building. A strong wall today called by the Samaritans the "Twelve Stones" lies north of the area. This wall is situated opposite to the northern gate of the precinct. In the eastern part of the cultic precinct, the eastern wall of the precinct was uncovered. In it a southern and a northern gate were uncovered. A fortress stood guard on its northern side. The best account of the inconsistency between Josephus' account and the archaeological evidence collected by Magen is J. Frey, "Temple and Rival Temple – The Cases of Elephantine, Mt. Gerizim, and Leontopolis," in B. Ego, A. Lange and P. Pilhofer (eds.), *Gemeinde ohne Tempel: Community Without Temple*, WUNT 118, Tübingen 1999, pp. 180–186. See on the Samaritans in the Hellenistic period U. Rappaport, "The Samaritans in the Hellenistic Period," in A. D. Crown and L. A. Davey (eds.), *New Samaritan Studies III and IV: Essays in Honour of G. D. Sixdenier, Studies in Judaica* 5, Sydney 1995, pp. 281–288. On the Samaritan Temple see R. T. Anderson, "The Elusive Samaritan Temple, *BA* 54,2, 1991, pp. 104–107. See the excavation reports of Magen. Y. Magen, "Mount Gerizim and the Samaritans," in E. Alliata and F. Manns (eds.), *Early Christianity in Context, Monuments and Documents*, SBFCM 38, Jerusalem 1993, pp. 91–148, Y. Magen, "Israele: un tempio come il Tempio," *Archeo* 128, 1995, pp. 30–38. See also Y. Magen, "Mount Garizim," *Christian Archaeology in the Holy Land, New Discoveries*, Jerusalem, 1990, pp. 333–342. On the first stage of the Temple see Y. Magen, and E. Stern, "Archaeological Evidence for the First Stage of the Samaritan Temple on Mount Gerizim, *Israel Exploration Journal* 52,1, 2002, pp. 49–57. On the inscriptions found in the Samaritan Temple see Y. Magen, and J. Naveh, "Aramaic and Hebrew Inscriptions of the Second Century BCE at Mount Gerizim," *Atiqot* 32, 1997, pp. 9–17. Magen and Naveh, however, argue for a beginning of the Samaritan Temple in the days of Ezra and Nehemia. On the Samaritans and Qumran see E. and H. Eshel, "Dating the Samaritan Pentateuch's Compilation in Light of the Qumran Biblical Scrolls," *Emanuel*, 2003, pp. 215–240.

[46] See Richardson, *Herod King of the Jews*, pp. 245–247.

[47] The Temple Scroll (11QT), one of the most important of the Dead Sea Scrolls, describes the Temple that shall be erected in Jerusalem by the sect once it will be in power and the revised Temple service. The Temple Scroll, parts III–VII, is quite specific in its description of the Temple, the measurements of the Sanctuary, the Holy of Holies, the chambers and colonnades, and its two outer courts. The general outline of the Temple of the sectarians consisted of a huge building that spanned a vast area and included three concentric courts. The Inner Court, quite small, consisted of a square that measured 120 cubits on each side. The Temple, which stood in the middle, repeated the traditional tripartite plan. Various structures stood in the Inner Court. Some, such as seats for the priests, and tables in front of the seats, the House of the Laver (*beth*

2. Herod and the Rebuilding of the Temple

the Temple Scroll directly influenced Herod's building program. It is, however, possible that the enormous new Temple corresponded more directly to the dreams of the Essenes, and perhaps to those of the Dead Sea sectarians, than the previous Hasmonean Temple had done. Maier and Delcors propose the sectarian Temple as a source of inspiration for the Herodian Temple, albeit with some differences.[48]

Herod's Temple was not only influenced by the Jewish past, but also by Graeco-Hellenistic architecture as well. I would like to suggest two sources of inspiration from the Hellenic world, the Acropolis of Athens, specifically, and, more generally, the *anathemata*, a feature characteristic of all the Graeco-Roman

---

ha-kior), the House of the Utensils (*beth ha-kelim*) and the Slaughterhouse (*beth ha-mitbach*) had a clearly utilitarian function. Others, such as the Stairhouse, a structure called the "Ceiling (*makeret*) of the Twelve Pillars," and a Stoa (*parvar*) of Columns to the west of the *hechal*, had a more decorative function. The second Middle Court, called the Court of the Tribes of Israel, measured 480 cubits on each side. It had three gates on each side, totaling twelve gates, as the number of tribes of Israel. The third Outer Court called the Court of the Daughter and of the Strangers, measured no less than 1,600 cubits on each side. It had three gates on each side. See Vermes, *Dead Sea Scrolls*, pp. 139–141. See also Y. Yadin, *The Temple Scroll I*, Jerusalem 1983, pp. 177–197, 200–210, 211–215, 216–223, 224–230, 230–235, 235–239, 239, 241–248, 249–276. Yadin compares the Sectarian Temple to other Temples, such as the Temple of Solomon, the Temple of Ezekiel, as well as the Herodian Temple, and the Temple described in m, *Mid*. See Yadin, *Temple Scroll*, pp. 161–170. Yadin also demonstrated the contemporary Hellenistic origin of some elements, such as the towers, with a central staircase similar to Hellenistic towers excavated at Dor, and the inner peristyles of the courts. That the Temple Scroll is also a source for contemporary Hellenistic architecture is an idea likewise proposed by M. Broshi, who underlines some Hellenistic elements, such as the tower with spiral staircase, and the peristyle, pp. 19–20. See M. Broshi, "Visionary Architecture and Town Planning in the Dead Sea Scrolls," in D. Dimant and L. H. Shifman (eds.), *Time to Prepare the Way of Wilderness, Studies in the Text of the Desert of Judah, Volume XVI*, Leiden 1985, pp. 9–23. J. Maier proposed as the main inspiration for the sectarian Temple the Vision of Ezekiel, but also the actual, more Hellenized Temple, restored by Simon the Just, at the time of Antiochus III. See J. Maier, "The Architectural History of the Temple in Jerusalem in the Light of the Temple Scroll," in G. J. Brooke (ed.), *Temple Scroll Studies, JSPSup. 7*, Sheffield 1989, pp. 23, 33–35. Maybe a real building, the Late Hellenistic-Hasmonean Temple in Jerusalem, inspired the Dead Sea sectarians.

[48] According to Maier, the Middle Court of the sectarian Temple more or less corresponds to the Court that measured 500 cubits described in m, Mid. 2, 1 and to the actual pre-Herodian, Hellenistic Square of 280 sq.m. in the central part of the Temple Mount. Maier also makes a comparison between the sectarian Temple courts and the courts of the Herodian Temple. He compares the Outer Court to the Square of 210 sq.m. in the Herodian Temple, the Middle Court to the Court of Men, and the Inner Court to the Court of Priests of the Herodian Temple. Finally, according to Maier, the Temple Scroll's Temple has a tendency to expand off-limits areas. On the contrary, the Herodian Temple has an inclusive tendency to restrict the cultic area. See Maier, "Architectural History of the Temple," pp. 23–63. Delcor is even more extreme in his conclusions. According to him there are striking similarities between the Temple Scroll and the Herodian Temple. The reason is that the Essenes took an important part in helping Herod; Delcor proposes that Menahem the Essene played a role in convincing the population regarding the rebuilding of the Temple. Thus, Essenes priests influenced Herod's reconstruction. See M. Delcor, "Is the Temple Scroll a Source of the Herodian Temple," in G. J. Brooke (ed.), *Temple Scroll Studies, JSPSup. 7*, pp. 67–85.

sanctuaries. Like Augustus and the Forum of Mars Ultor, Herod was inspired by the perfect classical architecture of the Acropolis of Athens. Josephus is most helpful in showing that, like Augustus, Herod was sensitive to the influence of Classical Greece. Thus the statues of Rome and of Augustus in the Temple of Caesarea Maritima were inspired by Classical models.[49] It seems to me that the Temple Mount in Jerusalem was thus rebuilt as a modern version of the Acropolis. In the Greek city, the acropolis played a mainly religious role, while the *agora* fulfilled a more secular one. In Jerusalem, however, although the Temple Mount fulfilled both the roles of acropolis and *agora-forum* simultaneously, its primary task was religious rather than secular. Thus it seems to me that one of the primary sources of inspiration probably was the Acropolis of Athens, and not just an *agora* or a *forum*. Herod endowed the Temple Mount with a sacral function, architecturally inspired by the Athenian Acropolis. How did the architecture of the Athenian Acropolis influence the Herodian conception of the Temple Mount? In the case of Augustus, the classical influences are clear.[50] Herod, however, could not copy any iconographic elements, since human images were forbidden, at least in the Temple area. So what did Herod take from the Acropolis of Athens? The main architectural influence appears to be expressed in the use of optic corrections. The external wall of the *temenos* of the Temple Mount was built using the same optic corrections used in the building of the Parthenon, and to the best of our knowledge, only the Parthenon's columns and the Temple Mount outer *temenos* employed such optical effects.[51] There is another feature of the Temple, exhaustively treated by Sanders, which is shared by all the pagan temples, Greek and Roman alike, but which is a feature originating in Greece, and before in the

---

[49] See Josephus, *BJ* I, 414. Thus, the statues of Rome and of Augustus in the temple of Caesarea Maritima were inspired by the statues of Hera in the Heraion at Argos by Polyclitus, and of Zeus Olympius in the Temple of Zeus at Olympia by Phidias.

[50] In the Temple of Mars Ultor the element adopted from the Acropolis was the caryatids, inspired by the Erechtheum. In the Ara Pacis the frieze itself was inspired by the internal frieze of the Parthenon that depicted the Panathenaic Procession. See K. Galinsky, *Augustan Culture, An Interpretative Introduction*, Princeton (N. J.) 1996, pp. 146–147.

[51] The most renowned optical correction is *entasis*. This is a slight convexity given to a column shaft, tower, etc. This device was a corrective to an optical illusion, when straight lines and right angles were seen from a certain distance against the background of the sky. A straight-sided column seen against a background of light would appear thinner in the middle than on the top and bottom. The Parthenon was not the only building where *entasis* was applied, but in it the use of *entasis* was much emphasized. Vitruvius, *On Architecture* III, 10–13 also wrote about *entasis*. See A. W. Lawrence, *Greek Architecture*, Harmondsworth 1987, pp. 222–223. I do not believe that *entasis* was used in the columns of the Herodian *temenos* as it is a characteristic of the Doric order. The Corinthian order was selected for the Herodian *temenos*. Today it is possible to see the application of optical corrections on the southwestern corner on the Temple Mount, where each course of Herodian hewn stones juts inwards three centimeters more than the course under it. See also J. M. Hurwit, *The Athenian Acropolis, History, Mythology, and Archaeology from the Neolithic Era to the Present*, Cambridge 2000, pp. 167–168; fig. 131 shows the optical corrections of the Parthenon as a whole.

2. Herod and the Rebuilding of the Temple

Ancient Near East. These are the *anathemata*, or *ex voto*, most of which came from the state and consisted of spoils of war. From the Hasmonean period onward, there must have been an enormous quantity of these. Other *ex voto* were personal, such as the golden chain of Agrippa I.[52] These immediately bring to mind Pausanias' descriptions of Delphi, Olympia, and the Acropolis of Athens, with the *ex voto* described in detail.[53]

It is important to compare Herod's Temple Mount to Greek-Hellenistic and Near Eastern cultic precincts, including Punic contemporary and earlier cultic precincts. The best example of a monumental non-Hellenic, Hellenistic sanctuary is the huge Sanctuary and Temple of Eshmun in Carthage.[54] The Temple of Eshmun can be compared to both the earlier Late Hellenistic-Hasmonean structures and the Herodian Temple Mount. In both cases, the sanctuary dominated the city, and both also consisted of a mixture of native and Hellenistic styles, though in the Punic sanctuary the native element probably predominated. In the surrounding Near East there are other interesting examples of urban sanctuaries that display characteristics similar to those of the Temple Mount. Similar urban conceptions are evident at Nabataean Petra in the Temple of Qasr al Bint;[55] at Palmyra in the Sanctuary of Bel; at Damascus in the huge Sanctuary of Zeus; and at Ba'albek in the Sanctuary of Jupiter Heliopolitanus. Hesberg emphasizes some features common to the Jerusalem Temple precinct and the great contemporary eastern sanctuaries of Bel and Nebo in Palmyra, and Zeus in Damascus. All of these cover huge areas; all have irregular features; and all are an expansion and reconstruction of older sanctuaries. In addition, all of these have a rectangular precinct and a huge altar, and the temples stood in the middle. These sanctuaries, however, lack the main characteristics of the Herodian Temple Mount – the forum plan and the basilica. Thus, a better parallel for these sanctuaries would be the Late Hellenistic-Hasmonean Temple Mount, rather than the later Herodian structure. The only exception is the Temple of Jupiter Heliopolitanus, which was built, like the Herodian Temple Mount, using the same Phoenician style in carving the huge stones.

The main source of inspiration for Herod's Temple Mount, however, was neither Jewish nor Greek-Hellenistic, but Roman. It is important to emphasize that while the primary function of the Temple Mount was religious, its second-

---

[52] See Josephus, *AJ* XIX, 294.

[53] See Sanders, *Judaism, Practice and Belief*, p. 85. See also Pausanias, *Description of Greece*, passim.

[54] On the Temple of Eshmun at Carthage see M. H. Fantar, *Carthage, la cité punique*, Paris 1995, p. 71 and p. 80.

[55] On the Qasr al Bint see Hesberg, "Significance of the Cities in the Kingdom of Herod," p. 12. On the Sanctuary of Bel in Palmyra see M. A. R, Colledge, *The Art of Palmyra*, London 1976, pp. 26–27. On the Sanctuary of Zeus see J. Sauvaget, "Le plan antique de Damas," *Syria* XXVI, 1949, pp. 314–358. On the Sanctuary of Jupiter Heliopolitanus in Ba'albek see F. Ragette, *Baalbek*, Park Ridge (N. J.) 1980.

ary function was secular, and hence the contemporary Roman Forum was the primary architectural complex influencing the Herodian *temenos*. There are other elements of Roman architecture that also influenced the Herodian Temple Mount, all connected to the forum, such as the *cryptoportica*, the basilica, and the mathematical relationship between the various architectural elements. Thus the most important influence on Herod's construction on the Temple Mount was the contemporary building agenda of Augustus in Rome. This plan consisted of the building of the Forum Iulium and the Temple of Venus Genitrix, originally begun by Iulius Caesar; the erection of the Forum of Augustus and the Temple of Mars Ultor; and the erection of various buildings in the Roman Forum, which included the Temple of Divus Iulius, the Actian and Parthian arches, the Basilica Iulia, and the Campus Martius complex, which included the Ara Pacis, the Horologium Solare, and the Mausoleum of Augustus.[56]

Jacobson suggests that the main motivation for the Roman plan of the Temple Mount was purely accidental,[57] but I would argue instead that Herod clearly had strong admiration for Rome and what it represented. As explained in Chapter II, Herod was without doubt a pioneer in bringing Roman Imperial architecture to the East and establishing it there. He could have rebuilt the Temple Mount in a Hellenistic style that was no less grandiose than that of Roman Imperial architecture – and that was still fashionable in the East – but he chose, instead, to rebuild the Temple Mount using new Roman building methods that had been introduced during this period in Augustan Rome and opting to construct Roman-style buildings and follow a Roman general plan. The Herodian model is thus firmly rooted in the Roman West rather than in the Hellenistic East.

First of all, in enlarging the Temple Mount, Herod built the southern wing on superimposed arches, covered by vaults. In other words, Herod used an element similar, but not identical, to *cryptoportica*, which were present in his construction at Sebaste,[58] an element that had been introduced at that time in Roman Imperial architecture. *Cryptoportica* were such a new element that they were not even used in contemporary Augustan Rome, but were found in the slightly later imperial *fora* in the Western provinces, such as in Arelate (Arles) and Narbo (Narbonne) in Gallia. As will be detailed below, Herod also introduced, all along the southern wing of the Temple Mount, a Roman building with a long architectural tradition, the basilica. True, the Herodian Royal Stoa was still a mixture of the Hellenistic *stoa* and a Roman basilica. Its northern wing was open, like the

---

[56] See Zanker, *Augusto ed il potere delle immagini*, pp. 29, 117 on the Forum Iulium, pp. 122–123 and 215–219 on the Forum of Augustus, pp. 87–88, on Augustus' intervention in Rome's Forum and pp. 127–128 and 131–135 on the Campus Martium complex, which included the Ara Pacis, the Horologium Solare and the Mausoleum of Augustus.

[57] As Solomon erected a temple in the Syro-Phoenician style, so Herod's sanctuary was a Roman forum. See D. Jacobson, "Herod's Roman Temple," *BAR* 28, 2, 2002, p. 19.

[58] See on the cryptoportica of the Temple of Augustus at Sebaste E. Netzer, "The Augusteum at Samaria Sebaste, A New Outlook", *Eretz-Israel 19*, 1987, pp. 97–105 (Hebrew).

inner wing of a *stoa*, but inside it was built like a basilica, with an inner colonnade on all sides. Furthermore, the plan of the sanctuary followed the general outline of a contemporary Roman forum, whose general outline consisted of a rectangular-shaped square, surrounded by a colonnade. Two types of buildings dominated the complex, a basilica and a temple. Generally the basilica stood on one of the short sides. In the middle, or on one of the short sides, generally in front of the basilica, stood a temple or a group of temples. Jacobson notes that the Temple Mount incorporates some of the characteristics of the earlier Roman sanctuaries in Latium, such as the Temple of Fortuna Primigenia at Praeneste, the Temple of Jupiter Anxur at Terracina, and the Temple of Hercules Victor at Tibur. These sanctuaries shared the following characteristic elements with the Temple Mount: twin symmetrical entrances, a centrally placed temple, and enclosing colonnades.[59]

Ward-Perkins suggests, as an alternative model, an Eastern interpretation of the Roman *forum*, underlining the similarity to the contemporary Caesareum of Cyrene and of Alexandria.[60] Both have a rectangular plan with a temple in the middle and a basilica on one of the short sides. The Caesareum was, in fact, an adaptation of Roman imperial *fora* as they were built in the West. Herod, however, had never visited Alexandria or Cyrene. I believe that the Western *fora* in Gaul and Spain are a far more plausible model. All of these *municipia* were in fact colonies settled by Augustus' and Agrippa's veterans, and thus the plans of these cities could have been familiar to Herod from his visits to Rome.[61] The *fora* of Glanum and Arelates in Gaul and of Tarragona in Spain, all dated to the Augustan period,[62] make use of the same features seen at the Temple Mount, as well as at the Herodian Temples at Caesarea Maritima and Sebaste – a precinct with a central or a side temple and a basilica. The *forum* included both the civic and the religious centers of the *municipium*. Jacobson also suggests another Roman element, this time mathematical. Though the interior of the Herodian Temple was tripartite, consisting of *ulam*, *hechal*, and *dvir*, as prescribed by the Bible, on the exterior it gave the illusion of a huge cube, 100 cubits on each side, though in fact it was actually T-shaped. The cube was the perfect Pythagorean number ten, (10 cubits × 10 cubits). These are aesthetic principles derived from classical architecture. Thus the Herodian Temple itself was symmetrical, which, in the Classical World symbolized mathematical harmony.[63]

---

[59] See Jacobson, "Herod's Roman Temple," pp. 22–23. See also Hesberg, "Significance of the Cities in the Kingdom of Herod," p. 12.

[60] See J.B. Ward-Perkins, *Roman Imperial Architecture*, Harmondsworth 1981, p. 366. See also D. Bahat, *The Illustrated Atlas of Jerusalem*, Jerusalem 1990, p. 44.

[61] On Augustan Gaul and Spain see R. MacMullen, *Romanization in the Time of Augustus*, New Haven (Conn.) 2000, passim.

[62] See P. Gros, *L'architecture romaine 1, Les monuments publics*, Paris 1996: Glanum: p. 224, fig. 269; Tarragona, p. 230, fig. 278, p. 353, fig. 410; Arelate, p. 231, fig. 280.

[63] See Jacobson, "Herod's Roman Temple," p. 25.

In conclusion, it is important to emphasize that a further feature common to cultic architecture in both Rome and Jerusalem was the Hellenization of the outer forms. This was reflected mainly in the exterior of the cultic building and in the use of Greek styles, in this case the Corinthian style, which completely dominated Rome itself and Roman Italy during the Augustan period and which very quickly became widespread in the Western provinces. Native architectural concepts, however, continued to dominate the interior of the temple buildings both in Rome and Jerusalem. The Herodian Temple thus continued to reflect the tripartite division of the Solomonic Temple, and the Roman temple conserved the Etrusco-Italic division of interior space.

B. The Temple and the Temple Mount.

The Temple Mount sanctuary, which made such a strong impression in Rabbinic literature,[64] is described in detail by Josephus.[65] The Herodian sanctuary made an outstanding impact, not least because of its topographical position, dominating the city. Moreover the site itself was sanctified by a long tradition of cult and worship. The Herodian Temple was separated from the rest of the urban grid by means of a podium, a huge structure (cfr. figure VI, 1). In this architectural composition, the Temple formed the culminating point of an extended architectural arrangement.[66] The fully rebuilt Temple Mount became the center of Jewish public life in Jerusalem, and the Temple itself became the center of Jewish pilgrimage from all around the *oikoumene*. It was a magnificent creation, no doubt the greatest *temenos* in classical antiquity. The building of the Temple Mount complex began around 20–19 BCE, with most of the work ending nine years later, around 11–10 BCE, though maintenance and repairs continued until some years before the great revolt.[67] Josephus gives an impressive description of the beginning of the work.[68]

---

[64] See TB, *Sukkah* 51 b, and TB, *B. Bat.* 4 a. See also m. '*Abod. V*, 7.

[65] The Temple Mount is described by Josephus in the *AJ* XV, 380–425, and in *BJ* V, 184–227. The Tractate *Mid.* of the Mishna is dedicated to the description of the Temple building. *Mid.* is one of the oldest tractates in the Mishna; the description is generally considered a realistic one, though some scholars claim it to be idealized. See m, *Mid*. Sanders argues for Josephus, *BJ* V, 212, as the best description of the Temple. See Sanders, *Judaism, Practice and Belief*, p. 59. On the Herodian Temple see also D. Bahat, "The Herodian Temple," in *CHJ, The Early Roman Period III*, 1999, pp. 38–59. Bahat presents a complete collection of sources, p. 38. The part dedicated to the history of the Temple from Herod's death to the destruction in 70 CE, pp. 38–43 is important. The archaeological remains and the Temple occupy most of the paper, pp. 43–58.

[66] See Bahat, *Atlas of Jerusalem*, pp. 42–43.

[67] See Schürer, *History of the Jewish People I*, p. 292. Josephus, however, in *BJ* I, 211, wrote that Herod began building the Temple in the fifteenth year of his rule (23–22 BCE). Perhaps he is referring to the beginning of preparations for building. It is probable that Herod began work on the Temple Mount only in 20–19 BCE. This would have coincided with the arrival of

2. Herod and the Rebuilding of the Temple

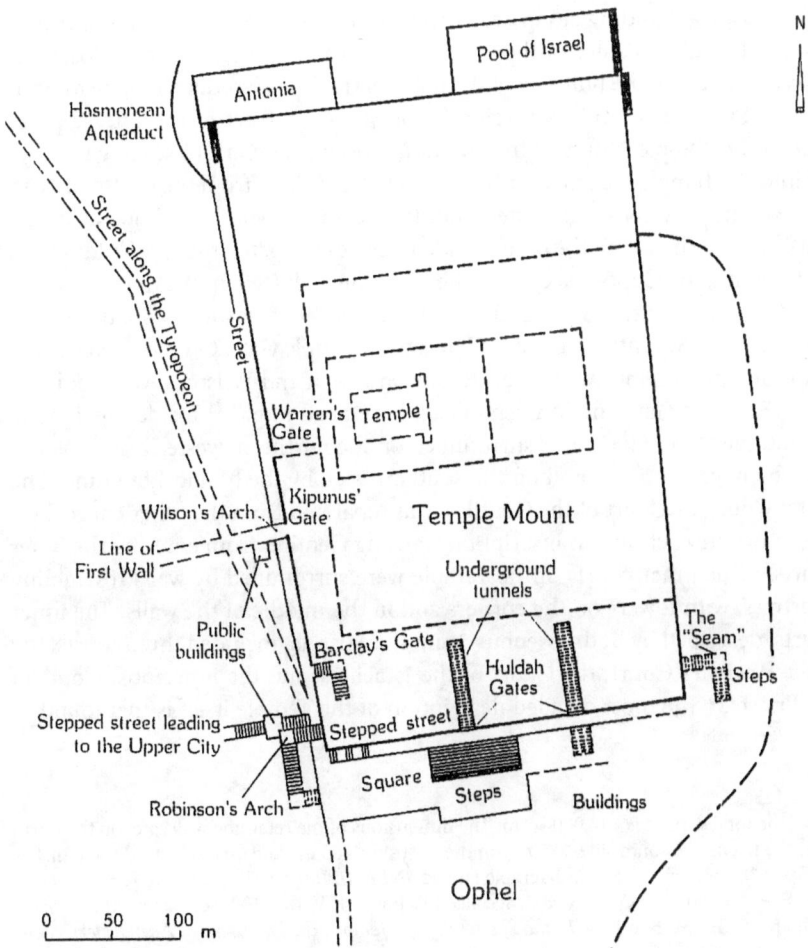

Figure VI, 1 – Plan of the Temple Mount from *The New Encyclopedia of Archaeological Excavations in the Holy Land* II, Jerusalem, "Plan of the Temple Mount as built by Herod, p. 738, Courtesy of the Israel Exploration Society, Jerusalem.

The plan of the Herodian Temple Mount consisted of a rectangular *temenos* erected around a mountain crest and surrounded on three sides by porticoes,

---

Augustus in Syria in the spring or summer of 20 BCE, according to Dio, *Roman History* 7, 6. If Josephus counted the years from 40 BCE, when Herod ruled from Sebaste, the Temple works indeed would have begun in 20–19 BCE. If Josephus counted the years from 37 BCE, when Herod conquered Jerusalem, the work would have begun in 17–16 BCE. According to Josephus, *AJ* XV, 423, after the completion of the Temple, a great festival was arranged, on the anniversary of Herod's accession to the throne.

[68] See Josephus, *AJ* XV, 391–397.

with a basilical building along nearly the entire southern side. The Temple itself was erected at the center of the *temenos*, closer to the western side.[69] Josephus describes in detail the building of the outer part of the Herodian Temple Mount. Archaeological data contributes significantly to reconstructing the outer appearance of the Temple Mount.[70] In *Antiquities* Josephus describes seven gates that led into the Temple Mount: four from the west and three from the south. In *War*, however, he describes eight gates from the north and south, and one from the east.[71] The Mishna,[72] on the other hand, describes five gates: the two Hulda Gates in the south, the Cuponius Gate in the west, the Tadi Gate in the north, and the Susa Gate in the east. Two walled-up gates are visible today in the southern wall of the Temple Mount: the Double Gate and the Triple Gate. On the western wall of the Temple Mount, two arches, Robinson's Arch and Wilson's Arch, and two gates, Barclay's Gate and Warren's Gate, have been found.[73] Inside the Temple Mount, the Outer Court was surrounded on the northern, western, and eastern sides by huge porticoes and on the southern side by the basilical building. The Outer Court, or Court of the Gentiles, was separated from the other courts by a screen or *soreg* bearing an inscription warning Gentiles from entering the inner courts.[74] The inner courts of the Temple were surrounded by walls resembling a fortress, with towers on the corners and in the middle of the walls. The inner courts, described by both Josephus[75] and the Mishna, included three courts, the outer Women's Court, the Court of the Israelites, and the innermost Court of the Priests.[76] The most detailed description of the Temple itself is that found in

---

[69] The total surface is 144,000 sq. m. The dimensions of the retaining walls are: on the north side, 315 m.; on the south side, 280 m.; on the west side, 485 m.; and on the east side, 460 m. See H. Geva, "Jerusalem, the Second Temple Period," *NEAHL II*, Jerusalem 1992, p. 735.

[70] See Josephus, *AJ* XV, 398–400. See also Josephus, *BJ* V, 184–190. See Bahat, *Atlas of Jerusalem*, p. 46. See M. Ben Dov, *In the Shadow of the Temple, the Discovery of Ancient Jerusalem*, Jerusalem 1982, p. 84.

[71] See Josephus, *AJ* XV, 410–411. See also *BJ* V, 201–206.

[72] m, *Mid.* I, 3.

[73] See Geva, "Jerusalem, the Second Temple Period," pp. 735–736. See also Josephus, *BJ* II, 5.

[74] See Josephus, *AJ* XV, 417–418. Two fragments of the inscription in Greek have been found. The inscription reads: "No foreigner shall enter within the balustrade of the Temple, or within the precinct, and whosoever shall be caught shall be responsible for his death that will follow in consequence of his trespassing." See Geva, "Jerusalem, the Second Temple Period," p. 344. On the warning inscription of Herod's Temple see mainly E. Bickerman, "The Warning Inscription of Herod's Temple," *JQR* XXXVII, 1947, pp. 387–405. See also A. M. Rabello, "The Lex de Templo Hierosolymitano Prohibiting Gentiles from Entering Jerusalem's Sanctuary," in *The Jews in the Roman Empire: Legal Problems, From Herod to Justinian*, Aldershot 2000, IIIa–IIIb. Rabello stresses that this law dated from Herod's reign, and not, as thought by other scholars, to subsequent Roman rule.

[75] On the various courts see Josephus, *AJ* XV, 410–421. See also Josephus, *BJ* V, 190–200.

[76] See Bahat, *Atlas of Jerusalem*, p. 42.

the Tractate *Middot* in the Mishna.⁷⁷ There are several discrepancies between Tractate *Middot* and Josephus' description of the Temple, and there are even differences in certain details reported in Josephus' two works, *War* and *Antiquities*. The sources agree as to the overall structure, despite the discrepancies.⁷⁸ The façade of the Temple can be reconstructed, according to Avi-Yonah,⁷⁹ using the silver tetradrachmas and didrachmas coined by Bar Kokhba during the Second Revolt, from 132 to 135 CE, as a model.⁸⁰

The Royal Stoa, described by Josephus, was composed of three parts, a central hall and two side aisles, with pillars that supported its ceiling. The two side halls or aisles were of equal width, but narrower than the central hall, in addition to being about half its height. The southern wall of the Temple Mount sealed the southern side of the building, but its northern side had openings facing onto the Temple Mount esplanade.⁸¹ As previously stated, the Royal Stoa more closely resembled a Roman basilica than a Greek stoa. The only difference is that while a basilica is closed on all four sides, the Royal Stoa was open on the long inner side. This huge structure was probably the largest basilica in the Roman world, longer than the contemporary Basilica Julia and the later Basilica Ulpia.⁸² According to Netzer, the main aim of the Royal Stoa was to emphasize Herod's position as a secular ruler on the Temple Mount. It seems to me that Herod probably sat as supreme judge in the Royal Stoa. As I have posited earlier, Herod as king was also

---

⁷⁷ The Temple described in *Mid.* is probably the one built by Herod the Great in 20–19 BCE. According to Neusner the tractate describes an imaginary building. See J. Patrich, "The Structure of the Second Temple – A New Reconstruction," *Ancient Jerusalem Revealed*, Jerusalem 1994, p. 260.

⁷⁸ On the Temple façade see Josephus, *BJ* V, 207–214; on the interior of the building see 215–222; on the exterior of the building see 222–224. See also L. I. Levine, "Josephus' Description of the Jerusalem Temple: War, Antiquities, and Other Sources," *Cathedra* 77, 1995, pp. 3–17. See also Patrich, "Structure of the Second Temple – A New Reconstruction," p. 260.

⁷⁹ See M. Avi-Yonah, "The Second Temple," *Sepher Yerushalayim*, Tel Aviv-Jerusalem 1956, pp. 392–419.

⁸⁰ The tetradrachm shows the Temple façade. According to Barag, the stylized figure between the columns is a representation of the Showbread Table. According to Barag, the didrachm that apparently depicts the façade of a building with two Corinthian columns, in fact shows the gates of the Temple. See D. Barag, "The Showbread Table and the Façade of the Temple on Coins of the Bar-Kokhba Revolt," *Ancient Jerusalem Revealed*, Jerusalem 1994, pp. 272–276. According to Y. Meshorer, the building shown on the Bar Kokhba tetradrachm is the Temple, but it is entirely idealized. See Meshorer, *Ancient Jewish Coinage II*, pp. 138–141. Another iconographical source is the paintings of the third century synagogue at Dura Europus. The façade of the Temple is slightly different from the building on the Bar Kokhba tetradrachm. See R. Hachlili, *Ancient Jewish Art and Archaeology in the Land of Israel, Handbuch der Orientalistik*, Leiden 1988, p. 27.

⁸¹ See Josephus, *AJ* XV, 411–417. See also Ben Dov, *Shadow of the Temple*, pp. 124–125. The Royal Stoa, a more developed form of the stoa, was designed to roof a broad area. Since the length of wooden beams was necessarily limited, the portico was shaped as a central hall with two side aisles. The central hall was generally built to a greater height than the aisles to accommodate windows. See Bahat, *Atlas of Jerusalem*, p. 43. On the Royal Portico, see also Sanders, *Judaism, Practice and Belief*, pp. 64–70.

⁸² See C. A. Carpiceci, *Roma, com'era 2000 anni fa*, Firenze 1981, pp. 19–22, 50, 147.

the supreme judge, and since the Roman basilica was the traditional location of law courts, and it is therefore possible that the shape of the Royal Stoa suggests its possible use as a tribunal. Thus it seems to me that the Royal Stoa, located on the Temple Mount, was a better suited and far more impressive place for Herod to seat in judgment, than were his royal palaces in the city. Moreover, since Herod was not a priest, he had no access to the Temple itself, the most important building in Jerusalem. Therefore the erection of the Royal Stoa, where Herod could sit as supreme judge, probably emphasized his status on the Temple Mount.[83]

Thus we may conclude that the Temple Mount enterprise offered solutions to Herod's two major problems. Because the Temple had a clear political and religious meaning for the Jews as the main symbol of their independence, Herod thus transmuted it into a religious symbol for his Jewish subjects, devoid of any political meaning. For the Jews, Herod was the king who built not only the most beautiful sanctuary that the Jews had ever known, but also the greatest sanctuary in the entire *oikoumene*. Since Herod himself now chose the high priest, the key figure in the Temple cult, the Temple as a religious center rested firmly in his hands. Because Herod was not of priestly lineage and therefore had no access to the Temple itself, he wanted to demonstrate his power to his Jewish subjects, even in their most sacred place, and, as Netzer has suggested, therefore he erected the Royal Stoa, from which he could dominate the Temple Mount as secular king.

3. The Synagogue in Judaea: A Civic Center

Previously in the chapter, we discussed the Temple, the religious center of the Jewish people. King Herod did not just rebuild the Temple Mount in its entire splendor, but indeed he succeeded in supervising and dominating its organization as well. However did Herod as well succeed in controlling the synagogue? As the Temple, the synagogue was a religious institution: it is called *proseuche* or House of Prayer. However the synagogue served also as *synagoge* or House of Assembly, the main public building in Jewish cities, towns and villages. In fact, as we shall see, the synagogue in the Herodian and in the Late Second Temple Period fulfilled not solely a religious function, but administrative, juridical, and social tasks as well.

According to the literary sources, there is no hint that King Herod controlled the synagogue, a peripheral institution, far away from the center, but none the

---

[83] Herod, as king, the high priest, and the members of the *Synedrion/Sanhedrin* enjoyed an exclusive standing on the Temple Mount, each at a different location. Thus Herod as king dominated the Temple Mount from the Royal Stoa, the high priest dominated the Temple Mount from the Temple itself, while according to Rabbinic tradition, the Sanhedrin sat in the so called Chamber of Hewn Stone. According to Josephus the Chamber of Hewn Stone was the seat of the *boulē*. See Bahat, *Atlas of Jerusalem*, pp. 36, 53, 114.

less very important. Most of the examples that can be helpful describe a slightly later period. And yet I suggest that it is quite probable that King Herod controlled the synagogue as institution. However first of all it is important to examine the position of the *proseuche/synagoge* in first century CE Judaea.

Together with the Temple, the synagogue was already a respected institution in Herodian Judaea that had begun to flourish during the Hasmonean period[84]. According to Netzer, the most ancient synagogue is a huge rectangular building found near the Hasmonean Palace in Jericho.[85] The presence of this institution in a royal palace is of great interest.

The development of the synagogue, as *proseuche* or House of Prayer, such as building dates and epigraphic evidence, took place during the Herodian and late Second Temple period. During this time the synagogue was not an alternative to Temple worship, but rather, a supplement to it. Sanders is thus correct in arguing that during the Second Temple period, after the Temple itself, the synagogue provided the other main focal point of religious life for the Jews. The home provided another such focal point, though to a lesser extent.[86] Levine nicely summarizes the various functions fulfilled by the synagogue during the Second Temple period as a community center, as a locale where communal meals were held, and as a place of punishment. Schools also were located in synagogues. The synagogue was also a religious institution, its main activity being public readings from the

---

[84] The origin of the synagogue is a much disputed topic. According to Levine, the First Temple City Gate, where the city elders met to make justice and decisions, was probably an important element in the development of the synagogue. There is disagreement over when this institution began to develop, whether in the Babylonian Diaspora, in Yehud in the Persian period or in the Hellenistic East. See L. I. Levine, *The Ancient Synagogue, The First Thousand Years*, New York 2000, pp. 19–41. Levine also argues that the synagogue does not appear in Judaean sources of the Persian and Hellenistic periods, but only in the Hasmonean period (pp. 31–41). Levine argues that the courses of Levites and priests were organized outside Jerusalem at the beginning of the Second Temple period, for Torah reading around a communal building when not serving in the Jerusalem Temple. See Levine, *Ancient Synagogue*, p. 36.

[85] See E. Netzer, "A Synagogue from the Hasmonean Period Recently Exposed in the Western Plain of Jericho," *IEJ* 50, 2000, pp. 203 ff.

[86] See Sanders, *Judaism, Practice and Belief*, p. 48. See also E. P. Sanders, "Common Judaism and the Synagogue in the First Century," in S. Fine (ed.), *Jews, Christians, and Polytheists in the Ancient Synagogue, Cultural Interaction during the Greco-Roman Period*, London 1999, pp. 1–17. Sanders argues for a possible origin of the synagogue in the Greek Diaspora, examining the extant documents, mainly from Asia Minor, in which the Jewish communities ask the Gentile cities for various rights, including a place of assembly. The place of assembly, mentioned together with other rites including the observance of sacred rites, the study of the Law of Moses, special dietary requirements, and the Sabbath rest, is thus seen by Sanders as an element essential for Judaism in the Diaspora. Sanders shows that the Diaspora Jews had their own synagogues in Jerusalem. Accordingly Sanders postulates that Diaspora pilgrims introduced the synagogue in Judaea. Another possibility raised by Sanders is that Jews living far away from Jerusalem built synagogues as they could not join the Temple cult regularly. Sanders also argues for twice and thrice daily prayers at home during the week and in the synagogue on the Sabbath. Sanders concludes his article stressing that the community rather than the Rabbis or the Pharisees ran the synagogue.

Torah and Haftaroth, or from the Prophets. However, the synagogue was also a center for study and educational activities, a place where sermons were delivered, where Targumim or Aramaic translations were read to the public, and perhaps where communal prayer was held.[87] However the communal and religious elements of the synagogue will not be discussed in this chapter,[88] as the synagogue as a religious center had been already much discussed.

As I wrote before, I wish to propose that the synagogue may have been the main administrative building of Judaea's cities and villages, with a clear civic function and not just a religious purpose or significance. To support my thesis I will use Josephus' description of the *proseuche* of Tiberias, as well as archaeological data. All this data, however refers to a latter period, well in the middle of the first century CE. Josephus refers to the synagogue of Tiberias as the *proseuche*, which served as the main setting for the assembly of the *boulē*, or city council of Tiberias. This building, probably the main synagogue of Tiberias, is described as a very large structure, the seat of the *boulē*, or city council, and one in which deliberations were held on Sabbath morning, in addition to religious services and prayers, thus fulfilling the traditional role of the synagogue as a "house of prayer

---

[87] On the Synagogue as community center see Levine, pp. 128–134. See also Josephus, *Vita* 271–98, 331, and *AJ* XIV, 235, 259–261. As a place for communal meals, see Levine, *Ancient Synagogue*, pp. 129–132, who bases his thesis mainly on later Rabbinic sources. On the synagogue as place of punishment see Levine, *Ancient Synagogue*, p. 132. See also Matt 10: 17–18; Mark 13: 9; Luke 21: 12 and 12: 11; Acts 22: 19. On schools in the synagogues see Levine p. 133–134. See also JT, *Megillah*, 3, 1, 73 d; JT, *Ketub*. 13, 35 c, BT, *Ketub*. 105 a. On the synagogue as a religious institution see Levine, *Ancient Synagogue*, pp. 134–159. On Torah reading see Levine, *Ancient Synagogue*, pp. 142. See A. Baumgarten, "Torah as a Public Document," *Studies in Religion* 14, 1, 1985, pp. 17–24. See also Josephus, *Apion* 2, 175, *AJ* XVI, 43; Philo, *Embassy* 156; *Dreams* 2, 127; Luke 4: 16–22, Acts 13: 14–15 and 15: 21, t., *Sukkah* 4: 6. On Haftaroth or reading from the Prophets see Levine, *Ancient Synagogue*, pp. 142–143. See also Luke 4: 17–19; Acts 13: 14–15, 27. t., *Meg.* 3: 1–9. On study and education in the synagogue see Levine, *Ancient Synagogue*, pp. 144–145. See also Philo, *Moses* 2, 216 and *Spec.* 2, 62–63. On sermons see Levine, *Ancient Synagogue*, pp. 145–147. See also Luke 4: 20–21; Acts 13: 15; Philo, *Moses* 2, 215; *Hypot.* 7, 13. On Targumim see Levine, *Ancient Synagogue*, pp. 147–151. On communal prayer see Levine, *Ancient Synagogue*, pp. 151–159. See also S. C. Reif, "The Early Liturgy of the Synagogue," *CHJ, The Early Roman Period* 3, Cambridge 1999, pp. 326–358.

[88] See also on Second Temple period synagogues L. Levine, "The Second Temple Synagogue, The Formative Years," in L. I. Levine (ed.), *The Synagogue in Late Antiquity*, Philadelphia 1987, pp. 7–31. See also L. I. Levine, "The First Century CE Synagogue in Historical Perspective," in B. Olsson and M. Zetterholm (eds.), *The Ancient Synagogue from Its Origins until 200 CE: Papers Presented at an International Conference at Lund University, October 14–17, 2001 (Coniectanea Biblica. New Testament Series, 39)*, Stockholm 2003, pp. 1–24. See also H. C. Kee, "Defining the First-Century CE Synagogue; Problems and Progress", *NTS* 41, 4, 1995, pp. 481–500. On the relationship between the synagogue and the Qumran sectarians see E. Eshel, "Prayer in Qumran and the Synagogue," in B. Ego, A. Lange and P. Pilhofer (eds.), *Gemeinde ohne Tempel: Community Without Temple*, *WUNT* 118, Tübingen 1999, pp. 323–334. Eshel argues that the Sages of Yavne transformed the synagogue, a Diaspora institution, from a place of study into a place of prayer. Moreover, the institution of fixed prayers, composed by Jewish groups who fled Jerusalem, such as the Qumran sectarians, were adopted by the Yavne Sages.

3. The Synagogue in Judaea: A Civic Center 309

and Torah reading."[89] Another possible role of the *proseuche* of Tiberias, however, which is not mentioned by Josephus, was that of a court of law. Although the *boulē* and the city magistrates dominated city life, there were other important authorities such as judges, who probably also administered justice in the same building in which the assembly convened. All these city magistrates, *boulē* members as well as judges were members of the ruling class.

Josephus describes the *proseuche* of Tiberias as a "huge building, capable of accommodating a large crowd,"[90] and this building is probably described in later Talmudic literature, though Rabbinic literature is somewhat problematic.[91] However, two *dyplastoon* buildings within a Jewish context did exist at the end of the Second Temple Period and may have served as source for the plan of the *proseuche* of Tiberias. The first building was Herod's Royal Stoa, described above, while the second building was the main synagogue of Alexandria.[92] It seems to

---

[89] See Josephus, Vita 277. Josephus calls it *"megiston oikema"*, a huge building, and then he adds that the building is capable of accommodating a large crowd. See Josephus, Vita 279 on the *proseuche* of Tiberias as seat of the *boulē*, or city council. See Josephus, Vita 278–279 on deliberations held on Sabbath morning in the *proseuche* of Tiberias. See Josephus, Vita 294–295 on service and prayers held in the *proseuche* of Tiberias. Josephus further describes this building as the site of various assemblies held in Tiberias at the beginning of the Great War in 66 CE, See Josephus, Vita, 280–284.

[90] See Josephus, Vita 277.

[91] The Jerusalem Talmud certainly mentions a building called "the synagogue of the *boulē*." See TJ, Šeqal. 7:5, 50 c. A synagogue of Tiberias is mentioned in m., ʿErub. 10: 10. See also Y. Hirschfeld, *Roman, Byzantine, and Early Muslim Tiberias: A Handbook of Primary Sources*, Tiberias 2005, pp. 10–12. Only the late Midrash on Psalms describes the synagogue of Tiberias. This is probably the same building mentioned by Josephus, as a huge building. Rabbinic sources thus describe this building as a *dyplastoon* building, or a basilica with two concentric rows of columns. See Midr. on Pss 93.
Midr. on Pss 93 is dated to the ninth century CE, and it was written after the terrible earthquake of 749 CE leveled the region. Is the building described a reflection of reality or merely a reflection of the *Royal Stoa* of the Temple, a part of the Temple well known by the Sages? It is worthy of note the word *dyplastoon*. The Midrash on Psalms uses a technical term that was totally obsolete in Late Antiquity and in the Middle Ages. Is it possible that this term may be a reflection of an earlier reality?

[92] The other *dyplastoon* building, the synagogue of Alexandria, mentioned by Philo as a huge building, is well-known also from a different Rabbinic source, the Babylonian Talmud, earlier than the Midrash on Psalms. See TB, *Sukkah* 51B. On the Alexandria Synagogue see also Philo, *Legat*. 134, where the building is called *"megiste"* and *"perisemotate."* The fact that the same type of building is described in two different sources points to the probable authenticity of the Rabbinic sources, as Hacham also points out in his article. See N. Hacham, "From Splendor to Disgrace; On the Destruction of Egyptian Jewry in Rabbinic Literature", *Tarbiz* LXXII, 4, 2003 (Hebrew), pp. 463–488. The building described by Rabbinic sources is also a huge *dyplastoon* basilica. Clearly this building, which displays Roman characteristics, was erected after the Roman conquest of Egypt in 31 BCE, but before 41 CE, when the pogroms suffered by the Jewish community of Alexandria would probably have made the erection of such a huge and beautiful building impossible. The plan of the synagogue of Alexandria appears to have originated in the Caesareum of Cyrene (excavated) and in that of Alexandria (not excavated). See Ward-Perkins, *Roman Imperial Architecture*, p. 366. See also Bahat, *Illustrated Atlas of Jerusalem*, p. 44. See also N. Bonacasa and S. Ensoli (eds.), *Cirene, Centri e monumenti dell'Antichita'*, Milano 2000,

me that Antipas (or Agrippa I/Agrippa II) erected the *dyplastoon* at Tiberias in imitation of Herod's Stoa Basilike and perhaps also the *dyplastoon* of Alexandria. The building in Tiberias, like the Royal Stoa in Jerusalem, was probably part of a porticoed courtyard. This building was most likely no longer in use at the beginning of the fourth century, since by then, a new basilica had been constructed in the center of Tiberias,[93] quite different from the building that is described in Talmudic sources. Antipas also erected other buildings in Tiberias, including a stadium, a palace, and city walls, in imitation of similar Herodian buildings.[94] In conclusion, it seems to me that the *proseuche* of Tiberias, a *dyplastoon* building used as the seat of the *boulē* and as a synagogue, followed the layout of the Roman basilica.

As noted in Chapter V, in towns and villages there were different authorities than in the great cities.[95] Where did these magistrates sit in judgment? It seems to me that they were seated in a public building. Were there two main public buildings in each village, one with a secular function, housing the local court of law and one serving as the house of prayer, the *proseuche* or synagogue? Or was only one building was used for both purposes? Not only did big cities in Judaea during the Second Temple period have a main public building with multiple functions, but towns and villages did as well. Public buildings, for instance, have been excavated at Kiriath Sefer and at Gamla, and these were shaped like the Late Classic-Hellenistic *bouleuteria*, thus following a Greek-Hellenistic model. These buildings are quite similar to the Late Classical-Hellenistic *bouleuteria*, such as the ones at Priene and at Miletus.[96] Foerster, followed by Maoz,[97] was the first to

---

pp. 90–96. This synagogue was apparently not financed by a Herodian ruler, because it stood in Egypt, which was the personal property of the Roman Emperor, ruled through the *praefectus Aegyptii*, a member of the equestrian class. Senators could visit Egypt only after receiving the express permission of the Emperor. Thus, a Herodian act of *euergetism* could have been seen as interference by the Imperial authorities. Moreover Josephus does not mention the building in the lists of buildings erected outside Judaea by King Herod. It seems that only the family of the *alabarch* would have been capable of financing that building. See Josephus, *BJ* V, 205 and *AJ* XVIII, 159–160, 259, XIX 276, XX, 100 on Alexander the *alabarch*, leader of the Jewish community of Alexandria.

[93] See Y. Hirschfeld, *Roman, Byzantine, and Early Muslim Tiberias: A Handbook of Primary Sources*, Tiberias 2005, p. 38. See also Y. Hirschfeld, *Antiquity Sites in Tiberias*, Jerusalem 1991, pp. 11–12.

[94] See Josephus, *AJ* XVIII, 36–38, on the foundation of Tiberias; *Vita* 64–69 on Antipas Palace; *BJ* III, 537–540, *Vita* 90–92 on the stadium; and *BJ* III, 447–461 on the city walls.

[95] Josephus wrote that the main authority lay in the hands of the seven appointed magistrates, the seven elders who formed the lowest court, and they were found in towns and villages. Their main task was to settle legal cases. Moreover, Josephus asserts that two Levites had to be co-opted by the local courts, together with the seven judges. See Josephus, *AJ* IV, 214, and *AJ* XVI, 203.

[96] On the *bouleuterion* of Miletus see K. Kästner, *Pergamon Museum, Griechische und Römische Architektur*, Mainz 1992, pp. 56–58.

[97] This subject was Foerster's Ph.D. thesis. However Foerster did not regard the Hellenistic *bouleuterion* as the only source of inspiration, citing also the *pronaoi* of the Eastern pagan

3. The Synagogue in Judaea: A Civic Center

highlight the relationship between the early synagogue buildings of the Second Temple period, the Zealots' synagogues at Masada and Herodium, and the Greek *bouleuterion*. The excavators identified these buildings as *bouleuteria* – shaped "synagogues." I would like to suggest that these buildings, shaped as *bouleuteria*, had a multiple function, serving not merely as synagogues, but as the place of assembly for the town or village elders during the week and as the seat of the local court as well. I shall use the term *"bouleuterion* – shaped" to describe these buildings, since *bouleuterion* indicates a structure housing the *boulē*, or city council, numbering sometimes hundreds of members. Clearly the term is unsuitable for describing the place of assembly for town or village elders in towns and villages where they scarcely numbered more than ten individuals, and thus I believe that the term *"bouleuterion* – shaped" is far more appropriate.

The examples at Kiriath Sefer and Gamla were similar in form to the Hellenistic *bouleterion* and are reminiscent of Hellenistic *bouleteria* from Asia Minor. Each of these buildings occupies a central position in its respective settlement and has been identified as a synagogue by the excavators. I would like to suggest that the apparent absence of other public buildings at these sites probably indicates that these should be regarded as multipurpose public structures, and not only as synagogues. The main civic building in towns and villages thus followed the earlier Hellenistic model of the *bouleterion*. This is probably in contrast to the examples in major cities which were modeled after the Roman basilica, as in Tiberias.

The Gamla "synagogue," one of the two main buildings excavated in the town,[98] consists of a building that was erected as late as the beginning of the first

---

temples such as those at Dura Europus. See G. Foerster, *Galilean Synagogues and their Relationship to Hellenistic and Roman Art and Architecture*, Ph. D. Thesis, The Hebrew University of Jerusalem, Jerusalem 1972. When he published the article, Foerster had only Gamla as a model. The synagogues at Masada and Herodium were two halls transformed by the Zealots into synagogues, but these were not initially planned as synagogues. Foerster links the plan of the "Galilean" synagogues to that of the Roman basilica as a further stage in the development of synagogue architecture. See G. Foerster, "Architectural Models of the Greco-Roman Period and the Origin of the "Galilean" Synagogue," in L. I. Levine (ed.), *Ancient Synagogues Revealed*, Jerusalem 1981, pp. 45–48. On the relationship between the Zealot's synagogue at Masada and the *bouleuterion*, see Y. Yadin, "The Excavations of Masada 1963/64," *IEJ* 15, 1965, pp. 78–79. However, Maoz, analyzing the synagogue of Gamla, which, in contrast to the Zealot's synagogues at Herodium and Masada, was built as such, saw the *telesterion* and the *bouleuterion* as its primary sources of inspiration. See Z. Maoz, "The Synagogue of Gamla and the Typology of the Second Temple Period Synagogues," in L. I. Levine (ed.), *Ancient Synagogues Revealed*, Jerusalem 1981, pp. 35–41.

[98] On the Gamla "synagogue" see Hachlili, *Ancient Jewish Art and Archaeology*, pp. 84–85. In the last few years another public building had been excavated at Gamla. This building, in Area S, is shaped like a short basilica. See D. Syon and Z. Yavor, "Gamla 1997–2000", in *'Atiqot* 50, 2005, pp. 16–21. See also D. Syon, "Gamla, Old and New," *Qadmoniot* XXXIV, 1, 2001, pp. 17–19 (Hebrew). The excavators suggested the possibility that this building could have served as a synagogue as well. It seems to me, however, that the building is extremely similar to the main hall of the Roman *principia*, found in permanent Roman military camps dated to the

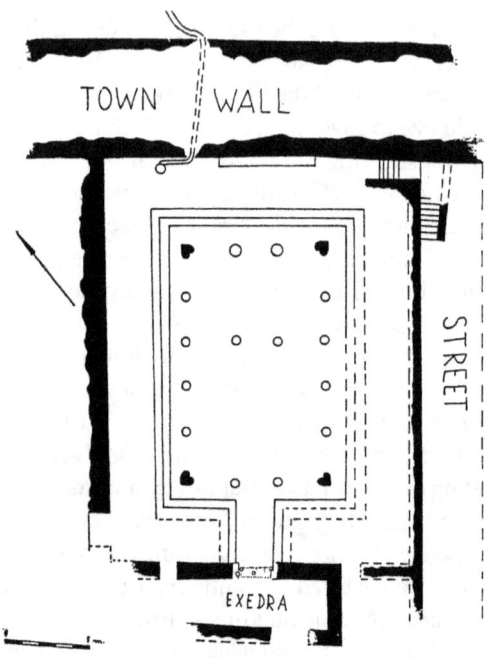

Plan of the synagogue

Figure VI, 2 – Gamla Public Building from S. Gutman, "The Synagogue at Gamla," L. Levine (ed), *Ancient Synagogues Revealed*, Jerusalem 1981, p. 31, Courtesy of the Israel Exploration Society, Jerusalem.

century CE, though a mid-first-century-BCE foundation, sometime between the reigns of Alexander Jannaeus and Herod, has also been proposed (cfr. figure VI, 2). Although it is not the only public building in the town, it is the only one that could have served as the seat of the elders, as a court of law, and as a synagogue. The building itself is rectangular and lies adjacent to the western city wall. The main feature is a peristyle of fourteen columns which surrounds the main hall on all four sides. A stepped cistern, just west of the main entrance to the synagogue,

---

Flavian-Hadrianic period. Thus, it was, perhaps, a structure erected to host the city governor on behalf of King Agrippa. There he could have convened his own court of law, in opposition to the court of law formed by the city elders. According to Josephus, *Vita* 46–47, Philip son of Jacimus, King Agrippa II's *eparch*, was wounded by rebels and found refuge near Gamla, sending orders to members of the garrison of Gamla to join him. Evidently, Gamla hosted a small royal garrison. It is possible that the basilica was the residence of the royal commander of the Gamla garrison. Later, Josephus (*Vita* 58–61) writes that Philip son of Jacimus, entered Gamla and remained there as temporary governor of the fortress-city. On the *principia* see A. Johnson, *Roman Forts of the First and Second Century AD in Britain and the German Provinces*, London 1983, pp. 123–152.

3. The Synagogue in Judaea: A Civic Center

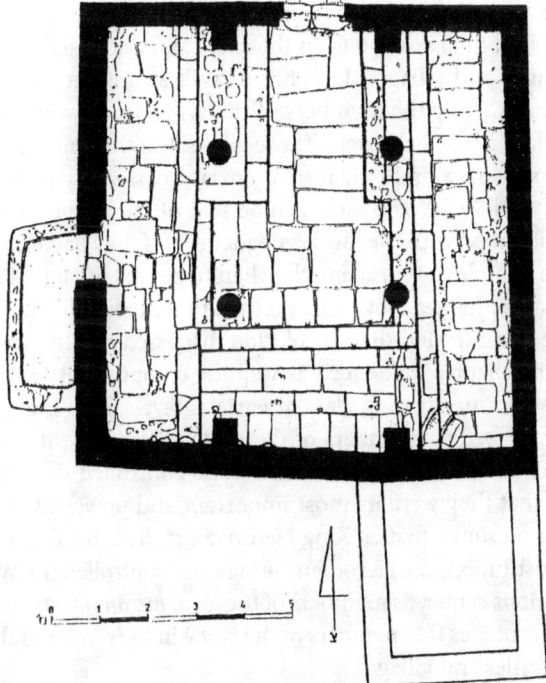

Figure VI, 3 – Plan of the Synagogue of Kiryat Sefer from Y., Magen, Y., Zionit, and E., Sirkis, "A Jewish Village and Synagogue of the Second Temple Period", *Qadmoniot* XXXII, 1 (117) 1999, p. 28, in B. Zissu, *Rural Settlements in the Judaean Hills and Foothills From the Late Second Temple Period to the Bar Kokhba Revolt*, Thesis submitted for the Degree "Doctor of Philosophy", The Hebrew University, Jerusalem, 2001 (Hebrew), fig. 15. Courtesy of Dr. B. Zissu.

may have been used as *mikveh*, but it dates from the period of the First Jewish Revolt. East of the main synagogue hall are several rooms, one of which may have had an opening into the main hall and contained benches. This may have been used as a study room.[99]

The building at Kiriath Sefer, dated to early first and second centuries BCE, was erected in the most prominent part of the settlement (cfr. figure VI, 3). The building was a square structure. The hall contained four columns with Doric-like capitals. The building was offset from the surrounding complex and was abandoned in the aftermath of the Bar Kokhba Revolt.[100] However, it is important to emphasize that the building at Kiriath Sefer served the population of a very small village.

---

[99] See Levine, *Ancient Synagogue*, pp. 51–52.

[100] See Levine, *Ancient Synagogue*, pp. 65–66. See also Y. Magen, Y. Zionit, and E. Sirkis, "A Jewish Village and Synagogue of the Second Temple Period," *Qadmoniot* XXXII, 1 (117) 1999, pp. 26–28.

Therefore as we argued the synagogue in first century CE Judaea served not only as *proseuche*, but also as *boulē* in the cities and as the seat of local court of law in small cities and villages. Josephus as well as archaeology was useful in establishing that. Clearly the members of the synagogues were part of the ruling class of Judaea at various levels. Those who sat in the *boulē* of Tiberias were more important than the rich villagers than sat in assembly in the synagogues of Gamla or Kiriath Sefer. The same can be said of the members of the various *ma'amadoth* identified with the local synagogue[101]. If they had enough free time to spend in the Temple of Jerusalem, they had to be well enough if not members of the ruling class of Judaea. But what was then the situation in Herodian Judaea? It seems to me that the Herodian revolution discussed in Chapter V and at the beginning of the chapter influenced as well the composition of the synagogue. As Herod created a new ruling class at various levels, new high priest, a new lay aristocracy, as well as members of the provincial gentry, it is probable that the members of the new Herodian ruling class controlled the synagogue, just for the reason that they were its most important and powerful members. Thus it is possible to presume, that as King Herod controlled the Temple as religious center and as institution, the Herodian ruling class controlled the synagogue as a peripheral religious center, as members of the local *ma'amad*, and as a peripheral administrative center as the members of the *boulē* in the city, or of the local court of law in small cities and villages.

And yet here were indeed in first century CE Judaea synagogues that served only as a religious and communitarian institution, and those were the synagogues erected by the various Jewish communities or groups from the Diaspora in Jerusalem.

Epigraphic evidence, such as the inscription of the Synagogue of Theodotus[102] and Acts,[103] clearly shows that the various Diaspora communities in Jerusalem had their own synagogues to serve the various *politeumata*, at least during the pilgrimages. Thus, there were the synagogues of the Liberti, of the Cyreneans, of the Alexandrians, and of the communities of Asia and Cilicia. These synagogues were modeled on their counterparts in the Greek Diasporas and were, in fact, community centers. The hierarchy of the various officials, the *archisynagogoi* and *presbyteres*, also reflects that of Diaspora synagogues. It seems to me that the creation of Diaspora synagogues was mainly an indirect consequence of Herod's rebuilding of the Temple as a House of all Nations and as a center of Pilgrim-

---

[101] See Chapter IV.
[102] See Levine, *Ancient Synagogue*, pp. 52–58. See also J. S. Kloppenborg, "Dating Theodotos ("CIJ" II 1404)," *JJS* 51,2, 2000, pp. 243–280. On synagogues in Jerusalem see Acts 24: 12, 22: 19, and 26: 11. See also R. Riesner, "Synagogues in Jerusalem," *The Book of Acts in its Palestinian Setting*, R. Bauckham (ed.), Grand Rapids 1995, pp. 179–210. On Herod and the Diaspora Jews see M. Stern, *The Kingdom of Herod*, pp. 92–96.
[103] See Acts 6: 9.

age for the whole Diaspora. It was Herod that rebuilt the Temple and therefore strengthened the tie between Judaea and the surrounding Jewish Diaspora. Once more, although most of the evidence is later, it seems to me that this trend, the erection of Diaspora House of Prayers and community center in Jerusalem, begun in the Herodian Period. Although Herod did not directly sponsor the erection of Diaspora synagogues in Jerusalem, however these synagogues answered to the Herodian ideal of relationship between center and Diaspora.

4. Herod and the Pagan Cults

Outside of Judaea proper, Herod patronized all of the cults of the Gentile Greeks. He financed the restoration of the Temple of Apollo at Rhodes, he renewed the Olympic Games at the shrine of Zeus Olympius at Olympia, and he participated in the construction of various temples at Nicopolis[104] (see Chapter I). Inside his kingdom, in Caesarea Maritima, Sebaste, and Paneas, Herod erected for his Gentile subjects only temples dedicated to the Imperial cult. Was this an act of pragmatism in favor of the Gentile subjects, or was it is only a symbolic act, through which Herod emphasized his ties with Rome? I believe that it does not appear to have been an act of tolerance toward his Gentile subjects, since, were that the case, other temples dedicated to local and Greek gods would have been built during Herod's reign. The evidence that we have for Caesarea Maritima and Sebaste indicates otherwise. With the exception of the temples dedicated to the Imperial cult, no other temples dedicated to other gods were built during Herod's reign, or under the rule of his sons. Paneas is an exception. The Temple of Augustus was erected there as part of a *temenos* consecrated to Pan, but Paneas and the surrounding area were not originally part of Herod's kingdom, having been ceded by Augustus. It is possible that Herod did not intervene in the pagan cults of the local Gentile population, though even here Herod did not erect any pagan shrine, with the exception of the Temple of Augustus. Thus the main difference between Paneas and Caesarea Maritima and Sebaste is that in the former, the existing pagan cult was not promoted, while in the latter two, all forms of pagan cult were forbidden, with the exception of Imperial cult. Thus, at Caesarea Maritima the only cultic precinct dated to the Herodian period is the Temple of Rome and Augustus. All of the other pagan shrines were erected after Caesarea Maritima became a Roman provincial city in 6 CE. It is interesting to note that the earliest cultic building erected by the Roman procurators was the well-known Tiberieum, erected by Pontius Pilatus, once more a temple dedicated to the Imperial cult. Only second century coins show the variety of pagan cults in Caesarea Maritima. In Sebaste, another temple, the Temple of Kore has been excavated, but it is post-

---

[104] See MacMullen, *Romanization in the Time of Augustus*, p. 20.

Herodian. The proliferation of pagan cults in Sebaste is dated by the city-coins to post-70 CE and is associated particularly with the reign of Hadrian. At Paneas, both excavations and numismatic evidence point to the Temple of Augustus as the only city temple for a long period, during the rule of Herod and that of his dynasty, under Philip, Agrippa I, and Agrippa II. It is possible that Herod wished to please Augustus, while being careful not to displease his Jewish subjects. It is likewise conceivable that Herod's pragmatism in the erection of temples in which Rome and the Emperor were worshipped[105] was regarded by his Jewish subjects as a mere political gesture towards Rome, devoid of any religious significance, and thus not as an introduction of paganism into the kingdom.

In the Temple itself there were sacrifices on behalf of the emperor.[106] A Gentile, Agrippa, inaugurated the Temple, as we have already seen. Neither Josephus, nor Philo, nor Talmudic sources ever mention the erection of temples dedicated to Rome and Augustus as a despicable act on the part of Herod, nor was he ever condemned for doing so. When Josephus mentioned in *Antiquities* that Herod introduced foreign practices among the Jews, clearly he was not referring to the Imperial cult intended for Herod's Gentile subjects. The situation in Jerusalem and Rome was similar with respect to the Imperial cult, where a shrine was dedicated to Iulius Caesar only after his death. During Augustus' lifetime only the *Fortuna Augusti* was worshipped. This religious feature, the building of cultic edifices in honor of the Roman emperor, was found only outside of Rome and Jerusalem, since the two cities were violently opposed to it from an ideological perspective. However, in both Rome and Jerusalem, prayers were offered for the ruler.

Josephus wrote that the Temple of Roma and Augustus, raised upon a mound overlooking the harbor, was remarkable for both its setting and its beauty and that it was visible from a great distance to those entering the harbor.[107] As Vitruvius suggests, the Temple of Roma and Augustus faced the sea. As the characteristic Roman temple illustrated by Vitruvius, the Temple of Roma and Augustus was built on a podium.[108] Of the huge Temple only few architectural fragments have survived.[109] It is possible, however, to reconstruct a structure similar to that of Sebaste. The Temple closely followed the rules or *modula* dictated by Vitruvius.

---

[105] We have already discussed the imperial cult in Chapter I. See S. R. Price, *Rituals and Power, The Roman Imperial Cult in Asia Minor*, Cambridge 1984, passim.

[106] Price distinguishes between sacrifices for the emperor, which were undoubtedly made in the temples of Caesarea Maritima, Sebaste, and Paneas, and sacrifices on behalf of the emperor that were offered in Jerusalem. See Price, *Rituals and Power,* pp. 209–210. See also Philo, *Legat,* 349–367.

[107] See Josephus, *BJ* I, 414.

[108] See Y. Porath and J. Patrich, "The Caesarea Excavation Project – March 1992–June 1994," *Excavations and Surveys in Israel 17,* 1998, pp. 45–46.

[109] The Temple was 20.5 m. high. It was hexastyle with a width of circa 31 m. It had a total façade of 27–30 m. See L. C. Kahn, "King Herod's Temple of Roma and Augustus at Caesarea

The Temple of Apollo Sosianus, erected between the years 20–5 BCE, probably inspired Herod's temple at Caesarea. Another possible source of inspiration was the Temple of Mars Ultor, whose construction ended only in 2 BCE, after Herod's death.[110] Clearly, Herod's Temple of Rome and Augustus was larger and much more impressive than its contemporary sources of inspiration in Rome, and it was clearly much higher. The Roman podia, moreover, were generally low. Herod's Temple of Roma and Augustus dominated both the city and the view of the city from the sea, towering above the other buildings in the city, with the exception of the Drusion lighthouse. In comparison, the Temple of Mars Ultor was enclosed in the forum of Augustus, and the neighboring Theatre of Marcellus dwarfed the Temple of Apollo Sosianus. It is important to underline once more Herod's and Augustus' shared classical inspiration. Like Augustus in building the Temple of Mars Ultor, Herod also reverted to fifth century Attic classicism. The models for the statues of Rome and Augustus were Phidias' statues of Zeus Olympius at Olympia and of Hera at Argos. This time Herod expressed his classicism in the artistic source for the Temple's statues, rather than in the optical corrections of the building, as in the Jerusalem Temple Mount.

As Josephus attests,[111] Herod also erected the Temple of Augustus that dominated the urban landscape of Sebaste (cfr. figure VI, 4). At the beginning of the third century CE, during the Severan period, it was repaired and partly rebuilt.[112] As at Caesarea Maritima, the Temple of Roma and Augustus was built of local calcareous stone and was covered by white stucco. At Sebaste, however, the Temple of Augustus was built within a cultic precinct or forecourt and did not stand alone, as at the Temple at Caesarea Maritima. It nonetheless dominated the precinct, since it was built on an elevated podium. The Temple precinct at Sebaste included a forecourt surrounded by colonnades north of the Temple. The Temple stood on the podium and had a wide octastyle façade, facing north.[113] While the Temple of Rome and Augustus at Caesarea Maritima shared certain elements with Augustus's Temple of Mars Ultor, the cultic precinct and the Temple of Augustus at Sebaste followed the plan of Iulius Caesar's Forum Julii and of the Temple of Venus, though in Augustan Rome, temples did not project outside the precinct. A characteristic shared by the Temple of Augustus at Sebaste and the Jerusalem Temple Mount was the use of *cryptoportica*, as at Arles and elsewhere in Gallia and Hiberia.

Maritima," in A. Raban, and K. Holum, (eds.), *Caesarea Maritima, a Retrospective after Two Millennnia, DMOA* XXI, Leiden 1996, pp. 135–142.

[110] See Kahn, "King Herod's Temple of Roma and Augustus," p. 142.

[111] See Josephus, *AJ* XV, 298.

[112] See E. Netzer, "The Augusteum at Samaria Sebaste, A New Outlook," *Eretz-Israel* 19, 1987, pp. 97–105.

[113] The Temple façade measured 21.8 m, and was 35 m. long. See D. Barag, "King Herod's Royal Castle at Samaria-Sebaste," *PEF 125*, 1993, pp. 3–17.

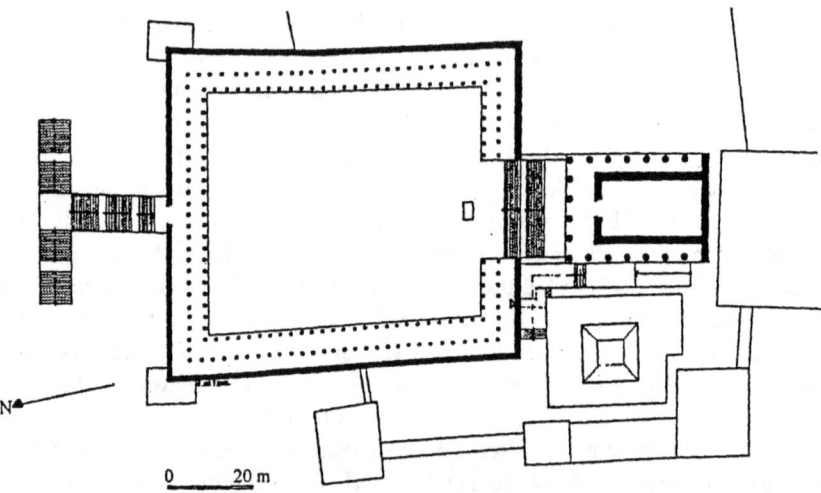

Figure VI, 4 – Plan of the Temple of Augustus at Sebaste from E. Netzer, "The Augusteum at Samaria Sebaste, A New Outlook", *Eretz-Israel 19*, 1987, pp. 97–105 (Hebrew), Courtesy of Professor Emeritus Ehud Netzer, The Hebrew University of Jerusalem.

The Temple of Augustus at Paneas is part of the sacred compound dedicated to Pan. Only part of the *temenos* has been uncovered by Maoz. Originally the structure was dominated by a cave dedicated to Pan, surrounded by a sacred oak forest. From Herod's reign and onward, in front of the grotto and around it, various temples and ceremonial courtyards were erected from the end of the first century BCE through the first half of the second century CE, along a 70-m.-long ledge. The buildings identified are, from west to east, the Temple of Augustus; an elevated courtyard where four niches were carved and decorated, added by Philip or Agrippas I in the first half of the first century CE; an additional Temple dedicated to Zeus Heliopolitanus and built in 100 CE; an elevated courtyard dedicated to Nemesis; and a structure whose use is unclear. According to Maoz, the remains of a structure opposite the mouth of the cave are part of the Temple of Augustus, erected by Herod in 19 BCE. The Temple consisted of a tetrastyle structure, with columns topped by Ionic capitals. Only the front of the structure was decorated with columns. The Temple was apparently not built on a podium, as Roman temples generally were. According to Jacobson, Herod's Temple at Paneas was similar to Augustus' Temple at Pula.[114]

---

[114] See Josephus, *AJ* XV, 363. Maoz's excavations were conducted from 1988 to 1993. On Paneas see J. F. Wilson (ed.), *Rediscovering Caesarea Philippi: The Ancient City of Pan*, Malibu (Cal.) 2001, pp. 8, 16. See also Jacobson, "Herod's Roman Temple," pp. 21–22. According to Jacobson, Herod's Temple at Paneas, depicted on coins, is similar to Augustus' Temple at Pula. Both have a tetrastyle façade. The coins minted by Philip depict on the obverse the Temple of

The similarities between the Temple Mount in Jerusalem and the two other Herodian temples, the Temple of Rome and Augustus in Caesarea Maritima and the Temple of Augustus in Sebaste are interesting. First, these sanctuaries depend upon a Roman model. The Herodian sanctuaries or temples are completely separated from the towns in which they are located by means of huge walls. This is true both of the royal city of Jerusalem and of the Herodian foundations of Caesarea and Samaria. The Temple Mount sanctuary dominates Jerusalem, and, similarly, the Temple of Augustus at Sebaste stood on top of the acropolis hill and was built as part of the royal castle. In front of it, a large precinct was erected. The visual effect created by this sanctuary was very similar to the visual effect created by the Temple Mount sanctuary in Jerusalem. The Temple of Rome and Augustus at Caesarea, built on a podium, dominated the harbor complex, Sebastos, and the entire city when viewed from the sea. All of these structures – the Temple Mount, the Acropolis and the Temple of Augustus at Sebaste, and the harbor of Sebastos and the Temple of Rome and Augustus at Caesarea – were isolated from the city by walls.[115]

5. Conclusions

The Temple cult and Jewish religion during the Herodian Period shared many features in common with the neighboring Mediterranean world. As we have seen, the high priest and the priests who directed the Temple services – who comprised the ruling class of Hasmonean Judaea, and to a far lesser degree, the ruling class of Herodian Judaea – shared much in common with the Greek and Roman aristocracy. The main difference between the priesthood in Judaea and in Greece and Rome was that, while in Judaea the priesthood was the main hereditary element that defined the aristocracy as such, in Greece and Rome priesthood was an elective or co-opted prerogative of the aristocracy. The Herodian Period is characterized by a temporary demotion of the high priest – now chosen from Diaspora families and thus less influential in Judaean affairs – and of the priests as an aristocracy, since Herod promoted other individuals coming from different sources. This process is quite similar to Augustus' revolution in Rome, with the creation of a new ruling class coming from the Roman traditional senatorial aristocracy, the equestrian order, and the Italic municipal aristocracy.

It was during this period that Jewish traditional holidays assumed a more "classical" character. New holidays were added, such as Hanukkah, Nicanor Day, and Purim. Both Hanukkah and Nicanor Day, days that celebrated the victories

---

Augustus and on the reverse the head of Philip, or of Augustus, or the jugate heads of Augustus and Livia. See. Meshorer, *Treasury of Jewish Coins,* pp. 85–90 and pls. 50–51.

[115] See Hesberg, "Significance of the Cities in the Kingdom of Herod," pp. 12–13.

of the Maccabees, had a strong classical character. We should recall that the Temple cult was a state cult – that of the Jewish realm itself – with obvious parallels to the Olympian cult in Greece and the Capitoline cult in Rome. While the cult in a single and exclusive Temple was a unique characteristic of the monotheist Jews in polytheistic surroundings,[116] both the sacrifices and the feasts were events common to the Graeco-Roman world throughout the Mediterranean. Thus, although the rationale behind the sacrifices and the rules that governed them, such as the *olah* sacrifice, were indeed different, as were the various ceremonies during a holy convocation, the general appearance of the cult was probably quite similar everywhere, the most obvious difference being the absence of cultic statues in the Jerusalem Temple. So, although they were not entirely identical, the Temple and the cult in Herodian Jerusalem appeared, at least superficially, to be similar to the temples and ceremonies in classical-Hellenistic Athens, Late Republican and Augustan Rome, and Punic Carthage. There was clearly room within this Hellenistic *koinos* for the Temple of Jerusalem, where the Living God, Who had no graven images or iconographic representations, dwelt.

The Herodian Temple reflected architectural features coming from a Jewish tradition, such as the division in surrounding courtyards, and those deriving from the Greek-Hellenistic World, such as the use of *enthasis* and *anathemata*. The most dominant influences, however, come from the Roman West, including the general shape of the *temenos* as a Roman forum and the use of various architectural elements stemming from the Roman tradition, such as the basilica. Moreover, it is necessary to emphasize that the Temple was a classical building with both religious and public functions, and that the Temple Mount assumed this function during the Late Hellenistic Period. During the Hasmonean period it was the *agora*, and during the Herodian period it became the *forum* of Jerusalem.

The Jewish synagogue in Judaea had a dual function, as a cultic building, for Torah reading, and as public building, in its guise as the seat of the *boulē* and other magistrates. The synagogue-*proseuche* was the essence of the administration and self-government of the Jewish cities and villages, as were the *bouleterion* in the Greek East and the Roman *curia* in the West.

Last but not least, Herod erected three temples dedicated to the Imperial cult in the Gentile areas of the kingdom. All of these temples present primarily

---

[116] See G. Bohak, "The Impact of Jewish Monotheism on the Greco-Roman World," *Jewish Studies Quarterly* 7,1, 2000, pp. 1–21. Bohak argues for a minimal impact of Jewish monotheism in the classical world. Bohak analyzes the issues in the political sphere, in the religious sphere, among Greek and Roman intellectuals and in the social sphere. Bohak thus shows that in the political sphere the Jews left virtually no trace; in the religious sphere Jewish monotheism made very little impression before the spread of monotheism; Greek and Roman intellectuals did not show any particular interest in the peculiar Jewish God, nor did they fully understand accommodation with the surrounding pagan world. Clashes between Jews and Greeks were an exception.

Roman features, such as the use of a *podium*. Since no other temples dedicated to various pagan divinities are known to have been erected or to have functioned in Herod's Judaea, it is possible to suggest that the Imperial cult had a political resonance, signifying allegiance to Rome, rather than indicating tolerance towards the Gentile subjects.

VII. The Herodian City

1. The Herodian Dynasty and the City

This chapter is dedicated to the Herodian city, which has already been discussed in some detail in the previous chapters. The city defenses were dealt with in the chapter dedicated to the Herodian army; its political bodies and administration were analyzed in the chapter dealing with legislation and jurisprudence in the Herodian kingdom; and finally, the huge sanctuaries found in the Herodian cities were analyzed in the chapter surveying the various religions of Herod's kingdom. Nevertheless, the subject is far from exhausted.

Thus, in this chapter, I would like to focus on specific subjects, the most important of which is the relationship between the Herodian dynasty and the city, with a specific emphasis on analyzing the city building that was so characteristic of Herod's rule. Herod not only expanded Jerusalem, but created other cities in the Jewish and Gentile areas of his kingdom, such as Caesarea Maritima, Sebaste, and Paneas. Thus, in the Herodian Period, Judaea began a serious process of urbanization, and Herod's sons, particularly Antipas, continued this process.

Following this analysis, I would like to examine the general urban features of the Herodian cities such as Jerusalem, Caesarea Maritima, and Sebaste, comparing them to those of the most important Classical cities. I shall also try to answer the all-important question of whether the Herodian cities should be considered Classical cities.

The last part of this chapter is dedicated to the analysis of various elements of Jerusalem, the most important of the Herodian cities. This will entail an examination of the demography of Jerusalem and an attempt to establish the position of Jerusalem among the Classical cities. Was it, for example, a large metropolis, such as Rome or Alexandria, or a much smaller city? I shall then evaluate two highly important urban features of the public face of Herodian Jerusalem – the water supply infrastructure and the leisure buildings – which were developed extensively during the Herodian Period. Did the water supply of Jerusalem and the leisure buildings erected there mirror the situation in other cities of the Hellenistic East or Augustan Rome? The chapter will close with an investigation of the private buildings of Herodian Jerusalem, mainly the patrician mansions excavated in the Herodian Quarter.

Herod's rule marked a watershed period in urban development with respect to the Jewish subjects in his kingdom.[1] Prior to Herod, it would be correct to say that the only Jewish city was Jerusalem. Even so, it did not entirely meet the criteria of a *polis*, being more of a royal city with no civic political bodies. With the accession of Herod to the throne, the situation changed dramatically. Though still a royal city, Jerusalem acquired all of the political trappings of the Greek *polis*, most notably the *boulē*. Herod also developed other cities, such as Caesarea Maritima, based on the model of Alexandria. Sebaste was another royal city, but with a clear-cut Greek character, since its population was composed entirely of Gentiles. Like Caesarea Maritima, Sebaste had no civic political bodies. The status of Paneas remains unclear, but it was probably a royal city, similar to Caesarea Maritima and Sebaste. Herod also created other smaller urban foundations, such as Herodium and Machaerus, which developed into real cities, even without having the status of *poleis*. The same can be said of two other cities that were founded in Judaea, Antipatris and Phasaelis.[2] Although these cities did not have the status of *poleis*, they were created as urban centers. Finally, the various urban centers of Judaea, such as Jericho and 'En Gedi, probably developed as well, as small cities. By the end of Herod's rule, Judaea was already an urbanized region with a full-fledged *polis*, two royal cities – albeit one totally Gentile – and various other urban centers.

This situation is not, however, a characteristic of Herodian Judaea alone. All of the client-kings of Rome tried their best to develop the urban network of their kingdoms.[3] For a king to develop Hellenistic cities, and therefore to provide his kingdom with an urban foundation, meant being part of the Mediterranean

---

[1] On the other hand, Gentile urbanism was well developed. Thus, in the Persian period Phoenician cities in the north and Philisto-Arab cities in the south dominated the coast of the Land of Israel. The advent of Hellenism brought a new level of urban development not only along the coast, but also in the interior and in Transjordan. The new Ptolemaic and Seleucid foundations in the interior shared the same common Greek culture with the Graeco-Phoenician cities of the coast. The Hasmoneans put an abrupt end to this development. However in 63 BCE Pompey and in 57 BCE Gabinius refounded most of these cities, after the dismemberment of the Hasmonean kingdom. With the exception of the coastal cities of Ascalon and Ptolemais, never under direct Hasmonean or Herodian rule, all the other coastal cities, as well as the cities in the interior, such as the cities of the Decapolis, developed only after 70 CE. These cities reached their peak in the middle of the second century CE like most of the cities in the Roman Empire. See D. Sperber, *The City in Roman Palestine*, Oxford 1998 and Y. Meshorer, *City-Coins of Eretz-Israel and the Decapolis in the Roman Period*, Jerusalem 1985.

[2] Josephus as well as archaeology is our main source. On Herodium see Josephus, *BJ* I, 265, 419, III, 55, on Machaerus see *BJ* III, 46, VII, 171–189 on Antipatris see *AJ* XVI, 143 and *BJ* I 99, 417, on Phasaelis see *AJ* XVI 145, *BJ* I, 418. On Antipatris and Phasaelis see also A. Kasher, *Jews and Hellenistic Cities in Eretz-Israel, Relations of the Jews with the Hellenistic Cities during the Second Temple Period*, TSAJ 21, Tübingen 1990, pp. 206–208. Kasher argues for their Gentile character.

[3] On the cities in the Eastern Roman Empire and their development see A. H. M. Jones, *Cities of the Eastern Roman Provinces*, Oxford 1998, passim. See also M. Sartre, *L'Orient Romain*, Paris 1991, mainly pp. 121–190.

Graeco-Roman *oikoumene*. Herod's death and the division of the kingdom did not stop the process of urbanization of the Jewish population. The *tetrarch* Herod Antipas continued the development of Jewish urbanism within the borders of his kingdom, founding Tiberias on the shores of the Sea of Galilee,[4] and that city, like Jerusalem, clearly had the character of a royal city as well as that of a *polis* with its *boulē*. Tiberias was not, however, the only city of Herod Antipas' kingdom. Sepphoris also most likely became a royal city, although its exact character is unclear, as is that of Livias.[5] Thus, under the rule of Herod Antipas, Galilee became even more urbanized than Judaea proper. It is true that the two *poleis*, Tiberias and Sepphoris, had a mixed Jewish-Greek population, but the Jews comprised the majority.

Judaea itself, now under the Roman procurators and prefects, also continued its urban development. It is during this period that Caesarea Maritima also became a *polis* with a city council, but in Caesarea Maritima the Jewish element was still very strong and was probably reinforced during the short reign of King Herod Agrippa I.[6] Thus, on the eve of the Great War against Rome in 66 CE, the province of Judaea, as well as the kingdom of Herod Agrippa II, was significantly urbanized, and the area was not different from Phoenicia, coastal Syria, and Asia Minor. It is clear that the Jews aspired to transform themselves from a rural society into a more urbanized one, just like the Greeks in the East. In Herod the Great the Jews found the man who would enable them to realize their aspirations.

2. The Urban Features of the Herodian City

The Herodian cities had certain urban features in common, like most of the Classical cities. Some of these, such as Jerusalem and Sebaste, had an acropolis and a lower city. Most were surrounded by city walls, and some of the cities presented a Hippodamian plan, as in Caesarea Maritima and Tiberias. Sanctuaries, royal palaces, and public and leisure buildings, such as theaters and hippodromes, dominated the urban landscape. I shall attempt to analyze the general urban

---

[4] On Tiberias's foundation see A. Kasher, "The Foundation of Tiberias and its Function as the Capital of the Galilee", *Idan* 11, 1988, pp. 3–11.

[5] On the foundation of Tiberias see Josephus, *AJ* XVIII, 36–38, *BJ* II, 168. On Sepphoris see *AJ* XVIII, 27. On Livias see *BJ* II, 168. Tiberias was indeed a *polis* in Late Antiquity also. The same can be said of Sepphoris as both maintained a *boulē*. On the *boulē* of Sepphoris and Tiberias in Late Antiquity see D. Goodblatt, "The Political and Social History of the Jewish Community in the Land of Israel, c. 235–638" in S. T. Katz (ed.), *CHJ IV, The Late Roman-Rabbinic Period*, Cambridge 2006, pp. 404–431. In this period, however, other magistrates as the *strategoi*, or *duoviri*, are mentioned as heading the *boulē*, now much more similar to the Western *Curia*. See TJ, *Yoma*, 1. 2. 39 a. On Jewish *bouleutes* appearing in Rabbinic sources see also TJ, *Môed Qaṭ*. 2. 3. 81 b, TJ, *Pèah*, 1. 16 a, TJ, *Ḥag.*, 3. 48 c – TJ, *Šabb*. 12. 3. 13 c and TJ, *Pesh*. 4. 1. 30 c.

[6] See Meshorer, *City-Coins of Eretz-Israel and the Decapolis*, p. 20 and K.G. Holum, *King's Herod's Dream, Caesarea on the Sea*, New York 1988, pp. 111–112.

features of Jerusalem, Caesarea Maritima, and Sebaste, the three best-known Herodian cities, together with Tiberias and Sepphoris, which were established by Herod Antipas, and to compare them to those of other Classical cities. How much do these cities have in common?

Herodian Jerusalem was without any doubt the most important of all the Herodian cities.[7] The most striking feature of Jerusalem was its city walls. There were three defensive city walls – the First Wall, on the south, encompassing most of the city; the Second Wall, constructed during the reign of Agrippa I; and the northernmost Third Wall. Jerusalem's walls were no different than those of other Classical cities.[8] The other two key features of the city that immediately drew attention were the two city centers that dominated Jerusalem from the east and the west – Herod's huge palace on the west, defended on the northwest by the three towers of Hippicus, Mariamme, and Phasael; and the huge Temple Mount *temenos* on the east, comprising a forum, with its huge southern basilica and the only sanctuary in the city, defended on its northwestern corner by the Antonia. The Herodian palace and the Antonia were not the only royal palaces. Somewhere near the northern part of the First Wall, not far from the Temple Mount, stood the older fortified Hasmonean palace. Jerusalem was clearly a royal city, replete with all these palaces.

Certain features of the *polis* were clearly evident here. The Temple Mount plan had much smaller parallels in Caesarea, Alexandria, and Cyrene.[9] The visitor would find a theater and a hippodrome that could be also utilized for gladiatorial games. A *gymnasium* with the *xyston* would also be seen in the city. Another feature that the visitor would note was a huge aqueduct in Roman style, quite unknown in the East during that period, that ensured Jerusalem's water supply, together with a siphon. All around the city were monumental tombs that shared Late Hellenistic features common to other monuments in the East and in Roman Italy, most of these belonging to the city's priestly aristocracy. The city was not constructed along any grid, but Rome and Athens, the two Classical cities *par excellence*, also lacked a Hippodamian plan.[10]

---

[7] On Jerusalem walls see Josephus, *BJ* V, 136–159, on Herod's main palace see *BJ* V, 177–182, on Herod's towers see *BJ* V, 156–176, on the Antonia see *AJ* XVIII, 91–95 and *BJ* V, 238–246, on the Temple Mount see *AJ* XV, 380–425, and *BJ* V, 184–227.

[8] Hellenistic Carthage displayed the same feature, a triple defensive wall, described by Appian, which defended the city from the land. See M. H. Fantar, *Carthage, La cité punique*, Paris 1995, p. 44.

[9] See on Alexandria and Cyrene Ward-Perkins, *Roman Imperial Architecture*, p. 366.

[10] On Athens and Rome lacking a Hippodamian plan see P. Connolly, *The Ancient City, Life in Classical Athens and Rome*, Oxford 1998. Moreover, like Athens and Rome, Jerusalem was built on hills, and the Hippodamian grid would not have been easily accommodated by their topography. Of the well known classical cities with hilly topography, only Priene had a Hippodamian plan. But here the urban grid was clearly an exceptional accomplishment of the urbanist. On Priene see J. Raeder, *Priene – Funde aus einer griechischen Stadt, Bilderhefte der Staatlichen Museen Preussicher Kulturbesitz Berlin*, Berlin 1983, pp. 8–9.

2. The Urban Features of the Herodian City

Figure VII, 1 – Air Photograph of the Model of Second Temple Period Jerusalem, Jerusalem, Museum Israel, Courtesy of Albatross.

In Jerusalem, as in Athens, Alexandria, Rome, and other Classical cities, there was a clear division into quarters (cfr. figure VII, 1). In Jerusalem this division was dictated by topography, encompassing the Lower City, divided in two by the Tyropoeon Valley; the Upper City, which extended east of Herod's palace and dominated the Lower City; the northern commercial quarter, enclosed by the Second Wall; and the new Bezetha quarter, enclosed by the Third Wall (cfr. figure VII, 2). As in Rome, the quarters of Jerusalem were mixed, and rich and poor lived together. It is true that the Upper City was the generally preferred residential quarter of the aristocracy, though not exclusively so, since poor people

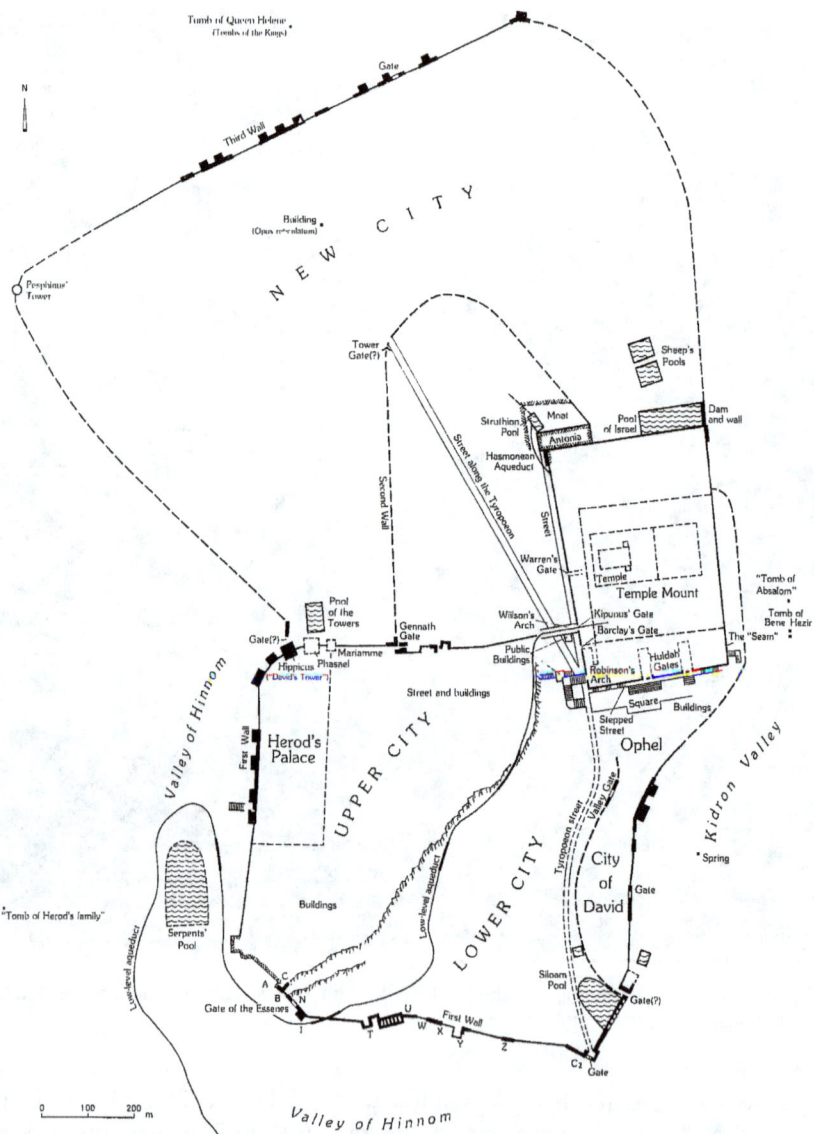

Figure VII, 2 – Plan of Second Temple Jerusalem from *The New Encyclopedia of Archaeological Excavations in the Holy Land* II, Jerusalem, p. 718, Courtesy of the Israel Exploration Society, Jerusalem.

2. The Urban Features of the Herodian City

lived there side by side with the aristocracy. Queen Helena of Adiabene erected her palace in the Lower City.[11]

In brief, the tourist would note the lack of temples and statues, as well as the lack of an urban grid, but he would also observe that of all the Eastern cities, Jerusalem could claim many Roman features, such as aqueducts and a *forum*. To sum up, it is not possible to remove Jerusalem from the category of Classical cities only because of its lack of statues and temples. The Classical city, even if it had more than one temple, was dominated by one major sanctuary, such as the Parthenon in Athens, the Capitolium in Rome, the Temple of Artemis at Ephesus, the Temple of Athena at Pergamum, or the Serapeum at Alexandria. The other city temples were generally not main features of the Classical city. Thus it is possible to say that Jewish Jerusalem was a Classical city – and a modern one at that.

Caesarea Maritima was the harbor city of Judaea.[12] The huge harbor, Sebastos, was entered past the Drusion tower, which was smaller than the Pharos, but nonetheless impressive (cfr. figure VII, 3). Docks lined the harbor and extended under the huge Temple of Augustus, the Augusteum, which towered over the city in the same way that the Serapeum dominated Alexandria. The harbor quarter around the docks would also have been the commercial quarter, where shops, commercial enterprises, mainly maritime, and brothels would have been found. The seashore was dominated by the huge hippodrome in the south, where Herod's huge palace stood, probably with some features common to the Ptolemies' palaces. The theater was situated in the southwestern part of the city. The city probably had a grid plan, and it is possible that, like Alexandria, the city was divided into quarters. An aqueduct conveyed water from the north to the city, and city walls surrounded the entire land side of the city, giving it the shape of a half-circle, the *clamys*, as at Alexandria. It is possible to conclude that, of all the Classical cities, Caesarea Maritima had many features in common with Alexandria, the greatest city in the Mediterranean at the time, such as the harbor, the

---

[11] On the quarters of Jerusalem see Levine, *Jerusalem*; on the Lower City, pp. 319–326; on the Upper City, pp. 335; on the northern commercial quarter, pp. 335–337, on the Bezetha quarter, pp. 337–340. We do not know if Josephus' quarters correspond to an administrative subdivision of the city. Nor do we know how these quarters were administered. Moreover, we know little about the division of the classical city in general into quarters. From classical Athens we are well acquainted with the Kerameikos quarter, which was outside the city walls. We know from Strabo that Alexandria was divided in four quarters, Α, Β, Γ, Δ. On Alexandria see A. Bernard, *Alexandrie des Ptolemées*, Paris 1995, pp. 17–18. For Rome the picture is clearer. Republican Rome was divided in four *regiones*, or administrative subdivisions. These were under the care of the two *curulis* and *plebis aediles*. Later, in 7 BCE Augustus divided Rome in fourteen *regiones*. This division was probably linked to Italy's division into new administrative regions. The supervision of each region was entrusted to a *praetor*, a *tribunus plebis*, or an *aedilis*. The regions were subdivided into *vici*. Under Augustus there were 265 *vici*, each with 4 *vicomagistri*. See O. F. Robinson, *Ancient Rome, City Planning and Administration*, London 1992, pp. 9–13.

[12] On the foundation of Caesarea Maritima see Josephus, *AJ* XV, 331–341, on Sebastos see *AJ* XV, 334–338 and *BJ* I, 411–413, on the Temple of Roma and Augustus see *AJ* XV, 298.

Figure VII, 3 - Air Photograph of Caesarea Maritima, Courtesy of Albatross.

2. The Urban Features of the Herodian City

grid plan, the royal palace on the promontory, the main temple that dominated the harbor, and the hippodrome.[13]

Sebaste was no less impressive than Caesarea Maritima.[14] The acropolis with the Temple of Rome and Augustus, together with Herod's palace fortress, dominated the landscape, towering above the city. The rest of the city, surrounded by a wall, stood on the slopes below the Acropolis. A main colonnaded street, traversing the entire city from north to south, was the main feature. The city had a hippodrome, which stood near the agora-forum. Clearly the wide street that cut the city in two would have suggested Antioch on the Orontes, one of the Seleucid royal cities.[15]

The architectural foundation of Antipas were no less striking, although much smaller. Seen from Mount Bereniki, the elongated city of Tiberias, erected on the shores of the Sea of Galilee, would have been far more impressive.[16] Surrounded by walls that extended to and encompassed sections of the surrounding hills, the city was probably characterized by a grid and a main colonnaded street that bisected the city lengthwise. The seaside palace of King Herod Antipas, the huge synagogue-*bouleterion*, and the theater were the most dominant elements in the city. As at Caesarea Maritima, both Jews and Greeks lived in the city, though the former clearly comprised the main segment of the population. There were no temples there.

Sepphoris, the first capital city of Herod Antipas' kingdom, had features similar to those found at Sebaste. The acropolis towered over the lower city, and the royal palace was very likely located there. Netzer believes that a small pagan temple stood on the acropolis, perhaps a Tiberieum, dedicated to the emperor who always showed kindness and friendship to King Herod Antipas. There was also a theater on the slopes below the acropolis. It seems that the dwellings of the Jewish population, most of them with underground *mikwaoth*, were concentrated on the acropolis. We do not know much about the appearance of the lower city during this period. Did a wall surround it? Did a main colonnaded street bisect it, as in the later Late Roman city? Was it built following an urban grid?

---

[13] On Alexandria see Bernard, *Alexandrie*, pp. 13–18, 46–60, 74–87, 90–93.
[14] On Sebaste see Josephus, *AJ* XV, 292–298; also *BJ* I, 403.
[15] On the stoas of Antioch see Josephus, *AJ* XIV, 148 and *BJ* I, 425. See also C. Kondoleon, "The City of Antioch: An Introduction", in *Antioch, The Lost Ancient City*, Princeton (NJ), 2000, p. 9.
[16] On Tiberias see Josephus, *AJ* XVIII, 36–38, on the foundation of Tiberias; *Vita* 64–69 on Antipas Palace; *BJ* III, 537–540, *Vita* 90–92 on the stadium; and *BJ* III, 447–461 on the city walls.

3. Jerusalem, a Classical City

A. Demography

Since there is not enough data on the other Herodian cities, this section will deal mainly with Jerusalem. It is important to understand to which group of Classical cities Jerusalem belonged. Was the city in the same class as Alexandria, Rome, Ephesus, and Antioch – the largest cities in the Roman Empire – or did it rank with such cities as Athens, Pergamum, Rhodes, and the various cities of Ionia, or perhaps with the smallest *poleis* of the East, such as Ptolemais or Ascalon, or with *municipia* in the West, such as Pompeii? Demography can provide an answer here, though the demography of the Classical city is not an exact science. Useful examples are Athens, Carthage, Alexandria, Rome, and Pompeii.[17]

There are various problems in establishing the population of Jerusalem. Literary sources are not particularly helpful, and thus archaeological data must provide the details.

According to Shanks, Jerusalem developed into a large city during the Late Hellenistic Period and in the first century, until 70 CE. Thus, from the end of the Persian Era to the beginning of the rule of John Hyrcanus I, the population of the city was stable. During the Late Persian and Hellenistic Periods, the population of the city numbered approximately 5,000, spread out over an area of 30 acres. This was a small number that put Jerusalem among the smallest *poleis* and urban centers. Its real growth began during the Hasmonean Period, following the construction of the First Wall. During the Hasmonean Period, the population would have been approximately 30,000–35,000, covering an area of 165 acres. Jerusalem had developed and transformed itself into the capital of a larger kingdom, with its population increasing tenfold. The civil wars that followed probably brought an abrupt end to the growth of the city. Under Herod, however, the city began to grow once more, and at this time the Second Wall was probably added. During

---

[17] The total population of Athens amounted to 500,000 in the fifth century BCE. See P. Connolly, *The Ancient City, Life in Classical Athens and Rome*, Oxford 1998, p. 14. Carthage in 149 BCE it had a population of around 575,000 in the city itself and the chora, with around 125,000, perhaps double that number, living within the city walls. On Carthage see D. Hoyos, *Hannibal's Dynasty, Power and Politics in the Western Mediterranean, 247–183 BC*, London 2003, pp. 28–29, 225–226. Alexandria also had a population of 300,000 to 500,000 persons. See P. Ballet, *La vie quotidienne à Alexandrie, 331–30 avant J.-C.*, La Vie Quotidienne, Paris, 1999, pp. The population of Late Republican Rome was around 250,000 persons. In the Augustan period it probably remained stable, after years of civil wars. However it reached a peak of 2,000,000 in the late first century to early second century CE. On the other hand, as we know that Rome had around 46,602 insulae or blocks, and that each insula could contain around 40 persons, we arrive at approximately 1,000,000 persons. Thus at its peak Rome's population ranged from 1,000,000 to 2,000,000. See Connolly, *Classical Athens and Rome*, pp. 125, 143–144. Pompeii, a typical Italic municipium, had a population of no more than 8,000–10,000, only 60% of which were free citizens. See P. Connolly, *Pompeii*, Oxford 1990, p. 18.

the Herodian Period, the population is estimated to have been 40,000, spread out over an area of 230 acres. Under Archelaus, the Roman prefects, and Agrippa I, years of peace enabled the city to continue to expand. Agrippa I erected the Third Wall, whose main purpose, among others, was to protect the new population. The years between the death of Agrippa I and the beginning of the Great War in 66 CE were years of slower growth, and the new quarters between the Second and Third Walls were scarcely inhabited. The city's growth is reflected demographically. Around 44 CE, when the city occupied an area of 450 acres, the population is estimated to have been 80,000–90,000 in number.[18]

Most scholars are only interested in the demography of first century Jerusalem and not that of the earlier periods. Thus Jeremias, Avi-Yonah, Broshi and Levine consider the demography of Jerusalem primarily on the eve of the war against Rome. Jeremias, for instance, has estimated that there was a population of 25,000 in first century Jerusalem. At the other extreme, Avi-Yonah has estimated a population of 250,000 on the eve of the city's destruction in 66 C.E, using Josephus and Tacitus as sources.[19] According to Broshi, the population of Jerusalem may be estimated on the basis of the area of the city. Broshi therefore reach the number of 100,000 people living in Jerusalem in 66 CE circa. Jerusalem thus belonged to a group of larger cities of the Classical World.[20] According to Levine, because the new area encompassed by the Third Wall was not densely populated, assuming that it contained half the population of the rest of the city, there were between 60,000 and 70,000 people living in Jerusalem. Thus, according to Levine, Jerusalem qualifies as being in the second rank of provincial cities, the first tier being Rome, Alexandria, Antioch, Pergamum, and Ephesus, all of them huge metropolises during the Augustan Period.[21] Thus, following Broshi, Jerusalem was one of the largest cities of antiquity, together with Athens, Alexandria, and Rome. Physically, Jerusalem was not as large in area as Rome or Alexandria.

---

[18] See H. Shanks, *Jerusalem, An Archaeological Biography*, New York 1995, p. 123.

[19] Thus Josephus, presents interesting data concerning the number of pilgrims who came to Jerusalem for the holidays each year: at least 2,500,000–3,000,000. See Josephus, *AJ* II, 280 and *BJ* VI, 423–425. Josephus also writes that around 1,000,000 persons fell in the siege of Jerusalem. Tacitus gives a figure of 600,000. We know that on the eve of the war many pilgrims were trapped inside the city, and that could have been half of the population of the besieged city. Presuming that half of the persons who fell in the siege were pilgrims, albeit no more as the war probably disrupted pilgrimages, we thus arrive at 500,000 according to Josephus or 300,000 according to Tacitus as the actual population of Jerusalem on the eve of the war. See Josephus, *BJ* VI, 420–426 and Tacitus, *Histories* V, 12, 3.

[20] See M. Broshi, "Estimating the Population of Ancient Jerusalem," *BAR* 4, 1978, pp. 10–15. Some scholars do not accept Broshi's reconstruction of the city's population. Most scholars, such as Reinhart, accept Broshi's estimate of the city's population as approximately 100,000 at the eve of its destruction.

[21] See L. I. Levine, *Jerusalem, Portrait of the City in the Second Temple Period (538 BCE–70 CE)*, Philadelphia 2002, pp. 340–343.

There is no data on Caesarea Maritima, though a plausible estimate can be made. If Pompeii, with a theater seating 5,000, had a population of 10,000, it is probable that Caesarea Maritima, with a theater seating 4,000, had a population of fewer than 8,000 people.[22]

B. The Water Supply

The story of Jerusalem's water supply until the time of the Hasmoneans was similar to that of other Near Eastern cities. The Canaanite city's water shaft was supplemented by two water reservoirs during the Iron Age – the Siloam Pool at the outlet of the Tyropoeon Valley, and the Birket el-Hamra east of the city. A water tunnel was also created inside the city. In Classical Greece wells and cisterns were also the main sources of water for the city.

Only during the Hellenistic period were real water conduits constructed. These aqueducts, called siphons, were underground conduits, concealed for safety, with strong, fitted terra-cotta pipes in rock-cut or masonry channels.[23] During the Hasmonean Period two projects were started to assure an adequate water supply for the city's population and for pilgrims. The first was the erection of a network of public reservoirs built to capture rainwater and take advantage of the newly built siphons. Second, the Hasmoneans built the first aqueduct, the Low Level Aqueduct[24].

The Romans were the real innovators in urban water supply. One characteristic of the Roman aqueducts is that they could be built on arches, thus bringing the water from a distance of tens of kilometers from the city.[25] The Roman aqueducts greatly influenced the development of the water supply in Jerusalem during the Herodian Period. It was Herod, however, who brought the Jerusalem water supply to its apogee by considerably expanding the original water supply of the

---

[22] See Connolly, *Pompeii*, pp. 22, 68, 70.

[23] See R. E. Wycherley, *How the Greeks Built Cities, The Relationship of Architecture and Town Planning to Everyday Life in Ancient Greece*, New York 1976, pp. 198–209.

[24] The Hasmoneans expanded the Siloam Pool and hewed Solomon's Pool east of the City of David, located near First Wall (Josephus, *BJ* V, 145). Their main project, however, was the creation of several cisterns on the Temple Mount itself. The Low Level Aqueduct was a siphon that originally consisted of two tunnels. It ran for 21 km from the lowest of Solomon's Pools near Bethlehem to the Temple Mount, passing over Wilson's Arch into a huge cistern system inside the Temple Mount and to the south of it. The Hasmonean aqueduct is thus a typical example of a Hellenistic siphon. See Levine, *Jerusalem*, pp. 213–214.

[25] Frontinus in his book on aqueducts boasts that the Romans did not built as beautiful temples as the Greeks, but did construct useful aqueducts. Characteristic of the Roman aqueducts is that they could be built on arches, thus bringing the water from tens of kilometers distance from the city. See Connolly, *Classical Athens and Rome*, Oxford 1998, pp. 130–133. See also Robinson, *Ancient Rome, City Planning and Administration*, p. 96, 98–99. See also Strabo, *Geography* V, 3, 8. In the Imperial period the administration of water supply was under the *curatores aquarum*, or water commissioners, established by Augustus to continue Agrippa's work.

city through the use of both Greek-Hellenistic and Roman methods, as in all of his other building enterprises. First, Herod renewed and expanded the existing Siloam Pool and Solomon's Pools, that had probably been damaged by the civil wars and neglect. He also had various other pools excavated, including the Tower Pool or Hezekiah's Pool, the Struthion Pool, the Probatic Pool or Bethseda, the Israel Pool, and the Serpent Pool, north, south, and west of the Temple Mount.[26] The purpose of these pools was not only to serve the city, but the pilgrims as well. When Herod expanded the Temple Mount, making it the greatest sanctuary of the Classical World, he realized that the *temenos* would require an enormous water supply, since purity was a very important concern in the Temple cult. Moreover, Herod also elongated the Low Level Aqueduct, adding a new part, known as the High Level Aqueduct, which runs from the upper sections of Solomon's Pools to the Upper City. This aqueduct probably followed a Roman model and was built on arches. Herod also added a short conduit from Wadi Biyar to Solomon's Pools, following a straight route, mostly through hewn tunnels that were 3 m. high.[27] The Herodian aqueducts were completed by Pontius Pilate.[28] It is important to reiterate that the Jerusalem water supply was not only necessary for the needs of the city itself, but also to enable observance of the rules of purity in the Temple and to accommodate the needs of the flocks of pilgrims who arrived in the city each year.

Jerusalem was not the only beneficiary of Herod's engineers, however. Herod also furnished Caesarea Maritima with a water supply, building the eastern aqueduct, a high level aqueduct that was nearly 13 miles long, originating in a spring in the Mount Carmel range. This conduit was partly constructed over a series of arches and partly hewn into bedrock. Only the easternmost aqueduct, still visible today, is Herodian; the westernmost segment was constructed by Hadrian. Thus, the two major cities of Herodian Judaea, Jerusalem and Caesarea Maritima, boasted far more advanced water supply systems than existed in any

---

[26] In the Herodian period there were eight pools that supplied water to Jerusalem. Three pools were situated to the north of the Temple Mount: the Birket Israel, the Betheseda Pool, that consisted of a pair of pools, identified with the Probatica of John 5: 2-4; the third pool was the Struthion Pool (Josephus, *BJ* V, 467). West of Temple Mount were three pools, Hezekiah's Pool (Josephus, *BJ* V, 468), the Mamillah Pool, and the Birket es-Sultan, to be identified with the Serpent's Pool (See Josephus, *BJ* V, 108). South of the Temple Mount were the Birket el-Hamra Pool See Levine, *Jerusalem*, pp. 213-214.

[27] Much had been written on Jerusalem's water supply. The most relevant material comes from A. Mazar, who distinguishes three phases in the development of the city's water supply under the Hasmoneans, Herod, and Pontius Pilate. See A. Mazar, "The Aqueducts of Jerusalem", Y. Yadin (ed.), *Jerusalem Revealed, Archaeology in the Holy City 1968-1974*, Jerusalem 1976, pp. 25-40. See also A. Mazar, "A Survey of the Aqueducts Leading to Jerusalem", in D. Amit (ed.), *The Aqueducts of Ancient Palestine*, Jerusalem 1989, pp. 169-195. See also Levine, *Jerusalem*, pp. 213-216.

[28] The Roman prefect extended the High Level Aqueduct. Josephus in *BJ* II, 175 writes of an aqueduct 400 furlongs in length. In *AJ* XVIII, 60 Josephus writes of an aqueduct 200 furlongs in length.

of the other cities in the Greek East, though they were inferior to those of the average Roman *municipium* in the West.

C. *The Leisure Buildings*

Leisure buildings, such as bath houses, theatres, hippodromes, and amphitheatres, are a main component in the texture of the Hellenistic and Roman cities. No leisure buildings are documented in Jerusalem before the Herodian Period, nor in the Late Hellenistic and Hasmonean Period, with the exception of the *gymnasium*, which has already been discussed in Chapter II. The Herodian Period was a turning point in this respect, and thus bathhouses were probably built, as well as a theatre and hippodrome documented by Josephus.

The first type of building to be discussed is the bath house. This building developed in the Hellenistic East[29] and reached its peak in Late Republican Augustan Rome.[30] It is important to emphasize that the Herodian baths in the various palaces, already discussed in Chapter II, were clearly something new in the Greek East. But, did Herodian Jerusalem have public baths? Both archaeological and literary sources can provide the answer to this question. A series of public ritual baths has been excavated south of the Temple Mount, and it is possible that these were a combination of *mikwe* and public bath. This would not have been an exceptional situation. In the Herodian palace, a bathhouse is always combined with a *mikwe* that takes the place of the *frigidarium*. At least two different literary sources suggest the mundane atmosphere of these ritual baths. The first source, Leviticus Rabba, depicts Hillel the Elder going somewhere to give rest to his body, not only to his soul. Where else could Hillel the Elder have gone, other than to a public bath, to rest his weary bones? The second source, a New Testament Apocrypha, already discussed in Chapter II, shows a dialogue between Jesus and a priest, who purified themselves in a *mikwe* together with *hetairai* and flute girls. Apparently, the establishment with the *mikwe* offered regular bath services, like any other bathhouse in Rome or in Campania.[31] But who built these buildings, the king or some private *euergetes*? That we do not know.

---

[29] The best source on baths and bathing in classical antiquity is F. Yegül, *Baths and Bathing in Classical Antiquity*, Cambridge (MA) 1995. Public baths developed as part of the *gymnasium* only in the early Hellenistic Period, see pp. 11, 14–17, 24–27.

[30] In Roman Italy the first bath buildings appeared in Campania as parts of private dwellings. The examples from Pompeii, a bath combined with a *palaestra*, all date to around the beginning of the first century BCE. The 33 BCE census of Agrippa reported 170 *balneae* or bath buildings in Rome. Agrippa was also the first to erect a monumental bath building, the Thermaea of Agrippa, in 25 BCE. This bath building became the model for the successive huge Roman bath buildings. See Yegül, *Baths and Bathing*, pp. 57–65, figs. 57–65, p. 66, fig. 68, p. 67, fig. 69, and p. 67, fig. 70, pp. 134–136, figs. 143–147.

[31] See Lev Rabbah 34, 3 in Hadas-Lebel, *Hillel*, p. 29. In later generations Sages continued to go

3. Jerusalem, a Classical City

When Herod erected theaters and hippodromes in Judaea, and even an amphitheater in Jerusalem, at least according to Josephus, most of these buildings had already been part of the Classical heritage of the Greek and Hellenistic *polis*[32] and of the Roman *municipium* for hundreds of years.[33] Herod's leisure buildings celebrated his ambitions and accomplishments as ruler of such Hellenistic cities as Jerusalem, Caesarea Maritima, and Sebaste. Once more, these buildings represented a major connection with the architecture of Augustan Rome, which Herod admired so much.[34] According to Josephus, Herod built a theater and an amphitheater-hippodrome[35] in Jerusalem, the kingdom's capital, though these are buildings that have not survived. Most scholars agree that Jerusalem's theater was a stone building. Patrich, however, suggests a wooden structure. According to Patrich the structure in Jerusalem was a Roman theater similar to the one in stone at Caesarea Maritima, but constructed of wood.[36] Caesarea Maritima also was furbished with a theater and a hippodrome. At Sebaste, Herod erected a hippodrome, and finally, for his court at Jericho, Herod erected a structure that served as both theater and hippodrome. Herod's son Herod Antipas erected theaters at Sepphoris and at Tiberias (cfr. figure VII, 4). Thus, on the eve on the Great War against Rome, Herodian Judaea had numerous leisure buildings

---

to a public bath. Thus Rabban Gamliel II of Yavne frequented pagan public bath, decorated with statues at Ptolemais. See m. *'Abod. Zar.* I, 1. See J. Jeremias and W. Schneemelcher, "Oxyrhynchus Papyrus 840, in W. Schneemelcher (ed.), *New Testament Apocrypha I, Gospels and Related Writings*, Louisville (KY) 1991, pp. 94–95. On the other hand, Levine is skeptical, to say the least, regarding the presence of public baths at Jerusalem. See Levine, *Jerusalem*, pp. 329–330.

[32] It is important to emphasize that in the Greek world theatrical representations, tragedies and comedies as well as mimes were parts of religious ceremonies. See Connolly, *Classical Athens and Rome*, pp. 14.

[33] Until the construction of the Theater of Pompey, temporary leisure buildings in wood were erected almost every year by the future aediles or by any other Roman magistrates who wanted to influence the votes of the plebe in elections with spectacular games. In this period, Roman terminology for leisure buildings is still not clear. The Roman wooden and early stone theaters served for both theatrical representations, generally comedies, and gladiatorial games. It should be underlined that in Late Republican Rome both the theatrical representations and the gladiatorial games had already lost the religious flavor they had in the earlier period. See M. Grant, *Gladiators*, New York 1995, pp. 9–28.

[34] Roller, *Building Program of Herod the Great*, p. 91.

[35] See Josephus, *AJ* XV, 268–291 on the theater and amphitheater; on the hippodrome see Josephus, *AJ* XVII, 255, *BJ* II, 44.

[36] Many sites have been suggested for Jerusalem's theater. Two of the proposed sites are extra-mural, between Abu Tor and the Valley of Hinnom and near Burj Qibrit. Both sites have yielded negative archaeological results. Reich and Billig suggested the area between Robinson Arch and Wilson Arch, where marble theater seats were found in secondary use. The area of Ummayad Palace III, near the Dung Gate, had been suggested as the site of the hippodrome. See R. Reich and Y. Billig, "A Group of Theatre Seats Discovered near the Southwestern Corner of the Temple Mount", *IEJ* 50, 2000, pp. 175–184. The marble theater seats found in secondary use near Robinson's Arch would thus not have belonged to the Herodian theater, but rather to the odeon of Aelia Capitolina. See J. Patrich, "Herod's Theatre in Jerusalem, A New Proposal", *IEJ* 52, 2002, pp. 231–239.

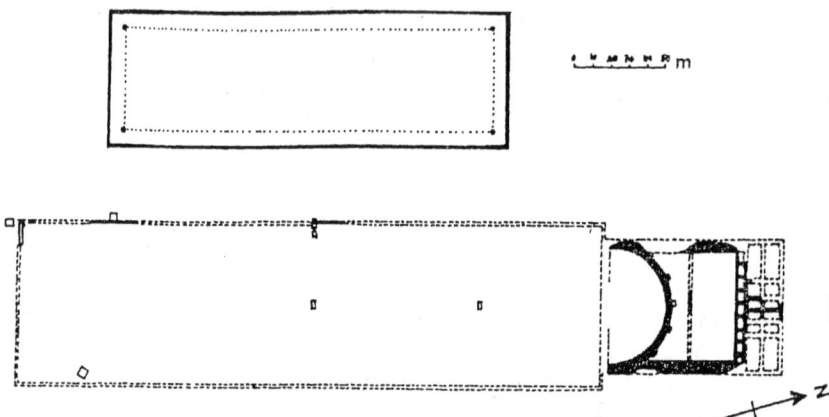

Figure VII, 4 – Plan of the Hippodrome at Jericho and the Stadium at Samaria from E. Netzer, *The Winter Palaces and the King's Estate in Jericho, Jericho, Kardom Series*, Jerusalem 1983 (Hebrew), Courtesy of Professor Emeritus Ehud Netzer, The Hebrew University of Jerusalem.

concentrated not only in the Gentile areas, such as Sebaste, but also in the mixed areas, such as Caesarea Maritima, and in the Jewish cities of Jerusalem, Sepphoris, and Tiberias. Herod also introduced games, to be held every five years in honor of Augustus, in both Jerusalem and Caesarea Maritima.[37] These games were to be celebrated in the new leisure buildings.

The purpose of the amphitheater-hippodrome is quite obvious. Its primary use was for chariot racing, and Josephus writes that there were races with chariots drawn by two, three, or four horses.[38] Also – and this was a Greek rather than Roman tradition, since the Romans were not interested in such games – there were wrestlers who competed naked, according to Greek tradition.[39] The hippodrome-amphitheater was also used for gladiatorial games, clearly a Roman innovation. Josephus is quite clear as to the types of entertainment for which the amphitheater was used, including *venationes*, or hunting displays involving wild beasts, and gladiatorial duels.[40]

The purpose of the theater is less obvious. Were the theatrical plays of Ezekiel the Tragedian shown to the Jerusalemite masses? Did Moses and Pharaoh appear on the stage? That appears quite unlikely. If so, Josephus would not have complained so vociferously about the foreign taste of the theater productions.

---

[37] On Jerusalem's games see Josephus, *AJ* XV, 268, On Caesarea's games, see Josephus, *AJ* XVI, 138 and *BJ* I, 415.

[38] See Josephus, *AJ* XV, 271. As far as we know from various reliefs and mosaics, mainly from Rome and North Africa, in the Roman period only four horses drew chariots, which were thus called *quadrigae*.

[39] See Josephus, *AJ* XV, 269.

[40] See Josephus, *AJ* XV, 273–275.

The best way to answer this question is to compare what happened to the theaters in Rome and in the Greek East during this period, which may allow us to draw some inferences regarding Jerusalem. The Greek theater of the Hellenistic Period had evolved considerably from the traditional theater of Classical Athens. The tragedies of Aeschylus, Sophocles, and Euripides no longer comprised the bulk of the plays performed. Comedy had also evolved from the political satire of Aristophanes to the comedies of Menander, which had a clear social and psychological emphasis. The mime would gradually take over the stage, particularly in comedies. The same thing occurred in Late Republican Rome, where the comedies of Plautus and Terence were no longer a focus of interest, and the audience also preferred the mime. Since the mime consisted mostly of performances with strong pornographic content, this would explain Josephus' protest if such performances also took place in Jerusalem. Surely musical contests in the best Greek tradition were also held in the theater.[41]

How did the kingdom's population react to Herod's leisure buildings? The reaction of the Jewish population of Jerusalem, as reported by Josephus,[42] is interesting. Most of the Jews' main concern, as underlined by Levine,[43] was not over the erection of leisure buildings or the institution of the games. According to Josephus, although these leisure buildings were completely foreign to Jewish tradition, most of the Jews objected mainly to the possible presence of cultic images on the building, and less to the bloody games held in the hippodrome-amphitheater. Herod probably located his entertainment buildings outside the city, according to Roller, and he did not decorate them with images, thus minimizing their offensiveness to Judaism.[44] Still, a small group conspired against Herod to defend the "customs of the countryland." The conspirators were caught and executed.[45] The reaction of the Jewish public was certainly not unique, but is reflected in the Greek East and in men of culture such as Seneca.[46]

---

[41] See Josephus, *AJ* XV, 270.

[42] See Josephus, *AJ* XV, 268–291.

[43] On the reaction of the Jews to the Herodian entertainment buildings in Jerusalem, see Levine, *Jerusalem*, pp. 201–206.

[44] See Roller, *Building Program of Herod the Great*, p. 191. Avi-Yonah located these buildings inside the city.

[45] See Josephus, *AJ* XV, 281–291.

[46] In the Greek East, although any city of importance could boast a theater, amphitheaters were not erected. This may show the distaste of the Greek public for gladiatorial contests. And yet the discovery at Ephesus of tombstones of gladiators and the fact that theaters were also used for gladiatorial contests, as in Rome prior to the erection of the Flavian amphitheater, shows that also the Greek East had its share of gladiatorial games and venationes. A second century episode shows Smyrna's Jews quite willingly to attend the death sentence ad bestias of the local Christian bishop, Polycarpus, in the local arena. Diaspora Jews probably enjoyed this kind of mass entertainment in the same way as their Greek or Roman counterparts did. On the other hand, part of the priestly class, as well as the Pharisee masters, probably condemned these shows. But once again, their dislike was shared by Greek and Roman men of culture, such as Seneca. See

It is noteworthy that permanent leisure buildings were introduced during the same period in Rome, such as the Theater of Pompey,[47] and in Jerusalem. In Augustan Rome many leisure buildings were constructed, although their exact purposes were not defined. Theaters were used for both shows and gladiatorial games. The first real amphitheater built in Rome was the Flavian Amphitheater, built after 71 CE, though in Campania, as the Pompeii amphitheater attests, these buildings were already erected in the first century BCE. The most important leisure buildings erected in Augustan Rome were the Circus Maximus, restored by Augustus himself, the Theater of Marcellus, the Theater of Balbus, and the Thermae of Agrippa, already discussed.

Thus in both Augustan Rome and Herodian Jerusalem, this period marked a new era for leisure buildings. In Augustan Rome, leisure buildings were erected for the first time as permanent stone structures. Augustus restored the Circus Maximus, and several *euergetes* erected many new, permanent leisure buildings in Rome over the course of a few years. Agrippa constructed the first huge thermal establishment in Rome, and Marcellus and Balbus built theaters that could be used for both theatrical and gladiatorial shows. Only Augustus' family and political allies erected these buildings, with the exception of the Circus Maximus. Augustus probably approved the construction of such buildings, but did not want to offend the wishes of the conservative Senate.

Augustus completely transformed the Republican leisure policy, dictated by the wishes of the Senate, albeit defied by Pompey and Caesar. Mainly in the later part of his rule, only members of his family could sponsor games. Thus, the Roman magistrates no longer had this demagogic means of influencing the population during elections. This marked the beginning of the *panem* and *circenses* method used by Roman emperors to win the hearts of the *plebs*. The advantage of this was that no one could continue to compete with the emperor.[48]

In Herodian Jerusalem, Herod erected leisure buildings for the first time, except for the *gymnasium* built in 175 BCE. In Jerusalem, unlike Rome, the establishment of leisure buildings and the games were a total innovation. Herod's construction of these buildings had a twofold purpose – to reinforce the Hellenistic culture of Jerusalem, and to procure the good will of the population through games, as Augustus had done in Rome. Herod probably succeeded in achieving both, though the Jewish public differed slightly from the Roman *plebs*. Thus, in both Rome and Jerusalem, permanent leisure buildings built in stone were

---

M. Polycarpii 12. 2. See also R. Lane Fox, *Pagans and Christians, in the Mediterranean world from the Second Century AD to the Conversion of Constantine,* Harmondsworth 1986, pp. 472, 485.

[47] In Rome theaters were built of wood prior to the erection of Pompey's theater in 55 BCE. The first to build a permanent stone theater in Rome was Pompey, the warlord pillar of the Senate. See Zanker, *Augusto e il potere delle immagini,* p. 25.

[48] See C. W. Weber, *Panem et Circenses, La politica dei divertimenti in massa nell'antica Roma,* Milano 1986.

erected for the first time. The ruler's wish to reinforce his personal position was the main motivation in both cases. In this, Herod acted as a true royal *euergetes*. His quinquennial games in honor of Augustus combined the best of Greek and Roman traditions, and he brought athletes and musicians from all over the Greek world to compete in Jerusalem and Caesarea Maritima. He also brought professional gladiators from the Roman West, to fight against condemned criminals, or at least to teach them, and his gladiatorial games not only introduced this Roman tradition to Judaea, but probably to the entire Greek East as well.

D. *The Private Buildings of Herodian Jerusalem*

This section will examine the mansions of Herodian Jerusalem, since private buildings were an integral part of the city's residential and architectural texture. Were the mansions of the upper classes of Herodian Jerusalem similar to the Greek *oikos*[49] or to the Roman *domus*, or did these preserve native features?[50]

In the Land of Israel during the Hellenistic Period, a Greek Hellenistic tradition of private buildings, similar to those erected in the surrounding Hellenistic world, existed side by side with a native tradition dating back to the Bronze Age. Some of the private dwellings in the Land of Israel during the Hellenistic Period, such as those at Philoteria and Marissa, appear to have adopted most of their features from the Greek private house, particularly with respect to their rectangular shape, their central courtyard, and the use of the *oikos*. There were no mosaic pavements, however, and the use of columns and verandas was also extremely rare. Most mansions, however, still conserved native features, such as

---

[49] Greek and Hellenistic houses were square shaped, built around a courtyard, though mansions generally had a peristyle. The main room was the *androon* or the *oikos*, where symposia were held. During the fourth century BCE and in the Hellenistic period this room was generally decorated with mosaic floors and painted walls in the First Eastern Style, while the rest of the house was generally not decorated. The women's section of the house, the *gynecaeum*, generally occupied part of the upper floor. On the Greek house see E. Walter-Karydi, *The Greek House, The Rise of Noble Houses in Late Classical Times*, The Archaeological Society at Athens Library 171, Athens 1998. Walter-Karydi brings examples from fourth century BCE Athens, Eretria, Pella, Priene, and second century BCE Delos. She underlines the common plan, also reflected in Hellenistic houses in the Land of Israel at Philoteria and Marissa, as well as the use of First Style wall painting and pebble bichrome mosaics to decorate the *androon* or *oikos*.

[50] The upper classes of Roman Italy inhabited the *domus*, a private dwelling one or two stories high that, though evolved from an Italic prototype, by the second century BCE had adopted all the trappings of the Hellenistic mansion including a peristyle courtyard. See A. G. McKay, *Houses, Villas, and Palaces in the Roman World*, London 1975, pp. 14–64 on *domus* from Pompeii and Herculanum. J. R. Clarke, *The Houses of Roman Italy 100 BC–AD 250, Ritual, Space and Decoration*, Berkeley 1991, is dedicated mainly to interior decoration. Finally, P. Zanker, *Pompeii, Public and Private Life*, Cambridge (MA.) 1998, pp. 135–206, is in part dedicated to the development of private housing in Italic and Roman Pompeii.

the mansions found on Mount Garizim.[51] In Jerusalem, the private dwellings erected during the Hasmonean Period were later renovated during the Herodian Period. These houses, constructed around a central courtyard, maintained native elements and were probably not dissimilar to the private houses excavated on Mount Garizim. It is interesting that the Roman settlements of Pompey and Gabinius left their traces on the private houses of Samaria, where the shape of the contemporary Roman *domus* influenced the private dwelling.[52] Thus, though the *atrium* is missing from the houses in Samaria, the peristyle does appear.

Urban dwellings with a private character, dated to the Herodian Period proper, have been excavated only in Jerusalem. Private buildings belonging to the new Herodian secular ruling class have not been found, but all of these houses appear to have belonged to the priestly aristocracy. Some of these buildings were erected during the Hasmonean Period, though most were erected after 37 BCE, during the Herodian Period, and remained more or less in their present state, since throughout the early Roman Period these mansions were seldom modified. The priestly aristocracy continued to reside in them until 70 CE.

During this period the buildings were only slightly modified. Were these structures, belonging to the priestly upper class, influenced in the same way as the Herodian court by the new trends coming from the outer Mediterranean world, or was such an influence felt in them to a lesser extent? Most of these houses, excavated by Avigad, were found in the Herodian Quarter, which was part of the Upper City where the Hasmonean palace, the palace of King Herod, and the mansion of Ananias the high priest were located.[53] The remains of at least six mansions were uncovered. Originally these were situated on the slope of the hill that faced the Temple Mount. Five of these mansions were grouped together in the eastern part, and one was located in the western end. The mansions were constructed roughly at the same time. The common element is a north-south/east-west orientation, with only the Western House differing slightly from this orientation. No streets have been discovered between the mansions, with the exception of closed lanes, and we may surmise that the main streets were probably

---

[51] The private houses of Philoteria and Marissa show clear Greek influence, while those of Ashdod and Mount Garizim have a native character. Third century houses in the Land of Israel, which show Greek influence, appear roughly to correspond to fourth century BCE examples in Greece, such as those in Athens and Olynthus. See R. Arav, *Settlement Patterns and City Planning, 337–301 BCE*. British Archaeological Reports, International Series 485, Oxford 1989. On Philoteria see R. Hestrin, "Beth Yerah", *NEAEHL I*, 1993, pp. 255–259. On Marissa see A. Kloner, *Marissa*, Jerusalem 1996. See also A. Kloner, Marissa, *NEAEHL III*, 1993, pp. 951–957. On Mount Garizim see Y. Magen, "Mount Garizim", *Christian Archaeology in the Holy Land; New Discoveries*, Jerusalem, 1990, pp. 333–342.

[52] On Building A in Insula IV at Samaria see Crowfoot, Kenyon, and Sukenik, *The Buildings at Samaria*.

[53] On the Herodian Quarter in Jerusalem see N. Avigad, *Discovering Jerusalem*, Jerusalem 1980, pp. 83–146. See also N. Avigad, *The Herodian Quarter of Jerusalem, Wohl Archaeological Museum*, Jerusalem 1989.

situated outside the excavated area. Likewise, there was no trace of the mansions' monumental façades. Generally the houses had two stories, with the living rooms on the ground floor and the service rooms in the basement. Some of the mansions had a second story. Two of them were particularly large, and these had a central internal courtyard surrounded by groups of rooms. One of the mansions definitely had a Hellenistic Roman peristyle, but its plan could not be established during the excavations. The houses were built on terraces, along the slope of the hill, from west to east. The quality of the building material was generally good, with the foundations built directly on bedrock and with walls built of hewn stones placed in one or two rows. The outer side of the stone blocks, covered by stucco, was often roughly hewn. The houses had various water installations, which included cisterns, pools, bathtubs, and ritual baths. Often the bathrooms of the mansions were paved with mosaics. The ritual baths differed from those described in the Mishna.[54] Deep cisterns provided the main water reserve.

The Western House consisted of a basement with water installations, which consisted in a bathroom, and two *mikwaoth* preceded by a vestibule, together with service rooms (cfr. figure VII, 5).[55]

The remains of a house with a peristyle, called the Peristyle Building, were also excavated. Perhaps the peristyle was part of a palace, or of a mansion, built in a similar way to the contemporary *domus* excavated in Pompeii.[56]

The Middle Block is a large complex of rooms belonging to two mansions, divided by a common wall which is oriented north-south. The pavements of the mansions were on different levels. The rooms found in the second building included an *oikos* and a bathhouse which included a large *mikwe*.[57]

The original plan of the Great Mansion, later referred to by Avigad as the Palatial Mansion, consisted of a rectangular building with an internal central courtyard. Two stories were discovered – a basement with service rooms and water installations, and the ground floor, which consisted of a central courtyard,

---

[54] The *mikwaoth* described in the Mishna had to hold 40 *seah* (750 liters) of spring or rain water. The Mishnaic *mikwaoth* were also three cubits deep. As this condition is difficult to observe, *mikwe* water could be purified if connected to ritually pure water. Thus, a second pool or *otzar*, which held pure water, was built near the immersion pool. Both pools were connected by a hole or a pipe inserted in the partition wall between the *otzar* and the immersion pool. This method allowed the use of the water of the immersion pool, purified with the water of the *otzar*, for ritual bathing. The baths discovered in the Herodian Quarter lacked the *otzar*. The model most often used consisted of a pool excavated in bedrock with steps, covered by a barrel vaulted ceiling built of hewn stones. The steps and the pool were covered with gray waterproof plaster. Two of the ritual baths had two entries, the first to descend for purification and the other to leave the pool after ritual immersion. Sometimes the two entries were separated by a low, built partition. Another characteristic of the *mikwaoth* excavated in the Herodian Quarter is a basin to wash the feet before ritual immersion. The *mikwaoth* were probably filled and emptied manually. See Avigad, *Discovering Jerusalem*, pp. 139–143.

[55] On the Western House see Avigad, *Herodian Quarter*, pp. 23–29.

[56] On the Peristyle Building see Avigad, *Herodian Quarter*, pp. 32–38.

[57] On the Middle Block see Avigad, *Herodian Quarter*, pp. 48–56.

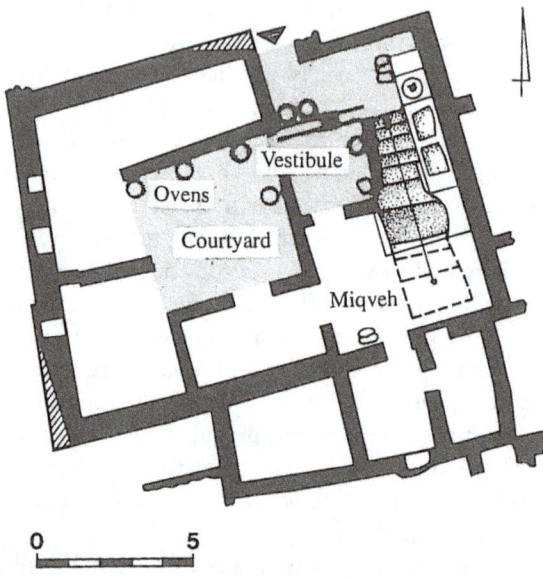

Figure VII, 5 – Plan of the "Herodian House" from Y. Hirschfeld, *The Palestinian Dwelling in the Roman-Byzantine Period, Studium Biblicum Franciscanum, Collectio Minor 34*, Jerusalem 1995, p. 58, fig. 34, Courtesy of the Israel Exploration Society, Jerusalem.

the *oikos*, and various residential rooms. The *oikos*'s walls were plastered in the First Eastern Style, while the ceiling was decorated with molded plaster. The rooms included a vestibule decorated with polychrome mosaics, and a room with frescoes in the Pompeian Third Style (cfr. figure VII, 6).[58]

The Burnt House was discovered north of the Palatial Mansion at the corner of Tiferet Israel and Misgav Ladach streets. This mansion, according to Hirschfeld, can be seen as representative of the smaller courtyard house, in the same way as the Palatial Mansion is representative of the larger type. The mansion had a central small courtyard. Only the basement of this mansion, which included a kitchen and a ritual bath, has been excavated.[59] The House of Caiaphas is situated in the area today occupied by the Armenian Quarter.

---

[58] On the Palatial Mansion see Avigad, *Herodian Quarter*, pp. 57–76. Jaeckle claims that this was the Hasmonean palace of Jerusalem. But the mosaics, frescoes, plastered ceiling, as well the general shape suggest a later Herodian date. The Hasmonean Palace, located nearby, would have been similar to the fortified palace of Jericho, a kind of *tetrapyrgion*, which shared much with the Attalid palaces of Pergamum. See Chapter II above. See R. Jaeckle, "Das Prätorium des Pilatus in Jerusalem", *DJ* 2 1990, pp. 59–72.

[59] On the Burnt House see Avigad, *Discovering Jerusalem*, pp. 120–139. One of the weights bears the inscription "property of the son of Katros". The family of Katros is mentioned in the Talmud as one priestly family that served in the Temple (BT, *Pesh.* 57 a, t. *Menah.* 13: 21).

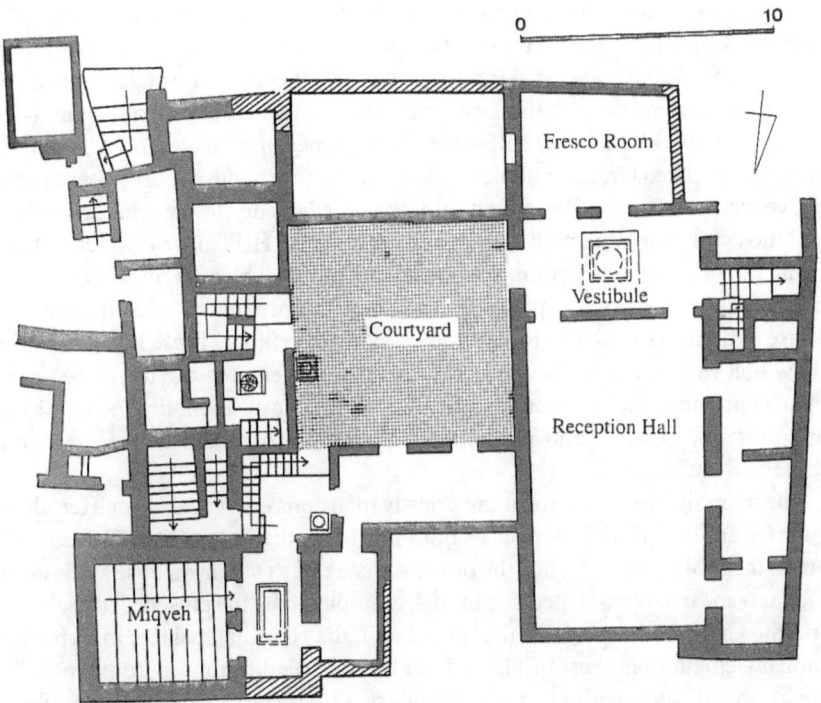

Figure VII, 6 – Plan of the Palatial Mansion from Y. Hirschfeld, *The Palestinian Dwelling in the Roman-Byzantine Period, Studium Biblicum Franciscanum, Collectio Minor 34,* Jerusalem 1995, p. 61, fig. 37, Courtesy of the Israel Exploration Society, Jerusalem.

A luxurious residential area was discovered on Mount Zion. The region was probably heavy populated, and thus, some of the houses probably had two and sometimes even three stories. With respect to this luxurious area, two building phases can be distinguished during the Herodian Period. Remains of water installations – such as cisterns, pools, and *mikwaoth*, some of them constructed, some excavated into bedrock, as well as the remains of masonry – were discovered in the area during the excavations. An important discovery is a fragment of painted stucco depicting a bird on an architectural-floral background of trees, garlands, and buildings. The panel follows the Second Pompeian Style. It is important to emphasize that none of these figures was supposed to be common in the artistic repertoire of the Second Temple Period Jewish population.[60]

---

[60] On the House of Caiaphas see M. Broshi, "Excavations in the House of Caiaphas, Mount Zion," in Y. Yadin (ed.), *Jerusalem Revealed, Archaeology in the Holy City, 1968–1974,* Jerusalem 1976, pp. 57–60.

Based upon comparison of the urban dwellings excavated in the Herodian Quarter, Herodian palaces, and contemporary private dwellings from Roman Italy and the Hellenistic East, it is possible to say that private housing in Herodian Jerusalem presents striking similarities to the Hellenistic East and to Roman Italy, though a native character is still evident. Two types of houses, those showing a more pronounced Greek or Roman influence, and those with a more pronounced native form, are found. Both the houses with Hellenistic-Roman characteristics and those following the native tradition display clear Hellenistic characteristics. Thus, the *oikos*, the reception room, the bathhouse, which obviously included ritual baths, as well as wall paintings and floor mosaics that decorated the bathhouse and the *oikos*, can be found in most of the dwellings. These houses clearly show that the local priestly aristocracy had fully integrated the urban tastes of their contemporaries in Rome and in the Greek East. Their urban mansions had mosaics, frescoes, and plaster ceilings in the most important rooms, and contained baths.

The main difference between the priestly mansions excavated in the Herodian Quarter and the Herodian palaces does not lie in the degree of Hellenization, but in the model chosen. Thus the priestly aristocracy evidently chose an Eastern Mediterranean Greek-Hellenistic model, exemplified by the presence of the *oikos* and the Greek bathhouse. On the other hand, the Herodian palaces incorporate similar elements, but these originated in a Western Mediterranean Romano-Italic environment, such as the Roman bathhouse. Other elements, such as the floor mosaics and the wall paintings, in both cases follow the same source of inspiration, probably dictated by King Herod. Thus in both cases the floor mosaics derive from an Eastern Greek model and follow the Hellenistic tradition. The wall paintings, at first, follow the Eastern First Style, but later, the Pompeian Second and Third Styles are found. This feature is reflected in the small objects used by the owners, such as glass vessels and Terra Sigillata – which were not present during the Hasmonean Period – together with their own local Hasmonean traditions. The Jewish identity of the owners is highlighted by the presence of ritual baths and the use of stone vessels. Ritual baths were not a unique characteristic of the priestly aristocracy and are also found in Herodian palaces, as well as in villages.

As usual, we do not know anything of the more modest urban dwellings of the Jerusalem proletariat. Were these similar to the Roman *insulae*, or housing blocks that were three, four, or five stories high[61]? It appears that that is quite unlikely in this period, at least, since there are no known *insulae* anywhere in the Greek East. Still, the information that archaeology – in addition to the literary sources – pro-

---

[61] In Rome the lower classes lived in *insulae* or multi-story apartment blocks, built around a central courtyard. The ground floor generally housed shops. On the *insulae*, mainly ones found at Ostia, see McKay, *Houses, Villas, and Palaces*, pp. 80–99. See also Connolly, *Classical Athens and Rome*, pp.134–150.

vides on late Second Temple Period Jerusalem serves to emphasize overwhelmingly the degree to which it belongs to the urban Mediterranean World.

4. Conclusions

During the Herodian Period, Judaea began a process of urbanization, starting with Herod's renovation of Jerusalem and continuing with the rebuilding of Caesarea Maritima and Sebaste by Herod's sons, primarily Antipas, who founded Tiberias. Thus the process of urbanization in Herodian Judaea reflected that of the surrounding Classical world.

The Herodian city was quite similar to the other Classical cities, and this designation applies not only to Caesarea Maritima and Sebaste, which were cities with a Gentile population, but also to Jerusalem and Tiberias. All of the physical components of the Classical city, such as the city wall, the Hippodamian grid, the colonnaded street, public buildings such as temples and basilicas, leisure buildings such as bath houses, theatres, and hippodromes, are all found in the Herodian city. However, in the Herodian cities the Roman elements are more prominent than in other parts of the Hellenistic East.

Although it was smaller than Rome, Alexandria, and Ephesus, Jerusalem, in particular, manifests a demographic growth that brings the Herodian cities into the same arena with the most important urban centers of the Classical world. The water system of Jerusalem evolved during the Hasmonean Period following the Hellenistic model of the siphon, and the aqueducts erected by Herod clearly followed a Roman model. In addition, the leisure buildings found in Herodian Jerusalem, such as the bath houses, theatre, and amphitheatre, found their counterparts in the wide Hellenistic Roman world, especially in the Roman world.

The private mansions of the Herodian upper class in Jerusalem present, for the first time, such Mediterranean characteristics as peristyle courtyards, wall paintings, mosaic floors, and Hellenistic baths, although the general layout still follows native trends. In the private domain, however, the influence comes from the Hellenistic East and not from Rome.

It is thus possible to conclude that the Herodian city, no matter where its influences derived from – the East or the West – was a supremely Mediterranean entity.

VIII. Herod's Burial

1. The Death of King Herod

This chapter will discuss King Herod's death, his testament, and his funeral. Herod's funeral and burial followed Jewish, as well as Hellenistic, practices, and his monumental tomb at the Foot of Herodium also accorded with Jewish burial customs of the period under consideration and recalls other Jewish monumental tombs. It seems that Herod also erected a monument in front of Damascus Gate, a monument mentioned by Josephus that closely imitated the shape of Augustus's mausoleum in Rome. Last but not least, this chapter will attempt to resolve the issue of how Herod was buried, whether in a sarcophagus or in an ossuary, the latter being a burial custom that came into vogue during this period. This issue was probably elucidated by the discovery, during excavations during the summer of 2007 at the Lower Herodium, of various fragments of a sarcophagus that Netzer attributes to King Herod.

The last decade of Herod's rule was a rather unhappy one for the king.[1] During these last years, he was physically ill[2] and needed to spend part of his time at the thermal springs of Callirhoe.[3] In fact, his physical suffering was so great that he actually attempted suicide.[4] Because of his physical condition, the old king probably could not devote sufficient time to the affairs of state, and the mental stress that he suffered from, together with his physical pain, resulted in an unbalanced mind. This became clear not only to his more intimate courtiers, but also to his subjects and neighbors, who understood that the Jewish king had gone mad.[5] The historical literature, which is quite hostile to Herod, details peculiar actions attributed to the dying king, and we may posit that his last, disturbed acts clearly stem from his mental state, rather than from his allegedly cruel character. For example, according to Josephus,[6] Herod called Salome and Alexas and ordered his soldiers to jail a multitude "of illustrious men coming from every village" in

---

[1] On the last years of Herod's rule see Josephus, *AJ* XVI, 356–404 and XVII, 1–192 and *BJ* I, 552–665.

[2] See Josephus, *AJ* XVII, 146.

[3] See Josephus, *AJ* XVII, 168–172. See also *BJ* I, 656–658.

[4] See Josephus, *AJ* XVII, 183–184.

[5] Sartre reports a Safaitic inscription "the year that Herod went mad." See Sartre, *Alexandre à Zénobie*, p. 784.

[6] See Josephus, *AJ* XVII, 175–180, 193 and *BJ* I, 659–660, 666.

the hippodrome of Jericho. Once his death was announced to the multitude, the soldiers were instructed to execute the people who had been assembled there by shooting them with arrows. Herod thus intended that his funeral would be remembered by an impressive act of public mourning. Instead of rejoicing at the king's death, the populace would mourn, if not for the king, at least for those who had been executed in the hippodrome. Once the king was dead, however, Salome and Alexas freed the prisoners and dismissed the soldiers. Is this story true? Probably not, since the episode appears to be too much like a *topos*. In fact it seems far too similar to the episode described in the Fourth Book of Maccabees, when the Jews of Alexandria were jailed in the hippodrome, to be trampled by elephants under order of Ptolemy IV. A miracle saved them, just as the Jews jailed in the hippodrome of Jericho were saved by the intervention of Salome and Alexas. Josephus is not alone in reporting a cruel command issued by a dying king.

Another instance of Herod's insanity before his death is Matthew's description of the slaughter of the innocents, or the slaying of infants.[7] Last but not least, Megillath Ta'anith reports the day of Herod's death as a day of rejoicing, because the king had hated the sages. The *scholium*, in fact, calls the king "a murder of sages." According to Noam, the *scholium* refers to the affair of the eagle and the successive execution of Judas and Matthias, rather than to the planned mass murder in the hippodrome of Jericho.[8] The truth is probably that Herod did not jail anyone in the hippodrome, nor did he give orders for the slaying of the infants. All of these actions are *topoi* intended to illustrate the tyrant's extreme and radical actions. Had Herod indeed ordered something like the execution in the hippodrome or the slaughter of the innocents, all known sources would have reported it. Instead, each source reports a different episode or event.

To the visible relief of his subjects, the old king died in 4 BCE,[9] probably somewhere between the second half of March and the beginning of April.[10]

---

[7] See Matt 2, 16–18.

[8] See Noam, *Megillat Ta'anit*, p. 261. See also Josephus, *AJ* XVII, 149–167 and *BJ* I, 648–655.

[9] Of what did Herod die? The symptoms are described in detail by Josephus: muscular weakness; mild fever; intolerable itch over the entire body; strong pains in the colon from ulcerations of the entrails; transparent swellings around the feet as in dropsy; malignancy in the abdominal area; putrefaction of the phallus, thereby creating worms; orthopnea or difficulty breathing; disagreeable breath; dyspnea or frequent gasping; spasms in all limbs, of unendurable force; fainting and turning the eyes up as though dead when immersed in warm oil; melancholy and enragement; inability to take food due to overpowering pains; sustained convulsions; cough; and attempted suicide. Modern diagnoses propose various possibilities, such as poisoning, cardio-renal failure, liver cirrhosis, sexually transmitted disease, cancer of the bowels, diabetes mellitus, cancer of the pancreas, amoebic dysentery. See N. Kokkinos, "Herod's Horrid Death", *BAR* 28, 2, 2002, pp. 28–35. According to Dr. Jan Hirshmann, Herod died of chronic kidney disease complicated by a rare form of genital gangrene called Fournier's gangrene.

[10] See Josephus, *AJ* XVII 213 and *BJ* II, 10.

1. The Death of King Herod

Did Herod's subjects rejoice upon their ruler's death? Josephus is silent on this subject. According to Josephus, both the people and the soldiers acclaimed Archelaus king and promised him their goodwill,[11] but celebrating the advent of a new king is still a far cry from rejoicing at the death of his predecessor. On the other hand, the Hebrew *scholium* of Megillath Ta'anith is positive on the subject. There is, however, a problem, since the information provided by Josephus and that which is furnished by Megillath Ta'anit do not correspond.[12] It seems to me that royal subjects who had not been personally wronged would have had no motive to rejoice at Herod's death. On the contrary, times had been good under the old king, and the future was unclear. Most of Herod's subjects probably mourned their king sincerely, as evidenced by the fact that his funeral procession was not disturbed by any incidents. Herod left behind an extensive kingdom that was faced with political uncertainty, despite its strong economy. As we know, his

---

[11] See Josephus, *BJ* I, 670. However *AJ* XVII, 195 reports only the soldiers' acclamation, not that of the multitude.

[12] Is Herod's death reported in *Megillath Ta'anit* as a holiday? Accordingly, Herod's death must be celebrated on the seventh of Kislev. This is a holiday because Herod hated Israel (the second of Shevath is likewise a holiday because of King Alexander Jannaeus' death). In the Aramaic text the seventh of Kislev is mentioned as a holiday. According to the Hebrew *scholium*, it commemorates the death of Herod. It is important to add that in the Aramaic text another day of rejoicing appears: the second of Shevath. According to the Hebrew *scholium* it commemorates the death of Alexander Jannaeus. However as indicated above, Josephus in *AJ* XVII, 213 and *BJ* II, 10 reports that Herod died not long before Passover, as Archelaus after seven days of mourning prepared the Temple for Passover. According to Graetz, the Hebrew *scholium* switched the dates of Alexander Jannaeus' and Herod's deaths. But there still remain ten weeks before Passover. According to Zeitlin, the seventh of Kislev is too far away. Zeitlin stresses that Josephus, in *AJ* XVII, 167 reports that not long before Herod's death there was an eclipse of the Moon. In 4 BCE it fell between March 12-13. Passover was on April 11. Thus, Herod died between 13 March and April 4. According to Zeitlin, *Megillat Ta'anit* thus commemorates another event. See I. Zeitlin, *Megillat Taanit as a source for Jewish Chronology and History in the Hellenistic and Roman Periods*, Ph.D. Thesis, Philadelphia 1922, pp. 100–101. See also Noam, *Megillat Ta'anit*, pp. 260–261, where Noam brings alternative events, such as the death of Antiochus Eupator, or the beginning of the Hasmonean rebellion at Modi'in. The problem of the eclipse is quite relevant, according to D. Schwartz. Although D. Schwartz stresses not one, as it appears from Josephus's reading, but two eclipses, the first and more impressive around the Day of Atonement of 5 BCE, the night between the 15 and 16 of September 5 BCE Josephus mentions this eclipse in *AJ* XVII, 167. The second eclipse occurred before Passover, the night between the 12 and 13 of March 4 BCE Schwartz nonetheless accepts the date of Herod's death between the second half of March and the beginning of April. The date of Passover was the night between the 12 and 13 of April 4 BCE Josephus then reports in *AJ* XVII, 213 ff. and *BJ* II, 100 ff. riots that occurred during Passover, following Herod's death. Thus, it is clear that Herod died before Passover. According to Schürer, Herod died between the eclipse of March 13 and mid April (Passover). Schwartz stresses that the eclipse of September was so impressive that Herod, thinking it a bad omen, had the high priest, Joseph son of Ellemus, disqualified and dismissed on the Day of Atonement. See also D. Schwartz, "Joseph Ben Illem and the Date of Herod's Death", in D. Schwartz (ed.), *Studies in the Jewish Background of Christianity*, WUNT 60, Tübingen 1992, pp. 156–167. Moreover the *scholium* is not clear as to whether of Herod's subjects rejoiced of his death, or if this was an *a posteriori* celebration.

realm erupted once more in civil unrest that necessitated the intervention of the Romans.[13] In retrospect, it is obvious that the king's last years left his subjects with bad memories, and his rule, which for the most part had been positive, was judged by posterity in a negative light. Moreover, both the civil unrest and the short unhappy reign of Herod's successor, Archelaus, contributed significantly to strengthening the unhappy recollection of the last years of his rule, and that memory somehow extended to Herod's entire reign.

2. The Burial of King Herod

A. Herod's Funeral

Josephus describes the funeral procession of King Herod in detail in both *War* and *Antiquities*, with minor differences.[14] The first part of the impressive ceremony was the reading of the king's testament. Ptolemy, who was the king's seal-bearer, was the only possible candidate for reading the testament. However, the king's prime minister argued that the king's testament was merely an expression of his wishes and that it was necessary to await Augustus' sanction, since only upon the Roman ruler's approval could the royal testament be enforced. There were two good reasons for this situation. First, as a Roman citizen, Herod was *cliens* of Augustus, and second, he was *socius et amicus populi romani*. After the reading of the testament, only Archelaus was acclaimed as Herod's successor, and not Antipas and Philip as well, since Archelaus appears to have been in a hurry and did not wish to wait for the emperor's fiat. Moreover, Herod had died in Jericho,[15] and Archelaus appears to have had the body brought to Jerusalem, the future capital of the part of the kingdom bequeathed to him. The soldiers stationed there were Archelaus' men and were not under his two brothers' command. The soldiers, who were divided into units, promised goodwill to the new king and the same readiness to serve him as they had formerly demonstrated to Herod. The acclamation was concluded with a prayer to God to assist the new ruler. This combination of Macedonian military acclamation and Jewish prayer is noteworthy and may have been a tradition going back to the last Hasmonean rulers. The acclamation was followed by the funeral procession, probably at the main palace in Jerusalem, where the king took his last breath. From there, it passed through the main gate of the Second Wall, the same spot where Herod had had his cenotaph erected. From Jerusalem the procession arrived at Herodium, which Herod had selected because it was the site where his royal adventure had

---

[13] See Josephus, *AJ* XVII, 206–298.
[14] See Josephus, *AJ* XVII, 195–200 and *BJ* I, 667–673.
[15] See Josephus, *AJ* XVII, 173 and *BJ* I, 659.

begun in 40 BCE, with the suicide of his brother.[16] The king was buried in a monumental tomb at the foot of the fortress.

Josephus describes the funeral procession in detail. The king's body was draped in purple and carried on a golden bier studded with precious stones. He wore a diadem and a crown of gold, and a scepter was placed in his right hand. Herod's sons and relatives followed the bier, with the entire army, divided according to units, behind them. Among these, first came the entire royal bodyguard with the picturesque foreign mercenaries in their exotic attire – the Thracians, Germans and Galatians – followed by the rest of the army. Five hundred servants carrying spices followed the army. Although the body was immediately buried, according to Jewish Law,[17] and hence there was no foul odor of decomposition that needed to be covered up, the burning spices, as part of the trappings of royal pomp, added an aura of solemnity. The funeral procession paraded on the grounds of the stadium in front of Herodium.

The funeral of Herod did not end with the sealing of the Tomb and the dispersion of the procession, however. Archelaus, the main heir, mourned his father until the seventh day after his death, in accordance with Jewish law. Once again, however, Macedonian and Jewish traditions were combined. Josephus' description shows in detail the extent to which a Jewish king behaved like a Hellenistic ruler, heir to Alexander the Great, and to what degree Jewish law was observed. The reading of the testament and the funeral procession clearly follow a Hellenistic model. For the kings of Macedonia and Pergamum, as well as for the Seleucids and Ptolemies, royal funerals probably followed a similar pattern. Herod's funeral procession was modeled on the funeral procession of Alexander the Great, replicating it in considerable detail, which comes as no surprise, since Herod the Great saw himself as the last of Alexander's Diadochi, which in fact he was. Curtius Rufus describes the last moments of Alexander, which bear a similarity to the last moments of Herod. The only difference is that no funeral games were prepared for Herod,[18] or perhaps Josephus simply neglected to mention them. Jewish law did not forbid such games, but perhaps Archelaus did not allow them to take place. The funeral procession itself imitated the funeral procession of Alexander the Great from Babylonia to Alexandria, as confirmed

---

[16] See Josephus *AJ* XIV, 365, 367, 369, 371, 379 and *BJ* I, 271–272, 274–275, 418 on Phasael's death, and XVI, 144 on the monument erected by Herod on the spot.

[17] On mourning in Jewish Law in the Second Temple Period and later the best reference is the tractate *Semahoth*, a collection of baraithoth dealing with the law of mourning compiled by R. Eliezer Ben Zadok. In this tractate are discussed *ossilegium* as well as the use of coffins, funerary practices that were common in the late Second Temple Period. See *Sem.* IV, 4, 19, V, 1 and VI–VII on laws of mourning, and IX on the custom of rending his own garments as emblematic of mourning. On burning articles at the funeral of kings see *Sem.* VIII, 5–6.

[18] See Curtius Rufus, *History of Alexander* X. Curtius describes the last moments of Alexander.

by Diodorus Siculus' detailed description of a ceremony quite similar to Herod's funeral procession.[19]

Nonetheless, Herod was a Jewish ruler and his funeral strictly followed Jewish Law. First, the body was buried as soon as possible and did not lie in state. Any other Hellenistic dynast's body would have been left exposed on his bier for some days, so that his family, courtiers, and soldiers could have paid their last respects, as in the case of Alexander the Great. Second, as we shall see, Herod was buried in a Jewish tomb, and sacrifices were not offered to his soul. Finally, his first heir, Archelaus, mourned his father for seven days, in accordance with Jewish law. Herod thus died as he had ruled, following both Jewish and Hellenistic-Macedonian traditions.

B. *Herod's Tomb*

As indicated above, Herod's attitude towards life was reflected in his death. Two monumental buildings epitomized his ideology: Herod's Tomb at Herodium and Herod's *cenotaphium* in Jerusalem. Herod was buried in a monumental tomb at the foot of Upper Herodium that was very similar to contemporary monumental tombs in Jerusalem. However, the *cenotaphium* facing today's Damascus Gate stood as a clear exception among the panorama of funerary buildings in Herodian Judaea, since it was a clear imitation of Augustus' mausoleum in Rome and probably a final gesture of homage, on Herod's part, to the Roman Empire.

According to Netzer, Herod was buried in a typical Jewish tomb at the foot of Herodium, near the spot where his brother Phasael committed suicide and where Herod, suddenly alone, embarked on his royal career (cfr. figure VIII, 1). According to Netzer, there are two elements that identify the spot as Herod's monumental tomb: the open area and the remains of a monumental building facing it in Lower Herodium. The open area, similar to a hippodrome, was the same spot used for Herod's funeral procession. The building, a rectangular structure made of hewn stone, faced this area and was oriented along the same axis. The façade probably consisted of a Doric style *distyle in antis*, topped by a pyramid. The inner part of the building was decorated with niches faced by Corinthian columns standing on pilasters. The interior walls were probably covered by frescoes, and the ceiling was covered in stucco decoration. A *mikweh* stood in front of the tomb. Since no tomb was discovered inside, it probably lay underground.[20]

---

[19] Diodorus Siculus, *History* XVIII, 26–28 gives an accurate description. See also R. Lane Fox, *Alexander the Great*, Harmondsworth 1987, pp. 477–478.

[20] This open area, located in the Lower Herodium, consisted of a surface that measured 350 × 30 m. The remains of a Doric architrave, consisting of a triglyph and a metope decorated with a relief depicting a rosette with sixteen petals were essential in reconstructing the monumental façade and in confirming the nature of the building. See Netzer, *Palaces of the Hasmoneans and*

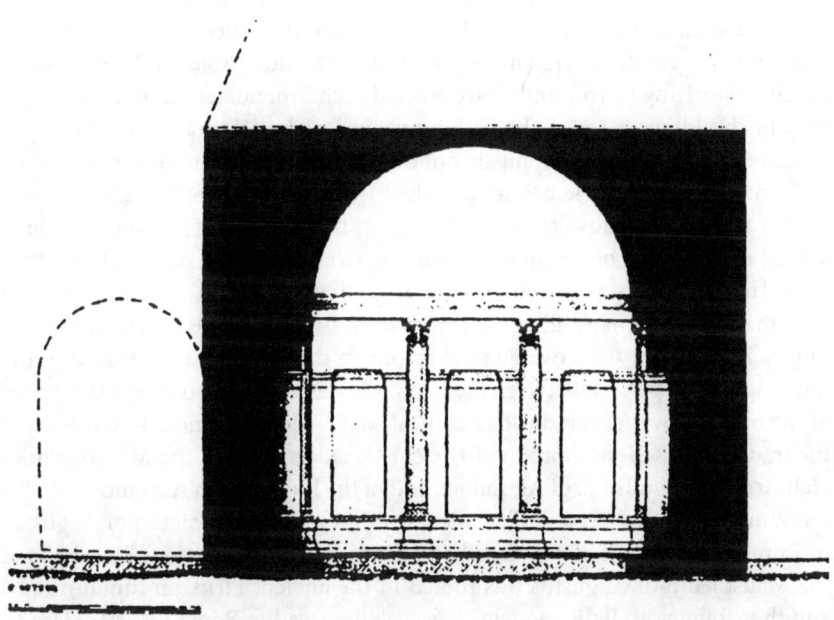

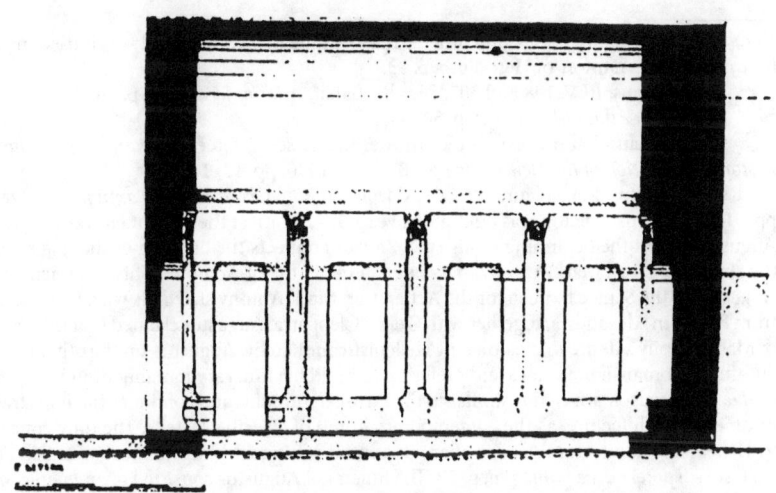

Figure VIII, 1 – Herod's Tomb in the Lower Herodium from E. Netzer, *The Palaces of the Hasmonaeans and Herod the Great*, Jerusalem 2001, p. 115, fig. 151, Courtesy of Professor Emeritus Ehud Netzer, The Hebrew University of Jerusalem.

Josephus mentions a monument,[21] which stood 250 m. north of the Damascus Gate. The remains of this structure in *opus reticulatum*, which points to the Herodian Period, were discovered in 1879 by Konrad Schick. Professor Netzer points out that only King Herod could have erected such a monumental structure, since only his buildings, such as the bath house in Jericho III, make use of an *opus reticulatum*. Moreover Josephus is quite clear that the monument was erected by Herod, calling it "Mnemeion." Clearly it was not a tomb, but its shape was so similar to that of a mausoleum that it suggests the function of a cenotaph, which served the purpose of reminding future generations of the might of the dead king. The cenotaph was a circular structure with two peripheral walls, one inside the other. The internal walls were constructed using the *opus reticulatum* technique. The exterior was covered in cut stone in the style commonly used in the buildings of the period. Between the two walls was a vaulted roof, and the center of the building was covered with a conical roof.[22] Herod's cenotaph was built in the tradition of self-celebration of Hellenistic rulers, such as the Mausoleum of Halicarnassus, the Tomb of Alexander, and of the Ptolemies in Alexandria.[23] This monument was also very similar in conception to the Mausoleum of Augustus in Rome.[24] There was, however, a basic difference in conception. The shape of the Mausoleum of Augustus was rooted in the ancient Etruscan tumuli-tombs and thus follows an Italic model that was widespread in Roman Italy.[25] Herod's building, a copy of a Roman sepulchral structure, does not fit the panorama of Jewish monumental tombs at the beginning of the Common Era. Herod's building was, then, an imitation of a Roman structure, alien to its surroundings, a final symbol of his admiration of Roman culture. Like the funeral and burial

---

Herod the Great, pp. 105–108. Still other scholars argue that King Herod was buried inside the base of the eastern tower of Herodium, p. 33.

[21] See Josephus, *BJ* V, 108 and 507. See also Bahat, *Atlas of Jerusalem*, p. 50.

[22] See Bahat, *Atlas of Jerusalem*, p. 50.

[23] On the mausoleum of Alexander in Alexandria see P. Green, *Alexander to Actium, The Historical Evolution of the Hellenistic Age*, Berkeley 1990, pp. 13–14.

[24] On Augustus' Mausoleum see C. A. Carpiceci, *Roma, com'era 2000 anni fa*, Firenze 1981, pp. 91–93. The mausoleum was built in the years 32–28 BCE at the peak of Herod's reign, when Augustus was at the beginning of his rule. Zanker connects the building of the mausoleum to the struggle against Mark Antony that ended in the Battle of Actium. In his testament, read by Augustus to the Senate to push for the Actian war, Mark Antony stated his wish to be buried far from Rome, in Alexandria, together with Queen Cleopatra. Augustus claimed that this was proof of Mark Antony's desire to create a new Hellenistic monarchy. Augustus, on the other hand, was faithful to Roman-Italic values and preferred to build his funerary monument in Rome, as *dux Italiae*. The mausoleum is thus similar to the Etruscan tumulus and continues the Italic tradition in funerary architecture, as the contemporary Tomb of Caecilia Metella. The only concessions to Hellenistic architectural tradition are its central setting and huge dimensions. See Zanker, *Augusto e il potere delle immagini*, p. 79. The funeral of Augustus consisted of an *apotheosis*. The apotheosis of Augustus is described by Suetonius, *Augustus* II, C. It is also described in detail by Dio Cassius in the *Roman History* LVI 34, 42–43. According to Dio, Numerius a Roman senator was rewarded because he swore that he had seen Augustus ascending to heaven.

[25] See on tumuli H. Von Hesberg, *Roemischen Grabbauten*, Darmstadt 1992, pp. 94–113.

of Herod, which presented Hellenistic-Macedonian elements mixed with Jewish tradition, Augustus' funeral and burial followed both a native Romano-Italic tradition tempered with Hellenistic elements. Both were inspired by the world of Hellenistic kingship. Even in death, both Herod and Augustus followed in the footsteps of Alexander the Great, whose vision unified the entire Mediterranean and the East. However, while the East slowly escaped from the embrace of Greek civilization, the Mediterranean did not, and both Herodian Judaea and Augustan Rome were Mediterranean countries.

C. Herod's Burial. Sarcophagus or Ossuary?

It is clear then that Herod's monumental tomb at the foot of Herodium reflected a common practice among the upper classes in Judaea. But, how was King Herod buried, in a sarcophagus or in an ossuary? Although King Herod was buried in a sarcophagus, during the last years of his reign a new trend in burial customs developed, namely the use of ossuaries. The Jews living in Judaea during the Hasmonean Period continued earlier burial traditions that dated back to the First Temple Period. As in earlier periods, the remains of the deceased were deposited in a burial chamber, and after decomposition of the flesh, the remains were transferred to a large communal charnel.[26] The first step in the evolution of Jewish burial customs was the introduction in Hasmonean Judaea of burial in *loculi* or *kochim*.[27] This type of burial, present in the Tomb of Jason, may be a reflection of Sadducee ideology.[28] The Sadducee denial of physical resurrection was not a total denial of the survival of the individual's soul after death. Thus, to-

---

[26] See L. Y. Rahmani, "Ossuaries and Ossilegium (Bone Gathering) in the Second Temple Period", in H. Geva (ed.), *Ancient Jerusalem Revealed, Expanded Edition 2000*, Jerusalem 2000, p. 193.

[27] This burial custom began in Ptolemaic Alexandria, spread from there to Marissa in the third century BCE and then to Jerusalem at the end of the third century or at the beginning of the second century BCE. Jason's Tomb in Jerusalem presents the use of *kochim*. In m., *B. Bat.*, 6, 8, are given the ideal proportions of the *kochim*. In most of the *kochim* tombs, after a year's time, "12 *yerachim*" in Mishna vocabulary, the bones of the deceased were gathered from the *koch* and deposited individually on the pavement of another room, as in Jason's Tomb, used as repository. See A. Kloner, "Burial Customs of the Jews at the time of the Hasmoneans", *In the Days of the Hasmoneans*, Jerusalem 1995, pp. 214–215.

[28] According to Josephus and other sources, the Sadducees had no belief in life after death, since it had no scriptural foundation. Thus, there was no need for an individual burial of the body of the deceased. On the contrary, the impressive façades of the tombs and the inscriptions, such as the one of the Tomb of Bene Hezir, reflect a strong materialistic view. The only tangible evidence of a man after he departed from his world was his deeds in life. Thus, a burial monument that would immortalize those deeds through its opulence and through an inscription that would remind the passerby of the deeds of the deceased is the best guarantee of immortality. To be immortal is thus to be remembered forever. See m. *Sanh.* 10: 1; Josephus, *BJ* II, 165; Matt 22–23, Luke 20: 27; BT, *Sanh.* 4b. See also Rahmani, "Ossuaries and Ossilegium", p. 193.

ward the end of the Hasmonean Period, the custom of burying the dead in coffins developed. Wooden coffins, sometimes decorated, were found both at ʿEn Gedi and Jericho and are dated to the Hasmonean Period. In Jericho such coffins were used for individual primary burial, while in ʿEn Gedi it appears that they sometimes contained more than one individual, the later inhumations probably being those of individuals related to the first person who had been interred. According to Barag, those buried in the coffins found at ʿEn Gedi were recently converted Idumaeans who probably still maintained their native burial customs.[29] The best parallel to the coffins found at ʿEn Gedi are those that were excavated at the Abusir necropolis in Ptolemaic Egypt from 1902 to 1904 by Watzinger, which are dated to the beginning of the Hellenistic Period.[30]

During the Herodian Period, the wooden coffins evolved into beautiful stone sarcophagi, evidently inspired by those of Augustan Rome. These sarcophagi made use of similar elements, including the use of local stone and the shape of the sarcophagus itself and of the generally vaulted lid and decoration, when present. The decoration generally consisted of reliefs depicting a row of rosettes repeated on the lid. A particularly beautiful sarcophagus from the Tomb of the Nazirite depicts spreading leaves of acanthus intermingled with vines and bunches of grapes, a motif commonly found on the sarcophagi of Augustan Rome. Plain and decorated sarcophagi were found in the Herod's Family Tomb, the Tomb of the Kings, the Tomb of the Nazirite, and the Tomb of Nicanor. Other sarcophagi dating from this period were found out of context.[31] The stone sarcophagi from Herodian Jerusalem are quite similar to contemporary sarcophagi from Augustan Rome. The sarcophagi from both Jerusalem and Rome display the use of a frame all along the long side of the coffin and the use of relief decoration, including many similar elements, such as the use of rosettes and acanthus leaves. Another characteristic motif appearing on the Roman sarcophagi of the Augustan Period

---

[29] On the late Hasmonean coffins from ʿEn Gedi see G. Hadas, "Nine Tombs of the Second Temple Period at ʿEn Gedi", ʿAtiqot 24, Jerusalem, 1994. See also B. Mazar, "ʿEn Gedi – The First and Second Season of Excavations, 1961–1962", Atiqot 5, 1966, p. 5, and N. Avigad, "Expedition A – Nahal David", IEJ 12, 1962, pp. 182–183. The dead were evidently brought into the cemetery inside the coffins. See TJ, Ber. 3, 6 b, and Naz. 7, 56 c describe coffin bearers. On the Jericho wooden coffins see R. Hachlili, "A Second Temple Period Necropolis in Jericho", BA 43, 1980, p. 235, and R. Hachlili, "Jewish Funerary Customs during the Second Temple Period in Light of the Excavations of the Jericho Necropolis", PEQ 115, 1983, pp. 110–125.

[30] See C. Watzinger, Griechische Holzsarkophage aus der Zeit Alexanders des Grossen, Ausgrabungen der Deutschen Orient Gesellschaft, Leipzig 1905, pp. 24–38.

[31] The sarcophagus from Queen Helena's Tomb is today in the Louvre Museum. See L. Y. Rahmani, "Sarcophagi of the Late Second Temple Period in Secondary Use", in H. Geva (ed.), Ancient Jerusalem Revealed, Expanded Edition 2000, Jerusalem 2000, pp. 232–234. Two sarcophagi were found in the Tomb of the Nazirite. See Avigad, "Architecture of Jerusalem in the Second Temple Period", pp. 66–67. Also in the Tomb of Nicanor two sarcophagi were found. See Rahmani, "Sarcophagi of the Late Second Temple Period", pp. 232–234. On these sarcophagi out of context see Rahmani, "Sarcophagi of the Late Second Temple Period", pp. 232–234.

are *bucrania* between flanking garlands, though this motif was too pagan to be used on Jewish sarcophagi from Judaea.[32]

Toward the end of the reign of Herod, a new method of inhumation appeared in Judaea – the ossuary – which quickly spread to all of the Jewish areas of the kingdom and was found side by side with sarcophagi, although, soon enough, ossuaries clearly predominated. This method of interring the dead remained in use through the end of the Second Temple Period in Jerusalem, but in Southern Judaea and in Galilee ossuaries were still in use at the beginning of the second century ce and at the beginning of the third century CE.[33] Why the ossuary as a burial practice supplanted the sarcophagus is not clear. After years of researching this subject, Kloner is still not sure what brought this new fashion into vogue. According to Rachmani, the use of ossuaries was theologically motivated by the belief in physical resurrection described in the Book of Ezekiel. According to Greenberg, however, it is not certain whether the relevant passage of Ezekiel was seen in early Jewish exegesis as a literal resurrection of the dead or merely as a vision or parable.[34] It may not, therefore, have been the theological justification for the introduction of ossuaries. Other scholars, such as Rubin, connect this new practice to the demographic expansion of Jerusalem in the late first century BCE and the first century CE, since most of the ossuaries date from 40–30 BCE, until the time of the destruction of the city in 70 CE. According to Rubin, the ossuaries were widespread in Jerusalem because they were a less expensive burial practice

---

[32] On Roman sarcophagi from the Augustan period see G. Koch and H. Sichtermann, *Römische Sarkophage, Handbuch der Archäologie*, München 1982, pp. 36–41. There are at least four sarcophagi decorated with a framed relief on the long side, the Sarcophagus Caffarelli at Berlin (N. 3), the sarcophagus from Ariccia (N. 7), the sarcophagus from Ostia Antica (N. 8), and the sarcophagus from Pisa (N. 10).

[33] See Rahmani, *Ossuaries and Ossilegium*, p. 195.

[34] In the Hasmonean period, the physical resurrection of the body as well as that of the soul became part of Jewish beliefs on the netherworld. See 2 Macc. 7, 9–23 and 14, 46, the woman's speech to her sons. According to the woman, the wicked will have no part in the resurrection of the body. See also the 2 Macc. 12, 39–45, which reports Judas Maccabaeus's speech to his troops. According to Rachmani, this idea was still present much later and, it seems, mainly among the Pharisees. Thus only at the end of the Herodian period, or more probably afterwards, the Pharisees, whose creed already included the belief in the afterlife (Josephus, *AJ* XVIII, 14) also stressed the physical resurrection of the body as part of their doctrinaire beliefs. Their source of inspiration was, according to Rachmani, the Vision of Ezekiel (37: 1–14). It was in the last years of the Second Temple period that the Book of Ezekiel definitively entered the Jewish canon, with the encouragement of the School of Hillel. See Rahmani, *Ossuaries and Ossilegium*, p. 192. Greenberg stresses that the earliest Jewish exegesis interpreted Ezek 37: 1–14 not as the depiction of a literal resurrection of the dead, but according to R. Eliezer (BT, *Sanh.* 92b) as a vision, or according to R. Judah (BT, *B. Bat.* 15a) a parable. Thus according to both exegeses it is not a narrative of reality. See M. Greenberg, *Ezekiel, The Anchor Bible* I–II, New York 1983, p. 3 (I), and pp. 749–751 (II). Today this passage is seen as a parable of the restoration of Israel. According to Josephus, *AJ* X, 79 Ezekiel wrote two books. Greenberg points out that the book can be divided in two parts, the first dedicated to prophecy of doom, and the second to visions of consolation.

than the sarcophagi, which necessitated digging a new burial chamber or an entire *loculus*.[35] It is quite possible, though not certain, that the practice of burial in ossuaries or *ossilegium* was first developed among the Pharisees, or at least was first accepted by them. Later Rabbinic sources analyze it in depth. It was so widespread toward the end of the Second Temple Period that it is obvious that not only Pharisees, but also Sadducees and Jews not belonging to any particular sect, used *ossilegium*.[36]

The *ossilegium*, described in the Mishna, consisted of secondary burial. The body of the deceased was brought to his tomb and was deposited on a bench under an *arcosolium*. There the body was left to decay for an entire year. After this period, a member of the family, generally one of the sons, came to gather the bones and put them in an ossuary. The ossuary was then closed and deposited in a *loculus* or *koch*. It seems that the same ossuary was sometimes used for gathering the bones of more than one individual, evidently including the bones of close relatives.[37] Ossuaries are found in family tombs in a special chamber, often in the hindmost and lowest chamber.[38] The rectangular ossuaries were generally produced using local limestone. Although most of the ossuaries were undecorated, some were ornamented, the most common decorative pattern being a central triglyph with two flanking rosettes. Some of the ossuaries bear the name of the deceased in Hebrew, Aramaic, and sometimes Greek.[39] It should be emphasized

---

[35] See N. Rubin, "Secondary Burials in the Mishnaic and Talmudic Periods: A Proposed Model of the Relationship of Social Structure to Burial Practice", in I. Singer (ed.), *Graves and Burial Practices in Israel in the Ancient Period*, Jerusalem 1994, pp. 248–269. Rubin's article is mainly anthropological. However Rubin also points to the burial of two persons in the same ossuary as originating in a problem of space. See pp. 262–264 and pp. 267–268.

[36] According to Rabbi Akiva, the judgment of the unrighteous in the Gehenna shall endure twelve months, see m., *Nez.* 2, 10. See Rahmani, "Ossuaries and Ossilegium", p. 194. A very good example of an ossuary used by a Sadducee is the ossuary that probably belonged to Caiaphas, the archetype of the Sadducee high priest in the New Testament. See L. Z. Greenhut, "The Caiaphas Tomb in Northern Talpioth", in H. Geva (ed.), *Ancient Jerusalem Revealed, Expanded Edition 2000*, Jerusalem 2000, pp. 219–222.

[37] Ossilegium is described in the m., *Sanh.* 6, 5–6. The disintegration of the sinner's body is the condition a priori for physical resurrection, See BT, *Sanh.* 47 b, BT, *Šabb.* 152 a, BT, *Roš Haš.*17 a. After this period, the bones can be collected and the deceased can rest, see *Sem.t* 12, 7, 9. It seems that the son collected the bones of his own father and put them in the ossuary. Thus, according to Rabbi Meir "It's a day of joy for a man to collect the bones of his father and mother;" see JT, *Môed Qaṭ.* 1, 5; 80 c. See Rahmani, "Ossuaries and Ossilegium," p. 194.

[38] See Rahmani, "Ossuaries and Ossilegium," p. 195.

[39] The ossuaries' chronology must be divided according to the centers of production. At Jerusalem the peak of production was from 20 BCE to 70 CE, at Jericho, from 5–10 CE to 70 CE. In the surroundings of Jerusalem, production continued till 135 CE. This is a carved inscription, most often in Hebrew or Aramaic, using Hebrew square characters. However some inscriptions are in Greek, and some in both Hebrew and Greek. See Rahmani, "Ossuaries and Ossilegium". On the ossuary and its ornamentation, see pp. 196–197. On the motifs of ossuary ornamentation, see pp. 198–203. There were geometric rosettes, gabled entrance (*nefesh* of the Tomb), palm trees, Ionic columns, amphorae, ashlar motifs. See also L. Y. Rachmani, *A Catalogue of Jewish Ossuaries, in the Collections of the State of Israel*, Jerusalem 1994.

that ossuaries, like sarcophagi, were part of a common tradition in the Mediterranean world. Greeks and Romans mainly incinerated their dead, in a tradition going back to the earlier periods of Greek history. Homer's heroes, for example, were burned on a funeral pyre. In Roman Italy the Villanovians incinerated their bodies. Both in Greece and Rome a burial tradition was developed whereby the ashes were deposed in a small box, called *larnax* in the Greek world[40] and *urna* in the Roman West. Thus, during the Herodian Period, the custom of burying the ashes of the dead in boxes, or *urnae*, was still widespread in Rhodes, in the Greek East, and in Roman Italy, particularly in Rome and Etruria. There are various ossuaries from Herodian Judaea that show a clear similarity to Roman *urnae* of the Augustan Period. The best example is an ossuary found on Mount Scopus, belonging to "Joseph son of Hananiah the scribe," according to the inscription. The ossuary is decorated with reliefs, like the *urnae* of Rome.[41] Moreover, the ornamentation itself – acanthus flowers, clusters of grapes, and rosettes – reflects similar sculpted decoration on *urnae* from Rome.[42] Other examples of ossuaries imitating Roman *urnae* are decorated as if they were small houses or palaces. There is, for example, an ossuary depicting an Ionic portico on its front side panel. Another ossuary, whose front side panel is shaped like a palace façade or, more probably, like a theatre, is decorated with gates-niches topped by alternating arched or triangular pediments.[43] The arched lid is shaped like the roof of a building. There are *urnae* from Augustan Rome shaped like palaces or houses, sometimes with the lid modeled like a tiled roof.[44]

The burial practices current in Rome did not fully reflect the various trends of Roman Italy. An interesting example is Volterra, an Etruscan city where the local aristocracy continued to bury their dead in cinerary urns that continued an artistic tradition dating back to the Hellenistic Period. Cinerary urns, decorated with reliefs depicting episodes from Greek mythology, mainly the Trojan War, continued during the Augustan Period. It is probable that Maecenas's Etruscan

---

[40] The Greeks had other slightly different ways of disposing of the ashes of their dead. In the Geometric period, amphorae were used as ash repositories (also sometimes by the Villanovians). In Hellenistic Alexandria the so-called Hadria vases, shaped as *hydriai* were used as ashes repositories. The most beautiful example of a *larnax* is the golden box decorated with the Argead six-pointed star found in the Tomb of Philip II at Vergina. On the golden *larnax* see M. Andronikos, *Vergina, The Royal Tombs and the Ancient City*, Athens 1989, pp. 166–167, fig. 135, and p. 169, fig. 136.

[41] See V. Susman, "A Jewish Burial Cave on Mount Scopus", in H. Geva (ed.), *Ancient Jerusalem Revealed, Expanded Edition 2000*, Jerusalem 2000, pp. 226–230.

[42] There are three good examples of Roman *urnae*, decorated in relief with acanthus leaves, clusters of grapes and rosettes, from the Augustan period found in Roman Italy. An *urna* from Vercelli (N. 16), an *urna*, today at Hever Castle (N. 21) and a *urna* from the Palazzo dei Conservatori at Rome (N. 29). See Koch and Sichtermann, *Römische Sarkophage*, pp. 41–58.

[43] See A. Kloner, "An Ossuary from Jerusalem Ornamented with Monumental Facades", in Geva, H. (ed.), *Ancient Jerusalem Revealed, Expanded Edition 2000*, Jerusalem 2000, pp. 235–238.

[44] See Koch and Sichtermann, *Römische Sarkophage*, pp. 41–58.

family, for example, was buried in this type of urn.[45] Thus, during the Augustan Period there was no such a thing as a single Roman funerary custom that prevailed throughout Roman Italy, nor was there was such a thing as a single Greek burial custom. Greeks, widespread in the eastern Mediterranean, incinerated their dead. Afterward, the ashes were buried under a gravestone painted or decorated in relief – as in Attica, in continental Greece, and in Asia Minor – or in a vase – as in Alexandria – or in funerary urns – as in Rhodes.

The burial customs of Judaea must therefore be seen and understood in perspective.[46] What is really Jewish is the fact that the body of the deceased was not burned, rather than the use of ossuaries. The Jews, who were forbidden by their tradition to incinerate their dead, adopted the burial custom of *ossilegium*, as well as a repository, the ossuary, very similar to the Roman *urnae*. Is there a connection *a priori* between Jewish *ossilegium* and the custom of incinerating the dead widespread in Augustan Rome? One possibility is that because wood was so expensive in Judaea, a funeral pyre was out of the question. Thus the Jews evolved a rather unpleasant burial custom, similar to the practices most widespread in contemporary Greece and Rome, an interesting, although somehow cynical, notion. But if *ossilegium* evolved *a posteriori* from a complex theology of the physical resurrection of the body developed during an earlier time frame – a theory which has still not been confirmed – then it is obvious that it was a local development that was not subject to foreign influence. The vast majority of the ossuaries do not show any trace that would indicate imitation of a foreign object similarly utilized, such as the Roman *urna*. The shape and incised decoration of most of the ossuaries rule out this possibility.

What probably happened is that when some of the richest members of the ruling class of Judaea, who were more open to foreign influence, adopted burial in ossuaries instead of sarcophagi, the shape of these objects much more strongly reflected the influence of the *urnae* of Augustan Rome. The possibility remains, however, that exactly the opposite occurred, and that the *ossilegium* developed *a priori*, and only later, when the custom became pervasive, did it receive *a posteriori* theological sanction, if indeed it ever received such sanction. In this context, it is important to recall that this funerary custom appeared in Herod's time, while the Book of Ezekiel, the ostensible catalyst to this development, was included in the Jewish canon by the Pharisees many years after Herod's reign,

---

[45] On Volterra in the Roman period see E. Fiumi, *Volterra etrusca e romana*, Pisa 1976. With Augustus, Volterra became one of the *municipia* of the VII *regio*, or Etruria. See also G. Cateni and F. Fiaschi, *Le urne di Volterra, e l'artigianato artistico degli Etruschi*, Firenze 1984, pp. 32–33, fig. 52, p. 132. An unpublished funerary urn from Etruria in the Bible Lands Museum in Jerusalem is attributed, according to the inscription, to a Cilnius, member of Maecenas's family.

[46] Rubin also points to a possible Roman influence. See Rubin, "Secondary Burials in the Mishnaic and Talmudic Periods", p. 263.

slightly before the destruction of the Second Temple. In other words, the question remains open.

Finally, it is always possible to claim a parallel but unrelated development of these phenomena in Augustan Rome and Herodian Jerusalem. The beginning of systematic burial in urns in Rome and in ossuaries in Jerusalem may also have been prompted by the sudden urban development of both cities. The introduction of a new burial technique corresponds to the demographic boom, as suggested by Rubin. This does not mean that Rome or Jerusalem influenced each other, but rather, that for different reasons, both in Rome and in Jerusalem, a similar solution was found to a common problem. Thus, there are arguments for and against both possible explanations – local development as opposed to foreign influence. For our purposes, it is sufficient to stress here the extent to which the burial customs of Herodian Judaea were not only similar to those of the Greek world, but even more so to those of Augustan Rome.

As Netzer's discovery in the summer of 2007 demonstrated, Herod was buried in a sarcophagus. In any event, burial in ossuaries was still not widespread during Herod's rule, and a dying ruler would have been unlikely to adopt this new trend. Besides, burial in a sarcophagus would have been more impressive than burial in an ossuary, since sarcophagi were far more expensive than ossuaries. Also, it is important to point out that Herod's family was buried in sarcophagi, and last but not least, nowhere is it recorded that Archelaus, Antipas, or Philip ever collected the bones of their father.

3. Conclusions

In this final chapter I have analyzed not merely the funeral and the monumental tomb of King Herod, but the actual burial practices of the period in question. As a Hellenistic king, Herod's funeral procession was similar to that of Alexander the Great, intermingled with various Jewish elements. Herod's body was buried in a monumental tomb at the foot of Herodium, in a tomb that was not only similar to other monumental Jewish tombs belonging to members of the ruling class of Judaea during the Hasmonean and Herodian Periods, but that also recalled tombs belonging to the ruling class of the Hellenistic Eastern Mediterranean. Moreover, in the first century CE, there were funeral monuments extant in Jerusalem that were influenced not only by funerary monuments typical of the surrounding East Greek world, but by Roman funerary monuments. The influence of Roman funerary customs on the ruling class of Judaea perhaps began with Herod's round funerary monument, similar to Augustus' mausoleum in Rome.

It is important to understand that not only monumental tombs, but the concept of burial itself influenced the funerary customs of Judaea from the Late Hellenistic Period and onward. Thus Jews began using *loculi* as well as sarcophagi to bury their dead. Indeed, wooden sarcophagi found at 'En Gedi, dating from the Hasmonean Period, as well as stone sarcophagi coming from Herodian Jerusalem, were strongly influenced by contemporary wooden sarcophagi from Ptolemaic Egypt and stone sarcophagi from Augustan Rome. Even the use of ossuaries, a custom that began to be prevalent only at the end of the Herodian Period, shows a certain similarity to the utilization of funerary *urnae*, a practice widespread in Augustan and Julio-Claudian Rome, with the obvious difference being that the bones of the deceased were collected in the ossuary, while ashes were placed in the funerary *urna*. Thus, even in the most intimate and conservative of customs – funerary practices – a certain Mediterranean atmosphere pervades Herodian Judaea.

4. Appendix I:
Monumental Tombs of the Hasmonean and Herodian Period: A Comparative Analysis

Herod's monumental tomb at the foot of Herodium undoubtedly reflected a trend in Judaea, one that was already apparent in the Hasmonean era and that continued during the Herodian Period.[47] Most of the monumental Jewish tombs from Jerusalem present similar traits. The façades consisted of a *monostyle* or more often a *distyle in antis* in Ionic style, topped by a Doric architrave and frieze. A *nefesh*, or "soul," generally in the form of a pyramid, topped the tombs. These tombs reflect the general trend of the Hellenistic and Roman periods throughout the Mediterranean basin. Herod's Tomb at the foot of Herodium is representative of a typology widely diffused in Hasmonean and Herodian Judaea. The Tomb of the Maccabees in Modi'in, erected by Simon, was clearly similar in conception to the Tomb of Herod at Herodium. While the Maccabees' tomb has not survived, it is described in the First Book of the Maccabees and by Josephus.[48] The façade of the tomb consisted of a portico, dominated by a frieze depicting warships and topped by seven pyramids. The most similar funerary monument is a contemporary Numidian mausoleum at Simitthus in Tunisia, dated to 148–118 BCE. A similar mausoleum stands at Nabataean Suweida in Syria, though it is dated much later.[49] Jason's Tomb in Rechavia in Jerusalem probably dates to the rule

---

[47] The best and most updated work on the Jerusalem necropolis is A. Kloner, B. Zissu, *The Necropolis of Jerusalem in the Second Temple Period*, Jerusalem 2003.

[48] See 1 Macc 13: 27–32 and Josephus, *AJ* XIII, 211.

[49] Like the Tomb of the Maccabees in Modi'in, the more impressive Numidian mausoleum had two stories with columns topped with a carved frieze showing various trophies of weapons. See F. Rakob, *Simitthus I, Die Steinbrueche und die antike Stadt*, Mainz 1993. The tomb from Suweida in Syria is, perhaps, Nabataean. The Greek inscription dates the monument to the end of the first century BCE. See D. M. Krencker, and W. Zschietzschmann, *Roemische Tempel in Syria I, Denkmaler Antike Architektur 5*, Berlin 1938, pp. 52–54. See also E. M. Meyers (ed.), "Suweida",

4. Appendix I: Monumental Tombs of the Hasmonean and Herodian Period 365

of Alexander Jannaeus and presents similar, though not identical, features, such as the Doric *monostyle in antis*, an architrave, and the pyramid that topped the tomb.[50] This type of structure, consisting of a façade topped by a pyramid, separated from the architrave by an Egyptian cavetto, was common throughout the Mediterranean. Similar tombs or Dado tombs, topped by a pyramid, can be found in Hellenistic Cyrene.[51] Other examples come from Punic North Africa at Dougga, Kroub, Sabratha, Sigga, and Sumaa.[52] There are also similar mausolea from late Seleucid Syria, such as ones at Hermel in Lebanon and Kalat Fakra in Syria,[53] although their exact dates are far from certain. The Tomb of Bene Hezir in the Kidron Valley, also dated to the Hasmonean Period, presents similar characteristics: a Doric façade consisting of a *distyle in antis*. Perhaps the adjacent so-called Tomb of Zechariah was the *nefesh* of that tomb, but it dates to the Herodian Period and thus was built some generations later. Another possibility, according to M. Ben Dov, is that the *nefesh*, probably a pyramid, was carved on the top of the Bene Hezir Tomb, but has not survived. The adjacent Tomb of Zechariah dates to the Herodian Period; however, the shape of the tomb, topped by a pyramid, continues an earlier Eastern trend.[54] This type of tomb, called "aedicula type" by Von Hesberg, was prevalent in the Roman West. Similar examples are the Torre de los Scipiones in Tarragona in Spain, the monumental tombs of Villayosa and Daimuz, and the Tomb of the Flavii in Kasserine in Tunisia.[55]

The Oxford Encyclopedia of Archaeology in the Near East 5, New York 1997, pp. 111–112 and A. Sartre, "Architecture funeraire en Syrie", in *Archeologie et histoire de la Syrie II, Schriften zur Vorderasiatischen Archaeologie I*, Saarbrueck 1989, p. 439.

[50] Jason's Tomb is situated in the Rechavia quarter of Jerusalem. See L. Y. Rachmani, "Jason's Tomb", *IEJ 17*, 1967, pp. 61–100. See also G. Foerster, "Architectural Fragments from Jason's Tomb", *IEJ 28*, 1978, pp. 152–156.

[51] See Bonacasa and Ensoli, *Cirene*, p. 162. The Dado tomb from Zawani is a good example.

[52] It is not known whether the monument from Dougga was a tomb or merely a funerary monument. A certain 'Ateban,' who is named in the inscription, must have been a Numidian king or prince during the third or second century BCE. See H. Lauter, *Die Architektur des Hellenismus*, Darmstadt 1986, pp. 216–217. The Lybio-Punic mausoleum of Sabratha is dated to the second century BCE. See Lauter, *Architektur des Hellenismus*, pp. 216–217. The tombs from Sigga and Sumaa are simpler. See Lauter, *Architektur des Hellenismus*, pp. 216–217. On the Tomb of Kroub see P. Gros, *L'architecture romaine II, L'architecture romaine 2, Maisons, palais, villas et tombeaux*, Paris 2001, p. 418, fig. 497.

[53] The Mausoleum at Hermel in Lebanon, once Phoenicia, was probably built about the turn of the second and first centuries BCE. See Krencker and Zschietzschmann, *Roemische Tempel in Syria I*, pp. 52–54. The Tomb of Kalat Fakra in Syria probably dates to the first century CE and is therefore later than the period under consideration. See Krencker and Zschietzschmann, *Roemische Tempel in Syria I*, pp. 52–54.

[54] On the Tomb of Bene Hezir see N. Avigad, *Ancient Monuments in the Kidron Valley*, Jerusalem 1954. On the Tomb of Zechariah see Avigad, *Ancient Monuments in the Kidron Valley*.

[55] See Von Hesberg, *Römische Grabbauten*, p. 149, n. 90. On the Tombs of Villayosa and Daimuz see Gros, *L'architecture romaine II*, p. 416, fig. 493).

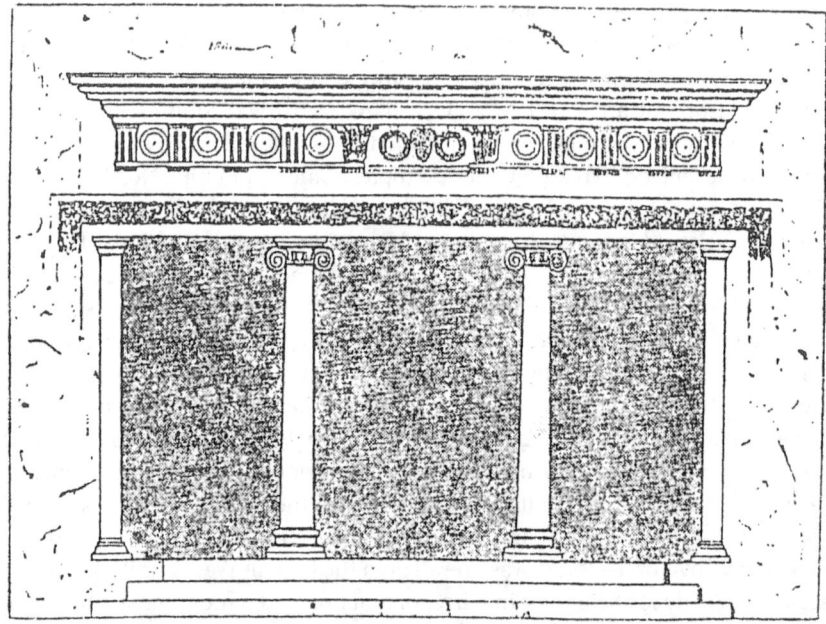

Figure VIII, 2 – Reconstruction of the façade of the Tomb of the Kings from N. Avigad, "The Architecture of Jerusalem in the Second Temple Period," in Y. Yadin, *Jerusalem Revealed, Archaeology in the Holy City, 1968–1974*, Jerusalem 1976, p. 19, Courtesy of the Israel Exploration Society, Jerusalem.

During the Herodian Period and afterwards, this trend continued, with the addition of Roman influence. The best known and most impressive monumental tomb of Jerusalem was the so-called Tomb of the Kings, the Tomb of Queen Helena of Adiabene and her sons (cfr. figure VIII, 2). This tomb was constructed some forty years later than the Tomb of Herod at Herodium, but the style is quite similar. Situated north of the Old City, the tomb is described by Josephus as having a façade that consisted of an Ionic *distyle in antis*, topped by a Doric frieze. The *nefesh* consisted of three pyramids that once topped the tomb. As in the Tomb of the Hasmoneans, each pyramid symbolized one of the three deceased, Queen Helena and her two sons Monobazus and Izates.[56] Most of the other monumental tombs were quite similar, consisting of a mixed classical façade with Ionic columns, a Doric frieze, and sometimes an Egyptian cavetto. In other words, the style that began during the Hasmonean Period remained

---

[56] On the Tomb of the Kings see Josephus, *AJ* XX, 95. See also N. Avigad, "The Architecture of Jerusalem in the Second Temple Period", in Y. Yadin (ed.), *Jerusalem Revealed, Archaeology in the Holy City, 1968–1974*, Jerusalem 1976, p. 17. See also A. Kloner, "The "Third Wall" in Jerusalem and the "Cave of the Kings" (Josephus War V 147)", Levant 18, 1986, pp. 121–129.

4. Appendix I: Monumental Tombs of the Hasmonean and Herodian Period

Figure VIII, 3 – Reconstruction of the façade of the Tomb of 'Umm –el -Amed (from N. Avigad, "The Architecture of Jerusalem in the Second Temple Period," in Y. Yadin, *Jerusalem Revealed, Archaeology in the Holy City, 1968-1974*, Jerusalem 1976, Courtesy of the Israel Exploration Society, Jerusalem.

unchanged.[57] Though its façade has not survived, the Herod's Family Tomb located near the King David Hotel in Jerusalem is a good example of this type of tomb and has been described by Josephus.[58] A monument stood before the entrance, which was closed by a rolling stone. The façade of the Tomb of the Frieze on Shmuel Ha Navi Street in Jerusalem has survived, though it remains in poor condition. This tomb had a simple entrance decorated with a Doric frieze and a Corinthian cornice.[59] The Tomb of Nicanor on Mount Scopus presents the same characteristics. Once more, the façade consisted of a *distyle in antis*. The Tomb of Umm el-'Amed is probably the best conserved of this group of tombs, and its façade consists of a *distyle in antis* of two Ionic columns faced by two pillars, with two more pillars at the corners (cfr. figure VIII, 3). The entire façade was decorated with ashlars.[60]

During the Herodian Period there were other trends in tomb architecture that exhibited a strong Western influence and that were quite different from Herod's

---

[57] See Avigad, "Architecture of Jerusalem in the Second Temple Period", p. 17.
[58] On Herod's Family Tomb see Josephus, *BJ* V, 108 and *AJ* XII, 507. See also Avigad, "Architecture of Jerusalem in the Second Temple Period", p. 17.
[59] On the Tomb of the Frieze see N. Avigad, "The Rock-Carved Facades of the Jerusalem Necropolis", *IEJ* 1, 1950-51, pp. 96–109.
[60] On Tomb of Umm el-'Amed see L. Y. Rachmani, "Jewish Rock-Cut Tombs in Jerusalem", *Atiqot* 3, 1964, pp. 93–120.

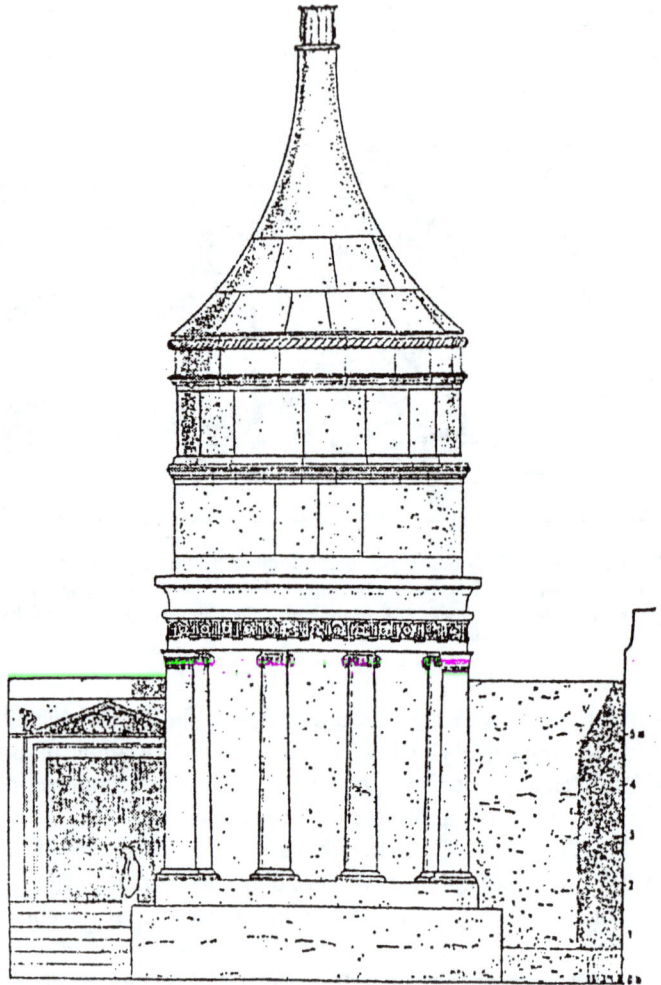

Figure VIII, 4 – Reconstruction of the Monument of Absalom (from N. Avigad, "The Architecture of Jerusalem in the Second Temple Period," in Y. Yadin, *Jerusalem Revealed, Archaeology in the Holy City, 1968–1974*, Jerusalem 1976, p. 17, Courtesy of the Israel Exploration Society, Jerusalem.

Tomb at the foot of Herodium. The so-called Tomb of Absalom, also in the Kidron Valley not far from the Tomb of Bene Hezir and the Tomb of Zechariah, displays such influence (cfr. figure VIII, 4). The tomb consists of a lower structure decorated with engaged Ionic columns, a Doric frieze, and an Egyptian cornice, topped by a drum and a cone.[61] This tomb recalls a vogue clearly popular in

---

[61] On the Tomb of Absalom see Avigad, *Ancient Monuments in the Kidron Valley*.

4. Appendix I: Monumental Tombs of the Hasmonean and Herodian Period

the Roman West, the tomb of the aedicula type. It is thus similar to Tomb of the Astacids in Pompeii, to the Tomb of Aefionius Rufus at Sarsina, and to the Mausolée des Julii in St. Remy (Glanum). Other similar tombs are the Nettuno Tomb and the Tomb of Publicius in Cologne.[62]

A third trend, probably regional, is followed by the Two Storeys Tomb, situated on Shmuel Ha Navi Street in Jerusalem. Two stories, each framed with half columns and topped by an architrave, characterize the façade. Were the Khazneh, the Corinthian Tomb, and the Deir at Petra the primary source of influence for this tomb? In fact, the main source of inspiration did not come from Nabataean Petra, but from Ptolemaic Egypt, where this façade was used for palace architecture rather than for tombs. The Thalamegos, or the yacht of Ptolemy IV, and the later façade of the Casa delle Colonne at Ptolemais may have been the main source of inspiration. Alternatively, a Western component, the Second Pompeian Style of painting, with its depiction of architectural elements, is possibly an alternative source of inspiration.[63] The recently excavated Aceldama Tombs, belonging to the family of the High Priest Ananias (6–15 CE), are another example. Josephus explicitly writes that the Tomb of Ananias the High Priest was situated at the southern end of the Hinnom Valley. Its monumental façade consisted of a triple gate, whose central gate was higher than those flanking it and was topped by a conch. Over it stood a superstructure, or *nefesh*, which has not survived.[64] Once more, the source for this monument was probably the Greek East, though the conch that topped the central gate was a local element, reproducing the conch that topped the main gate of the Temple itself. Since the person buried there had been a high priest, the Temple was an obvious source of inspiration.

Finally, there were other much simpler monumental tombs, characterized by a gabled pediment that topped an undecorated façade. The pediment was generally decorated with floral motifs, clusters of grapes, and acanthus leaves. The Tomb of Jehoshafat in the Kidron Valley, adjacent to the Tomb of Absalom, is a good

---

[62] See Von Hesberg, *Römische Grabbauten*. The Tomb of the aedicula type consists of a high basement, a cube framed by Corinthian columns on the corners, architrave and frieze and topped by a cone. On the Tomb of Aefionius Rufus at Sarsina see p. 129, no. 74. On the Mausolee des Julii see p. 129, no. 75. On the Nettuno, Tomb p. 134, no. 78. On the Tomb of Publicius at Cologne, see pp. 142–143, no. 85.

[63] On the Tomb of Two Storeys see Avigad, "The Rock-Carved Facades of the Jerusalem Necropolis", pp. 96–109. A possible source of inspiration for this tomb could be monumental tombs from the Necropolis of Cyrene. In the Hellenistic period a new typology appears which reproduces the courtyard of the house, hewn in the rock facing the main façade, also hewn in the rock, or partly hewn and partly built using hewn stones. The facade thus could be a simple surface with the entrance gate, or a more complicated portico with real or half columns. Sometimes the facade had two stories. Thus developed the typology which S. Stucchi calls "false facade," or with *scaena frons* not hewn in the rock but completely free standing. See Bonacasa and Ensoli, *Cirene*, pp. 158–163.

[64] On the Aceldama Tombs see Josephus, *BJ* V, 504–507. See also G. Avni, L. Z. Greenhut, T. Ilan, "Three New Burial Caves of the Second Temple Period in Aceldama", *Ancient Jerusalem Revealed, Expanded Edition 2000*, Jerusalem 2000, pp. 206–218.

example of such tombs.⁶⁵ The Tombs of the Sanhedrin in the Sanhedria neighborhood present similar characteristics.⁶⁶ The nearby Tomb of the Cluster Grapes northeast of the Tombs of the Sanhedrin, is another fine example.⁶⁷

5. Final Conclusions

In this work I undertook a general analysis of Herodian Judaea and of its ties with the Classical world, beginning with Augustan Rome, then the center of power, and followed by the main centers within the Mediterranean basin and in the Hellenistic East.

In the book I argue that Herod looked to Augustus as an ideal model, worthy of imitation; both men indeed had many things in common. Each began his political career at a very young age. Both not only brought an end to a long and bloody period of civil war in their own countries, but the blessing of many years of peace as well. Both created a new regime, different from its predecessor.

We may well ask why the Romans supported Herod, and the answer is found in the fact that, on the whole, Herod was a successful ruler who enjoyed, for a certain period at least, the tacit support of the majority of his subjects. That Herod's success was greatly appreciated in Rome is indicated by the fact that while in Augustus's *Res Gestae* Armenia is mentioned as a serious source of trouble, Herodian Judaea is conspicuously absent. Evidently Herod was a guarantor of internal and external peace to the Roman overlords. On the other hand, if Herod had been problematic and distasteful to his subjects, the Romans would have deposed him in favor of another ruler or taken direct control of Judaea, as they did with Archelaus.

I also contend that Herod pushed Judaea toward a major Hellenization, albeit with many elements more akin to Rome than to the surrounding Hellenistic East. But the Herodian program of Hellenization was not something really new or a break with past, as it continued a previous policy begun by the Hasmoneans. Hasmonean Judaea could already be considered a Mediterranean society. Herodian society was also permeated by a general trend, not only toward Hellenization but more specifically, Romanization, forced or spontaneous. However, contrary to Hellenisation, this was a feature common only to the ruler and to the ruling class. Herodian Jerusalem was thus quite similar to Augustan Rome and to other contemporary Greek cities in the East.

---

⁶⁵ On the Tomb of Jehoshafat see Avigad, *Ancient Monuments in the Kidron Valley*.
⁶⁶ On the Sanhedrin Tombs see Rachmani, *Atiqot 3*, pp. 93–120.
⁶⁷ On the Tomb of the Cluster Grapes see Rachmani, *Atiqot 3*, pp. 93–120. See also on simpler tombs A. Kloner, B. Zissu, "The "Cave of Simon the Just" and "The Minor Sanhedrin", Two Burial Complexes from the Second Temple Period in Jerusalem", in L. V. Rutgers (ed.), *What Athens Has to Do with Jerusalem, Essays in Honor of Gideon Foerster*, Leuven 2002, pp. 125–149.

More specifically I analyzed various facets of Herodian Judaea. I began with an analysis of Herod's ideology. To understand both Herod's rule and ideology, it is necessary to examine it in the light of the ideology of the earlier Kings of Israel and Judah, the Hasmonean rulers, the Hellenistic monarchs, and of course, Augustus himself. It is simplistic to define Herod's rule as that of "another Hellenistic despot/tyrant." It is true that Herod's ruling ideology followed the tradition of the Hellenistic absolute ruler, which was slightly different from the somewhat theocratic Hasmonean rule. However there are other equally important constituents. Like all the other Hellenistic rulers and, to a certain extent, Augustus, Herod's public personality was molded on the figure of Alexander the Great and the early Macedonian monarchs. Like Alexander the Great and other Hellenistic monarchs, Herod emphasized the mythical divine origin of his power. Alexander presented himself as a descendant of both Heracles and Achilles. The other Hellenistic potentates did the same. For example, the Seleucids claimed a tie with Apollo. Augustus too was celebrated as a descendant of Aphrodite and Aeneas. Herod, a Jewish king, could not trace his origins to a pagan deity. It seems, however, that his ideology of rule vis-a-vis his Jewish subjects was modeled after the legendary rule of Solomon, the Temple builder and peaceful king. Herod modeled himself on a figure from the Jewish past, but he followed a Hellenistic cultural model in defining the relationship with the far away "mythical" past. Thus the model for Herod's Solomon must not be searched in the Bible, but it can be found in writings such as those of the Jewish Hellenistic author Eupolemus, who reconstructed the Jewish Biblical past, using the methods of Greek historiography and literature. In this choice of an ideological model for rule, Herod was at an advantage in comparison to the Hasmoneans in that, unlike them, he was a secular figure rather than a priest-king. In contrast to the absolute rule of the Hellenistic rulers and Herod Augustus' rule stands as "primus inter pares" and his maintenance, at least in form, of the old Republican system. Augustus' authority was theoretically based on both his moral *auctoritas* and ruling *potestas*. There are, nevertheless, various practical similarities between Herod's and Augustus' rule. The rule of both was based upon consensus within the army. The limitation of Herod's absolute rule can be found in his foreign policy. Herod was also *socius et amicus* of the Senate and Roman People and his foreign policy was thus limited by Rome's wishes. However, what Herod could not achieve by the force of arms he achieved through diplomacy, at which he was as brilliant as Alexander had been at war. One of the main characteristics of a Hellenistic ruler was his role as *euergetes*. Herod's behavior as *euergetes* and his *philotimia* must be compared to that of other Hellenistic rulers and of Augustus. In his *philotimia* Herod was probably one of the greatest, if not the greatest, Hellenistic ruler. His buildings projects within his kingdom and abroad appear to have been unsurpassed. Herod's *philotimia* spanned the eastern Mediterranean: Olympia, Sparta and Athens in Greece; Rhodes and Coos in Asia Minor; and Antioch in Syria. In various building projects, such as at Nicopolis, Herod celebrated Augustus. The buildings erected by Herod in Jerusalem and by Augustus in Rome are of the same type. However, while Herod was free to dominate Jerusalem as sole *euergetes*, in Rome Augustus had to share his glory as *euergetes* with members of his family, political allies and even political enemies. An interesting parallel between both Augustus and Herod is that they drew the inspiration for their building projects from the Athenian Golden Age. It is also useful to draw a comparison between Herod and Juba II of Mauritania: both were client kings, in their Romanization and in their nativism and, of course, in their relationship with Augustus.

Then I analyzed the court and the palatial setting. Like all other Hellenistic rulers, Herod maintained a royal court. The court was the main medium by which the king's ideological message and wishes were transmitted to his subjects. Thus, the primary task of the royal court was to serve as the ruling and administrative center of the kingdom and to display Herod's power in all its opulence. This section of my book is devoted to analysis of the structure, activities and mechanisms of the Herodian royal court. Herod's court appears to have been based upon the royal court of Alexander the Great and those of other early Macedonian rulers, even if, for practical reasons, the closest similarities can be found in the Ptolemaic and, to a lesser degree, the Seleucid courts (although our impressions may be skewed by the fact that we know much more about the court of the Ptolemies than that of the Seleucids). The hierarchy of Herod's court can be reconstructed. At the head of the court stood King Herod, surrounded by his family, which included his relatives, his wives and sons. The *philoi* or courtiers were divided into an inner circle, dominated by Herod's ministers Ptolemy and Nicolaus, and an outer circle connected to Herod's sons. Other members of the court were visitors, intellectuals, dynasts, and political envoys as well as Herod's military household and his domestic staff. Herod's court was completely different from that of Augustus, still entrenched in the values of the Roman Republic. Later, however, during the rule of Claudius, something similar to the Late Hellenistic royal courts emerged at Rome with the creation of an imperial bureaucracy (imperial *liberti* with important governing and administrative tasks in the imperial bureaucracy were not found before this).

I have also analyzed the position of Jerusalem as an alternative center of independent Greek culture in the East, outside direct Roman control, following the decline of Alexandria. The Herodian court also appears to have become a center of Greek learning and culture, where numerous Greek men of culture could be found. These included the statesman and historian, Nicolaus of Damascus, as well as Philostratus, Crinagoras, Iraenaeus, and Ptolomaeus. After the fall of Ptolemaic Alexandria, all of these Greek men of culture found a haven in Herodian Jerusalem, and their literary output is mentioned by various sources. Thus Herod, a Jewish king, invited Greek intellectuals to come to his court to pursue their literary achievements safely and successfully, in an environment of Greek culture, and for a time his court became, in fact, an important center of Greek culture. It seems to me that Herod's decision to make his court into a center of Greek culture influenced the development and appreciation of Greek culture within the ruling class of Judaea in the long term. Thus, in an Appendix, I have argued for the existence of the well known *gymnasium*, mentioned in the *Fourth Book of Maccabees*, during the Herodian period. This institution stood in Jerusalem side by side with other educational institutions, where the ruling class of Judaea could pursue traditional Jewish education. This *gymnasium* education, based on knowledge of Classical rhetoric, could prepare the young members of the ruling class to fill future positions in Herod's court, army, and administration. It is important to note, however, that this *gymnasium* did not serve the members of the Herodian royal family. Herod's sons, Alexander, Aristobulus and Antipater, as well as Herod's grandson, the future Agrippa I, were educated in Rome at the court of Augustus or in the house of Asinius Pollio. Moreover, the influx of Greek-speaking Diaspora Jews brought to Judaea a wider and deeper knowledge of the Septuaginta. Thus there was probably a Jewish Greek-speaking public in Judaea which was interested in Jewish culture in Greek. Yet under Herod's rule, the Jewish literary tradition, written in Hebrew for an exclusively Jewish public and represented, for example, by the Psalms of Solomon, continued to flourish. But this culture was also well imbued with Greek cultural values and certain knowledge of the surrounding Hellenistic Roman world. As the Dead Sea Scrolls clearly show, the sectarian community at Qumran knew well enough who the Romans, the Kittim, were. The long term cultural consequences were a strengthening of Jewish culture expressed in Greek that continued to develop until the Bar Kochba Revolt. After Herod's death, Herod Antipas strengthened Greek culture in Galilee through the foundation of Tiberias. On the other hand, Agrippa I continued to strengthen Greek culture in Jerusalem. Agrippa II probably continued this process until the time of his death. The consequences of this process, namely the possibility of learning the basic tenets of Greek education, are exemplified in the figures of Josephus and Justus of Tiberias. It is possible to say, then, that both Josephus and Justus are the consequence of Herod's cultural establishment. A basic knowledge of Greek language and culture enabled Josephus, as well as such members of the Judaean ruling class as Justus of Tiberias, not only to communicate with the Roman administration and the Imperial power, but also fostered literary achievement in Greek. Both Josephus and Justus wrote on Jewish history and culture for a wider Gentile public. Yet they were the product of a cultural tradition that flourished in Judaea, and not in the Alexandrian Diaspora. Thus, although Josephus complained that he needed the help of assistants to write the *War* in Greek (*Against Apion* I, 50) and, later, his *Antiquities* (XX, 262–263), his achievements in Greek are unquestioned.

Much may be learned concerning the day-to-day functioning of Herod's royal court from his royal palaces and residences, the physical setting of the court. The palatial structures in the Land of Israel during the Hellenistic period, mainly the Hasmonean palaces, provided Herod with a local source of inspiration, together with the palatial structures of the Ptolemies and the Seleucids as well as the Roman urban domus and villa. An in-depth analysis of the plans and functions of Herod's palaces can aid us in understanding the machinery of Herod's court. Herod's palaces indeed underline the similarity of his court to those of the other Hellenistic rulers, again, of the Ptolemies in particular. The Herodian palaces are analyzed in detail: the two main royal palaces, Jerusalem and Jericho, the palaces in the Greek areas, Caesarea Maritima and Sebaste, and the various other palaces including Masada and Herodium. In the conclusion a comparison with the modest Mansion of Augustus on the Palatine is likewise helpful in understanding the different position of Herod as a supreme ruler recognized de jure and de facto, as compared to Augustus, primus inter pares, whose de facto power was based only on his *auctoritas* and *potestas*. Finally, the influence of Herodian palatial architecture on imperial villas and palaces is analyzed.

The Army of King Herod had been analyzed next. Herod was both a Hellenistic ruler and an ally of Rome. The external defense of his kingdom was in the hands of a mobile army composed of Jews, who formed its bulk, and Gentile mercenaries, such as Gauls and Ituraeans. It is difficult to calculate the total number of soldiers serving in the Herodian army. The organization of Herod's army for the most part followed a Hellenistic model, with special emphasis on cavalry. There were, however, various Italic or Roman officers at the head of the army. Thus, heavy infantry and engineering units were probably organized along Roman lines. Herod's army included a royal guard, light and heavy cavalry, light and heavy infantry, and various engineering units. Herod's army *poliorcetica* was therefore well developed. It followed the latest trends developed in Rome, as the siege of Jerusalem clearly demonstrates. All the city walls and major fortifications of the Herodian kingdom had artillery machines. The Herodian army successfully fought a civil war as well as two wars of conquest against the Nabataeans and participated as an auxiliary force of the Roman army in a campaign in Arabia.

Herod's kingdom was also protected by static defenses consisting of both fortifications and colonies. The kingdom had very few fortified cities, including Jerusalem, Caesarea Maritima, and Sebaste. The city fortifications were built according to Hellenistic techniques, however in some cases the gates and the towers followed a Roman model, common in the West from Augustus onward. The major fortifications in the Herodian kingdom included city fortifications, as at Sebaste; tetrapyrgia, such as the Antonia, Upper Herodium and Machaerus; and smaller castles, mainly concentrated in Judaea, such as Masada. These fortifications, guaranteeing both a local and a more comprehensive defense of the kingdom, also served as royal residences and as administrative centers. Various small forts and towers ensured the protection of the borders. Most of these fortifications had an earlier Hellenistic (Ptolemaic, Seleucid, or Hasmonean) origin and were partly rebuilt, partly left by Herod. The bigger fortifications display clearly Hellenistic characteristics, and some, like Upper Herodium, may be considered as paradigmatic of Hellenistic military building technology. Smaller fortifications, however, conserve a strong native character. These fortifications probably also served the imperial defense. In case of a Parthian invasion, such fortifications would have been intended to stop or at least delay a possible advance toward the Roman province of Egypt. The military colonies played an important role in the defense of the Herodian kingdom, both in the midst of native hostile populations, such as the colonies built in the northern regions of the kingdom, and to strengthen the borders, such as the colonies founded in the south. No colony was ever founded in Judaea. Then I deal with Herod's military fleet. The fleet was at first based in Joppa, later in the huge military harbor of Sebastos at Caesarea Maritima. Herod's warships also patrolled the Sea of Galilee and the Dead Sea.

Herod's administrative system was based on two different models. The first model was the priestly *ma'amad* and the *mishmereth*, which were the basic administrative units for the Jewish areas. The second model was the administrative organization of Coile Syria under the Ptolemies and the Seleucids, as well as the administrative division of the Jewish State under the Hasmoneans. Herod's kingdom comprised various ethnic elements, such as Jews living in Judaea, Galilee, and Idumaea; Samaritans; Greeks living in various urban agglomerations on the coast and in the interior; and various nomadic populations living in the northern regions of the kingdom. Although there was a clear-cut administrative hierarchy of officials, each region was administered in a different way, with the respective areas divided into different types of administrative circumscription. The various administrative officials in each region probably had different powers. One of the purposes of Herodian administration was the taxation of the country's populations. Although according to some scholars the tax rate was high, greater than 50%, it seems that Herod used much of his own private revenues for the Kingdom's expenditures, thus lowering the level of taxation of his subjects. Moreover Herod taxed mainly the upper class. As an ally of the Romans, Herod did not pay any tribute to Rome. Herod also developed a social program to help the lower strata of the population, made destitute by years of civil war. The land in Herod's kingdom was divided into royal lands, on which were established royal estates as well as colonies, and privately owned lands. Privately owned lands were characterized in the Jewish areas by the presence of manors as well as villages. Successful taxation depended upon a flourishing and developed economy. The economic resources of the Herodian kingdom were the same as those of the other Mediterranean lands making up the Roman Empire. Herod's main economic resource throughout the kingdom was agriculture. Crops included a variety of grains, grapes and olives, the most important products of the Herodian kingdom. These were the main products of Mediterranean agriculture. It is important to analyze agricultural production, which may have been influenced by the latest developments in Roman Italy: widespread introduction of villas, side by side with small landholders. Herod also possessed various royal estates, another common feature in the Hellenistic kingdoms and in the Roman Empire. After agriculture, manufacture was the other main component of the ancient economy. The Herodian kingdom produced a variety of different manufactured products, including glass, perfume, stone products in Jerusalem, and pottery. Commerce also played a very important part in the development of the Herodian kingdom. The existence of both local and international trade (both maritime and overland, e.g., spice routes) is related by archaeological and contemporary literary sources.

In the Appendix to this chapter, I have argued that during the Herodian Period there was a shift in Judaea towards the development of the Greek language. Judaea was a polyglot society; various languages were spoken and written in Herod's kingdom by the various ethnic groups which comprised it, including Aramaic, Hebrew, and of course Greek. Of these three languages it is Greek that developed the most and that reached a zenith. Herod minted coins with legends only in Greek. Most of the monumental inscriptions, both public and private, dated to Herod's rule, are in Greek. Even on the Temple Mount, rebuilt by Herod, various monumental inscriptions in Greek have been found, and of further significance, Greek became the dominant language of the ruling class of Judaea – Greek was the spoken and written language at Herod's court, in his army and administration. The main reasons for the development of Greek in Herodian Judaea were that under Herod's rule Judaea became a vital part of the surrounding Hellenistic civilization of the Mediterranean East, his kingdom became an important element in the geopolitics of the Roman Empire in the age of Augustus, and, last but not least, there was a significant influx into the kingdom of Greek-speaking Jewish pilgrims from various Mediterranean countries.

Next I have analyzed the ruling bodies of Herodian Judaea. As in the Hellenistic kingdoms and from the time of Augustus' reign and onward in the Roman Empire, the primary source of law in the Herodian kingdom was the ruler himself, and thus it is important to analyze Herod's relationship to the ruling class of Judaea. Like Augustus, Herod tried to create a new ruling class that was totally devoted to his dynasty. I therefore analyzed the relationship between Herod and the various political parties, the Sadducees, the Essenes, and the Pharisees, as well as the Herodians. In the second part of the chapter, I analyzed Herod's influence upon the various legislative bodies of the kingdom. The diverse ethnic composition of the Herodian kingdom presupposes distinct legislative bodies for each segment of the kingdom's population. My analysis began with Judaea proper. The political constitution of Herodian Judaea included the *ekklesia*, or popular assembly, the *boulē*, or the city – senate, found in Jerusalem and later in Tiberias from the rule of Antipas onwards, and the *synedrion-Sanhedrin*, whose composition and power I have attempted to define. Outside Judaea and the other regions where Jews resided, it seems that Greek law dominated. This is probably true concerning the various Gentile *poleis* such as Caesarea Maritima and Sebaste, but was also true for the various regions inhabited by indigenous populations, such as the Ituraeans in the northern part of the kingdom, who were neither Jewish nor Greek. In an Appendix, I have also discussed the Law on Thieves which was enacted by King Herod, which is the only example of a law which can be dated to the rule of King Herod with a certain measure of accuracy.

The cults of the Herodian Kingdom have then been analyzed. First I analyzed the high priest and the temple bureaucracy. Herod defined anew the figure of the High Priest, until then the spiritual and political ruler of Judaea. Herod was the first native ruler who appointed and dismissed high priests at will. The typical Herodian High Priest came from a small number of Diaspora families from Babylonia and Alexandria. This neutralized the high priest's political and religious influence in Jewish society. I also analyzed the cult in the Herodian Temple, both the traditional holidays and mainly the new holidays such as Hanukka and Purim, introduced in the Late Second Temple Period. Herod presented himself to the Jews as the builder of the Temple. The Jewish Temple was the only cultic building in Judaea. Before Herod, it underwent a major process of restoration in the late Hellenistic Period and under the Hasmoneans, when the *temenos* was transformed into an agora. Herod entirely rebuilt the Temple Mount. There were various sources of inspiration for Herod's building project: Jewish models such as the Temple described in the Book of Ezekiel, and Graeco-Roman models as the Periclean Acropolis of Athens, and of course the contemporary Roman fora, which much influenced the Herodian Temple Mount. It is also important to compare the Temple Mount *temenos* to Hellenistic and Roman as well as contemporary Near Eastern cultic buildings. It should be emphasized that the Herodian Temple was the greatest *temenos* in Classical antiquity. A comparison of the religious architecture of Herodian Jerusalem with that of Augustan Rome reveals that Hellenization is a feature common to cultic architecture in both cities, mainly reflected in building exteriors. Native architectural conceptions still dominated the interior portions of the temples in Rome and Jerusalem. Both Augustus and Herod, albeit for different reasons, were inspired in their building projects by Periclean Classicism. Moreover there is a clear similarity between the religious policy of Herod in Jerusalem and that of Augustus in Rome. The latter also underlined his *pietas* in restoring or constructing various religious buildings in Rome. In this chapter I also analyze the synagogue of Herodian Judaea, which I see not just as a house of prayer or a community center, but as a civic center with the same functions as the Greek *bouleterion*. Outside Judaea proper, Herod patronized the cults of his Gentile subjects. The erection of various Gentile cultic buildings inside the kingdom, at Sebaste, Caesarea Maritima, and Panias, is a clear indication of Herod's pragmatism. It is interesting to note, however, that the only Gentile temples erected inside the kingdom were dedicated to the imperial cult. It is possible that Herod did so in order to please Augustus without offending his Jewish subjects. Perhaps Herod's pragmatism was seen by the Jewish sects as only a political gesture toward Rome, void of any religious significance and thus, not as an introduction of paganism to the kingdom.

The Herodian City had been analyzed next. In this section, I analyze the influence of Herod's dynasty on the urban landscape of the kingdom. The Herodians deeply changed the nature of the Jewish areas of the kingdom, with the erection of new cities or the development of existing ones. Next I compare the various urban features of Herodian Jerusalem to those of other Hellenistic and Roman cities. Jerusalem possessed most of the typical public buildings associated with such cities, such as water supply and various leisure buildings such as theaters, amphitheaters, hippodromes and bath-buildings. The prototypes for these buildings, however, did not originate in the Hellenistic East, but in Augustan Rome. A significant similarity between the two cities is that leisure buildings were introduced in both cities during the same period. The task of these buildings was the same in both cities. However, in Rome, Augustus had all the leisure buildings erected by his family and political allies so as not to upset the Senate. In Jerusalem, as he did not face organized opposition, Herod was, of course, the only *euergetes* for leisure buildings. Private housing in Jerusalem, both of the wealthy as well as more modest buildings, also presents striking similarities with that of the Hellenistic East as well as Augustan Rome.

I have concluded my book with Herod's burial. Herod's attitude toward life was also reflected upon his death. His funeral procession was modeled after that of Alexander the Great, the model for all of the Hellenistic kings. Two monumental buildings epitomized Herod's ideology: Herod's cenotaph in Jerusalem and Herod's tomb at Herodium. The former stands as an exception in the panorama of funerary buildings in Herodian Judaea, as it was a clear imitation of Augustus' mausoleum in Rome and probably a final homage of Judaea's ruler to the Roman ruler. However, Herod was buried in a monumental tomb at the foot of Upper Herodium that was very similar to contemporary monumental tombs in Jerusalem as well as in the classical Mediterranean. In this chapter, I also discuss whether Herod was buried in a sarcophagus or in an ossuary. I likewise stress the similarity between the burial customs of Herodian Jerusalem and Augustan Rome.

Bibliography

Primary Sources

Josephus and Philo

Niese, B., and Destinon, J.v., *Flavii Josephi opera edidit et apparatus critico instruxit Benedictus Niese*, Berlin 1887–1895 (Greek Text).
Josephus I–IX, tr. Feldman, L. H., Marcus, R., and Thackeray, H.S, Cambridge (Mass.) 1926–1965.
Philo Complete Works I–X, tr. Colson, F. H., and Whitaker, G. H., Cambridge (Mass.) 1929–1939.

Apocrypha and Pseudepigrapha

Charlesworth, J., (ed.), *The Old Testament Pseudepigrapha*, Garden City (N. Y.), 1983.

Dead Sea Scrolls

Vermes, G., *The Dead Sea Scrolls in English*, Harmondsworth 1987.

Rabbinic Literature

Broude, W. G., *Pesikta De-Rab Kahana, R. Kahana's Compilation of Discourses for Sabbaths and Feastal Days*, London 1975.

פסיקתא רבתי דרב כהנא, מה׳ י.י. מנדלבוים, ניארק תשמ״ז.

Danby, H., trans., *The Mishna*, London 1933.

משנה, הפירוש למשנה, מה׳ ח. אלבק, תל אביב תשכ״ש.

Epstein, I., *The Babylonian Talmud*, London 1961.

תלמוד בבלי, בני ברק תשכ״ח (1960).

Freedman, H. and Simon, M., *Midrash Rabbah* I–IX, London 1983.

מדרש רבה, מה׳ מ.א. מירקין, תל אביב תשל״ב (1975).
מדרש בראשית רבה, מה׳ י. תיאודור וח. אלבק, ירושלים תשכ״ה (1965).
מדרש ויקרא רבה, מה׳ מ. מרגליות, ירושלים תשל״ב.

Neusner, J., *Sifre' to Numbers, An American Translation and Explanation* I–II, Atlanta (Ga.) 1986.

ספרי על במדבר, מה׳ ש. האראווייץ, ירושלים תשכ״ו.

Hammer, R., *Sifre: A Tannaitic Commentary on the Book of Deuteronomy*, New Haven (Conn.), 1986.

ספרי על ספר דברים, מה׳ א.א. פינקלשטיין, ניו יורק תשכ״ט.
Neusner, J., trans., *The Tosefta*, New York 1977–86.
תוספתא, מה׳ ש. ליברמן, ניו יורק תשט״ז – תשמ״ה.
תוספתא, מה׳ מ.ש. צוקרמנדל, ירושלים תשכ״ז.
Neusner, J., Sifra, *An Analytical Translation* I-III, Atlanta (Ga.) 1988.
ספרא, מה׳ מ. איש שלום וש. האראוויץ, ברעסלויא תרע״ה (1915).
Schwab, M., *Le Talmud de Jérusalem*, Paris 1977.
תלמוד ירושלמי, בני ברק תש״ס.

Greek Literature

Appian, *Roman History*, tr. White, H., Cambridge (Mass.) 2002.
Aristotle, *Athenian Constitution et al.*, tr. Rackham, H., Cambridge (Mass.) 1938.
Aristotle, *Politics*, tr. Rackham, H., Cambridge (Mass.) 1972.
Arrian, *History of Alexander* et al. I-II, tr. Rev. Iliff Robson, E., Cambridge (Mass.) 1954.
Dio Cassius, *Roman History*, I-IX, tr. Cary, E., Cambridge (Mass.) 1954–1961.
Diodorus Siculus, *History* I-XII, tr. Walton, F. et al., Cambridge (Mass.) 1984.
Plutarch, *The Parallel Lives* I-XI, tr. Perrin, B., Cambridge (Mass.) 1988.
Strabo, *Geography* I-IX, tr. Jones, H. L., Cambridge (Mass.) 1960–1969.
Thucydides, *The Peloponnesian War* I-IV, tr. Smith, C. F., Cambridge (Mass.) 1975–1980.

Latin Literature

Caesar, *Alexandrian, African, and Spanish Wars*, tr. Way, A. G., Cambridge (Mass.) 1954.
Caesar, *Civil Wars*, tr. Peskett, A. G., Cambridge (Mass.) 1979.
Caesar, *Gallic War*, tr. Edwards, H. J., Cambridge (Mass.) 1986.
Cato and Varro, *De Re Rustica*, tr. Ash, H. B., and Hooper, W. D., Cambridge (Mass.) 1999.
Columella, *De Re Rustica* I-III, tr. Ash, H. B., et al., Cambridge (Mass.) 1941–1955.
Curtius, Q., *History of Alexander* I-II, tr. Rolfe, J. C., Cambridge (Mass.) 1946.
Frontinus, *Aqueducts*, tr. McElwain, M. B., Cambridge (Mass.) 1961.
Horace, *Odes and Epodes*, tr. Bennett, CE, Cambridge (Mass.) 1939.
Horace, *Satires, Epistles, Ars Poetica*, tr. Fairclough, H. R., Cambridge (Mass.) 1961.
Livy, *History of Rome* I-XIV, tr. Foster, B. O., et al., Cambridge (Mass.) 1999.
Ovid, *The Art of Love and Other Poems*, tr. Mozley, J. H., Cambridge (Mass.) 1957.
Ovid, *Fasti*, tr. Frazer, Sir J. G., Cambridge (Mass.) 1951.
Ovid, *Metamorphoses* I-II, tr. Miller, F. J., Cambridge (Mass.) 1984.
Pliny, *Natural History* I-X, tr. Rackham, H., Cambridge (Mass.) 1938–1963.
Suetonius, *Twelve Caesars* I-II, tr. Rolfe, J. C., Cambridge (Mass.) 1959–1964.
Tacitus, *Histories* I-II, tr. Moore, C. H., Cambridge (Mass.) 1925–1931.
Tacitus, *Annals* I-II, tr. Jackson, J., Cambridge (Mass.) 1937.
Velleius Paterculus and Res Gestae Divi Augusti, tr. Shipley, F. W., Cambridge (Mass.) 1961.
Virgil, *Eclogae and Georgicae* I-II, tr. Fairclough, H. R., Cambridge (Mass.) 1978.
Vitruvius, *De Architectura* I-II, tr. Granger, F., Cambridge (Mass.) 1931–1934.

Roman Law

Gaius, *The Institutes*, tr. W. M. Gordon and O. F. Robinson, London 1997.
Justinianus, *Corpus Iuris Civilis, Digesta*, tr. A. Watson, Philadelphia 1985..
Justinianus, *Corpus Iuris Civilis, Institutes*, tr. P. Birks and G. McLeod, London 1998.

Modern Literature

VV. AA., *The Athenian Agora, A Guide to the Excavations and Museum*, American School of Classical Studies at Athens, Athens 1990.
Aharoni, Y., and Amiran, R., "Excavations at Tel Arad, Preliminary Report on the First Season, 1962", *IEJ 14*, 1964, pp. 131–147.
Aharoni, Y., "Tel Beersheba", *IEJ 24*, 1974, p. 271.
Aharoni, Y., *Carta's Atlas of the Bible*, Jerusalem 1974.
Aharoni Y., and Avi-Yona, M., *The MacMillan Bible Atlas*, Toronto 1993.
Alexander, P. S., "Jewish Elements in Gnosticism and Magic", *CHJ, The Early Roman Period 3*, Cambridge 1999, pp. 1052–1079.
Alon, G., "The Attitude of the Pharisees toward Roman Rule and the Herodian Dynasty", *Scripta Hierosolymitana 7*, 1961, pp. 53–78.
Anderson, G., *Sage, Saint and Sophist: Holy Men and their Associates in the Early Roman Empire*, London 1994.
Anderson, R. T., "The Elusive Samaritan Temple, *BA 54,2*, 1991, pp. 104–107.
Andronicos, M., *Delphi*, Athens 1983.
Andronicos, M., *Vergina The Royal Tombs and the Ancient City*, Athens 1989.
Arav, R., *Settlement Patterns and City Planning, 337-301 BCE*, British Archaeological Reports, International Series 485, Oxford 1989.
Ariel, D. T., "Tel Istaba", *IEJ 38*, 1988, pp. 30–35.
Arnaud, P., "Le Forum d'Auguste", *Roma Antiqua, envois des architectes français (1788-1924: Forum, Colisée, Palatin)*, Rome 1985.
Arnould, C., *Les arcs romains de Jérusalem, Architecture, décor et urbanisme*, Novum Testamentum et Orbis Antiquus 35, Göttingen 1997.
Avigad, N., "The Rock-Carved Facades of the Jerusalem Necropolis", *IEJ 1*, 1950–51, pp. 96–109.
Avigad, N., *Ancient Monuments in the Kidron Valley*, Jerusalem 1954 (Hebrew).
Avigad, N., "Expedition A-Nahal David", *IEJ 12*, 1962, pp. 182–183.
Avigad, N., "The Architecture of Jerusalem in the Second Temple Period", in Yadin, Y., (ed.), *Jerusalem Revealed, Archaeology in the Holy City, 1968-1974*, Jerusalem 1976, pp. 14–20.
Avigad, N., *Discovering Jerusalem*, Jerusalem 1983.
Avigad, N., *The Herodian Quarter of Jerusalem, Wohl Archaeological Museum*, Jerusalem 1989.
Avi-Yonah, M., "The Second Temple", *Sepher Yerushalayim*, Tel Aviv-Jerusalem 1956, pp. 392–419. (Hebrew).
Avi-Yonah, M., "The Hasmonaean Revolt and Judah Maccabee's War against the Syrians", in *The World History of the Jewish People 6, The Hellenistic Period*, New Brunswick 1972, pp. 147–182.

Avi-Yonah, M., "Jerusalem in the Hellenistic and Roman Periods", in *The World History of the Jewish People 7, The Herodian Period*, New Brunswick 1975, pp. 207–248.

Avi-Yonah, M., "Jewish Art and Architecture in the Hasmonaean and Herodian Periods", in *The World History of the Jewish People 7, The Herodian Period*, New Brunswick 1975, pp. 250–261.

Avi-Yonah, M., *Carta's Atlas of the Period of the Second Temple, the Mishnah and the Talmud*, Jerusalem 1974.

Avni, G., Greenhut, L., Ilan, T., "Three New Burial Caves of the Second Temple Period in Aceldama", *Ancient Jerusalem Revealed, Expanded Edition 2000*, Jerusalem 2000, pp. 206–218.

Bahat, D., *The Illustrated Atlas of Jerusalem*, Jerusalem 1990.

Bahat, D., "The Herodian Temple", in *CHJ, The Early Roman Period 3*, 1999, pp. 38–59.

Ball, W., *Rome in the East, The Transformation of an Empire*, London 2000.

Ballet, P., *La vie quotidienne à Alexandrie, 331-30 avant J.-C.*, La Vie Quotidienne, Paris, 1999.

Balty, J. C., *Guide d'Apamée*, Bruxelles 1981.

Bar-Adon, P., "Philoteria", *IEJ 4*, 1954, pp. 128–129.

Barag, D., "King Herod's Royal Castle at Samaria-Sebaste", *PEF 125*, 1993, pp. 3 -17.

Barag, D., "The Showbread Table and the Facade of the Temple on Coins of the Bar-Kokhba Revolt", *Ancient Jerusalem Revealed*, Jerusalem 1994, pp. 272–276.

Barag, D., "New Evidence on the Foreign Policy of John Hyrcanus I", *INJ 12* 1994, pp. 1–12.

Barclay, J. M., *Jews in the Mediterranean Diaspora, From Alexander to Trajan (323 BCE– 117 CE)*, Edinburgh 1997.

Bar-Ilan, M., "Literacy among the Jews in Antiquity", *Hebrew Studies 44* (2003), pp. 217–222.

Bar-Kochva, B., *The Seleucid Army*, Cambridge 1976.

Bar Kochva, B., "Manpower, Economics, and Internal Strife in the Hasmonean State", in Van Effentere, H., (ed.), *Armées et fiscalité dans le monde antique, Colloque National du CNRS No. 936*, Paris 1977, pp. 167–195.

Bar-Kochva, B., *Judah Maccabaeus. The Jewish Struggle against the Seleucids*, Cambridge 1989.

Bar-Kochva, B., "The Battle between Ptolemy Lathyros and Alexander Jannaeus in the Jordan Valley and the Dating of the Scroll of the War of the Sons of Light", *Cathedra 93*, 1999, pp. 7–57 (Hebrew).

Barr, J., "Hebrew, Aramaic and Greek in the Hellenistic Age", in *CHJ 2, The Hellenistic Age*, Cambridge 1989, pp. 79–114.

Batey, R. A., *Jesus and the Forgotten City, New Light on Sepphoris and the Urban World of Jesus*, Grand Rapids (Mi) 1991.

Baumgarten, A. I., "On the Legitimacy of Herod and his Sons as Kings of Israel", in *Jews and Judaism in the Second Temple, Mishna and Talmud Period, Studies in Honor of Shmuel Safrai*, Jerusalem 1993, pp. 31–37 (Hebrew).

Baumgarten, A. I., "Who Were the Sadducees? The Sadducees of Jerusalem and Qumran", in *The Jews in the Hellenistic-Roman World, Studies in Memory of Menahem Stern*, Jerusalem 1996, pp. 393–411 (Hebrew).

Baumgarten, A. I., *The Flourishing of the Jewish Sects in the Maccabean Era, An Interpretation*, Supplements to the Journal for the History of Judaism 55, Leiden 1997.

Baumgarten, A. I., "Literacy and the Polemics surrounding Biblical Interpretation in the Second Temple Period", in Kugel, J. L., (Ed.), *Studies in Ancient Midrash*, Cambridge (Mass.) 2001, pp. 27-41.

Baumgarten, A. I., "The Pharisees", in *Common Judaism, or a Plurality of 'Judaisms' in Late Antiquity, The State of Debate, The Thirteenth School in Jewish Studies*, Jerusalem, May 13-16 2003. Paper not published.

Baumgarten, J., "The Calendar of the Book of Jubilees and the Temple Scroll", *VT 37*, 1987, pp. 71-78.

Beit-Arieh, I., *Tel 'Ira, A Stronghold in the Biblical Negev*, Tel Aviv University, Institute of Archaeology, Monograph Series No. 15, Tel Aviv 1999.

Ben-Arieh, S., "The "Third Wall" of Jerusalem", *Ancient Jerusalem Revealed, Archaeology in the Holy City 1968-1974*, Jerusalem 1976, pp. 60-63.

Ben Dov, M., *In the Shadow of the Temple, the Discovery of Ancient Jerusalem*, Jerusalem 1982.

Ben Dov, M., *Historical Atlas of Jerusalem*, New York (N. Y.) 2001.

Bell Dinsmoor, W., *The Architecture of Ancient Greece*, London 1985.

Ben Shalom, I., *The School of Shammai and the Zealot' Struggle against Rome* (Hebrew), Jerusalem 1993.

Benovitz, M., "Herod and Hanukkah", *Zion 68*, 1, 2003, pp. 6-15 (Hebrew).

Bernard, A., *Alexandrie des Ptolemées*, Paris 1995.

Berquist, J. L., *Judaism in Persia's Shadow, A Social and Historical Approach*, Minneapolis, 1995.

Betz, O., "The Essenes", *CHJ, The Early Roman Period 3*, Cambridge 1999, pp. 444-471.

Bickerman, E., *Institutions des Seleucides*, Paris 1938.

Bickerman, E., "The Warning Inscription of Herod's Temple", *JQR 37*, 1947, pp. 387-405.

Bickerman, E., *Chronology of the Ancient World, Aspects of Greek and Roman Life*, London, 1980.

Bickerman, E., *The Jews in the Greek Age*, Cambridge (Mass.) 1988.

Billows, R. A., *Antigonos the One-Eyed and the Creation of the Hellenistic State*, Berkeley 1997.

Biran, A., and Cohen, A., "Aroer in the Negev", *Eretz-Israel 15*, 1981, pp. 250-273 (Hebrew).

Blackman, D., "Naval Installations", in *The Age of the Galley, Mediterranean Oared Vessels since pre-classical Times*, London 1995, pp. 224-234.

Bloedhorn, H., and Hüttenmeister, G., "The Synagogue", in *CHJ, The Early Roman Period 3*, Cambridge 1999, pp. 267-298.

Boethius, A., *Etruscan and Early Roman Architecture*, Harmondsworth 1990.

Boffo, L., *Iscrizioni greche e latine per lo studio della Bibbia*, Brescia 1994.

Bohak, G., Asenath's Honeycomb and Onias' Temple; The Key to "Joseph and Asenath", *WCJS 11, A*, 1994, pp. 163-170.

Bohak, G., "CPJ III, 520; the Egyptian Reaction to Onias' Temple, *JSJ 26,1*, 1995, pp. 32-41.

Bohak, G., "The Impact of Jewish Monotheism on the Greco-Roman World", *JSQ 7,1*, 2000, pp. 1-21.

Bohak, G., "The Ibis and the Jewish Question: Ancient "Anti-Semitism" in Historical Context", in Mor, M., (ed.), *Jews and Gentiles in the Holy Land in the Days of the Second Temple, Mishna and Talmud*, Jerusalem 2003, pp. 27-43.

Bonacasa, N., and Ensoli, S., (eds.), *Cirene, Centri e monumenti dell'Antichita'*, Milano 2000.
Bonfil, R., "On Judaea and Jerusalem in the Letter of Aristeas", *Beth - Mikra 49, 2*, pp. 131-142 (Hebrew).
Bowersock, G. W., "Eurykles of Sparta", *JRS 51*, 1961, pp. 112-118.
Bowersock, G. W., *Roman Arabia*, Cambridge (Mass.) 1994.
Bowersock, G. W., "Augustus and the East: the Problem of the Succession", in Millar, F., and Segal, E., (eds.), *Caesar Augustus, Seven Aspects*, Oxford 1994, pp. 169-189.
Bowersock, G. W., "The Pontificate of Augustus", in Raaflaub, K. A., and Toher, M., (eds.), *Between Republic and Empire: Interpretations of Augustus and his Principate*, Los Angeles (Ca.), 1990, pp. 380-394.
Bowman, A. K., *Egypt after the Pharaohs 332 BC-AD 642*, London 1986.
Bowsher, J., "The Nabataean Army", *The Eastern Frontier of the Roman Empire*, BAR International Series 553 (1), 1989, pp. 19-30.
Bradley, K., *Slavery and Society at Rome, Key Themes in Ancient History*, Cambridge 1994.
Brooten, B. J., "The Jews of Ancient Antioch", in *Antioch, The Lost Ancient City*, Princeton (N. J.), 2000, pp. 29-39.
Broshi, M., "Excavations in the House of Caiaphas, Mount Zion", in Yadin, Y., (ed.), *Jerusalem Revealed, Archaeology in the Holy City, 1968-1974*, Jerusalem 1976, pp. 57-60.
Broshi, M., "Visionary Architecture and Town Planning in the Dead Sea Scrolls", in Dimant, D., and Schiffman, L. H., (eds.), *Time to Prepare the Way of Wilderness, Studies in the Text of the Desert of Judah, Volume 16*, Leiden 1985, pp. 9-23.
Broshi, M., "The Diet of Palestine in the Roman Period", *IMJ 5*, 1986, pp. 41-56.
Broshi, M., "Estimating the Population of Ancient Jerusalem", *BAR 4*, 1978, pp. 10-15.
Broshi, M., and Eshel, H., "A Messiah before Jesus Christ", *Tarbiz 60, 1* 2002, pp. 1-33 (Hebrew).
Brown, P., *Poverty and Leadership in the Later Roman Empire*, in *The Menahem Stern Jerusalem Lectures*, Hanover (NH) 2002.
Browning, I., *Palmyra*, Park Ridge (N. J.), 1979.
Browning, I., *Jerash and the Decapolis*, London 1982.
Browning, I., *Petra*, London 1982.
Bruneau, P. (ed.), *Delos, île sacrée et ville cosmopolite*, Paris 1996.
Burkert, W., *Greek Religion*, Cambridge (Mass.) 1998.
Burrell, B., "Palace to Praetorium: The Romanization of Caesarea", in Raban, A., and Holum, K., (eds.), *Caesarea Maritima, a Retrospective after Two Millennia, DMOA 21*, Leiden 1996, pp. 228-245.
Bury, J. B., and Meiggs, R., *A History of Greece*, London 2001.
Campbell, J., "The Qumran Sectarian Writings", *CHJ, The Early Roman Period 3*, Cambridge 1999, pp. 798-822.
Canfora, L., *The Vanished Library, A Wonder of the Ancient World*, Berkeley Los Angeles 1989.
Carcopino, J., *Daily Life in Ancient Rome, The People and the City at the Height of the Empire*, Harmondsworth 1985.
Carcopino, J., *Giulio Cesare*, Milano 1993.
Carpiceci, C. A., *Roma, com'era 2000 anni fa*, Firenze 1981.
Carr, E. H., *What is History?* Harmondsworth 1961.
Cary, M., and Scullard, H. H., *A History of Rome*, London 1986.

Casson, L., *Ships and Seafaring in Ancient Times*, London 1994.
Cateni, G., and Fiaschi, F., *Le urne di Volterra, e l'artigianato artistico degli Etruschi*, Firenze 1984.
Chauveau, M., *L'Egypte au temps de Cléopâtre - 180-30 av. J.-C., La Vie Quotidienne*, Paris 1997.
Chauveau, M., "Clergé et temples: rites, richesse et savoir", in *La gloire d'Alexandrie, Musée du Petit Palais*, Paris 1998, pp. 187-192.
Charron, A., "Les Ptolémées et les animaux sacrés", in *La gloire d'Alexandrie, Musée du Petit Palais*, Paris 1998, pp. 192-201.
Charron, A., "La sculpture en Égypte à l'époque ptolémaique", in *La gloire d'Alexandrie, Musée du Petit Palais*, Paris 1998, pp. 170-180.
Cheesman, G.L., *The Auxilia of the Roman Imperial Army*, Chicago 1975.
Clarke, J.R., *The Houses of Roman Italy 100 BC-AD 250, Ritual, Space and Decoration*, Berkeley 1991.
Clarke, J.R., *Looking at Lovemaking, Constructions of Sexuality in Roman Art*, Berkeley 1998.
Coarelli, F., *Rom, Ein archäologischer Führer*, Mainz 2000.
Coates, J., "The Naval Architecture and Oar Systems of Ancient Galleys", in *The Age of the Galley, Mediterranean Oared Vessels since pre-Classical Times*, London 1995, pp. 127-141.
Cohen, B., "Civil Bondage in Jewish and Roman Law", *Louis Ginzburg Jubilee Volume*, New York 1945, pp. 113-132.
Cohen, B., *Jewish and Roman Law 1*, New York 1966.
Cohen, S.J.D., "The Temple and the Synagogue", *CHJ, The Early Roman Period 3*, Cambridge 1999, pp. 298-316.
Colledge, M.A.R., *The Art of Palmyra*, London 1976.
Colter, W., "The Collegia and Roman Law: State Restrictions on Voluntary Associations", in Kloppenborg, J.S., and Wilson, S.G., (eds.), *Voluntary Associations in the Graeco-Roman World*, London 1996, pp. 74-89.
Connolly, P., *The Roman Army*, London 1976.
Connolly, P., *Hannibal and the Enemies of Rome*, London 1978.
Connolly, P., *The Greek Armies*, London 1977.
Connolly, P., *Living in the Time of Jesus of Nazareth*, Oxford 1983.
Connolly, P., *Pompeii*, Oxford 1990.
Connolly, P., *The Roman Fort*, Oxford 1991.
Connolly, P., *The Ancient City, Life in Classical Athens and Rome*, Oxford 1998.
Corbo, V., "Macheronte, la regia fortezza erodiana", *LA 29*, 1979, pp. 315-326.
Cotton, H.M., and Geiger, J., *Masada, The Yigael Yadin Excavations 1963-1965: Final Reports, 3, The Latin and Greek Documents*, Jerusalem 1989.
Croom, A.T., *Roman Clothing and Fashion*, Charleston (S.C.) 1988.
Crowfoot, J.W., and Kenyon, K.M., and Sukenik, E.L., *The Buildings at Samaria*, London 1942.
Dalby, A., and Grainger, S., *The Classical Cookbook*, London 1996.
Damati, E., "The Palace of Hilkiya", *Qadmoniot 15*, 1982, pp. 117-121 (Hebrew).
Daniel, B., "Les 'Hérodiens' du Nouveau Testament sont-ils Esséniens", *Revue de Qumran 6*, 1967-1969, pp. 31-53.
Daniel, B., "Nouveaux arguments en faveur de l'identification des Hérodiens et des Ésseniens", *Revue de Qumran 7*, 1969-1971, pp. 397-402.

Dar, S., *Landscape and Pattern. An Archaeological Survey of Samaria, 800 BCE-636 CE*, Debevoise (N.C.) 1986.
Dar, S., *Landscape and Pattern, BAR International Series*, Oxford 1986.
Dar, S., "Agriculture and Agricultural Produce in Eretz-Israel in the Roman-Byzantine Period", in Kasher, A., Oppenheimer, A., Rappaport, U., (eds.), *Man and Land in Eretz-Israel in Antiquity*, Jerusalem 1986, pp. 81-148 (Hebrew).
Dar, S., "The Estate of Ptolemy, Senior Minister of Herod", in Stern, M. (ed.), *Jews and Judaism in Second Temple, Mishna, and Talmud Period*, Jerusalem 1993, pp. 38-50 (Hebrew).
Dar, S., "The Agrarian Economy in the Herodian Period", *The World of the Herods and the Nabateans, An International Conference at the British Museum*, London 2001, pp. 17-18.
Daube, D., "Rabbinic Methods of Interpretation and Hellenistic Rethoric", *HUCA 22, 1949*, pp. 239-264.
Davies, J. K., *La Grecia Classica*, Bologna 1983.
Delcor, M., "Le temple d'Onias en Egypte", *RB 75*, 1968, pp. 188-205.
Delcor, M., "Is the Temple Scroll a Source of the Herodian Temple", in Brooke, G. J., (ed.), *Temple Scroll Studies, JSPSup. 7*, Sheffield 1989, pp. 67-85.
Del Ponte, R., *La Religione dei Romani*, Milano 1992.
Di Vita, A., and Di Vita-Evrard, G., *Lybia, The Lost Cities of the Roman Empire*, Cologne 1999.
Doran, R., "The High Cost of a Good Education", in Collins, J. J., and Sterling, G. E., (eds.), *Hellenism in the Land of Israel*, Notre Dame (Ind.), 2001, pp. 90-100.
Dueck, D., *Strabo of Amasia, A Greek Man of Letters in Augustan Rome*, London 2000.
Dupont, F., *La vie quotidienne du citoyen romain sous la République*, Paris 1989.
Eck, W., "Senatorial Self-Representation: Developments in the Augustan Period", in Millar, F., and Segal, E., (eds.), *Caesar Augustus, Seven Aspects*, Oxford 1994, pp. 129-169.
Eck, W., *The Age of Augustus*, Oxford 2003.
Eder, D., "Augustus and the Power of Tradition: the Augustan Principate as a Binding Link between Republic and Empire", in Raaflaub, K. A., and Toher, M., (eds.), *Between Republic and Empire: Interpretations of Augustus and his Principate*, Los Angeles (Ca.), 1990, pp. 71-122.
Edersheim, A., *The Temple, Its Ministry and Services As They Were at the Time of Jesus Christ*, Grand Rapids (Mi.), 1997.
Elior, R., "Enoch son of Jared and the Solar Calendar of the Priesthood in Qumran", *Von Enoch bis Kafka, Festschrift für Karl E. Gräzinger zum 60. Geburtstag*, Wiesbaden 2002, pp. 25-42.
Elsner, J., "Cult and Sculpture: Sacrifice in the Ara Pacis Augustae", *JRS 81*, 1991, pp. 50-61.
Ephron, J., "The Psalms of Solomon, The Hasmonean Decline and Christianity", in *Studies on the Hasmonean Period 6*, Leiden 1987, pp. 219-286.
Ephron, J., "The Great Sanhedrin in Vision and Reality", in *Studies on the Hasmonaean Period 7*, Leiden 1987, pp. 290-336.
Ephron, J., "The Deed of Simon Son of Shatah in Ascalon", in Kasher, A., (ed.), *Canaan, Philistia, Greece, and Israel: Relations of the Jews in Eretz-Israel with the Hellenistic Cities (332 BCE-70 CE)*, Jerusalem 1988, pp. 298-320 (Hebrew).
Errington, R. M., *A History of Macedonia*, Berkeley (Ca.) 1993.

Eshel, E., "Prayer in Qumran and the Synagogue", in Ego, B., Lange, A., and Pilhofer, P., (eds.), *Gemeinde ohne Tempel: Community Without Temple*, WUNT 118, Tübingen 1999, pp. 323–334.

Eshel, H., "Some Notes concerning High Priests in the First Century CE", *Zion* 64, 4, 1999, pp. 495–504 (Hebrew).

Eshel, E., and Erlich, Z. E., "The Fortress of Acraba in Kh. Urmeh", *Cathedra* 47, 1988, pp. 17–24 (Hebrew).

Eshel, H., and E., "Dating the Samaritan Pentateuch's Compilation in Light of the Qumran Biblical Scrolls", *Emanuel*, 2003, pp. 215–240.

Eshel, E., and Eshel, H., "4Q471 Fragment 1 and Ma'amadot in the War Scroll", in Trebolle Barrea, J., and Vegas Montaner, L., (eds.), *The Madrid Qumran Congress 3, Proceedings of the International Congress on the Dead Sea Scrolls, Madrid 18–21 March 1991*, Leiden 1991, pp. 617–618.

Falk, D. K., "Prayer in the Qumran Texts", CHJ, *The Early Roman Period 3*, Cambridge 1999, pp. 852–877.

Falk, Z. W., *Introduction to Jewish Law of the Second Commonwealth 1*, Leiden 1978.

Fantar, M. H., *Carthage, La cité punique*, Paris 1995.

Fantham, E., "Images of the City: Propertius New-Old Rome", in Habinek, T., and Schiesaro, A., (eds.), *Roman Cultural Revolution*, Cambridge 1997, pp. 122–135.

Faure, P., *La vie quotidienne des armées d'Alexandre, La Vie Quotidienne*, Paris 1982.

Favro, D., *The Urban Image of Augustan Rome*, Cambridge 1996.

Feldman, L. H., "The Identity of Pollio, the Pharisee, in Josephus", *JQR* 49, 1958–59, pp. 53–62.

Feldman, L. H., *Jew and Gentile in the Ancient World*, Princeton (N. J.), 1993.

Feldman, L. H., "Asinius Pollio and Herod's Sons", in *Studies in Hellenistic Judaism*, in Arbeiten zur Geschichte des Antiken Judentums und des Urchristentums 30, Leiden, 1996, pp. 52–56.

Feldman, L. H., "Josephus (CE 37–c. 100)", CHJ, *The Early Roman Period 3*, Cambridge 1999, pp. 901–922.

Ferguson, J., *The Religions of the Roman Empire, Aspects of Greek and Roman Life*, Ithaca (N. Y.) 1994.

Fiensy, D. A., *The Social History of Palestine in the Herodian Period: The Land is Mine*, Studies in the Bible and Early Christianity 20, Lewiston (N. Y.) 1991.

Fiumi, E., *Volterra etrusca e romana*, Pisa 1976.

Fleischer, R., "Hellenistic Royal Iconography on Coins", in *Aspects of Hellenistic Kingship*, Studies in Hellenistic Civilisation 7, Aarhus 1996, pp. 28–41.

Finkelstein, I., and Silberman, N. A., *The Bible Unearthed, Archaeology's New Vision of Ancient Israel and the Origin of its Sacred Texts*, London 2001.

Fittschen, K., "Wall Decorations in Herod's Kingdom: Their Relationship with Wall Decoration in Greece and Italy", *Judaea and the Greco-Roman World in the Time of Herod in the Light of Archaeological Evidence*, Abhandlungen der Akademie der Wissenschaften in Göttingen N. 215, Göttingen 1996, pp. 139–163.

Fitzmyer, J. A., "The Languages of Palestine in the First Century AD.", in Fitzmyer, J. A., (ed.), *A Wandering Aramean: Collected Aramaic Essays*, Missoula (Mt.), 1979, pp. 29–56.

Fiumi, E., *Volterra etrusca e romana*, Pisa 1976.

Flacelière, R., *La vita quotidiana in Grecian el secolo di Pericle*, Milano 1983.

Foerster, G., *Galilean Synagogues and their Relationship to Hellenistic and Roman Art and Architecture*, Ph. D. Thesis, The Hebrew University of Jerusalem, Jerusalem 1972 (Hebrew).
Foerster, G., "Studies in the History of Caesarea Maritima", in Fritsch, C. T., (ed.), *The Joint Expedition to Caesarea Maritima I, BASOR, Supplemental Studies No. 19*, (1975).
Foerster, G., "Architectural Fragments from Jason's Tomb", *IEJ 28*, 1978, pp. 152–156.
Foerster, G., "Architectural Models of the Greco-Roman Period and the Origin of the "Galilean" Synagogue", in Levine, L. I., (ed.), *Ancient Synagogues Revealed*, Jerusalem 1981, pp. 45–48.
Foerster, G., *Masada 5, The Yigael Yadin Excavations 1963–1965, Final Reports, Art and Architecture*, Jerusalem 1996.
Foerster, G., "Hellenistic and Roman Trends in the Herodian Architecture of Masada", *Judaea and the Greco-Roman World in the Time of Herod in the Light of Archaeological Evidence, Abhandlungen der Akademie der Wissenschaften in Göttingen N. 215*, Göttingen 1996, pp. 55–72.
Forrest, W. G., *A History of Sparta, 950–192 BC*, London 1968.
Förtsch, R., "The Residences of King Herod and their Relations to Roman Villa Architecture", in *Judaea and the Greco-Roman World in the Time of Herod in the Light of Archaeological Evidence, Abhandlungen der Akademie der Wissenschaften in Göttingen N. 215*, Göttingen 1996, pp. 73–120.
Foss, C., *Roman Historical Coins*, London 1990.
Fox, R. L., *Alexander the Great*, Harmondsworth 1987.
Foxhall, L. and Lewis, A. D. E., *Greek Law in Its Political Setting: Justifications Not Justice*, Oxford 1996.
Frey, J., "Temple and Rival Temple – The Cases of Elephantine, Mt. Gerizim, and Leontopolis", in Ego, B., Lange, A., and Pilhofer, P., (eds.), *Gemeinde ohne Tempel: Community Without Temple, Wissenschaftliche Untersuchungen zum Neuen Testament 118*, Tübingen 1999, pp. 171–203.
Fritsch, G. T., "Herod the Great and the Qumran Community", *JBL 74*, 1955, pp. 173–181.
Frova, A., *Scavi di Caesarea Maritima*, Milan 1965.
Funk, R. W., "The 1957 Campaign at Beth-Zur", *BASOR 150*, 1958, pp. 8–20.
Gabba, E., *Republican Rome, The Army and the Allies*, Berkeley 1976.
Gabba, E., "The Finances of King Herod", *Greece and Rome in Eretz Israel*, Jerusalem 1990, pp. 160–168.
Gabba, E., "The Historians and Augustus", in Millar, F., and Segal, E., (eds.), *Caesar Augustus, Seven Aspects*, Oxford 1994, pp. 61–89.
Gabba, E., "The Social, Economic and Political History of Palestine 63 BCE–CE 70", *CHJ, The Early Roman Period 3* Cambridge 1999, pp. 94–168.
Gabrielsen, V., "The Athenian Navy in the Fourth Century BC", in *The Age of the Galley, Mediterranean Oared Vessels since pre-classical Times*, London 1995, pp. 234–240.
Gafni, I. M., "Punishment, Blessing or Mission – Jewish Dispersion in the Second Temple and Talmudic Period", *The Jews in the Hellenistic-Roman World, Studies in Memory of Menahem Stern* Jerusalem 1996, pp. 229–251 (Hebrew).
Galili, E., "Raphia, 217 BCE, Revisited", *SCI 3*, 1976–77, pp. 52–127.
Galinsky, K., *Augustan Culture, An Interpretative Introduction*, Princeton (N. J.) 1996.
Gardiner, P., *Theories of History*, New York 1959.
Geagan, D. G., "The Athenian Constitution after Sulla", *Hesperia Supplements 12*, Princeton (N. J.) 1967.

Geertz, C., *Local Knowledge, Further Essays in Interpretative Anthropology*, New York (N. Y.) 1983.

Geiger, J., "Herod and Rome: New Aspects", *The Jews in the Hellenistic-Roman World, Studies in Memory of Menahem Stern*, Jerusalem 1996, pp. 134–137 (Hebrew).

Geva, H., "Jerusalem, the Second Temple Period", *The New Encyclopedia of Archaeological Excavations in the Holy Land 2*, Jerusalem 1992.

Gianfrotta, P. A., "Harbor Structures of the Augustan Age in Italy", in Raban, A., and Holum, K., (eds.), *Caesarea Maritima, A Retrospective after Two Millennia, DMOA 21*, pp. 65–77.

Gibbs, J. G., and Feldman, L. H., "Josephus' Vocabulary for Slavery", *JQR* 76, 4, 1986, pp. 281–310.

Gichon, M., "Idumaea and the Herodian Limes", *IEJ* 17, 1967, pp. 27–42.

Gichon, M., "Roman Bath-Houses in Eretz-Israel", *Qadmoniot 11*, 1978 (Hebrew).

Gichon, M., "En Boqeq", *NEAEHL 2*, pp. 395–396.

Ginzburg, C., *History, Rhetoric, and Proof, The Menahem Stern Jerusalem Lectures*, New York 1999.

Ginzburg, C., "Just One Witness", in S. Friedlander (ed.), *Probing the Limits of Representation, Nazism and the "Final Solution,"* Cambridge (Mass.) 1992, pp. 82–96.

Ginouvès, R., *I Macedoni, da Filippo II alla conquista romana*, Milano 1993.

Glatzer, N., *Hillel the Elder, The Emergence of Classical Judaism*, New York 1966.

Gleason, K., "Ruler and Spectacle: The Promontory Palace", in Raban, A., and Holum, K., (eds.), *Caesarea Maritima, a Retrospective after Two Millennia, DMOA 21*, Leiden 1996, pp. 208–227.

Glessmer, U., "Calendars in the Qumran Scrolls", in P. W. Flint and J. C. VanderKam (eds.), *The Dead Sea Scrolls after Fifty Years, A Comprehensive Assessment II*, Leiden 1999, pp. 213–278.

Golb, N., "The Dead Sea Scrolls and pre-Tannaitic Judaism", *CHJ, The Early Roman Period 3*, Cambridge 1999, pp. 822–852.

Goldin, J., "The Three Pillars of Simon the Righteous", *PAAJR* 27, 1958, pp. 43–58.

Goodblatt, D. M., "The Talmudic Sources on the Origins of Organized Jewish Education", *Studies in the History of the Jewish People and the Land of Israel 5*, 1980, pp. 83–103 (Hebrew).

Goodblatt, D. M., *The Monarchic Principle, TSAJ 38*, Tübingen 1994.

Goodblatt, D., "The Political and Social History of the Jewish Community in the Land of Israel, c. 235–638" in S. T. Katz (ed.), *CHJ IV, The Late Roman-Rabbinic Period*, Cambridge 2006.

Goodman, M., *The Ruling Class of Judaea, The Origins of the Jewish Revolt against Rome AD 66–70*, Cambridge 1987.

Goodman, M., "The Roman Identity of Roman Jews", *The Jews in the Hellenistic-Roman World, Studies in Memory of Menahem Stern*, Jerusalem 1996, pp. 85*–101*.

Goodman, M., "Galilaean Judaism and Judaean Judaism", *CHJ, The Early Roman Period 3*, Cambridge 1999, pp. 596–618.

Gracey, H. M., "The Armies of the Judaean Client Kings", *The Defence of the Roman and Byzantine East*, Oxford, BAR, 1986, pp. 311–323.

Graham, A. J., *Colony and Mother City in Ancient Greece*, Chicago 1983.

Grant, M., *Herod the Great*, New York 1971.

Grant, M., *Gladiators*, New York 1995.

Green, P., *Alexander to Actium, The Historical Evolution of the Hellenistic Age*, Berkeley 1990.
Greenberg, M., *Ezekiel, The Anchor Bible 1-2*, New York 1983.
Greenfield, J.C., "Languages of Palestine, 200 BCE-200 CE", in Paper, H.H., (ed.), *Jewish Languages, Theme and Variations*, New York 1978, pp. 143-154.
Greenhut, L., "The Caiaphas Tomb in Northern Talpioth", in Geva, H. (ed.), *Ancient Jerusalem Revealed, Expanded Edition*, Jerusalem 2000, pp. 219-222.
Griffin, M.T., *Nero, The End of a Dynasty*, London 1984.
Griffin, J., "Augustus and the Poets: Caesar qui cogere posset", in F. Millar and E. Segal (eds.), *Caesar Augustus, Seven Aspects*, Oxford 1994, pp. 189-219.
Grimm, G., *Alexandria, Die erste Königsstadt der hellenistischen Welt*, Mainz 1998.
Grimm, G., "Le Sérapéion", in *La gloire d'Alexandrie, Musée du Petit Palais*, Paris 1998, pp. 94-98.
Gros, P., *Aurea Templa, recherches sur l'architecture religieuse de Rome à l'époque d'Auguste, Bibliothéque des Écoles Françaises d'Athénes et de Rome 231*, Rome 1976.
Gros, P., *L'architecture romaine 1, Les monuments publics*, Paris 1996.
Gros, P., *L'architecture romaine 2, Maisons, palais, villas et tombeaux*, Paris 2001.
Gruen, E.S., *The Last Generation of the Roman Republic*, Berkeley (Ca.), 1974.
Gruen, E.S., "The Imperial Policy of Augustus", in Raaflaub, K.A., and Toher, M., (eds.), *Between Republic and Empire: Interpretations of Augustus and his Principate*, Los Angeles (Ca.), 1990, pp. 395-416.
Gruen, E.S., "The Origins and Objectives of Onias' Temple", *SCI 16*, 1997, pp. 47-70.
Gruen, E.S., *Heritage and Hellenism, The Reinvention of Jewish Tradition, Hellenistic Culture and Society 31*, Berkeley (Cal.) 1998.
Gruen, E.S., *Diaspora; Jews amidst Greeks and Romans*, Cambridge (Mass.) 2002.
Gunneweg, J., Perlman, I., Yellin, J., *The Provenance, Typology and Chronology of Eastern Terra Sigillata, Qedem 17*, Jerusalem 1983.
Gunneweg, J., Perlman, I., Yellin, J., "Pseudo-Nabatean Ware and Pottery of Jerusalem", *BASOR 262*, 1986, pp. 77-82.
Gurval, R.A., *Actium and Augustus, The Politics and Emotions of Civil War*, Ann Arbor (Mich.), 1995.
Habicht, C., *Athens from Alexander to Antony*, Cambridge (Mass.), 1999.
Hacham, N., "From Splendor to Disgrace; On the Destruction of Egyptian Jewry in Rabbinic Literature", *Tarbiz* LXXII, 4, 2003 (Hebrew), pp. 463-488.
Hachlili, R., "A Second Temple Period Necropolis in Jericho", *BA 43*, 1980, pp. 235-240.
Hachlili, R., "Jewish Funerary Customs during the Second Temple Period in Light of the Excavations of the Jericho Necropolis", *PEQ 115*, 1983, pp. 110-125.
Hachlili, R., *Ancient Jewish Art and Archaeology in the Land of Israel, Handbuch der Orientalistik*, Leiden 1988.
Hadas, G., "Nine Tombs of the Second Temple Period at 'En Gedi", *'Atiqot 24*, Jerusalem, 1994 (Hebrew).
Hadas-Lebel, M., *Hillel, Un sage au temps de Jésus*, Paris 1999.
Hammerschmidt, E., "Königsideologie im Spätantiken Judentum", *ZDMG 113*, 1963-64, pp. 493-511.
Harari, M., "Un punto di vista archeologico sulla lettera di Aristea", *Studi Ellenistici 2*, 1987, pp. 96-106.
Hayward, C.T.R., The Jewish Temple at Leontopolis; A Reconsideration", *JJS 33,1-2*, 1982, pp. 429-443.

Head, B. V., *A Guide to the Principal Coins of the Greeks*, British Museum Department of Coins and Medals, London 1959.
Head, D., *Armies of the Macedonian and Punic Wars, 359 BC to 146 BC*, Goring-by-Sea 1982.
Heilmeyer, W. D. (ed.), *Kaiser Augustus und die verlorene Republik*, Berlin 1988, pp. 13–291.
Hengel, M., *Judaism and Hellenism. Studies in their Encounter in Palestine during the Early Hellenistic Period*, London 1974.
Herbert, S. C., *Tel Anafa, Final Report on Ten Years of Excavation at a Hellenistic and Roman Settlement in Northern Israel, Part 1*, JRA Supp. Series No. 10, Ann Arbor, 1994.
Herr, M. D., "The Historical Significance of the Dialogues between Sages and Roman Dignitaries", *Scripta Hierosolymitana* 22, 1971, pp. 123–150.
Herr, M. D., "The End of Jewish Hellenistic Literature: When and Why?", *The Jews in the Hellenistic-Roman World, Studies in Memory of Menahem Stern*, Jerusalem 1996, pp. 361–379 (Hebrew).
Herzog, Z., "Settlement and Fortification Planning in the Iron Age", *The Architecture of Ancient Israel, from the Prehistoric to the Persian Period*, Jerusalem 1992, pp. 231–274.
Von Hesberg, H., *Römische Grabbauten*, Darmstadt 1992.
Von Hesberg, H., "The Significance of the Cities in the Kingdom of Herod", *Judaea and the Greco-Roman World in the Time of Herod in the Light of Archaeological Evidence, Abhandlungen der Akademie der Wissenschaften in Göttingen*, Göttingen 1996, pp. 9–27.
Hezser, C., *Jewish Literacy in Roman Palestine*, TSAJ 81, Tübingen 2001.
Hezser, C., "Jewish Literacy and the Use of Writing in Late Roman Palestine", in Kalmin, R. L., and Schwarz, S., (eds.), *Jewish Culture and Society under the Christian Roman Empire, Interdisciplinary Studies in Ancient Culture and Religion*, Peeters 2003, pp. 149–195.
Hezser, C., "The Social Status of Slaves in the Talmud Yerushalmi and in Graeco-Roman Society", in Schäfer, P. (ed.), *The Talmud Yerushalmi and Graeco-Roman Culture* III, TSAJ 79, Tübingen 2003, pp. 91–137.
Hezser, C., "Slaves and Slavery in Rabbinic and Roman Law, in Heszer, C. (ed.), *Rabbinic Law in its Roman and Near Eastern Context*, TSAJ 97, Tübingen 2003, pp. 133–176.
Hezser, C., "The Impact of Household Slaves on the Jewish Family in Roman Palestine", *JSJ* 34, 4, 2003, pp. 375–424.
Hirschfeld, Y., *The Palestinian Dwelling in the Roman-Byzantine Period*, SBF, Collectio Minor 34, Jerusalem 1995.
Hirschfeld, Y., "The Early Roman Bath and Fortress at Ramat Hanadiv near Caesarea", in *The Roman and Byzantine Near East: Some Recent Archaeological Research*, JRA Supp. Series 14, 1995, pp. 28–54.
Hirschfeld, Y., *Ramat Hanadiv Excavations, Final Report of the 1984–1998 Seasons*, Jerusalem 2000.
Höckmann, O., "Schiffahrt zwischen Alpen und Nordsee", in *Römer zwischen Alpen und Nordmeer*, Mainz 2000, pp. 264–269.
Hoehner, H. W., *Herod Antipas, A Contemporary of Jesus Christ*, Grand Rapids (Mi) 1980.
Hölbl, G., *A History of the Ptolemaic Empire*, London 2001.
Holum, K. G., *King's Herod's Dream, Caesarea on the Sea*, New York 1988.
Hopkins, K., *Conquerors and Slaves: Sociological Studies in Roman History* I, Cambridge 1978.

Hornbury, W., "Women in the Synagogue", *CHJ, The Early Roman Period 3*, Cambridge 1999, pp. 358–402.
Horowitz, J., "Town Planning of Hellenistic Marisa ", *PEQ 112*, 1980, pp. 93–111.
Hoyos, D., *Hannibal's Dynasty, Power and Politics in the Western Mediterranean, 247-183 BC*, London 2003.
Humphrey, J. H., "Amphithetrical Hippo-Stadia", in Raban, A., and Holum, K., (eds.), *Caesarea Maritima, A Retrospective after Two Millennia, DMOA 21*, Leiden 1996, pp. 121–129.
Hurwit, J. M., *The Athenian Acropolis, History, Mythology, and Archaeology from the Neolithic Era to the Present*, Cambridge 2000.
Hurwit, J. M., *The Acropolis in the Age of Pericles*, Cambridge 2004.
Ilan, T., *Jewish Women in Graeco-Roman Palestine, TSAJ 44*, Tübingen 1995.
Ilan, T., *Integrating Women into Second Temple History, TSAJ 76*, Tübingen 1999.
Isaac, B., "Trade Routes to Arabia and the Roman Army", *Roman Frontier Studies 12 1979, 3, BAR International Series 71*, Oxford 1979, pp. 889–901.
Innes Miller, J., *The Spice Trade of the Roman Empire, 29 BC to AD 641*, Oxford 1969.
Isser, S., "The Samaritans and their Sects", *CHJ, The Early Roman Period 3*, Cambridge 1999, pp. 569–596.
Jackson, B. S., "The Divorces of the Herodian Princesses: Jewish Law, Roman Law or Palace Law?", in *International Josephus Colloquium*, Rome, 21–24 September 2003 (Unpublished Paper).
Jacobson, D., "The Anchor on the Coins of Judaea", *BAIAS 18*, 2000, pp. 73–81.
Jacobson, D., "The Roman Client Kings: Herod of Judaea, Archelaos of Cappadocia, and Juba of Mauretania", *PEF 133*, 2001, pp. 22–38.
Jacobson, D., "Herod's Roman Temple", *BAR 28*, 2, 2002, pp. 19–23.
Jaeckle, R., "Das Prätorium des Pilatus in Jerusalem", *DEI 2*, 1990, pp. 59–72.
Japp, S., *Die Baupolitike Herodes des Großen, Internationale Archäologie 64*, Rahden 2000.
Jaubert, A., "Le Calendrier des Jubilés et la secte de Qumran: ses origins bibliques, *VT 3*, 1953, pp. 250–264.
Jeremias, J., *Jerusalem in the Time of Jesus: An Investigation into Economic & Social Conditions during the New Testament Period*, Philadelphia 1969.
Jeremias, J., and Schneemelcher, W., "Oxyrhynchus Papyrus 840", in Schneemelcher, W., (ed.), *New Testament Apocrypha 1, Gospels and Related Writings*, Louisville (Kent.) 1991, pp. 94–95.
Johnson, A., *Roman Forts of the 1st and 2nd centuries AD in Britain and the German Provinces*, London 1983.
Johnston, D., *Roman Law in Context, Key Themes in Ancient History*, Cambridge 1992.
Jones, A. H. M., *The Herods of Judaea*, Oxford 1967.
Jones, A. H. M., *The Greek City, From Alexander to Justinian*, Oxford 1984.
Jones, A. H. M., *Cities of the Eastern Roman Provinces*, Oxford 1998.
Junkelmann, M., *Die Legionen des Augustus, Der römische Soldat im archäologischen Experiment, Kulturgeschichte der Antiken Welt 33*, Mainz 1994.
Kahn, L. C., "King Herod's Temple of Roma and Augustus at Caesarea Maritima", in Raban, A., and Holum, K., (eds.), *Caesarea Maritima, a Retrospective after Two Millennnia, DMOA 21*, Leiden 1996, pp. 135–142.
Kaltsas, N., *Ancient Messene*, Athens 1989.
Kaminka, A., "Hillel's Life and Work", *JQR 30*, 1939–40, pp. 107–122.

Kasher, A., "The War of Herod against the Nabateans", *Proceedings of the National Academies of Sciences*, 7, 4, 1986, pp. 109-142 (Hebrew).
Kasher, A., *Jews, Idumaeans and Ancient Arabs*, TSAJ 18, Tübingen 1988.
Kasher, A., "The Foundation of Tiberias and its Function as the Capital of the Galilee", *Idan* 11, 1988, pp. 3-11 (Hebrew).
Kasher, A., *Jews and Hellenistic Cities in Eretz-Israel, Relations of the Jews with the Hellenistic Cities during the Second Temple Period*, TSAJ 21, Tübingen 1990.
Katzoff, R., "Philo and Hillel on Violation of Betrothal in Alexandria", *The Jews in the Hellenistic-Roman World, Studies in Memory of Menahem Stern*, Jerusalem 1996, pp. 39-57 (Hebrew).
Kaufman, D. J., "The Dead Sea Scrolls and the Oniad High Priesthood", *Qumran Chronicle* 7,1-2, 1997, pp. 51-63.
Kee, H. C., Defining the First-Century CE Synagogue; Problems and Progress, *NTS* 41,4, 1995, pp. 481-500.
Keppie, L., "The Roman Army of the Later Republic", in *Warfare in the Ancient World*, Hackett, J., (ed.), New York 1989, pp. 169-191.
Keppie, L., *The Making of the Roman Army, from Republic to Empire*, London 1998.
Klausner, J., "The First Hasmonaean Rulers: Jonathan and Simeon", in *The World History of the Jewish People 6, The Hellenistic Period*, New Brunswick 1972, pp. 183-207.
Klausner, J., "John Hyrcanus I", in *The World History of the Jewish People 6, The Hellenistic Period*, New Brunswick 1972, pp. 211-221.
Klausner, J., "Judah Aristobulus and Jannaeus Alexander", in *The World History of the Jewish People 6, The Hellenistic Period*, New Brunswick 1972, pp. 222-241.
Klausner, J., "Queen Salome Alexandra", in *The World History of the Jewish People 6, The Hellenistic Period*, New Brunswick 1972, pp. 242-254.
Klausner, J., "The Economy of Judaea in the Period of the Second Temple", in *The World History of the Jewish People 7, The Herodian Period*, New Brunswick 1975, pp. 180-205.
Klawans, Z. H., *An Outline of Ancient Greek Coins*, New York 1982.
Kloner, A., "The "Third Wall" in Jerusalem and the "Cave of the Kings" (Josephus War V 147)", *Levant* 18, 1986, pp. 121-129.
Kloner, A., "Marissa", *NEAEHL* 3, 1993, pp. 951-957.
Kloner, A., "An Ossuary from Jerusalem Ornamented with Monumental Facades", in Geva, H., (ed.), *Ancient Jerusalem Revealed, Expanded Edition 2000*, Jerusalem 2000, pp. 235-238.
Kloner, A., "Burial Customs of the Jews at the time of the Hasmonaeans", *In the Days of the Hasmonaeans*, Jerusalem 1995, pp. 211-218 (Hebrew).
Kloner, A., *Marissa*, Jerusalem 1996.
Kloner, A., "Columbaria in Jerusalem", in Schwartz, J., Amar, Z., and Ziffer, I., (eds.), *Jerusalem and Eretz Israel*, Tel Aviv 2000, pp. 61-66.
Kloner, A., "The Economy of Hellenistic Maresha", in Archibald, Z. H., , Davis, J., Gabrielsen, V., Oliver, G. J., (eds.), *Hellenistic Economies*, London and New York 2001, pp. 103-131.
Kloner, A., *Maresha Excavations Final Report I: Subterranean Complexes 21, 44, 77*, Jerusalem 2003.
Kloner, A., Zissu, B., "The "Cave of Simon the Just" and "The Minor Sanhedrin". Two Burial Complexes from the Second Temple Period in Jerusalem", In Rutgers, L. V., (Ed.) *What Athens Has to Do with Jerusalem, Essays in Honor of Gideon Foerster*, Leuven 2002, pp. 125-149.

Kloner, A., Zissu, B., *The Necropolis of Jerusalem in the Second Temple Period*, Jerusalem 2003.
Kloppenborg, J. S., "Collegia and Thiasoi: Issues in Function, Taxonomy and Membership", in Kloppenborg, J. S., and Wilson, S. G. (eds.), *Voluntary Associations in the Graeco-Roman World*, London 1996, pp. 16-31.
Kloppenborg, J. S., "Dating Theodotos ("CIJ" II 1404)", *JJS 51,2*, 2000, pp. 243-280.
Knigge, U., *The Athenian Kerameikos, History - Monuments - Excavations*, Athens 1991.
Knohl, I., *The Messiah before Jesus*, Jerusalem 2000.
Koch, G., and Sichtermann, H., *Römische Sarkophage, Handbuch der Archäologie*, München 1982.
Kokkinos, N., *The Herodian Dynasty, Origins, Role in Society, Eclipse, JSPSup. 30*, Sheffield 1998.
Kokkinos, N., "Herod's Horrid Death", *BAR 28, 2*, 2002, pp. 28-35.
Kondoleon, A., "The City of Antioch: An Introduction", in *Antioch, The Lost Ancient City*, Princeton (NJ) 2000, p. 9.
Krause, C., *Villa Jovis, Die Residenz des Tiberius auf Capri*, Mainz 2003.
Krencker, D. M., and Zschietzschmann, W., *Römische Tempel in Syria 1, Denkmaler Antike Architektur 5*, Berlin 1938.
Kuhrt, A., "The Seleucid Kings and Babylonia: New Perspectives on the Seleucid Realm in the East", in *Aspects of Hellenistic Kingship, Studies in Hellenistic Civilisation 7*, Aarhus 1996, pp. 41-55.
Kuttner, A. L., *Dynasty and Empire in the Age of Augustus, The Case of the Boscoreale Cups*, Berkeley (Cal.) 1995.
La Penna, A., *Introduzione in Virgilio, Bucoliche*, Milano 1983.
La Rocca, E., *Ara Pacis Augustae, in occasione del restauro della fronte orientale*, Roma 1983.
Landau, T., "Power and Pity, The Image of Herod in Josephus BJ", *International Josephus Colloquium*, Rome 21-24 September 2003 (Unpublished Paper).
Lane Fox, R., *Alexander the Great*, Harmondsworth 1987.
Langlois, C. V., and Seignobos, M. J. C., *Introduction to the Study of History*, London 1912.
Lauter, H., *Die Architektur des Hellenismus*, Darmstadt 1986.
Lawrence, A. W., *Greek Architecture*, Harmondsworth 1957.
Le Bohec, Y., *L'esercito Romano*, Roma 1993.
Lehmann, J., "Le procès d'Hérode, Saméas et Pollion", *REJ 24*, 1892.
Leon, H. J., *The Jews of Ancient Rome*, Peabody (Mass.) 1995.
Levi, M. A., *Pericle*, Milano 1980.
Levi, M. A., *Augusto e il suo tempo*, Milano 1986.
Levick, B., *Claudius*, London, 1993.
Levick, B., *Vespasian*, London, 1999.
Levine, L. I., "The Political Struggle between Pharisees and Sadducees in the Hasmonean Period", in Oppenheimer, A., Rappaport, U., and Stern, M., (eds.), *Jerusalem in the Second Temple Period, Abraham Shalit Memorial Volume*, Jerusalem 1980, pp. 61-83 (Hebrew).
Levine, L. I., "From the Beginning of Roman Rule to the End of the Second Temple Period", in Stern, M., (ed.) *The History of Eretz-Israel 4, The Roman-Byzantine Period, The Roman Rule from the Conquest to the Bar Kochba War (63 BCE-135 CE)*, Jerusalem 1987 (Hebrew).

Levine, L. I., "The Second Temple Synagogue, The Formative Years", in Levine, L. I. (ed.), *The Synagogue in Late Antiquity*, Philadelphia 1987, pp. 7–31.

Levine, L. I., "Josephus's Description of the Jerusalem Temple: War, Antiquities, and Other Sources", *Cathedra 77*, 1995, pp. 3–17 (Hebrew).

Levine, I. L., "Unity and Diversity in Ancient Judaism: The Case of the Diaspora Synagogue", *The Jews in the Hellenistic-Roman World, Studies in Memory of Menahem Stern*, Jerusalem 1996, pp. 379–393 (Hebrew).

Levine, L. I., *Judaism and Hellenism, Conflict or Confluence?*, Seattle 1998.

Levine, L. I., *The Ancient Synagogue, The First Thousand Years*, New York 2000.

Levine, L. I., *Jerusalem, Portrait of the City in the Second Temple Period (538 BCE–70 CE)*, Philadelphia 2002.

Levine, L. I., "The First Century CE Synagogue in Historical Perspective", in Olsson, B. and Zetterholm, M. (Eds.), *The Ancient Synagogue from Its Origins until 200 CE: Papers Presented at an International Conference at Lund University, October 14–17, 2001 (Coniectanea Biblica. New Testament Series, 39)*, Stockholm 2003, pp. 1–24.

Levine, L. I., The First-Century Synagogue; Critical Reassessments and Assessments of the Critical, in Edwards, D. (ed.) *Religion and Society in Roman Palestine, Old Questions New Approaches*, London 2004, pp. 70–102.

Lewis, N., *The Documents from the Bar – Kochba Period in the Cave of Letters, Vol. 2, Greek Papyri*, Jerusalem 1989.

Liddell Hart, B., *A Greater than Napoleon, Scipio Africanus*, London 1926.

Lieberman, S., *Hellenism in Jewish Palestine*, New York 1994.

Lightstone, J., *The Commerce of the Sacred, Mediation of the Divine among Jews in the Graeco Roman Diaspora, Brown Judaic Studies 59*, Chico (Ca.) 1984.

Ling, R., *Roman Painting*, Cambridge 1992.

Lintott, A., *Imperium Romanum, Politics and Administration*, London 1993.

Luce, T. J., "Livy, Augustus, and the Forum Augustum", in Raauflaub, K. A., and Toher, M., (eds.), *Between Republic and Empire, Interpretations of Augustus and His Principate*, pp. 123–138.

Luttwak, E. N., *La grande strategia dell'impero romano*, Milano 1991.

MacDonald, W. L., *The Architecture of the Roman Empire 1*, New Haven (Con.) 1986.

MacMullen, R., *Paganism in the Roman Empire*, New Haven (Conn.) 1981.

MacMullen, R., *Romanization in the Time of Augustus*, New Haven (Conn.) 2000.

Magen, Y., *The Industry of Stone Vessels in Jerusalem in the Second Temple Period*, Jerusalem 1988.

Magen, Y., "Mount Garizim", *Christian Archaeology in the Holy Land; New Discoveries*, Jerusalem 1990, pp. 333–342.

Magen, Y., "Mount Gerizim and the Samaritans", in Alliata, E. and Manns, F. (eds.), *Early Christianity in Context, Monuments and Documents*, SBFCM 38, Jerusalem 1993, pp. 91–148.

Magen, Y., "Israele: un tempio come il Tempio", *Archeo 128*, 1995, pp. 30–38.

Magen, Y., and Naveh, J., "Aramaic and Hebrew Inscriptions of the Second Century BCE at Mount Gerizim", *'Atiqot 32*, 1997, pp. 9–17.

Magen, Y., "Excavations at the Damascus Gate", *Ancient Jerusalem Revealed, Expanded Edition 2000*, Jerusalem 2000, pp. 281–287.

Magen, Y., and Stern, E., "Archaeological Evidence for the First Stage of the Samaritan Temple on Mount Gerizim, *IEJ 52,1*, 2002, pp. 49–57.

Magen, Y., Zionit, Y., and Sirkis, E., "A Jewish Village and Synagogue of the Second Temple Period", *Qadmoniot 32, 1 (117)*, 1999, pp. 25-32 (Hebrew).
Maier, J., "The Architectural History of the Temple in Jerusalem in the Light of the Temple Scroll", in Brooke, G.J., (ed.), *Temple Scroll Studies, JSPSup. 7*, Sheffield 1989, pp. 23-35.
Mantel, H.D., *Studies in the History of Sanhedrin*, Cambridge 1961.
Mantel, H.D., "The High Priesthood and the Sanhedrin in the Time of the Second Temple", in *The World History of the Jewish People 7, The Herodian Period*, New Brunswick 1975, pp. 264-274.
Maoz, Z., "The Synagogue of Gamla and the Typology of the Second Temple Period Synagogues", in Levine, L.I., (ed.), *Ancient Synagogues Revealed*, Jerusalem 1981, pp. 35-41.
Marsden, E.W., *Greek and Roman Artillery, Historical Development*, Oxford 1969.
Martin, L.H., *Hellenistic Religions, An Introduction*, Oxford 1987.
Mason, S., *Flavius Josephus on the Pharisees, A Composition - Critical Study, Studia Post Biblica*, Leiden 1991.
Mass, M., "People and Identity in Roman Antioch", in Kondoleon, C. (ed.), *Antioch, The Lost Ancient City*, Princeton (N.J.), 2000, pp. 13-23.
Maxwell Miller, J., and Hayes, J.H., *A History of Ancient Israel and Judah*, Philadelphia 1986.
Mayer, L.A., *The Third Wall of Jerusalem, An Account of Excavations*, Jerusalem 1930.
Mazar, A., "The Aqueducts of Jerusalem", in Yadin, Y., (ed.), *Jerusalem Revealed, Archaeology in the Holy City 1968-1974*, Jerusalem 1976, pp. 25-40.
Mazar, A., "A Survey of the Aqueducts leading to Jerusalem", in Amit, D., (ed.), *The Aqueducts of Ancient Palestine*, Jerusalem 1989, pp. 169-195 (Hebrew).
Mazar, A., *Archaeology of the Land of the Bible 10.000-586 BCE*, New York 1990.
Mazar, B., "'En Gedi - The First and Second Season of Excavations, 1961-1962", *Atiqot 5*, 1966, p. 5 (Hebrew).
Mazar, B., *Kingship in Ancient Israel, Biblical Israel, State and People*, Jerusalem 1992.
McKay, A.G., *Houses, Villas, and Palaces in the Roman World*, London 1975.
McLaren, J.S., *Power and Politics in Palestine. The Jews and the Governing of their Land, 100 BC-AD 70, JSNT Supplement Series 63*, Sheffield 1991.
McNicoll, A.W., *Hellenistic Fortifications, From the Aegean to the Euphrates, Oxford Monographs on Classical Archaeology*, Oxford 1997.
Mélèze Modrzejewski, J., *The Jews of Egypt, From Ramses II to Emperor Hadrian*, Philadelphia 1993.
Mendels, D., *The Rise and Fall of Jewish Nationalism*, New York 1992.
Meshorer, Y., "A Stone Weight from the Reign of Herod", *IEJ 20*, 1970, pp. 97-98.
Meshorer, Y., *Ancient Jewish Coinage 1, Persian Period through Hasmonaeans*, New York 1982.
Meshorer, Y., *Ancient Jewish Coinage 2, Herod the Great through Bar Cochba*, New York 1982.
Meshorer, Y., *City-Coins of Eretz-Israel and the Decapolis in the Roman Period*, Jerusalem 1985.
Meshorer, Y., *The Coinage of Aelia Capitolina*, Jerusalem 1989.
Meshorer, Y., *A Treasury of Jewish Coins, From the Persian Period to Bar Kokhba*, Jerusalem 2001.
Meyers, E.M. et al., *Sepphoris*, Winona Lake (Ind.) 1992.

Meyers, E. M.(ed.), "Suweida", *The Oxford Encyclopedia of Archaeology in the Near East 5*, New York 1997, pp. 111–112.
Meyers, E. M., "Recent Archaeology in Palestine: Achievements and Future Goals", *CHJ, The Early Roman Period 3*, Cambridge 1999, pp. 59–75.
Mielsch, H., *Die römische Villa*, München 1987.
Mierse, W., "Augustus' Building Program in the Western Provinces", in Raauflaub, K. A., and Toher, M. (eds.), *Between Republic and Empire, Interpretations of Augustus and His Principate*, pp. 308–325.
Milik, J. T., *The Book of Enoch: Aramaic Fragments of Qumran Cave 4*, Oxford 1976.
Millar, F., "State and Subject; the Impact of Monarchy", in Millar, F. and Segal, E., (eds.), *Caesar Augustus: Seven Aspects*, Oxford 1984, pp. 37–60.
Millar, F., *The Emperor in the Roman World*, Ithaca (N. Y.) 1992.
Millar, F., *The Roman Near East 31 BC–AD 337*, Cambridge (Mass.) 1993.
Millar, F., "The Roman City State under the Emperors, 29 BC–AD 69", in *Rome, the Greek World and the East I, The Roman Republic and the Augustan Revolution*, London 2002, pp. 360–377.
Millard, A., *Reading and Writing in the Time of Jesus*, New York 2000.
Momigliano, A., *Studies in Historiography*, London 1966.
Momigliano, A., *Alien Wisdom*, Cambridge 1976.
Momigliano, A., "The Rhetoric of History and the History of Rhetoric: On Hayden White's Tropes", *Ottavo contributo alla storia degli studi classici e del mondo antico*, Storia e Letteratura, Roma 1984, pp. 49–59.
Mommsen, T., *The Provinces of the Roman Empire from Caesar to Diocletian 1*, Chicago 1974.
Mooren, L., "Über die ptolemaischen Hofrangtitel", *Studia Hellenistica 16 (1968), Antidorum W. Peremans Sexagenario Ab Alumnis Oblatum*, Louvain 1968, pp. 161–180.
Morel, J. P., "L'artigiano", *L'uomo romano*, Bari 1993.
Morrison, J. S., *Greek and Roman Oared Warships, 399-30 BC*, Oxbow Monograph 62, 1996.
Murray, O., *La Grecia delle origini*, Bologna 1983.
Murray, O., "Hellenistic Royal Symposia", in *Aspects of Hellenistic Kingship, Studies in Hellenistic Civilisation 7*, Aarhus 1996, pp. 15–28.
Nakman, D., *The Halakhah in the Writings of Josephus*, Ph. D. Thesis submitted for the Degree "Doctor of Philosophy", Bar-Ilan University, Ramat Gan 2004 (Hebrew).
Nappo, S., *Pompeii, Guide to the Lost City*, London 1998.
Naveh, J., *Early History of the Alphabet*, Jerusalem 1987.
Negev, A., *Masters of the Desert, The History of the Nabateans*, Jerusalem 1983 (Hebrew).
Netzer, E., "Cypros", *Qadmoniot 8*, 1975, pp. 54–61 (Hebrew).
Netzer, E., "Herod's Building Projects: State Necessity or Personal Need? A Symposium", *The Jerusalem Cathedra 1*, 1981, pp. 48–80 (Hebrew).
Netzer, E., *Greater Herodium, Qedem 13*, Jerusalem 1981.
Netzer, E., "The Winter Palaces and the King's Estate in Jericho", in *Jericho, Kardom*, 1983 (Hebrew).
Netzer, E., "The Augusteum at Samaria Sebaste, A New Outlook", *Eretz-Israel 19*, 1987, pp. 97–105 (Hebrew).
Netzer, E., *Masada 3, The Yigael Yadin Excavations 1963-1965, Final Reports, The Buildings, Stratigraphy and Architecture*, Jerusalem 1991.

Netzer, E., "The Palaces built by Herod – A Research Update", *Judaea and the Graeco Roman World in the Time of Herod in the Light of Archaeological Evidence, Abhandlungen der Akademie der Wissenschaften in Göttingen*, Göttingen 1996, pp. 28–54.

Netzer, E., "The Hasmonaean Palaces in Palaestine", in Hoepfner, W. and Brands, G. (eds.), *Basileia – Die Palaeste der Hellenistischen Koenige*, Mainz, 1996, pp. 203 208.

Netzer, E., "The Promontory Palace", in Raban, A., and Holum, K., (eds.), *Caesarea Maritima, a Retrospective after Two Millennia, DMOA 21*, Leiden 1996, pp. 201–207.

Netzer, E., "A Synagogue from the Hasmonean Period Recently Exposed in the Western Plain of Jericho", *IEJ 49*, 1999, pp. 203–221.

Netzer, E., *The Palaces of the Hasmoneans and Herod the Great*, Mainz 1999.

Netzer, E., *The Palaces of the Hasmonaeans and Herod the Great*, Jerusalem 2001.

Netzer, E., *Hasmonean and Herodian Palaces at Jericho 1, Final Reports of the 1973–1987 Excavations*, Jerusalem 2001.

Netzer, E., *Hasmonean and Herodian Palaces at Jericho 2, Final Reports of the 1973–1987 Excavations*, Jerusalem 2004.

Netzer, E., "The Cities in Herod' the Great's Realm", in *Die Stadt als Grossbaustelle, Deutsches Archäologisches Institut*, Berlin 2004.

Neugebauer, O., "Appendix A" to M. Black, *The Book of Enoch or I Enoch*, Leiden 1985, pp. 386–419.

Neusner, J., *The Rabbinic Tradition about the Pharisees before 70, I*, Leiden 1971.

Neusner, J., *From Politics to Piety: The Emergence of Pharisaic Judaism*, Providence (R. I.) 1973.

Nicolet, C., *Le métier de citoyen dans la Rome républicaine*, Paris 1976.

Nicolet, C., "Augustus's Government and the Propertied Classes", in Millar, F., and Segal, E., (eds.), *Caesar Augustus, Seven Aspects*, Oxford 1994, pp. 89–129.

Nielsen, I., *Hellenistic Palaces, Tradition and Renewal, Studies in Hellenistic Civilisation 5*, Aarhus 1995.

Noam, V., *Megillat Ta'anit, Versions, Interpretation, History*, Jerusalem 2003 (Hebrew).

Oliver, J. H., *Marcus Aurelius: Aspects of Civic and Cultural Policy in the East, Hesperia Supplements 13*, Princeton (N. J.) 1970.

Olmstead, A. T., *History of the Persian Empire*, Chicago 1948.

Ostrow, G. E., "The Augustales in the Augustan Scheme", in Raaflaub, K. A., and Toher, M., (eds.), *Between Republic and Empire: Interpretations of Augustus and his Principate*, Los Angeles (Ca.), 1990, pp. 364–379.

Papahatzis, N., *Ancient Corinth, The Museum of Corinth, Isthmia and Sicyon*, Athens 1984.

Papathanassopoulos, G., *The Acropolis, Monuments and Museum*, Athens 1977.

Parente, F., "Onias III' Death and the Founding of the Temple of Leontopolis", in Parente, F. and Sievers, J. (eds.), *Josephus and the History of the Greco-Roman Period, Essays in Memory of Morton Smith, Studia Post Biblica 41*, Leiden 1994, pp. 69–98.

Parente, F., "Le témoignage de Théodore de Mopsueste sur le sort d'Onias III et la fondation du temple de Léontopolis", *REJ 154,3-4*, 1995, pp. 429–436.

Parker, R., *Athenian Religion: A History*, Oxford 1996.

Pastor, J., *Land and Economy in Ancient Palestine*, London 1997.

Patrich, J., "The Structure of the Second Temple – A New Reconstruction", *Ancient Jerusalem Revealed*, Jerusalem 1994, pp. 260–272.

Patrich, J., "Herod's Theatre in Jerusalem, A New Proposal", *IEJ 52*, 2002, pp. 231–239.

Peremans, W., and Van't Dack, E., *Prosopographia Ptolemaica 6, La cour, les relations internationales et les possessions exterieures, la vie culturelle, nos. 14479–17250*, Studia Hellenistica 17, Louvain 1968, p. xv.

Perowne, S. G., *The Life and Times of Herod the Great*, London 1956.

Pollini, J., "Man or God: Divine Assimilation and Imitation in the Late Republic and Early Principate", in Raaflaub, K. A., and Toher, M., (eds.), *Between Republic and Empire: Interpretations of Augustus and his Principate*, Los Angeles (Ca.), 1990, pp. 334–363.

Pollitt, J. J., *Art in the Hellenistic Age*, Cambridge 1986.

Porath, Y., and Patrich, J., "The Caesarea Excavation Project – March 1992 – June 1994, Expedition of the Antiquities Authority", *Excavations and Surveys in Israel 17*, Jerusalem 1998, pp. 39–41.

Préaux, C., *Le monde hellenistique, La Grèce et l'Orient 323–146 av. J. C., I–2*, Paris 1997.

Price, S. R. F., *Rituals and Powers, The Roman Imperial Cult in Asia Minor*, Cambridge 1984.

Pritchard, J. B., *The Times Atlas of the Bible*, London 1987.

Raaflaub, K. A., "Opposition to Augustus", in Raaflaub, K. A., and Toher, M., (eds.), *Between Republic and Empire: Interpretations of Augustus and his Principate*, Los Angeles (Ca.), 1990, pp. 417–454.

Raban, A., and Hohlfelder, R. L., "The Ancient Harbors of Caesarea Maritima", *Archaeology 34*, 1981, pp. 56–60.

Rabello, A. M., "Herod's Domestic Court? The Judgement of Death for Herod's Sons", in *Jewish Law Annual 10*, Boston 1992, pp. 39–56.

Rabello, A. M., "Civil Justice in Palestine from 63 BCE to 70 CE", in Katzoff, R., Petroff, Y., and Shaps, D., (eds.), *Classical Studies in Honor of David Sohlberg*, Ramat Gan 1996, pp. 293–306.

Rabello, A. M., "The "Lex de Templo Hierosolymitano", Prohibiting Gentiles from Entering Jerusalem's Sanctuary", *Christian News from Israel 21,3*, 1970, pp. 28–32.

Raditsa, L. F., "Augustus' Legislation Concerning Marriage, Procreation, Love Affairs and Adultery," in *Principat: Recht, ANRW 2, no. 13*, 1980, pp. 278–339.

Radt, W., *Pergamon, Geschichte und Bauten einer antiken Metropole*, Darmstadt 1999.

Ragette, F., *Baalbek*, Park Ridge (N. J.) 1980.

Rachmani, L. Y., "Jewish Rock-Cut Tombs in Jerusalem", *Atiqot 3*, 1964, pp. 93–120 (Hebrew).

Rachmani, L. Y., "Jason's Tomb", *IEJ 17*, 1967, pp. 61–100.

Rachmani, L. Y., *A Catalogue of Jewish Ossuaries, in the Collections of the State of Israel*, Jerusalem 1994.

Rachmani, L. Y., "Ossuaries and Ossilegium (Bone Gathering) in the Second Temple Period", in Geva, H., (ed.), *Ancient Jerusalem Revealed, Expanded Edition 2000*, Jerusalem 2000, pp. 191–205.

Rachmani, L. Y., "Sarcophagi of the Late Second Temple Period in Secondary Use", in Geva, H., (ed.), *Ancient Jerusalem Revealed, Expanded Edition 2000*, Jerusalem 2000, pp. 232–234.

Raeder, J., *Priene – Funde aus einer griechischen Stadt, Bilderhefte der staatlichen Museen preussicher Kulturbesitz Berlin*, Berlin 1983.

Rainbow, P. A., "The Last Oniad and the Teacher of Righteousness", *JJS 48,1*, 1997, pp. 30–52.

Rajak, T., *Josephus, The Historian and His Society*, London 2002.

Rajak, T., "Josephus as Historian of the Herods", *The World of the Herods and the Nabateans, An International Conference at the British Museum*, 17–19 April 2001 (Paper Unpublished).
Rakob, F., *Simitthus 1, Die Steinbrüche und die antike Stadt*, Mainz 1993.
Ramage, N., and Ramage, A., *The Cambridge Illustrated History of Roman Art*, Cambridge 1991.
Rankov, B., *The Praetorian Guard*, London 1994.
Rankov, B., "Fleets of the Early Roman Empire, 31 BC–AD 324", in *The Age of the Galley, Mediterranean Oared Vessels since pre-classical Times*, London 1995, pp. 78–85.
Rappaport, U., "La Judée et Rome pendant le règne d'Alexandre Jannée", *REJ, Historia Judaica* 78, 1968, pp. 329–342.
Rappaport, U., "The Hasmonean State and Hellenism", *Tarbiz* 60, 1991, pp. 481–490 (Hebrew).
Rappaport, U., "The Samaritans in the Hellenistic Period", in A. D. Crown and L. A. Davey (eds.), *New Samaritan Studies III and IV: Essays in Honour of G. D. Sixdenier, Studies in Judaica* 5, Sydney 1995, pp. 281–288.
Rappaport, U., "Social Stratification, Political Structure and Ideology on the Eve of the Destruction of the Second Temple", *The Jews in the Hellenistic-Roman World, Studies in Memory of Menahem Stern*, Jerusalem 1996, pp. 147–167 (Hebrew).
Rathbone, D., "The Grain Trade and Grain Shortages in the Hellenistic East", in Garnsey, P., and Whittaker, C. R., *Trade and Famine in Classical Antiquity*, Cambridge 1983, pp. 46–48.
Ravid, L., "The Book of Jubilees and its Calendar – A Reexamination", *Dead Sea Discoveries* 10,3, 2003, pp. 371–394.
Redde, M., *Mare Nostrum, Les infrastructures, le dispositif, et l'histoire de la marine militaire sous l'Empire Romain, Bibliotheque des 'Ecoles Françaises d'Athenes et de Rome 260*, Rome 1986.
Regev, A., *The Sadducees and their Halakhah, Religion and Society in the Second Temple Period*, Jerusalem 2005 (Hebrew).
Reich, R., and Billig, Y., "A Group of Theatre Seats Discovered near the South-Western Corner of the Temple Mount", *IEJ* 50, 2000, pp. 175–184.
Reif, S. C., *Judaism and Hebrew Prayer, New Perspectives on Jewish Liturgical History*, Cambridge 1998.
Reif, S. C., "The Early Liturgy of the Synagogue", *CHJ, The Early Roman Period* 3, Cambridge 1999, pp. 326–358.
Rey-Coquais, J. P., "Une inscription du Liban-Nord", *MUSJ* 47, 1972, pp. 96–97.
Rey-Coquais, J. P., "Syrie Romaine de Pompée à Dioclétien", *JRS* 68, 1978, pp. 44–73.
Richardson, L., *A New Topographical Dictionary of Ancient Rome*, Baltimore (Ma.) 1996.
Richardson, P., *Herod King of the Jews and Friend of the Romans*, Columbia (S. C.) 1996.
Richardson, P., "Early Synagogues as Collegia in the Diaspora and Palestine", in Kloppenborg, J. S., and Wilson, S. G., (eds.), *Voluntary Associations in the Graeco-Roman World*, London 1996, pp. 90–109.
Riesner, R., "Synagogues in Jerusalem", in Bauckham, R. (ed.), *The Book of Acts in its Palestinian Settings*, Grand Rapids 1995, pp. 179–210.
Ritterling, E., "Legio", in Paulys, *Realencyclopaëdie der Classischen Alterturmswissenschaft* XII, 2, Stuttgart 1925.
Rivkin, E., "Beth Din, Boule, Sanhedrin: A Tragedy of Errors", *HUCA* 46, 1975, pp. 181–199.

Robinson, O. F., *Ancient Rome, City Planning and Administration*, London 1992.
Roitman, A., "From Dawn to Dusk Among the Qumran Sectarians" in Roitman, A., (ed.), *A Day at Qumran, The Dead Sea Sect and Its Scrolls*, Jerusalem 1997, pp. 19-20.
Roller, D. W., *The Building Program of Herod the Great*, Berkeley 1998.
Romeopulos, K., *Leucadia – Archaia Mieza*, Athens 1997.
Rosenfeld, B., "The Boundary of Gezer Inscriptions and the History of Gezer at the End of the Second Period", *IEJ 38*, 1988, pp. 235-245.
Rostovtzeff, M. I., *The Social and Economic History of the Hellenistic World*, Oxford 1986.
Rostovtzeff, M. I., and Fraser, P. M., *The Social And Economic History of the Roman Empire*, Oxford 1963.
Rozenberg, S., *Enchanted Landscapes, Wall Paintings from the Roman Era*, Jerusalem 1993.
Rozenberg, S., "The Wall Paintings of the Herodian Palaces at Jericho", in *Judaea and the Greco-Roman World in the Time of Herod in the Light of Archaeological Evidence, Abhandlungen der Akademie der Wissenschaften in Göttingen N. 215*, Göttingen 1996, pp. 121-139.
Rowley, H. H., "The Herodians in the Gospels", *JTS 41*, 1940, pp. 14-27.
Rubin, N., "Secondary Burials in the Mishnaic and Talmudic Periods: A Proposed Model of the Relationship of Social Structure to Burial Practice", in Singer, I., (ed.), *Graves and Burial Practices in Israel in the Ancient Period*, Jerusalem 1994, pp. 248-269 (Hebrew).
Rutgers, L. V., *The Jews in Late Ancient Rome: Evidence of Cultural Interaction in the Roman Diaspora, Religions in the Graeco-Roman World*, Vol. 126, Brill 1995.
Safrai, S., "The Ritual in the Second Temple", *Sepher Yerushalayim*, Tel Aviv – Jerusalem 1956 (Hebrew).
Safrai, S., "The Temple and the Divine Service", in *The World History of the Jewish People 7, The Herodian Period*, New Brunswick 1975, pp. 284-332.
Safrai, Z., "The Influence of Demographic Stratification on the Agricultural and Economic Structure During the Mishnaic and Talmudic Periods", in Kasher, A., Oppenheimer, A., Rappaport, U., (eds.), *Man and Land in Eretz-Israel in Antiquity*, Jerusalem 1986, pp. 20-48 (Hebrew).
Safrai, Z., *The Economy of Roman Palestine*, London 1994.
Safrai, Z., and Lin, M., "Geva in the Hasmonean Period", *Cathedra 69*, 1993, pp. 18-36 (Hebrew).
Salmon, E. T., *Roman Colonization under the Republic*, Ithaca (N. Y.) 1970.
Salmon, E. T., *A History of the Roman World, 30 BC to AD 138*, London 1987.
Salza Prina Ricotti, F., *Ricette della cucina romana a Pompei*, Roma 1993.
Sanders, E. P., *Judaism, Practice and Belief 66 BCE-66 CE*, London 1992.
Sanders, E. P., *The Historical Figure of Jesus*, London 1993.
Sanders, E. P., "Common Judaism and the Synagogue in the First Century", in S. Fine (ed.), *Jews, Christians, and Polytheists in the Ancient Synagogue, Cultural Interaction during the Greco-Roman Period*, London 1999, pp. 1-17.
Sartre, A., "Architecture funeraire en Syrie", in Dentzer, J. M. and Orthmann, W., *Archeologie et histoire de la Syrie II, La Syrie de l'époque achéménide à l'avènement de l'Islam, Schriften zur vorderasiatischen Archaeologie 1*, Saarbrücken 1989.
Sartre, M., *L'Orient Romain*, Paris 1991.
Sartre, M., "Les metrokomiai de Syrie du Sud", *Syria 76*, 1999, pp. 197-222.
Sartre, M., *L'Asie Mineure et l'Anatolie d'Alexandre à Diocletien, IVe siècle av. J.-C. – IIIe siècle ap. J.-C.*, Paris 1995.

Sartre, M., *D'Alexandre à Zénobie, Histoire du Levant Antique, IVe siècle av. J.-C. – IIIe siècle ap. J.-C.*, Paris 2001.
Sauvaget, J., "Le plan antique de Damas", *Syria 26*, 1949, pp. 314–358.
Schalit, A., *King Herod, Portrait of a Ruler*, Jerusalem 1962 (Hebrew).
Schalit, A., "Die Herodianischen Patriarchen und der Davidische Herodes", *ASTI 6*, 1967–68, pp. 114–123.
Schalit, A., "Domestic Politics and Political Institutions", in *The World History of the Jewish People 6, The Hellenistic Period*, New Brunswick 1972, pp. 255–288.
Schalit, A., "The Fall of the Hasmonaean Dynasty and the Roman Conquest", in *The World History of the Jewish People 7, The Herodian Period*, New Brunswick 1975, pp. 26–44.
Schalit, A., "The End of the Hasmonaean Dynasty and the Rise of Herod", in *The World History of the Jewish People 7, The Herodian Period*, New Brunswick 1975, pp. 44–71.
Schalit, A., *König Herodes, Der Mann und Sein Werk*, Berlin 2001.
Schallmayer, E., *Hundert Jahre Saalburg, Vom Römischen Grenzposten zum Europäischen Museum*, Mainz 1997.
Schäfer, P., "From Jerusalem the Great to Alexandria the Small"; The Relationship between Palestine and Egypt in the Graeco-Roman Period, in Schäfer, P., (ed.), *The Talmud Yerushalmi and Graeco-Roman Culture I, Text and Studies in Ancient Judaism 71*, Tübingen 1998, pp. 129–140.
Schaper, J., "The Pharisees", *CHJ, The Early Roman Period 3*, Cambridge 1999, pp. 402–428.
Scherrer, P., *Ephesos, Der neue Führer, Österreichisches Archäologisches Institut*, Wien 1995.
Schiffmann, L. H., *Reclaiming the Dead Sea Scrolls, The History of Judaism, the Background of Christianity, the Lost Library of Qumran*, Philadelphia 1994.
Schmidt-Colinet, A., *Palmyra, Kulturbegegnung im Grenzbereich*, Mainz 1995.
Schremer, A., "Papyrus Se'elim 13 and the Question of Divorce intended by Women in Ancient Jewish Halakha", *Zion 63*, 4, 1998, pp. 377–390 (Hebrew).
Schürer, E., *The History of the Jewish People in the age of Jesus Christ 1–3*, Edinburgh 1987.
Schwartz, D., "Josephus and Nicolaus on the Pharisees", *JSJ 14*, 1983, pp. 151–171.
Schwartz, D., "Agrippa I, The Last King of Judaea", *TSAJ 23*, Tübingen 1990.
Schwartz, D., "On Sacrifices by Gentiles in the Temple of Jerusalem", in Schwartz, D. (ed.), *Studies in the Jewish Background of Christianity, Wissenschaftliche Untersuchungen zum neuen Testament 60*, Tübingen 1992, pp. 102–116.
Schwartz, D., "Joseph Ben Illem and the Date of Herod's Death", in Schwartz, D. (ed.), *Studies in the Jewish Background of Christianity, Wissenschaftliche Untersuchungen zum neuen Testament 60*, Tübingen 1992, pp. 156–167.
Schwartz, D., "Ishmael ben Phiabi and the Chronology of Provincia Judaea", in Schwartz, D. (ed.), *Studies in the Jewish Background of Christianity, WUNT 60*, Tübingen 1992, pp. 218–242.
Schwartz, D., "Hillel and Scripture; from Authority to Exegesis", in Charlesworth, J. H. and John, L. L. (eds.), *Hillel and Jesus, Comparative Studies of Two Major Religious Leaders*, Minneapolis 1997, pp. 335–362.
Schwartz, D., "Jewish Sources on the Herods", in *International Conference at the British Museum, "The World of the Herods and the Nabataeans,"* held between 17–19 April 2001.

Schwartz, S., "Language, Power and Identity in Ancient Palestine, *Past and Present 148*, 1955, pp. 3–47.
Schwartz, S., *Josephus and Judaean Politics, Columbia Studies in the Classical Tradition 18*, Leiden/New York 1990.
Schwartz, S., *Imperialism and Jewish Society, 200 BCE to 640 CE*, Princeton (N.J.) 2001.
Scott, J.C., *Domination and the Arts of Resistance – Hidden Transcripts*, New Haven 1990.
Sear, D.R., *Greek Imperial Coins and their Values, The Local Coinages of the Roman Empire*, London 1991.
Seaby, H.A., *Roman Silver Coins, I. Republic to Augustus*, London 1978.
Segala, E. and Sciortino I., *Domus Aurea*, Milano 1999.
Sekunda, N., *The Army of Alexander the Great*, London 1984.
Sekunda, N., *Hellenistic Warfare*, in Hackett, J., (ed.), *Warfare in the Ancient World*, New York 1989, pp. 130–135.
Sekunda, N., *The Seleucid Army*, Stockport 1994.
Sekunda, N., *The Ptolemaic Army*, Stockport 1994.
Sekunda, N., *Early Roman Armies*, London 1995.
Sekunda, N., *Republican Roman Army 200–104 BC*, London 1996.
Sekunda, N., *The Spartan Army*, London 1998.
Sekunda, N., *Greek Hoplite, 480–323 BC, Weapons, Armour, Tactics*, London 2000.
Sellers, O.R., *The Citadel of Beth Zur*, Philadelphia, 1933.
Shanks, H., *Jerusalem, An Archaeological Biography*, New York 1995.
Shatzman, I., "Artillery in Judaea from Hasmonaean to Roman Times", *The Eastern Frontier of the Roman Empire, BAR International Series 553 (2)*, 1989, pp. 461–484.
Shatzman, I., *The Armies of the Hasmonaeans and Herod, TSAJ 25*, Tübingen 1991.
Shatzman, I., "The Army of the Sons of the Light in the War Scroll (1QM)", in *The Jews in the Hellenistic and Roman World, Studies in Memory of Menachem Stern*, Jerusalem 1996 (Hebrew).
Sherwin-White, S., and Kuhrt, A., *Hellenism in the East: The Interaction of Greek and Non-Greek Civilizations from Syria to Central Asia after Alexander*, Berkeley 1990.
Sherwin-White, S., and Kuhrt, A., *From Samarkhand to Sardis, A New Approach to the Seleucid Empire*, Berkeley 1993.
Shuckburgh, E.S., *Augustus Caesar*, New York 1995.
Shutt, R.J.H., "Letter of Aristeas, A New Translation and Introduction, in Charlesworth, J.H. (ed.), *The Old Testament Pseudepigrapha*, Garden City (N.Y.), 1983, pp. 7–11.
Silver, A.H., *A History of Messianic Speculations in Israel, From the First through the Seventeenth Centuries*, New York 1927.
Simon, E., *Augustus, Kunst and Leben in Rom um die Zeitenwende*, München 1986.
Smallwood, E.M., "The Diaspora in the Roman Period before CE 70", *CHJ, The Early Roman Period 3*, Cambridge 1999, pp. 168–192.
Smith, M., "The Gentiles in Judaism 125 BCE–CE 66", *CHJ, The Early Roman Period 3*, Cambridge 1999, pp. 192–250.
Smith, M., "The Troublemakers", *CHJ, The Early Roman Period 3*, Cambridge 1999, pp. 501–569.
Smith, R.R.R., *Hellenistic Sculpture*, London 1991.
Southern, P., *Augustus*, London 1998.
Speidel, M., "The Roman Army in Judaea under the Procurators", *Ancient Society 13/14*, 1982–1983, pp. 233–240.
Spengler, O., *The Decline of the West*, New York 1926.

Sperber, D., *The City in Roman Palestine*, Oxford 1998.
Stemberger, G., "The Sadducees – their History and Doctrines", *CHJ, The Early Roman Period 3*, Cambridge 1999, pp. 428–444.
Stern, E., *Material Culture of the Land of the Bible in the Persian Period, 538–332 BC*, Jerusalem 1982.
Stern, E., "The Walls of Dor", *IEJ 38*, 1988, pp. 6–14.
Stern, E., "The Phoenician Architectural Elements in Palestine during the Late Iron Age and the Persian Period", *The Architecture of Ancient Israel, from the Prehistoric to the Persian Period*, Jerusalem 1992, pp. 302–304.
Stern, E., *Dor Ruler of the Seas*, Jerusalem 1994.
Stern, M., "The Reign of Herod", in *The World History of the Jewish People 7, The Herodian Period*, New Brunswick 1975, pp. 71–117.
Stern, M., "The Herodian Dynasty and the Province of Judaea at the End of the Period of the Second Temple", in *The World History of the Jewish People 7, The Herodian Period*, New Brunswick 1975, pp. 124–176.
Stern, M., *Greek and Roman Authors on Jews and Judaism 1, From Herodotus to Plutarch*, Jerusalem 1976.
Stern, M., "The Herodian Dynasty and the Roman Empire after Herod's Death", in M., Stern (ed.), *Nation and History, Studies in the History of the Jewish People*, Jerusalem 1983, pp. 55–71 (Hebrew).
Stern, M., "The Treaty between Judaea and Rome in 161 BCE", *Zion 60*, 1986, pp. 3–28 (Hebrew).
Stern, M., "Thrakides, on the Epithet of Alexander Jannaeus in Josephus and Syncellus", in Amit, M., Gafni, I., and Herr, D. M. (eds.), *Studies in Jewish History, The Second Temple Period*, Jerusalem 1990, pp. 125–128 (Hebrew).
Stern, M., *The Kingdom of Herod*, Tel Aviv 1992 (Hebrew).
Stern, S., *Calendars and Community, A History of the Jewish Calendar 2nd Century BCE–10th Century CE*, Oxford 2001.
Stockton, D., *The Classical Athenian Democracy*, Oxford 1990.
Strack, H. L., and Stemberger, G., *Introduction to the Talmud and Midrash*, Minneapolis (Minn.) 1992.
Sussman, V., "A Jewish Burial Cave on Mount Scopus", in Geva, H., (ed.), *Ancient Jerusalem Revealed, Expanded Edition* 2000, Jerusalem 2000, pp. 226–230.
Sydenham, E. A., *The Coinage of the Roman Republic*, London 1952.
Syme, R., *The Roman Revolution*, Oxford 1939.
Syme, R., *The Augustan Aristocracy*, Oxford 1986.
Tagliamonte, G., *Guida Archeologica*, in H. Mielsch, *La villa romana*, Firenze 1987, pp. 170–205.
Talcot Parsons, E. F. and Smelser, N., *Economy and Society*, London 2003.
Talcot Parsons, E. F., *Structure and Process in Modern Societies*, Glencoe (Ill.) 1960.
Talmon, S., "The Calendar of the Covenanters of the Judaean Desert", in Rabin, C. and Yadin, Y. (eds.), *Aspects of the Dead Sea Scrolls, SH 4*, 1958, pp. 162–169.
Talmon, S., and Knohl, I., "A Calendrical Scroll from a Qumran Cave: Mismarot Ba, 4Q321, in Wright, D. P. Freeman, D. N. and Hurvitz, A. (eds.), *Pomegranates and Golden Bells: Studies in Honor of Jacob Milgrom*, Winona Lake (Ill.) 1995, pp. 267–301.
Taylor, J. E., "A Second Temple in Egypt; The Evidence for the Zadokite Temple of Onias", *JSJ 29,3*, 1998, pp. 297–321.
Tcherikover, V., "Was Jerusalem a Polis", *IEJ 14*, 1965, pp. 61–78.

Tcherikover, V., "The Hellenistic Environment: The Political Background", in *The World History of the Jewish People 6, The Hellenistic Period*, New Brunswick 1972, pp. 5-32.
Tcherikover, V., "The Hellenistic Environment: The Cultural Background", in *The World History of the Jewish People 6, The Hellenistic Period*, New Brunswick 1972, pp. 33-50.
Tcherikover, V., "Hellenistic Palestine: The Political Situation from 332 to 175 BCE", in *The World History of the Jewish People 6, The Hellenistic Period*, New Brunswick 1972, pp. 53-86.
Tcherikover, V., "Hellenistic Palestine: Social Conditions", in *The World History of the Jewish People 6, The Hellenistic Period*, New Brunswick 1972, pp. 87-114.
Tcherikover, V., "Hellenistic Movement in Jerusalem and Antiochus' Persecutions", in *The World History of the Jewish People 6, The Hellenistic Period*, New Brunswick 1972, pp. 115-144.
Tcherikover, V., *Hellenistic Civilisation and the Jews*, Philadelphia 1979.
Tellegen-Couperus, O., *A Short History of Roman Law*, London 1993.
Thomas, J. A. C., *Textbook of Roman Law*, Amsterdam 1976.
Thomson, F. H., *Archaeology of Greek and Roman Slavery*, London 2003.
Thubron, C., *The Seafarers, The Ancient Mariners*, New York 1981.
Todd, S. C., *The Shape of Athenian Law*, Oxford 1993.
Toynbee, A., *A Study of History*, New York 1934-1961.
Tsafrir, Y., and Magen, Y., "The Desert Fortresses of Judaea in the Second Temple Period", *The Jerusalem Cathedra 2*, 1982, pp. 120-145 (Hebrew).
Tsafrir, Y., and Magen, Y., "Two Seasons of Excavations at the Sartaba - Alexandrium Fortress", *Qadmoniot 17*, 1984, pp. 26-32 (Hebrew).
Turcan, R., *Vivere alla corte dei Cesari*, Firenze, 1991.
Turcan, R., *Les cultes orientaux dans le monde romain*, Paris 1992.
Turcan, R., *The Gods of Ancient Rome, Religion in Everyday Life from Archaic to Imperial Times*, Edinburgh 2000.
Urbach, E., *The Halakhah, Its Sources and Development*, Tel Aviv 1996.
de Vaux, R., *The Institutions of the Old Testament, Vol. 1 - Social Institutions*, New York 1961.
de Vaux, R., *Ancient Israel I*, New York 1965.
Vermeule, C. C., *Roman Imperial Art in Greece and Asia Minor*, Cambridge (Mass.) 1963.
Wacholder, B. Z., "Greek Authors in Herod's Library", *Studies in Bibliography and Booklore 5*, 1960, pp. 104-109.
Wacholder, B. Z. and Wacholder, S., "Patterns of Biblical Dates and Qumran's Calendar, "The Fallacy of Jaubert's Hypothesis", *HUCA 66*, 1995, pp. 1-40.
Wachsmann, S., *The Sea of Galilee Boat, An Extraordinary 2000 Year Old Discovery*, New York 1995.
Wallace-Hadrill, A., "Mutatio Morum: The Idea of a Cultural Revolution", in Habinek, T., and Schiesaro, A., (eds.), *Roman Cultural Revolution*, Cambridge 1997, pp. 3-22.
Wallbank, F. W., *The Hellenistic World*, London 1992.
Walter-Karydi, E., *The Greek House, The Rise of Noble Houses in Late Classical Times, The Archaeological Society at Athens Library, 171*, Athens 1998.
Ward-Perkins, J. B., *Roman Imperial Architecture*, Harmondsworth 1981.
Warry, J., *Warfare in Classical World*, London 1980.
Wasserstein, A., "Notes on the Temple of Onias at Leontopolis", *ICS 18*, 1993, pp. 119-129.
Watson, G. L., *The Roman Soldier*, Ithaca (N.Y.) 1969.

Watzinger, C., "Griechische Holzsarkophage aus der Zeit Alexanders des Grossen", *Ausgrabungen der deutschen Orient Gesellschaft*, Leipzig 1905.
Weber, C. W., *Panem et Circenses, La politica dei divertimenti in massa nell'antica Roma*, Milano 1986.
Webster, G., *The Roman Imperial Army*, London 1985.
Weinberg, S., "Tel Anafa, the Hellenistic Town", *IEJ 21*, 1971, pp. 86–109.
Weinryb, E., *Historical Thinking, Issues in Philosophy of History*, Tel Aviv 1987 (Hebrew).
White, H., "Historical Emplotment and the Problem of Truth," in S. Friedlander (ed.), *Probing the Limits of Representation, Nazism and the "Final Solution,"* Cambridge (Mass.) 1992, pp. 37–53.
White, H., *Metahistory, The Historical Imagination in Nineteenth – Century Europe*, Baltimore (Mar.) 1993.
Wiedemann, T., *Greek and Roman Slavery*, Baltimore 1981.
Wilcox, P., *Rome's Enemies 3, Parthians and Sassanid Persians*, London 1986.
Will, E., *Histoire politique du monde hellénistique, 323 -30 av. J.-C.*, Paris 2003.
Williams, M., "The Contribution of Jewish Inscriptions to the Study of Judaism", *CHJ, The Early Roman Period 3*, Cambridge 1999, pp. 75–94.
Wilson, J. F. (ed.), *Rediscovering Caesarea Philippi: The Ancient City of Pan*, Malibu (Cal.) 2001.
Winsor-Leach, E., "Horace and the Material Culture of Augustan Rome", in Habinek, T., and Schiesaro, A., (eds.), *Roman Cultural Revolution*, Cambridge 1997, pp. 105–121.
Wise, M. O., "Languages of Palestine", in Green, J. B., McKnight, S., and Marshall, I. H., (eds.), *Dictionary of Jesus and the Gospels*, Downers Grove (Ill.) 1992, pp. 434–444.
Wise, T., *Armies of the Carthaginian Wars 265-146 BC*, London 1982.
Worsley, P., *The Trumpet shall Sound, A Study of "Cargo" Cults in Melanesia*, New York 1968.
Wright, G. R. H., "The Archaeological Remains at El-Mird in the Wilderness of Judaea", *Biblica 42*, 1961, pp. 1–21.
Wycherley, R. E., *How the Greeks Built Cities, The Relationship of Architecture and Town Planning to Everyday Life in Ancient Greece*, New York 1976.
Yadin, Y., *The Scroll of the War of the Sons of the Light Against the Sons of Darkness. Edited with Introduction and Commentary*, London 1962.
Yadin, Y., "The Excavations of Masada 1963/64", *IEJ 15*, 1965, pp. 1–120.
Yadin, Y., *The Temple Scroll, Text and Commentary 1*, Jerusalem 1983 (Hebrew).
Yavetz, Z., *Augustus, The Victory of Moderation*, Tel Aviv 1994 (Hebrew).
Yavetz, Z., "The Res Gestae and Augustus's Public Image", in Millar F., and Segal, E., (eds.), *Caesar Augustus, Seven Aspects*, Oxford 1994, pp. 1–37.
Yeguel, F., *Bath and Bathing in Classical Antiquity*, Cambridge (Mass.) 1995.
Zanker, P., *Il Foro di Augusto*, Rome 1984.
Zanker, P., *Augusto e il potere delle immagini*, Torino 1989.
Zanker, P., *Pompeii, Public and Private Life*, Cambridge (Mass.) 1998.
Zanker, P., *The Mask of Socrates, The Image of the Intellectual in Antiquity*, Berkeley (Cal.) 1995.
Zaphiropoulou, P., *Delos, Monuments and Museum*, Athens 1983.
Zeitlin, I., *Megillat Taanit as a Source for Jewish Chronology and History in the Hellenistic and Roman Periods*, Ph. D. Thesis, Philadelphia 1922.
Zeitlin, I., "The Assumption of Moses and the Bar Kokhba Revolt", *JQR 38*, 1947-48, pp. 1–45.

Zissu, B., "Two Herodian Dovecotes: Horvat Abu Haf and Horvat 'Aleq", in *The Roman and Byzantine Near East: Some Recent Archaeological Research, JRA, Supp. Ser Number 14*, 1995, pp. 56–69.

Zissu, B., *Rural Settlements in the Judaean Hills and Foothills From the Late Second Temple Period to the Bar Kokhba Revolt*, Thesis submitted for the Degree "Doctor of Philosophy", The Hebrew University, Jerusalem, 2001 (Hebrew).

Index of Sources

Bible

Exod
22, 1   277
22, 2–3 276
22, 3   278

Num
24, 17   32

Deut
17, 16   26
23, 19   95

1 Kgs
3, 5–14   26
3, 15–28 26
5, 9–14   26
6, 1–7, 2 292
6, 1–38   26
7, 1–12   26
7, 13–50 26
7, 13 – 7 292
7, 51   292
8, 1   289
9, 15   26
10, 26   26
11, 1–4   26
11, 5–10 26

2 Kgs
1, 32–38   23
11, 12–20 23

Ezek
1, 10   42
17, 7   42
37, 1–14   359
40, 5–43, 2 292

Prov
31, 30   290

Esth
9, 19–20 290

Ezra
1, 7–11   292
3, 2–3, 8 292
8   292
6, 1–2   292
6, 3–6   292

1 Chr
23–28   198

2 Chr
35, 65   198

Apocrypha and Pseudepigrapha

Tobit
5, 4   221

Sir
38, 27–28   233

50, 1–4   293

T. Mos.
6, 2–9   257

Let. Arist		13, 1–16, 24	30
81	67	13, 27–32	364
84–101	293	14, 7	214
172–186	67	14, 24	30
205	37	16, 4	140
		16, 15	178
1 Macc.			
2, 1–6, 17	30	2 Macc.	
4, 6	140	7, 9–23	359
4, 36–61	288	10, 3–9	288
7, 5–50	289	12, 3	144
8, 23–29	53, 130	12, 39–45	359
9, 23 -12: 53	30	14, 1–15	289
9, 50–2	157	14, 36	289
9, 62	157	14: 46	359
10, 65	201	15, 36	289
10, 88–9	214		
11, 33	199	4 Macc.	
12, 1–23	130	12	131
12, 8–9	214	12, 19–24, 35	86
12, 21–23	44	12, 35	86

Dead Sea Scrolls

Pesher Nahum (4QpNah) 258
Community Rule (1QS), 5–8 269

Josephus

BJ		I, 138–140	103
I, 31–40	30	I, 150	266
I, 38	130	I, 151	81
I, 48–49	30	I, 156	39, 160, 187
I, 50–54	30	I, 166	160, 187
I, 54–69	30	I, 170	200, 256
I, 61	135	I, 181	34
I, 63	199, 200	I, 194	53
I, 64	39	I, 199	263
I, 76	76	I, 203–216	134
I, 85–106	31	I, 211–213	55
I, 88	135	I, 241	76
I, 99	324	I, 248–357	34
I, 104–105	187	I, 262	76
I, 107–119	33	I, 265	324
I, 113	69	I, 266	178
I, 120–178	33	I, 271–272	353

Index of Sources

I, 274–275	353	I, 381–385	140, 150
I, 276	214	I, 382	135
I, 280	85	I, 383–384	138
I, 290	135	I, 396	214
I, 290–360	148	I, 396–397	54, 184
I, 291	148	I, 398–400	54
I, 292–294	135	I, 399	54, 210
I, 294	178	I, 401	39
I, 297–299	148	I, 403	139, 166, 188, 189, 214, 331
I, 302	137		
I, 303	137, 145	I, 408 – 414	39
I, 304	181	I, 411 – 413	191, 329
I, 304–308	140	I, 414	298, 316
I, 305	136, 137	I, 415	338
I, 307	149	I, 416	185
I, 308	183	I, 417	324
I, 309–314	149	I, 418	214, 324, 353
I, 314	207	I, 418–421	112
I, 314–316	137, 145	I, 419	324
I, 317	137, 145	I, 422	28, 45
I, 317–320	148	I, 422–428	43
I, 319	259	I, 424	45
I, 323	138	I, 425	44, 45, 46, 331
I, 323–325	142	I, 426–428	43
I, 326	259	I, 427	43
I, 327	137	I, 428	45, 46, 210
I, 329	137, 146, 149	I, 432–433	76
I, 329–330	140	I, 433	79
I, 364 – 365	39	I, 437	34
I, 343–344	140	I, 448	76, 81
I, 344	34	I, 450	81
I, 346	138, 146	I, 452	81
I, 349	137	I, 452–454	81
I, 354–356	140	I, 453	81
I, 357	267	I, 454	81
I, 357–358	149	I, 455	81
I, 358	260	I, 456	81
I, 359	205	I, 473	85
I, 361–362	209, 214, 215	I, 457–466	81
I, 364–365	149	I, 483	214
I, 364–385	149	I, 488–492	90
I, 366	135	I, 513–533	82
I, 366–367	150	I, 529	90
I, 367	143	I, 532	88
I, 367–369	148	I, 535	82, 142
I, 371	135	I, 538	274
I, 373–379	135, 141	I, 547	91
I, 380	150	I, 552–565	349

I, 557	82	II, 69	85, 184, 215
I, 562	76, 77, 82	II, 74	142, 147
I, 562–563	75	II, 77	142
I, 563	77	II, 76–77	139
I, 563	77	II, 77	142
I, 564–569	274	II, 80–92	256
I, 571	253, 257	II, 86	205
I, 574–577	151	II, 94–98	209
I, 576	134	II, 100	351
I, 576–577	88	II, 141	40
I, 588	77	II, 165	357
I, 590	76	II, 167	214
I, 592	87	II, 168	56, 161, 325
I, 599	77	II, 175	335
I, 599–600	82	II, 183	56
I, 637–638	85	II, 204–222	56
I, 646	83	II, 236	136, 147
I, 648–650	253, 256, 266	II, 252	202
I, 648–655	350	II, 280	235
I, 656–658	349	II, 331	263
I, 659–660	349	II, 344	169
I, 662	142	II, 405	263
I, 664	83	II, 500	136
I, 666	349	II, 531	142
I, 667–669	85	II, 544	136
I, 667–673	352	II, 566	142
I, 670	351	II, 599	265
I, 670–673	112	II, 615	265
I, 672	88, 144	II, 629	202
II, 1–2	23	II, 639–641	263, 265
II, 4	205	III, 35–43	202
II, 5	304	III, 36	139, 188, 189
II, 10	350, 351	III, 43	217
II, 14–24	85	III, 46	324
II, 16–18	209	III, 54–55	199, 202
II, 21	87, 94	III, 55	169, 324
II, 40	140	III, 66	136
II, 41	209	III, 68	196
II, 44	337	III, 97	136
II, 52	134, 142, 147	III, 408	191
II, 55	139, 188, 189, 201	III, 447–461	310, 331
II, 56	167	III, 509	232
II, 57	214	III, 537–540	310, 331
II, 58	142, 147	IV, 144	130
II, 59	188, 214	IV, 413	202
II, 63	142, 147	IV, 469	231
II, 66	140	IV, 481	232
II, 67	135	V, 467	335

Index of Sources

V, 108	335, 356, 367	IV, 214	274, 310
V, 136–159	326	VI, 17–23	190
V, 142–145	163	VIII, 1–211	28
V, 146	163	VIII, 21	28
V, 145	334	VIII, 22–25	28
V, 147–150	163	VIII, 61–129	28
V, 154	265	VIII, 130–140	28
V, 156–159	163	VIII, 150	28
V, 156–176	119, 169, 326	X, 79	359
V, 158–159	163	XI, 304–312	295
V, 159	163	XII, 141	293
V, 160	163	XII, 142–144	203
V, 177–182	109, 326	XII, 126	85
V, 184–190	304	XII, 160–228	13
V, 184–227	302, 326	XII, 169–184	203
V, 190–200	304	XII, 225–228	44
V, 201–206	304	XII, 261–264	201
V, 205	310	XII, 265 – 353	30
V, 207–214	305	XII, 307	140
V, 211	302	XII, 313–314	140
V, 212	302	XII, 326	30
V, 238–246	119, 169, 326	XII, 417–419	157
V, 267	143	XII, 507	367
V, 347	143	XIII, 1 – 61	30
V, 358–359	143	XIII, 15–17	157
V, 467	335	XIII, 26	157
V, 468	335	XIII, 64–71	295
V, 504–507	369	XIII, 73	295
V, 507	356	XIII, 80–196	30
V, 532	263, 264	XIII, 102	199
VI, 68	136	XIII, 127	199
VI, 172	136	XIII, 164–170	178
VI, 238	142	XIII, 211	364
VI, 354	265	XIII, 215	200
VI, 421	235	XIII, 230	30
VI, 420–426	333	XIII, 230–300	30
VI, 423–425	333	XIII, 227	130
VII, 5	136	XIII, 273	214
VII, 8	171	XIII, 275	39
VII, 171–177	175	XIII, 288–298	30
VII, 177	143	XIII, 301–319	31
VII, 225	136	XIII, 320	68
VII, 280–300	119	XIII, 320–404	31
VII, 420–436	295	XIII, 323	68
		XIII, 337	140
AJ		XIII, 338	181
II, 280	333	XIII, 357	185
IV, 68–73	206	XIII, 378	140

Index of Sources

XIII, 380	68	XIV, 361	178
XIII, 382	187	XIV, 365	353
XIII, 383	69	XIV, 367	353
XIII, 387–388	295	XIV, 369	353
XIII, 395–397	187	XIV, 371	353
XIII, 396	181, 200	XIV, 372	214
XIII, 397	200	XIV, 377	85, 87
XIII, 398	69	XIV, 379	353
XIII, 405–432	33	XIV, 385	22
XIII, 407	68	XIV, 394	135
XIII, 417	182	XIV, 394–491	148
XIII, 422	157	XIV, 396–397	135
XIII, 422–424	182	XIV, 400	135
XIII, 424	69	XIV, 400	135
XIV, 1	76	XIV, 406–408	148
XIV, 1–104	33	XIV, 411	137
XIV, 8	214	XIV, 413	136, 142, 145, 149
XIV, 10	69, 214	XIV, 413–414	137
XIV, 37	69	XIV, 414	148, 181
XIV, 43	191	XIV, 415	136, 137, 145
XIV, 76	39	XIV, 416	137
XIV, 78	34	XIV, 419	183
XIV, 79	69	XIV, 421–430	149
XIV, 82	69	XIV, 431–432	137, 145
XIV, 84	69	XIV, 433	207
XIV, 90–91	262	XIV, 434	137, 145
XIV, 93	69	XIV, 435–436	148
XIV, 121	19, 39	XIV, 436	259
XIV, 137, 143–144	53	XIV, 438	142, 148
XIV, 143–144	263	XIV, 447	137
XIV, 145–148	53	XIV, 448–450	142
XIV, 147	45, 46	XIV, 449–450	138
XIV, 148	45, 46, 331	XIV, 450	259
XIV, 149–155	44	XIV, 452	137, 146, 149
XIV, 156–184	134	XIV, 452–455	141
XIV, 158–184	55	XIV, 458	135
XIV, 163	214	XIV, 462	22
XIV, 163–184	267	XIV, 465–467	141
XIV, 172–174	254	XIV, 466	142
XIV, 175–176	254	XIV, 467	35, 76
XIV, 177–184	134	XIV, 468	137, 138, 146
XIV, 235	308	XIV, 472	136
XIV, 259–261	308	XIV, 476	163
XIV, 268–269	55	XIV, 482–486	40
XIV, 280	190, 193	XIV, 483–484	141
XIV, 300	76	XIV, 489–490	149
XIV, 330–XV, 10	34	XV, 1	260
XIV, 353	76	XV, 2–4	40

… *Index of Sources*

XV, 3–4	253, 254	XV, 260	87
XV, 5	35, 205, 209, 215, 251	XV, 260–263	253, 256
XV, 5–7	215	XV, 264	205
XV, 22	284	XV, 267	94
XV, 23	76	XV, 268	338
XV, 31	79	XV, 268–291	337, 339
XV, 31–41	35	XV, 269	338
XV, 31–34	284	XV, 270	339
XV, 34	79, 284	XV, 271	338
XV, 39–41	284	XV, 273–275	338
XV, 41	79, 284	XV, 281–291	339
XV, 51–56	80, 284	XV, 292–298	166, 331
XV, 53–56	103	XV, 293–296	139, 188
XV, 56	284	XV, 294	139, 188, 189, 214
XV, 64	80, 284	XV, 296	139, 188, 189, 214
XV, 91	200	XV, 298	317, 329
XV, 96	209, 214, 215	XV, 299–316	205, 211
XV, 106	209, 214, 215	XV, 303	206
XV, 107	205	XV, 314	211
XV, 108–160	39, 149	XV, 320	77, 285
XV, 109	205	XV, 320–322	285
XV, 111–112	150	XV, 322	284
XV, 112	143	XV, 324	169
XV, 115–119	148	XV, 331–341	39, 110, 165, 329
XV, 121–122	103	XV, 334–338	191, 329
XV, 127–146	140	XV, 342	80
XV, 132	209, 214, 215	XV, 343	62, 201
XV, 148–154	140	XV, 343–348	54
XV, 148–160	150	XV, 344	201
XV, 173	267	XV, 354	54
XV, 174	93	XV, 360	201, 210
XV, 184	89, 90	XV, 362	201
XV, 185–186	183	XV, 363	318
XV, 187–194	57	XV, 365	206
XV, 190	53	XV, 365–369	133, 195
XV, 215–217	184	XV, 367	40
XV, 216	201	XV, 368–370	252, 254
XV, 217	54, 201, 214	XV, 370	253, 254
XV, 223–226	90	XV, 372	252
XV, 226–227	90	XV, 373–379	252
XV, 228–231	72, 74	XV, 378	253
XV, 236–237	87	XV, 378	253
XV, 250	142	XV, 380–425	302, 326
XV, 252	86, 87	XV, 385	26, 292
XV, 252–260	87	XV, 385–386	292
XV, 252–266	86	XV, 391–397	303
XV, 253–255	142	XV, 398–400	304
XV, 254	201	XV, 410–411	304

Index of Sources

XV, 411–417	304, 305	XVI, 321	85
XV, 417–418	245, 247, 304	XVI, 332	86, 142
XV, 423	303	XVI, 333–355	151
XVI, 1–5	276	XVI, 343	210
XVI, 11	80	XVI, 354	86
XVI, 12–14	112	XVI, 356–357	274
XVI, 13	57, 183	XVI, 356–404	349
XVI, 14–15	48	XVI, 357	267
XVI, 16–22	194	XVI, 387	91
XVI, 29–31	85	XVI, 393–394	266
XVI, 32–57	85	XVI, 394	81, 183
XVI, 43	308	XVI, 401	81
XVI, 65	206	XVII, 1–192	349
XVI, 86	81	XVII, 10	86
XVI, 97	80	XVII, 19–22	75
XVI, 104–122	81	XVII, 21	77
XVI, 127–129	81	XVII, 24	146
XVI, 128	210	XVII, 24–26	189
XVI, 132–135	81	XVII, 25	206
XVI, 133	80, 81	XVII, 31	202
XVI, 138	338	XVII, 31	202
XVI, 142–143	214	XVII, 41	258
XVI, 143	324	XVII, 41–45	254, 255, 257
XVI, 145	214, 324	XVII, 41–46	253
XVI, 146	43	XVII, 42	207, 253
XVI, 146–148	43	XVII, 42–45	258
XVI, 149	43	XVII, 53	82
XVI, 179–184	27	XVII, 58–59	201
XVI, 190–191	81	XVII, 61	201
XVI, 191	85	XVII, 68	76
XVI, 203	8, 274, 310	XVII, 69	90
XVI, 207	214	XVII, 70–77	87
XVI, 235	88	XVII, 73	91
XVI, 241–245	91	XVII, 78	82, 285
XVI, 242–243	91	XVII, 79	90
XVI, 243	87	XVII, 89	274
XVI, 257	85, 87	XVII, 99	85
XV, 271–299	151, 188	XVII, 99	85
XVI, 273	81	XVII, 115–162	116
XVI, 278	264	XVII, 146	349
XVI, 279	210	XVII, 149–167	350
XVI, 285	139, 188	XVII, 154–155	204
XVI, 291	210	XVII, 162	293
XVI, 292	147, 188	XVII, 164	285
XVI, 299	85	XVII, 166	285
XVI, 302–309	82	XVII, 167	351
XVI, 312	88	XVII, 168–172	349
XVI, 319	90	XVII, 172–176	254

Index of Sources

XVII, 173	352	XVIII, 27	161, 325
XVII, 174–179	116	XVIII, 31	56
XVII, 175–180	349	XVIII, 34	284
XVII, 183–184	349	XVIII, 36	56, 167
XVII, 184	142	XVIII, 36–38	161, 168, 188, 310, 325, 331
XVII, 188–190	83		
XVII, 193	349	XVIII, 60	335
XVII, 193–194	86	XVIII, 91–95	119, 169, 326
XVII, 193–195	116	XVIII, 109–126	153
XVII, 195	85, 351	XVIII, 130–131	73
XVII, 195–200	352	XVIII, 136	77
XVII, 197	22	XVIII, 149	265
XVII, 198	88, 144	XVIII, 159–160	310
XVII, 199	137	XVIII, 249	135
XVII, 200	23	XVIII, 252	56
XVII, 204–205	205	XVIII, 259	310
XVII, 206–298	134, 352	XVIII, 374	135
XVII, 213	350, 351	XVIII, 378	135
XVII, 219	86	XIX, 1–273	56
XVII, 219–228	85	XIX, 276	310
XVII, 221–222	209	XIX, 293–295	23
XVII, 225	87	XIX, 294	299
XVII, 226	94	XIX, 356	194, 272
XVII, 240–248	86	XIX, 365	136
XVII, 250	77	XX, 11	263, 264, 267
XVII, 251	140	XX, 95	366
XVII, 253	209	XX, 98	136
XVII, 255	337	XX, 100	136
XVII, 266	135, 137, 139, 145, 147	XX, 122	147
XVII, 270	139, 142, 201	XX, 131	85
XVII, 271	167	XX, 194	264
XVII, 275–276	137, 147	XX, 199–200	267
XVII, 277	188, 202, 214	XX, 208	285
XVII, 283	137, 147	XX, 216–218	268
XVII, 286	136	XX, 223	285
XVII, 289	85, 184, 215	XX, 247–248	79, 284
XVII, 294	137, 147		
XVII, 297	139, 142	*Vita*	
XVII, 299–314	256	40	202
XVII, 305–307	209	46–47	312
XVII, 307	215, 251	58–61	312
XVII, 308	205	64–69	310, 331
XVII, 313–316	88	69	265
XVII, 315–316	86	90–92	310, 331
XVII, 318–320	209	121	136
XVII, 339	285	203	202
XVIII, 3	285	214	136
XVIII, 14	359	219	214

418   *Index of Sources*

271–98	308	*Apion*	
277	309	1, 2	227
278–279	309	1, 112–120	25
279	309	1, 198–200	293
280–284	309	2, 49	86
294–295	309	2, 118	282, 290
296	265	2, 175	308
331	308		
407	142		

Philo

Flacc.		*Mos.*	
6, 40	56	2, 215	308
		2, 216	308
Hypoth.			
7, 13	308	*Somn.*	
		2, 127	308
Legat.			
37, 294–297	57	*Spec.*	
134	308	2, 62–63	308
156	308	4, 7	278
349–367	316	4, 11–12	279

New Testament

Matt		*Luke*	
2, 16–18	350	4, 16–22	308
10, 17–18	308	4, 17–19	308
12, 22–29	258	4, 20–21	308
20, 2, 9–10, 13	221	12, 11	308
20, 8	223	16, 1–8	223
22, 15–22	261	20, 20–26	261
22, 16	260	20, 27	357
22–23	357	21, 12	308
26, 57, 59	269	23, 50	261
Mark		*John*	
1, 38	217	5, 2–4	335
3, 6	260, 261		
8, 15	261	*Acts*	
12, 13	260	4, 5	269
12, 13–17	261	4, 15	271
13, 9	308	6, 9	314
14, 53, 55, 64	269	6, 12	269
15, 43	263	13, 14–15	308

13, 15	308	23–35	110
13, 27	308	24, 10	284
15, 21	308	27, 1	147
22, 5	269	30	269
22, 19	308		

Rabbinic Literature

m. *Demai* 3, 1	223	m. *Šeb.* 1, 2	198
m. *Ma'as'*. 5, 8	236, 238	m. *'Abod. Zar.* 1, 1	337
m. *Šabb.* 14, 4	231	m. *'Abod. Zar.* 5, 7	302
m. *Šabb.* 22, 2	238	m. *'Abot* 1, 4	38
m. *'Erub.* 5, 6	223	m. *'Abot* 1, 10–11	254
m. *'Erub.* 10, 10	309	m. *Menaḥ.* 8, 6	229
m. *Pesh.* 3, 1	236, 238	m. *'Arak.* 6, 5	217
m. *Šeqal.* 6, 4	24	m. *'Arak.* 9, 3	217
m. *Ta'an.* 4, 2	198	m. *'Arak.* 9, 6	181
m. *Ta'an.* 4, 8	290	m. *Ker.* 1	250
m. *Meg.* 1, 1	217	m. *Ker.* 3, 7	235
m. *Meg.* 1, 1–2	234	m. *Parah* 3, 5	284
m. *Meg.* 2, 3	217	m. *Kelim* 1, 7	217
m. *Meg.* 3, 6	234	m. *Kelim* 17, 12	236, 238
m. *Ḥag.* 2, 2	268	m. *Neg.* 6, 1	236, 238
m. *Ketub.* 13, 10	217	m. *Nidd.* 2, 7	229
m. *Naz.* 2, 10	360	m. *Makš.* 7, 3	238
m. *Soṭah* 1, 3	275	m. *Yad.* 1	94
m. *Soṭah* 2, 1	238		
m. *Soṭah* 9, 1	268	*Sem.* 4, 4, 19	353
m, *Soṭah*, 9, 15	284	*Sem.* 5, 1	353
m. *Qidd.* 2, 3	217	*Sem.* 6–7	353
m. *B. Meṣi'a* 4, 6	217	*Sem.* 12, 7, 9	360
m. *B. Meṣi'a* 5, 8	223		
m. *B. Meṣi'a* 8, 6	217	t. *Ber.* 4, 14	231
m. *B. Bat.* 2, 5	231	t. *Šeb.* 7, 10–15	198
m. *B. Bat.* 4, 7	223, 224, 231	t. *Sukkah* 4, 6	308
m. *B. Bat.* 5, 3	231	t. *Ta'an.* 1, 7	275
m. *Sanh.* 1, 1–3	275	t. *Meg.* 3, 1–9	308
m. *Sanh.* I, 4	274	t. *Ḥag.* 2, 9	268
m. *Sanh.* 1, 5	268	t. *Ketub.* 13, 20	234
m. *Sanh.* 1, 6	274	t. *B. Meṣi'a* 3, 20	235
m. *Sanh.* 2, 1–2	269	t. *Sanh.* 7, 1	268
m. *Sanh.* 2, 4	250	t. *Hor.* 13, 2, 8	32
m. *Sanh.* 4, 4	268	t. *Menaḥ.* 13, 21	344
m. *Sanh.* 6, 5–6	360	t. *Neg.* 6, 3	231
m. *Sanh.* 10, 1	357		
m. *Sanh.* 11, 2	268	JT	
m. *Sanh.* 11, 4	275	*Ber.* 3, 6b	358

Pēah, 1, 16a	325	Ḥag. 16b	252, 268
Šeb. 6, 1	215	Ketub. 105a	308
Ma'ass´. 4, 1	230	Qidd. 18a	277
Šabb. 12, 3, 13c	325	Qidd. 66a	32
Pesḥ. 4, 1, 30b	198, 325	B. Bat. 3b	256
Šeqal. 7, 5, 50c	309	B. Bat. 4a	302
Yoma, 1, 2, 39a	325	B. Bat. 15a	359
Ta'an. 4, 2, 67d	198	Sanh. 4b	357
Meg. 3, 1, 73d	308	Sanh. 17b	217
Meg. 3, 74a	274	Sanh. 47b	360
Môed Qaṭ. 1, 5, 80c	360	Sanh. 49a	250
Môed Qaṭ. 2. 3. 81b	325	Sanh. 72b	277
Ḥag. 2, 2	268	Sanh. 82a	262
Ḥag. 3, 48c	325	Sanh. 92b	359
Yebam. 8, 8d	223	'Abod. Zar. 8b	32
Ketub. 13, 35c	308	'Abod. Zar. 36b	262
Naz. 7, 56c	358	'Abod. Zar. 50b	233
Sanh. 8, 8, 26	277	Hor. 13a	32
Hor. 3, 9–48b	32	Ḥul. 91b	235
		Bek. 55a	275
BT		Ker. 5b	24
Šabb. 13a	217	Ker. 111b	238
Šabb. 15a	32		
Šabb. 21a	288, 290	Siphri Deut	
Šabb. 30b	238	10	214
Šabb. 31a	94	41	214
Šabb. 56a	250	85	214
Šabb. 104a	275		
Šabb. 152a	360	Sifre Deut	
Pesḥ. 55b	233	118	277
Pesḥ. 57a	344	157–162	252
Yoma 9a	284	162	78
Yoma 35b	221		
Sukkah 51b	302, 309	Gen. Rabba 99	235
Roš Haš. 17a	360	Exod. Rab. 23, 13	42
Ta'an. 21a	217	Lev Rab. 34, 3	336
Meg. 26a–b	275		
Mo'ed Qaṭ. 13b	233	Midr. on Pss 93	309

Classic Authors

Greeks		Roman History VIII, 96	192
		Syrian Wars 10, 62	197
Appian			
Roman History V, 75	201	Aristotle	
Roman History VIII, 14	192	Politica II, 11, 1–14	265
		Politics III, 8, 2	250

Index of Sources

Arrian
Anabasis of Alexander I, 1 — 38
Anabasis of Alexander I, 12 — 27

Dio Cassius
Roman History 7, 6 — 303
Roman History 42, 38, 2 — 92
Roman History 51, 22, 2–3 — 27
Roman History 53, 2, 1–2 — 211
Roman History 54, 24, 4–7 — 191
Roman History 56, 34, 42–43 — 356
Roman History 65, 9, 2 — 258
Roman History 66, 6. 2 — 263
Roman History 59, 14, 1 — 218

Diodorus
History XVIII, 26–28 — 354
History XVIII, 74, 3 — 273
History XIX, 85 — 144

Diogenes Laertius
Life of the Philosophers V, 52 — 92
Life of the Philosophers V, 58 — 92

Greek Anthology 7, 645 — 93

Homer
Odyssey XIX, 111–114 — 37

Isocrates
To Daemonicus 36 — 38, 250
Evagoras 41 — 38
Nicocles 15 — 38
Nicocles 19 — 36
Nicocles 22 — 38

Philostratus
Life of Apollonius of Tyana I, 24 — 27

Plutarch
Life of Demetrius 42 — 38
Life of Mark Antony 80 — 93
Life of Sulla 26 — 92
Short Sayings of Kings and Commanders 189d — 92
On Exile 601 — 92

Polybius
History V, 10 — 36
History V, 11 — 38
History V, 70, 6–12 — 181
History VI, 41–42 — 144
History XIII, 3 — 38
History XIV, 5 — 144
History XVIII, 16 — 37
History XVIII, 41, 3 — 36
History XXVIII, 18 — 38
History XXX, 31, 10–12 — 210

Strabo
Geography V, 3, 8 — 334
Geography VIII, 6 — 192
Geography X, 2, 2 — 47
Geography XI, 2–3 — 190
Geography XVI, 1 — 232
Geography XVI, 2, 4 — 197
Geography, XVI, 2, 40 — 112, 178, 181, 187
Geography XVI, 2, 41 — 231
Geography XVI, 2, 400 — 171
Geography XVI, 4, 22–24 — 151
Geography XVI, 3, 763 — 103
Geography XVII, 1, 8 — 92
Geography XVII, 1, 8, 793–794 — 67
Geography XVII, I, 46 — 92
Geography XVII, 1, 53 — 151

Theocritus
Idillia XV, 8 — 67

Latin

Caesar
Gallic War VII, 69–74 — 142

Cicero
Ad Atticum 4, 10 — 92
Philippicae 5, 14 — 272
Philippicae 8, 27 — 272
Pro Balbo 28–30 — 272

Columella
De Re Rustica II, VII — 231

De Re Rustica II, VIII, 3–5   231

Curtius Rufus
History of Alexander X   353

Horace
Epist. II, 184   214

Livius
History of Rome XXX, 5   144

Martialis
Epigrammata VIII, 36   125

Persius
Saturae 5, 176–184   290

Pliny
NH V, 14, 70   202
NH IX, 60–62   234
NH XII, 54, 11–124   231
NH XII, 115–118, XIII, 44–46   103
NH XII, 118   209
NH XIII, 44   230
NH XVI, 25   232
NH XXX, 4   92

Pompeius Trogus
Historiae Philippicae 36, 31   231

Res Gestae Divi Augusti
4, 19   27
25, 2   255
26, 3   61
27   55
34, 3   61

Seneca
De Beneficiis 2, 20   36
Epistulae ad Lucilium, 88, 37   92
Epistula Moralia 47   290
Epistula Moralia 95   290

Statius
Silvae IV, 2, 18   125

Stobaeus
Florilegium VII, 61, 10   250

Suetonius
Augustus, 40, 2   212
Augustus, 60   49
Augustus, 72   124
Augustus, 72, 2   124
Augustus 100, 3   61, 356
Tiberius, 14   258
Tiberius, 65, 6   126
Nero, 31   125
Vespasianus 18   212
De Grammaticis 17   124

Tacitus
Ann. II, 55   272
Ann. IV, 67   126
Ann. XV, 42   125
Hist. II, 78, 1   258
Hist. V, 6   230, 231
Hist. V, 12   232
Hist. V, 12, 3   333

Varro
De Re Rustica 3,7   231

Virgil
Aeneid VI, 853, p. 61

Vitruvius
Architecture I, 5   156
Architecture III, 10–13   298
Architecture V, 12   192
Architecture X, 10–15   143

Roman Law

Gaius
Institutes III, 183–188   277
Collatio VII, 1   277

Justinian
Digesta 47. 18.2   277

Church Fathers

Eusebius
Prep. Ev. 9, 34, 19   25

Orosius
Historiae adversum
Paganos VI, 15, 31   92

Syncellus
Ecloga Chronographica I, 558–559   187

M. Polycarpii 12, 2   339

Index of Modern Authors

Aharoni, Y. 180
Alon, G. 180, 253
Amiran, R. 180
Anderson, G. 27
Anderson, R. T. 296
Andronicos, M. 43, 361
Arav, R. 155, 342
Ariel, D.T. 187
Arnould, C. 163
Avigad, N. 163, 233, 234, 237, 238, 293, 342, 343, 344, 358, 365, 366, 367, 368, 369, 370
Avi-Yonah, M. 198, 199, 200, 201, 202, 305, 333
Avni, G. 369

Bahat, D. 109, 163, 169, 301, 302, 306, 309, 356
Ballet, P. 67, 266, 273, 332
Bar-Adon, P. 155
Barag, D. 30, 109, 112, 167, 214, 305, 317
Bar-Kochva, B. 76, 131, 133, 144, 214
Barr, J. 246
Baruch, Y. 176, 178
Baumgarten, A.I. 7, 8, 15, 16, 252, 256, 257, 258, 259, 308
Beit –Arieh, I. 180
Ben-Arieh, S. 163
Ben Dov, M. 305
Bell Dinsmoor, W. 43
Ben Shalom, I. 255, 256
Benoit, P. 241
Benovitz, M. 288, 290
Bernard, A. 109, 192, 329, 331
Bickerman, E. 1, 7, 8, 38, 67, 70, 197, 282, 293, 304
Billig, Y. 337
Billows, R.A. 8, 9, 36, 273
Biran, A. 180, 242
Blackman, D. 192

Bliss, F.J. 224
Bohak, G. 295, 320
Bonacasa, N. 52, 309, 365, 369
Bonfil, R. 294
Bowersock, G.W. 87, 282
Bradley, K. 213
Brooten, B.J. 46
Broshi, M. 91, 228, 253, 297, 333, 345
Brown, P. 42
Brunt, P.A. 212
Burkert, W. 287
Burrell, B. 110
Bury, J.B. 265

Canfora, L. 92, 93
Carpiceci, C.A. 305, 356
Carr, E.H. 11
Cary, M. 53, 54, 55, 228, 250, 265
Casson, L. 195
Cateni, G. 362
Chauveau, M. 29, 213
Charron, A. 29
Charlesworth, J. 240, 257
Cheesman, G.L. 133, 146, 147
Clarke, J.R. 96, 341
Clarysse, W. 244
Von Clausewitz, K. 147, 151
Cohen, A. 180
Cohen, B. 277
Colledge, M.A.R. 299
Connolly, P. 142, 143, 144, 145, 156, 192, 287, 326, 332, 334, 337, 346
Corbo, V. 175
Cotton, H.M. 232, 237, 341
Cross, F.M. 242
Crowfoot, J.W. 155, 167, 342

Dalby, A. 91
Damati, E. 224
Daniel, B. 252

Index of Modern Authors

Dar, S. 14, 153, 183, 184, 215, 220, 228
Davies, J.K. 265
Delcor, M. 295, 297
Del Ponte, R. 287
Di Vita, A. 265
Di Vita-Evrard, G. 265
Dinsmoor, W.B. 293
Doran, R. 130
Dueck, D. 93
Dupont, F. 122

Eck, W. 208
Edersheim, A. 286
Ensoli, S. 52, 309, 365, 369
Erlich, Z.E. 184
Eshel, E. 198, 241, 242, 308
Eshel, H. 198, 253, 283

Fantar, M.H. 299, 326
Feldman, L.H. 16, 57, 255
Fiaschi, F. 362
Fiensy, D.A. 222
Fisher, M. 178
Fleischer, R. 70
Finkelstein, I. 26
Finkelstein, L. 261
Fittschen, K. 10, 107
Fitzmyer, J.A. 242, 246
Fiumi, E. 362
Flacelière, R. 265
Foerster, G. 10, 105, 119, 121, 168, 171, 310, 311, 365
Förtsch, R. 10, 106, 107, 156
Foxhall, L. 16
Frey, J. 295, 296
Fritsch, G.T. 168, 253
Frova, A. 166
Funk, R.W. 177

Gabba, E. 14, 54, 205, 206, 209, 210, 212
Gabrielsen, V. 192
Galinsky, K. 6, 8, 50, 61, 62, 123, 125, 298
Gardiner, P. 4
Geagan, D.G. 272
Geertz, C. 108
Geiger, J. 14, 22, 212, 232, 237, 241
Geraty, L.T. 241, 242
Geva, H. 245, 304

Gianfrotta, P.A. 193
Ginouvès, R. 43
Ginzburg, C. 12
Gleason, K. 111
Goldin, J. 38
Goodblatt, D.M. 249, 261, 262, 264, 266, 268, 269, 271, 325
Goodman, M. 13, 220, 251, 260, 261, 283
Gracey, H.M. 134, 178, 189, 196
Grainger, S. 91
Grant, M., 2, 3, 337
Green, P. 37, 356
Greenberg, M. 358
Greenfield, J.C. 241, 246
Greenhut, L. 360, 369
Griffin, M.T. 43
Grimm, G. 29
Gros, P. 127, 156, 301, 365
Grottanelli, C. 89
Gruen, E.S. 8, 25, 250, 295
Gunneweg, J. 233, 237

Habicht, C. 272
Hacham, N. 309
Hachlili, R. 169, 305, 311
Hadas, G. 358
Hadas, M. 293
Hadas-Lebel, M. 255, 336
Hammerschmidt, E. 29
Harari, M. 294
Harrington, D.J. 242
Hayes, J.H. 26
Hayward, C.T.R. 295
Head, B.V. 30, 31, 42
Head, D. 140, 144, 145
Hengel, M. 1, 130, 197, 203, 236, 243
Herbert, S.C. 103
Herr, M.D. 69, 94
Herzog, Z. 155, 180
Von Hesberg, H. 46, 298, 319, 356, 365, 369
Hestrin, R. 243, 247, 342
Hirschfeld, Y. 185, 221, 224, 309, 310
Hirschmann, J. 350
Höckmann, O. 193
Hoehner, H.W. 75
Hohlfelder, R.L. 192
Hölbl, G. 67

Holum, K.G. 166, 325
Hopkins, K. 213
Horowitz, J. 155
Hoyos, D. 265, 332
Hurwit, J.M. 298

Ilan, T. 369
Isaac, B. 178, 245
Innes Miller, J. 238

Jacobson, D. 60, 300, 301, 318
Jaeckle, R. 344
Jeremias, J. 286, 333, 337
Johnson, A. 144, 312
Jones, A.H.M. 2, 3, 204, 324

Kahn, L. C. 316, 317
Kaltsas, N. 156
Kaminka, A. 255
Kasher, A. 135, 149, 150, 152, 159, 178, 220, 256, 272, 273, 324, 325
Kästner, K. 310
Kaufman, D. J. 295
Kee, H.C. 308
Kenyon, K.M. 166, 167, 342
Keppie, L. 140, 142, 143
Klausner, J. 204, 220, 221, 223, 227, 229, 231, 232, 233, 235, 236, 238
Klawans, Z.H. 33
Kloner, A. 230, 241, 242, 342, 357, 361, 366, 370
Kloppenborg, J.S. 314
Knigge, U. 156
Knohl, I. 253
Koch, G. 359, 361
Kokkinos, N. 1, 3, 72, 73, 74, 75, 76, 77, 79, 86, 127, 212, 350
Kondoleon, A. 46, 331
Krause, C. 126
Krauss, S. 290
Krencker, D.M. 364, 365
Kuhrt, A. 29, 67, 273

La Penna, A. 63
Landau, Y.H. 243
Landau, T. 20
Langlois, C.V. 4
Lane Fox, R. 27, 39, 339, 354

Lapin, H. 275
Lauter, H. 294, 365
Lawrence, A.W. 155, 298
Le Bohec, Y. 136, 140, 142, 143
Lehmann, J. 255
Levi, M.A. 19
Levick, B. 76, 124, 258
Levine, B.A. 241
Levine, L.I. 129, 251, 265, 283, 288, 289, 290, 305, 307, 313, 314, 329, 333, 334, 335, 339
Lewis, A.D.E. 16
Lewis, N. 214, 241
Lieberman, S. 94
Lightstone, J. 27
Lin, M. 214
Lintott, A. 208, 272

Macallister, R.A.S. 224, 242
MacDonald, W.L. 125
MacMullen, R. 8, 50, 59, 190, 301, 315
Magen, Y. 163, 178, 183, 221, 234, 242, 29, 313, 342
Maier, J. 297
Mantel, H.D. 262, 267, 268
Maoz, Z. 311
Marsden, E.W. 143, 156
Mason, S. 254, 258
Maxwell Miller, J. 26
Mayer, L.A. 163
Mazar, A. 26, 335
Mazar, B. 22, 243, 245, 358
McKay, A. G. 341, 346
McLaren, J.S. 271
McNicoll, A.W. 155, 163
Meiggs, R. 265
Mélèze Modrzejewski, J. 295
Mendels, D. 195, 196, 291
Meshorer, Y. 22, 24, 30, 31, 32, 33, 34, 35, 40, 41, 42, 58, 190, 191, 193, 194, 195, 211, 234, 235, 242, 243, 245, 262, 264, 273, 319, 324, 325
Mielsch, H. 126, 225
Milik, J.T. 241
Millar, F. 55, 267
Millard, A. 94, 242, 243, 244, 245, 247
Momigliano, A. 1, 6, 12, 293
Mooren, L. 8

Morrison, J.S. 193
Murray, O. 71, 265

Nakman, D. 277, 278
Naveh, J. 32, 241, 242, 243, 296

Netzer, E. 97, 98, 99, 101, 102, 103, 105, 106, 109, 110, 112, 116, 118, 119, 120, 122, 153, 158, 169, 171, 178, 193, 214, 300, 307, 317, 354
Nielsen, I. 8, 65, 66, 67, 69, 96, 97, 98, 99, 101, 102, 103, 106, 107, 110, 112, 114, 116, 120, 124, 125, 156, 160, 169
Noam, V. 289, 290, 350, 351

Oliver, J.H. 272
Olmstead, A.T. 65
Oppenheimer, A. 220
Oren, E.D. 244
Orieux, C. 244

Papahatzis, N. 50
Papathanassopoulos, G. 44
Parente, F. 295
Pastor, J. 14, 205, 206, 207, 209, 210, 211, 212, 214, 215, 220, 222, 229, 230, 231
Patrich, J. 305, 316, 337
Peremans, W. 67
Perlman, I. 233, 237
Perowne, S.G. 2, 3
Pestman, P.W. 244
Peters, J.P. 244
Pollini, J. 63
Pollitt, J.J. 109
Porath, Y. 110, 316
Préaux, C. 29, 36, 37, 38, 39, 67, 250, 265, 273, 275
Price, S.R.F. 50, 51, 52, 316

Raban, A. 192
Rabello, A.M. 263, 273, 274, 304
Radt, W. 50, 294
Ragette, F. 299
Rachmani, L.Y. 191, 242, 243, 244, 357, 358, 359, 360, 365, 367, 370
Raeder, J. 326
Rainbow, P.A. 295
Rainey, M. 180

Rajak, T. 5, 20, 94, 240
Rakob, F. 364
Rankov, B. 145, 192, 195
Rappaport, U. 30, 32, 53, 191, 220, 244, 296
Rathbone, D. 229
Redde, M. 192, 195
Regev, A. 252, 284
Reich, R. 337
Reif, S.C. 308
Rey-Coquais, J.P. 215
Richardson, P. 1, 3, 56, 83, 84, 124, 187, 252, 253, 256, 260, 261, 284, 296
Riesner, R. 314
Riklin, S. 184, 258
Rivkin, E. 270
Robinson, O.F. 329, 334
Roller, D.W. 43, 44, 45, 46, 47, 49, 77, 85, 86, 87, 88, 91, 93, 94, 107, 337, 339
Romeopulos, K. 41
Rosenbaum, J. 241
Rosenfeld, B. 86
Rostovtzeff, M.I. 6, 8
Rozenberg, S. 116
Rowley, H.H. 260
Rubin, N. 360, 362
Rutgers, L.V. 11

Safrai, S. 198, 264, 275, 285, 286
Safrai, Z. 214, 217, 218, 223, 228, 229, 230, 231, 232, 235
Salza Prina Ricotti, F. 91
Sanders, E.P. 204, 206, 231, 252, 253, 266, 271, 286, 293, 299, 302, 305, 307
Sartre, A. 365
Sartre, M. 153, 190, 197, 203, 208, 209, 215, 216, 221, 225, 232, 234, 275, 324, 349
Sauvaget, J. 299
Schalit, A. 2, 3, 28, 29, 31, 62, 140, 198, 199, 200, 201, 204, 255, 262
Schallmayer, E. 144
Schäfer, P. 295
Scherrer, P. 50
Schick, K. 356
Schiffmann, L.H. 240, 241, 246
Schneemelcher, W. 95, 337

Schürer, E. 2, 19, 31, 32, 33, 34, 56, 201, 206, 261, 262, 264, 268, 269, 270, 272, 286, 302
Schwartz, D. 6, 8, 13, 28, 31, 32, 56, 254, 257, 283, 288, 351
Schwartz, S. 10, 15, 16, 20, 94
Sciortino I. 125
Scott, J.C. 256
Scullard, H.H. 53, 54, 55, 228, 250, 265
Sear, D.R. 30, 60
Segala, E. 125
Seger, J.D. 241
Seignobos, M.J.C. 4
Sekunda, N. 8, 9, 66, 136, 140, 143, 145, 147
Sellers, O.R. 177
Shanks, H. 293, 333
Shatzman, I. 14, 133, 135, 136, 137, 138, 139, 140, 141, 145, 146, 147, 153, 165, 166, 167, 169, 177, 178, 180, 181, 182, 183, 184, 185, 187, 188, 195
Sherwin-White, S. 29, 273
Shuckburgh, E.S. 55, 194
Shutt, R.J.H. 294
Sichtermann, H. 359, 361
Silberman, N.A. 26
Sirkis, E. 221, 313
Smelser, N. 15
Smith, R.R.R. 127
Southern, P. 50, 51, 55, 277
Spengler, O. 11
Sperber, D. 324
Stern, E. 155, 296
Stern, M. 53, 69, 202, 267, 293
Sukenik, E.L. 163, 166, 167, 342
Sussman, V. 361
Sydenham, E.A. 57
Syme, R. 61, 251, 283
Syon, D. 311

Tagliamonte, G. 225
Talcot Parsons, E.F. 15
Taylor, J. E. 295
Tcherikover, V. 262, 270
Tellegen - Couperus, O. 250
Thiersch, H. 244
Thomas, J.A.C. 277

Thomson, F.H. 213
Todd, S.C. 90, 208
Toynbee, A. 11
Tsafrir, Y. 178, 183
Turcan, R. 124

Vandorpe, K. 244
Van't Dack, E. 67
de Vaux, R. 65, 78, 241
Vermes, G. 269
Vico, G.B. 4

Wacholder, S. 94
Wachsmann, S. 193
Walter-Karydi, E. 341
Ward-Perkins, J.B. 125, 301, 309, 326
Warry, J. 195
Wasserstein, A. 295
Watzinger, C. 358
Weber, C.W. 340
Webster, G. 140
Weill, R. 245
Weinberg, S. 103
Weinryb, E. 4, 11
White, H. 12
Wiedemann, T. 213
Wilcox, P. 146
Will, E. 8, 123, 266
Wilson, J.F. (ed.) 318
Wise, M.O. 246
Wright, G.R.H. 178
Wycherley, R.E. 334

Yadin, Y. 241, 297, 311
Yardeni, A. 241, 242
Yavetz, Z. 150
Yavor, Z. 311
Yegül, F. 107, 336
Yellin, J. 233, 237

Zanker, P. 6, 8, 11, 27, 50, 51, 123, 124, 125, 300, 340, 341
Zeitlin, I. 351
Zionit, Y. 221, 313
Zissu, B. 176, 217, 218, 223, 224, 231, 370
Zschietzschmann, W. 364, 365

Index of Names and Subjects

Abila 187, 200, 202
Abr Naharain 197
Abu Haf (Horvat Abu Haf) 231
Abu Shawam (Khirbet Abu Shawam) 217
Abusir 358
Achaemenids 65, 66, 176, 197, 199, 218
Achaia (See Greece*)
Achiab 73, 74, 139, 141, 201
Achilles 27, 371
Acrabata 169, 199, 200, 202, 217
Acrabatena (See Acrabata*)
Actium 46, 55, 56, 58, 87, 144, 149, 151, 158, 183, 356
Aeneas 61, 63, 371
Aeschylus 339
Adiabene 358, 366
Adora 199
Agaba (See Gabae*)
Aegae 66
Aelia Capitolina 46, 163
Aelianus 136
Aeschylus 339
Africa 46, 60, 227, 238, 243, 365
agoranomos 235, 264, 265
Agrippa (Marcus Vipsanius Agrippa) 45, 47, 48, 55, 56, 57, 102, 105, 116, 123, 125, 183, 185, 190, 194, 301, 316, 336, 340
Agrippa I (Marcus Iulius Agrippa I) 1, 6, 8, 21, 23, 40, 56, 58, 74, 76, 79, 81, 103, 110, 127, 153, 159, 161, 163, 196, 245, 260, 261, 272, 283, 299, 310, 312, 316, 318, 325, 326, 333
Agrippa II (Marcus Iulius Agrippa II) 20, 21, 40, 56, 58, 76, 103, 127, 196, 213, 215, 245, 257, 260, 267, 284, 310, 312, 316, 325, 373
Agrippium (See Anthedon*)
'Ain Feshkha 194
Rabbi Akiva 360

Akkaron 199, 200, 214
'Aleq (Horvat 'Aleq) 231
Alesia 142
Alexander (son of Aristobulus II) 69
Alexander (son of Herod) 13, 35, 57, 62, 77, 79, 80, 82, 86, 87, 88, 89, 90, 183, 266, 274, 278, 373
Alexander III 74
Alexander the Great 1, 2, 5, 19, 20, 21, 27, 31, 32, 33, 36, 39, 47, 60, 62, 65, 78, 94, 95, 134, 140, 141, 145, 229, 353, 354, 356, 357, 363, 371, 372, 378
Alexander Balas 91, 282
Alexander Jannaeus 11, 31, 32, 33, 34, 35, 37, 40, 68, 69, 70, 72, 78, 103, 115, 178, 181, 182, 185, 191, 196, 198, 199, 200, 204, 227, 242, 243, 244, 262, 295, 312, 350, 365
Alexander Severus 127
Alexandra (Hyrcanus II's daughter) 68, 89, 183
Alexandria 46, 47, 48, 51, 52, 77, 85, 86, 91, 92, 93, 103, 109, 110, 168, 192, 210, 238, 251, 260, 265, 283, 284, 285, 293, 301, 309, 323, 324, 326, 327, 329, 332, 333, 347, 351, 353, 356, 357, 361, 362, 372, 373, 377
Alexandria, Caesareum 301
Alexandria, Harbour and Pharos 192, 193
Alexandria, Serapeum 48, 329
Alexandrium (Sartaba) 89, 157, 176, 183
Alexas (See Hilkyia*)
Alexas of Laodicea 86
amarkalim 286
Amathus 188, 199, 200, 202, 262
Amrit 293
Anafa (Tel Anafa) 103, 237
Ananel 251, 284
Ananias 283, 342, 369
Ananias son of Nedebaeus 284

Ananus 267
anathemata 297, 298, 299, 320
Anatolia (See Asia Minor*)
Anchises 62
Andromachus 90, 91
annona 210, 211
Anthedon 54, 184, 185, 200, 214
Antigonids 43, 65, 67, 262, 273
Antigonus Monophthalmos 8, 36, 37, 108
Antigonus III 92
Antioch on the Orontes 45, 47, 48, 51, 103, 109, 118, 156, 331, 332, 333, 371
Antioch Seleucia 200
Antiochus II 91, 156
Antiochus III Megas 92, 140, 141, 203, 243, 262, 293, 296, 297
Antiochus IV Epiphanes 43, 46, 54, 78, 91, 145, 282, 293, 351
Antiochus V 244
Antiochus VII 31
Antipas (Herod Antipas) 1, 21, 76, 77, 79, 81, 83, 84, 87, 94, 102, 139, 153, 159, 161, 167, 196, 202, 208, 209, 245, 260, 265, 310, 323, 325, 326, 331, 337, 347, 352, 363, 373, 376
Antipater (Herod father) 19, 53, 55, 62, 69, 72, 74, 213, 214, 263
Antipater (Herod son) 13, 79, 81, 82, 83, 84, 86, 87, 90, 373
Antipater III 74
Antipater IV 74
Antipater Gadiad 84, 86
Antipater son of Jason 130
Antipater of Samaria 90
Antipatris (Tel 'Afeq) 185, 214, 324
Antiphilus 84, 87, 91
Antonia Maior 56
Aosta (Augusta Praetoria) 156
Apherims 199, 200
Aphrodisias in Caria 49, 51
Apollo Actium (Games of) 47
Apollonia 184, 200
Apollonius Rhodius 92
Apollonius of Tyana 259
'Aqav (Horvat 'Aqav) 224
Aqed (Khirbet el-'Aqed) 217
Aquileia 81
Aquincum 110

Arabia 133, 148, 151, 238, 374
Arad (Tel Arad) 178, 180, 217, 224
Arad Valley 218
Aratus 92
Aramaic language 240, 241, 242, 243, 244, 245, 246, 247, 308, 360, 376
Arameans 85
Arbel (See Arbela*)
Arbela 137, 145, 200, 202
Archelaus (King of Cappadocia) 60, 79, 80, 81, 84, 86, 87, 267, 274
Archelaus (Herod Archelaus) 1, 21, 23, 41, 58, 83, 84, 85, 86, 102, 110, 134, 139, 147, 190, 193, 195, 196, 209, 245, 256, 272, 274, 283, 333, 351, 352, 353, 363
archisynagogos 275, 314
archon 264, 265
arcosolium 360
Arelate (Arles) 300, 301, 317
Aretas IV 152, 153
Areopagus 272, 276
Arretium 237
Areus 44
Argaeads 31, 32, 33, 36, 65, 66, 68
Argos 298, 317
aris 221
Aristeus of Emmaus 263
Aristobulus (Jewish writer) 130
Aristobulus (son of Herod) 13, 35, 57, 62, 77, 79, 80, 81, 82, 83, 86, 87, 88, 89, 90, 183, 274, 278, 373
Aristobulus II 19, 33, 68, 68, 70, 74, 79, 81, 103, 150, 158, 191
Aristobulus III (brother of Mariamme the Hasmonean) 79, 123, 284
Aristotle 92
Armenia 55, 370
'Aroer (Tel 'Aroer) 176, 178, 180, 217, 224
Arsacids 1
Arsinoë (See Anafa*)
Ascalon 28, 72, 127, 184, 191, 194, 229, 236, 238, 324, 332
Ascanius 62
Asclepiodotus 136, 147
Ashdod 83, 200
Asia (Province of) 52, 87, 194, 208, 210
Asia Minor 27, 28, 45, 49, 145, 156, 168, 190, 208, 215, 221, 223, 225, 227, 229,

232, 234, 237, 238, 239, 240, 275, 308, 311, 314, 325, 362, 371
Athenion 150
Athens 37, 44, 49, 50, 51, 52, 90, 92, 156, 192, 207, 208, 210, 236, 237, 265, 273, 276, 281, 294, 320, 326, 327, 329, 332, 333, 339, 341, 342, 371
- Acropolis 44, 49, 298, 299, 377
- Agora 43, 127
- Parthenon 49, 298, 329
- Piraeus192
Attalids 43, 67, 69
Attalus I 36, 37, 39, 40, 43
Attalus II 43
Attica 362
auctoritas 61, 374
Augustus (Caius Iulius Caesar Octavianus Augustus) 2, 5, 19, 21, 23, 39, 44, 47, 48, 50, 51, 52, 53, 54, 55, 56, 57, 58, 59, 60, 61, 62, 63, 65, 66, 78, 80, 81, 82, 83, 84, 85, 86, 87, 88, 89, 90, 91, 92, 93, 105, 115, 122, 123, 124, 125, 126, 133, 142, 144, 145, 149, 150, 151, 152, 153, 158, 190, 190, 193, 195, 201, 205, 207, 209, 210, 211, 212, 214, 215, 230, 237, 251, 254, 255, 256, 267, 277, 278, 282, 283, 284, 298, 300, 301, 303, 316, 317, 318, 319, 329, 338, 352, 354, 356, 357, 363, 370, 371, 372, 374, 376, 377, 378
Auranitis 54, 159, 187, 201, 202, 208, 215, 228
Av beth – din 268
Avdat 237
Avtalion 255
'Azeqa (Tel 'Azeqa) 217
Azotus 184

Ba'albek, Sanctuary of Jupiter Heliopolitanus 225, 299
ba'alei nechasim 222
Baba Ben Butha 256, 257
Babatha 241
Babylonia 26, 29, 39, 251,260, 283, 284, 353
Babylonian Jews 146, 189, 232, 284, 307, 377
Bacchides 157

Balbillus (Tiberius Claudius Balbillus) 258
Balbus (Lucius Cornelius Balbus) 340
Bagoas 90, 258
Baiaea, Temple of Mercurius 116
balnea (See bathhouse Roman*)
balsam 209, 230, 240
Bar Kochba 11, 33, 218, 241, 242, 245, 305, 313, 373
basilike ge (royal land) 213, 214, 215, 216
Batanaea 54, 139, 146, 159, 187, 188, 189, 201, 202, 208, 210, 215, 228
Bathhouse Roman 336, 346, 347
Bathyllus 90
Bathyra 189, 190
Beersheba (Tel Beersheba) 178, 180
Beersheba Valley 218
Ben Sira 293
Benjamin area 218
Berenice I 74, 79, 80, 82, 83
Berenice II (Lagid queen) 92
Berytus 28, 267, 274
Beth Hillel (See Hillel*)
Beth Shammai (See Shammai*)
Bethar 217
Bethbatzi 157
Betharamatha 102, 187, 188, 200, 202, 325
Bethfage 233
Beth Govrin (See Marissa*)
Beth ha-Keren 199, 200
Bethel 157
beth din 268, 274, 275
Bethhoron 157
Bethlehem 334
Bethleptenpha 169, 217
Betholethephene (See Bethleptenpha*)
Beth Saida 233
Beth Shean (see Scythopolis*)
Bethsur 140, 157, 159, 177, 199, 200, 202
Bible 301
Bithynia 237
Bocchus III 58
Boethus 77, 251, 284, 285
Bosporus 194
boulē 249, 250, 263, 264, 265, 266, 269, 272, 306, 308, 314, 320, 325, 376
bouleterion 265, 310, 311, 320, 377
Brundisium 239

Brutus (Marcus Iunius Brutus) 19
Byblos 28, 127
Bythinia 51

Caesarea Maritima 39, 46, , 47, 48, 54, 58, 59, 60, 88, 158, 160, 161, 163, 166, 167, 168, 184, 185, 190, 191, 194, 200, 202, 203, 209, 210, 214, 224, 232, 233, 237, 247, 250, 272, 273, 281, 298, 315, 323, 324, 325, 326, 329, 334, 337, 338, 341, 347, 374, 375, 377
- Drusion tower 316, 329
- Herod palace 73, 97, 98, 99, 100, 101, 102, 106, 108, 110, 111, 126, 127, 329, 374
- hippodrome 329, 337
- praetorium (See Caesarea Maritima, Herod palace*)
- Sebastos harbor 105, 186, 191, 192, 193, 329, 375
- Temple of Roma and Augustus 48, 298, 301, 315, 316, 317, 319, 329, 377
- theatre 329, 337
- Tiberieum 315
- water supply 329, 335
Caesarea of Mauritania 59, 60
Callimachus 92
Callirhoe 349
Campania 336, 340
Canatha 150
Capernaum 221
Capharsaba 185
Capo Sorrento (Villa of) 107
Cappadocia 87, 88, 267, 274
Capri 126
Capri, Villa Jovis 107, 126
Caracalla (Marcus Aurelius Antoninus) 215
Caria 51
Carmel (Mount Carmel) 200, 229, 335
Carthage 192, 264, 265, 299, 320, 326, 332
Carthage, harbor 192
Carthage, Temple of Eshmun 299
Cassander 273
Cassius 190, 193
Cassius (Gaius Cassius Longinus) 19, 56, 57
Celer (architect) 125

Chersones 223
China 238
Chios 45
choker 221
chora 216
chrematistes 275
Christians 291
Cicero (Marcus Tullius Cicero) 61, 92
Cilicia 45, 210, 237, 314
Cilicians 135, 196,
Claudius (Tiberius Claudius Nero Germanicus) 56, 58, 90, 123, 153, 263, 267, 372
Cleanthes of Assos 36
*clementia*61
Cleopatra VII 5, 13, 33, 46, 53, 54, 56, 61, 80, 85, 86, 115, 144, 149, 10, 158, 205, 209, 356
Cleopatra (Herod wife) 75, 77, 79, 83
Cleopatra Selene 60
clipaeus virtutis 61
coffins (see sarcophagi*)
Coile Syria 37, 55, 197, 203, 375
Colonia Claudia Ara Agrippiniensium (Köln) 110, 369
columbaria 231, 240
comitia 266, 267, 276
Coos 45, 87, 88, 127, 371
Coponius 235
Corinth 50, 52
Corinthus 88
Costobar 74, 79, 86, 87, 141, 201, 205, 256
Council of the Hasmoneans 262
Council of the Jews 32, 262, 263
Crete 110
Crimea 160
Crinagoras 87, 88, 93, 372
Crus (L. Cornelius Lentulus) 87
Cumanus (Ventidius Cumanus) 284
Curtius Rufus (Quintus Curtius Rufus) 353
Cuthea (See Samaria*)
Cypros (Nuseib el-Aweishiret) 108, 119, 178, 231, 237
Cypros II 79
Cypros III 74, 79, 81
Cyprus 210, 236
Cyrenaica 238

Cyrene 51, 52, 301, 326, 365, 369
Cyrene, Caesareum 51, 52, 301
Cyrrus 140
Cyzicus 51

Dacia 146
Dagon 178
Daimuz 365
Damascus 45, 85, 299
Damascus, Sanctuary of Zeus 299
Damascus Document 295
Dan 242
Daphne 294
Darius III 295
David 22, 24, 25, 26, 27, 28, 31, 32, 65, 78
Day of Atonement 288, 351
Dead Sea 102, 108, 119, 193, 232, 240, 373, 375
Decapolis 54, 161, 176, 184, 185, 186, 201, 214, 242, 273, 324
dekaprotoi 265
Delos 210, 341
Delphi 43, 299
Demetrias 156
Demetrius (Hellenistic-Jewish writer) 130
Demetrius I 91
Demetrius III Eucareus 140
Demetrius (Herod courtier) 84, 87
Demetrius Phalerus 92, 273
Demetrius Poliorcetes 37, 38, 40, 144, 168
Demosthenes 92
Diadochi 32, 37, 60
Diaspora (Jewish Hellenistic) 11, 21, 283, 285, 291, 307, 309, 314, 315, 339, 350, 373, 377
Didymus (Arius Didymus) 92
dies herodis 289, 290
dikasteria 275
Diodorus Siculus 354
Diogenes 68, 69
dioikeitai 275
Diophantus 90
Diospolis 25, 150, 187
Dios (See Diospolis*)
Diotogenes 250
Dium (See Diospolis*)
Docimium

Domitian (Titus Flavius Domitianus) 58, 123, 125
domus 106, 113, 122, 341, 342
Dor 155, 184, 191, 194, 200, 297
Dora (See Dor*)
Doris 75, 76, 81
doryphoroi 88, 144
Dositheus 74
Dositheus of Cleopatrides 84, 86
Dougga 365
Drusilla 58
Dura Europus 110, 119
Dydima (Asia Minor) 293

Ecclesiastes 25
Egypt 25, 29, 33, 39, 46, 54, 92, 146, 147, 150, 213, 229, 230, 236, 238, 284, 295, 309, 364
ekklesia 249, 250, 261, 262, 263, 266, 267, 276, 275, 376
ekklesia megale 262, 266
Rav Eliezer Ben Zadok 353
Elionaeus son of Cantheras 283
Elis 43
Elpis 75, 77
Emesa 140
Emmaus 140, 157, 169, 178, 202, 217
'En Boqeq 214, 224
'En Gedi 171, 199, 200, 202, 209, 214, 217, 218, 230, 274, 324, 358, 364
Ephesus 49, 50, 51, 52, 329, 332, 333, 347
Ephesus, Temple of Artemis 329
Ephraim area 218
epikephalion (poll tax) 203, 204, 206, 208
episkopoi 275
epitropos 263
Eratosthenes 92
Eretria 341
Esdraelon Valley 209, 214, 215
Esebonitis 187, 188, 189
Essenes 4, 40, 249, 252, 253, 297, 376
'Ethri (Horvath 'Ethri) 217, 218
Etruria 361
Etruscans 356, 361, 362
euergetes (*euergetism**)
euergetism 42, 45, 50, 51, 210, 211, 336, 340, 371, 372

Index of Names and Subjects

Eumenes I 273
Eumenes II 43, 54, 92
Eupolemus 24, 25, 130, 246, 371
Eupolemus son of Joannes 130
Euphorion 92
Euripides 339
Eurycles 44, 47, 82, 87, 88, 90
Evaratus (C. Iulius Euaratus) 88
Ever ha-Yarden (See Transjordan*)
Ezechias (the robber) 254
Ezekiel 292, 297, 359, 362, 377
Ezekiel the Tragedian 130, 338
Ezra 296

Firdusi (Khirbet Firdusi) 183, 184
Fréjus (Forum Iulii) 194
Frontinus (Sextus Iulius Frontinus) 334

Gabae 69, 139, 182, 189, 202, 214, 215, 229
Gabara 200, 202
Gabinius (Aulus Gabinius) 54, 160, 185, 187, 200, 201, 262, 274, 324, 342
Gadara 54, 184, 185, 187, 200, 201, 202, 214
Gadora (Tell Jadur) 188, 199, 200
Gaius (Roman jurist) 276
Gaius Caesar 49, 56
Gaius (Gaius Caesar Germanicus "Caligula") 23, 27, 56, 58
Galatians 67, 88, 144, 145, 353
Galestes 69
Galil (See Galilee*)
Galilee, Upper: p. 200, 202
Galilee 34, 55, 58, 83, 137, 138, 148, 153, 160, 176, 181, 182, 188, 189, 199, 200, 201, 202, 207, 208, 213, 214, 217, 218, 220, 222, 227, 228, 229, 231, 236, 242, 259, 262, 278, 325, 359, 375
Gallia 300, 301, 317
Gallus (G. Cornelius Gallus) 92, 133, 148, 151, 153
Gamala 199, 200, 202, 310, 311, 312, 314
Gamaliel II 223, 257, 337
Gamla (See (Gamala*)
Gamalitis 153
Garizim (Mount Garizim) 294, 295, 342
Gauls 134, 135, 374

Gaulanitis 83, 159, 201, 202, 215, 217, 218, 222, 228
Gaza 54, 178, 184, 185, 194, 200, 201, 209, 210, 214, 229, 273
Gazara 26, 86, 177, 200, 214, 217, 241
Gelithon 200,
Gennesareth (Valley of Gennesareth) 236
Gerasa 46, 185, 187, 200
Gerizim (Mount) 242
Germans 88, 134, 144, 145, 353
Germania Superior 110, 146
gerousia 261, 262
Gessius Florus 263
Gezer (Tel Gezer - See Gazara*)
Giladitis 199, 200, 201
Gindarus 137
gizbarim (*gazophylakes*) 286
Giv'at Sha'ul 177
Glanum 301, 369
Glaphyra 79, 80, 87
Goded (Tel Goded) 224
Golan (See Gaulanitis*)
Gophanitica (See Gophna*)
Gophna 169, 202, 217
Gortyn 110
Gratus 139, 142, 147
Gratus (Valerius Gratus) 284
Great Revolt (See Jewish War*)
Greece 49, 50, 52, 27, 212, 227, 229, 281, 287, 298, 320, 362, 371
Greek language 1, 240, 241, 242, 243, 244, 245, 246, 247, 360, 376
Greeks 135, 206, 375
Gush Halav 181, 229
gymnasium 101, 129, 130, 131, 264, 265, 326, 336, 340, 373
gymnasiarch 264, 265

Hadom ha-Shomron 218
Hadrian (Publius Aelius Traianus Hadrianus) 316, 335
Halasarna 88
Halicarnassus 156, 356
halike (Dead Sea salt tax) 206
Hannibal 5
Hanukka 281, 288, 289, 290, 319, 377
Har ha-Melech 214
Hasdrubal 144

Hasmoneans 1, 2, 14, 19, 25, 28, 29, 30, 31, 32, 34–35, 39, 42, 48, 53, 65, 67, 68, 74, 75, 70, 72, 73, 76, 78, 79, 82, 89, 102, 109, 133, 134, 135, 157, 158, 159, 160, 163, 175, 178, 181, 184, 187, 191, 193, 195, 198, 199, 200, 201, 202, 203, 204, 206, 209, 207, 211, 212, 213, 214, 218, 239, 244, 245, 249, 250, 256, 262, 263, 281, 282, 284, 285, 286, 287, 288, 289, 290, 292, 293, 294, 295, 297, 299, 307, 319, 324, 332, 334, 335, 336, 342, 346, 351, 352, 357, 358, 364, 365, 366, 374, 375
hazanim 275
Hazor 26
Hebrew language 240, 241, 242, 243, 244, 245, 246, 247, 360, 376
Hebron 178, 218, 224, 242
Hebron, Haram el-Khalil 28
Hecataeus of Abdera 329
Heftzibah 243
Helena of Adiabene 358, 366
Heliopolis (Egypt) 295
Heliopolis, Temple of Zeus (see Ba'albek, Sanctuary of Jupiter Heliopolitanus*)
Hephaestion 27, 95
Heracleides 53
Heracles 371
Hermel 365
Herod the Great:
Herod and the heritage of the House of David 22–28
Herod and the heritage of the Hasmoneans 28–36
Herod as Hellenistic king 36–42
Herod as *euergetes* 42–52
Herod as Client King of Rome 52–58
Herod compared to Juba II 58–60
Herod and his brother and sisters 73–75
Herod and his wives 75–78
Herod and his offspring 78–83
Herod and his cultural circle 91–95
Herod and his portrait 127–129
Herod and his army 133–134
Herod as military commander 141
Herod and the administrative division of his kingdom 200–203
Herod's income 208–210

Herod's social program 210–213
Herod's royal land and royal estates 213–216
Herod's legal position as ruler of Judaea 249–251
Herod and the Sadducees 251–252
Herod and the Essenes 252–253
Herod and the Qumran sect 253
Herod and the Pharisees 253–259
Herod and the *Herodians* 259–261
Herod and the boulē 263–266
Herod and the ekklesia 266–267
Herod and the *Synedrion-Sanhedrin* 267–272
Herod and the high priest 282–285
Herod and the rebuilding of the Temple 291–302
Herod and the Pagan cults 315–319
Herod's death 349–352
Herod's funeral 352–354
Herod's tomb 354–357
Herod II 79, 82
Herod III 79
Herod IV (Herod son) 74, 79
Herod IV of Chalcis 79, 81
Herod VI 74
herodeioi 259
Herodians 249, 251, 259, 260, 261
Herodias 76, 79, 82, 83, 153
Herodium 73, 105, 168, 169, 202, 217, 231, 311, 324, 349, 352, 353, 354, 357, 364, 368, 374
Herodium, Lower Herodium 97, 98, 99, 100, 102, 107, 108, 112, 349, 354
Herodium, Upper Herodium 98, 99, 102, 107, 108, 119, 121, 122, 169, 175, 354, 374, 375, 378
Heshbon 139, 199
Hever (Nahal Hever) 241
hever ha-yehudim (See Council of the Jews*)
Hezekiah 25
Hiberia (see Spain*)
Hiericus (See Jericho*)
Hieron of Syracuse 27
Hilkiya 74, 84, 86, 349, 350
Hillel the Elder 94, 254, 255, 289, 290, 336, 359

Hippicus 95
hippodrome 101
Hippos 184, 187, 200, 214
Hiram 28
Hispania (see Spain*)
Homer 94, 361
Horace (Quintus Horatius Flaccus) 62
horin 261
Horvath 'Eleq 176, 185
Horvath Mesad 177
Horvath Salit 176, 180
House of David (See David*)
Hyrcania (Khirbet el-Mird) 178
Hyrcanus the Tobiad 103
Hyrcanus II 19, 33, 35, 44, 48, 53, 55, 57, 68, 69, 70, 72, 74, 76, 79, 103, 115, 127, 150, 157, 158, 191, 214, 243, 263, 257, 295

Idumaea 74, 83, 86, 138, 139, 145, 146, 149, 159, 160, 176, 178, 179, 180, 188, 189, 190, 199, 200, 201, 202, 209, 224, 227, 228, 260, 262, 278, 375
Idumaeans 135, 139, 147, 149, 176, 188, 189, 215, 242, 261
Iliad 94
India 238
insula 346
Ionia 45, 85
Ionians 67
Iopicas (See Joppa*)
ir 217
'Ira (Tel 'Ira) 177, 180, 217
Iranians 67
Irenaeus 93, 94, 372
ish har ha-bayt (*ish ha-bayt*) 286
Ishmael son of Phabes 284
Isocrates 250
Israel (See Judaea*)
Israel (Ancient) 22, 65, 250
Israel (Land of Israel - see Judaea*)
Italy 10, 106, 193, 213, 220, 224, 228, 229, 237, 238, 239, 240, 326, 336, 346, 361, 362, 376
Ituraea 54, 215, 278
Ituraeans 135, 146, 149, 158, 188, 196, 374
Iulius Caesar (Caius Iulius Caesar) 5, 19, 20, 27, 34, 48, 49, 50, 51, 53, 55, 57, 61, 62, 92, 125, 126, 142, 250, 262, 316, 317, 340
iustitia 61
Izates 366

James 267
Jamnia 56, 83, 184, 199, 200, 202, 210, 223, 243, 308
Jason 78, 129, 282
Jehuda (First Temple Period Judaea – See Israel (Ancient*)
Jericho 23, 103, 135, 137, 157, 159, 169, 177, 178, 188, 194, 199, 200, 202, 209, 214, 230, 231, 236, 237, 262, 307, 324, 350, 352, 358
Jericho, Hasmonean palaces 69, 105, 103, 177, 307, 344
Jericho, Herod's palaces 73, 100, 101, 102, 168, 374
Jericho, hippodrome 350
Jericho, First Winter Palace 97, 98, 112, 113, 114
Jericho, Second Winter Palace 115, 116
Jericho, Third Winter Palace 97, 98, 106, 107, 109
Jerusalem 23, 26, 31, 35, 37, 39, 41, 57, 63, 67, 69, 83, 88, 89, 91, 93, 101, 102, 103, 134, 135, 138, 142, 148, 149, 157, 158, 160, 165, 166, 169, 177, 178, 199, 200, 202, 203, 212, 229, 231, 232, 233, 234, 235, 236, 237, 242, 250, 259, 262, 265, 267, 272, 286, 290, 293, 294, 295, 298, 302, 303, 307, 308, 314, 315, 316, 323, 324, 325, 326, 327, 333, 340, 341, 345, 346, 347, 349, 352, 354, 356, 357, 358, 359, 361, 363, 364, 365, 366, 367, 369, 370, 372, 374, 377, 378
- Aceldama Tombs 369
- amphitheatre-hippodrome 338
- Antonia 97, 100, 102, 108, 119, 158, 168, 169, 175, 326
- Baris 294
- Bezetha 327, 329
- Chamber of Hewn Stone 268, 270
- Gichon Spring 23
- *gymnasium* 129, 130, 131
- Hasmonean Palace 326
- Herod's Family Tomb 358, 367

Index of Names and Subjects

- Herod Palace 73, 98, 99, 101, 108, 109, 168, 326, 342, 374
- Herodian Quarter 323, 342, 343, 344
- Hinnom Valley 369
- Kidron Valley 293, 365, 369
- Royal Stoa 105, 300, 305, 306, 309, 310
- Synagogue of Theodotus 245, 314, 315
- Temple 48, 94, 234, 265, 281, 283, 285, 286, 287, 288, 289, 290, 291, 292, 293, 294, 295, 296, 297, 298, 301, 302, 304, 305, 306, 314, 315, 319, 320, 351
- Temple Mount 23, 26, 105, 157, 158, 243, 245, 268, 281, 284, 291, 292, 293, 296, 298, 299, 300, 301, 302, 303, 304, 305, 306, 317, 319, 326, 329, 332, 335, 342, 376, 377
- theatre 337, 338, 339
- Tomb of Absalom 368, 369
- Tomb of Bene Hezir 243, 357, 365, 368
- Tomb of the Cluster Grapes 370
- Tomb of the Frieze 367
- Tomb of Jason 357, 364
- Tomb of Jehoshafat 369
- Tomb of the Kings 358, 366
- Tomb of the Nazirite 358
- Tomb of Nicanor 358, 367
- Tombs of the Sanhedrin 370
- Tomb of Umm el-'Amed 367
- Tomb of Zechariah 293, 365, 368
- Two Storeys Tomb 369
- Tower of Hippicus 39, 95, 102, 119, 169, 326
- Tower of Mariamme 102, 119, 158, 169, 326
- Tower of Phasael 102, 119, 158, 169, 326
- Tower of Psephinus 158, 163
- Walls 158, 159, 161, 162, 163, 326, 327, 332, 333, 352
- Water Supply 326, 334, 335,
- *xistos* 130, 131

Jesus 272, 336
Jesus son of Phabes 284, 296
Jewish War (66–70 CE) 6, 48, 218, 224, 241, 243, 245, 246, 253, 260, 263, 283, 313, 325, 333, 337
Jezreel Valley (See Esdraelon Valley*)
Jib'it (Horvath Jib'it) 217

Joash 22, 23
Joazar son of Boethus 284, 285
Jonathan 30, 53, 78, 157, 199, 200, 246
John Hyrcanus I 30, 31, 33, 53, 69, 135, 196, 199, 210, 242, 244, 246, 282, 296, 332,
Joppa 135, 137, 177, 184, 191, 200, 202, 210, 214
Jordan 160
Jordan Valley 214, 229, 230
Joseph (Herod uncle) 73, 74
Joseph II (Herod brother) 74, 145
Joseph III 74
Josephus (Flavius Josephus) 5–6, 28, 43, 44, 65, 68, 72, 75, 76, 81, 87, 100, 109, 110, 119, 130, 133, 136, 137, 138, 141, 142, 143, 147, 148, 149, 150, 159, 161, 165, 171, 188, 196, 191, 196, 206, 208, 221, 246, 252, 253, 254, 256, 257, 258, 259, 260, 263, 264, 265, 266, 267, 268, 269, 270, 271, 273, 274, 276, 277, 278, 279, 287, 291, 293, 295, 296, 302, 303, 304, 305, 312, 314, 316, 317, 324, 329, 333, 337, 339, 349, 351, 352, 353, 356, 366, 367, 373
Joseph son of Ellemus 284, 285, 286, 338, 351
Joseph son of Camei (Camydus) 283
Joseph of Arimathea 263
Joseph the Tobiad 13
Joseph and Asenath 295
Josiah 25
Jotopata 181
Juba II 58, 59, 60, 68, 372
Jucundus 88
Judaea 1, 3, 7, 8, 9, 10, 15, 16, 30, 34, 53, 54, 55, 78, 80, 81, 83, 87, 89, 116, 148, 149, 152, 159, 176, 177, 178, 181, 197, 199, 200, 201, 202, 203, 208, 212, 213, 215, 220, 222, 224, 227, 228, 229, 230, 232, 234, 235, 242, 245, 246, 247, 251, 252, 261, 262, 263, 267, 269, 273, 274, 275, 276, 278, 281, 283, 285, 287, 290, 291, 307, 308, 310, 314, 319, 321, 323, 324, 325, 341, 357, 359, 364, 370, 371, 373, 374, 375, 376, 377, 378
Judaism 1, 3, 339
Judas (Eagle Affair) 256, 350

Judas Aristobulus I 31, 78
Judas Maccabaeus 25, 29, 30, 53, 78, 140, 157, 246, 289, 359
Judeideh 103
Jugurtha 148
Julias 202
Julio-Claudians 51, 56, 76, 77, 364
Justus of Tiberias 246, 373

kablan 221
Kafr Haris 183, 184
Kafr Laqif 183, 184
Kafr Sur 183
Kalat Fakra 365
Karawat Beni Hasan 229
Kasserine 365
katolikin (*katholikoi*) 286
kefar 217
Kefar Buraq 229
Kefar Hanania 233
Kefar Shihim 233
Kefar Signa 229
kerach 217
Khafira (Khirbet el-Khafira) 217
King's Highway: p. 159, 182, 183
Kiriath Sefer) 217, 218, 221, 310, 311, 313, 314
kochim 357, 360, 363
Köln (See Colonia Claudia Ara Agrippiniensium*)
kome 197, 217, 239
komogrammateus 197, 204
el – Kôm (Khirbet el – Kôm) 241, 242
Kroub 365

Labeo 276
Lacedaemon (See Sparta*)
Lagids (See Ptolemies*)
laocrites 275
Laodicea 48, 140
larnax 361
Latin language 240, 247
Law on Thieves 276, 277, 278, 279
Lebanon 160, 365
Lebanon (Mount) 137, 146, 149, 181
Lemba 200
Leontopolis (Tell El Yahudiye) 284, 294, 295, 296

Leptis Magna 45, 193
Letter of Aristeas 293, 294
Leucadia 41
Livia (Julia Augusta Livia Drusilla) 56, 58, 81, 122, 123
Livias (See Betharamatha*)
Livy (Titus Livius) 62, 93
loculi (see *kochim**)
Lucius Caesar 56
Lucullus (Lucius Licinius Lucullus) 92
Lycia 45, 210
Lycon 91
Lydda 169, 185, 199, 200, 202, 214, 217, 229
Lydians 67
Lysimachus (Herod courtier) 85, 87

ma'amad 198, 199, 200, 307, 314, 375
Maccabees 1, 7, 30, 320, 364
Maccabees (Fourth Book of) 350, 373
Macedonia 36, 41, 52, 54, 66, 67, 68, 69, 262, 353,
Machaeras 137, 145, 148, 149, 259
Machaerus 119, 171, 188, 200, 202, 324, 374
Maecenas (Gaius Cilnius Maecenas) 122, 123, 361
Maenemus 252
Malichus (Hasmonean courtier) 69
Malthace 75, 77, 79, 83
Marcellus (Marcus Claudius Marcellus) 340
Marcus Aurelius (Marcus Aurelius Antoninus) 208
Mariamme the Hasmonean 13, 35, 74, 75, 76, 79, 80, 81, 84, 89, 90, 183, 214, 274
Mariamme II 75, 77, 79, 82, 84, 285
Mariamme III 79, 83
Mariamme IV 74
Mariamme V 79, 81
Marion of Tyre 181
Marissa 72, 199, 200, 202, 213, 230, 241, 242, 341
Marius (Gaius Marius) 19
Mark Antony (Marcus Antonius) 5, 13, 19, 22, 35, 39, 46, 47, 54, 55, 56, 57, 59, 85, 61, 62, 86, 113, 119, 125, 137, 138,

Index of Names and Subjects

142, 148, 149, 150, 151, 205, 255, 284, 356
Masada 73, 98, 102, 108, 119, 158, 159, 168, 171, 231, 232, 237, 242, 244, 283, 311, 374
- Northern Palace 99, 100, 106, 107, 120, 121, 126
- Western Palace 97, 98, 99, 100, 105, 106, 119

ma'aser 206
Matthias (Eagle Affair) 256, 350
Mattathias Antigonus 19, 33, 34, 37, 69, 74, 112, 135, 148, 149, 207, 215, 252, 256, 259, 284
Matthias son of Theophilus 284, 285, 286
Mauretania 58
Mauretania Caesarensis 147
Mazaeus (libertus of Augustus) 50
Mazor 231
Medeba 200
Megiddo 26
Megillath Ta'anith 350, 351
Melas 87, 88
Memphis 127
Menander: p. 339
Menander (Jewish historian) 25
Rav Menashiah 24
Menelaus (high priest) 282, 294
meridarch (See *meridarchia**)
meridarchia 198, 199, 201, 202, 239
Meron 230
Messalina 76
Messalla (Marcus Valerius Messalla Corvinus) 122
Messalina (Valeria Messalina) 76
metropolis 198, 202
Mezad (Horvat Mezad) 224
Michal (Tel Michal) 185
Migdal 193
Migdal Zeboaya 233
Migdol (See Tarichaeae*)
mikwe 95, 217, 224, 331, 336, 343, 344, 345
Miletus 238
Misenum 193, 194
mishmereth 198, 202, 286, 375
Mithridates (libertus of Augustus) 50

Mithridates VI (King of Pontus) 37, 43
Mizpah 199, 200
Mnesiptolemus 91
Moabitis 199, 200
Modein 218, 351
Modein, Tomb of the Maccabees 364
Modi'in (See Modein*)
Monobazus 366
Mordechai's Day (See Purim*)
municipium 216, 336, 337
el-Murak (Khirbet el-Murak) 224
Murabba'at (Wadi Murabba'at) 241
Murcus 190, 193
Mytilene 88

Nabataea 159
Nabataean War (First) 39, 57, 135, 138, 141, 143, 148, 149, 150, 151
Nabataean War (Second) 55, 148, 151, 152, 153, 159, 209, 210
Nabataean language 242
Nabataeans 1, 39, 76, 85, 134, 138, 139, 144, 150, 152, 153, 155, 158, 181, 187, 189, 190, 195, 196, 206, 209, 210, 233, 364, 374
Narbata 199, 200, 202
Narbo (Narbonne) 300
nasi 268
Negev 160, 178
Nehemia 296
Neleus of Coriscus 92
Nero (Nero Claudius Caesar Augustus Germanicus) 43, 56, 125
Netofah 230
Nicaea 51
Nicanor 289
Nicanor Day 288, 289, 319
Nicodemus 69
Nicolaus of Damascus 5, 20, 26–27, 39, 72, 84, 85, 87, 93, 94, 105, 141, 152, 153, 246, 254, 255, 258, 278, 372
Nicomedia 51
Nicopolis 46, 47, 52, 372
Nicopolis, temenos of Apollo 46, 315
Nîmes (Nemausus) 156, 163
Numenius son of Antiochus 130
Numidia 58
Numidians 364, 365

Obadas 152, 210
Obestimm 193
Octavian (See Augustus*)
Odissey 94
'Ofarim 183, 184, 224
oikos 224, 341, 344
Olympia 43, 44, 52, 298, 299, 315, 317, 371
Olympias (daughter of Herod) 74
Olympic Games 43, 315
Olympus (Herod ambassador) 85, 86
Oniads 32, 38, 78, 249, 261, 284, 285, 293
Onias I 44
Onias III 78, 282, 294, 295, 296
Onias IV 25, 294, 295
Oresa 178
Orine (See Jerusalem*)
Oronaim 200
ossilegium 360, 362, 363
ossuaries 357, 359, 360, 361, 362, 363, 378
Ostia 193

palaestra 101
Pallas (Herod wife) 75, 77, 79
Palmyra 46
Palmyra, Sanctuary of Bel 299
Palmyra, Sanctuary of Nebo 299
Pamphylia 210
Paneas 39, 58, 83, 102, 103, 106, 159, 202, 281, 315, 316, 318, 323, 377
Paneas, Temple of Augustus 58, 318, 377
Pannonia 110, 146
Paphos 236, 237
parnese ha-zedakah 275
Parthia 282, 284
Parthians 1, 34, 55, 146, 155, 158, 195, 196, 214
Passover 287, 351
Patroclus 27
Pausanias 299
Pegae (Tel 'Afeq) 185
Pella 341
Pella (Decapolis) 185, 187, 200, 202
Peloponnesus 44
Pelusium 38, 238
Pentateuch (see Torah*)
Pentecost 287, 288

Peraea 74, 102, 187, 188, 199, 200, 208, 214
Pergamum 44, 50, 51, 52, 54, 69, 92, 109, 265, 273, 332, 333, 353
Perseus (Stoic philosopher) 36
Perseus (Antigonid king of Macedonia) 36
Persia 66, 238
Persius (A. Persius Flaccus) 290
Petra 121, 144, 153, 178, 236, 237, 299, 369
Petra, Corinthian Tomb 120, 369
Petra, Deir 120, 369
Petra, Khasneh 120, 369
Petra, Temple of Qasr al Bint 299
Petronius (*praefectus* of Egypt) 211
Phabatus 88, 90
Phaedra (Herod wife) 75, 77, 79
Phallion (Herod's uncle) 74
Pharathon 157
Pharisees 4, 27, 28, 30, 31, 32, 60, 68, 69, 90, 207, 249, 251, 253, 254, 255, 256, 257, 258, 259, 261, 270, 268, 269, 270, 271, 272, 287, 289, 294, 307, 359, 360, 362, 376
Phasael 74, 112, 354
Phasael II 74, 81
Phasael III 79
Phasaelis 83, 210, 214, 324
Phasaelus 45
Pheroras 13, 73, 77, 79, 87, 90, 102, 183, 188, 201, 207, 214, 258, 259
Phidias 298, 317
Philadelphia (Decapolis) 48, 150, 185, 187
Philip (Herod Philip) 1, 21, 40, 58, 77, 79, 83, 84, 102, 209, 363
Philip I (son of Herod) 79, 139, 153, 316, 318, 352
Philip II of Macedonia 36, 42, 43, 65, 66, 68, 76, 78, 361
Philip V (Antigonid ruler) 38
Philip son of Jacimus 312
philoi 69, 70, 71, 74, 84, 96
Philo of Alexandria 276, 277, 309
Philonides 91
Philostratus 93, 94, 372
Philoteria 155, 341
philotimia (See *euergetism**)

Phoenicia 24, 25, 28, 227, 234, 243, 293, 325, 365
Phoenician language 243
phoros (soil tribute) 203, 204, 206
Phrygians 67
phylarches 273
pietas 61, 377
Pisidians 135, 196
pistoi 275
Pitholaus 69
Plautus (Titus Maccius Plautus) 339
Plutarch (L. Mestrius Plutarchus) 40
Polemon I of Pontus 33
polis 216, 217, 336, 337, 377
Pollio 28, 40, 253, 254, 255, 256, 259
Pollio (Gaius Asinius Pollio) 57, 62, 63, 373
Polybius 36, 94, 136, 137, 144, 147, 265
Polyclitus 298
Pompeii 234, 332, 334, 336, 340, 341, 369
Pompeii, House of Faun 114
Pompeii, House of Menander 122
Pompeii, Villa di Diomede 120
Pompeii, Villa dei Misteri 120
Pompey (Gnaeus Pompeius Magnus) 1, 33, 49, 54, 57, 62, 72, 125, 126, 158, 160, 171, 185, 201, 211, 220, 262, 291, 324, 340, 342
Pontius Pilatus 335
Pontus 37, 194
Popilius Laenas (Publius Popilius Laenas) 54
Portus 193
Praeneste, Temple of Fortuna Primigenia 301
Priene 326, 341
pronoetai 275
Proverbs 25
proseuche (House of Prayer) 306, 307, 308, 309, 314, 320
proskynesis 66
Pseudo-Hecataeus 292, 296
Ptolemais (Akko) 28, 48, 135, 155, 191, 194, 236, 324, 332
Ptolemais (Lybia) 120, 369
Ptolemies 8, 25, 29, 30, 36, 37, 42, 43, 65, 67, 70, 72, 73, 76, 78, 84, 85, 91, 92, 93, 96, 109, 140, 141, 144, 145, 147, 150, 155, 157, 184, 196, 197, 201, 203, 209, 213, 214, 218, 234, 273, 275, 282, 293, 324, 356, 357, 372, 374, 375
Ptolemy (Herod' *epitropos*) 84, 85, 215, 260, 352, 372
Ptolemy (Nicolaus of Damascus brother) 87
Ptolemy I Soter 92
Ptolemy II Philadelphus 67, 92, 293, 294
Ptolemy IV Philopator 37, 92, 121, 140, 350
Ptolemy VI 294
Ptolemy IX 127, 129
Ptolemy X (Lathirus) 127, 129, 140, 181
Ptolemy son of Thraseas 243
Ptolomaeus (historian) p. 94, 372
Pula 318
Punic language 243
Purim 281, 288, 290, 319, 377
Putaeoli 193, 239
Punta Campanella (Villa of) 107

Qasr e-Leja 183, 184, 224
Qumran 240, 242, 296, 297, 308, 373
Qumran Sect 253, 291, 296, 297

Rabbis (See Sages*)
Rabirius 125
Raepta 152
Ragaba (See Gabae*)
Ramat ha-Nadiv 224
Ramathain 199, 200
Raphia 37, 140, 200
Rass (er-Rass) 183
Ravenna 193, 194
Rhine 193
Rhodes 31, 45, 52, 53, 54, 56, 87, 210, 245, 332, 361, 362, 371
Rhodes, Temple of Apollo Pithius 45, 315
Rhinocorura 200
Roman army 133, 138, 140, 142, 143, 145, 147, 148, 149, 151, 196
– *auxilia*: p. 139, 151
– legions: p. 137, 138, 140, 196
Rome 2, 6, 11, 21, 45, 47, 48, 53, 57, 62, 63, 65, 80, 81, 88, 91, 92, 93, 110, 124, 125, 140, 207, 208, 209, 211, 212, 213, 250, 256, 265, 267, 270, 281, 282, 283,

284, 287, 302, 316, 320, 323, 326, 327,
329, 332, 336, 337, 339, 340, 346, 347,
349, 358, 361, 362, 363, 364, 370, 371,
377, 378
- Actian Arch 51, 300
- Ara Pacis 49, 123, 298, 300
- Augustan regions 329
- Basilica Iulia 300
- Basilica Ulpia 305
- Campus Martius 110, 300
- Capitolium 329
- Circus Maximus 111, 340
- Domus Augustana (Imperial Palace) 125
- Domus of Augustus 111, 112, 124, 126, 374
- Domus Aurea 125
- Farnesina Villa 121, 126
- Flavian Amphitheater 339, 340
- Forum 51, 300
- Forum of Augustus 49, 122, 298
- Forum Iulium 300, 317
- Horologium Solare 300
- House of Livia 124
- Mausoleum of Augustus 300, 354, 356, 357, 362, 378
- Palatine 124, 125
- Parthian Arch 51, 301
- Temple of Apollo Palatinus 125
- Temple of Apollo Sosianus 317
- Temple of Divus Iulius 51, 300
- Temple of Mars Ultor 300, 317
- Temple of Venus Genitrix 300, 317
- Theatre of Balbus 340
- Theatre of Marcellus 340
- Theatre of Pompey 110, 337, 340
- Thermae of Agrippa 335, 340
- Water supply 334
Romema on the Carmel 181
Roxane 79
Rufus 139, 142, 147
Rujm el-Hamiri 178, 224
Rusazus 59
Rusguniae 59

Saalburg 144
Sabratha 365

Sadducees 4, 80, 222, 249, 251, 252, 257, 270, 271, 272, 289, 357, 360, 376
Sages 307, 309
Saint Rémy (See Glanum*)
Salampsio 79, 81
Saldae 59
Salit (Horvat Salit) 224
Salome (Herod sister) 56, 73, 79, 80, 83, 86, 90, 256, 258, 349, 350
Salome II 79
Salome Alexandra 19, 33, 39, 40, 68, 69, 70, 76, 140, 251
Samaria 41, 55, 75, 83, 137, 139, 145, 155, 159, 176, 182, 183, 184, 188, 189, 199, 201, 202, 209, 214, 215, 224, 227, 228, 229, 234, 237, 295, 342
Samaritans 84, 161, 200, 242, 294, 295, 296, 375
Samaritis (See Samaria*)
Sameas 40, 253, 254, 255, 256, 259
Sanaballetes 295
Sanhedrin (See *synedrion-Sanhedrin**)
Sappinas 84, 87
sarcophagi 357, 358, 359, 360, 363, 378
Sarsina 369
Saturnalia 289, 290
Saturninus 152, 274
Scipio Africanus (Publius Cornelius Scipio Africanus Maior) 62, 144
Scipiones 122
Scythians 156, 160
Scythopolis (Tel Istaba) 185, 187, 200, 229
Sea of Galilee 190, 193, 194, 232, 260, 325, 331, 375
Sebaste 39, 47, 48, 57, 81, 89, 102, 158, 159, 160, 166, 167, 168, 184, 190, 202, 203, 250, 272, 281, 303, 315, 316, 317, 323, 324, 325, 331, 337, 338, 347, 377
Sebaste, Acropolis Palace 108, 112, 331, 374
Sebaste, Temple of Augustus 167, 300, 301, 317, 319, 331, 377
Sebastenoi 137, 139, 142, 147
segan (*strategos tou ierou*) 285, 286
seganim (*strategoi*) 286
Seleucia on Tigris 47, 119
Seleucids 8, 29, 30, 33, 36, 37, 42, 43, 46, 47, 65, 66, 67, 70, 72, 73, 76, 78, 84, 91,

92, 96, 109, 140, 141, 144, 145, 157, 175, 184, 197, 199, 201, 203, 204, 206, 207, 208, 209, 213, 214, 234, 239, 243, 273, 282, 324, 372, 374, 375
Seleucus of Syria 258
Seneca (Lucius Annaeus Seneca) 339
Sepphoris 102, 148, 161, 167, 176, 199, 200, 202, 262, 325, 326
Senate (Roman) 53, 54, 61, 276, 287, 337, 338, 371, 378
Settefinestre (Villa of) 107, 224
Seuthas 156
Seven Town Elders 274, 275
Severus (architect) 125
Sextus Caesar (Sextus Iulius Caesar) 55, 56
Sextus Pompeius (Sextus Pompeius Magnus Pius) 19, 62
Sabbath 243, 272, 287, 307
sganim 261
Shammai 94, 254, 255, 256, 290
Sha'ar ha-'Amaqim 182
Sharon Plain 185, 215, 229
Sharuhen 180
Shechem 182
Shemaya 255
Shephela 215, 218
Shifkon 229
Shilo (Tel Shilo) 217
Sidon 28, 229, 238
Sigga 365
Silas the Jew 181
Silo 148, 149
Simitthus 364
Simon (the Just) 293, 297
Simon II (Oniad high priest) 38
Simon the Hasmonean 30, 53, 78, 130, 140, 267, 364
Simon son of Boethus 82, 251, 284, 285
Simonides 92
Sinai 24
Sinope 194
Sirmione 126, 127
sitones 264
Smyrna 339
socher 221
Soemus of Ituraea 88, 89
Sokho 217

Solomon 22, 23, 24, 25, 26, 27, 28, 34, 60, 62, 63, 65, 78, 289, 292, 297, 371, 373
Song of Songs 25
Sons of Baba 253, 256
Sophocles 339
Sosius (Gaius Sosius) 138, 149
Souron 25
Spain 224, 227, 237, 301, 317
Sparta 52, 87, 371
Sperlonga (Villa of Tiberius) 107
Spello 156
Sphaerus of Borysthenes 36
Spice Route 150, 151, 152, 178, 181, 209, 227, 238, 239, 240
Stoics 36, 122
Strabo 46, 92, 159, 171, 187
strategos 197, 199, 272
Strato 92, 151
Straton Tower (See Caesarea Maritima*)
Suetonius (Gaius Suetonius Tranquillus) 124
Sulla (Lucius Cornelius Sulla Felix) 44, 62, 92, 250
Sukkot (See Tabernacles*)
Sumaa 365
Sunium 49
Suweida 364
Syah 45, 127
Sycion 37
Syllaeus 88, 90, 151, 152, 153
symposium 71
synagogue 281, 306, 307, 308, 309, 310, 311, 312, 313, 314, 315, 316, 320, 377
synedrion 262, 267, 268, 269, 270, 271, 273, 274
synedrion-Sanhedrin 249, 250, 263, 264, 267, 268, 269, 270, 271, 272, 276, 306, 376
Syphax 144
Syracuse 27, 156
Syria 24, 28–29, 54, 55, 88, 140, 148, 153, 210, 215, 221, 225, 229, 238, 239, 240, 243, 267, 275, 303, 325, 364, 365, 371
Syria (modern) 160

Tabernacles 31, 287, 288, 289
Tabor (Mount Tabor) 181, 200
Tacitus (Publius Cornelius Tacitus) 333

Targumim 308
Tarichaeae 200, 202, 232
Tarragona 301, 365
Tarsus 236, 237
Tekoa 229
Tell (Khirbet et-Tell) 183, 184
Temple Scroll 293, 296, 297
Tephon 157
Terentius (Publius Terentius Afer) 339
Terra Sigillata 234, 236, 237, 346
Tero 91, 266
Terracina, Temple of Jupiter Anxur 301
terumah 206
tetrapyrgion 155, 156, 157, 168, 175, 176, 196
Thamna 157, 169, 202, 217
Thamnitica (See Thamna*)
Thamnatha (See Thamna*)
Thapsus 58
theatre 101
Theophilus 25
Theophrastus 92
thermae (See Bathhouse, Roman*)
Thracians 88, 134, 135, 144, 145, 353
Tiberias 58, 102, 159, 161, 167, 202, 263, 265, 308, 309, 311, 314, 325, 326, 331, 337, 338, 347, 373, 376
– Antipas Palace 331
– city walls 167, 168, 331
– *dyplastoon* 309, 310
Tiberius (Tiberius Iulius Caesar Augustus) 81, 140, 167, 258, 267
Tibneh 217
Tibur, Temple of Hercules Victor 301
Tigranes II 140
Tigranes III 55
Timagenes 140
Timarchus 53
Timgad (Thamugabi) 46
Titus (Titus Flavius Sabinus Vespasianus) 56, 58, 263
Tivoli 107
Tobiads 13
toparch (See *toparchia**)
toparchia 197, 198, 199, 200, 201, 202, 217, 235, 239, 274
Torah 38, 94, 270, 276, 281, 288, 293, 308, 309, 320

Torre Astura (Villa of) 107
Trachonitis 54, 83, 139, 147, 152, 187, 188, 189, 201, 202, 208, 215, 228
Trans-Jordan 35, 159, 176, 187, 188, 324
Trasyllus 258
Tripolis 28
tryphe 67, 72
Tryphon (Herod courtier) 91, 266
Tubusuctu 59
Tufaniyeh (Khirbet el- Tufaniyeh) 181
Tunisia 364, 365
Turas (Horvath Turas) 217
Turin (Augusta Taurinorum) 156
Turnus 61
Tyrannius 92
Tyrannus 88
Tyre 25, 28, 229, 234

Umm el-'Amdan (Khirbet Umm el-'Amdan) 217, 218
uparchoi 265
'Urmeh (Khirbet el 'Urmeh) 183, 184
urnae 361, 362
'Uza (Tel 'Uza) 178, 180

Vaphres 25
Varus (Publius Quinctiulius Varus) 256
Varro (Marcus Terentius Varro) 92
Vedio Pollio (Villa of) 107
Ventidius (Publius Ventidius Bassus) 145, 148
Vergina 361
Verona 156
Vespasian (Titus Flavius Sabinus Vespasianus) 56, 58, 258, 272, 294
Via Maris 184, 185
Villanovians 361
Villayosa 365
Virgil (Publius Vergilius Maro) 61, 62
virtus 61
Vitellius (L. Vitellius) 153
Volterra 361, 362
Volumnius 142
Vouni 119

Wood Offering 290

xyston 131, 265, 326

Yahud (Khirbet el-Yahud) 193
Yattir (Nahal Yattir) 176
Yavne (See Jamnia*)
Yehuda (See Judaea*)
Yehuda ha-Nasi 215

Zadokites 286, 295
Zama 144

Zamaris 139, 189, 215
Zealots 311
Zenodorus 54, 278
Zenodotus of Ephesus 92
Zerubabel 292
Zeus 42
Zoara 200
Zoilus of Dora 191

www.ingramcontent.com/pod-product-compliance
Lightning Source LLC
Chambersburg PA
CBHW052049290426
44111CB00011B/1668